D1188480

RICH HERRIN
A Head Coach
Ahead Of His Time

MATT WYNN

WORDS MATTER
P U B L I S H I N G
OUR WORDS CHANGE THE WORLD

This Book is dedicated to my dad ...
Mack Wynn (1944-2021)

The best dad a guy could have

I love you Dad...This is for you

Table of Contents

Foreword

Our team entered the first game of the Honolulu Shootout with a (6-1) record. We were athletic at every position. Inside, we had three Saluki Hall-of Famers (Ashraf Amaya, Rick Shipley and Jerry Jones.) Our first game in the tournament was against the Silver Streaks of Chaminade University. The Streaks were known for their stunning upset of number one Virginia and Ralph Sampson in 1982, but that was years ago. We were clearly the better team and I noticed our size advantage as soon as we took the floor for pre-game warm ups.

When the game started, I took my usual place near the end of the bench to wave the towel and offer encouragement. As expected, we jumped out to a quick 10-2 lead before the Streaks called a time-out. After the timeout, Chaminade scored a basket and then hustled back to a soft 2-1-2 defense, daring us to shoot the ball. Our guards struggled to hit shots and the Streaks climbed back into the game to take a two-point lead. Coach Herrin called a timeout to make adjustments. This was it. If I was ever going to play, this was the situation. Our team needed a shooter to pull the defense out of the zone.

After the timeout, I took my place on the bench and mentally prepared myself for the opportunity I had been waiting for. I could feel it coming. I tightly gripped a white towel to dry my sweaty palms and bloody fingers. I have a terrible habit of biting the skin around my fingers when I'm nervous. If you want to know my anxiety level, just look at my fingers. On this night, I had chewed my thumbs to a bloody pulp as I waited to see if Coach Herrin would pull the trigger.

Clank! Another missed shot. Coach had seen enough. As if it was his last option, he walked by me and grumbled, "Matt…let's go…get Freddie!" I quickly jumped up and tore my warm-ups off and raced to the scorer's table. This was it. My heart pounded and I took deep breaths as I rubbed my bloody fingers on the trunks of my uniform. There was only one thing on my mind; hit that first one.

In our first offensive possession, we ran a very simple play called "stationary". I took my place on the right wing and split the gap between the top and bottom defenders of Chaminade's soft 2-1-2 zone. Point guard, Sterling Mahan, penetrated the gap between the top defenders and passed me the ball. I was wide open. I looked inside and pitched the ball back to Mahan at the top of the key. With frustration, Sterling placed the ball on his hip and shot me a stern look and said, "Shoot the ball!" Again, he charged the gap of the defense and zipped me the ball. With no hesitation, I let it fly. I knew it was good when I let it go. As a shooter, there is no greater feeling. The ball ripped thru the net and out of the corner of my eyes I could see my buddies on the bench jump to their feet to cheer for one of their own. As I darted down the floor to play defense, a bolt of energy ran through my body.

I ended up scoring 14 points in the game and the breakthrough solidified my spot as the Salukis' designated three-point shooter for the remainder of my college career. It was my greatest moment in basketball. This was my Coach Herrin moment. Let me explain.

Before Rich Herrin accepted the head coaching position at SIU-C, he was a legendary high school coach in my hometown of Benton, Illinois. At Benton, he accumulated 521 coaching victories establishing himself as one of the greatest high school basketball coaches in the country. He arrived at Benton in 1960 and left when Southern Illinois University lured him to Carbondale to coach the basketball Salukis in '85. Coach Herrin left Benton my sophomore year in high school, but I did get the chance to play for him in college at SIU.

When I first arrived at Southern Illinois University in the fall of 1987, I was a red-shirt walk-on. It was an embarrassing title that gave proof that I was at rock bottom. My red-shirt year (1987-88) was tough. By NCAA rule, red-shirts were not eligible to appear in games. My parents paid for my first year of college tuition and I focused on improving my strength and quickness. I only dressed for home games and when the team was on the road, I locked myself into my dorm room and listened to legendary broadcaster, Mike Reis, call the game. I was clearly the last guy on the team.

In the spring of my red-shirt season, Coach Herrin called my dorm room and said, "Matt come on over to the Arena, I want to talk to you." Upon arriving, he grabbed my hand and pulled my thumb back in an awkward position and cackled when I started to show weakness. He looked at me with a wide grin and said, "I could still whip you." This was his way; always sparring with you, exploiting a weakness, making a joke. He then told me to have a seat. He looked at me and said, "Biggin…you've worked pretty hard…we're going to put you on scholarship." I was stunned. I rose out of the chair and offered my hand and said, "Thank you, Coach." He shook my hand and quickly snapped, "I didn't give you anything…you earned it." I raced back to my dorm room to call my parents. It was a nice thing to say to my parents; Mom, Dad, my college is good, it's paid for. All those nights I spent by myself shooting the ball, the camps, the goal my grandpa put up in our driveway; in a way, the scholarship justified all of it. The free ride was certainly a relief to my parents, but it did not translate to playing time.

In my second year (athletically, my freshman year), I appeared in only eight games and scored five points. At the end of the season, we received a plaque that displayed a picture of the team with our names under the picture. I found satisfaction in seeing my picture on the plaque and then looked to find my name…it wasn't there. My name wasn't engraved on the plaque. This was the proof of my insignificance. I needed to see my name on that plaque. Why? Because it was the only evidence I could point to as being a college basketball player. I certainly had no quality playing time to boast of. I had no stats. Nothing but zeros. Being told by my coaches that I was helping the team with my good attitude and hard work was getting old. The no-name on the plaque was hurtful, but it also served as motivation. I needed to contribute. I needed to prove my worth, if not to the team, then at least to myself.

This is why that moment against Chaminade was so special. I had to earn it. It didn't come easy. Yes, I hit the shot and certainly worked hard to put myself in that position, but it was Coach that provided that opportunity. Due to the urging of his brother Ron, and also Saluki Assistant, Ron Smith, Coach Herrin allowed me the opportunity to walk-on at SIU. He saw in me something more than I saw in myself. I knew him growing up. I went to all of his camps. I played for him in college and even coached the Benton Rangers for seven seasons.

As a youngster, I had front row seats to Coach Herrin's teams and witnessed some of the most exciting high school basketball games in the country. Through the game of basketball, Coach was able to make an impact on the lives of so many of his players. Coach Herrin's twenty-five years at Benton were special. He had incredible teams. How did he do it? What was it like to play for Coach Herrin in the glory days of the Benton

Rangers? How was he able to win consistently in the rugged South Seven Conference? Which teams were his best? Who were the players that built the program? Hundreds of players played for Rich Herrin at Benton, Illinois and hundreds tell their stories. Get ready, gang…this is the story of Rich Herrin and his Benton Runnin' Rangers!

CHAPTER ONE

Brotherly Love - Rich & Ron

"See…I had a great big brother." – Rich Herrin

The intercom blared; "All basketball players please report to the gymnasium for a short meeting." The announcement came with about thirty minutes left in the school day. I was a sophomore in high school. I gathered my books and slowly walked to the west end of the school. I had no idea what the meeting was about. My first thought was that Coach Herrin wanted to meet with us about our schedule for the summer. I wasn't quite sure, but as I approached the gym, I saw my teammates and a few adults standing to the side. Coach Herrin waited patiently for all of us to gather. The mood was quiet and sullen. Coach looked uncomfortable and I could sense immediately that this meeting was not about our summer schedule. He began to speak…but his voice broke. He paused for a moment, regathered himself and said, "I wanted to be the first to tell you guys…I accepted the head coaching position at SIU this afternoon. It was a tough decision and I wanted you guys to be the first to know. It has nothing to do with you guys…it's a new challenge." He spoke to each one of us and shook our hands. That was it. He was gone.

After the shell shock of his announcement, the attention focused on who was going to be his replacement. We had a solid team returning. The head basketball job at Benton High School was one of the most coveted jobs in the state of Illinois. There was speculation about Dave Luechtefeld from Okawville and Dick Corn from Pinckneyville, but ultimately the BCHS board hired Coach's brother, Ron.

Ron Herrin was a coaching legend himself. He coached at Olney High School and his Tigers had the Rangers' number in the late seventies. Much like his brother, Ron Herrin loved the game. The first time I met Ron Herrin, I immediately liked him. I trusted him. Think of the courage it took for Ron Herrin to take the Benton job after his younger brother. He didn't flinch. Looking back, I believe I got the sweetest deal. I had the opportunity to play for Ron in high school and Rich in college. After coaching at Benton, he became a volunteer assistant coach at SIU and helped his little brother. Later in my life, when I was coaching at Meridian High School, I would get handwritten letters of encouragement in the mail from Ron. That was the type of man he was and that was who his little brother looked up to. Rich Herrin idolized his older brother and Ron always steered him in the right direction. Unfortunately, Ron Herrin passed away in the spring of 1997, leaving a huge void in Rich's life.

During one of our interviews, Coach Rich Herrin mentioned that he was in the St. Louis Sports Hall of Fame. So I Googled the Hall of Fame site and found his membership biography. I began reading the bio and then scrolled down to the bottom of the page and noticed there was an eight-minute video showing his induction interview. I clicked play. The emcee of the ceremony introduced Coach Herrin; Coach then left his seat at the table and walked to center stage to do a short interview with the emcee.

The emcee described how Herrin put together three 20-win seasons at SIU and then got snubbed by the NCAA in 1990 with a team that was 26-7. The emcee asked, "How did you feel about being snubbed?" Rich then replied, "I came down pretty hard on the NCAA selection committee." The emcee then explained that the '93 Salukis made the tournament and the selection committee rewarded them with Duke in the next round. Coach laughed and said it was his fault. "I should have kept my mouth shut the year before." Everyone laughed.

Then the emcee asked a question that completely caught Coach Herrin off guard. The emcee said, "When you finally won the tournament and all the players are gathered at center court for a picture, I remember you were standing by your brother"…when Coach Herrin realized the question was about his brother, he was so touched that he could not continue. The emcee gave him some time to collect himself. Coach paused, and then he tried to go on by saying, "See, my brother was a student of the game." Coach then began to cry and sat up in his chair and raised his hands and said, "I'm sorry, I'm sorry." He then regathered himself and somehow finished by making everyone laugh.

It was hard for me to watch. Coach wanted his brother to be there more than anything in the world, and he knew he wouldn't have been there without his big brother. Coach loved his brother. Ron is his soft spot. The interview can be seen on the St. Louis Sports Hall of Fame site.

The story of Rich Herrin cannot be told without a clear understanding of the strong bond he shared with his big brother Ron. Rich followed Ron's lead from the time he was a young boy until Ron's death in 1997. Ron Herrin was the best big brother a guy could have. Having played for Ron Herrin in high school for two years, it was touching to hear the people that were closest to him describe his impact on them. Ron was a straight arrow. He understood the difference between right and wrong at an early age. He was a friend to all people and he was sincere in his actions. His little brother Rich watched his every move and admired all of these qualities.

I picked up the phone one afternoon to call the person that knew Ron Herrin the best, his wife Mary Lou. I've known Mary Lou since they moved to Benton in the summer of 1985. Mary Lou was not only Ron's wife, she was his best friend. They met in college in what Mary Lou would say was an act of providence. At the time, Mary Lou was a seventeen-year-old freshman at McKendree College, from Metropolis, Illinois. As a freshman at McKendree, Mary Lou was chosen as Homecoming Queen and, as her roommate Norma told her, "The Queen must have a date." Mary Lou recalled the first time she met Ron.

Mary Lou Herrin: *Ron and I met at McKendree College in the fall of 1950. At the time, I was a seventeen-yea- old freshman and Ron was a junior. He was a big man on campus because he was an athlete, earning ten letters* (four in basketball, and three each in football and track). *I had seen him around, but had never spoken to him, although I always thought he was attractive. My first impression of him was that he was a ladies' man, and that did not appeal to me at all.*

Our first date came about in an unusual manner, and really only happened because I was, quite frankly, desperate. In late October that year, much to my surprise I was selected as a candidate for Homecoming Queen. At that time, I didn't have a steady boyfriend, but had accepted an invitation to attend the festivities with a young man from Chicago who often played the piano in the student lounge. He was an excellent musician and I was attracted to him for that reason, but we had never dated, and didn't know each other well at all.

I was elected Homecoming Queen so you can imagine my shock when he called on the morning of the game and left a message with my roommate Norma that he had to cancel. Apparently, he had heard through the grapevine that I didn't drink, which did not fit in with his plans. When Norma delivered the news to me that day, I was shocked and humiliated at the prospect of attending the banquet and dance without an escort. Norma, quick thinking and practical, almost immediately came up with a solution for my problem. She had known Ron for years (they were both preacher's kids) and she offered to call him to see if he would step in as my escort. She told me that he was a great guy, assured me that I had a mistaken perception of him, and thought I would really like him. Since beggars couldn't be choosers, I quickly agreed to let her call him. Lucky for me, Ron was both available and willing to step in and come to my rescue.

That afternoon, as luck would have it, Ron was injured in the football game and had to hobble in on crutches to escort me to the dance that night. Yet we somehow managed to get by, and the Chicago pianist was not missed at all. And so began the romance of Ron Herrin and Mary Lou Hard which lasted until his death forty-seven years later.

In the Bible, Jesus says that we are to "Love thy neighbor as thyself" (Mark 12:31). Every time I hear this Bible verse, I think of Ron Herrin. He was an amazing human being that had flaws just as we all do, but he excelled in loving people well. Ron gave people the benefit of the doubt. He was kind and friendly to all that knew him. He was sensitive to those around him. He was not only a good big brother, but he was a good husband and great father to his children; Sara, Jim, Kim and Sue. The children reminisced about their childhood memories of their father, who always had time for them.

Sara Herrin (Ron's oldest daughter): *I never saw or heard Dad treat a woman inappropriately ---he wasn't that kind of man -- which is one reason I enjoy this memory. One evening -- after Mom had gone to bed -- Dad and I were sitting on the sofa watching t.v. The show "Maude" came on (it must have been in re-runs since it was late night). When Adrienne Barbeau, who played Maude's daughter, came into the scene, Dad made a noise like "hubba-hubba" (Andrienne Barbeau was well-endowed and attractive in a sexy way). Dad then noticed my surprised reaction, and we both started laughing. I think* *his reaction to Ms. Barbeau's appearance was partly in jest, but that he also thought she was hot.*

Jim Herrin (Ron's son): *In the fall of my senior year, I decided that I did not want to play basketball. My senior class was loaded with talent and I really would not have seen much playing time at all. I had gone to Mom first with my decision so she could prepare Dad for what I wanted to do. That night, Dad came home late from a meeting and I was already in bed, but still awake. Dad came down to my room and we had a nice talk about my not playing basketball that season. I told him that I wanted to concentrate on track during the winter. I told Dad that I would run twice a day during the winter leading up to track season and I did. I would get up every morning before school and run three miles and then run with the rest of the track team after school. I know that Dad was disappointed that I did not play, but he was very positive and supportive of my decision. Actually, I had a pretty good season running on some winning relay teams (two-mile and four-mile relays) and finished fourth in the NEC Conference Meet in the mile run. The next fall, when I was at McKendree for my freshman year of college, I received a letter from Dad telling me how proud he was of the hard work that I put into my senior year of track.*

Kim Herrin (Ron's youngest daughter): *I can't just name one memory because there are too many, so I have a compilation of Ronny memories. Mean moo cow… a quick explanation of MMC is Dad got on his hands and knees and became a mean cow. We would run around him and he would try to grab us and bring us in to his mean moo cow pen. I loved that game. The monster hide-and-seek game… We would hide upstairs and Dad would come try to find us. He acted like a Frankenstein-type monster as he walked around the room searching for us. We also never knew how long it would be before he came upstairs. It could be two minutes or could be ten minutes…the anticipation was part of the fun. Loved it! As we got older I really enjoyed the twenty dollar handshake: Dad would have a twenty dollar bill hidden in his hand, and he would slide it into your hand as he hugged you and shook your hand.*

Sue Herrin Vennard (Ron's third child): *One time, when we were a little older, we got in some trouble for something we had done. Dad was pretty upset with us, so he took us, one by one, into an ERHS classroom, leaving the other three kids waiting, and listening, in the hall. First, we could hear a loud spanking sound, followed by an impassioned "Ouch!" That went on for a couple of minutes until finally, the punished child would come limping out of* *the room, rubbing his or her behind as if it were very sore. The anticipation of getting that spanking was excruciating, but Dad being Dad, he didn't really spank any of us. That noise turned out to be him slapping the desk really hard with a book. Each of us kids went along with his plan by doing some excellent acting, both with our yelps and also the way we exited the room, looking down at the floor, not making eye contact with our siblings, appearing very traumatized by the whole event.*

Darryl Vennard (Ron's son-in-law): *One weekend when the Herrin family was getting together in Benton, Ron asked me if I wanted to accompany him while he ran a few errands. Naturally, I said, "Sure," always glad for the opportunity to spend a little time with my father-in-law. We drove to West Frankfort to pick up some donuts and entered the shop from the employees' entrance. As we walked through the kitchen, a young man with Down's Syndrome yelled out to him, Hey, Coach!" When Ron stopped to talk to him, he began beaming from ear to ear. Ron said, "Do you still work here?" and the boy laughed and responded proudly, "Every weekend, Coach Herrin." Ron then told him to be sure and work hard at school like he does at the donut shop, and the kid assured him that he was doing just that. Then Ron tousled his hair, and gave him a little shoulder rub before we went on in to get our donuts. While we were there, Ron talked to every person in the shop. When we left, he gave the dishwasher the business one last time. "You better keep doing your homework, I'm going to check up on you!" Ron warned in a soft and gentle manner. "Don't worry, I will, Coach." I'll never forget that kid's smile as we walked out. Everyone wanted time with Ron, and he gave the most time to the admiring special needs dishwasher. That is who Ron Herrin was to me.*

Ron was also in the running for Best Grandpa. He loved to play and pull practical jokes on his two grandchildren, Matthew and Nick. Regretfully, he never got the chance to meet Ben and Cam. He would have loved them, and they would have loved him more.

On top of being such a devoted family man, Ron Herrin was a very good basketball coach in his own right. In thirty-five seasons of coaching high school basketball, he compiled a record of 578 wins and 372 losses. He coached five years at Freeburg High School with a record of 93-43. He guided Freeburg to three District Championships in basketball, and coached the baseball team to a second place finish in the state tournament in 1956.

In 1960, Ron accepted the head boys' basketball coaching position at Olney (East Richland) High School. Olney, Illinois is located in the center of Richland County in Southern Illinois. With a school enrollment of approximately 750 students, this placed Olney as a small AA school in Illinois when the two class system was adopted in 1972. The Tigers had to deal with Effingham, Paris and sometimes Mt. Vernon to advance in tournament play. Today, the gym at Olney has been named Ron Herrin Gymnasium in his honor.

In 1975, it was Ron's Olney Tigers that eliminated the state ranked Benton Rangers in the Sectional semi-finals and then defeated Effingham in the Sectional finals. It was the only game the Rangers lost in the 1975 season, finishing 27-1.

Rich Herrin: *Ron had a good basketball team…Dunbar tore his knee up and couldn't play. My brother stuck a triangle and two on us. They guarded Smith and Tabor and we couldn't score…give them credit…they did what they had to do to win the ballgame.*

This was Olney's first appearance in the "Sweet Sixteen" since 1942. The Tigers were defeated in the Super-Sectional by the East St. Louis Flyers. Tony Phelps was the second leading scorer and rebounder for the Tigers in 1975.

Tony Phelps: *Ron Herrin was my high school basketball coach, but he became a dear friend. Almost once a week when I was in college he sent me a letter. Because of this and many other things, I realized this was a man who really cared for me far beyond the basketball court. I was a teacher's aide for him when in high school. I watched him closely and I saw the passion he had for coaching. It didn't take long for me to desire that vocation. Now for forty years I have always coached something without a single year off. Ron was and is my inspiration.*

People that know Olney basketball history recognize the last name of Bussard. There was Rick, Terry and Larry. They were all very good players that played on memorable Olney teams. I had a chance to talk to Terry Bussard who was the leading scorer on the "Sweet Sixteen" team of 1975.

Terry Bussard: *I lost my father when I was very young. Ron was like a father figure to all of us. When I played for Ron our teams were always prepared. A* *lot of people remember what we did as seniors. What people don't realize is the season before we went to the Super Sectional we were 5-20. He had conversations with all of us and he really challenged us to turn it around. Under his leadership we were able to do that. I feel blessed that I had the opportunity to have Ron Herrin as my high school basketball coach. I coached a little bit after playing in college and I remember Ron always taking the time to sit down and talk basketball with me. He would write me personal letters to encourage me and they would always arrive at a time when I needed a good word. That is the kind of person Ron Herrin was.*

While Rich was at Benton building the Ranger program, Ron was at Olney coaching the Tigers. I love this bit of trivia. Rich and Ron played each other 16 times in their high school coaching career. They each finished 8-8. My early memories of Olney came at the Benton Invitational Tournament. I was nine years old in 1977-78 when I saw big blonde-headed Darnall Jones and his Olney Tigers square off against Johnny Fayne of the Carbondale Terriers. Those games still stand out as some of the greatest games I witnessed at Rich Herrin Gymnasium. After high school, Johnny Fayne and Darnall Jones became teammates at SIU-Carbondale. Darnall remembered those days.

Darnall Jones: *There were a couple of times we had to play Benton in the BIT… and I could just sense in Ron that there was a little bit more on the line when we faced off against Rich at Benton. We beat Benton a couple of times in that time period…you'll have to look that up. Before one of the Benton games, I remember we had a walk through and we were working on our underneath out of bounds plays. We only had about four or five plays and we went through them forever…finally I said something like, "Coach I think we got them down." He was playing his brother you know…I always remember that.*

Darnall admired how Ron handled all of the different personalities of his players. He admitted that he was sometimes the one that would not immediately fall in line, but Ron was very shrewd in dealing with him as a player.

Darnall Jones: *Ron was a very smart coach. He knew our personalities well and he knew who to get into and the players that needed encouragement. If I had a bad half, he understood that nobody was harder on themselves than me. He wouldn't single me out because he knew that about me. He might kind of* *bump into me on the way out of the locker room and just look at me like a father would his son. I would kind of always take it as Hey come on, you got to get it going.*

Much like his brother Rich, the game of basketball consumed most of his thoughts. Darnall delighted in telling a story about sneaking up behind Ron at church one Sunday.

Darnall Jones: *Growing up in Olney, I attended the St. Paul Methodist Church. Our family attended faithfully and Coach Herrin and his family were also members. Ron was a note taker….Always taking notes…beautiful penmanship…you know. I was probably in junior high, old enough to know that he was the basketball coach. The preacher was in the middle of his sermon and I saw Ron start taking notes. I was sitting in the pew behind him and leaned forward to see what he was writing. When I looked at his paper, all I saw was x's and o's…he was diagraming some plays. He was constantly thinking about ways to make his team better.*

My last question to Darnall was this; "Can you put into words the impact Coach Herrin made on your life?" Darnall paused a moment and then began to speak.

Darnall Jones: *I respected him as I would my father. He showed us how to be a man through his actions. I never heard him cuss…ever. He was about doing everything the right way. The impact and carry over he had on the lives of the guys that played for him is incredible. Matt, we had twelve or thirteen guys on our basketball team and all of them turned out to be successful. Ron had something to do with that.*

Big Darnall would go on to score close to 1,000 points in his college career at Southern Illinois University. Life after basketball has been very good; he is entering his thirty-ninth year as an agent for Country Companies Insurance. He now lives in O'Fallon, Illinois with his wife, Kim.

Ron was looked at by people in the Olney community much the way Rich was viewed in Benton. The town of Olney loved Ron Herrin and Tony Phelps remembers Ron's impact on the Olney community.

Tony Phelps: *Ron was highly respected in Olney. Not only did he bring winning teams to the court almost annually, but he was seemingly everyone's friend. He was so highly respected that in the late nineties the Olney high school gym was named in his honor.*

Today, Ron Herrin is the winningest high school basketball coach in the history of Olney High School. On his heels is current Tiger coach Rob Flanagan. Flanagan is one of the best high school basketball coaches in Southern Illinois and has embraced the legacy of Ron Herrin to teach his players about the rich history of Olney basketball.

Rob Flanagan: *When I got to Olney in '98 Ron had been gone for thirteen years. The people in town still talked about him with a great deal of respect and admiration. I got a picture of him and put it in my office. I tried to em-brace what he had done before me and let it help the program I was trying to build. We used the phrase 'Building a future from a historic past'! Ron was that past! Around 2004 we replaced the old letters that said 'Gymnasium' outside our facility with large orange letters that said 'RON HERRIN GYM'. I was very happy to get that done and have always loved coaching in a gym named after a legend. It was my way of honoring him. I have always felt like Ron was looking down from above enjoying Tiger basketball.*

When Rich left Benton High School to coach at Southern Illinois University, Ron accepted the job at Benton and coached five more seasons. In thirty-five seasons of coaching high school basketball, he earned a record of 578 wins and 372 losses. Ron is a member of the IBCA Basketball Hall of Fame.

Over the course of twenty-five years of coaching at Olney, many of Ron Herrin's players went on to become teachers and coaches. As a high school player, Dave Gray moved from Bridgeport to Olney for his senior year and looked forward to playing for Coach Herrin. Dave loved the game of basketball and he and his father thought that Olney would be a good fit. When Dave arrived for his first day of school at Olney, Ron Herrin noticed him and introduced himself. Dave laughed as he recalled their first meeting.

Dave Gray: *The gym wasn't open in the summer so this is really the first time I talked to Coach Herrin. He introduced himself and immediately asked, "Are you planning on playing basketball?" I said, "Yes." He then said, "Good, we* *have cross country practice today after school, I expect you to be there." I said, "Coach I don't have any clothes for practice." Coach then said, "Don't worry about it, I've got clothes for you."*

We started the 1964 season a little shaky. We won the first two games of the year but we really didn't play well. We had a really good team. Jim Corrona was our point guard and Rick Franklin was a solid player, among others. I was 6'5" but I was more comfortable facing the basket and my teammate Gene Piper was about 6'2" and he had always played with his back to the basket. From the first day of practice Ron assumed because I was 6'5" he would play me with my back to bucket and he moved Gene out on the floor. Gene and I were just not comfortable at our positions and we weren't playing well. I decided to talk to Coach Herrin about it and he listened to us and changed our positions. Then we just took off and won a lot of games and played so much better. My point is he listened to us and not all coaches did that in 1964.

After playing for Ron Herrin, Dave Gray went on to become a coaching legend at Norris City-Omaha-Enfield High School. Gray coached the Fighting Cardinals from 1974 to 2001. He ended his coaching career with a 432-284 record (.603). He is the winningest basketball coach in Norris City history and won back-to-back Sectional titles in 1989-1990. The 1990 team placed third in the State Tournament, finishing with a record of 31-2.

Dave Gray: *I believe Ron Herrin influenced me to coach athletics, not just basketball. He believed that it was important for kids to compete in different sports. Ron also coached track and cross country, he wasn't just a basketball coach. When I arrived at Norris City in 1974, I made it a point to encourage all of our basketball players to run track or play baseball and we had to build a track program by recruiting kids that were walking the halls at school. I always remember something Coach Gene Hale from Harrisburg told me. He said, "Your track program is an indication of how good your athletic program is."*

The 1964 Olney Tigers went on to win the Regional Championship and finish with a record of 20-8. Gray's teammates on the '64 Olney team, Jim Corrona and Rick Franklin, would also spend the rest of their lives teaching and coaching the game of basketball. Jim Corrona became somewhat of a journeyman and had coaching stints in Albion, Wapella, Effingham, Salem and Vandalia. He also coached at Cincinnati Christian University until the program was dropped. He was then hired by the NBA to organize and instruct basketball camps overseas. He is now coaching at Wayne City, Illinois and the players love his enthusiasm and passion for the game. I remember Coach Corrona at the old TMI basketball camps when I was growing up for his energy and passion. Rick Franklin went back to Olney and has coached more than forty years at Olney Junior High. Dave Gray, Jim Corrona and Rick Franklin are all part of the Ron Herrin coaching tree that went on to influence the lives of so many through the game of basketball.

Dave Gray is now retired and lives with his wife Joyce in Norris City, Illinois. They have two children, Clay and Melissa. Clay was a standout player at Norris City and played for his father on the third place team of 1990. He went on to play basketball at Union University in Tennessee.

On Saturday, May 10, 1997, Ron and Mary Lou Herrin wandered next door to a neighbor's house for an informal graduation party. Ron was engaged in a conversation with former Ranger and next door neighbor, Denny Smith. At the time, Ron was no longer coaching high school basketball. He was helping his brother at SIU and faithfully attending Cardinal baseball games with his wife Mary Lou. He made the comment to Smith that he had been having headaches. Ron then rose from his lawn chair and walked to the side of the yard where he suddenly collapsed. Emergency personnel were called to the scene. Ron was then flown by an emergency helicopter to Barnes Jewish Hospital in St. Louis, Missouri.

Rich and Sue Herrin had just returned home from a much needed getaway. As they were unloading their luggage from the car, the phone rang. Sue answered the phone and Rich could tell by the urgency in Sue's voice that this wasn't an ordinary call. Judy Dixon, a close family friend from Benton, delivered the news that Ron Herrin had collapsed at a graduation party at his neighbor's home. It wasn't good. Rich and Sue were in a state of shock. They had just seen Ron days earlier, and he was the picture of health. Rich and Sue jumped into the car and headed for the hospital. Sue said silent prayers for Ron to herself and she also worried about Mary Lou and their children. Upon arriving at the hospital, doctors had just told Mary Lou that Ron had lost brain function. He had suffered a brain aneurysm. Ron Herrin was pronounced dead at 4:30 a.m. Sunday, May 11, 1997. Ron was sixty-seven years old.

Sue Herrin: *It was a horrible blow to Rich. He and Ron were about as close as two brothers could possibly be. They had the exact same interests all their lives, and Ron had always been such a support for Rich in whatever he attempted. Of course he was the only surviving member of his immediate family, and it left a big hole in Rich's heart. So many times later he would say to me, "I'd just like to call and talk to my brother. It was heart-breaking.*

Terry Bussard: *I was living in Salt Lake City, Utah when Ron passed away. My mom called me and said, "We lost him." I knew who she meant and it was simply devastating for me, I had a really hard time with his death.*

I'm so thankful Ron was my high school basketball coach. We always had a good relationship and we won games together. Ron Herrin was one of the finest human beings I've ever known in my life. He had a tremendous impact on my life and I remember that Sunday when I got the call about his death. My good friend and former teammate, Brad Wills, called me with the news that Coach had passed. I put down the phone, went outside, dropped the tailgate on my truck, lay back in the bed…and cried. It was one of the saddest days of my life.

The visitation was held at the Benton Methodist Church where Ron and Mary Lou attended. People were wrapped around the church waiting to pay their respects to the family. It was completely silent as former players, coaches and friends waited their turn to pay their respects. I stood in line with my wife and I remember standing in front of a man named Ricky Nix. Ricky had a tire repair shop north of town for years. Over the years, Ricky had become a very close friend of both Rich and Ron. They joked with each other and Ricky was just always pleasant to be around and they would frequent his shop often. It was an overcast day, Ricky wore all black and he had sunglasses on to hide his tears.

There was a feeling at Ron's visitation of deep sorrow. I believe the sadness came from a deep need to keep him here with us. We were not ready to let him go because Ron Herrin brought God's light to all that knew him. Upon entering the church there was a full sized picture of Ron doing what he loved the most; coaching. The picture showed Ron standing in the coach's box with a towel draped around his shoulder calling timeout. When I saw the picture…it was too painful and I forced myself to look away.

Sue Herrin Vennard (Ron Herrin's daughter): *Over the course of the last few days, I've had countless people tell me that Dad was their hero that they wish they had lived their lives more like he lived his. Nearly 1,500 people came to the church to pay their respects and tell us how much they loved Dad. Most of them waited in line for at least ninety minutes. Many told us their hearts were broken. Many more were too broken up to talk. Chris Carr, the former Saluki player and member of the NBA Minnesota Timberwolves, brought one of his jerseys and asked us to bury it with Dad. Chris told us Dad has been like his second father. We also placed in the casket mementos from Olney, Benton, SIU and McKendree College. We put in a Cardinals hat because Dad loved the Cards. He went to two games in the final week of his life, both victories. My five-year-old son never missed going to a home opener with Grandpa.*

Sara Herrin (Ron's oldest daughter): *The day before he died, Dad called me at work. I was out of the office that day, but he left a message which was, essentially, "I just called to say I love you." Dad did that sort of thing a lot -- he didn't need a reason to call or write. He just wanted us to know he loved us and was thinking of us.*

Kim Herrin (Ron's youngest daughter): *At Dad's visitation, I'll never forget how many people came. There was a long line of people outside the church waiting to come in and pay their respects. So many people told stories of Dad stopping by to see them at work or home on a regular basis and making them laugh and playing pranks on them. Dad made a lot of people feel like they were his best friend. I remember that someone even said that at the visitation. I think it was Ricky Nix.*

The following day was the funeral. The funeral service was officiated by Reverend Randy Grimmett and Ron was put to rest at the Masonic and Odd Fellows Cemetery in Benton, Illinois. There were hundreds of people gathered at the cemetery and they all witnessed something they would never forget. The moment was surreal and it was as if Ron was looking down on his friends and gave them all one last sign to make them feel better. Larry Miller was a good friend of Ron's and he remembered this moment well.

Larry Miller (Good friend of Ron's who spoke at Ron's memorial service): *The moment his casket was lowered in the ground. Simultaneously,* *we looked up in the sky and saw a rainbow around the sun. Mary Lou described it as a "basketball going through a hoop." Some people said it was merely a sundog but the fact remains that it's the only one I've ever seen, it came at a highly symbolic moment, it expressed Ron's personality, and it lightened every heart--just the effect Ron would focus his will on causing. So people can say what they want about "merely a sundog" but I think--all things considered--it was Ron doing what he could for the people he loved. Why should death change that?*

Mary Lou has been without Ron for twenty-three years now. Since Ron's death she has lived quietly in Benton and is an active member of the Benton Methodist Church. She has developed many close relationships and makes it a point to stay in touch with her children. Each year her four children set aside some time each summer to come to Benton and visit. She loves to see her grandchildren and wishes that Ron could be there right in the middle of it all. Near the end of our conversation I asked her, "What are the things that you most admired about Ron?" There was a pause on the phone, and I thought that I might have asked the wrong question. She then said, "Matt, can I answer this by e-mail? I think I can give you a better answer."

Mary Lou Herrin: *It is interesting how the answer to this question changes with time. When we first met in college, I was attracted to Ron for his looks, his athleticism, his popularity on campus and the fact that he smelled good. As the years went by, I appreciated that Ron was a loving father, an attentive husband, and a good person. He was faithful in his church attendance and while he didn't talk a lot about being a Christian, it was evident in the way he treated others.*

Throughout our time together, I witnessed Ron interacting with people from all walks of life. Of course, he had special relationships with his players, often keeping in touch with them long after they played for him, especially those who became coaches themselves. He always went the extra mile to help them, whether with career advice or a personal problem. However it wasn't just athletes that Ron made time for. He was particularly kind to people who were mentally or physically challenged. He seemed to go out of his way to give those with special needs the extra attention that seemed to mean so much to them and their families.

Ron definitely had an extraordinary way of connecting to people. His interest in helping others was both sincere and altruistic. He wasn't doing these

things for appearances, nor did he ever brag about all of his good deeds...
much of that I learned about after his death. It was truly amazing how many
people that I scarcely even knew reached out to me to share a story about how
Ron had helped them (or their son or daughter) in some way. In most cases I
was unaware of these relationships. I knew I had married a good man, but the
impact he had on so many lives was even more than I had realized.

The story of Rich Herrin really begins with his older brother of three years, Ron. It is doubtful that there are two brothers that ever had a deeper affection for one another than Rich and Ron. Growing up, Rich followed his older brother everywhere and you could seldom see one without the other. As Rich got older, he followed him to McKendree, and he then followed Ron's pursuit of coaching basketball. Ron was the big brother that all of us would want and he served as Rich's protector throughout his life. Ron loved his little brother and was never jealous or resentful of his successes. He was a competitive person by nature, but he was able to put his relationship with his brother first, and basketball second. During the interviews for this book, I spoke to Rich Herrin more than one hundred times to dig information from him. Rich mentioned Ron in almost every conversation and there were times he would get choked up on the other end of the phone. Sensing this, I immediately shifted the conversation a different direction. Rich Herrin misses Ron each and every day. He loved his big brother.

Rich (1) and Ron Herrin (5) in Dieterich, Illinois in 1934.
(Ron Herrin family collection)

Ron and Rich at Amwoco Boy Scout Camp in 1946.
(Ron Herrin family collection)

Ron gladly stepped in as Mary Lou's date when she was crowned
homecoming queen at Mckendree College in the fall of 1951.
(Ron Herrin family collection)

Ron Herrin was a three sport athlete (Football, Basketball & Track)
at Mckendree College. *(McKendree College)*

Ron and Mary Lou were married on May 21st, 1952.
(Ron Herrin family collection)

Ron spent two years in the military and was assigned to Fort Gordon in Augusta, Georgia during the Korean War. *(Ron Herrin family collection)*

Ron guided Freeburg to a district championship in basketball in 1956 and then that spring led the Baseball team to a 2nd place finish in the state tournament. *(Ron Herrin family collection)*

Herrin guided the Olney Tigers to a 20-8 season and a Regional Championship in 63-64. Dave Gray is #31 and Rick Franklin is #51. Jim Corrona is the first player on the left. *(Olney East Richland High School)*

Ron Herrin and family in the late 60's. Standing from L-R is Sara Herrin, Mary Lou and Ron. Sitting from L-R is Kim, Sue and Jim.
(Ron Herrin family collection)

Tony Phelps played on the great Olney team of '75 and credits his decision to become a teacher and coach to Ron Herrin.
(Olney- East Richland High School)

Darnall Jones led the great Olney teams of the late 70's and is still the career leader in points (1573) and rebounds (818). (Olney-East Richland High School)

The 1978 team finished 21-7 and won a sectional. (Olney-East Richland High School)

The legendary match-up of Darnall Jones and Johnny Fayne of Carbondale lives on in BIT lore. Jones and Fayne later became teammates at SIU. *(SIU)*

After playing for Ron Herrin in High School, Rick Franklin was inducted into the IHSA Basketball Hall of Fame in 2011. He is now entering his 51st season as the head coach at Olney Jr. High. *(Olney- East Richland High School)*

Ron and Rich played 16 times and ironically both finished with an 8-8 record. *(Ceasar Maragni)*

Coach Rob Flanagan has carried the torch well at Olney. Flanagan needs 11 more wins to pass Ron Herrin as the winningest coach in Olney history. *(Olney- East Richland High School)*

Ron was a great basketball coach but an even better grandpa.
Here he is photographed with his oldest grandson,
Matthew in 1988. *(Ron Herrin family collection)*

Ron and Mary Lou in the early 90's while
serving as an assistant coach at SIU. *(SIU)*

Ron and Rich were as close as brothers could possibly be. Here they are in the mid-90's coaching together at SIU. *(Ron Herrin family collection)*

A picture of what is now "Ron Herrin Gymnasium" in Olney, Illinois. *(Matt Wynn)*

CHAPTER TWO

The Son of a Methodist Minister
(1933–1956)

"See…I was a little more ornery than my brother." – Rich Herrin

I arrived at the Herrin's home just before 9:a.m. Their house is nestled in the back of a quiet neighborhood sandwiched between the homes of Kyle and Kristy, the two youngest Herrin children. Coach Herrin is now retired after completing a coaching career that spanned more than sixty years. I knocked on the back door and Sue quickly greeted me with a smile. Sue Herrin is the best. She is all class. She said, "Matt, it's so nice to see you. Please come in. Can I get you something to drink?" I declined and began to explain the book to Sue. I knew there was no way I could begin to write this book without her blessing. She was with Coach through it all, and I needed her approval. As we were talking, Coach Herrin rounded the corner. He was dressed in a purple McKendree College shirt and khaki shorts. He looked me up and down and then uttered "Golly, you're bigger than a skinned mule." Translation: "I'm glad to see you!" Now, this has been a common phrase he has greeted me with for years. Sue looked down and shook her head and quietly said "Rich." I just laughed and tried to visualize a skinned mule and then snapped out of it.

Sue led us to a sitting room on the east side of the house. Coach's hair was neat and combed to the side and he sat back in his chair with a cup of coffee. I think we both felt a little awkward at first. It then dawned on me that for as much as I had been around Coach, I couldn't ever recall being in a room alone with him. When we were together it was always in the presence of others. I could tell he felt this same uneasiness. Coach broke the ice and asked, "Why do you want to write this book?" Coach was eighty-seven years old and he wanted to get the elephant out of the room as quickly as possible. Before I could answer he said, "You know, I had three of my former players from Okawville visit me about a week ago, and you know why?" I didn't say anything and waited until he answered his own question. He looked at me and said, "Because they don't think I'll be here much longer." I'm usually not very quick, but I was ready for his question. I looked him in the eye and said "First, your story needs to be told. You have a great story. I saw your teams play, I went to your camps and I played five years for you at SIU. We have been in over a thousand practices and shoot arounds together and competed in over 150 games." I then paused and said "I know enough about you to put it on paper." He grinned and said, "Let's do it."

I knew it was necessary that I set some ground rules for the interview. Coach is notorious for starting with a certain topic and finishing somewhere you never thought the conversation would go. My preacher Sammy Simmons calls it "chasing rabbits". So I asked him to try to stay close to the conversation and only answer the questions. My direct request surprised him, because I've never really directed him to do anything; he fired back and said, "Oh, going to tell me what to do...huh?" It was classic coach because he just couldn't simply comply. He had to get that dig in there. We laughed and he said, "I'll do whatever you want me to big guy ...go ahead." Coach loves to kid and play. I dated my wife, Trudee, all through college at SIU and he knew her well. When he addressed us together, he would first say "Hey, that's not the same girl I saw you with last week." That was his way of greeting us and he must have said it more than ten times to us in college. I realized it's those little nuances about Coach that make him so endearing.

After the groundwork was set, I threw a barrage of questions at him that really tested his long term memory. Questions like; what was your father like? Can you describe your house in Flat Rock? Can you tell me about your mother? I could tell he embraced the challenge of taking his mind back to the 1930's in Flat Rock, Illinois. The conversation was amazing and he told me things about himself that we had never discussed before. I couldn't write fast enough and there were times I had to slow him down. He followed the ground rules well and delivered answers without hesitation. I sat back and took it all in and then tried to put it into words.

Rich Herrin came into the world on April 6, 1933, in West Liberty, Illinois. Homer and Florence Herrin beamed as they held their new baby boy. The Herrin's already had one son, Ron, who was three years of age. Ron was excited to have a little brother and he often helped his mother Florence take care of Rich.

Homer Herrin was a Methodist minister and it seemed the Herrins were always on the move. In 1937, the family lived in a small community called Flat Rock, Illinois in a two story white house that was connected to his father's church by a sidewalk. On the first floor, Ron and Rich shared the same room and slept in the same bed. There was a small kitchen, a sitting area and their parents' bedroom. In the summer, there was no air conditioning, but fans oscillated to allow for some air flow. The house was heated by a wood stove and there were no indoor bathrooms. The top story of the home was vacant, one big space. To utilize the space, Homer hung a rim in the top floor of the house so Ron and Rich could play basketball. This was Rich's first memory of the game of basketball. He was four years old. Ron's friends would come over to play basketball, and Rich would always be the odd man out because he was the youngest but Ron would hold the ball and refuse to let play begin unless his little brother was included. This was Ron Herrin. Ron always protected his little brother and Rich followed him wherever he went. It was rare to see one without the other.

The Herrin boys grew up in a loving and supportive family. Rich described his father Homer as honest, fair, demanding, supportive and quiet. He was a man of little emotion and rarely showed affection to even his family. But there is no doubt that Homer was a good provider and a loving father. Rich knew his dad loved him because Homer never missed any of his games. He was always there, always available. By the time Rich and Ron were born, Homer had a life experience that gave light to his stern personality.

As a young man, Homer R. Herrin was drafted to fight in World War I. After basic training, he was sent to Europe and saw action in a battle that took place in France. The Great War was fought in trenches and the conditions were brutal. More soldiers in World War I died of disease and dysentery than in combat. On this day in France, Homer Herrin was engaged with the German army when he heard the cry of one of his fellow soldiers. "Gas"! Homer had been trained for this moment. He reached for his gas mask but was having trouble placing it on correctly. Mustard gas kills by blistering the lungs and throat if inhaled in large quantities.

Its effect on masked soldiers, however, was to produce terrible blisters all over the body as it soaked into their woolen uniforms. Homer Herrin was overcome by the gas and he woke up in a field hospital. He spent a month in recovery with orders to return to his battalion. When he left the field hospital to find his battalion, he got lost. For six weeks, he wandered the countryside of France begging for food and sleeping in barns. He eventually found an American unit and survived the war. There were over 100,000 US soldiers killed in World War I, but Homer Herrin was not one of them. He would survive the war, but Rich believed his experience in the Great War left a lasting impression on him.

The Herrin family still has the original letters that Homer wrote Florence, his wife-to-be, from World War I. Homer starts each letter with the greeting, "Dear Friend". True to his personality, there are no affectionate words used to describe what he may be feeling. Learning that his father dated his mother for eight years before proposing, Rich needled his dad by asking, "Dad, did Mom have to propose to you?" Homer then looked down and met eyes with young Rich and said, "None of your business." Coach laughed as he told me that story.

When Homer returned from the war, he boarded a train to attend college in Indianapolis. He was the son of a preacher himself and graduated with a degree in religion. While attending Indiana Central University, he found time to play on the baseball team. He was a quality pitcher and recorded wins against Notre Dame, Purdue and the University of Indiana.

Homer grew up in Claremont, Illinois and lived two miles from a girl named Florence Heckler. Claremont is located on the outskirts of Olney, Illinois. Homer and Florence would see each other and when Homer returned from World War I they married. It is sometimes said that opposites attract, and in this case, it was the truth. Florence was outgoing and she more than made up for Homer's quiet demeanor. She was affectionate to both Ron and Rich. Florence was heavy set with long brown braids and she handled the budget. She was an extremely good cook and was very resourceful and found ways to stretch the money. Rich said this about his mother; "She flat ran the show…I'll tell you that right now."

Rich remembers that she could be strict and demanding. He laughed at a story that he felt summed up the difference between his and Ron's personality. The boys were always outside playing and Florence would step outside the house and call them to supper. If they arrived too late, she would be waiting with a peach tree switch. Rich recalled, "When mom switched us, Ron wouldn't say anything, but I would always say something smart and get another one." Rich shrugged his shoulders and said, "See...I was a little more ornery than my brother." Rich loved his mother and made it clear that he remembers the family as "very close knit".

Coach was quick to point out that he and Ron were baptized in a creek by their father. Ron and Rich were preacher kids ("P.K.'s") and there were certain things they were not allowed to do. They were not allowed to go to the movie theater with their friends or play organized sports on Sundays. He admitted that his parents were good examples and since his dad was a minister, they were at church whenever the doors were open. Rich said, "Our parents expected us to do what was right....if we didn't... there were consequences."

It was common for Methodist ministers to always be on the move and that was definitely the case for the Herrin family. The Herrins lived in Dieterich for two years and then moved to Flat Rock. The family then moved to St. Francisville and then to Cisne. Finally, the family settled in Bridgeport where Rich and Ron graduated high school. Even though the moves were not far in distance, this had to be a tough adjustment for Ron and Rich. When I asked Rich about the moving, he said, "It's just the way it was...and I'll say this, we had one good move...and that was to Bridgeport."

The toughest move for Rich was the move to Cisne to start the fifth grade. Rich said, "I got my tail whipped by the school bully." When I asked him specifics about the incident, his elephant-like memory kicked into full gear and he quickly said, "The kid's name was Dean Powell and we later became good friends." I couldn't believe that he could remember the incident with such detail.

He told a story that indicated how competitive he and Ron were at an early age. He recalled that while living in Cisne the family had chickens. Rich said that he chose a brown-legged hen and Ron chose a white-legged hen, and they kept a record of which chicken could lay the most eggs. I asked, "Who won?" Rich said they both claimed the victory and I asked, "How could that be?" He laughed and then grumbled, "Ron's chicken laid an egg every day but they were small...my chicken laid an egg every other day...but the egg was big." I had to laugh when Rich muttered after the story, "I still think I had the better chicken."

Charlie Mix was Rich's junior high coach at Cisne. Coach Mix was inexperienced but young Rich liked his style. Rich said, "He gave us the freedom to play." As a player, Rich appreciated this new found freedom to express himself on the floor and became a firm believer that basketball is more enjoyable for the players, coaches, and especially the fans when the players are allowed to play with freedom. He would later adopt this basketball philosophy of freedom and expression as his motto. Herrin said, "Nobody wants to see a slow game...and the players enjoy a fast game... It's got to be fun."

He played on the seventh grade team as a fifth grader and the eighth grade team as a sixth and seventh grader. In those days the ball had raised laces, and if bounced directly on the laces, it took an awkward bounce. At Cisne, Rich wore the number 22 and fell in love with the game of basketball. He and Ron played all of the time.

When Rich finished the seventh grade at Cisne, his dad talked to the family about the possibility of moving to Bridgeport. Rich thought nothing about the possible move but Ron was adamant they should go. He was well aware of the size of Bridgeport's gymnasium and heard nothing but good things about its basketball program. Ron quickly piped in and said, "Dad...I wouldn't mind moving to Bridgeport at all."

Bridgeport was the home of the most spacious gymnasium in Southern Illinois. The gym seated over 4,000 people and Bridgeport played host to more sectional tournaments than any other town in the state. Rich knew it was a good move when he first walked into the gymnasium. At the time, Ron was a junior and Rich was an eighth grader.

At Bridgeport, a watershed moment occurred in the lives of both Rich and Ron. Ron was a senior and Rich a freshman when they first played for Frank "Doc" Hunsaker. Coach Hunsaker took on the name of "Doc" because as a boy he drove a horse and buggy for his uncle who was a doctor. There was something much different about Doc Hunsaker. He was a student of the game and a very good teacher. For example, Doc liked guards setting screens on big men because the defense could not switch the screens. If the defense switched it would create a mismatch. This was a revolutionary thought at the time because the game was still evolving. Doc had creative offensive patterns and he was the originator of a play called "little box". The play was part of our offense when I played at Southern. Doc was demanding. Rich said, "I was half scared of him." Both Ron and Rich grew to love coach Hunsaker.

As a freshman, Rich played on the frosh/soph team, while Ron, a senior, was the star player on the varsity team. As a sophomore Rich played junior varsity basketball. As a junior, Rich made the starting lineup and played alongside four very talented seniors. His junior year, Bridgeport was ranked eighteenth in the state, but lost to Lawrenceville in the Regional Championship. It was a disappointing loss because they had beaten Lawrenceville twice during the regular season.

At the end of his junior season, Coach Hunsaker left Bridgeport to accept the football and basketball head coaching positions at Robinson, Illinois. Rich's senior year at Bridgeport was a good one, but coincidently it would be Robinson that knocked off the Bulldogs in the semi-final of the Regional Tournament.

Rich graduated from Bridgeport High School in 1951. Later in life, Doc Hunsaker invited Rich and Ron with their wives for a weekend getaway to his summer home in Holten, Michigan. Doc would later say that both Rich and Ron were in the top five athletes he ever coached. Frank "Doc" Hunsaker was inducted into the Illinois Basketball Coaches Hall of Fame in 1978. He passed away of natural causes in 1990.

McKendree College (1951-1955)

Rich followed his brother to McKendree College in Lebanon, Illinois. It was the fall of 1951, and his college roommate was his big brother Ron. Ron was a senior and very well known on the McKendree campus. Ron played football, basketball and ran track at McKendree and earned ten varsity letters. Rich explained that he and Ron were not recruited like the athletes of today. Rich explained that education was important to his father and he expected both of them to go to college after high school. Homers Methodist church in Bridgeport supported McKendree college with financial donations and P.K.'s (preacher's kids) got a tuition break. McKendree College it would be.

Rich loved McKendree and rooming with his older brother helped him transition to being away from home. Rich took his classes seriously and excelled in the classroom. He also began to improve as a basketball player. As a freshman, Rich started three games with his brother. Rich shared a funny story he referred to as the "brotherly love" incident that happened in a game against Eureka College. Evidently, both Ron and Rich started the game and Rich scored seven of the first eleven points of the game. All of Rich's points had come from assists by his brother Ron. Rich was then subbed out of the game. He jogged to the bench and grabbed a towel. Team statistician, Jim Reddon, looked down at Rich and said, "I like teamwork but looks to me there is a little brotherly love going on." Rich fumed, but he kept it too himself. The next day, as part of a campus job, Rich and Ron were painting the cafeteria. Rich told Ron what had happened and Ron dropped the paint brush immediately to go look for Jim Redden. Upon finding Redden, Ron quickly confronted him with Rich's story. Redden said it was true and quickly apologized.

In his third year at McKendree, Coach was in a very serious automobile accident. I asked Coach, "Can you tell me what you remember about the night of that car crash?" I then said, "I totally understand if you don't want to talk about it." He met my eyes and said, "I'll tell you what I remember." He paused for a moment and the grimace on his face said it all.

Coach told me that the accident occurred during the fall of his junior year. The McKendree basketball team had a scrimmage game at Centralia. There were two games. Rich was going to get a ride after the game from teammate Virgil Motsinger. The problem was Virgil played in the first game and Rich was to play in the second game. Virgil asked Rich, "Can you get a ride with someone after your game? I'm going to go on." Rich told Virgil, "Go ahead and go, I'll find a ride." After the game, Rich crawled into the car with teammate Van Musgrave. Musgrave had a new '53 white Ford. There were six players in the car, three in the front and three in the back. Rich said that he sat in the middle of the front seat. Musgrave agreed to take Rich to Mt. Vernon to meet his parents, Homer and Florence. It was approximately 10:00 p.m. and Musgrave was racing well over the speed limit. He came up behind a driver that was going slow. There was a viaduct ahead and Musgrave began to pass. As Musgrave's car began passing they could see lights in the on-coming traffic lane. Musgrave's car was moving at a speed of 65 mph on contact, and it was a violent collision. Coach told me, "The only thing I remember was the fear before impact. I didn't wake up until approximately 2:00 p.m. the next afternoon. I suffered a broken right leg and left arm, along with a broken jaw." I asked Coach, did anyone die?" He looked down and said, "One boy died months after the crash and the driver of the other car did not make it." Rich did not finish the season and received a medical red-shirt.

With Ron now graduated and married, Rich's new roommate was George "Tip" Butler. As a senior in high school, Butler was the leading scorer of the North Egyptian Conference. Rich spent much of his time practicing on his own and his game improved by leaps and bounds.

During this time, he became close friends with college teammate, Rich Stein. Stein lives in O'Fallon and is a retired teacher and junior high basketball coach. Stein remembers Rich well as a player at McKendree College.

Rich Stein (McKendree Teammate): *Rich was as hard-nosed a player as you could find. He was a great competitor and a great rebounder for his size. He was the toughest player I ever played with.*

Head coach Hugh Redden left McKendree after Rich's freshman year. The Bearcats hired coach James E. Collie to replace Reddon. Rich enjoyed playing for Coach Collie. Rich's senior year, the Bearcats hosted Blackburn and the game was played at the New Baden High School gym. It was a game that Rich would never forget. That night he set a single game McKendree scoring record of 47 points. Rich Stein played in the game and remembers it well.

Rich Stein: *At the start of the third quarter Coach Collie called a timeout and he ordered Rich to go to the end of the bench to get a drink. He wanted Rich to leave so he could talk to us without Rich being present. Coach Collie was aware that Rich had a shot at the scoring record…he told us to look for him if possible. Rich didn't force any shots, he just played.*

Rich's senior season at McKendree was a memorable one. The team won the league and the Bearcats received a nomination to the NAIA Illinois State Tournament. McKendree reached the final four where they matched up against Wheaton College. Wheaton College was the defending NAIA state champions and entered the game with a record of 25-1. Wheaton College defeated McKendree in the semi-final matchup by just eight points.

In the spring of 1956, Rich Herrin graduated from McKendree College with honors. He double majored in chemistry and physical education. It was now time for Rich to "find his life's work".

Sue Herrin

There is a popular saying that states: "Behind every good man is a great woman". This statement applies to Rich Herrin. There were many decisions Herrin made during his life but the decision to marry Sue Herrin proved to be his greatest. Sue Herrin was in college at Southern Illinois University when Rich first accepted the job at Okawville High School.

During our interview at his home, I asked Coach how they met and he craned his neck back and hollered, "Sue…Suzy!" I was tickled and he glared at me and said, "Quit laughing at me…I can still whip you!" Sue came into the room and Coach said, "Matt has a question for you." Sue sat down and I asked her how she and Rich first met. They looked at each other and kind of chuckled and she told me the story.

Sue Herrin: *It would have been October of 1956 and I was dating a guy named Larry Grove. I had four tickets to an SIU football game and I asked Larry to go and it just so happened that Larry Grove knew Rich, so he asked Rich to go. It was my job to find Rich a date, which was kind of hard to do. I never could find Rich a date so he just came to Carbondale with Larry?. He was kind of the third wheel. We had a nice time and Larry and I happened to break up. Time went by and Rich had a night class at Benton. It was a botany class. He left class and went to a phone booth and called me at my sorority house. He asked me on a date. Our first date was at the old Orpheum Theater in Marion. It used to sit where the civic center sits now. I believe that was January of 1957. He proposed in August and we got married December 21, 1957.*

The former Sue Cooksey was a native of Marion, Illinois. She had two sisters and one brother and recalled that her family was very close. Her father was Benjamin Harvey Cooksey and her mother went by Elizabeth Keller Cooksey. Sue remembered her father as always upbeat and in a good mood. He was known as "Sunshine" to his friends. Sue was very close to her mother Elizabeth. Elizabeth stayed at home with the children and was an excellent cook. She was also a very accomplished seamstress. Sue recalls her making most of the clothing for the children and even the dresses she wore to high school homecomings and proms. Sue Cooksey Herrin was the homecoming queen at Marion High School in 1954.

While speaking to coach Dave Luechtefeld on the phone, he said something really profound. Dave and I were talking about Sue, and he broke in quickly to make the following point.

Coach Dave Luechtefeld: *Coach Herrin and I are very alike in one way. We both picked good wives. I have a wonderful and supportive wife (Flo) and I certainly see that in Sue. The fact that our wives bought into the life of being a coach's wife made it so much easier.*

Sue Herrin was Rich's greatest supporter. I asked Sue about the challenges of being a coach's wife and she took her time with the answer.

Sue Herrin: *There are many challenges to being a coach's wife. First of all, if your husband is a dedicated coach, which mine was, he is going to spend a lot of time away from home. Between practices, games, attending lower-level games, scouting, etc., most coaches are gone nearly every night. Rich was. I'll admit…I questioned a lot of those demands on his time. Rich was also A.D. which only added more time away. Our children were also in a lot of athletic activities, which took a lot of our time. I will have to say, between teaching, cooking, laundry, attending games, and all the other things expected of a mom, it was a full-time job. Of course there is always the criticism a coach and his family have to endure, but the fun we had through the years with the great teams and fans outweighed all of that. The years went pretty fast, and I would do it all over again if I could.*

Although the Herrin family shared Coach with so many people, there is nobody that knew him better than Sue. I asked Sue this question; what is something about Coach Herrin that others wouldn't know? She paused and carefully put together her answer.

Sue Herrin: *He could come across as harsh sometimes…maybe…but he was a softy at home…especially as he got older. He also liked to do other things than just basketball. He liked to hunt, fish, boat and wood working. He didn't like to watch t.v. or read. He liked activity. He also loved to camp…we would do that when the boys were young. Later on, he loved being on his tractor or his lawn mower…he didn't like to sit.*

All of the children loved their mother and were quick to give credit to Sue for all of their dad's successes.

Rod Herrin: *When it comes down to it Dad was a great guy…but the one thing some people don't realize is that he wouldn't have been the kind of man he was without Mom. He would tell you that too…he loved Mom as much as she loved him. The two of them together were unbelievable. Mom is the best.*

Randy Herrin: *My mom was 100% supportive of my dad. She sat at so many games and did it wholeheartedly. She supported us at every level of our life. Dad was the coach and the big man and all, but she ran the house* *and kept all of us grounded. And Dad needed that. She was the glue in our family. Mom is one of the strongest women I've ever seen. What you see is what you get. She is one of the sweetest yet toughest ladies there are...she was the rock.*

Kyle Herrin: *Mom definitely ran the show. She didn't take any crap either. I have the best mom a guy could have. She didn't teach for ten years because she focused on raising us. She was always there. She went to too many games and she was probably tired of that but she was always there supporting Dad. Dad was gone quite a bit...especially with the athletic director's job. My dad was so lucky to have her...I have an incredible mom and I was blessed to have the parents that I had.*

Kristy Herrin: *Dad was gone a lot...you know...it was really the three of us because the boys were so much older. I almost felt like an only child. I think there were times that Mom wished that Dad was home more often...but she was quieter...much more reserved. I've seen her get really fired up before. There were times that our vacations were centered on recruiting trips to Chicago and even Los Angeles. We got lost in a few neighborhoods...it was kind of scary. But Mom was the backbone...she did so much and she was my go-to person for anything that I was struggling with emotionally.*

In June, 2020, Sue brought Coach Herrin to our home in Benton and dropped him off. Coach was not driving at the time. Coach walked into the house and quickly commented, "You hanging meat in here." I'm a sweat hog and we keep it about 68 degrees in the house. I should have known better. I said, "Coach, do you want a blanket?" He popped back, "I hope to tell you I do." So I grabbed him a yellow blanket and he sat on the couch and fielded questions wrapped in a blanket with only his head peeking over the top. I asked him if he wanted something to drink and he barked, "Yeah, I want some hot chocolate!"

As the day came to an end, I said, "Coach, I can take you home." He said, "Ok, let me call Sue to tell her." As we climbed into my car, Coach dialed Sue's number. There was no answer. I asked him a question...but he didn't answer. He tried to call again for Sue...no answer. Then I could see that he was worried. He then called his granddaughter who lives near their home to go over and check on her. He called her number again... no answer. I realized there was to be no conversation until he found Sue. Finally, Sue called...and you could just see this feeling of relief come over him. He then went right back to our conversation with much enthusiasm and his whole mood came alive. He found Sue.

Rich Herrin: *Sue is tremendous…she was always supportive…She always knew what to say and when to say it. I overachieved when I found my wife… just like you did.*

Homer and Florence Herrin were loving parents to
Rich and Ron. *(Ron Herrin family collection)*

The Herrin family lived in Cisne, Illinois during the World War II
years of the early 40's. *(Ron Herrin family collection)*

As a 7th grader at Cisne, Illinois, Rich chose to wear 22 in honor of
his boyhood idol Dwight "Dike" Eddleman of Centralia.
(Rich Herrin family collection)

Rich and Ron had great respect for their high school coach,
"Doc" Hunsaker. *(Ron Herrin family collection)*

As a senior at Bridgeport High School in 1951, Herrin earned
the nickname "Bull" for his tenacious rebounding and hustle.
(Rich Herrin family collection)

George "Tip" Butler was Herrin's good friend and roommate at
McKendree College. *(McKendree College)*

Rich Stein was a Herrin's teammate at Mckendree and they became life-long friends. *(McKendree College)*

Rich and Sue Herrin married on December 21st, 1957. *(Rich Herrin family collection)*

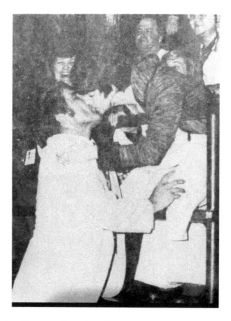

Sue was Rich's best friend and greatest supporter. The Herrin's celebrate a big win in the late 70's. *(Rich Herrin family collection)*

Rich and Sue's picture in the SIU media guide in '92. (SIU)

The Herrin family (Circa 1988). Sitting L-R Coach Herrin, Kristy, and Sue. Standing L-R Kyle, Rod and Randy. *(Rich Herrin family Collection)*

CHAPTER THREE

First Stop… Okawville

"Coach Herrin was ahead of his time" – Dave Luechtefeld

My junior year of high school, a car load of my buddies and I road-tripped to St. Louis to watch the Cardinals. On the trip to the game we pulled off on the Okawville exit and decided to eat at the Hen House. We all jumped out of the car and raced in to get a bite to eat. The waitress sat us in a booth by a wall and then gave us our menus. I knew what I wanted and just started studying the place. Near our booth were some black and white pictures of older Okawville basketball teams. I love that kind of stuff, so I went over to get a closer look. The first thing that struck me was the records of the teams; 1957-22-6, 1958-27-2, 1959-23-5, 1960-23-4. Wow! I said to myself, those are some strong teams. I then started reading the names of the players. I found Dave Luechtefeld and knew he was the present coach at Okawville. His son Jeff was my age and he was a good player. I also saw the name Herbie Dingwerth. I thought, maybe this is Doug's dad. These were familiar names to me. I scanned the caption to look for the coach's name. To my surprise, it read, "Coach Rich Herrin". I studied the young coach in the back row just to make sure it was the same Rich Herrin that I knew. He was younger and thinner but it was him. I remember thinking to myself, how old is this guy? That was the first time I realized that Coach Herrin had begun his coaching career at Okawville High School.

Obviously, the Rockets had talent, but I was curious how Coach had landed in Okawville. So I asked Coach Herrin, "How did you get the Okawville job?" He grinned and then told me the story.

It was the spring semester of Rich's senior year at McKendree College. The Bearcats had just been eliminated in the final four by Wheaton College. To earn a little extra spending money, Rich went to Lebanon High School to referee a sophomore basketball tournament. Later that day, he officiated a game between Okawville and Trenton. When he grabbed the ball to start the center jump, he was amazed at the size of the young man jumping center for Okawville. As the game got underway, he noticed that Okawville was pretty talented. The young man that jumped center that day for the Flares was Dave Luechtefeld. Luechtefeld was big and he could play. Herrin noticed him immediately. He then noticed a scrappy guard that could really shoot it. There was a break in the action and Herrin went to the official book to get the names of some of the Okawville players. He found the name Herb Dingwerth by the corresponding number. Then there was another that caught his eye, a player by the name of Loyd Karmeier. The young Rockets made an impression on Herrin. They had players coming.

In the summer of 1956, Ron Herrin was teaching and coaching at Freeburg and learned the Okawville basketball job was open. He gave his little brother a call. Rich had just graduated from McKendree and was job hunting. Rich remembered the young Rockets and was interested. He knew the pieces were in place to win at Okawville.

When Rich found out about the job opening, he asked Coach Collie to go with him to Okawville to inquire about the job. Okawville principal L.L. McDaniel informed Rich they were going to hire that night. It was late July and school was approaching. Rich realized he had a problem. He had to take Coach Collie back to Lebanon and then get back to Ashley to find a suit to wear to the interview. He was living with his parents in Ashley, Illinois at the time. There was just no way he could make it back to Ashley and then to Okawville. He raced back to Lebanon and dropped off Coach Collie and then sped to his big brother Ron's house in Freeburg. Ron gave Rich one of his best suits to wear for the interview.

Principal McDaniel was older and looked like the typical high school principal of the time. Rich would later learn that Mr. McDaniel was less than supportive of athletics but he needed a job and Okawville needed to hire quickly. The Okawville Board of Education hired Rich

Herrin by a unanimous vote. He would follow his brother, who was at Freeburg, and be a teacher and basketball coach. It was his first job and he was excited.

Rich Herrin: *I knew the job was very good because I knew about Dave Luechtefeld, Herbie Dingwerth and Loyd Karmeier. What I didn't know was that Stan Luechtefeld was going to be a freshman and they had another brother named Gerald. There was some talent…*

Rich pulled into town with his home on a trailer. The Rockets had a very good season the year before under head coach Wayne Nelson. Nelson was a good basketball coach and the players were really sad to see him go. Rich would have to prove himself.

Okawville is a community of German immigrants that have very distinguished surnames. In its heyday, Southern Illinoisans from a wide area sojourned here, enjoyed its mineral baths, and drank copious amounts of water from a spring. In the late 19th century, Okawville was a prominent spa community. The first Okawville Springs Hotel was established in 1867. The town is located in the northwest region of Washington County and is about forty-three miles southeast of St. Louis. Today, it is an agricultural community but there are many people that make the commute to St. Louis for their employment. The town has a population of about 1,400 people. The average enrollment at Okawville High School is approximately 175-200 students.

When Coach Herrin arrived at Okawville in 1956, he was surrounded by people that placed work above everything, including basketball. The school's gymnasium was extremely small. There were only bleachers on one side and the walls crowded the out of bounds lines on the ends and one sideline. The gym held 200 people. Between 1956 and 1960, the Rich Herrin-coached Rockets would use their size and small gym to their advantage to post a perfect 39-0 record at home.

Today, the Rockets have a state of the art facility that holds more than 2,800 people. Here is an amazing fact about the Okawville basketball program: there have only been two head basketball coaches since 1962. Coaching stability is a big reason the Rockets have been so successful over a long period of time. Dave Luechtefeld took over the Rockets program in 1962 and left in 2000. In thirty-eight seasons, Dave Luechtefeld had an amazing record of 738-348. He won nine Regional Championships along with seven Sectional Championships. He coached teams that finished third in the state tournament in 1980 and second in 1987. He is the Rich Herrin of Okawville.

Another reason for the basketball success in this small town is talent. Okawville has had some great players. McLeansboro coach Curt Reed once told me, "There are three things that make a good basketball coach." He paused and looked very serious at me and said, "First, you got to have talent." I could agree with that so I nodded my head. He paused and looked at me sternly again and asked, "You know what number two is?" I shook my head no. He said, "Number two…you got to have talent." By now he made his point, but he went on to finish his story, "and number three…you got to have talent." The Rockets had talent.

Most importantly, basketball is important to the people of Okawville. For the people of Okawville, basketball is a common thread in the community. The fans are knowledgeable and take great pride in their team. As is the case with most small towns, the school serves as the identity of the community. People make it a priority to attend the games. Young boys grow up with dreams of being a Rocket and so the cycle goes.

I called Dave Luechtefeld at his home in Okawville, Illinois. Coach Luechtefeld was kind and gracious with his time. I asked him this question: What was special about playing for Coach Herrin?

Dave Luechtefeld: *I've never known anybody more dedicated to basketball. Other than his family, all he could think about was basketball.*

He then went on to tell me a story that confirms his "eat, sleep and drink" attitude about basketball.

Dave Luechtefeld: *There was a time we were at a coaches' meeting…I forget where it was. Brad Weathers, Dick Corn, Coach Herrin and myself were sitting at this table talking about basketball. You know…that is all Coach really wants to talk about. So Coach Herrin gets up to go to the bathroom and I told Brad and Dick," When he comes back, let's talk about something other than basketball and see how long it takes before he changes the conversation back to basketball." Coach Herrin comes back and sits down and we started in on some random subject…I can't remember. He was quiet for about thirty seconds and then interrupted us and veered the conversation back to basketball. We just laughed…and he just looked at us.*

Dave Luechtefeld and his brothers grew up on a dairy farm and work came first. He had two brothers; Stan and Gerald. All three were very good basketball players. Dave was the oldest brother and their father's name was Sidney Luechtefeld. In 1957, Sidney came down with tuberculosis. Dave was a junior. Their mother, Vera, helped the boys pick up the slack left in Sidney's absence. They milked cows early in the morning before school and late into the night. Dave remembers that his father was a wonderful man and a tough guy. Nothing got in the way of work.

Dave and Stan went on to play college basketball at St. Louis University. Dave's sons, Jeff and Ryan, along with his daughter, Donna, played basketball at Saint Louis University. Dave's oldest son, Keith, was a Division III All-American at Illinois Wesleyan. Saint Louis University did a very classy thing in 2011 and inducted Dave and his three children into the Billiken Hall of Fame. Stan Luechtefeld, Dave's younger brother, was also inducted. Dave recalled how he always thought Coach Herrin was ahead of his time.

Dave Luechtefeld: *When he first came to Okawville he just outworked people. Coach Herrin was ahead of his time because most basketball coaches at that time were just doing it for a little extra money. There weren't a lot of guys that made coaching basketball a profession. I guess Duster Thomas at Pinckneyville…Trout at Centralia….Changnon at Mt. Vernon. It was Rich's profession. He wanted to be a basketball coach. Today it's very different. Most coaches today make it a profession…they go to clinics…they work at it. It wasn't that way with all coaches at that time.*

Dave's younger brother, Stan, was a sophomore on the 1958 Rockets. Stan was a very good player and followed his brother Dave to Saint Louis University to play for the Billikens. He recalled the first time he ever laid eyes on Coach Herrin.

Stan Luechtefeld: *I remember when Coach Herrin came to our house for the first time. We lived on a farm and we were all out working. He came driving up in a Studebaker, I believe. He got out of the car and started talking about basketball. My dad looked him in the eyes and said, "I don't think the boys will be playing this year." Coach Herrin was kind of stunned and beside himself. I think Dad was joking but it was hard to tell. As time went on we all played and enjoyed playing for Coach Herrin.*

The biggest negative at Okawville during the Rich Herrin years is that basketball in Illinois was a one-class system. The Rockets had to get by Centralia in the Regional Tournament to advance to a Sectional. Along with Centralia, there were other quality teams in the region such as Breese, Nashville and Mt. Vernon. It was difficult to advance in State Tournament play for a small school like Okawville. It would take a very special team to advance. The 1958 Rockets were special.

The '58 Rockets featured four very good players led by floor general Herbie Dingwerth. Herbie's older brother Don was an All-State player in 1955. Herbie did his duty by pumping the ball inside to the Luechtefelds, but he could also score.

Rich Herrin: *Herbie could play…I didn't realize how good Herbie really was until I got to Benton. He was as good as the best point guards I had at Benton. He could really play…he ran the show for us.*

In our phone interview, Herbie was a delight. He enjoyed reminiscing about the 1958 season and spoke with gratitude when asked about the impact Coach Herrin had on his life.

Herbie Dingwerth: *I was one of nine children and my mom raised us all. My senior year Coach Herrin gave me three pair of tennis shoes because we wore the same size. He knew I needed those shoes. He did a lot for me. He is really the reason I went to college. Coach Herrin talked me into living with a host family (the Coe Family) when I went to junior college in Centralia. I played one year there and then went to Murray State to get a teaching degree. I wanted to teach and coach.*

After graduating from Murray State with a teaching degree, he returned to Okawville and was hired to teach junior high science and coach basketball and baseball. He would serve as the junior high basketball coach from 1963-2001. Herb taught the fundamentals at the junior high level and played a key role in helping build the great Rocket basketball program.

The Rockets had a solid season in 1957, finishing 22-6. They were eliminated in the District Tournament by Breese 50-44. In that season, there was a game that was noteworthy. The Rockets defeated Vergennes by a score of 129-51. In that game, Dave Luechtefeld set a single game scoring record of 64 points. Herbie Dingwerth remembered the game.

Herbie Dingwerth: *I remember that Coach Herrin knew that he could possibly get the scoring record and he told us that nobody can shoot in the fourth quarter except David. I stole the ball one time and was out ahead of everybody and waved David down the floor and then shoveled it to him so he could score.*

In 1958, the Rockets were ready to make a run at the State Championship. Along with Dave Luechtefeld, Herbie Dingwerth and Stan Luechtefeld, there was Loyd Karmeier. Karmeier was a very good rebounder and defender. He was the second leading free throw shooter on the team behind Herbie Dingwerth.

Loyd Karmeier: *Coach Herrin was always intense and he was a great student of the game. He loved and lived basketball. I remember he would always kick the bleacher if we made a mistake.*

Loyd Karmeier grew up much like the Luechtefeld brothers. He lived on a dairy farm and work came before basketball. He had wonderful parents that worked hard and were a good example. Judge Karmeier would graduate from Okawville in 1958 and attend the University of Illinois. He first wanted to be an engineer but then went to law school. He would practice law for twenty-two years in Washington County. He would later become the States Attorney and he is currently serving as an Illinois Supreme Court Justice. He now lives in Nashville, Illinois and will soon be celebrating his 55th wedding anniversary. He has two daughters and six grandchildren. Loyd admitted that Coach Herrin was a positive influence in his life. I asked, "In what ways?"

Loyd Karmeier: *He was a good example to us in that he worked hard. He was extremely dedicated and was always pursuing a goal.*

The Rockets opened the much anticipated '58 basketball season with a win over Valmeyer 80-45. Early in the season, the Rockets beat a tough Columbia team, 62-53. The team won the Clinton County Tournament by defeating Mulberry Grove 36-33 and entered Regional play with a record of 25-1. As the Regional Tournament drew near, the town grew excited with anticipation. Unfortunately, Stan Luechtefeld was not feeling good and this is where the story gets interesting.

Stan Luechtefeld: *I was sick and not feeling well…it was right before the Regional Tournament was to begin. My brother David took me to the doctor to get some medicine. When we were coming home Dave was going as slow as he could and it was icy on the roads. The roads were turtle-backed with steep ditches. We slid off the road and the car turned over. We both crawled out of the car. I had the medicine bottle open and it was all over the car. We got a ride to Coach Herrin's trailer and then eventually got home.*

After the car accident, Stan's fever spiked to 103 and he was under doctor's orders not to play in the Salem Regional. The Rockets made it to the Regional finals by defeating Sandoval and then Mater Dei. Basketball powerhouse, Centralia, was next up. Stan was the second leading scorer and rebounder on the team, but he was unable to play. The Rockets played well, but did not have enough fire power to beat Centralia. The Orphans won the game 64-60 in a packed house at Salem. Today, all of the players believe that with Stan, they would have won. It was a tough break.

Herbie Dingworth: *I believe we would have won with Stan…No doubt about it. We sure didn't get any breaks from the officials that night either.*

Centralia had roughly 700 more students than Okawville. This was a frustration that went on for a long time. With that being said, Dave went on to tell me one of his favorite memories in his long coaching tenure at Okawville.

Dave Luechtefeld: *A memorable moment for me is when we beat Centralia in 1970 in the Regional Championship. It was still a one-class system in 1970 and Centralia had won seventy-five straight regional games before we beat them. We then beat Mt. Vernon in the Super-Sectional and went to the State Tournament. That was pretty exciting.*

After Dave Luechtefeld retired from coaching in 2000, he served as a Republican member of the Illinois Senate, representing the 58th District from September, 1995, until January 2017.

Today, Dave's younger brother, Stan Luechtefeld, lives in St. Louis County, Missouri. He lives with his wife Judy and they have two children. His son Steve works in sales and his daughter Debbie is a doctor of psychiatric medicine. I thought this was a true and gracious statement that Stan Luechtefeld said in our interview.

Stan Luechtefeld: *I think it's great that you're writing a book about Coach Herrin. He certainly deserves it. You know who else needs a book? my brother David.*

I learned a great deal while researching the basketball history of the Okawville Rockets. As I researched the numbers, I just could not get over Dave Luechtefelds success and longevity (1962-2000) as a coach. It is incredible. To give you a historical perspective, he began at Okawville when John F. Kennedy was President and left the last year of Bill Clinton's term.

Coach Jon Kraus has picked up where Coach Luechtefeld left off and the program is thriving. Kraus was a solid guard at Okawville in the early nineties and he played under Dave Luechtefeld.

I love the story that Herb Dingwerth told me about the tennis shoes and he was adamant to point out that it was Herrin who really encouraged him to go to college. Dingwerth coached at the Junior High at Okawville for thirty-eight years also. Think about how many lives have been touched by Dave Luechtefeld and Herbie Dingwerth. At Okawville, Rich Herrin left his lasting mark through the long and successful coaching careers of Dave Luechtefeld and Herbie Dingwerth who influenced the lives of so many young men that played in the Rockets program.

Since 1956 at Okawville High School, including the Herrin Years, the boys basketball program has a record of 1265-611 (.674 winning percentage). They have one State Championship in 2018, two second place finishes (1987 and 2017) and one third place finish in 1980. Today, the Okawville Rockets remain one of the most successful high school basketball programs in the State of Illinois.

Coach Herrin in his first year at Okawville in the fall of 1956.
(Rich Herrin family collection)

In 1958, Dave Luechtefeld led the Rockets to an impressive 27-2 season. He
would later coach the Rockets from 1962-2000 amassing 738 wins. *(Okawville
High School)*

Stan Luechtefeld came down with mono and didn't play in the '58 Regional
Tournament. Stan was a force in the paint and later
played at St. Louis University along with his big brother Dave.
(Okawville High School)

Herrin had many great point guards and believed Herbie Dingwerth ranked as
one of the best point guards he ever coached at the
high school level. *(Okawville High School)*

Loyd Karmeier started on the great '58 team and is now serving as an Illinois
Supreme Court Justice. *(Okawville High School)*

Herrin's first great high school team was the '58 Rockets who were
nipped by Centralia in the Regional Championship. The team
finished 27-2. (Okawville High School)

Dave Luechetefeld became a coaching legend at Okawville High School and later served as an Illinois Senator.

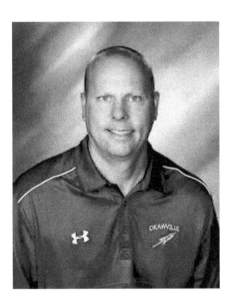

Jon Kraus replaced Dave Luechtefeld as the Rockets head coach in the fall of 2000 and has kept the Okawville basketball machine thriving. *(Okawville High School)*

CHAPTER FOUR

The Miracle Run of the
'61 Rangers

"I think winning the Super-Sectional in '61 was the spark that set Rich's career on fire." – Sue Herrin

Rich Herrin sat anxiously outside the board room at Benton High School waiting his turn. Benton High School principal Mr. Herbert Mundell then cracked the door and motioned him into the room. As Herrin took his seat, the board members studied his every move. The smell of cigarette smoke wafted through the room as Herrin confidently fielded all of the questions from the seven BCHS board members. He was young and in formal dress, complete with a tie. He carried an impressive resume into the room. In four seasons at Okawville, Herrin had not lost a home game and compiled a jaw-dropping 95-17 record. He interviewed that night with a nothing-to-lose attitude knowing that if he wasn't hired, he would simply return to Okawville and keep winning games. He felt no pressure. Rich Herrin was one of the best young coaches in Southern Illinois and his success at Okawville spoke for itself.

Herrin knew very little about Benton, Illinois. He had heard of the great football player and shotput state champion John Bauer, but that was about it. Before he interviewed for the Benton job, he did some digging and came to the conclusion that Benton had potential. Herrin was impressed that the school had a last hour athletic period which was a sure sign that the administration valued athletic participation. Last hour athletics meant basketball practice at Benton began at 2:30 and players that lived in "feeder" communities (Ewing, Akin, and Logan) were transported home by bus after practice. It served as a great way to ensure that boys living in the country could participate in athletics, and Herrin liked the concept. Benton also played in the old South Seven Conference which was the toughest league in Southern Illinois. The Conference at the time featured Benton, Centralia, Harrisburg, Herrin, Marion, Mt. Vernon and West Frankfort. Carbondale would later be added to the conference. He was also keenly aware of the history of the conference, especially in basketball. He knew that Arthur Trout coached thirty-seven seasons at Centralia, beginning in 1914, and led the Orphans to three State Championships. Herrin also knew of Stan Changnon's back-to-back State Championships in 1949-1950 with the Mt. Vernon Rams. On a more personal note, Benton was closer to Bridgeport (Rich's family) and Marion (Sue's family) than Okawville. All of these factors made Benton an attractive job.

Coach Rich Herrin: *There were seven board members in the room along with Herbert Mundell and Claude Rhodes. I taught with a man named Russell Weger at Okawvill. He taught agriculture. He was married to Mike McCarty's sister. That was my only connection to Benton. John Cherry told me the underclassmen at Benton were pretty good. There were eighteen applicants for two jobs ...I really felt the interview went well. I felt I had it when I left.*

After the interview, Principal Mundell instructed Herrin that he would receive a phone call later that evening informing him of the board's decision either way. Herrin interviewed well. President of the board, Mike McCarty, pushed for Herrin and in a unanimous decision, Rich Herrin was hired as the new basketball coach at Benton High School. The board was impressed with Herrin, and why wouldn't they be? Besides his incredible coaching record, he could bring youth and ambition to an aging BCHS faculty and staff. He was also the son of a Methodist minister, which couldn't hurt. The board didn't take long to decide. Moments later, Herbert Mundell picked up the phone and called Rich Herrin to offer him the head basketball job at Benton High School. Herrin quickly accepted. Little did he know, but with that simple phone call, Herbert

Mundell changed the course of the community of Benton for the next twenty-five years.

Sue Herrin: *Rich and I lived in a trailer the entire time we lived in Okawville, so when he got the Benton job, we packed up our home and went to Benton. Rich and his dad pulled the trailer down, and Rodney, our one-year-old son, Grandma Herrin and I took our station wagon. It was packed to the gills on top, and when we arrived in Benton around lunchtime we pulled into the Dog and Suds north of town to get a bite to eat. Being so excited at arriving in Benton, I forgot I had stuff on top of the station wagon, and when I pulled under the canopy I knocked out all of the lights in the Dog and Suds. People came running and hollering from every direction. I was so embarrassed! What a grand entrance into my new home. Especially in front of my relatively new mother-in-law. We rented a small lot on Beatrice Street one block south of the high school on which to put our trailer. It was very convenient for Rich as he could just walk down to the school and gym. We lived there for a year. We then bought the Dairy Treet and moved our trailer to North Main behind the Dairy Treet.*

Before Rich Herrin accepted the basketball job at Benton High School there were some lean years. Under the guidance of Ralph Davison, the Rangers recorded a dismal 68-101 from 1954-1960. The 1959 Rangers did manage to win twenty games and win the Sectional Tournament. They were led by captains Vic Tasky and Jeff Ferguson. In the trophy case at Rich Herrin Gymnasium, there is a classic team picture of the '59 Rangers in the locker room after the victory. The game nets drape around the necks of Tasky and teammate Jeff Ferguson as the Rangers celebrate the victory. This was the lone bright spot in six years and Ranger fans were ready for winning basketball on a more consistent basis.

Today, there are a total of fifteen maroon banners that line the east end rafters at Rich Herrin Gymnasium. These banners represent all the Ranger teams that qualified for the State Tournament. From top to bottom, the banners display the state finish, the year and the team record. Most of the team records are impressive. For example, the '66 team was 31-1, and the '67 team was 30-1. The '33 Rangers are the winningest team in school history with a record of 35-1. The banner displaying the '61 team record of 17-13 naturally piques the curiosity of the Basketball fan. What happened? How did this team get to the Elite Eight? The improbable run of the '61 Rangers set the table for what would be twenty five years of Ranger basketball dominance. The '61 team has a story similar to the underdog town of Hickory, in the classic basketball movie "Hoosiers."

Unfortunately, Vic Tasky and Jeff Ferguson were out of high school eligibility after their "Sweet Sixteen" run of 1959. The question was this: who were the '60-'61 Rangers? When the Rangers opened practice, one thing was for certain; the team was young. Most of the returning players were incoming juniors with very little varsity experience. Mark Kern, Gene Miller and Bill Kerley were the only three seniors returning from a 7-20 season in 1959-1960. Herrin liked the junior class of Wiley Hall, Terry Thomas, Tom Whittington, Bobby Orchid, Ronnie Head, Ernie Duckworth and Dean Manis. The only sophomore on the team was Robert Crawford.

The 1960-1961 school year started in late August at Benton Consolidated High School. To those that remember it, old Benton High School was an architectural wonder. The school's presence gave incoming freshman the feeling they were part of something much larger than junior high. The school had a grand entrance sandwiched between two enormous concrete columns. The floors of the common areas and hallways were solid marble. In the classrooms, twelve-foot ceilings gave way to planked hardwood floors. At this time, there was no air conditioning in public schools but each classroom had giant windows that teachers could crank open to take in wafts of fresh air. The two-story brick school had a majestic look from the outside and a cozy nostalgic feel on the inside. The school featured wide hallways that were lined with class pictures of Benton alumni. It was common to see groups of students stopped in the hall pointing out relatives that had graduated years ago. The school itself was something the Benton people were proud of and was a large part of the fabric of the community.

When Coach Herrin arrived at Benton in the fall of 1960, he was oblivious to the appearance of the school. He had one thing on his mind; winning basketball games. Upon entering the school for the first time, Herrin made a bee line to the gym that would become his sanctuary, and where he would spend countless hours. To be politically correct, the gym is now called "The East Gym." Back in the day, it was affectionately known as the "Cracker Box." It was the home of the Rangers until the new gym was built to start the 1973-1974 school year.

The gym was an old WPA project built after World War II, and the word "sturdy" is an understatement. Everything about the gym is solid, including the old wooden floor that has very little give. Upon entering the gym for the first time, Herrin is excited for what the future holds but he must first turn his attention to football. He has also been hired to be the assistant football coach under Jim Lynch.

Coach Rich Herrin: *Jim Lynch was a solid football coach and I enjoyed coaching football. A lot of people don't realize I coached football…but I coached football at Benton for almost as many years as basketball. Several of my basketball players played football and this is where I really got my first look at them.*

Herrin discovered that five key players of the '61 Basketball Rangers also played football; seniors Gene Miller and Ernie Duckworth along with juniors Terry Thomas, Bobby Orchid and Wiley Hall. They were key players on a 6-3 football team. Herrin immediately took notice of junior quarterback, Wiley Hall.

Coach Rich Herrin: *Wiley was wiry strong. He was athletic and pretty tough. He was our quarterback in football and I coached the backfield. Ernie Duckworth was also a part of that backfield. Wiley did things as a basketball player that didn't always show up in the scorebook. He was a great leader for us along with Thomas.*

Wiley Hall stood at a lanky 6'0" and wore a flat top along with a determined countenance. Hall was the quarterback of the football team and became the point guard on the basketball team. He was a leader among his peers and had a good first impression of Herrin when he first arrived.

Wiley Hall (junior Point Guard '61): *Rich was in one word - refreshing. He gelled with us immediately. At the young age of twenty-seven, Rich knew a lot about basketball. He got us in shape by running drills and more drills balanced with skills and strategy sessions. He wanted us to understand the game of basketball. He was a good man. The players loved him and I never heard anyone speak ill of him.*

Ron Head, a junior forward, recalled his memorable first meeting with Coach Herrin. Ron still credits his experience as a player under Coach Herrin as invaluable for preparing him for the Marine Corps.

Ron Head (junior Forward '61): *Funny story...the first time I met Coach Herrin was in the boiler room of the high school and I was talking to the janitor, killing time so I didn't have to go back to class. Coach Herrin was going around the school introducing himself individually to all the players. When he left, I turned to the janitor and commented; Golly ...he is an old sucker ain't he? Coach was only twenty-seven, but I was a kid, you know.*

Junior Terry Thomas played in the backcourt with Wiley Hall and filled the shooting guard position on the team. Terry recalled his experience about what it was like to play for Coach Herrin.

Terry Thomas (Guard '61): *Coach Herrin was pretty tough and he didn't put up with any nonsense. It was pretty obvious he was intense and his sole purpose was to win basketball games. You had to respect him for that. It was funny, he would kind of track us at night and make sure we were getting home at a good time and I remember kidding him and saying, "Don't you have anything better to do?" Geez, I'm sixteen years old you know.*

The season opener came quickly. Due to the annual Turkey Day football game against West Frankfort, the Rangers had only one week of basketball practice before their first game. Benton and West Frankfort are the two largest communities in Franklin County. The Turkey Day Game was always the last football game of the season. The annual Turkey Day game was the Franklin County Super Bowl of its time between county rivals, Benton and West Frankfort. Most importantly, it was a Thanksgiving tradition from 1916 to 1983. The game was played so late in November that it nearly ran into basketball season. After the last Turkey Day football game was played in 1983, Benton had 34 victories to West Frankfort's 31.

Coach Rich Herrin: *I thought the Turkey Day game was a good thing until the football playoffs came along. The Turkey Day game did not affect basketball. I wanted to play games. I usually had at least seven days to get ready for the season and that was enough time. I wanted to play.*

On Tuesday, December 6th, the basketball Rangers loaded the bus and headed for Christopher for the opener of the '61 season. The players were expected to wear a collared shirt and jeans. Many wore their letter jackets with a white letter "B" on the left chest. All eleven players wore a tight flat top or a crew cut.

The '61 Rangers took the floor in their visiting maroons. They sported a t-shirt uniform top with white stripes across the shoulders. Large white numbers were displayed on the front and back of the top. The shorts were high with a belt around the waist with Benton inscribed on the side panels. All of the players wore maroon and white tube socks tucked inside their white canvas Converse high-tops. The Rangers thumped the Bearcats by a score of 78-33 giving Herrin his first coaching victory at Benton High School. Sophomore Robert Crawford led the Rangers with 18 points followed by senior Mark Kern who chipped in 14. Senior Gene Miller also had 11 points.

The Rangers spent Wednesday and Thursday preparing for the conference opener at Mt. Vernon. Changnon Gymnasium was the home of the Mt. Vernon Rams and it provided a unique basketball venue. The word "Gymnasium" etched in the aged brick greeted fans as they entered the gym. The trophy case in the front lobby presented a glimpse of the program's storied history. The bright orange banners high in the rafters provided a constant reminder of the Rams' unbelievable back-to-back titles in '49-'50. The gym was beautifully built and had a very nostalgic feel. The gym floor was so small that it played under the rules of a restraining line. A restraining line is used in gyms with tight space around the floor to allow enough room for the ball to be passed in-bounds. If fans had seats on the front row, it is likely they were scolded by a referee to move their feet off the floor. The cheerleaders were close, the fans were close, and it could be 15 degrees outside but 95 degrees in the gym. The locker rooms were old and outdated. Ranger fans called it the "Pit", some calling it the "snake pit". The people of Mt. Vernon loved their basketball and Changnon Gymnasium served home to legendary games between the Rangers and Rams.

The Rams were heavy favorites, especially at Changnon Gymnasium. On this Friday night, the game was back and forth. The Rams pulled away at the end to win 43-39. The young Rangers played well, but just didn't win. Mark Kern was a senior on the '61 team. I once heard him tell a story about the bus ride home from Mt. Vernon after that loss. The story stuck with me. Kern said, "you know…we were upset about losing…but we played pretty well. We were just kind of talking among ourselves in the back of the bus…I guess it got a little too loud. Coach Herrin was in the front of the bus, stewing about the loss." Coach Herrin marched to the back of the bus and said, "Hey, what's going on?" Kern said, "No one said anything." Coach then said, "You know I expect to beat Mt. Vernon.

There was nothing we could say to that…he was right." Kern said. "That really made an impression on me because…he was right. Coach said the right thing at the right time." Kern and his '61 teammates then realized the expectations were going to be higher. Kern said, "it's one thing to say that…but we all really felt he believed it. In my mind, that moment on the bus set the tone for that year." Kern was a guard and would play a big role off the bench. He was tough and hard-nosed.

There is perhaps no one on the team that best represented the toughness and resiliency of the '61 team more than senior Gene Miller. If any of the Rangers could choose one person to be in a foxhole with, it would be Gene Miller. As a high school senior, Miller was 6'0" tall and weighed 190 pounds. He was a fierce competitor and a product of old Midwestern values.

Gene Miller (Forward '61): *Look, I grew up in the country and my mom had me start school early so I could eat. I had three older brothers and three older sisters. I was the youngest, and to make my way in the world I developed an attitude that I would not allow myself to be defeated. Also, we lived in a more nurturing society in those times than today. The whole town helped me, they looked after me and they honored my achievements in athletics. I'm thankful for that.*

Herrin practiced the Rangers hard and Wiley Hall remembers the Rangers style of play all too well.

Wiley Hall (Junior Guard '61): *I just remember that Rich gave us the freedom to be ourselves on the floor. He conditioned us well and we were a very good team defensively. The way I remember it, we could shut teams down. Most teams in Southern Illinois played at a slow pace and ran more of a ball control offense. I remember that if a team scored on us we would get it out of the net quickly and attack and he encouraged that. We were a running team - don't get me wrong, we had our plays, but our style in '61 was different than a lot of teams we played. I believe it helped us win games.*

Terry Thomas was a key contributor to the success of the team. Coach Herrin recalled his memory of Terry Thomas.

Coach Rich Herrin: *Terry was ornery…He didn't take anything off of anybody…He just gave us toughness from the guard position…He could also shoot it.*

Over Christmas break, the Rangers were eliminated in the second game of the Centralia Tournament by the host Orphans, 76-46. On February 3rd, the Herrin Tigers came to Benton for a conference game. The Rangers were on a two-game skid after losing to Marion and West Frankfort. Their record stood at 7-9. Earlier in the practice week, the Rangers had been doing shooting drills and Herrin noticed that Hall and Thomas were always partners. Herrin walked over and told them to find different shooting partners for the rest of the week. As the week continued, he noticed Hall and Thomas ignored his request. In all fairness, Thomas and Hall probably thought it wasn't a big deal. Rich Herrin needed to get the team's attention and he made a bold move. He benched Terry Thomas and Wiley Hall for the entire Herrin game. Ernie Duckworth and Gene Miller started in their place. As so often happens in coaching, sometimes the basketball gods reward tough coaching decisions. Ernie Duckworth had the "game of his life" and scored ten points in a thrilling 54-53 win over Herrin. Gene Miller chipped in four. Message sent.

Ernie Duckworth: *I do remember that me and Gene Miller played that night.*

Wiley Hall (Junior Point Guard '61): *I remember Coach Herrin got upset at me and Terry. We were on the bench and he just didn't play us. He later told me and Thomas that there were other people on the team and we needed to include everyone.*

Ernie Duckworth went to Belle Rive Junior High and moved to Benton his freshman year of high school. He liked his teammates at Benton. In football, Ernie played in the backfield with Terry Thomas and Wiley Hall. Coach Herrin coached the backs and they became familiar with each other during football season.

Ernie Duckworth (Junior Guard '61): *I enjoyed Coach Herrin and we played our hearts out for him. He was honest with us and he had a good work* *ethic. A lot of our guys were hard workers and I give Coach a lot of credit for instilling that in us.*

After the Herrin game, the Rangers were routed by Harrisburg and Centralia. Centralia's Herb Williams was possibly the best player in the South Seven Conference in '61.On February 14th the DuQuoin Indians came to town. The Indians played a sagging defense to closely guard Whittington and Crawford. Junior guard Bobby Orchid made the Indians pay by scorching the nets for 22 points. Orchid scored 14 points in the third quarter and the Rangers won big 66-49.

Terry Thomas (Junior Guard '61): *Bobby was a straight up kid and a good teammate. He worked at it…he became a very good shooter…Rich and Bobby were close…he was kind of like a father figure to Bobby, you know.*

Bobby Orchid (Junior Guard '61): *Coach Herrin lived in a trailer on West Main behind the Dairy Treet when he and Sue first moved to town. He was young and didn't have a lot of money so he was always trying to make money on the side. In the fall of that first year, the freshmen and sophomores played football on Monday and Tuesday nights. He would referee these football games as a way to make a little money. I think he liked me because I worked hard. He would ask me to ride with him to these games. One time, we were going to a game and he flips me the football rules book…he wanted me to quiz him on the right mechanics to the calls. He was worried he didn't know the hand signals for some of the calls. So I said off-sides! He then took his hands off the steering wheel and gave me the off-sides call. This went on for a while and he would completely take his hands off the wheel to show me the correct mechanics of a call. He was the driver's ed teacher you know…Gosh, I thought to myself. I am going to die.*

Bobby Orchid wore number 20 and he lived on West Adams Street down the road from Newhouse Lumber. The Newhouse Lumber building still stands to this day. He was an only child and spent long hours as a young boy entertaining himself by shooting the basketball. In '61, Orchid was a solid player and was the hero to many young grade school players. He remembered one encounter he had with one of his young admirers.

Bobby Orchid (Junior Guard '61): *When I was in high school we walked places you know…not everybody had their own car. I would be walking home from school or practice and I would always see this kid shooting around by himself. He was maybe a fourth-grader. He knew I played basketball for the Rangers and every once in a while I would stop and shoot with him…or maybe give him some pointers. I really didn't think anything of it…I was just trying to be nice. The kid ended up in the NBA.*

The fourth grade boy that Bobby Orchid graciously showed some attention was Doug Collins. Collins would later become the most celebrated basketball player in Benton History. He was the first team college All-American at Illinois State. Collins was a member of the USA Olympic basketball team in 1972 and was the number one pick in the NBA draft of 1973. He would play nine seasons for the Philadelphia '76ers. Collins was a four-time NBA All-Star. Doug Collins wore number 20 at Benton High School, Illinois State, and with the Philadelphia '76ers.

In 2008, Collins returned to Benton and was the featured speaker at the annual Methodist Men's Basketball banquet. Collins was introduced by Dr. Bill Dixon who is still a very close friend to Coach Herrin. In one part of his speech, Collins turned to the players and spoke passionately about always doing things right, because there are youngsters watching your every move. To drive the point home, he told the story of what it meant to him when Bobby Orchid took the time to shoot with him when he was a kid. Doug smiled and said, "Bobby Orchid was my favorite player. I chose to wear number 20 on every team I played on in honor of my boyhood hero, number 20 Bobby Orchid."

On February 17th, the Rangers traveled to McLeansboro to play the Foxes. The Foxes were solid and led by point guard David Lee. Mcleansboro native and local basketball coach/historian, Tom Wheeler, was also a member of the Foxes. On this night, the Rangers beat the Foxes 70-56 behind 21 points from sophomore center Robert Crawford. Tom Whittington chipped in with 20 points. The Rangers then defeated Murphysboro at home 60-45 behind by Bobby Orchid's 17 points. After the Murphy game, Coach Herrin made the decision to start four juniors (Hall, Thomas, Orchid, and Whittington) and sophomore center Robert Crawford. Wiley Hall remembered the move.

Wiley Hall (Junior Guard '61): *We were all about 6'0" to 6'3". I think Rich felt as if we were the five that played the best together. Our guys off the bench were great also.*

The last regular season game for the Rangers came on February 25th against the Centralia Orphans. Senior players Mark Kern, Bill Kerley and Gene Miller were honored before the start of the varsity game. The Rangers trailed 35-21 at halftime before the Orphans pulled away for an easy victory. The Rangers finished the regular season with an unimpressive 11-12 record.

The Miracle Run in '61 (State Tournament Play)

The Rangers opened Regional play on March 1st, at West Frankfort against Galatia. Tom Whittington led the Rangers' attack with 18 points and Wiley Hall chipped in 13. The Rangers made it look easy and won the game 63-38.

Next up for the Rangers would be the West Frankfort Redbirds. The birds had beaten the Rangers twice during the regular season. West Frankfort featured junior Bob Brown. Brown scored 44 points in two games against the Rangers and is still one of the most celebrated players in West Frankfort basketball history. The score was tied after the first quarter at 17. At halftime the Rangers were ahead 32-30. Defensively, Bobby Orchid was doing everything he could to stop Brown, but he still put up 17 points by halftime.

The Rangers found themselves down by two points going into the fourth quarter of play. A resilient Ranger team held on to win 59-57. In the locker room, the Rangers celebrated the upset, but knew they had to defeat Johnston City that Friday night to win the Regional Championship. Brown ended the night with 27 points and proved to be the best player on the floor, but the team effort and balanced scoring of the Rangers prevailed. Herrin believed the win over West Frankfort gave the team a much needed boost of confidence.

Rich Herrin: *There wasn't any doubt about it...the WF game gave us confidence to play against Johnston City. See... Johnston City beat us during the regular season and they had a really good player named Litton.*

A large crowd jammed into Max Morris Gymnasium for the Regional final. The Benton cheerleaders formed two lines and the Ranger fans rose to their feet as their young Rangers took the floor sporting their flat-tops and flashy warm-up tops that formed a "V" in the front. Most importantly, the West Frankfort victory gave the Rangers a swagger and confidence they so desperately needed. Herrin and longtime assistant Harry Stewart walked to the bench behind the team. Herrin and Stewart were young and wore close military flat-tops. They were in good physical condition and they looked like coaches that meant business. Johnston City then took the floor. The two teams warmed up and occasionally glanced down at the other end of the floor to study their opponents.

The Rangers held a slim one point lead at halftime. In a tough contest, the Rangers held on to win the game 56-53. The young Rangers were starting to find themselves just at the right time. It was a happy ride home on the bus, and the team received a fire truck escort around the Benton public square. Rich Herrin would make this victory circle around the square more than any other coach in Benton history. The players urged the bus driver to go a little slower so they could savor the moment. Young and old gathered at the Benton public square to show support. Bobby Orchid recalls what it was like to be a basketball player in Benton in 1961.

Bobby Orchid (Junior Guard '61): *We had a soda fountain-type restaurant on the square called Battles Grill. Mr. Battle was a big Ranger fan and he hung pictures up in his restaurant of all the great players and teams. He hung our picture in there and that was a big thrill to go into a restaurant when you are eighteen years old and see your face on the wall. There was definitely a recognition from people in the community if they knew you played basketball.*

The Rangers advanced to the Eldorado Sectional to play Carmi. This was a good draw for the Rangers. Carmi came into the game at 13-11 and surprised themselves by advancing to the Sectional. The Rangers won the game 58-50 to advance to play the McLeansboro Foxes in the Sectional Championship. The Mcleansboro game was a tight game that went down to the wire. Bobby Orchid drew a charging foul late in the game and went to the line and hit two key free throws to lead the Rangers to an exciting victory. Entering the post season with a record below .500, the Rangers did the impossible. They were Sectional champions. Sophomore Robert Crawford led the scoring attack. Tom Whittington remembered Robert Crawford as a solid player.

Tom Whittington (Junior Forward '61): *Bobby could really shoot it...He was a good jumper but I remember him as more of a catch and rise up type player.*

The '61 Ranger team had now taken the tiny coal mining town by storm. Coal miners were trying to get off work to go to the game. Those that couldn't would have to settle for the radio broadcast. People scrambled for tickets. When the students returned to school on Monday there was an aura of excitement in the building. There was certainly a bounce in the step of the players as they strode through the hallway finding it hard to focus on school. The Rangers needed one more win to get to the State Tournament. Standing in their way was Belleville High School. Belleville was a big school and greatly outnumbered Benton in enrollment. Entering the game, the Maroons outsized Benton at each position and were the heavy favorite. The Super-Sectional would be played at Max Morris Gymnasium in West Frankfort.

A capacity crowd overflowed to the balcony as the Rangers and Maroons were ready to tip off the '61 Super-Sectional. The Rangers got off to a good start and led 12-11 at the end of the first quarter. In the second quarter a crazy thing happened. The scoreboard blew a fuse and play was stopped. The powers that be could not get the clock back to work. So imagine this; there is no working game clock that shows the score or the time for the rest of the game. The clock would be operated by a stop watch and the score was kept at the scorer's table. It was bizarre, but Junior forward Ron Head felt that this worked to the Rangers advantage.

Ron Head (Junior Forward '61): *You know, I really think that helped us. The last thing we needed to be doing was watching the scoreboard. They were the favorites, and it kind of took the pressure off of us in a way. We just played, man!*

In athletics, the phrase "being in the zone" is used when a player or team is so locked in that everything goes right. On this night in West Frankfort, the Rangers' team was "in the zone". The Rangers' played mistake-free basketball and shot the ball with deadly accuracy from the field.

Rich Herrin: *It may have been the greatest game I ever had a team play.*

Late in the game, the Rangers spread the floor late to control the clock. As the Ranger fans watched, they could see the growth and maturity in a team that had a very shaky regular season. It was all coming together at the right time. An official at the scorer's bench indicated that time had elapsed and bedlam ensued. Rangers fans rushed the floor and celebrated with their conquering heroes. It would be a night the young Rangers would always remember. Sue Herrin looked on and cheered as she held young Rodney in her arms. Belleville fans left the game in disbelief.

Sue Herrin: *The fans went wild and all came pouring out on the floor. We were all kind of in a state of shock.*

An excited Ranger team gathered in the locker room located in the underbelly of Max Morris Gymnasium. They hugged each other and celebrated. The Rangers quickly gathered for a team picture. Herrin threw his arms around Ron Head and Mark Kern in elation and smiled for the camera. Wiley Hall and Bobby Orchid have the victory nets draped around their necks with the heavy sectional trophy displayed on the floor in front of the team. Terry Thomas and Tom Whittington look as if they are already thinking about the next game. In the back row, Ernie Duckworth leans in and has his hand draped around longtime coach Glen "Doc" Truelove. Bobby Crawford is kneeling in the front and has a big smile on his face knowing he has two more years of basketball eligibility.

Gene Miller is wearing number 53 and is kneeling in the front with his arm resting on his leg. Miller has a smile on his face. He looks like a chiseled marine veteran as he takes it all in. Gene Miller was an outstanding football player and he liked to compete. He brought toughness and helped the Rangers with his hard-nosed play off the bench. Coach Herrin remembers the important role Gene played on the team.

Rich Herrin: *Gene was tough…His first sport was football but he was a great competitor…he helped us win basketball games and he was well liked by everyone.*

Big Bill Kerley has his arm draped around assistant coach Harry Stewart, and is smiling from ear to ear. Bill was a sophomore when he celebrated with Vic Tasky and Jeff Ferguson after the sectional victory of 1959. Tom Whittington remembers Bill Kerley.

Tom Whittington (Senior Forward '61): *Bill was a great guy to be around…He was a hard worker and a great teammate…he had some knee problems as a sophomore…but he stuck it out.*

As local newspaper writers waited outside the locker room, the Cinderella Rangers took a little extra time showering. Rich Herrin fielded questions from the writers and quickly shuffled his young Rangers on the bus for the short six-mile ride north. The bus was louder than usual. Some players rehashed the game, while some were bombarded with thoughts of what it was going to be like playing in the state tournament. The team bus made its way to Route 37 North and headed for Benton. As the bus approached the outskirts of town, fire trucks waited. The bus stopped south of town and a local fireman peeked into the bus and said, "Coach, looks like we're going to do this again."

Fire trucks turned their lights on and then the sounds of sirens filled the air. The sirens served warning to the hundreds of fans gathered at the Benton Public Square that the team was close. As the bus approached the square, the players sat up in their bus seats and craned their necks out of the bus windows. Seas of people all ages filled the square, and some BCHS teachers came out to show support. Many of the students wore heavy coats and some wore the traditional letter jackets. The players could hear their girlfriends yelling their names amongst the noise. Some of the players' parents had congregated in a section in the middle of the square. They were filled with pride as they met eyes with their sons for a brief second as the bus wound its way around the square. Grade school boys waved to their heroes. It was a Norman Rockwell scene that is only found in small communities. This night would be something the '61 Rangers would remember for the rest of their lives.

Sue Herrin: *I think one of the absolutely most exciting moments in Rich's high school coaching career was when we won the Super-Sectional tournament in West Frankfort in '61 to go to the State Tournament. I had grown up in Marion, which was quite a basketball town at that time…and "going to State" was really something. Since it was our first year in Benton, and we were playing a powerhouse like Belleville, winning that game was kind of unbelievable. The fans went wild and all came pouring out on the floor. We were all kind of in a state of shock. I feel like winning that game was kind of the spark that set Rich's career on fire. From then on we were all hungry to* *get back to State. A lot of little boys wanted to become Benton Rangers after that game.*

BCHS Principal Herbert Mundell liked his young coach and was excited about the team's success. The Rangers won the Super-Sectional on Tuesday night and Mundell had the unenviable job of urging faculty and students to go about business as usual on Wednesday and Thursday, with the first game of the State Tournament looming on Friday. It was an impossible task. The student body was in a basketball trance that they could not break until the State Tournament was to be played on Friday. Tom Whittington recalled the madness of it all.

Tom Whittington: *Honestly, getting to the State Tournament was not even in my mind when we started post season play in the Regional…But we took it one game at a time and found ourselves in the State Tournament.*

On Thursday morning, the players came to school with their bags packed for Champaign. Tucked in their duffle bags were their home and away uniforms, game warm-ups and white Chuck Taylors. They also took extra clothes and spending money given to them by their parents. Thursday would be shortened classes because the players were receiving a send-off pep session in the afternoon. The Cracker Box buzzed with excitement as students filed in to the pep session to find a seat. The cheerleaders performed a cheer and then the students rose to their feet as one giant army as the band played the school loyalty. The loyalty began with a heavy drum beat and every hand clapped in unison as the players sat in folding chairs in front of the stage and took it all in. The players were then introduced and Coach Herrin addressed the student body. Each player then grabbed their travel bags and hustled out the side doors of the gym. To provide maximum comfort, the players rode in groups of three to Champaign in cars donated by local car dealers.

On the trip up to Champaign, it was best the players not dwell on the school's State Tournament history. The Rangers had a third place finish in the State Tournament in 1933. The '33 team was led by star athlete Wilbur Henry, and coached by legendary coach Hubert Tabor. Tabor also coached football. Today, the Benton football field is named in his honor. On the drive north, nervous feelings came over the players when they thought too deeply about the upcoming game. The players found themselves having random conversations about anything but basketball to avoid over-thinking the game. Some players attempted to sleep on the way up. Rich Herrin was twenty-seven years old and he couldn't wait to play. His mind was racing about how to beat Peoria Manual.

The Rangers stayed in a small motel on the outskirts of Champaign. For some of the players, it was the first time they had ever stayed in a motel. The Rangers played the first game of the last State Tournament ever held at Huff Gymnasium. In 1961, there was a one-class system in basketball in the state of Illinois. This meant that the 17-12 Rangers were among the best eight teams in the entire state. The team went to sleep that night anxious for a day they would always remember.

The Rangers woke the next morning and grabbed a light breakfast. The team then traveled to a local junior high for a pre-game shoot around and walk-through. The team prepared to play a box-in-one defense. Peoria Manual had a player that was ruled ineligible, but they were still a much bigger team than the Rangers. After the shoot around, the team then headed to Huff Gymnasium. The Rangers looked out of the windows of their cars to catch their first glimpse of old Huff Gym. "There it is," a player said. The players were met at the door by tournament workers and led inside. Huff Gym was old and it lacked the adequate amount of locker room space to accommodate eight high school teams in one day. The Rangers were led into an empty racquetball court in the bowels of the old gym. A piece of paper was taped to the locker room door that read, "Benton Rangers."

Tom Whittington (Junior Forward '61): *I remember that when we first walked in Huff Gym I felt cold…I looked around and saw some doors wide open because the games were going to be televised throughout the state. Television equipment was being brought through the doors.*

The team began to get dressed and it was unusually quiet. Every player was thinking about the task at hand. Coach Herrin went over the game plan and then the Rangers walked down the hallway that led to Huff Gym. As they walked down the hallway, they could hear the crowd awaiting their arrival. Game officials waved the Rangers onto the floor. On Friday March 17, 1961, Wiley Hall and Ernie Duckworth led the Rangers on to the floor of Huff Gymnasium for the first game of the afternoon session of the 1961 Illinois State Basketball Tournament. The parents and families of the players were there early and chills ran down their spines as the Rangers took the floor.

The national anthem was played and the color guard was in full view. Sue Herrin was a nervous wreck, but she had seen her husband win 112 games and lose only 29 in five years of high school coaching. This gave her some solace. Ron Herrin was there. He wouldn't miss his little brother's coaching debut in the State Tournament. The starting line-ups were announced and the teams gathered at center court for the tip.

One thing is for sure, the next thirty-two minutes of basketball would be something that the Rangers would remember for the rest of their lives. Benton started quickly and played extremely well early in the game. At the beginning of the fourth quarter, the Rangers had a commanding lead and Benton fans started to think about making plans to stay over Friday to see the Rangers on Saturday. If the Rangers could win, they would meet Bogie Redman and the Collinsville Kahoks in the semi-finals. The Kahoks were led by Southern Illinois coaching legend Virgil Fletcher.

Wiley Hall recalled an incident that happened late in the game that speaks to the over-confident attitude of the young Rangers.

Wiley Hall (Junior Guard '61): *I do remember something that happened near the end of the game. Ask Terry about it, he will remember. As I recall, we were up about twelve with three minutes to go. There was a break in the play, you know….a foul was called or something. Terry Thomas walked by me closely and slapped me in the rear and leaned into my ear. He said, "Looks like we got this one in the bag."*

Terry Thomas (Junior Guard '61): *I remember it…That happened.*

Peoria Manual was in panic mode and they had to have the ball. They applied full-court pressure and the Rangers turned it over. The Rangers were usually a very good free throw shooting team but they tightened up, going 1-7 in the fourth quarter. The Rangers scored only three points in the fourth quarter and Manual tied the game at the end of regulation to send the game to overtime. At the end of regulation, the momentum had shifted to Manual as the Rangers felt like lambs headed for the slaughter. The Rangers did not score one point in the overtime. It was over. Coach Herrin and some of the players recall the end of the game as they remember it.

Bobby Orchid (Junior Guard '61): *I think Coach Herrin over the years has blamed himself for the loss but it was on us too. We missed some free throws down the stretch.*

When I asked Coach Herrin about the end of the game and what happened on that Friday afternoon, I sensed it was something that still bothers him.

Coach Rich Herrin: *I wish I would have had a little more experience… it was my fault. I told our players not to break the pressure by throwing long passes…I should have just let them play. We beat ourselves and it was tough to take.*

After the game, the Rangers returned to their locker room. The tears of defeat streamed down the cheeks of the young Rangers. The players showered and then dressed. The locker room was quiet as the players reflected on the season. The juniors were heartbroken but then slowly came around to the "we'll get 'em next year" attitude. Bobby Crawford was a sophomore and was visibly shaken, but he had two more opportunities to return to Champaign. The seniors were done. The loss was devastating and it would be something they would have to live with forever.

Gene Miller (Senior forward '61): *I didn't want to hear "We'll get 'em next year" from anybody. The seniors didn't have any more years left…It was over. I took the loss pretty hard.*

Bobby Orchid (Junior Guard '61): *I've never really shared this with anybody but this is a good story for you. I had this thing where I told myself that I wasn't going to wash my socks until we lost. So through the whole tournament run I never washed my socks. They kind of air-dried out you know…When we got beat by Peoria Manual that afternoon, I took a shower with my socks on…I didn't want to take them off. The loss was devastating.*

Rich Herrin: *After the game, the players left the locker room and I was crying. I stayed in the locker room long after the players left…I was immature…I didn't handle it very well. My brother and John Cherry finally got me to come out because I had to speak to the press.*

Benton fans were heartbroken and some were even moved to tears. Most of the Benton fans that made the trip climbed in their cars and returned home early Friday evening. The team stayed in Champaign that Saturday night and then headed down I-57 South early Sunday morning. It had been a special year. As the Rangers came into town, they were again met with a fire truck escort.

Tom Whittington (Junior Forward '61): *I just remember that I couldn't believe the people met us on the square after we lost...I just found it odd.*

Tom Whittington was from a generation when you were rewarded for winning, and not when you lost. The reception at the square caught him off guard, but it does indicate the love affair the town had with the team. The team had captured the hearts of everyone not only in Benton, but all of Southern Illinois.

When the season was over, Herrin reflected on what had been an unbelievable run. Taking nothing away from his team, he thought it was nice not having to beat Centralia or Collinsville to get to the State Tournament. In fact, there were many that believed the Illinois Basketball State Championship in 1961 took place when Collinsville defeated Centralia in the other Southern Illinois Super-Sectional. They may be right.

When reflecting on the season, Herrin laughed to himself about the needling he received from Dr. Bill Swinney when he first came to Benton. When Rich and Sue first moved to Benton, their house was on a trailer. The house was literally on wheels. They lived on North Main in the exact spot of the driver's license facility today. After settling in, Rich was introduced to Dr. Swinney. Folks in Benton just called him "Doc". He was short and heavy set. He always wore his glasses on the tip of his nose and looked over his glasses at you.

After hearing about Rich's house on wheels, Doc told Coach Herrin, "You are the smartest coach I know." Herrin stepped back and said, "Why?' Swinney said "Your house is on wheels, so when you get fired you can just move on to the next job." Doc Swinney was an important man in the community and the two would become good friends. In fact, Doc was my doctor growing up. William Swinney was special and God broke the mold when he made Doc.

The '61 school year came to an end in May. Seniors Mark Kern, Bill Kerley and Gene Miller walked across the stage to receive their high school diplomas. It had been a great start at Benton for Rich Herrin, and the three seniors would go on to be good workers, good husbands and good fathers.

Mark Kern stayed in the Benton area and became president of Rend Lake College. Rend Lake College grew immensely under his leadership. He and his wife Lana had five children that all graduated from BCHS; Frank, Erik, Brian, Jason and Megan. Brian was a solid point guard on the '92 team that placed third in state. Mark has since passed away and he is survived by his children and his second wife Pat.

Bill Kerley would also settle in Benton with his wife Sue. Bill worked in the coal mines until retirement. Bill and Sue were the parents of two boys; Mark and Scott. Both Mark and Scott played basketball at Benton, earning All-South honors. Mark was the starting center on the 1982 team that went to State. Scott led his Ranger teammates to the sectional championship his senior year in '88 before getting beat by Centralia. Bill has since passed away.

Gene Miller now lives in western Nebraska. After working for the Tennessee Valley Authority, he ventured west and made a career in conservation. Gene's wife, Brenda Sue, has passed away. Losing his wife was extremely difficult. Gene told me a story about his district track meet when he was a senior in high school.

Gene Miller: *I was running the half mile. I missed the qualifying time of 1:55 because a Herrin runner by the name of Steve Fisher cut me off. The same Steve Fisher that led the Michigan "Fab Five" to the Final Four in '92 and '93. After the race, I showed my frustration by taking off my track shoes and tossing them in a nearby trash can. It was my last race and I wouldn't need them anymore.*

Gene is proud of his daughter Kristen. He told me that Kristen turned out to be a very good half-mile runner in high school. At the time, Gene and his family lived in Montana. Kristen placed second in the State of Montana in the half-mile as a senior in high school. Gene cheered as she ran, and was exhausted when the race was over, feeling as if he had run every step with her. After Kristen received her second place medal, she met eyes with her father Gene. As a tribute to her father, she untied her shoes and tossed them in front of the podium. She knew the story about her father's last track meet, and with tears in his eyes, Gene Miller proudly stood and clapped for his daughter.

'62 Rangers

Juniors Wiley Hall, Terry Thomas, Bobby Orchid, Tom Whittington, and Ernie Duckworth returned in '62. Robert Crawford, the team's leading scorer, would also be back. In fact, for a brief time Crawford became Benton's all-time leading scorer, surpassing Ed Rice. His scoring record was broken by several great Rangers in the late 1960's. Crawford would never return to the State Tournament.

The expectations were high for '62 and the Rangers did not disappoint. It was a solid year, but unfortunately Wiley Hall and Terry Thomas both came down with mononucleosis toward the end of the season. The Rangers had a solid Centralia Tournament, but lost in the championship to the host Orphans by a score of 49-45. Robert Crawford was selected as a member of the All-Tournament team. The Rangers won the West Frankfort Regional by defeating Johnston City for the second straight season 44-31. Ranger fans lined the square as the '62 Rangers savored what would be their final victory lap around the square. The next week the Rangers traveled to Herrin to face Anna Jonesboro in the first game of the Sectional. The Rangers rolled 82-55. The team needed to win two more games to return to Huff Gym. The win advanced the Rangers to the Sectional final against Marion. Benton had beaten Marion twice during the season. Marion played well and held on to defeat the favorite Rangers by a score of 56-53. It was a tough loss.

The '62 Rangers then met for the last time in the locker room. Coach Herrin addressed the team. He could not hide his disappointment as he thanked the team and the seniors for two years of hard work and commitment. The Rangers boarded the yellow bus and went home. Most of the team would run track in the spring. Now that basketball was over, they began to think about what they were going to do with their lives after high school.

Coach Herrin: *It was tough to lose the '62 class…the '61 and '62 teams were my first two years…they created an excitement in our community. They were the guys that got the program going.*

Wiley Hall received a full ride basketball scholarship to Rice University. The first thing Wiley said on the phone was, "Coach Herrin really helped me get a scholarship at Rice." He enjoyed his days in Benton. He served in Vietnam and then became a med vac pilot. Wiley Hall was doing his daily crossword puzzle in California when I called him, and he gave me much insight into the season.

Terry Thomas received a full-ride basketball scholarship to Middle Tennessee University. He would room with teammate Tom Whittington. Terry still lives in Benton and made his living as a pharmaceutical representative. Terry is still married to his high school sweetheart and '62 BCHS homecoming queen, Ms. Mary Lou (Chance) Thomas. They have two children; Tara and Todd.

Tom Whittington would also receive a full-ride basketball scholarship to Middle Tennessee University. He became a teacher and coach. He lives with his wife Sue who was also a school teacher. He is an avid golfer and plays a lot with his son Todd. Tom doesn't age and he looks the same as he did thirty-nine years ago when he was my coach. He served as the seventh grade coach in Benton for seventeen years and taught school for more than thirty years.

Bobby Orchid received a full-ride basketball scholarship to Central Missouri University. Bobby Orchid became a navy pilot and flight instructor. At one time, he was stationed at Guantanamo Bay. He then worked for companies which included Nabisco, Frito Lay and Little Tikes. He also owned his own business for more than fifteen years. As a semi-retirement job, Bobby served as a general repairman at Hilton Head in South Carolina for years. He now resides in historic Anniston, Georgia.

Bobby Orchid (Junior Guard '61): *I played for two really good coaches at Central Missouri. Gene Bartow was a young and upcoming coach that later ended up at UAB. I really liked Bartow. He was intense and very fair. He didn't play favorites. Coach Bartow left at the end of my sophomore year. Joe B. Hall then replaced Bartow. He was rough. Joe B. Hall eventually left after I graduated and became an assistant for Adolph Rupp at Kentucky. I honestly believe my experience playing under Coach Herrin made my transition to coach Bartow much easier. They were alike in many ways.*

Ron Head went straight to the marines after high school. Ron created his own gospel album and he was the voice of the Rangers in the early 1980's. He still sings the national anthem at home Ranger basketball games. Ron sings from the heart. My wife once said, "I feel like we have a ten-point lead to start the game when Ron sings the anthem." Ron lives with his wife Judy (Short) Head in Benton. Ron's son, Chris, played on the '84 and '85 teams and works at the high school. Ron and Judy also have a daughter, Ginger.

Ernie Duckworth would go to SIU and then serve three years in the army as a switchboard operator for the President of the United States. Ernie worked in the coal mines for twenty-five years and then sold strawberries for fifteen years. He married Judy Tate. They are still happily married and run JED's (Judy and Ernie Duckworth's) farm, located east of Benton.

Robert Crawford received a full-ride scholarship to Tulane University. He then went into the marines and served his country in the Vietnam War. He went back to Benton and worked as a coal miner for years. Robert and his wife Betty moved the family to Mansfield, Texas. Robert passed away but is survived by his wife and two children; Angie and Bobby.

One thing is for sure, the '61 Rangers will always be remembered as the spark to the fire. The fire would blaze in '66 and '67, but these were the players that would inspire boys in Benton to get their basketball and spend hours on their own practicing. Rich Yunkus was a sixth grader at Washington elementary school when the Rangers upset the Belleville Maroons in the Super Sectional. He and his family tuned into the game on tape delay the next day to hear the upset. In five short years, Yunkus and his teammates would dominate Southern Illinois basketball in a way that Benton fans would never forget. Their inspiration would be the '61 team.

The town of Benton was never the same after BCHS Principal Herbert Mundell hired Rich Herrin. *(Benton High School)*

A young Rich Herrin pulls up his socks as he prepares for battle in the old "Cracker Box." *(Benton High School)*

Old Benton High School was a majestic site and is revered by
Benton Alumni. *(Benton High School)*

Rich, Sue and young Rodney in January, 1961.
(Rich Herrin family collection)

Coach Herrin made an impression on Mark Kern when he said, "I expect to beat Mt. Vernon." Kern later became a driving force behind the growth of Rend Lake College. *(Benton High School)*

Wiley Hall was the first great point guard of the Rich Herrin era. *(The WF Daily American)*

Terry Thomas provided the team with great shooting and physicality from the guard position. *(UPI)*

Gene Miller was a fierce competitor that gave the '61 Rangers some swagger off the bench. *(Benton High School)*

Tom Whittington let his rugged play in the post do his talking in '61.
(The WF Daily American)

Bobby Orchid wore 20 and was the idol of many youngsters in
Benton including Doug Collins. *(Vern Richey- Urbana Courier)*

Bobby Crawford was the leading scorer on the '61 team and graduated in '63 as Benton's All- Time leading scorer (1,313 points).

Benton rooters leap in ecstasy as their team sinks a huge bucket late against Belleville West in the '61 Super-Sectional. *(The WF Daily American)*

Bedlam ensued after the Rangers upset win against Belleville West.
(Paul Hickman)

State Bound in '61. *(Benton High School)*

This is why you play. Uninhibited joy breaks out in the under
belly of Max Morris Gymnasium after the win over
Belleville West. *(Paul Hickman)*

The '61 team started the utopic 25 year run of Rangers basketball.
(Paul Hickman)

Coach Herrin addresses the reception for the team after returning home from the loss to Peoria Manual in the State Tournament. *(Benton High School)*

The Miracle team of '61. Kneeling L-R Hall, Orchid, Whittington, Crawford, Thomas. Standing Coach Stewart, Duckworth, Miller, Kerley, Head, Kern, Coach Herrin. *(Paul Hickman)*

Doc Swinney told Herrin he was "the smartest coach he ever knew because his house was on wheels." *(Benton High School)*

The '62 team was solid. *(Benton High School)*

CHAPTER FIVE

Rich Yunkus

"I'll tell you this... Yunkus was pretty good." – Rich Herrin

My phone rang one recent morning about 9:30 a.m. I was away from the phone, and it rang three times before I could answer with, "Hello?" A voice on the other end grumbled, "You're about as fast as you were when I coached you." I laughed politely and Coach Herrin asked me if I needed some phone numbers of some of his former players. He then told me that he couldn't find his black book. The black book that coach is referring to is one of his most prized possessions. Inside the book is every phone number he has ever written down since about 1950 in no specific order. The phone numbers are correct but good luck finding the person you may be looking for. I have to chuckle as I visualize him searching for the numbers of the 1966 Rangers. Coach somehow veered the conversation to his college playing days and was on the subject of how he was a good rebounder for his size. I politely said yes a few times and then cut in, "Hey, I'm going to see Yunkus today." He went quiet for a second and then said;

Rich Herrin: *You can quote me on this. Rich Yunkus is one of the top five high school basketball players to ever play in the State of Illinois.*

Coach has always had a hard time with the pronunciation of Yunkus. He says "Yawnkus". There have been several occasions I have asked Coach about the top players he ever coached at Benton. Out of respect for all those that played for him, he has always avoided the subject of his best players. Besides, there were so many great players during his coaching run at Benton. On this day, I really tried to pin him down. "Come on Coach, who is your all-time starting five at Benton?" Usually there is no answer. Careful not to say too much, and knowing there would be no argument about his answer, he made this comment.

Rich Herrin: *I'll tell you this… Yunkus was pretty good.*

So I pressed on by asking him some questions. Obviously, Rich Yunkus was a great player. His jersey number number 40 is retired and hangs high in the rafters at Rich Herrin Gymnasium. I was too young to see Yunkus play but all of the old timers sing his praises. Growing up in Benton, I heard my Grandpa Wynn refer to the time period of 1966-1967 as the "Yunkus years". I then asked Coach Herrin why he felt like Rich Yunkus was one of the top players ever in the State of Illinois. He was ready for my question and quickly shot an answer back that was hard to argue.

Rich Herrin: *We were 61-2 in two years. We had back to back thirty-win seasons and he is a big reason for that. There can't be many players in the state that can say that…*

I arrived at Rich Yunkus' house at ten in the morning and was greeted by his wife Donna. The house is located on Bailey Lane and sits just southeast of the Dairy Queen in Benton. The home is eye-catching and very well kept. Every blade of grass is green and there are over 275 plants that have been meticulously cared for and perfectly placed around the house and walkways. There is a swimming pool in the back yard surrounded by a privacy fence. Rich and Donna like to travel and they have just built an unattached building that houses their mobile home. It is a beautiful day as I pull into their driveway. Donna led me thru the house into a large back room that is impossible to see from the front of the home. Large wooden beams line the ceiling and everything in the house is in perfect place. This has been the home of Rich and Donna Yunkus since 1972, but it has the look and feel of a new home.

Rich was sitting in a recliner watching television when I entered the room. During this time, he was recovering from hip surgery. The problems of aging joints and the wear and tear of many years of basketball have taken its toll. I sat on a couch across the room and Donna then took a chair as we began to talk. We spent the first part of our meeting talking about our families and then I explained my vision about the book.

The interview began at approximately 10:15 a.m. and I left the Yunkus home at 2:15 in the afternoon. I almost wanted to turn around and apologize for staying so long, but the conversation was so enlightening to me that I hustled home under the fear that I would forget something and began writing. There was much to take away from listening to Yunkus talk about the game of basketball. In front of me was a guy that scored 2,232 career points in only three years of college basketball at Georgia Tech. During this time, it was an NCAA Rule that incoming freshman were not eligible to play. Despite playing just three years and the absence of the three point shot, Yunkus remains the all-time scoring leader at Georgia Tech.

I knew Rich Yunkus but I never had the chance to really sit down and talk to him at any length. I was looking forward to our conversation for many reasons. I definitely wanted his perspective on Coach Herrin and his time as a Ranger, but I also wanted to gain insight on what really made him tick. He did not disappoint. As we spoke, the qualities that made him a high school and college All-American began to surface. There is no doubt that he had talent and was blessed with good size which helped his basketball career, but there was much more. I realized that Yunkus is a good husband, a good father to his two girls and someone that believes there is only one way to do things; the right way. He is a firm believer in hard work and preparation. Yunkus is very intelligent and has a cerebral approach to all that he does, including basketball. He does not waste time and there is a purpose for everything. There were times during our conversation that he would pause, as if not to ramble. He would then put together the right words and say something very profound. For example, we were talking about Coach Herrin's impact on so many people and he stopped me and made a very simple comment that had great meaning. In fact, it really summed up the theme of the book.

Rich Yunkus: *I believe Coach Herrin always thought that good athletes make good people.*

Rich Yunkus always struck me as a very private person. He is not someone I run into every day at the grocery store or randomly see at Walmart. He was a mystery to me, but all of my encounters with him have been cordial. After our conversation, I gained a greater appreciation for his personality. As a player, he admitted he was never a vocal leader or rah-rah type guy. He is quiet and introspective with a very analytical approach to life. Rich Yunkus chooses to speak through his actions. Also, I noticed by his meticulously kept house and yard, the careful phrasing of his answers and his somewhat quirky mental approach to the game that he is very much a perfectionist. He is not about just doing something the right way, he is about doing it perfectly.

Because of his low-key personality; it can be overlooked how good Yunkus really was as a basketball player. Before we get into awards and accolades, just know that Yunkus scorched Dave Cowens and the Florida State Seminoles for 41 points one night in 1970. Dave Cowens went on to play in the NBA for years as a member of the Boston Celtics, and was inducted into the NBA Hall of Fame in 1991. He scored more than 40 points five times that same season. I love the "Cowens thrashing" and it speaks to what kind of player Yunkus was. He was really good.

Yunkus was enshrined as a member of the State of Georgia Athletic Hall of Fame in 1998 along with predecessors Jackie Robinson, who was born in the Peach State before going on to stardom as the first black player in Major League Baseball; Morehouse College and Olympic hurdles champion Edwin Moses, NASCAR driver Bill Elliott and professional golfer Lyn Lott. He is the first, and only, Georgia Tech student to be inducted into their Hall of Fame immediately upon graduating. A high school and college All-America pick, Yunkus is also a member of the Illinois Basketball Coaches Association Hall of Fame. He is proud of his basketball career but has also excelled in the business world, but he is not one to toot his own horn or demand attention.

After his basketball career, Yunkus and his wife settled in Benton in 1972. He took over his father's business and proved to be very successful. Donna then became an elementary teacher who served the Benton community for more than twenty years. In 1993, he became a member of the Rend Lake College Foundation Board. Although he prefers to be low-key, Yunkus has given much back to the Southern Illinois area. He has served on the Rend Lake College Foundation Board of Directors for almost twenty-five years. During his stint as a board member, he was credited with being one of the driving forces behind making sure the RLC Murphy-Wall Pinckneyville Campus had the ability to offer a complete degree program to eliminate out-of-the-area student transportation costs to the Rend Lake campus. He also supported the construction of the Rend

Lake Children's Center with generous monetary donations and was the board member most responsible for building the best facility possible. In 2000, he became the ninth person to receive the Presidential Award from the RLC Foundation. Today, Yunkus holds memberships to the Benton Chamber of Commerce, Rotary Club and Elks Club. He is now seventy years old and quietly goes about his life devoting much of his time and energy to his family.

Obviously, the name Yunkus is not a common Benton surname. During the years of World War I, Rich Yunkus' grandparents fled Lithuania and settled temporarily in Scotland due to the destruction and chaos of the war. As so many Europeans did during this time, they then emigrated to the United States in search of opportunity. Rich's grandfather, Felix, eventually found work in Southern Illinois as a coal miner and he and his wife, Ada, settled in West City, Illinois.

Yunkus was born November 13, 1949, in Omaha, Nebraska. He was born the son of Tony and Donna Yunkus. Before junior high, the Yunkus family lived among a row of taverns in West City. West City is a tiny village contiguous to the west side of Benton. Rich remembers the taverns were full of good hard-working men that worked in the coal mines. The miners had different shifts and the taverns were open at all hours of the day. There was no mischief, just guys getting a cold beer after a hard day's work at the coal mine. He grew up in a one-story home with wooden shingles that were painted grey. The house was actually his grandmother's home that had been moved to this location after the construction of Interstate 57. In fact, the location of the original Yunkus home sat near the area of today's on-ramp to I-57 North toward Mt. Vernon. There was no air conditioning in the home, but Rich did have his own room. He lived with his parents along with his grandmother, Ada. Felix passed away when Rich was very young. Rich believes that his height was a genetic gift from his grandfather on the Yunkus side of the family.

The family later built a home at 406 West Fourth Street when Yunkus was in junior high. Rich fondly remembers his mother giving him a quarter and sending him to Peilo's Grocery store to get bread and he would keep the extra change to put in his piggy bank. He attended Washington Elementary School and he spent time with other boys in the neighborhood playing wiffle ball or riding bikes together.

Growing up in the 1950's in America, a young boy could not avoid the pull of baseball. Yunkus recalled playing most of his Little League games in the Bone Yard Woods area near the Benton Bocce Ball Club.

During this time, baseball was the sport of choice for most boys and it was common place to see neighborhoods peppered with groups of boys playing America's pastime. Rich's neighborhood was no different. Yunkus loved baseball and as a boy, it was his first love. His boyhood idol was Stan Musial, and he remembered times as a boy going with his dad to old Sportsman's Park in St. Louis to see his hero play. I found it intriguing that Yunkus would idolize Musial. Musial's family also emigrated to the United States from Europe, he was an amazing athlete with an odd last name and Stan was a believer in doing things the right way. Yunkus and Musial had some similarities.

Rich's parents, by all accounts, were loving and supportive. He was very quick to point out that his mother "ruled the roost". His father, Tony, was much more laid back. He then went on to tell me a story that was very telling of the influence his mother had in his life.

Rich Yunkus: *My seventh grade basketball coach was Bruce Jilek. In the seventh grade, we had two practices, one before school and one after school. The morning practice was more about fundamentals and Coach Jilek was a good fundamentals coach. I was physically very weak at this time. I couldn't do one pull up in P.E. class. We went to Herrin for a game, and everybody on the team played in the game but me. I came home and I was downhearted about the game and my father sympathized with me and said, "Why don't you just quit the team?" My mother came in and immediately said, "You are not quitting the team and I will drive you to practice tomorrow." My mom would not let me quit. She was a great influence in my life. Coach Jilek had a talk with me at the next practice and asked me this question; "Do you really want to play basketball?" It made me think, and I told him that I really wanted to play.*

Rich Yunkus was an only child, and he grew up in a world where he sometimes had to entertain himself, and being alone was just part of a life with no siblings. As an only child there is time to think for yourself, entertain yourself, and there's a tendency to gain a valuable degree of independence. In fact, Yunkus was quick to point out that basketball appealed to him because all you needed was a ball to get better. A boy could find a sort of peace and solace that only shooting a basketball could provide. Yunkus played basketball in junior high but enjoyed baseball more because he found himself on the field participating. He was a left-handed pitcher and when he wasn't pitching, he played first base. He didn't get really serious about basketball until his freshman year of high school.

Rich Yunkus: *I remember my dad put a pole in the ground in our back yard and he nailed a square wooden board to it and then attached the rim to the board. My grandmother knitted me a net. I bounced the ball on the surface of the ground which was a bare spot of dirt. I remember that someone told me that good shooters shot the ball off their fingertips. I remember shooting for hours and then looked at my hands and my fingertips would be dirty but my palms would be clean.*

As a freshman in high school, he was encouraged to go out for football by Coach Rich Herrin. Herrin believed Yunkus would grow, and he felt football would be a good way to toughen him up. When Yunkus began his freshman year of high school, he was 5'11" and weighed 111 pounds. Coach Herrin struggled to find shoulder pads that would fit his narrow shoulders. As the basketball season began, Coach Herrin met with freshman coach Woody Burnett and encouraged Burnett to work with Yunkus on a high shot release.

Rich Yunkus: *I really liked Coach Burnett. He was just a good guy. Coach Herrin wanted me to shoot the ball above my head. Because of my strength level, I shot the ball kind of off my shoulder. I was very weak and we would just get 6-8 feet in front of the basket and work on shooting the ball with the release above my head.*

As a sophomore, Yunkus went out for football again, but between his freshman and sophomore years he grew four inches. As a sophomore, he played at 6'5". In football, Yunkus was a tight end, but with his sudden growth, it was plain to see that his football days were numbered. In the middle of his sophomore football season, he began meeting Coach Herrin at the gym for individual basketball workouts. Yunkus chose not to play football after his sophomore year.

When basketball season started, he began the year practicing with the varsity team, but Coach Herrin decided to hold him back and play him on the sophomore level only. Coach Herrin believed that keeping Yunkus with the sophomores would allow him to gain strength and confidence. He was right. This decision proved to be critical in Yunkus' development and in his own words, Yunkus remembered his sophomore year as the "turning point". He spent that all-important year under the watchful eye of long-time Ranger assistant coach, Harry Stewart.

Rich Yunkus: *I loved playing for Coach Stewart. He was a great motivator and he gave us the freedom to play. I remember there was a time…I think we were playing DuQuoin. We had a terrible first half and DuQuoin wasn't very good. The score was close and Coach Stewart came into the locker room and picked up the chalk and started to write on the board and then just threw the chalk down and left. As players we waited for him to return, and then we heard the three minute horn…no Coach Stewart…then we heard the horn to start the second half. We all decided it best to return to the floor. There was Harry sitting on the bench waiting for us. He said, "Oh, you guys have decided to come and play the second half?" He knew there was nothing he could tell us with that chalk in his hand…he had to motivate us to play. I just remember when the second half started…that game was over in about two minutes because he pressed the right buttons.*

Harry Stewart would serve as Rich Herrin's assistant basketball coach throughout Coach Herrin's twenty-five year run at Benton High School. He was loyal and he knew the game. His players loved him, because he was real and he had a way of dressing a player down without making it personal. Coach Stewart had that unique ability to use humor as a way to impart wisdom. He could be intimidating, but he was a great motivator and understood young people. He was a master at button-pressing. Coach Stewart was there through it all, and he was a big part of the basketball success at Benton High School. He could sometimes act as an interpreter and he had a way of bringing a calm balance to the passionate approach of Rich Herrin.

I got the opportunity to play for Coach Stewart my freshman year. There were three freshman brought up late in the year to play on the sophomore team. I happened to be one of them. This incident happened in one of my first sophomore practices and it sums up how Coach Stewart dealt with tough situations.

We were in the middle of having a terrible practice one day after school. The first team couldn't score and it was frustrating for everybody…turning the ball over…bad shots…you name it. I was standing on the sideline watching all of this. Coach Stewart just observed and let this go on for a while until he finally had seen enough. He barked, "Hold up, stop…and don't move!" The sophomores stopped where they were at on the floor and just looked at him. Coach Stewart went silent for like 30 seconds…I remember thinking…what is he going to say? In a booming voice, he said, "Look around…somebody's going to get pregnant."

It took me a minute and then I understood his point. All of the players were standing next to each other and he was making the point that we had no offensive flow because we lacked proper floor spacing. But who says that? He didn't mention the correct basketball terminology of floor spacing…he used the word "pregnant", which he knew we would all remember. This was his genius. We smiled at each other…laughed a little bit…understood his point…and then finished with a good practice. He completely changed the whole mood and direction of that practice with that one comment….and all of us liked him more for it.

In an in-person interview, I asked Coach Herrin about Harry Stewart and he sat back in his chair and smiled. I could tell that he had a respect and love for Harry that only comes from winning and losing together for twenty five years. They had been through it all together.

Rich Herrin: *Harry was a great football coach. He knew the game of basketball. He made it fun and the players loved him….and he had their respect… He always had a way to lighten the mood. He was a good coach and a good man.*

Harry Stewart graduated from Benton High School and played college football at the University of South Carolina. He served as head football coach at Benton High School and won seventy-six games in the tough South Seven Conference over the course of fifteen seasons. He is also a member of the IHSA Football Coaches Hall of Fame. He passed away September 18, 2011. He was 81 years old.

Yunkus really came into his own as a player during his sophomore year. He gained valuable game experience and began to improve by leaps and bounds. He enjoyed Coach Stewart. He was having fun and gaining confidence and the sophomores were winning games. The future looked bright. Yunkus spent long hours in the gym, shooting on his own, and was quietly becoming a deadly shooter. One of his many quirks was that he had to achieve some sort of shooting goal before leaving the gym. He might set a goal of hitting fifteen elbow jumpers in a row before leaving the gym and he wouldn't leave until he hit fifteen in a row. It was this type of discipline and work ethic that made Rich Yunkus special. Yunkus began to see the fruits of his labor by scoring 40 points in one sophomore game. He was also self-aware enough to realize that basketball might be something he needed to focus on solely. After his sophomore year, Yunkus gave up baseball to put all his energy into basketball. At this time, Rich Yunkus may have been the best kept secret in the State of Illinois.

To set the stage for the dynasty years, the Rangers of '63 to '65 fought and scraped just to tread water in the always-tough South Seven Conference. The '63 Rangers captured yet another Regional Championship by defeating Johnston City, 72-61, for the third straight year at West Frankfort. The Rangers went on to win the first game of the Sectionals by defeating Sparta 52-47, before losing to the host Herrin Tigers in the Sectional Championship. The '63 Rangers finished the season with a 15-12 record. They were led in scoring by senior Robert Crawford, who finished a fine Ranger career. When Crawford walked across the stage on graduation night in 1963, he was the all-time leading scorer in Benton Ranger basketball history. He scored 1,313 points in his three years as a varsity player. Crawford was the leading scorer as a sophomore on the '61 team that made it to the State Tournament, and was a member of three Regional Championship teams. It was a nice career for Mr. Crawford. The other two seniors on the '63 team were guards Richard Morris and Larry Saxe.

The '64 team finished with a record of 11-14 and was one of only two teams in Rich Herrin's twenty-five years at Benton that finished below the .500 mark. In defense of the Rangers, their record can be deceiving. To indicate the teams' competitive play, nine of the fourteen Ranger losses were under a margin of five points. After three straight losses to the Rangers in the Regional finals, the Johnston City Indians finally defeated the Rangers 71-70 in the Regional Championship at Max Morris Gymnasium in West Frankfort. The game had a controversial ending that some of the old timers in Benton are still seething about. Junior Tom Appleton tipped the ball in at the buzzer, and it appeared the Rangers had won the game. The officials didn't have the nerve to make the call, so the decision was deferred to the scorekeeper, who claimed the shot didn't count. Ranger fans were livid. Unfortunately, that is how the 1964 season ended for the Rangers.

Rich Herrin: *We were able to watch the tapes and the ball was in the net at least three seconds before the horn sounded. I had ten to twelve people tell me we won that game.*

Senior Rich Adkins led the team in scoring and rebounding and finished a fine Ranger career. Other seniors on the '64 team were Clark Hunter, Mike Franklin, Warren Watson and Charlie Bennett.

The Rangers of 1965 finished one game above .500 with a record of 14-13. The team suffered from inconsistency and seemed to turn it up against good competition. After losing to a very average Harrisburg Bulldog team 67-50 on a Friday night, they came back to beat state ranked Centralia at Home 63-61. The '65 Rangers were led by seniors Tom Appleton, Bob Deitz, Tom Gulley and Tom Smothers. Senior guard Bob Deitz ended a fine career scoring a career 1,007 points which ranked him among the top scorers in Benton history at the time. At the end of the '65 season, Rich Herrin believed the best years at Benton were right around the corner; returning from the '65 team were seniors Jim Hill, Terry Heard, David Woodland, Kenny Payne and Jim Adkins. He liked this group of in-coming seniors and he would also have incoming juniors Jerry Hoover, John Burlison and Bill Lowery. Little did Herrin know that he would coach possibly the best high school basketball player in the state of Illinois for the next two years, Rich Yunkus.

Yunkus's parents, Tony and Donna, attended all of Rich's games.
(Rich Herrin family collection)

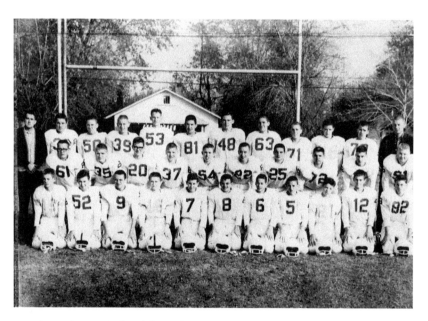

Rich Yunkus (53) played football as a freshman but came to understand that basketball would be his ticket. *(Benton High School)*

A picture of the fighting freshman in the winter of '63. Yunkus is 42.
(Benton High School)

Rich enjoyed his sophomore year under the guidance of Coach Harry Stewart.
(Rich Yunkus family collection)

Yunkus's textbook jump shot was a lethal weapon in the
Rangers offensive attack. *(Benton High School)*

Coach Herrin and Rich Yunkus are pictured after Yunkus's selection
on the '67 All American team. *(Benton High School)*

Being recruited with a steak dinner by Georgia Tech head coach, John "Whack" Hyder in the spring of '67. *(Rich Yunkus family collection)*

A picture of Yunkus with his parents and future wife, Donna, at the Georgia Tech recruiting dinner. The dinner was held at the old Benton Elks Club. *(Rich Yunkus family collection)*

While at Georgia Tech, Yunkus became one of the greatest college
players in the country. Here, he displays his deadly jump shot
that was almost impossible to block. (Rich Yunkus family collection)

Jerry West presents Yunkus with the Atlanta Tip-Off club
"Player of the year" award. (Rich Yunkus family collection)

The 62-63 Rangers finished 15-12 and won a Regional Championship. They
were led by one of Herrin's first great players at Benton,
Robert Crawford 30. *(Benton High School)*

From 63-65, Bob Deitz scored 1007 points and established himself
as one of the great Rangers of the 1960's. *(Benton High School)*

The '64 Rangers finished 11-14 and lost a controversial game to Johnston City in the Regional Championship. *(Benton High School)*

Rich, Rodney (5), Randy (3) and newborn Kyle in January of '64.
(Rich Herrin family collection)

The '65 Rangers finished 14-13 and were led by Tom Appleton, Bob Deitz and Tom Gulley. *(Benton High School)*

The Yunkus years of 65-67 cement the Rangers as one of the greatest high school basketball programs in the state of Illinois. Here is a picture of Yunkus at Georgia Tech. (Rich Herrin family collection)

CHAPTER SIX

Four Splinters and a Barrel

*"When we won the Centralia Tournament by beating Thornton,
I knew I was playing on a very special team."*
– All Stater, Jim Adkins

In the summer of 1965, IHSA rules prohibited coaches from instructing their players in the summer, but the Benton Gymnasium was open for the players to come in and play. Coach Rich Herrin opened the gym each morning of the week in the summer from 7:00 a.m. to 11:00 a.m., and on Monday, Wednesday and Thursday nights at 6:00 p.m. Herrin strongly encouraged his players to attend. The seniors usually organized the games by picking teams with whoever showed up to play. The games were to seven points and everyone played hard, there was no foolishness. There were disagreements about the score at times, but usually the only sounds in the gym were the squeaks of tennis shoes as the players cut and slashed. If you were on the winning team, your team stayed on the floor until beaten. The reward for winning was to play again because winning was important, especially at Benton.

Playing alongside Rich Yunkus was All-State forward Jim Adkins. Adkins was a senior who played limited minutes as a sophomore, but led the team in points and rebounds as a junior in '65. He played at 6'4" but standing next to Yunkus who was 6'7", their reach was nearly the same. Adkins had extremely long arms and a quick first step. He was very effective playing the back position of Benton's full court pressure. Adkins deflected balls and was agile enough to get back and defend the goal if the pressure was broken. Jim Adkins shared a telling story of the talent in open gym during those summer days of 1965.

Jim Adkins: *Terry Heard reminded me of a time when we were at open gym in the summer before our senior year. He asked me, "Jim…do you remember picking those teams in the summer open gyms and leaving little Dougie Collins out?" I did remember that. In all fairness Doug was just a freshman at the time. He rarely got picked to play in that summer of '65.*

The summer basketball program beginning in the mid-1960's served as a basketball training camp except there was one thing; no instruction from the coaches. The opportunity to play without being under the watchful eye of coaches gave the players a sense of independence and freedom that made the game fun. Also, this unsupervised structure of open gym allowed the players to spend time with one another and bond as teammates. Team chemistry is extremely important in basketball and the ability for a group of teenage boys to sacrifice their own selfish desires for the betterment of a team is much more attainable when they like each other. The 1966 Rangers definitely had talent, but they were friends off the floor as well.

Jim Adkins: *We were a very close team. We knew each other's strengths and we all played together well. The guys that didn't start were great contributors to the team. Coach Herrin would take us to All-Star games in Kentucky and we would go swimming at Lake Benton together as a group…We did some team-building things that helped our chemistry.*

Jim Adkins moved to Benton, Illinois at the beginning of his eighth grade year. His father James moved the family to Benton to find work in the coal mines. James went by the nickname of "Bones" because of his slender build. His mother's name was Lily Mae and the family lived across the street from the high school. The Adkins family had three boys; Rich, Jim and Roger that would be key contributors to the Ranger Basketball Program. Jim's older brother Rich played on the '64 team, and then younger brother Roger played on the great '71 team that advanced to State.

Jim was the middle brother, and upon moving to town he attended Webster Junior High and played for Coach Sherwood Pace. Jim proved to be one of the greatest high school players to ever play at Benton. As a senior, Adkins had one of the greatest single seasons in Ranger history in '66. Adkins loved to play on his own, and he spent long hours on the outdoor basketball courts improving his game. In high school, Adkins walked across the street and snuck into the East Gym to play. He often brought his Ranger teammates with him. Adkins was a gym rat and a coach's delight due to his deep love for the game. Adkins remembered watching the '61 team play when he first moved to Benton in the eigth grade. Coming into his senior season in '66, he felt like the team could be special.

Jim Adkins: *My freshman year…our class was very good and then when I played with my class as a sophomore we won our sophomore tournament. I really thought we had a chance to win a Regional and Sectional.*

Benton played Johnston City in the first game of the '66 season and won 90-53. The score is indicative of many games in '66. The Rangers would pounce on opponents early and there were many games the starters didn't get an opportunity to play in the fourth quarter because Coach Herrin refused to run up the score on the opponents. During my interview with Yunkus, he paused for a moment when he recalled his first varsity start.

Rich Yunkus: *I can still see that opening tip to start the '66 season against Johnston City. I can see it like it was yesterday. I was the only junior that started for us, but the seniors accepted me.*

This moment must have meant so much to Yunkus. He could have played varsity basketball as a sophomore but Coach Herrin held him back to improve and gain confidence. Finally, the opportunity to play varsity basketball had come, and even though he would later become a High School All-American, these first minutes of varsity basketball were special.

The '66 Rangers played a suffocating full court 1-2-2 press that gave opponents fits. Kenny Payne was at the point of the press and he was active. Affectionately nicknamed "Squirrel" by his teammates, he was quick and very hard-nosed. He never ran out of gas and brought an energy that rubbed off on his teammates. On defense, Ranger fans grew accustomed to Payne's whistle as he hawked the ball. I looked at Kenny Payne in the 1966 yearbook closely and thought of one word; quick. He just looked quick, and his teammates describe him in that way. Payne was a guy you wanted on your team, but not a guy you would want to play against.

Rich Yunkus: *I really got a kick out of Kenny at times. Coach Herrin could get pretty excited. You really had to be dialed in to understand all that was said. There would be times that we would leave the huddle and Kenny would turn to me and say: "Rich…what did he just say?"*

Unfortunately, Kenny Payne has passed away, but I recently saw his wife Mary Lou at the library. Mary Lou served Benton High School as a math teacher and is now retired. When I was first hired at Benton High School, she was in the final years of her teaching career. I told her about the project and we had a great conversation about the good 'ole days of 1966. She made this comment:

Mary Lou Payne: *Matt, did you ever hear the story about Kenny when we were playing Centralia his senior year? The official stopped the game and told Coach Herrin that he had to tell Kenny to quit whistling…because it was too distracting.*

We both laughed about the story and it made me think of what a great interview Kenny would have been for the book. Kenny certainly had the respect of all of his teammates due to his positive attitude and endless energy.

On the wings of the press were David Woodland and Terry Heard. Woodland and Heard were both smart players with enough athletic ability and discipline to force teams into a trap. The key to the press was Adkins and Yunkus who were the back men. The Rangers extended pressure below the free-throw line, and Yunkus and Adkins would creep up over the center line. As soon as a team passed the ball in-bounds, they were met with a hard trap. Adkins and Yunkus were athletic enough to anticipate passes for steals and easy buckets. They were also smart enough to know when to gamble and when not to. If the ball was passed up the floor, they could hustle back and guard the rim. If teams broke the pressure, then the Rangers most often fell back into a 1-2-2 half-court zone.

Dave Woodland: *Our back guys on the press were not just big, they were athletic. Yunkus and Adkins could anticipate bad passes.*

On the offensive end, the '66 Rangers played a double post offense. Adkins and Yunkus cross screened for each other and flashed to open areas of the lane. The game was officiated much differently than basketball today. The defensive player couldn't hand check and ride the offensive player out of the lane, so it was very advantageous to have size.

The starting cast of the '66 Rangers came to be known to many as "the four splinters and a barrel". The four splinters were Yunkus, Adkins, Woodland and Payne and the barrel being Terry Heard. Heard had a stocky build, and looked like a fullback, but he could play the game. He was not overweight, but very solid and extremely intelligent. He knew where every player was at all times. Heard was calm under pressure and didn't turn the ball over. He knew exactly where the ball needed to go on the offensive end of the floor. He and Kenny Payne complemented each other well at the guard positions. Heard could be vocal if he needed to, and he knew how to communicate with his teammates. He was the valedictorian of the BCHS class of '66. He never made a "B" in his high school academic career. Herrin gave Terry Heard high praise in an interview about the team.

Rich Herrin: *Terry would give me suggestions during the game and most players didn't do that…when he spoke, I listened, I'll tell you that right now. He was one of the smartest players I ever coached.*

David Woodland was also a key member of the '66 team. Woodland averaged 11.1 points per game and was the third leading scorer on the team behind Adkins and Yunkus. He was athletic enough to be bothersome on defense, but his value was his deadly perimeter shooting that opened up Benton's dominant inside game. Woodland was an intelligent player. He knew how to create passing angles and was very unselfish. There was almost a telepathic relationship he had with Yunkus and Adkins. He always knew where they were on the floor, and he could deliver the ball just at the right time to create scoring opportunities for the big men. Teammate Jim Adkins remembers Woodland's game well.

Jim Adkins: *I just remember Woodland being such a smart player. He played the wing and he had this thing where he would catch the ball and look back to Heard at the point like he was going to pass to him…and then he would throw it inside. He would actually move the defense just a little before he passed the ball inside. David was also a knockdown shooter.*

Depth off the bench came from three very talented juniors; Jerry Hoover, Bill Lowery and John Burlison. Senior Jim Hill would also be used at times if the Ranger big men were in foul trouble, but this was not often. Hoover, Lowery and Burlison would gain valuable experience as juniors more in practice than in games.

In 1966, Coach Herrin felt most comfortable with his main five on the floor and substituted only when necessary. Hoover eventually stepped in to run the show on the '67 team and would become one of the greatest point guards in Ranger basketball history. In fact, it would be fair to say that Hoover was the gold standard for all Ranger point guards after his graduation in '67. He was extremely quick and a very smart player.

Jerry Hoover: *That '66 team was a great team. In the Turkey Day Game, which is always the last game of the year against West Frankfort, I banged my knee up. My knee was swollen and I had water on my knee. I got off to a slow start in basketball in '66 and I played off the bench. Kenny Payne was a fun guy and Terry Heard was all business and they were really good players. We won thirty games, you know…I took my playing time where I could get it. I accepted my role and just did my best to help when I got an opportunity.*

Lowery was just a hard-nosed, gritty post player that did his job. He was an above average rebounder and a tough and crafty post defender. He was the type of guy that you needed to win big basketball games in the South Seven Conference.

Bill Lowery: *My skill sets in basketball were pretty limited. We each had roles to play and I played my role. I bought in to Coach Herrin's philosophy about hustle and that was really my role. I played as hard as I could. Coach Herrin told us that there would be nights that a great offensive player will get shut down by a great defensive player. There might be a night when a great offensive player overwhelms a great defensive player, but the ability to hustle and play at 110% can never be taken away.*

John Burlison became a great shooter and a key player on the '67 team. His shooting ability would open up the Ranger inside game of Fustin and Yunkus in '67. Another player off the bench for the Rangers was Mark McCutcheon who was a very good athlete in his own right. He excelled on the football field, and he was a skilled basketball player that sharpened the '66 Rangers every day in practice with his tough play. Hill was a great teammate and a standout football player for the Rangers. Senior Richard Tennant and junior Mike McGuire also provided tough play in practice.

A high school basketball team practices almost three times as much as they play. The quality of the practices is mostly determined by the effort of the team as a whole, and the chemistry among the group. Do the players work hard? Do they like each other? Do the reserves accept their role without causing problems? Also, are the reserves talented enough to push the starters in practice? The 1966 Rangers were a great practice team and the attitude and commitment of the reserve players was a big reason for the team's success.

Also, there has to be a coach that the players respect, that can organize practices and motivate players. Coach Herrin had the respect of his players and when you put all of these different dynamics together, it made playing basketball fun. In fact, it would be fair to say that had some of the reserves played in a different Southern Illinois town they would have received valuable playing time, or possibly could have been a starter. The Ranger reserves played on the number one team in the State of Illinois in 1966, so playing time was hard to come by. Obviously, winning had a great deal to do with how the players remember their experience, but it is not everything. The '66 Rangers had everything; they worked hard, they liked each other, they had a good coach and they had talent. They were a complete package. Junior reserve guard Mike McGuire remembers what he took away from his experience of playing basketball on that great Ranger team.

Mike Mcguire: *You know Mattie, every day in practice I got to play against the best players in the State of Illinois. When I was sitting on the bench, I sat by some of the greatest players that would ever play at Benton like Jerry Hoover. Those three years of playing basketball at Benton High school were some of the best years of my life.*

There were only two people in my life that ever called me Mattie. It was my Grandma, Molly Wynn, and Mike McGuire. Mike McGuire is one of my favorite people and he is a dedicated Ranger fan that still lives in town. His experience as a reserve on the team brought a different perspective to the story of the '66 Rangers. I loved it, because it was a perspective that I could relate to. I played high school basketball for the Rangers in '86 and '87. I played about every minute, but in college I had to adjust and I spent a lot of time on the bench. I kind of look back on my time on the bench at SIU much the way McGuire looks back at his time as a reserve at Benton. I didn't like the bench and I did everything in my power to play, but as I grew older, I saw the big picture. It was the experience and the journey that really counted, and I believe McGuire has also come to this conclusion.

Mike McGuire: *Mattie, a few years ago I was at the Benton Invitational Tournament. It was an early game and Benton wasn't playing and there wasn't much of a crowd. I saw Coach Herrin sitting on the bottom bleacher at the very end of what is usually the Ranger Bench. He was trying to look around the players and coaches that were blocking his view of the game. When I sat down, he said, "I need to move Mac, I can't see anything down here." McGuire saw his chance and smiled back at Coach Herrin and said, "I don't feel sorry for you one bit, now you know how I felt when I played for you." Coach Herrin leaned back and clapped his hands, cackling at the same time and said, "You got me big guy...you got me."*

Another reserve on the '66 team was senior Richard Tennant. Tennant's family moved to Benton the same time that Adkins came to Benton. The Tennant family came from West Virginia and Richard's father was a coal miner. He and Jim Adkins became best friends. I called him at his home in Crestview Florida where he now lives with his wife Pamela. Tennant said something very profound at the start of our conversation.

Richard Tennant: *I thought about that '66 season and I will just say this: I was just proud to be a member of that team and I would rather sit on the bench and be a part of a great team than play a lot on a terrible team.*

Reserve players like Tennant competed in practice every day, but their contributions didn't always show up in the newspaper. Tennant was about 6'1" and he found himself guarding the 6'7" Yunkus every day in practice. Tennant pushed and shoved for position and admitted he fouled Yunkus constantly, but he hoped that it made him a better player. Tennant was quick to point out that he was in the best physical shape of his life after fighting through the grueling practice regime of Rich Herrin.

Richard Tennant: *Coach Herrin's teams were always in great physical condition and I always thought this was one of his strengths as a coach.*

The home of the Rangers was called Benton Gymnasium. Yunkus and Adkins admitted that playing at home was to their advantage. Due to the small size of the Benton floor, the Rangers could use their size to harass teams into turnovers, and it sometimes seemed to opponents that the Rangers were playing with more than five players. They were everywhere. The gym at full capacity could only seat 1,200 fans. It was so tight along the sidelines that the Rangers played with a restraining line that they knew well, but could be confusing for the visiting team. There were a total of 400 reserved seats with about 200 running along the sidelines protected by a rigid black guard rail that separated the playing floor from the fans. Lowery remembered the old guard rails as yet another home-court advantage.

Bill Lowery: *We played in that old gym so much that we knew how to play on that court. I always thought that rigid rail down the sides of the floor gave us an advantage. Our opponents were scared of the rail because it had no give to it so they did their best to stay away from it. We practiced there every day and knew exactly where it was. If we went flying for a ball around the rail we simply grabbed it and pushed ourselves back into play.*

There were more reserved seats created when the legs of study hall chairs were removed and placed above the reserved chair seats. As the gym started busting at the seams with fans, more reserved seating was added on the ends. There were approximately 800 general admission seats that were first come-first served located in the corners of the gym. Portable bleachers were also set up for home games. Custodians set up risers on the stage to give a designated area for the Benton students. Fans seated in general admission were fearful of getting up to get popcorn because they knew they might lose their seat. When the gym was full of fans, it was extremely hot. Rich Yunkus loved playing in the friendly confines of the old Cracker Box.

Rich Yunkus: *That place would be packed to the gills. 90% of the fans were Ranger fans because it was so hard for visiting fans to get a ticket for the game. The gym would get hot and I enjoyed playing in the heat. I felt like I could get loose quicker, and I could breathe better in warmer conditions as opposed to the cold.*

The team benches were located in front of the stage on the north end of the floor, and there was a bird's nest in the northeast corner of the gym that seated the scorekeepers and statisticians. In 1966, Louis Eovaldi was the official time-keeper and Norman Carlile was the statistician. Louis Eovaldi served as a local judge and was a popular gentleman in the community. Today, the varsity baseball field at the Benton Park is named in his honor. Eovaldi was old school, and he didn't take any nonsense from anybody, even Rich Herrin.

Norman Carlile: *I remember in the old gym…Louis controlled the substitutions with a button he pushed in the crow's nest. He was a little late getting one of our guys substituted into the game…Coach Herrin came over and started complaining and Louis fired back, "Coach, you get back to the bench and coach your team…me and Mr. Carlile will take care of what goes on up here."*

BCHS biology teacher, H.M. Aiken, operated the concession stand located in the south lobby. The lobby was small and always crowded, with the smell of cigarette smoke and popcorn wafting through the air. There is a sort of basketball nostalgia that is still felt to this day when walking into Benton's East Gymnasium.

It was common to see Benton students and fans braving frigid temperatures and snowy conditions to secure a seat to the big games with Carbondale and Centralia. Many Benton fans were unable to get tickets and just chose to attend the road games where seats were easier to come by. Caravans of cars full of Benton fans accompanied the team bus on road trips, and there were often more Benton fans present than that of the host school.

Rich Yunkus: *I can still remember looking out of the back of the bus window and seeing just nothing but car headlights following us to and from games. We traveled well. When the team traveled we wore black slacks and a maroon sport coat, with a white shirt and black tie. A lot of teams did this at the time.*

After the Rangers defeated Johnston City in the opener, they played host to the Mt. Vernon Rams and won easily by a score of 82-59. Mt. Vernon's starting center was a player by the name of Danny Hester. Hester scorched the Rangers for 30 points, but the Rangers forced the Rams into turnovers and won the game easily. Danny Hester went on to be the starting center at LSU alongside his college teammate, Pete Maravich.

Jim Adkins told a great story about Maravich from his college days at the University of Alabama. After Adkins' high school career at Benton, he received a full-ride basketball scholarship to the University of Alabama, and the Crimson Tide played LSU on a regular basis.

Jim Adkins: *Do you know I guarded Pete Maravich and held him to 18 points?..In the first half...he was averaging something like 44 and at halftime my coach put someone else on him and he got 30 in the second half. He finished with 48 against us. He was something.*

Adkins enjoyed his playing days at Alabama and mentioned that he loved playing for legendary coach C.M. Newton. Adkins' voice came alive as he recalled his college visit to the University of Alabama.

Jim Adkins: *Coach Herrin flew to Tuscaloosa with me to visit Alabama. When we got on campus we went to the athletic office and the athletic secretary took us to meet the Alabama athletic director. It was Bear Bryant, the legendary football coach. When we walked into Coach Bryant's office his desk sat up on a platform and when you took a seat...he was always looking down on you. I was not familiar with him but Coach Herrin was well aware of who Bear Bryant was.... I will just say this...Coach Herrin always comes across as the guy most in charge but he was very reverent in the presence of Coach Bryant... it's something I always remembered.*

The Rangers were not really tested again until they traveled to play Marion. Marion featured guard Greg Starrick who was a phenomenal shooter. Starrick was a high school All-American and received a basketball scholarship to the University of Kentucky. He played one season for the Wildcats under the direction of legendary coach Adolph Rupp. Starrick then transferred to SIU for his final three seasons and was a standout player. He led the nation in free-throw percentage his junior and senior season. On this night in Marion, Starrick scored 31 points, but the Rangers prevailed 72-69. Jim Adkins scored 28 and Yunkus added 25. The Rangers were too big and too balanced for Greg Starrick and the Marion Wildcats.

Starrick was later selected by the Portland Trail Blazers in the tenth round of the 1971 the NBA draft (155th pick overall) and the Cleveland

Cavaliers in ninth round of the 1972 NBA draft (132nd pick overall, he did not play in league). After basketball, he remained familiar to many people in Southern Illinois by color commentating SIU basketball games alongside legendary broadcaster Mike Reis. When I interviewed Starrick, he asked me about the '66 team and when I said the name Jim Adkins he cut me off to say this:

Greg Starrick: *Oh, I remember Adkins well. That cat was really good…and so smooth around the basket.*

Before Christmas, the Rangers defeated Herrin and a very talented Carbondale team who were predominantly juniors. The Rangers were a perfect 6-0 heading into the Centralia Tournament.

The Centralia Tournament first began during the World War II year of 1942. It is a three-day tournament held between Christmas and New Year's featuring sixteen teams and attracting over 6,000 spectators each year. The tournament is a basketball extravaganza featuring some of the top teams in every area of the state. Each Christmas, Ranger fans flocked to the tournament in droves to see the Rangers play, and the tournament became the highlight event of the holidays. Older men from Benton would carpool to the tournament and stay all day and then discuss the teams and players on their forty-five minute ride home.

During this time, Trout Gym was the Mecca of high school basketball in Southern Illinois. The gym was named after Arthur Trout who coached at Centralia from 1914 to 1951. Trout's longevity and success at Centralia is incredible. Arthur Trout coached thirty-seven years at Centralia, compiling a record of 811-330. Coach Trout won three State Championships and placed in State three other times. During the mid-sixties, the Orphans were still the top team in Southern Illinois. Trout gym was much bigger than Benton's Gymnasium. Reserved seating lined the sidelines and ends of the court and general admission seats were tucked under the overhang of an upper balcony that went all the way around the gym. The Centralia student section was located behind the Centralia bench and it was called "The Orphanage". Rich Yunkus said it was his favorite gym to play in on the road.

Rich Yunkus: *It was an unbelievable atmosphere to play in. The tournament was very prestigious, it was warm like the East Gym and it was a great jump-*

ing floor. The smell of popcorn...and when it was packed it could really get loud. It was just a great basketball venue.

The Orphans got their unique nickname during the early 1900's when the boys basketball team advanced to the State Tournament. At the State Tournament, an announcer commented that the team looked like a bunch of orphans on the court because of their tattered uniforms. The name stuck.

The Rangers first entered the Centralia Tournament in 1954, but had never come away with a championship. Their best showing was 1962, when they placed second to the host Orphans. The '66 Rangers opened the tournament on Tuesday afternoon, December 28, 1965, against Lincoln Way, a team from up north. The Rangers rolled as Adkins led the way with 25 points and Yunkus added 24. In the quarter-finals the next day, the Rangers defeated Edwardsville 91-71. Yunkus dropped in 32 points, with Adkins adding 25. The game was over early and Herrin strategically substituted to rest the legs of his starters. Again, it was the full-court pressure that was creating easy scoring opportunities as the Rangers scored a whopping 169 points in the first two games of the tournament.

On Thursday, December 30th, the Rangers had to win in the semi-finals against the largest school of the tournament, New Trier. There are many factors that play into winning two basketball games in one day such as nutrition, rest, conditioning and the mental fortitude of being focused for sixty-four minutes of competitive basketball. In the semi-finals, the Rangers defeated the Trevians, 78-63, to set up one of the greatest championship games in tournament history. Senior guard Dave Woodland scored 18 points against New Trier and remembered the game well.

Dave Woodland: *Something I remember about the Centralia Tournament was we had to beat New Trier to play Thornton for the Championship. We played New Trier in the afternoon and they were a northern school that had about 5,500 students. Our enrollment was about 750 students. They had a big seven-footer with the last name of Rosenzweig. I just remember that Yunkus took him to school. Our expectation was to win regardless of the size of the school and the seven-footer. We expected to win, period.*

The Rangers were now a perfect 9-0 and were ranked number two in the State of Illinois. In the Championship game that night, the Rangers played number one Thornton. Thornton Township High School is located in Harvey, Illinois on the south side of Chicago. Thornton was 10-0. So, it was number one Thornton, from upstate vs. number two Benton, from downstate.

Basketball fans buzzed with anticipation about the championship matchup. The Benton fans that saw the semi-final against New Trier stayed in Centralia and ate a late lunch and passed the time until the evening session. Back at Benton, many Ranger fans listened to the semi-finals on the radio and then jumped in their cars that evening and raced 48 miles northwest to Centralia. They weren't going to miss it!

After the semi-final win, the Ranger players retreated to the team bus and went to a steakhouse in nearby Womack. The players needed to un-wind before the 7:30 championship match-up with Thornton. There are few times in our lives when we can vividly remember the happenings of a particular day. All of the Rangers I interviewed quickly recalled that cold, winter night in Centralia when they met Thornton in the finals.

Rich Yunkus: *The gym was packed and Thornton was very big and physical. I remember Kenny Payne got a big steal and an easy bucket…and the game kind of turned. Coach Herrin had us in great physical condition and you could just see it coming…we wore them down.*

Thornton had a 6'10" center by the name of Jim Ard who went on to play college basketball at the University of Cincinnati. Ard was drafted in the first round of the ABA draft and was the sixth overall pick of the Seattle Supersonics. He played in the ABA from 1970-1973 and had his debut in the NBA in 1974. Ard was a physical specimen and was the first player the average fan noticed because of his tremendous size. Jim Adkins re-membered his match-up with Jim Ard that memorable night in Centralia.

Jim Adkins: *Ard guarded me and he had trouble with me. I flashed through the lane a couple of times and would catch the ball and shot fake to lift him off his feet…and then raise up and shoot it. Sometimes I faced up and drove to the basket. He had trouble with me…so they moved Lamar Thomas on me, and I had a couple of inches on him…so I took him to the post.*

Lamar Thomas was the point guard on the Thornton team and was a great athlete. He had tremendous strength and quickness and went on to play Big Ten football at Michigan State University. The Rangers used their full-court pressure to harass the Wildcats into turnovers that led to easy baskets. The Rangers defeated Thornton, 70-63, and the victory is still regarded by some as the greatest win in Benton basketball history. After the game, the championship trophy was presented to the Rangers and then it was time to celebrate. It was a raucous locker room with congratulatory hugs being passed among players and coaches alike. The victory still lives in the memory of the Ranger players and proved so strong that it bonded the team for life. Later in life, players and fans alike passed the story of the great victory over Thornton to future generations. Rich Herrin had this to say about that special win over Thornton to win his first of a record six Centralia Tournament Championships:

Rich Herrin: *The Thornton game of '66 and the Belleville Super-Sectional game of '61 are probably the two most memorable games of my high school coaching career.*

Jim Adkins had an outstanding performance in the tournament, and was possibly the best player on the floor that night against Thornton. The Wildcats had no answer for his quickness and slashing ability around the rim. Adkins scored 30 points in the championship game and had ten rebounds to earn All-Tournament honors. Adkins was selected as the most outstanding player of the Centralia Tournament in '65. Rich Yunkus scored 19 points and tallied 12 rebounds, and was selected to the All-Tournament Team. David Woodland had a solid tournament by netting perimeter shots that opened up the inside game for the Rangers. Heard and Payne were solid as usual.

After showering and talking to sportswriters, the Rangers boarded the team bus. They were having the time of their lives. The players grouped up on the bus and rehashed moments of the game and then speculated if they would now be the number one ranked high school team in the state. The Coaches sat toward the front of the bus and discussed the game. Fans heading home from the game raced to the square to gather with those that listened on the radio to welcome the team back to town. On the outskirts of town, the team bus was escorted to the public square by fire trucks. As the bus circled the square, the townspeople of Benton celebrated a victory that will forever live on in Ranger lore. Benton, 70 – Thornton, 63.

When the Rangers returned to practice on Monday, January 3rd, things had changed. Yunkus and Adkins admitted that after beating Thornton they knew they were on a very special team. The Thornton win moved the Rangers up in the state rankings to number one.

For the first time since Herrin had arrived in Benton, people from the community began showing up to watch practice. Coach Herrin locked the gym doors to close practice to the public. There were some people like Claude Rhodes, Elmer Jenkins, Wilbur Vanhorn and Chubby Rice that he would allow to come in to watch the Rangers. Ranger fans were buying "Go Rangers" buttons, boots and even cowboy hats. The town was just crazy, and it was pretty special to be a basketball player in Benton at that time.

The Rangers were also getting good press. During this time, people followed their sports teams by reading the newspapers. During the era of the sixties and early seventies, Bob Tedrow was the sports writer for the Benton Evening News. The Benton Evening News served as the only newspaper in town and it was the news source for the townspeople of Benton. In his coverage of the team, Tedrow was knowledgeable and fair to the players and coaches. Tedrow had a good rapport with Coach Herrin; therefore, he gained unlimited access to the team. His writing was creative and he could really spin a story. He always sat near the end of the Rangers bench at home games and he started a popular sports column in the Benton Evening News called "From the Bench". The column provided inside information about the team and would even give the Benton townspeople information about universities who were interested in recruiting particular Rangers. The townspeople of Benton followed his writing. Tedrow's creative writing and inside information about the team brought the Benton public inside the journey of all the great Ranger teams, and it created a heightened awareness about basketball in the community. Tedrow's coverage lifted the basketball players to celebrity-like status. Not only did the young boys in town know the names of their favorite players, but older people that seldom went to the games could recite the names of the players and coaches. The people of Benton were well-informed about their favorite team.

Rich Yunkus: *I was at Battle's getting a bite to eat and I had my car with me. Jimmy Davis and John Malkovich were kind of wandering around Battle's. They were just kids in junior high. This is John Malkovich the actor. They asked me for a ride home and so I told them to get in the car and that I would take them home. I dropped them off and then they walked back to Battle's to get their bikes so they could ride them home. I guess they knew who I was… and just wanted me to give them a ride home.*

The Rangers also received state recognition from a writer by the name of Pete Swanson of the Evansville Courier. I found it interesting that when I opened the old statistic books that were kept by Norman Carlile, the phone number of the Evansville Courier was on the first page, front and center. It was Carlile's job to report the scores and statistics of the Ranger Games to the Evansville Courier after each contest. The Courier had a large Sports section in the Sunday edition of the paper. Swanson would take the scores and write glowing articles about Rich Herrin and the Benton Rangers. Swanson's favorable articles about the Rangers gave them statewide recognition. The articles not only shed light on the great teams, but it gave recognition to individual players in the area that may be talented enough to play at the college level. There is no doubt that Yunkus and Adkins were benefitting from the positive exposure created by the Evansville Courier. In fact, there were more Benton citizens receiving the Evansville Courier on Sundays than the Southern Illinoisan.

Coach Herrin knew that the team was getting a lot of notoriety, so he addressed it with his team one day after practice. Yunkus remembered Herrin told the team something that stuck with him the rest of his life.

Coach Herrin: *You guys are getting a lot of notoriety…Just remember, when you are in public, your actions…what you say…and what you do…because there is a little kid who idolizes you…they will do exactly what you say and do.*

When Yunkus told me this story, he was emotional, because this made a big impression on him. In this moment, I realized what a great influence Coach Herrin had on his life. All these years later, Yunkus still remembered the words of his high school basketball coach, and I'm sure he passed all of these truths to his daughters. When I asked Jim Adkins to describe Yunkus as a player, he paused and said this:

Jim Adkins: *Smooth…smooth! He moved smoothly and he had a smooth jump shot.*

Yunkus also was quick to point out that Adkins was a force to be reckoned with and a teammate that challenged him to raise his game.

Rich Yunkus: *When he got a lot of attention…then it was good for me and vice versa. We played off each other and we complimented one another well. There were nights after practice that Adkins and I would go home after prac-*

tice…get a bite to eat and then go to the gym and play one on one. I know it helped me…because I was playing against a very good player and I think it helped him also.

Yunkus and Adkins remain the greatest post-player duo in Benton basketball history. Each night, teams had to deal with two Division I players inside and it was hard to contain them both. Usually, one of them could not be contained. Yunkus averaged 22.6 points per game and 13.8 rebounds per game in '66. Adkins averaged 20.6 points per game and ten rebounds per game in '66. In my opinion, Jim Adkins is in the top ten Rangers of all-time. His statistics speak for themselves. Adkins went on to score 1,103 points in his high school career at Benton. The numbers are incredible; they truly were a dynamic duo in '65-'66.

It is also important to know that their numbers were within the structure of the team. Yunkus and Adkins were friends, and they did not resent each other's success. There was not a scoring or rebounding competition among them. They were team players. In fact, there were many games that Yunkus and Adkins did not play the fourth quarter because the score of the game was so lopsided. Bill Lowery remembered something that he really admired about Yunkus' game.

Bill Lowery: *Yunkus had amazing offensive skills around the basket…but he wasn't just a black hole. When the ball went to him in the post…he didn't automatically shoot it. If he felt a double team or the defense collapsed, he would pass the ball back out to a guard for a better shot. He was definitely our scorer, but he played team basketball.*

After winning the Centralia Holiday Tournament for the first time in Ranger history, the team put their efforts toward winning the South Seven Conference. The Rangers had never won the Conference in basketball since the league had been formed. Yunkus recalled something that he had never seen Coach Herrin do after winning the Centralia Tournament.

Rich Yunkus: *We played our games on Friday and Saturday nights so it was Coach Herrin's way to only take one game at a time. The weekend after the tournament we played Centralia on Saturday night. It was always our way of doing things to prepare all week for the Friday night game and then have a walk through the next day for the Saturday game. The idea was to take one game at a time and not get ahead of ourselves. During this week, we prepared*

for Centralia all week and just played Harrisburg on Friday night and won.
It's the only time I remember doing it in high school.

Coach Herrin's strategy for the weekend worked. The Rangers defeated
Harrisburg Friday night 73-58 and then beat Centralia Saturday night, at
Trout Gymnasium, by a score of 68-52. The Rangers then won the Quad
City Tournament in Fairfield and finished the month of January with a
perfect record of 8-0. The Rangers overall record stood at 18-0.

On February 12, 1966, the Centralia Orphans came to town. The
Rangers dismantled the Orphans, 75-54, in front of a packed house. Before the game, an older man walked into the gym with what looked to be
his son. Herrin noticed the two men immediately because of their size.
They were both tall. He assumed the boy was in college, and shifted his
focus to beating the Orphans and remaining undefeated. When the final
horn sounded, the teams shook hands and headed for the locker room.
Herrin was in good spirits. The Rangers won, but most importantly, they
played well. The team was moving in the right direction, and this was Herrin's thought as he began his walk to the locker room. As he approached
the door leading to the locker room, the tall man he remembered entering the gym before the game, stepped in front of him and said, "Coach, I
would like to talk to you." Herrin looked up at the man and said, "Let me
talk to my team and I'll be right up." Coach Herrin addressed the team,
and then headed upstairs. He was curious about his visitors.

When Herrin walked out of the locker room, he saw the two strangers sitting on the bottom row of the bleachers. As Herrin approached,
both of them rose to their feet. The young man towered over Herrin.
The father extended his hand and said, "Coach Herrin, my name is Joe
Fustin, and this is my son Greg. My son is a junior at Taylorville High
School, and we want to come to Benton and play basketball next year."
Coach Herrin had some key move-ins during his twenty-five years as
head coach of the Rangers and this is mostly how it happened. People
like winners, and when you start winning, you get attention. Joe Fustin
and his son had been tracking the Rangers. They knew of their number
one state ranking, they saw the Rangers beat Thornton, and they just
witnessed the Rangers take a good Centralia team behind the woodshed.
They had seen enough. They wanted to be a part of a winning program.
Joe Fustin also wanted his son to play for Rich Herrin. There are many
people from other towns that accused the Rangers of recruiting; some
have even dubbed the team the "Benton Strangers". As the program sus-

tained its success, there would be more. This process is summed up with this simple phrase: if you win, they will come. Herrin loved winning basketball games. Of course he wanted Greg Fustin to come to Benton in '67, but he first had to finish the '66 season. According to Herrin, after this brief conversation with the Fustins, there was no correspondence with the Fustin family until June of '66.

The Rangers final test of the season came when they played Carbondale, on February 19, 1966. The head coach of the Carbondale Terriers was John Cherry, and he had a very talented squad of mostly juniors. Carbondale featured players like L.C. Brasfield, Early "Peaches" Laster, and 6'9" center, Billy Perkins. The Terriers also had a fine point guard, Kenny Lewis, shooting guard Phil Gilbert, and forward Terry Wallace. The Rangers won the ballgame by a score of 65-61. Yunkus led the Rangers in scoring by netting 23 points, and Woodland chipped in 15. It was a happy bus ride home from Carbondale that night. The Rangers finished the conference season undefeated and captured their first South Seven Conference Championship in school history. With two games to play in the regular season, the Rangers record stood at a jaw-dropping 22-0. Perfect, just like Yunkus would prefer.

Ranger fans poured into the Cracker Box for the final home game of the regular season against the McLeansboro Foxes. It was senior night, and it would be the last time Ranger fans would see Adkins, Payne, Woodland, Heard, Hill and Tennant play. The six seniors were honored before the game. The Benton faithful had grown to love the seniors.

The Rangers led only 25-23 at halftime, and 48-44 to start the fourth quarter. Rich Yunkus was quietly putting together a game for the ages. Yunkus had 34 points going into the fourth quarter of play. The attention was on the game, of course. The Rangers did not want to lose their last home game and suffer their first loss of the year. Ranger fans stood and cheered as the Rangers pulled away and Herrin removed the starters late in the fourth quarter.

Upon being taken out, Terry Heard jogged toward the bench and manager Jon Battle tossed him a towel. Heard then found a seat on the bench next to sports writer, Bob Tedrow. Tedrow leaned over and whispered in Heard's ear, "Yunkus is one bucket away from the single season scoring record." Heard then got up and walked to Coach Herrin and told him what Tedrow knew. Yunkus was on the bench at the time and had no idea; he was oblivious to the circumstances. Coach Herrin shooed Heard away and sent him back to his seat on the bench. As Heard returned to his seat, Tedrow locked eyes with him and shrugged his shoulders as if to say, "That's all you can do, kid." With just minutes left in the game, Coach Herrin grabbed Yunkus by the shoulder and sternly said, "Get a bucket and I'm taking you out." Yunkus then entered the game and quickly hit a short baseline jump shot. Coach Herrin quickly removed Yunkus from the game, and he was replaced by senior Richard Tennant. Yunkus then jogged back to the bench with the BCHS single game scoring record of 45 points. Yunkus' single game scoring record stood for twenty-five years, before Jo Jo Johnson scored 47 points in 1992 against the Cairo Pilots. His teammates were happy for him and it would be a night he would never forget. In the last game of the season, the Rangers defeated Alan Crews and the DuQuoin Indians by a score of 68-54 to end the regular season at 24-0.

'66 State Tournament Play

The Rangers opened regional play at Max Morris Gymnasium in West Frankfort. Max Morris Gymnasium was always the preferred site of post-season tournaments in Southern Illinois because of its immense space. West Frankfort even managed to host Super-Sectionals during this time. Max Morris Gymnasium featured a lower bowl of seats just above the court and then a middle bowl of bleacher seating tucked directly underneath the balcony. The Gym can seat up to 4,000 people. It was first opened in 1950 and named after Max Morris, who was a great multi-sport athlete in the 1940's. He went on to play basketball and football at Northwestern University. The Rangers enjoyed unprecedented success during the sixties and seventies in post season play at Max Morris Gymnasium. The 1966 Rangers walked thru the Regional Tournament defeating the host Redbirds in the championship by a score of 61-45.

The Sectional was held at Davenport Gymnasium in Harrisburg, Illinois. Davenport looks like an airplane hangar with seating from the floor level into an upper level on both sides of the court. There is very little seating on the ends. There is quite a bit of court space behind the benches and the lighting is dim. The colors of purple and white are found everywhere, and the place is as sturdy as a WWII bunker.

The Rangers opened sectional play by squeaking out a nail biter against Danny Hester and the Mt. Vernon Rams. The Rangers led by four going into the fourth quarter, but the Rams were playing with house money. The pressure was on the Rangers. They had not been beaten. Mt. Vernon was loose, and they had nothing to lose, but the Rangers hung on. Adkins led the Rangers by scoring 23 points along with 17 from Yunkus. The Rangers defeated the Rams by a score of 55-49 to win the Harrisburg Sectional.

Rich Yunkus: *This one went right down to the wire and I remember when I got home…my dad told me that he went to the parking lot because he couldn't bear to watch it.*

The Sectional final was played on Friday night, March 11, 1966. During the day the players were in a complete fog at school. Again, the excitement of basketball season had trumped the need for a good education. Some of the players were trying to think about anything but the game and some thought only of the game. At school, students were finalizing their plans for the thirty-five minute drive east to Davenport Gymnasium that night. After first hour, the bell rang and as students passed to their next class, they cheered, and the halls were filled with young excited voices chanting, "RANGERS, RANGERS!" The students focused on getting through the school day and then racing to Harrisburg for the sectional final. The Rangers did not disappoint. The Rangers led Metropolis 34-26 at half-time and then stormed out of the locker room and outscored the Patriots 27-15 in the third quarter to win the game 79-64. To begin the third quarter, the Rangers forced turnovers, and played with renewed energy to surge ahead of the Patriots. Yunkus ripped the nets for 31 points, and the Patriots had no answer. Woodland also stepped up and dropped in 22 from long range.

After the game, the Rangers were presented with the Sectional Championship trophy. The Sectional Championship trophies of the sixties are my favorite. They are heavy and feature a basketball player in a passing motion. There is a gold plate in the front that reads; 1966 Sectional Champion. My second favorite trophy is the old South Seven Ball. It is a gold ball that sits on top of a solid wood block, with a plate that reads; South Seven Champ, and the year. The trophy is simple and to the point. What makes the trophies even more attractive is when there are many of them sitting side by side. The banners are nice, but in my opinion, the collection of trophies in the west foyer of Rich Herrin Gym is the greatest visual to Ranger basketball dominance. Remember, the '66 team was the first team to earn a South Seven Championship team trophy. Before

Herrin left Benton, his teams would win ten more South Seven Championships. Good basketball became the identity of the town, and after '66, the Rangers seemed to always be in contention to win the conference in basketball.

Funny story I have to tell you about my son Gehrig. He graduated in 2019 and played on three great Ranger teams. His junior year, the Rangers finished 31-3 and beat Marion and Carbondale to win the Regional Championship. They defeated Cahokia in the first game of the sectional, but then lost to Centralia. His senior year they were 25-6. He was fortunate to have great teammates and coaches (Ron Winemiller, Wade Thomas, Jason Hobbs and Casey Wylie). After he graduated, I took him to the Centralia Tournament to see some games. The tournament featured larger schools with players that were destined to play college basketball. Gehrig was impressed with the size and athleticism of the teams. I told him, "You know…we (the Rangers) won this thing six times." I took him into the front lobby of the new gymnasium. Centralia has done a great job of showcasing all of their basketball tradition in the lobby. It is a new gym complete with a new school. It is not the old Trout Gym that Yunkus spoke so affectionately of, but the new gym is very classy. We started looking at the trophies and I began walking him through some of Centralia's basketball history. We got to the South Seven Trophies and he made this comment: "Dad, I thought you said Centralia was really dominant…Where are all of those South Seven trophies that you like?" I then realized Centralia had a few of them sprinkled in their case, but not like we have. I proudly said, "They're all over at our place in the trophy case at Benton." We both laughed and kept looking around. I'll never forget that.

After winning the Harrisburg Sectional, the Rangers matched up against the Centralia Orphans in the Carbondale Super-Sectional. The Super-Sectional was played at the spacious SIU Arena in Carbondale. There is an old saying in sports that says, "It is hard to beat a good team three times." Some would say it is hard to beat a good team once.

Dave Woodland: *Coach Herrin had such a clear understanding of the game. He understood how to teach the game and he was a winner. He was very good at tweaking things if we happened to play a team more than once or twice.*

If the Rangers were to advance to the State Tournament, they would have to beat the Orphans a third time. Centralia had All-State guard Roger

Westbrook and they were a dangerous team despite the Rangers two regular season victories. The Orphans came prepared and they hung tough with the Rangers to the very end. The Rangers led by nine points going into the fourth quarter, but Centralia did not lie down. The Orphans outscored the Rangers by six in the fourth quarter, but it wasn't enough. The Rangers held on to win 46-43 in front of a sea of fans.

With most teams eliminated from State Tournament play, hordes of people packed the arena to watch the Orphans and the Rangers. The game was played on a Tuesday night and the Rangers bused home to a hero's welcome on the Benton square. Fans lined the streets as their beloved Rangers waved through the bus windows. What a feeling for the players. In three days, they would take the floor at the State Tournament in Champaign. This could be it. Herrin must have known that he may never have a more effective one-two punch than Yunkus and Adkins. It was possible for the Rangers to win it all, and everyone felt it. The town of Benton was consumed with the thought of winning their first basketball State Championship.

Coach Herrin took the Rangers to State in '61, and this experience set the precedent for the itinerary of events that occurred before Friday's game in Champaign. Like in '61, the student body returned to the basketball trance they had fallen into just five years earlier. Talk of the game, plans to get to the tournament, cheering between classes, and adults sipping their early morning coffee talking about nothing but basketball, summed up the week. The people of Benton read the articles of Bob Tedrow and found that virtually all of their conversations were about the Rangers. It was memorable for the school and the community. The excitement was electric.

Rich Yunkus was also excited. How could he not be? He was seventeen years old and all of this success and notoriety happened so quickly. Just a year ago, he was practicing with the sophomores. Now, the Rangers were ranked number one in the State of Illinois, and he was receiving college attention from about every major college in the country. He was just a junior. Remember, Yunkus walked to the beat of his own drum. It was not his way to live in the past and rehash games like so many people like to do. He told me a story that really gave me some insight into his mental approach to basketball.

Rich Yunkus: *My parents went to all of my games. They would often have couples over after the game and they would sit around and rehash the games. Go through all of the plays. I remember one time we had a home game and I* *came home after the game because Coach Herrin had a curfew for all of the players. When I got home, I walked into the house and everyone started asking me questions about the game. I was polite; I answered the questions because I knew I had to. But the next day, I told my mom I couldn't do that anymore. I couldn't talk about the game for another forty minutes. I just don't want to do that. When the game is over, it's over, and I don't want to talk about it anymore.*

After he told me this story, I really admired his thought process. There are a lot of athletes that sit around and talk about what happened in the past; Yunkus did not. Did Yunkus learn from his past experiences in order to improve his game? Absolutely! But he did not rest on his accomplishments or beat himself up for his mistakes. He learned and moved on. This type of approach is important to all people who are successful at what they do. What is next? The expectations of athletic performance is simple, "What have you done for me lately?" Yes, a player can score thirty points on Friday night, but it's also important he plays well on Saturday night. So after thinking about it, I admired his mindset of not living in the moment, but just moving on.

The '66 Rangers received a pep session on Thursday and then traveled north to a Ramada Inn, near Assembly Hall in Champaign. On the trip north, their minds wandered and many of the players let themselves imagine what it would be like to win the State Championship. The Rangers played the second game of the afternoon session against Galesburg. The team had a walk through scheduled in the morning at a nearby high school.

Jim Adkins: *I remember before the first game we took some photographs for the media and someone held up an iron because we were a pressing team. We went into a restaurant that weekend and ran into Dick Butkus. It was just a magical time.*

Rich Yunkus: *My grandmother packed my pork and beans that I always ate before games…and I remember that morning we ate in the hotel and I had to find someone to open that can of pork and beans for me. I got some funny looks.*

Mike McGuire: *I've got a story about the State Tournament, Mattie. The IHSA only allowed ten players on the bench during post season play in 1966. We had 12 players on the team. Me and two other players drew straws to see* *which tournament we would dress. I forget who the two other players were. I drew the long straw which meant I had my choice as to which tournament I would dress. I chose the State Tournament. Remember, if we would have gotten beat in the Regional or Sectional I wouldn't have dressed at all. That's how much faith I had in that team. I didn't think there was a team that would beat us, and fortunately it worked out. I got to dress in the State Tournament at Champaign against Galesburg. Something I will never forget.*

On March 18, 1966, at approximately 2:30 in the afternoon, the Rangers busted through a paper hoop decorated by the cheerleaders and ran on to the Assembly Hall floor. Junior Jerry Hoover led the Rangers onto the floor as the Rangers divided into two line lay-up shooting. Unfortunately, it was against IHSA rules for mascots to lead the team onto the floor. Seven-year-old Rod Herrin, (Coach's oldest son) had led the team onto the floor all year but all was not lost for young Rodney.

Rod Herrin: *They wouldn't let me run the team out because it was against the rules. But I remember when we went to state in '66...we stayed at a Ramada Inn and it had an indoor swimming pool...when you're little you know that is the thing...it was the first time I had ever stayed overnight in a hotel. That was a big deal.*

The adrenaline pumped through the veins of the players and Mike McGuire's heart skipped as he shot his first lay-up on the floor of Assembly Hall. Most high school players never get this thrill and McGuire was full of pride knowing that he made the right choice by choosing to dress in the State Tournament. It was the game within the game for McGuire, and he had outfoxed them all. He relished in the moment of playing at Assembly Hall in Champaign, Illinois.

The Silver Streaks of Galesburg came into the game with a record of 26-2. They were solid, and it would be a great coaching match-up featuring two of the best coaches in Illinois high school basketball, with Rich Herrin from Benton and Coach John Thiel from Galesburg. At the time, Coach John Thiel was a coaching legend in the State of Illinois. He was slightly older than Herrin and had been at Galesburg since 1955. He is still the winningest basketball coach in Galesburg history with an incredible record of 398-90 (.816 winning percentage). In 1966, the Silver Streaks were loaded. Galesburg was a very physical team and they had good size and strength. Their best player was Dale Kelley, who later went on to play Division I basketball at Northwestern University. This was a tough draw for the Rangers. Galesburg was no joke.

The Rangers were dressed in their maroon uniforms. The border of the Rangers shorts were lined in maroon and white. The shorts were very high, as was the style of the mid-sixties basketball trunk. The tank top sported thin straps that simply said Rangers arched across the chest with a maroon and white boarder with enlarged numbers on the front and back. In those days, the road uniforms were always dark with an odd number. For example, Rich Yunkus' number 40 is now retired at Benton High School, but in 1966, Yunkus wore number 40 only at home games. The home game uniform was always white. On the road, Yunkus wore a maroon jersey, number 41. This helped the officials report fouls knowing that the home team always wore even numbers, and the away team wore odd numbers. The Ranger players wore one of their shoelaces in maroon and one in white. All of the Ranger players were right-handed, with the exception of Yunkus, so they chose to wear the maroon shoestring on their right shoe. Naturally, with Yunkus being left-handed, he wore the maroon shoestring in his left shoe. The Rangers all sported short hair and some had fresh flat-tops received from the town barbers, Homer Jones and Dave Barnfield.

The town came out in force and gladly drove the three hours north to watch their beloved Rangers. Assembly Hall was huge and there was quite a bit of space behind the baskets that served as a tough shooting background for some players. The SIU Arena was similar in this regard, and the Rangers hoped for the same outcome. The Rangers stayed with their plan of a full-court 1-2-2 press. Why would they change anything now? They were 30-0. The Rangers started the game well, and settled in nicely against the Silver Streaks. Galesburg standout Dale Kelly came out firing, scoring 11 of the Streaks' 19 points in the first quarter, but the Rangers kept the pace and even pulled ahead by three at halftime (36-33).

Rich Yunkus: *Galesburg was physical and they were just a solid basketball team. We certainly didn't look past them. They were very good.*

In the third quarter, led by Kelley's 14 points, the Streaks surged ahead and held a lead of 54-46 entering the fourth Quarter. The court at Assembly Hall was a collegiate floor and it was certainly not the small, tight floor of the Cracker Box. The floor was spacious and the Rangers had a difficult time disrupting the Streaks with their full-court pressure. Also, Galesburg was really good. They were definitely the best team the Rangers played besides Thornton.

Jim Adkins: *I really felt like the size of the court at Assembly Hall kind of hurt us. Our press was not as effective. The floor was just bigger. I do remember at halftime having a feeling like, hey we got this.*

The Rangers showed their resolve by battling back and tying the game late. The Rangers had no answer for Dale Kelley, as he scorched the Rangers for 11 points in the fourth quarter. With the score tied at 71, he hit a shot with about five seconds left to seal the win. The Rangers quickly passed the ball in bounds and Jim Adkins heaved a long shot toward the rim that had a chance, but fell off the mark. It was over. Galesburg defeated the Rangers by a score of 73-71. Dale Kelly scored 31 points for the Silver Streaks. Dave Woodland ended his high school career by leading the Rangers in scoring with 25 points and Adkins chipped in 17 points and Yunkus added 15. The Streaks eventually played Thornton for the 1966 Illinois State Championship. The same Thornton team the Rangers defeated in the Centralia Tournament. Thornton won the ballgame 74-60 but the score was not indicative of the game. Thornton jumped out to a 47-25 halftime lead and never looked back.

When I asked Yunkus about the loss, he painted the picture of a tough defeat.

Rich Yunkus: *The locker room wasn't pleasant. When you win 31 in a row... you're not ready to get beat...but we all took it like men, you know. Galesburg was really good and we just got beat. On that day...a better team had beaten us. We didn't have anything to be ashamed of.*

This was Coach Herrin's second loss in the opening round of the State Tournament. In '61, he had to be coaxed out of the locker room by his brother Ron and fellow coach John Cherry to address the media. He was twenty-seven years old and was an emotional wreck after the gut wrenching defeat of '61. He locked himself in the locker room and cried. It is fair to say that although it was a very tough loss, Herrin himself had matured and had a better perspective on picking himself up off the mat. He was certainly not in a good mood following the game, but a more experienced and mature coach came out of the locker room to face the music. He fielded tough questions as he rehashed the game with reporters, and he graciously gave Galesburg credit for a game well played. There is an old saying in athletics that "you learn the most through your defeats" and you could certainly see the growth in Herrin's ability to move on after a tough loss. What hurt him the most at this time was the fact that it was over for the seniors. He loved his guys. Jim Adkins, Terry Heard, Dave Woodland, Kenny Payne, Jim Hill and Richard Tennant. They were good kids and Herrin enjoyed their company. Through their hard work and sacrifice the tradition of good basketball in the town of Benton would continue for years to come. Herrin knew '66 was special, and the finality of it was tough for everyone.

Most of the Benton fans that attended the game drove home that same day. They had anticipated a whole weekend away from home and a possible State Championship, but it just wasn't to be. Karen Young (Baker) is a member of the BCHS Class of '66, and she vividly remembered the disappointing ride home after the season ending loss against Galesburg.

Karen Young (Baker): *After the game me and my girlfriends hopped in the car and headed back to Benton. We were so disappointed. We went to all of the games. It was a quiet ride home and we were boo-hooing about the loss. On our way home we saw Kenny Tate and Mark Darnell broken down on the side of the road. We picked them up and took them back to Benton with us. We were crammed into the car like sardines. That basketball season was incredible, we were all into it!*

Karen still lives in Benton with her husband Fred. Their son Bryson was a standout player at Benton and graduated in 1989. She was the vice president of the class of 1966, and is diligent about organizing class reunions, so she became helpful in my search for phone numbers.

Mike McGuire recalled a conversation he had with Coach Herrin at the 50-year reunion for the Class of 1967. Coach Herrin and Sue make it a point to go to several of the old Benton class reunions. Coach loves to catch up with his former players. He is no longer coaching and he has a tendency to reflect back to certain decisions he made with feelings of melancholy. Over the course of twenty-five years at Benton High School, he made thousands of big decisions that directly affected young people. Should I keep this kid? Should I play this kid? Should I dress this kid? Should I discipline this kid? How should I discipline this kid? Herrin sometimes reflects back and fears that he may have been too harsh or maybe made a mistake that hurt someone. When he was younger, he was in the moment and just made the decision. Now, he's older and more reflective. He worries about the fairness of his decisions. Rich Herrin is human and he wasn't perfect. He made mistakes. I'm sure there are a few ex-players that are bitter at something he did, or did not do, and that comes with the territory. You're just not going to please everybody. Coach Herrin is getting older now and his time to say sorry is running out, and sometimes his mind dwells on these instances and it bothers him. Mike McGuire tells a great story about something that happened at the '67 class reunion that he will never forget.

Mike McGuire: *Coach Herrin cut me my senior year in '67. I think he had younger players that he felt like needed an opportunity to play and so 1966 was my last year of basketball. He saw me at the class reunion and called me over and apologized for cutting me. I could tell that it really bothered him and that he needed to say it. Mattie, I looked at him and said, "Coach you don't have anything to apologize for, those three years of playing basketball were the best years of my high school years. I got to play against the best of the best in the State of Illinois every day in practice and I want to thank you for that experience."*

McGuire had let this incident go long before the class reunion, but it still bothered Coach Herrin. Today, McGuire and Herrin are close and they like to spar with each other and tell stories. They laugh together, and you can tell they enjoy each other's company. Life is too short and there are no hard feelings about the '67 basketball tryouts. It's over.

Today, Coach Herrin's impact on the players of the 1966 team is evidenced by what their lives have become. Is Coach the sole reason for their success after basketball? Absolutely not! But during the players formative years; there was a coach in their ear, talking about the importance of hard work, unselfishness and doing things the right way. There was a coach motivating them to work toward a common goal and guiding them through a time in their lives they would never forget. All of these important life lessons were taught under the guise of basketball. The players were eager to talk about the past, but most importantly, they are all doing very well in the present.

Jim Adkins attended the University of Alabama on a full-ride basketball scholarship. Besides guarding Pete Maravich, he attended some of the home football games and saw legendary coach Bear Bryant in action on the sidelines. Adkins enjoyed his college experience and loved the area of Tuscaloosa. After serving a two year military commitment at Fort Bragg, North Carolina, he returned to Tuscaloosa and was a special education teacher for eight years. He later moved into an assistant principal's role and then would go on to work as a high school principal. He currently lives with his wife Deborah, who was also a teacher. They have one daughter, Amy, who is a teacher as well.

Kenny Payne married Mary Lou Gulley and remained in the Benton area. After high school, he served his country as a paratrooper in the U.S. Army from 1968 to 1970. Kenny sustained a life-changing injury in 1976. He was admired and respected by all in the way he adapted to his limitations. Kenny and Mary Lou have two boys; Doug and Chuck. Kenny remained a life-long Ranger fan and attended most of the home games. He was loved by his '66 teammates and respected for his energy and ability to always keep things light. Kenny was also the co-captain of the Ranger football team and was a great pole vaulter in track. Kenny passed away on April 16, 2016. He was sixty-seven years old.

Dave Woodland went on to play basketball at MacMurray College and played for a young Itchy Jones. Jones was a standout athlete at Herrin High School and would later be known by the people of Southern Illinois for leading the SIU baseball team to the College World Series. Woodland started as a certified public accountant but would later work in hospital administration and become the CEO and owner of a company in Nashville, Tennessee. Today, Woodland is retired and lives with his wife Susan in Nashville, Tennessee. He has one son, Chad who resides in Sesser. He is proud of his two grandsons, Clayton and Gavin.

Richard Tennant graduated from SIU in 1970 with a bachelor's degree in Zoology. After attending SIU, Tennant enlisted in the military. During his service in the United States Air Force he met his wife Pamela. While in the Air Force he advanced to second Lieutenant and then retired from the Air Force in 1992 as a Major. Tennant was a fun interview and he still stays in touch with his good friends, Jim Adkins and Terry Heard. He and his wife Pamela have one son, Francis.

Mike Mcguire served in the Vietnam War in 1969-1970. He drove a supply truck. When he returned from the war, he married his high school sweetheart Vickie and they settled in Benton. Mike worked for thirty-five years as a coal miner at Old Ben 24. He first served as an underground laborer and later became a mine examiner. Mike and Vicki have two boys;

Michael and Tyler, who both live in Benton. After retiring from the mines, Mike worked at the park as a groundskeeper. He is still very visible in the community and he relishes his role as a Grandpa to his five grandchildren. He loves basketball and still attends the games. He provided a great perspective to the story of the '66 Rangers.

In the spring of 1966, many of the basketball players were strongly encouraged to go out for track. Yunkus and Adkins would run and so would most of their basketball teammates. Herrin enjoyed track because there was a winner and a loser. A track meet is scored by points based on the finish places of each event. A track meet can be very competitive and Herrin loved the fact that a runner was either faster or not, could throw farther or not and could jump higher or not. There is very little subjectivity in track. He loved the strategy of determining what athletes should participate in what events, which is a key skill in being a good track coach. He saw to it that all the big men on the basketball team ran the high hurdles. In the 110 high hurdles the distance between the hurdles is 9.14 meters. Herrin would place the hurdles about ten meters apart to make his hurdlers stride out and extend. He enjoyed putting relay teams together and deciding which runners would receive the baton early or late in the exchange zone. He liked the fact that his basketball players were competing, spending time with one another and maintaining their physical condition. High school baseball in the State of Illinois was not yet a sport at Benton High School.

In 1966, the Rangers fielded close to fifty athletes on the track team, and most all of the key basketball players would come out. Many of the seniors that were done with their high school basketball careers made it a point to come out for track. Successful track teams are often based on the amount of athletes that are willing to come out for the team. For example, the fastest kid in Southern Illinois may be walking the halls, but if he doesn't come out for track nobody would ever know. Good track teams have good numbers and Coach Herrin and Coach Stewart were very good at persuading their athletes to run track. In fact, the 1976 Benton Ranger track team finished undefeated and was the South Seven champion against schools that had more enrollment and arguably better athletes, but the Rangers got the athletes out.

In the spring of 1966, Rich Herrin was a happy man. His basketball team just finished the season with a record of 31-1 and advanced to the State Tournament for the second time in six years. His players were all out for track and he knew that '67 would be a special year with the return of

Yunkus, and a solid group of incoming seniors. He also knew that it could really be good if that big Fustin boy would go ahead and move to Benton.

In early April, Coach Herrin got a call from Joe Brockett. Joe Brockett was a Benton native who was coaching at a junior high in Edinburg, Illinois. He called to see if Herrin could be the guest speaker at a basketball banquet for his junior high basketball team. Herrin accepted the invitation and thought it might be a nice getaway for him and Sue. Invitations to speaking engagements such as banquets or coaches clinics were becoming more frequent with the success of his Benton Rangers. Herrin looked at the map to find Edinburg and noticed that it was very close to Taylorville. Perfect, Herrin thought to himself. After speaking at the banquet, he planned to give Greg Fustin a visit. He had not told Sue his plans. Herrin enjoyed himself at the banquet. He encouraged the junior high boys at Edinburg to work hard and to listen to their coaches and teachers. He and Sue stuck around to speak to Joe Brockett after the banquet before leaving. Upon getting into the car, Herrin's mind shifted to meeting the Fustin family. He was curious when they were going to move to Benton. He had a lot of questions. Were the Fustins actually going to move? If so, when would they be moving to town? Did Greg have a tall younger brother? Did the father manage to get a job in the coal mines near Benton? There was much to talk about as Herrin raced for the Fustin home. Then something happened that really speaks to Coach Herrin's reverence of Sue.

Sue noticed they were not heading down Interstate 57 to Benton and asked, "Where are you going?" Rich, thinking nothing of it, and blinded by his basketball goggles said, "I'm going by the Fustins…if I can find their home." Sue looked at Rich and simply said, "Rich…I wouldn't do that. It's not the right thing to do." Rich thought about it, mumbled his justification for the visit, but ultimately turned the car around and headed back to Benton. He knew Sue was right. The bottom line is this; he didn't go. He would let the Fustins decide for themselves if they would move to Benton in '67, and he was crossing his fingers hoping they would.

A picture of Rich Herrin in the fall of 1965. *(Benton High School)*

Jim Adkins won the MVP of the Centralia Tournament in '65 and scored over 700 points his senior season. He was truly one of the great Rangers of all-time. *(Rich Herrin family collection)*

Kenny Payne was lightening quick and had the habit of whistling on the defensive end of the floor. *(Rich Herrin family collection)*

Coach Herrin admitted that when point guard, Terry Heard, had a suggestion; he listened. Heard was valedictorian of the class of '67 and had a tremendous basketball IQ. *(Rich Herrin family collection)*

Dave Woodland was the knockdown shooter that opened up
the Rangers inside game of Adkins and Yunkus.
(Rich Herrin family collection)

As a junior, Jerry Hoover played behind Terry Heard in '66 and
then burst on the scene as one of the top guards in Southern
Illinois in '67. *(Rich Herrin family collection)*

Bill Lowery provided hustle and physicality to the '66 team.
(Rich Herrin family collection)

Reserve player, Richard Tennant, made a profound statement in
our interview when he said; "I would rather sit on the bench for a
great team than play every second on a bad team."
(Rich Herrin family collection)

Mike McGuire said that playing basketball at Benton was
one of the greatest times of his life because every day he
practiced against some of the best players in the
State of Illinois. *(Rich Herrin family collection)*

What a picture! Herrin poses with the "Four Splinters and a Barrel."
From L-R Payne, Adkins, Herrin, Yunkus, Woodland and Heard.
(Rich Herrin family collection)

Another picture of the great 65-66 five sporting their team blazers and cowboy hats. *(Rich Herrin family collection)*

The Rangers used the small floor of the 'Cracker Box" to suffocate smaller opponents with their stifling 1-2-2 ball press. *(Rich Herrin family collection)*

Bill Lowery claimed the railing down the sidelines created a great home court advantage for the Rangers 1-2-2 pressure. *(Rich Herrin family collection)*

Centralia's Arthur Trout is still revered as one of the greatest basketball coaches in state history. At Centralia, Trout was 811-330 in 37 years with three state championships. *(Centralia High School)*

Old Trout Gymnasium in Centralia has provided Rangers fans
with many great moments. *(Centralia High School)*

The Rangers were popular among the town because of Bob Tedrow's
fair and thorough coverage in the Benton Evening News.
(Rich Herrin family collection)

Marion guard, Greg Starrick, was Southern Illinois' version of "Pistol" Pete in the 60's.

Yunkus battles Perkins for a rebound at Carbondale.
(Rich Herrin family collection)

A happy group of Rangers after their 79-64 Sectional Championship at
Davenport Gymnasium in Harrisburg. *(Rich Herrin family collection)*

Adkins slices to the basket against Centralia in the '66
Super-Sectional victory. *(Rich Herrin family collection)*

The Benton coaching staff walks to the locker room at halftime
with a 36-33 lead over Galesburg in the quarterfinal game of the
'66 state tournament. *(Rich Herrin family collection)*

The town poured out in droves to greet the Rangers on the square
after their return from the '66 state tournament.
(Rich Herrin family collection)

CHAPTER SEVEN

Benton Becomes a Basketball Town in '67

"It was just a magical time" – Joe Browning, Voice of the Rangers

During the long, hot summer of 1966 there were hundreds of race riots that took place throughout the country. The civil rights movement led by Martin Luther King forced the country to re-evaluate the famous words of Thomas Jefferson; "All men are created equal." At this time, there was also unrest about our country's participation in the Vietnam War. Each night, Americans tuned into the news on television about the war and began to question the purpose of our involvement in Vietnam. Anti-war protesters flooded the streets in great numbers in most American cities. Young Americans voiced their political beliefs more than ever and demanded that they be heard. Our country was changing, and on a much smaller scale, so was the town of Benton.

The town of Benton, Illinois in the 1960's fell in line with Norman Rockwell's vision of small town America. In 1967, the town of Benton had roughly 8,000 inhabitants. There was the historic Franklin County Courthouse nestled in the middle of the Benton Public Square that was lined with thrift shops, a drug store and several small diners. A popular hang-out for BCHS students was Battle's Grill on the southwest corner of the square. This classic soda fountain-type restaurant catered to high school students by serving soda and burgers, and lined its walls with pictures of all the great Ranger basketball teams. The citizens of Benton were friendly and hard-working. Most of the men worked in the coal mines and many of the women were now entering the workforce. Faith in God was important to the community, and Christian churches of various denominations were embedded in neighborhoods all over town.

The kids of Benton could be seen everywhere. Remember, technology was limited in those days and children spent much of their time outside. They could be seen on bikes, jumping rope, playing marbles and even just walking the streets. Most noticeable to all outsiders of Benton was the number of boys that could be found outside playing basketball. There were basketball rims everywhere. Basketball rims hung on the sides of garages, some hung from telephone poles, others from the sides of trees and some were even found in barn lofts. There were also outdoor courts at Logan School, Douglas School and Grant School. The sound of a bouncing basketball was as common as hearing a bird chirp or the engine of a car. The town had fallen in love with the game of basketball and young boys in Benton began to aspire to the possibility of one day playing for the Benton Rangers.

This basketball fever that took over the town of Benton in the 1960's began with the arrival of Rich Herrin and the success of his Benton Rangers. In his first season, the Rangers made an improbable run to the State Tournament in '61. In '66, the team won the Centralia Holiday Tournament and the South Seven Conference for the first time. In fact, after upsetting number one ranked Thornton, the Rangers were the top ranked team in the state for the remainder of the season. The '66 Rangers went 31-1 before being eliminated in the State Tournament by a tough Galesburg team. The people of Benton had confidence in their young basketball coach and they now began to expect good basketball teams. By 1967, the town of Benton had become a basketball-crazy community, and the town of Benton became known throughout the state as a basketball powerhouse.

In June of 1966, incoming juniors Danny Johnson and Bruce Taylor heard there was a new kid that moved in, and he was shooting baskets in the gym. Johnson and Taylor hurried over to the gym to get a glimpse of their new teammate. Johnson and Taylor may have been the first players to lay their eyes on Taylorville transfer, Greg Fustin.

Danny Johnson: *I have to say that when we first saw him...we couldn't believe it. He was big, but he couldn't dunk it. We kind of laughed at first... but then I have to tell you...he got better. He ended up really helping us in '67 because he was such a big body.*

I asked Johnson about Fustin's improvement and he was quick to say, "The coaches worked with him to make him better." "Raw" is the most polite way to describe Fustin's game when he first arrived in Benton in June of '66. He stood at a solid 6'8", but his footwork in the post needed work. In June of '66, he was far from ready to play in the South Seven Conference. Greg Fustin was going to be a senior. Needless to say, the challenge for Fustin was to improve his footwork and offensive skills in such a short amount of time. Coach Herrin worked long hours in the gym individually with Fustin in order to develop his game. He taught Fustin how to post up and use his 6'8" frame to his advantage. The Mikan drill forced Fustin to keep the ball high and improve his touch around the rim with either hand. Herrin motivated Fustin to "speed his motor up", and was relentless in urging him to rebound. Each drill had a purpose and was important in creating muscle memory and good habits on the offensive end of the floor. Later in the fall, Coach Herrin had Yunkus and Fustin play one-on-one against each other in the post. Fustin proved to be a good pupil, and his improvement was noticeable. By December, Fustin was game ready in the rugged South Seven Conference.

Team chemistry is another important element that plays into the complex dynamics of a move-in player. Would there be hard feelings if Fustin took playing time away from one of his teammates? The '67 Rangers were worried about winning games, and if Greg Fustin could help, so be it. All of the Rangers accepted Fustin and welcomed him as their teammate.

On July 15, 2020, I again made the short trek to the home of Rich Yunkus. I was really looking forward to our meeting because the ice had been broken. He fully understood the vision of the book and was totally on board. Again, Donna greeted me at the door and took me back to the living room area where we had met just weeks earlier. Yunkus had two great years ('66 and '67) at Benton and then an unbelievable career at Georgia Tech, so it was my idea to meet twice. There was just too much information for one sitting, so Rich was gracious enough to meet a second time. In the first visit, we focused on his family and his junior season of 1966. Today, the focus is on his senior year and his career at Georgia Tech. We made small talk for a while, but then went straight to his senior year of 1967. Before I could say anything, he looked at me and made this comment.

Rich Yunkus: *I kind of felt like our junior year, we had earned the number one ranking in the state when we beat Thornton at Centralia. Then, when the*

'67 season began, we were ranked pre-season number one in the state…and those expectations were kind of inherited. It was just different.

I really enjoyed talking basketball with Yunkus, because I found his basketball mind to be very cerebral. On the floor, Yunkus was efficient. There was just no wasted motion, and there was a purpose for everything he did on the floor. He is arguably the greatest high school player Benton has ever had, and he is left-handed. I asked Yunkus if he thought being left-handed was an advantage to him as a player. He thought for a moment, and gave me a great answer.

Rich Yunkus: *I always thought that being left-handed gave me two and sometimes three baskets a game. Basketball is a game of instincts. Most players are so used to defending right-handed players, their instincts will sometimes take over and they might play the wrong shoulder…just forgetting I was left-handed. I think it gave me four to six points a night.*

Yunkus also had the ability to be a good shot blocker, yet stay out of foul trouble. This rare combination is a great indication of his basketball IQ. There is a phrase used by coaches in the game of basketball today called "wall up". To wall up simply refers to the defensive player's ability to maintain a vertical defensive position with their hands straight up to avoid fouling the offense. Walling up requires the defender to display self-discipline by staying vertical and not fouling. Yunkus was walling up before the terminology came out. He realized that his size alone altered shots and rarely was in foul trouble. He did not revel in swatting the ball into the second row of the bleachers; he blocked shots by simply tapping the ball to himself, and then getting the ball to his guard. Bill Russell made the play famous. Why swat the ball out of bounds and have the offense take it out underneath their own goal, when you can just tap it to yourself and go the other way? Yunkus became a great shot blocker in '67. He shared his thought process on the art of blocking shots.

Rich Yunkus: *Whenever I attempted to block a shot, I always watched the offensive player's eyes. When the offensive player looked up to the rim…I jumped.*

Yunkus was also becoming a great rebounder. Thru constant play, he improved his ability to read the trajectory of a shot to determine where the ball would bounce off the rim. Yunkus was such a dominant rebounder in '67, that one long-time Benton Ranger fan took notice.

Bob Gariepy: *I graduated from Benton in 1957 along with my wife Nora Jane. When we first started going to the games we actually sat on the steps in the Southwest corner of the gym until Herbert Mundell got us reserved seats in the nearest section. Yunkus was such a great rebounder…that in '67…I came up with the "R-E-B-O-U-N-D" chant.*

When I played for Coach Herrin at SIU, he emphasized how important rebounding was each day in practice. There is no doubt that size and instincts play big in rebounding the basketball, but so does heart and tenacity. A rebound is essentially a loose ball, and it comes down to a determined fight to get the ball. Good rebounders are usually competitive and embrace the fight for the ball. Coach Herrin could motivate all players to go get the ball. Coach Herrin was a great motivator and his teams were very good at winning battles for loose balls and rebounds.

Harry Stewart explained the art of rebounding in very simple terms in one of my sophomore practices in '85. One day in practice, Coach Stewart grew so frustrated with our rebounding effort that he stopped practice. Again, there was a long silence. I knew something profound was about to be said. He bellowed, "Do you guys like pork chops?" We all kind of half-nodded our heads "Yes." He then said; "You've got to go after the ball like you're one of nine children…and Daddy just threw a pork chop on the table." It was classic Harry Stewart. I never forgot that advice, because it was both funny and true. He was right. This is exactly the effort and tenacity of a great rebounder.

There are so many different skills that make up the game of basketball that it can be easy to underestimate the value of a rebound. There is only one thing I felt Coach Herrin loved more than rebounding, and that was scoring. He loved to watch the ball go in the net, and he loved to play an up-tempo type of basketball. He fully understood that before his teams could run, they had to have the ball. In fact, all successful running teams are good rebounding teams. When I close my eyes and think back to our practices in the SIU Arena from 1987-1992, the word that Coach Herrin used the most was, "rebound!". There is no doubt that Yunkus and the '67 Rangers constantly heard him say the word, "rebound".

As a senior, Yunkus was a much more polished player than he was as a junior. With much hard work, he made himself a great shooter, but most importantly, he was much stronger. He just wasn't getting bumped around as much. Usually a player with superior physical strength translates into a more confident player.

It was also his second full season playing the back of the Rangers fierce full-court 1-2-2 press, and he was just better and more experienced. He was much improved in the area of anticipating errant passes and knew when to gamble and when not to. He had the athletic ability to sprint back to the goal to prevent easy baskets. He was like a goalie. In fact, Yunkus' ability to guard the basket allowed the Benton guards to turn up the ball pressure and overplay passing lanes. Sharpshooting Marion guard Greg Starrick remembered the Rangers well and he made a great point about Yunkus' ability to guard the rim.

Greg Starrick: *Rich Yunkus was such a great rim protector. Matt, how many times have you seen a guard get beat off of dribble penetration…and then get scored on. It happens in front of everyone and so the coach takes the guard that got beat out of the game, right? But, if you were Hoover or any of the Benton guards…you might get beat on dribble penetration…but there was a good chance that Yunkus would block the shot. Let's face it, a great shot blocker allows the guards to take more chances and overplay the ball. The guards know that if they get beat off the dribble…they have the shot blocker to bail them out of trouble.*

In '66, Yunkus and Adkins complimented each other well. With the loss of Adkins to graduation, the addition of Greg Fustin to the Ranger line-up in '67 was huge. The 6'8" Fustin gave the Rangers a rebounding advantage and another shot blocking presence. Most importantly, his presence took some defensive pressure off Yunkus. Now, there were two big men to guard and not just one, which made defending the Rangers a difficult task. More often, the presence of Yunkus greatly helped Fustin. Yunkus usually drew the top defender, which sometimes left the 6'8" Fustin with a player half his size guarding him. Benton Rangers sportswriter, Bob Tedrow, dubbed Yunkus and Fustin the "Twin Towers". Yunkus recalled his old teammate Greg Fustin.

Rich Yunkus: *Greg was low-key…he was easy going and quiet. When he first came to Benton he was raw…. He was a big body. He became a good offensive rebounder and every game he got a little better.*

How do you top 31-1 and a trip to the State Tournament? The expectations for the '67 team were extremely high. Yunkus was possibly the best player in the state and was the only returning starter. Heard, Woodland, Atkins and Payne were lost to graduation, but the Rangers reloaded. At the point guard position it would be senior Jerry Hoover. As a junior, Hoover came off the bench and played behind Heard and Payne, but he had game.

Rich Yunkus: *Jerry added an extra dimension to our offense. He kind of had an outgoing personality…He was quick and had good hands. He could shoot it and he was very up-tempo.*

As I looked at the '67 BCHS Yearbook, I came across a picture of Jerry Hoover and studied it closely. He looked like the all-American kid. Hoover wore a tight flat-top and was a member of every club in the school. He displayed a wide grin in every picture. Much like the look of Kenny Payne, you could assume he had some quickness by his athletic build. There was this fun energy about him that I'm sure radiated to those around him. I called Jerry at his home in Houston, Texas and we had a great conversation. The energy that I assumed about him revealed itself in our conversation, as he recalled his days as a Ranger.

Hoover moved to Benton in the fifth grade, and his father, Billy, owned a John Deere tractor dealership out east of town. Hoover's mother's name was Mary Francis and she served as a great fan and encourager to Jerry throughout his athletic career. The Hoovers lived in a white two-story house on a 500-acre farm on Route 14, complete with horses and cattle. He had two younger brothers and his father expected them to work on the farm. Jerry recalled that there was so much work to do in the summer that he didn't get to play Little League baseball. There was very little free-time growing up in the Hoover household. He recalled his first memories of Basketball in Benton.

Jerry Hoover: *When we first moved to Benton in the fifth grade, I went to Grant School. I was a Grant Green Gorilla. I do remember always trying to flirt with Betty Blondi, who was Bobby Blondi's sister. One day at recess, our principal, Perry Eisenhower, walked up to me and said, "You are going to be on our basketball team." He was the principal and the coach…and he was a great guy…a great competitor. I think because he was also our principal… there was nothing like getting a little positive feedback from Perry Eisenhower.*

Perry instilled in us the will to win. I remember we practiced outside on the courts behind Grant School, and I just loved to play. Behind our house there was a concrete slab left from a house that had burned down, and I would have my buddies over, and we would play all the time. I remember shoveling snow off of it in the winter so we could play. Anytime I could slip into a gym and play, I would. I was a gym rat!

One of the biggest compliments I felt Hoover received was from Danny Johnson. Johnson was a junior on the '67 team and played a key role in the team's success. When I was interviewing Johnson, we were talking about the '67 team and he cut in and said, "Have you talked to Hoover yet?" I told Danny that I had and then Johnson paused for a moment and made this comment:

Danny Johnson: *I liked playing with Jerry Hoover…He had a spirit about him and we worked well together when we trapped the ball. He was a good teammate.*

Hoover had fond memories of all of his coaches at Benton. In football, Jerry was a slot-back and the position allowed him to run and catch the football. He was a skilled football player, and enjoyed playing for Coach Harry Stewart and Coach Maurice Phillips.

In 1967, Coach Maurice Phillips was the Rangers' sophomore basketball coach. Phillips was a Benton High School graduate of 1954, and played college basketball at Erskine College with fellow Ranger Bob Johnston. Phillips began his coaching career at Benton in 1964 and served as assistant basketball coach through the sixties and into the seventies. Coach Phillips knew the game well, and deeply cared for his players. The players respected his basketball knowledge and his patient demeanor. He taught history at Benton High School and the students loved his easygoing personality, and his passion for Illinois history. Coach Phillips had a son that was born in '67, and according to Bob Tedrow's sports column; he named his second son Jerry, after Jerry Hoover. I called Coach Phillips at his home located south of town. He loves to work outside and is in great physical condition for a man in his eighties. I asked Coach Phillips to speak about Jerry Hoover, and this is what he told me:

Coach Maurice "Moose" Phillips: *Hoover was a great athlete that played all sports…He was very unselfish and he always put the team first. He was* *very serious about everything he did…He was a good leader through his actions. After he graduated, the family moved to Hopkinsville, Kentucky and I would go down and take him fishing.*

Coach Phillips later coached varsity football at Benton and is now retired. He, along with Coach Harry Stewart, proved to be instrumental in teaching and developing players at the underclassmen level.

Senior John Burlison started at the off-guard position in '67. Burlison lived on the South Side of Benton and attended Logan Grade School as a youngster. Growing up, he loved to play basketball and could be found playing on the outdoor courts with his friends at Logan School. As a junior in '66, Burlison played sparingly. As a senior in '67, he was suddenly thrust into the starting line-up of possibly the greatest Ranger team in school history. He responded. Burlison's ability to hit the outside jump shot provided a balanced attack to a team that at first glance, seemed to be strictly an inside team. The "Blonde Bomber" opened up offensive opportunities for the Twin Towers by hitting long jump shots. In '67, Burlison averaged 9.6 points per game, and was a solid defender. He complimented Hoover well at the guard position by spotting up and canning shots off of Hoover's ability to penetrate and kick.

At the small forward position, the Rangers started senior Bill Lowery. As a junior, Lowery was the first post player off the bench. Lowery grew up on the east side of town and attended Douglas School. Lowery was "blue collar". He was a tenacious rebounder and was able to guard players that were taller because of his physicality. Lowery's competitive fire and grit were key ingredients to the great recipe of the '67 Rangers. There were times that Coach Herrin would quickly substitute junior Danny Johnson into the game in Lowery's spot, but Lowery did his job and didn't complain. He proved to be a great team player and enjoyed playing for Coach Rich Herrin.

Bill Lowery: *Coach Herrin was a player's coach. There would be times after practice that he would play two-on-two…and three-on-three with us. He would get in there and mingle with us… but he could tow that line of interacting with us on a more personal level but still be our coach. We respected him.*

I was very curious about Lowery's take on Fustin moving over in '67. I assumed that the addition of another inside player may have cut into

Lowery's playing time. I asked Lowery this question: What were your feelings about Greg Fustin moving to Benton in '67?

Bill Lowery: *He worked in with us well. There were no issues with Greg at all. We all understood our roles and we knew that he could help us win games.*

There was no hesitation in his response and I came to the conclusion that every team needs a Bill Lowery. I remember Yunkus telling me a neat story about Lowery that really spoke to how different the player-coach relationship is today, compared to 1967.

Rich Yunkus: *Bill had a girlfriend that lived in the Ewing area and Coach Herrin had a curfew for the players on the weekends during the season. We played on Friday and Saturday nights. On Friday night our curfew was 10:30, because we had a game the next night. He would enforce the curfew by sometimes randomly checking on us. On Saturday night, we had a little later curfew of 11:30. After the game we might go uptown to get a soda, but Bill and his girlfriend couldn't stay long because he had to get her home and the get home himself. One day after practice, our whole team walked into Coach Herrin's office in the East Gym. We asked Coach Herrin if he would extend the curfew until 11:45 so Bill had enough time to get his girlfriend home by 11:30. He said, "No". Then we asked what if we all keep our curfew at 11:30 and Bill has a curfew at 11:45? I think he liked the fact that we were sacrificing our curfew for a teammate. He thought about and said, "Curfew's at 11:45 for all of you, but you better not break it."*

There are a few things that strike me about the story. First, there are not many coaches in today's age enforcing a curfew on their players. Also, it is neat to see the whole team try to help a teammate and it speaks to the respect that the players had for each other. The curfew story also sheds light on the expectations of being a Benton Ranger in 1967. Playing basketball for the Benton Rangers was a privilege, and there were expectations not only on the floor, but off of it as well. Lowery told me that he remembered the incident, and he gave me a funny response to the story.

Bill Lowery: *You know…I do remember that…but I will tell you this; Coach Herrin was the ruler and all. But the one guy I feared the most was my dad, and I sure wasn't going to break his curfew.*

Off the bench, the Rangers played juniors Danny Johnson, Dick Corn and Bruce Taylor. Danny Johnson made the team better instantly when he came into the game. He provided immediate energy and stifling defense. Johnson was an athlete. He had a quick first step and could jump out of the gym. As a junior, he thrived in the up and down pace of the game, and was a defensive juggernaut on the point of the full-court 1-2-2 pressure. Players of opposing teams feared a hard trap by Danny Johnson and Jerry Hoover.

Norman Carlile: *Danny Johnson was the best player I have ever seen at anticipating a bad pass…He just knew where the ball was going. On the offensive end…he was a slasher. Matt, he was just a tremendous player… Tremendous.*

As the back-up point guard, Dick Corn proved to be steady and dependable. Corn's minutes with the '67 club proved to be valuable in preparing him for the starting point guard position in '68. Junior Bruce Taylor was very capable off the bench at the post position. Early in the season, he provided the Twin Towers with a quick rest but his role expanded after Fustin's jaw injury. As a senior, Taylor was one of the better post players in Southern Illinois and provided the Rangers with much needed offense. The other players on the '67 team were juniors Dennis Miller, Mike Davey, David Choisser, and Gary Kearney.

At this time, it was typical that Midwest high school basketball was played at a slower, more methodical pace. In the off-season, Coach Herrin attended basketball clinics in the east and loved the wide open, creative style of East Coast basketball. The East Coast brand of basketball was played at a faster pace, and players played with more freedom. Herrin wanted his players to enjoy playing the game, and he felt players preferred a faster and more aggressive style of play. This would be the pace at which the Rangers practiced.

Practices were intense and up-tempo. The beginning of practice focused on fundamentals. The players were divided into small groups for what was called "station work". Each station focused on a different fundamental. There were stationary ball-handling drills along with change of direction dribble drills that focused on the cross-over, behind the back, between the legs and whirl dribble. As the players handled the ball they were coached to keep the ball low with their eyes up to see the floor. There were passing drills that included skills such as jump-stopping and pivoting. The second part of practice was a controlled scrimmage. The whole floor was in use, and Herrin used controlled scrimmages to interject key teaching points. He often played the first team against the second team, blowing the whistle only to teach or correct. Players were constantly in motion, keeping them in great physical condition. The Rangers rarely conditioned without the basketball. Coach Herrin called running without the ball, "cross country practice". He didn't believe in it, and he knew the players didn't enjoy it. He understood from his own playing experience that players would willingly run if the basketball was involved.

There was no standing around. Coach Herrin hollered out directives as play was happening, forcing players to think on their feet and remain "locked in" through moments of fatigue. The players liked the full-court drills where they could get the ball and go. Herrin believed the fast-tempo approach allowed players to work hard and have fun at the same time. Although Yunkus was 6'7" as a senior, he was not awkward. He could fill a lane and finish a transition play if the guard was crafty enough to get him the ball. The players chirped and communicated with one another. Every drill had purpose. The Rangers were expected to play in practice just as they would in a game. Unfortunately, the team was so dominant in '67 that they were pushed more in practices than some games. The Rangers played 31 games in the '67 season, winning 19 of those games by more than 20 points. They dominated basketball in Southern Illinois.

The Rangers' style of play was becoming well-known throughout the state. It was an aggressive brand of basketball that featured a suffocating full-court 1-2-2 pressure. If the opposing team broke the press, the Rangers then dropped back in a variety of half-court defenses that depended on the scouting report. Coach Herrin made every effort to gather information about the opposing teams. On off-nights, he scouted. He made telephone calls to his coaching friends to get information on the enemy. When the Rangers played home games, assistant coach Maurice Phillips slipped out of town to scout the next Ranger opponent. Coach Herrin loved to win, but most importantly, he loved to prepare to win.

The Rangers could see the fruits of their labor and the players all bought in. Working hard and winning games together created strong bonds among the players. In the sports world, this special connection among teammates is referred to as "team chemistry". The '67 team had talent plus chemistry, and it proved to be a deadly combination to Ranger opponents.

The team opened the season by playing Johnston City on December 2, 1966, at Benton. Fans piled in wearing cowboy hats, buttons and some even wore cowboy boots to show their enthusiasm. Rich Yunkus was a creature of habit, and he believed that mental preparation was just as important as physical preparation. Since his junior year, Yunkus made it a point to leave his home in West City no earlier than 7:00 p.m. for a home basketball game. He needed time to mentally prepare for battle and sitting on a hard bleacher watching a sophomore game did little to focus his mind on the game. On the nights of home games, his parents left for the games to get their seats, but Yunkus would depart for the gym at a later time. Yunkus drove to the gym by himself, and entered a side door to the gym. He would then then slip into the locker room and focus his mind on the game. Again, there was no wasted time, all business. It was his way, and it worked!

As the Ranger players took the floor, they had the look of a very good basketball team. Someone today might say they "passed the eye test". The Rangers had extraordinary size with Yunkus, Fustin, Taylor and Lowery. The guards of Hoover, Johnson, Burlison and Corn looked like young marines. The players all sported a clean flat-top to show solidarity. They were rated number one in the state when they took the floor and also had the look of a top-ranked team. The fans marveled as the Rangers effortlessly rose above the rim and dropped the ball in the hoop during two-line lay-ups. Johnston City did their best to look the part in their pre-game warm-ups, but they had to feel that they were in for a thrashing as they glanced toward the Rangers' end of the floor. Following the pre-game warmups, BCHS agriculture teacher, B.L Finley, announced the starting line-ups. Official timer Lou Eovaldi and scorekeeper Norman Carlile readied themselves in the crow's nest of the northeast corner as the ball was tipped to open to what some believed to be the greatest basketball season in Benton Ranger history.

The Rangers dominated the game behind 30 points from Rich Yunkus and 19 from Greg Fustin. The Twin Towers were too much for the Indians. Jerry Hoover ran the team nicely, and chipped in 14 points. Junior Danny Johnson scored just three points, but the energy he created in the Rangers' full court pressure was noticeable. Ranger fans were pleased with what they saw and Coach Herrin was happy with the team's play. The Rangers won the opener by a score of 83-59.

The dilemma for Coach Herrin in '67 was to figure out how to challenge the players and keep them sharp. The Rangers played as tough a schedule as you can play in Southern Illinois, but very few teams could test them. There were few situations where the team had to come from behind, or make a big play to win a game.

Rich Herrin: *I was a little concerned about the fact that we were not battle-hardened…It worried me because it was hard for us to get better…but this group really didn't need an edge…they practiced hard every day. They (the players) were pretty tough and they did things the right way…made my job pretty easy.*

Coach Herrin admitted that the second team of the Rangers was sometimes more competitive than their opponents. He also was quick to point out how the junior players like Danny Johnson, Dennis Miller, Dick Corn and Bruce Taylor benefitted from the intense competition with the seniors in practice.

Rich Herrin: *Our second team was pretty good…our juniors really got better in '67 because we had great practices and they played with great players like Yunkus and Hoover. We had a good team in '68…because of all those practices the year before.*

The Meridian Bobcats then came to town on December 10th, under the direction of legendary coach Jim Byassee. On this cold Southern Illinois night, the Rangers would be too much for the young Bobcats. The Rangers defeated Meridian 83-56 in the sold-out Cracker Box. Yunkus had his way by scoring 32 points, while Fustin chipped in 19.

The Rangers opened South Seven play by hosting Marion, and All-American guard Greg Starrick. Starrick was a senior and was an unbelievable high school talent. He had tremendous skills and played with unbridled creativity. He was an artist.

Danny Johnson: *Starrick was one of the best players I ever played against. I remember one time I cut off the baseline on him…and Hoover was a little late trapping him…he passed the ball behind his back to a teammate under the goal. I thought, wow!*

Starrick was the Southern Illinois version of "Pistol" Pete Maravich. As a senior, he scored 70 points against West Frankfort. He ended his high school career with 1,975 career points. I had the pleasure of interviewing Greg, and was excited to get his perspective of Coach Herrin and the Benton Rangers.

Greg Starrick (Marion Guard): *As a player, I loved the challenge of playing against Rich Yunkus and the Benton Rangers. Coach Herrin's teams played so hard and they were so fundamentally sound. Matt, Jerry Hoover was a really good player too. He had such a quick release...and he knew how to get Yunkus the basketball. Hoover had good quickness and could also shoot it...He was capable of going for 15 to 20 points on a given night.*

The Rangers were ready and defeated Marion by a score of 95-52 in a packed house at home. Starrick played well by scoring 30, but Yunkus netted 34, with Fustin adding 16.

Rich Herrin: *Greg Starrick was an incredible player...His father was a legendary coach and he grew up around basketball.*

In the northwest corner of the Cracker Box, Joe R. Browning did the play-by-play on WFRX for the '67 Rangers. Browning was my neighbor when I was a boy and I knew him well before he moved to San Diego, California in 1993. He became the Ranger play-by-play in 1961 and was the voice of the Rangers until 1975. Joe explained to me that the 1967 Ranger basketball team gained popularity in Southern Illinois because the Ranger games became part of a basketball double-header on WJPF. The first game was always the Herrin game, but the Benton game was tape delayed and would come on the radio immediately after the Herrin game as the second game of the double-header. Basketball fans in the area would be leaving their game of choice and turn the radio on and the Ranger game would just be starting.

Joe told me a funny story about a game that he completely lost. In '67, the Rangers won the Quad City Tournament Championship, but due to technical difficulties they had lost the tape of the game. Joe contacted Benton Evening News sportswriter, Bob Tedrow, and asked for his shot charts. Tedrow kept accurate and neatly written records of each game that allowed him to prepare his story for the paper complete with shot charts. Since the game was to be aired by tape delay the following day, Browning had the time to take Tedrow's shot charts to the station and recreate the game complete with crowd noise. He then returned Tedrow's shot charts the next morning. Joe just sat back and laughed at his re-created game, but it worked. He admitted that the motivation behind all his trouble was the great interest of his listeners. They wanted to hear the Rangers, and he might take some heat if he didn't provide the broadcast. Desperate times call for desperate measures and Browning delivered the all-important Ranger basketball game and all was right with the world. Joe and his wife Evelyn now live in Mesa, Arizona.

Joe Browning: *The thing that I remember about that '67 team was the atmosphere in the gym…I would go to Battle's Restaurant early Saturday morning with a game coming up that night…It was the closest thing to being a celebrity that I ever felt…I was the voice of the Rangers and the old men would come in and we would get lost in conversation about the team and by that time it's late afternoon. I would go home…clean up and go to the game. It was just a magical time.*

The Rangers then traveled to Herrin and defeated the Tigers 74-60 to set up a game that all of Southern Illinois had been anticipating; Benton at Carbondale. The Terriers were under the direction of legendary Coach John Cherry, and they were loaded. In '66, the Rangers beat the Terriers in both meetings, but Carbondale was a year away. L.C. Brasfield, Billy Perkins, Peaches Laster and Phil Gilbert were now seniors and they were looking forward to the highly touted Rangers' arrival to town. It was December 23, 1966, as Ranger fans caravaned to Bowen Gymnasium ready to face off with the fifth ranked team in the state, the Carbondale Terriers.

Carbondale led 14-13 after the first quarter before the Rangers battled back to a 28-25 halftime lead. After halftime, the Rangers played their best third quarter of the year, outscoring Carbondale 23-10. The Rangers stunned the Terriers with their pressure, and Burlison hit key perimeter shots to open up the inside game. The Rangers held on to win the game 66-48.

With Christmas just two days away, and the anticipation of defending their title in the Centralia Holiday Tournament, it was a happy bus ride home for the Rangers. Hoover scored 14 points in the second half and Fustin continued his steady play by chipping in 13. The Rangers were 5-0 and were playing like they were the best team in the state.

I knew former Terrier Coach John Cherry from my playing days at SIU. John Cherry is now 89 years old, and he spends much of his time caring for his wife of more than sixty years. Over time, Coach Cherry and Coach Herrin became close friends. Coach Cherry would sometimes be a guest of Coach Herrin's on some of our SIU road trips. John Cherry is one of the finest human beings I've ever met, and he spoke to me for close to two hours on the phone about his great '67 Terrier team. The starting point for our interview was this first meeting in Carbondale against the Benton Rangers. Coach Cherry remembered the game well, and that it changed their season.

John Cherry (Carbondale Coach): *Matt, I remember that first game with the Rangers very well. It was two days before Christmas…they just came into town and gave us a beating. Matt, that game ruined my Christmas that year, but I learned something about our team from that game. I wanted to play fast and I think the players did too. If you just looked at our team…you would think we would thrive in a fast-break type of game. A running style of basketball is fun, creative and just a beautiful thing to watch. When Benton came to town…we tried to play fast and run with them but the reality was we couldn't do it. We looked like a running team, but we couldn't beat good teams like Benton playing fast. We had to play slower and uglier. I remember coming in after Christmas before the Carbondale Holiday Tournament at the Arena. I met with the team and we all came to the conclusion that we had to be more patient…play a slower game on the offensive end of the floor. I was determined that teams that full-court pressed like Benton were no longer going to speed us up. Matt, we only had one player that could really dribble the ball without looking at it…and that was our point guard Kenny Lewis. He was the engine that really made us go. To attack full-court pressure from that point on we placed Kenny Lewis* (point guard) *and Phil Gilbert* (shooting guard) *across from each other and placed big 6'9" Billy Perkins in the middle of the floor. Peaches Lassiter and L.C. Brasfield were back. The guards would pass it back and forth and then if we couldn't pass the ball up the sideline, we would just lob the ball up to Billy and he would turn and pass it over the defense. It was methodical and ugly…but it worked for us. That week, we won the Carbondale Holiday Tournament by defeating Collinsville. Collinsville had a great ball press just like Benton and that win really sold our guys on the fact that we needed to be more patient. After the tournament, I felt like our team was gaining confidence and turning the corner.*

Benton opened the '66 Centralia Tournament with Salem, who was now coached by former Benton freshman coach Woody Burnett. It was a morning game and the Rangers won the game easily, 75-41, but did not play well.

After the game, Yunkus said the team stopped at the Hotel Langen-feld in downtown Centralia to eat lunch. The Rangers were the top team in the state at the time, and that kind of attention brings high expecta-tions. The Rangers were to play Highland the next afternoon and the Highland team happened to be dining in the same restaurant. Yunkus had knowledge that the Highland head coach made a remark about the Rangers sloppy afternoon performance against Salem. That hit a nerve with Coach Herrin. In an afternoon game at Centralia on December 30, 1966, the Rangers dismantled Highland and Yunkus believed the beating was a result of the remark made by the Highland head coach the previ-ous day. Yunkus admitted that Coach Herrin was always respectful of the opponent and knew when to "call the dogs off". In a time-out late in the game, Coach Stewart urged Herrin to take the starters out by saying qui-etly, "Remember Rich, we have two tough games tomorrow." Yunkus said it was the only time he saw Coach Herrin run the score up, but admits the Highland coach asked for it. When the game was over there was not the usual coaches' handshake. The final score was; Benton 109, Highland 56.

The Rangers then took care of Champaign Centennial by a score of 70-47 behind Greg Fustin's 25 points to set up the title game with the Homewood-Flossmoor Vikings. In the championship game, the Rangers defeated the Vikings by a score of 77-65 in business-like fashion. Yunkus scored 30 points and Fustin added 20 points as the Rangers claimed the victory. The Rangers were now 9-0 and had won the prestigious Centralia Tournament for the second straight year. Yunkus was named the Most Valuable Player of the tournament, and teammate Greg Fustin was an All-Tournament selection.

On Friday, January 6, 1967, the Rangers defeated Harrisburg 70-49, behind Yunkus' 27 points. Despite the win, it was a tough night for the Rangers and junior guard Danny Johnson. The night before the Harris-burg game, Johnson's mother took her own life. Johnson did not play that night at Harrisburg, and the team hurt for his loss. These were the words of Ranger sports writer Bob Tedrow, in the January seventh edition of the Benton Evening News following the Harrisburg game.

Bob Tedrow: "*But as exciting as the ball game might have been, last night's duel was overshadowed by the personal tragedy of Ranger regular Dan John-son, whose mother passed away the day before. The entire team as well as the whole of the Benton following felt a personal loss for the likeable young Johnson.*"

On Saturday night, the Rangers stunned the Orphans, 83-61. Again, Yunkus had a big night by scoring 34 points. Rich Yunkus was playing his best basketball. The jump shots were falling and his confidence was growing. As Yunkus swept the glass, Ranger fan Bob Gariepy, bellowed his infamous "R-E-B-O-U-N-D" chant that could be heard throughout the gym.

As the '67 season wore on, Greg Starrick and Rich Yunkus became two of the most highly touted basketball recruits in the country and they lived only twenty miles apart. There was definitely a friendly rivalry between the two players, and Starrick remembered his great battles against Yunkus and the Benton Rangers.

Greg Starrick (Marion Guard): *First of all, Rich Yunkus is a good personal friend of mine. At that time you just didn't see 6'8" guys stepping out on the floor and hitting perimeter shots. Yunkus was a stretch-four before the term was ever used. He had such a soft touch and he could really score the ball. He was a great talent on both ends of the floor. I definitely took it as a personal challenge every time we played the Rangers because of Rich. I'm sure Rich would say the same thing. Those were great times.*

The Rangers then traveled to Max Morris Gymnasium on January 13, 1967. The Redbirds did their best to hold the ball in an attempt to upset the heavily favored Rangers. The Rangers survived by winning 27-16, in a very uneventful game. The next night the Rangers traveled to Chagnon Gymnasium and defeated the Rams by a score of 81-49. The game was a beat down and it proved to people across Southern Illinois that the Rangers were the real deal. Yunkus had 29 points to lead the team again but it was the play of the guards that was exciting. Junior Danny Johnson was more assertive and scored 13 points along with Fustin. Hoover chipped in 12 points. The Rangers then swept the table at the annual Quad City Tournament in McLeansboro by winning three straight and defeating Fairfield in the championship game by a score of 76-51. The Rangers were 15-0 and most importantly the team was playing well.

Next on the schedule was the second battle with Greg Starrick and the Marion Wildcats. The Marion game was a crazy affair that would live on in Ranger lore. The infamous game between the Rangers and Wildcats took place on January 27, 1967, in Marion. It would be Starrick's last chance to get the Rangers, and it was the final meeting between the two high school All-Americans; Starrick and Yunkus. The Rangers came out hot and the game itself became a side note. The Rangers were ahead 49-19 at halftime and cruised to the 89-62 win.

It was what happened in the second quarter of the game that would always be remembered. According to Yunkus, late in the second quarter, Marion player Ed Thompson went up for a shot and Yunkus blocked the shot. Thompson then went up again and got stuffed again. As the Rangers retrieved the blocked shot, Thompson turned out of frustration and struck Fustin in the jaw. Fustin happened to be standing near the play. Yunkus believes it happened out of Thompson's frustration of getting blocked twice in a row. There is another story that Fustin had made an inappropriate remark to Thompson provoking him to lose his cool. Unfortunately, whatever happened on that night in Marion, Greg Fustin suffered a broken jaw and had to sit out the next four games due to injury.

Rich Herrin: *I knew his jaw was broken because he couldn't close his mouth… his lower jaw just kind of dangled there. Then I saw blood between his teeth.*

Stuart Schmidt, an official from West Frankfort, was right on top of the play and called Thompson with a technical foul and disqualified him from the game. Unfortunately, the incident proved to be a setback for both teams.

Greg Starrick: *It was an unfortunate incident for both teams. Thompson was suspended and we had to play without him and then the Rangers lost Fustin for a while.*

After the game, Fustin went to Barnes Hospital in St. Louis and underwent surgery for his jaw. The surgery was successful and Fustin returned to play out the rest of the season in a contraption that looked like boxing headgear to protect his jaw from further injury. Jerry Hoover recalled another incident in the game that brought on some good-humored teasing from his teammates.

Jerry Hoover: *I was guarding Starrick…and he was just an unbelievable player. I stole the ball at mid-court from him and went in for a lay-up. Starrick chased me to the goal and fouled me pretty hard and I hit my head on the floor. For a brief moment, I lost consciousness and my greatest supporter… Mary Francis Hoover (my mother) came down from the stands and actually found her way onto the floor and gave Starrick a dirty look. I took a lot of* *grief from my teammates because my mom came out on the floor in my defense. Mothers were not supposed to be out on the floor, you know?*

The next night, the West Frankfort Redbirds came to town under the direction of head coach Gene Earnest. It would be the Rangers first game without the services of senior, Greg Fustin. Basketball is certainly a team game, and even the slightest change in player personnel can cause a team to play differently. In the first half, it was all Redbirds. West Frankfort could not miss, and there looked to be a chink in the Rangers' armor. The team was tired from the Friday night wrestling/basketball game at Marion, and they were without Fustin. In Fustin's absence, Bruce Taylor received more minutes and did a fine job filling the void. It was noticeable to the Ranger fans that the team was in a tailspin. Fustin's injury and the state of things needed to be addressed and Herrin did just that at halftime. It was the first time all season the Rangers trailed at halftime. The score was: West Frankfort 46, Benton 36. Senior forward, Bill Lowery, remembered Coach Herrin's message at halftime.

Bill Lowery: *Coach Herrin came in and I think he sensed that we were frustrated. He gave us a few minutes to talk among ourselves and he then very calmly told us that if they continue to play like that, we might lose. He encouraged us to play harder and I remember some of us played so hard we were asking for rest. He believed we needed to run and that's what we did.*

The Rangers came out of the locker room with renewed energy and outscored the Redbirds 34-17 in the third quarter of play. The Rangers went on to win the game 98-84. In Fustin's absence, every player had to do more, but it was Yunkus' 40 points and 19 rebounds that were the difference in the game. Hoover stepped up with 18 points, Danny Johnson chipped in 16 and Bill Lowery came alive to score a season high 12 points in the second half. Great players have the ability to reach down and get a little extra. On this night, Yunkus refused to let the Rangers lose.

The West Frankfort game also told another story. The South Seven was loaded. On any given night, a team could get beat by any team in the league if they didn't play well. When West Frankfort came to Benton, they were the last place team in the conference. The Redbirds had guards Jeff Overturf and stand-out sophomore Kenny Griffin. Griffin scored 22 points behind leading scorer Tim Pollack, who had 26 points. Greg Hudgens and Dennis Dziadus were also very good players for the Redbirds. In

'67, there were just no patsies in the South Seven Conference; teams had to play every night.

Marion Guard Greg Starrick: *The South Seven Conference at that time was loaded with talent. I learned that how good you were as a team depended on how good the other teams were. I know that there were great crowds in Benton, but I can remember big crowds every night we played, it didn't matter where you were at. There were several players in the league that were high Division I players. We played on Friday and Saturday nights back then and we might have Benton come to town on Friday with Yunkus and Hoover and then have to go to Carbondale and play against Billy Perkins and L.C. Brasfield. The league was extremely competitive.*

On Friday, February 3, 1967, the Rangers defeated Herrin at home by a score of 90-65. The Rangers were led in scoring by John Burlison, who had a season-high 23 points. The press forced the Tigers into turnovers and the Rangers shot lay-ups. The Rangers were idle on Saturday night.

The following weekend, the Rangers hosted the Harrisburg Bulldogs. In other South Seven action that night, Marion hosted West Frankfort. Legendary Kentucky basketball coach Adolph Rupp saw an opportunity to watch two of the best high basketball players in the country. He decided to make the long trip from Lexington, Kentucky to Marion, Illinois. Rupp had his eyes on All-American guard Greg Starrick and All-American forward Rich Yunkus. Starrick remembered the night well.

Greg Starrick (Marion Guard): *It was known that Coach Rupp did not travel out of Kentucky often to see players. He came to Marion one night to watch me play. I was really nervous and didn't have a very good first half. At halftime, Coach Rupp got up and left. Do you know where he went? He went to Benton to watch Rich Yunkus.*

Brad Weathers was in junior high at the time and he remembered the '67 team well. He recalled the night that he spotted Coach Rupp in the Cracker Box.

Brad Weathers: *I just remember that Barney* (Mr. Genesio) *brought this older gentleman in the gym and sat him in Mr. Craddock's reserved seats. At first, I thought, "Who is this guy in the Craddocks' seats?" Then word got around that it was Coach Rupp from the University of Kentucky.*

After the Rangers win over Harrisburg, Coach Rupp spoke to Yunkus and his parents following the game. Yunkus was highly recruited from Division I schools all over the country, including UCLA, who dominated college basketball at the time.

Coach Rupp was extremely interested in both players, and on his way back to Lexington, he stopped by Starrick's home. Rupp knocked on the door and the Starricks invited him inside for a quick chat. Rupp asked Starrick, "How did your game finish?" Starrick replied, "We lost in double-overtime." Coach Rupp then said, "That's a shame...how many points did you score?" Starrick replied, "I had 70." Greg Starrick scored 70 points against West Frankfort and lost, but it is still one of the greatest individual scoring performances in IHSA history. Starrick attended the University of Kentucky before transferring home to SIU. Starrick had an outstanding college career. Yunkus passed on Kentucky and would become the greatest Georgia Tech basketball player in school history. They both played in the South Seven Conference.

It's important to note that all of the Ranger players benefitted from the college exposure created by Yunkus. Jerry Hoover made it a point to tell me in our interview that he received Division I exposure because college coaches might be at the game watching Yunkus, but accidentally see him also. Some coaches realized they had no shot at Yunkus and might say, "Hey, who is that point guard?" Jerry Hoover received a full-ride basketball scholarship to the University of Florida. Yes, the Gators. Hoover had an outstanding college career at Florida and eventually earned the starting point guard position. Let's just say this; major Division I basketball programs were well aware of Benton, Illinois.

The Rangers were 20-0 when the Centralia Orphans came to Benton on Saturday, February 11. The Rangers carved up the Orphans by a score of 74-53 led by Yunkus' game high 20 points. Hoover chipped in 18, and Johnson had 16 points. The Rangers were now 21-0.

On February 17, it was Benton vs. Carbondale II. Carbondale had only one loss and that was to the Benton Rangers two days before Christmas. The Rangers had gotten the best of Carbondale for the past two seasons, but the Terriers were playing good basketball and they were healthy. Fustin returned to the line-up but was still not in game shape from his four game lay-off, and Yunkus was also under the weather. In our interview, Yunkus never used mononucleosis as an excuse for anything. He rarely spoke about it. Late in the season he was diagnosed with mononucleosis and wasn't practicing regularly. This was a setback, but Yunkus did his best on game nights and played well.

Coach Herrin: *I should have sat him out of games down the stretch and let him recover…but I didn't. I should have…*

Coach Herrin was adamant in our interviews about the '67 season that Yunkus had lost some strength and was playing sick, yet to Yunkus' credit, he was very reluctant to admit how much his sickness really affected his play. He was not one to make excuses.

As legend has it, a funny incident happened during the week of the Carbondale game that is worth telling. On this week in late February, the Benton area received snow showers throughout the week with accumulations not severe enough to cancel school. Despite the student hopes of a "snow day", buses could still run and school continued as scheduled at Benton Consolidated High School. On Wednesday, February 15, Danny Johnson decided that he and good friend, Kenny Irvin, were going to have their own snow day.

Rich Herrin: *When I got to school that day Mr. Genisio told me that Johnson wasn't at school. I just went to his house.*

Danny Johnson: *Kenny was at my house and we decided that we weren't going to school that day. We saw Coach Herrin pull up in the driveway. He was pretty bold too…He didn't even knock on the door…he just came into the house. I jumped out from behind the door and scared him…He didn't like that much.*

Kenny Irvin: *He asked us what we were doing and I remember telling Coach that we tried to come to school but the snow was too deep…Coach Herrin replied, "Why aren't there any foot tracks in the snow?" Both of you guys get dressed…we are going to school!"*

The big day had finally come. Students at Benton High School that didn't know a basketball was round couldn't ignore the game. The game had everyone's attention. Remember, tickets for visiting teams coming to Benton were almost impossible to get and Carbondale was well aware of that. Knowing the difficulty of getting tickets, legend has it that Carbondale released school early allowing Terrier fans a chance to travel to Benton and jockey for good position in the ticket line. Somehow, Benton found out about Carbondale's early dismissal and BCHS Principal Barney Genisio immediately called for an early dismissal at Benton, giving the Benton students the head start in the fight for game tickets. Again, Brad Weathers remembered the "fight for a ticket" incident well.

Brad Weathers: *I'm in some class at Webster Junior High and they came across the intercom that school was going to dismiss early that day. As soon as school was out, I remember running from Webster Junior High to the high school to stand in line to get tickets for that game. We stood in line all day in the snow and I would have someone hold my place in line so I could get some hot chocolate at Chick's Market across the street. We got in to see that game and I think we sat on the stage. Our feet just dangled off the stage all over someone's coats below us- that's how packed in we were.*

I love this story. The fact that both schools dismissed early to gain an advantage for the game speaks to how important basketball was to these two Southern Illinois communities. These are the moments that many students remember the most about school. Hearing the story made me want to go back in time and live out the week. The number one Rangers against the number five Terriers in the Cracker Box in '67; are you kidding me?

When the game started that night, the energy in the gym was equal to a heavyweight fight. The anticipation was electric. Among the people of Benton, the game dominated every conversation and had already proven to be more important than education. Game introductions were spirited and then the players walked onto the floor; it may have been the most talented group of ten players to ever begin a game in Benton's tiny gymnasium. Carbondale started Kenny Lewis, a great ball handler and very sound in all facets of the game. Phil Gilbert was the off-guard and he was the Terriers outside shooting threat. L.C. Brasfield (6'3") was the small forward and he would go on to have a great career at SIU and would be a teammate of Greg Starrick. Early "Peaches" Laster (6'6") started at the power forward position and after high school played at the University of Utah. Louisville-bound Billy Perkins was the center, standing at 6'9"tall.

The Rangers walked onto the floor with Yunkus, Hoover and Fustin, who would later play Division I basketball. Burlison and Lowery were the other two Ranger starters, and they too played at the next level. After high school, Greg Fustin played at Rice University. Danny Johnson was the first man off the bench for the Rangers, and went on to play in a final four at Western Kentucky. Doug Collins was a sophomore and not dressing on the varsity team. He wouild later make a living playing professional basketball in the NBA. Southern Illinois was a hotbed for high school basketball at this time and it is safe to say that there was never more basketball talent in the historic South Seven Conference than in 1967.

Carbondale controlled the tip and the first bucket of the game was scored by Carbondale's L.C. Brasfield. There were few cheers for anything that Carbondale did right because they had clearly lost the ticket war. The Terriers led 12-8 after one quarter. In the second quarter, the cream rose to the top for the Rangers. Yunkus and Johnson teamed up to net 19 points to shift the momentum back to the Rangers. The Rangers led 28-26 at halftime.

It was clear that Carbondale was a much improved team from their first meeting before Christmas. The Terriers had only lost one game all year and that was to Benton, but most importantly they had found their identity. They were not trying to run and push the ball. They were playing slower, much more methodical and it was working.

To Benton's credit, Fustin suffered a broken jaw and Yunkus was not practicing regularly at this point, but the Rangers were still fighting. To Coach Herrin's credit, the Rangers were 21-0 at this point and they had not yet stumbled despite the giant bullseye on their back. The two heavyweights battled under the direction of two great high school basketball coaches. Nothing was going to be easy. The Terriers led 53-48 going into the fourth quarter and Brasfield had 22 points. L.C. was coming into his own as a player. The Rangers started the fourth quarter well with early buckets from Fustin and Burlison to force the game into overtime.

To start the overtime period, the score was tied at 65. The teams traded baskets in the overtime period. The overtime period against Carbondale was a coming out party for the talented junior guard. Johnson scored five points in the overtime and hit two crucial free throws to put the Rangers ahead, 71-69. Then the Terriers quickly tied the game at 71. With just .06 seconds left in the game, Johnson was fouled and went to the free throw line with a chance to give the Rangers a two-point advantage.

Danny Johnson: *I just remembered that I had played pretty well in the game and I hit the free throw that put us ahead and I was feeling pretty good, you know…And then…well I missed the second one and thought…Oh no…As I ran back on defense I thought, please don't make this shot…The ball just barely rimmed out, otherwise I would have been the goat.*

Coach Herrin was relieved after the game and credited his players for fighting back from a ten-point deficit at one point to keep their composure. It was clear that the gap between the Rangers and the Terriers was closing. For the Terriers, there were no moral victories taken from the game, but when the smoke cleared, they knew they would be ready if there was to be a third meeting.

John Cherry (Carbondale Coach): *I remember the game well. We lost in the Cracker Box but we played well…Phil Gilbert took the last shot in the corner and it just rimmed out.*

Benton improved to a perfect 22-0, and 13-0 in the South Seven Conference. With the win over Carbondale, the Rangers clinched the South Seven regular season championship, their second in a row. In fact, they had won 27 consecutive South Seven games, tying the record set by Centralia. If the Rangers could win at Chagnon the next night, they would set a new record of 28 consecutive conference victories. On to Mt. Vernon!

The Rangers completed a great weekend by winning at Mt. Vernon the next night, by a score 65-49. Danny Johnson led the Rangers with 19 points, ending a great individual weekend. John Burlison sizzled from the outside adding 17 points, and Yunkus chipped in 14. It is important not to overlook this win. Since the organization of the South Seven Conference in 1939, the Rangers had only won three times at Mt. Vernon. With that being said, the Mt. Vernon game was a huge win and it really showed the mental toughness of a team that was not as healthy as it could be, but still digging deep to meet all comers. The Rangers were the real deal. It would take a great effort to knock them off the stump. They were now 23-0, and a perfect 14-0 in the conference. They had run the table two years in a row in a very tough league, and despite being physically and mentally exhausted, the Rangers relished the moment on the ride home from Mt. Vernon. It was a happy bus ride home. The team now had to shift their focus to finishing the season strong to prepare for tournament play.

On Tuesday, February 21, 1967, the Rangers traveled to Mcleansboro and beat the Foxes by a score of 94-59. Yunkus put on a clinic in the post by shooting 16-24 from the field and finishing the game with 33 points. John Burlison played well, adding 19 points, and it was a good sign to see Fustin chip in with 14. The Rangers improved to 24-0 with only one home game remaining against the DuQuoin Indians.

Just before the DuQuoin game, the IHSA (Illinois High School Association) ruled that Marion Forward Ed Thompson would be suspended for the remainder of the season after striking Greg Fustin in the jaw. It was understood that the report did investigate possible reasons for the blow. Taking into account rumors that a racial comment may have played a role, the report said that Thompson was not called a name denoting a racial slur. Other Marion players were also questioned, and said they did not hear any name calling from either team.

On Friday, February 24, the DuQuoin Indians and All-State Player Alan Crews came to town for the final home game of the 1967 season. There were mixed emotions on this night. The home gym was packed. Ranger fans knew this would be the last time they would see the seniors; Yunkus, Hoover, Lowery, Burlison and Fustin. This group was part of two South Seven Championships, two Centralia Holiday Tournament Championships and two undefeated seasons at home. To show appreciation to the seniors for such a memorable season, the fans laid down a red strip of carpet for the Rangers' entrance onto the floor. Jerry Hoover then darted through the tunnel of cheerleaders as the Rangers took the home floor for the final time. The Rangers were ranked number one in the state and were undefeated. The home fans stood and clapped in support. Parents of the players and steadfast fans close to the team were emotional as B.L. Finley announced the introduction of the players. After the ball was tipped, the Rangers then took the Indians behind the woodshed and unleashed a brutal whipping. The energy in the building transferred to the team overwhelming the Indians. The Rangers won the ballgame by a score of 101-63 and finished the year a perfect 25-0.

'67 State Tournament Play

The team then opened Regional play at Max Morris Gymnasium in West Frankfort against the Christopher Bearcats. Yunkus was not scrimmaging in practice. Yunkus admitted not having the stamina he had at the beginning of the year. Point guard Jerry Hoover was recovering from a throat infection. Bill Lowery had a hairline fracture on the side of his left foot that he had suffered in practice. The fracture was annoying and limited his mobility. Greg Fustin was still in the process of regaining his stamina after his broken jaw. The Rangers were 25-0 but the season had taken its toll. The Rangers needed an easy one, and Christopher was just what the doctor ordered. Yunkus remembered the first game of the Regional well.

Rich Yunkus: *I just remember Coach Herrin told us before the game that the starters are going to play the first and third quarters and everyone else be ready in the second and fourth quarters. That's exactly what happened.*

The mighty Rangers dressed ten players and everyone scored. The final score was 109-32. The Rangers then defeated Waltonville by a score of 96-62. Jerry Hoover led the scoring attack with 20 points as five Rangers scored in double figures. The Rangers moved on to play the DuQuoin Indians in the Regional Championship. DuQuoin was a scary game because the Rangers won easily on senior night, but it was as if the Indians forgot to get off the bus. Besides All-State player Alan Crews, the Indians also featured future major league pitcher Don Stanhouse who was also a good basketball player. All of the Rangers knew that the second time around would be different, and it was. Despite a better effort from the Indians, the Rangers defeated the Indians 79-66 behind 30 points and 15 rebounds from Rich Yunkus.

Coach Herrin had now won six out of seven Regional Championships since his first season in 1961. To celebrate the Regional Championship, the Rangers were escorted around the square as the townspeople of Benton waved and shouted. The Benton Evening News featured a full page team picture of the victors posing behind their Regional Championship plaque. The headline read in huge letters, "28 Down And Six To Go." It was clear that the townspeople were thinking State Championship. In the picture the players are smiling, but the picture indicates relief more than jubilation. On to the Sectional!

In 1967, Eldorado played host to the Sectional Tournament and the Rangers matched up with the Mt. Carmel Aces. Rich Herrin had scouted Mount Carmel and made these comments in the Benton Evening News the night before the game:

Rich Herrin: *They are well built and strong and very aggressive. They play with great energy and enthusiasm.*

It was as if Herrin was looking into a crystal ball, because the Aces came out on fire. The Aces led at halftime by a score of 32-24 and remained on top going into the fourth quarter, 45-43. The Rangers did what great teams do; they ground out the win despite their lackluster performance. Late in the game, Yunkus demonstrated his smooth stroke and dropped shots from all angles and distances. He skillfully used the glass and was

4-5 from the free throw line. In a close call, the Rangers won by a score of 70-61, and advanced to face Ridgeway in the Sectional Championship.

The Sectional Championship was played on March 10, 1967. It was a David vs. Goliath match-up because of Ridgeway's small school enrollment compared to Benton's. Again, the Rangers started slow and Ridgeway led the game 29-28 after the first half. Yunkus struggled with only seven points, but answered the bell in the second half by scoring 15 to end the night with 22 points. The Rangers won the game by a score of 65-57, but just didn't play that well. Ridgeway center, Ronnie Stallings, was the player of the game and led all scorers with 30 points. The Rangers were elated and relieved. This is what they had worked for and they had won their last three games despite sickness and injury. There is a picture of the team in the Benton Evening news following the win. The Rangers are waiting patiently to be presented the Sectional trophy. At first glance, it's hard to tell by the body language and facial expressions of the players that they had just won the Sectional. They look exhausted more than elated. Coach Herrin is sitting in the middle of the players in deep thought and the players have the same look. Still, it was a Sectional Championship and it has only happened eleven times over the span of 115 years. There was much to celebrate.

After the Rangers won the Eldorado Sectional, they boarded the yellow school bus and headed back to Benton among a caravan of happy Benton fans. Again, the victory lap around the square is special to any Benton athlete that has ever been a part of it. It never gets old. The town has a tradition of celebrating their conquering heroes and this night would be no different. The fans greeting the team on the square were not concerned about injuries, sickness and lackluster play. The general thought was, "we won, so let the good times roll...let's celebrate." That is exactly what the team did. Danny Johnson loved being on that fire truck, and he expressed what that moment meant to him personally.

Danny Johnson: *The memory of being on that fire truck and people shouting your name and cheering for you was unbelievable. For me...at that time...it was a moment that validated me...I wish that my grandkids have that experience one day. The history of those moments...and to be a part of that.*

On this same night at the SIU Arena, the Carbondale Terriers shocked the Meridian Bobcats by a score of 70-45. It would be Benton (30-0) vs. Carbondale (26-2) in the Carbondale Super-Sectional at the newly built SIU Arena. It would be a game for the ages!

Battles Grill was a popular hang-out for the high school students. Battles highlighted the accomplishments of the basketball team by displaying pictures of the great teams and players. *(Bobbi Battle)*

Greg Fustin moved in from Taylorville to join Yunkus as Benton's Twin Towers. *(Benton High School)*

Rich Yunkus was the dominant player in Southern Illinois in 66-67.
(Benton High School)

Bob Gariepy and his wife Nora Jane were some of the
most loyal Rangers fans the town has ever known.
(Benton High School)

Coach Herrin using a little body language to guide the ball thru the net. Notice that the benches were on the end lines in the old "Cracker box."
(Benton High School)

Greg Starrick dribbles away from Benton pressure in the old Marion High School gym which is now the Junior Gym. *(Rich Herrin family collection)*

Jerry Hoover became the gold standard of point guards at Benton after his amazing season in 66-67. *(Benton High School)*

Danny Johnson was a junior in 66-67 and he provided a competitive energy on both ends of the floor. *(Paul Hickman)*

Coach Maurice Phillips was well respected in the Benton Community and provided solid coaching at the underclass level. *(Benton High School)*

John Burlison (the blonde bomber) provided the Rangers with deadly perimeter shooting that opened up Fustin and Yunkus inside. (Rich Herrin family collection)

Bill Lowery always played hard and gave the Rangers productive minutes in '67. (Benton High School)

Norman Carlile later became the 8th grade coach but in '67 he played the role of statistician and book keeper. Carlile loved the game. (Benton High School)

The voice of the Rangers, Joe Browning.
(Joe Browning family collection)

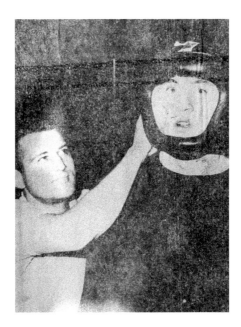

Herrin adjusts Fustin's head gear after Greg's broken jaw at Marion.
(Benton Evening News)

BCHS Principal Barney Genisio, gave Brad Weathers one of his greatest memories growing up when he shut down school early on Friday to allow Benton fans to beat Carbondale fans to the ticket line. *(Benton High School)*

Bento fans brave the weather to see the great match-up between Benton and Carbondale in the winter of '67. *(Benton High School)*

Danny Johnson hit one of two free throws late in the game to seal the Rangers classic victory over the Terriers in '67. *(Benton High School)*

Coach Herrin calls a timeout during the 66-67 season.
(Benton High School)

The Rangers receive their Sectional Championship Trophy after defeating
Ridgeway by a score of 65-57. *(Paul Hickman)*

CHAPTER EIGHT

Benton vs. Carbondale III

"Some called it the game of the decade." – Terrier Coach John Cherry

Some called it the game of the decade. The SIU Arena featured a college floor with a spacious shooting background behind both goals. It was not a great place to shoot the basketball and the hard floor sometimes made it tough for players to get loose. In my opinion, it was a hard place to play, and I spent five years of my life in that building.

Carbondale had already played four games in the Arena during the Carbondale Holiday Tournament. It had to feel like a home game for the Terriers. For the Rangers, the Arena wasn't the warm Cracker Box in Benton. Advantage…Terriers. On Tuesday, March 14, a sold out SIU Arena saw two of the greatest high school teams in Southern Illinois history go head to head. Ranger fans dressed in maroon and white and packed the Arena sporting white cowboy hats. Terrier fans also piled into the Arena wearing their school colors of black and white.

John Cherry (Carbondale Coach): *My assistant coach had scouted Benton eight times throughout the course of the year and I know Rich had scouted us numerous times. Both teams knew each other very well. There was a lot of hype around the game because they were the number one team in the state and we were the number three team in the state. Our only two losses were to Benton. Although they had beaten us twice, I felt like we were closing the gap…and only lost by one in the Cracker Box in Benton. You couldn't squeeze another person in the SIU Arena.*

Rich Herrin: *Carbondale was a great team and they had improved...Coach John Cherry did a great job with them. I first met Coach Cherry at a church camp playing softball in high school. He was very good friends with my brother and we became very good friends.*

The game was back and forth in the first half and the Rangers held a 27-26 lead at halftime. Yunkus had 11 and Johnson had eight at the break. The Terriers methodically broke the Rangers' pressure, as the college floor seemed to serve to Carbondale's advantage. The Rangers came out strong in the third quarter and then Bill Lowery hit a free throw to start the fourth quarter and the Rangers led 45-39.

Suddenly, the Rangers offense went cold. The Terriers came roaring back by scoring six unanswered points to tie the game at 45. Point guard Kenny Lewis scored an easy bucket to put Carbondale ahead for the first time in the game. Danny Johnson then made two quick field goals to put the Rangers up 49-48 before Carbondale center Billy Perkins scored to make it 50-49, in favor of Carbondale. Jerry Hoover sank two free throws on Benton's next possession to put the Rangers up 51-50. Unfortunately, this would be the last time the Rangers would hold the lead. Terrier guard Phil Gilbert made a short jump shot with 3:40 remaining and then added two free throws to put the Terriers ahead to stay at 54-51. Benton regained possession of the ball twice trailing by just three points, but couldn't score.

In basketball, momentum is important and some plays just have a way of changing the outcome of the game. After interviewing the players, they all agreed that the momentum of the game shifted to Carbondale's favor when Early "Peaches" Laster picked off a Ranger pass and delivered a thundering dunk that ignited the Carbondale faithful. When the final buzzer sounded, Carbondale had defeated Benton 59-53. A wild and frenzied Carbondale fan section rushed the floor to celebrate what they considered an upset.

Rich Yunkus: *It was not a big upset. Both teams were very good and I was devastated we lost...but they were just a good team and we got beat.*

All of the players experienced the defeat in their own way, but they had trouble putting it into words. Many of the players just said, "You know, you played, you've been in those locker rooms before," and I knew exactly what they meant. After the game, Bob Tedrow maneuvered his wheel chair near the Ranger locker room. He knew the players well, and in a way they all had gone on this magnificent ride together. Tedrow knew the ride was over. Tedrow summed up the mood of the locker room in his article in the next day's edition of the Benton Evening News.

Bob Tedrow: *Unless one could have gone into the dressing room after the game and have seen the tears, felt the sullen quietness and watched the boys each in his own way feeling the agony of defeat, the full impact could not be realized.*

Coach Herrin was visibly upset after the game, but was gracious and wished the Carbondale team luck at the State Tournament. He credited his boys on a wonderful season and expressed his appreciation for their effort despite the loss.

Coach Rich Herrin: *It was one of the most devastating losses I've ever experienced in my career... it was tough.*

Obviously, the loss was very tough but he had to be thinking about the special group that he would no longer have the opportunity of coaching. He may have been thinking that he missed his best chance to win a State Championship. He knew that in a town of 8,000 people, players like Yunkus, Hoover and Johnson are not going to be there year after year. Only Coach Herrin knows what he was thinking in those moments.

Benton Ranger mascot, eight-year-old Rodney Herrin, was completely distraught after the game for an entirely different reason.

Rod Herrin: *In '67 when we got beat by Carbondale in the Super-Sectional I cried because I wanted to go back to State and stay at the Ramada Inn. I wanted to swim. Just typical kid stuff, you know.*

When I was interviewing Rich Yunkus and it was time to let go of the '67 team, he made a point to express his appreciation and love for his old basketball coach. Yunkus became emotional as he expressed his feelings about Coach Herrin.

Rich Yunkus: *He never expected anything out of you that he didn't expect of himself. He had an unbelievable work ethic and led by example. He cared for you as a person... and not just an athlete.*

When he made this statement in our interview, Donna was in the room and she made this point.

Donna Yunkus: *I feel as if Coach Herrin is a part of our family. He still calls us and keeps up with us. He cares for us as people and he knows the names of our daughters and asks about them. He had a tremendous impact on Rich.*

Jerry Hoover was also quick to express his feelings about the opportunity of playing for Coach Herrin.

Jerry Hoover: *We didn't know how good we had it with Coach Herrin. We had nothing to compare it to. I mean…he was probably better than most all of our college coaches. He was such a great coach.*

After defeating the Rangers in the Super Sectional, Carbondale went on to defeat Collinsville for the second time by a score of 53-47 in the quarterfinal game of the State Tournament. They then defeated Rockford West by a score of 67-66 in overtime on a last second shot by L. C. Brasfield. The semi-final game was the second game of the afternoon session and Carbondale had to quickly come back and play Pekin. Pekin defeated the Terriers by a score of 65-49, to win the 1967 Illinois State Championship.

As I gathered research on the 1967 Rangers, I grew more familiar with the Carbondale team and enjoyed learning about their journey to the '67 State Championship. I loved interviewing former Terrier Coach John Cherry. I asked him about his team and he was very complimentary of all of his players. He has kept up with them much the way Coach Herrin has kept his relationships with his players.

Growing up in Benton, I've always heard Laster mentioned in old stories told by former Benton players. Laster was above average in skill and was big and physical. Peaches ended up playing Division I basketball at the University of Utah. So, out of curiosity, I wanted to know more about Peaches Laster. I asked Coach Cherry about Peaches and he chuckled and said, "I get that question a lot, everybody wants to know about Peaches." Maybe it's just the name Peaches, but I was intrigued and Coach Cherry told me a story that I had to include. It is a story about a coach and player that at first had their differences, but later grew to love each other.

John Cherry (Carbondale Coach): *When I got to Carbondale I was the freshman football coach and later became the varsity basketball coach. I enjoyed* *coaching football and it gave me a chance to develop a relationship with the players that I later coached in basketball. Peaches played football for me as a freshman and he could be difficult at times. He was about 6'2" as a freshman with some baby fat but he could move and I could see that he had potential. I had already coached his older brother in basketball and I had a good experience with him and the family. We made it through freshman football together and then basketball started. Peaches was a freshman and I was the varsity basketball coach at the time and he started being difficult with the freshman basketball coach. As the varsity coach, I called him into my office and told him to turn in his equipment and that he could wrestle in the winter. I was tired of putting up with him. He was caught off guard and he begged me to be back on the team but I didn't budge. After the incident took place, his older brother that once played for me came by the school and asked if I would come over to the house and speak to his parents about Peaches. The next day I dropped by Laster's house to talk to his parents. When I entered into the house the whole family was in the living room waiting on me - I'll never forget that. Peaches had four older sisters and they were in the room along with his older brother and his mother and father. Everyone was sitting down except Peaches, who was standing in a doorway to an adjoining room. Peaches father was a custodian at the high school and we knew each other. I think they thought I was a fair man. I then took my seat and his mother, who I grew to love, spoke first. She said, "Mr. Cherry, what seems to be the problem with Peaches?" I said, "He has been difficult to coach and I'm just not taking it anymore". Something to that effect. She then asked, "Can Peaches come out for the team as a sophomore?" I was no dummy. I wasn't trying to run Peaches off because I knew he could really help us later in basketball and it would be good for him to play. I told her, "I would welcome him back if he would straighten up." Mr. Laster then spoke up and said, "Mr. Cherry, you'll have no trouble out of Peaches." He then looked at his son and said, "Isn't that right Peaches?" Peaches quickly answered, "Yes, sir." And I'm telling you, after that day I had absolutely no trouble out of Peaches. It was definitely tough love at first, but our relationship grew and we got along well together. I stayed in touch with him for the rest of his life. Unfortunately, Peaches got Alzheimer's disease at the age of fifty-six and he lost his ability to speak. After the disease worsened and he lost movement, I would call him and the caregiver would put the phone to his ear. He could take information in and I wanted to bring him some joy. I remember saying, "Peaches do you remember that steal and dunk you got against the Benton Rangers in the Super-Sectional?" The caregiver told me that a big smile would come across his face. As the years passed, we grew to love each other.*

In my opinion, this is why John Cherry was a great high school basketball coach. He loved his players for a lifetime, and they loved him back. Cherry stepped down after the '67 season and remained in the area and was always a close friend to Coach Herrin. He coached eight seasons at Carbondale and accumulated a record of 132-80. According to Coach Cherry they have never spoken of the Super-Sectional, as some things are best left unsaid.

After the Super-Sectional loss, It was a sad bus ride home for the Rangers. The team boarded the bus and each player gazed out the bus windows, still in shock that it was over. The players were physically and emotionally exhausted and it took weeks for them to be able to reflect and really appreciate the special journey they had all shared. Following the loss to Carbondale, it seemed the school year was over to many students. There was a feeling of enormous letdown that the entire student body felt, yet school marched on.

Many of the seniors were in the process of deciding where they would attend college. The recruiting war for Rich Yunkus was intense and it was taking its toll on him. The attention included daily phone calls and visits from coaches across the country. New York Knicks player Bill Bradley penned a letter to Yunkus urging him to attend Princeton University. Yunkus received a letter from John Wayne to attend USC, and then weeks later the great John Havlicek lobbied for his services at Ohio State University. Duke University was also a school involved in the recruiting war.

Georgia Tech assistant coach, DeWayne Morrison, won the recruiting war because as Yunkus said, "He was no-nonsense and a straight shooter." Yunkus was not in awe of any one coach or school. He made the decision based on the school that fit him best, and it was Georgia Tech. The results speak for themselves. He made the right decision. Rich Yunkus is still the all-time leading scorer in Georgia Tech History and would earn an AP third Team All-American selection, in 1971. One of the greatest highlights of his college career was finishing runner-up to North Carolina in the National Invitational Tournament played at Madison Square Garden in 1971. Yunkus spoke highly of his college coach, Whack Hyder. He loved his experience at Georgia Tech and remains connected to the university. He was a high achiever academically and admitted he was ready to move on with his life despite being drafted in the third round by the Cincinnati Royals in the 1971 NBA Draft. He married his high school sweetheart Donna in 1972 and moved back to Benton, Illinois. After returning to Benton, he grew his father's business and was active in serving the Benton community. Rich and Donna reside in Benton. They have two daughters, Lindsay Yunkus Darnell, and Alicia Yunkus Wuebbles.

Guard John Burlison went on to play basketball at MacMurray College after high school. Burlison worked as a dentist in Benton for more than thirty-two years. His wife Christy is a retired teacher of thirty-four years. They have one son, Jared, who is a nuclear radiologist earning a degree from Vanderbilt University. John and Christy now live in Lake Havasu City, Arizona.

Point guard Jerry Hoover went on to play Division I basketball at the University of Florida. Hoover became the starting point guard and had a solid college career. After his graduation, the Hoover family moved away and Jerry seldom gets back to Benton, but is faithful to attend class reunions. He loved growing up in Benton, Illinois. Jerry is currently married to his wife Renee and he has three daughters; Natalie, Kinzie and Taylor. He mentioned that he enjoys spending time with his grandchildren. Jerry earned his undergraduate degree in business and exceled in banking, even serving as president of Texas Commerce Bank from 1981-1987. He then went back to school to earn his law degree and now has his own practice. He and his wife now reside in Houston, Texas.

Forward Bill Lowery attended Young Harris Junior College to play basketball and later transferred to Georgia Southern. Bill sold insurance in Carbondale and served as a layout technician at Maytag in Herrin for years. Lowery's son, John, served as a Captain in the navy and his daughter Nicole is in the restaurant business.

Center Greg Fustin attended Rice University on a basketball scholarship. Fustin later served in the Air Force and returned home and worked as a coal miner. He was employed by the Zeigler Coal Co. at the Spartan Mine. He married his wife Janis (Trout) Fustin in 1974. They had two boys; Vance and Lee. Greg Fustin passed away on November 12, 1994 in Barnes Hospital in St. Louis, Missouri. He was only forty-five years old.

A life size team picture of the '67 Rangers hangs in the west lobby of Benton's Rich Herrin Gymnasium. The black and white picture shows the Rangers in their home white uniforms. The team represents excellence and is the pinnacle of the glory years of the 1960's. Although the players are scattered all over the country, they certainly left their mark on the Benton basketball program. They are possibly the greatest team in a school full of basketball tradition. In '68, Danny Johnson and his Rangers will use the bar set by the '67 team to inspire great play and yet another South Seven Championship season. Hang on, because '68 is cray-zee!

Carbondale Coach John Cherry slowed his team down to play a more methodical tempo. It proved big. *(Carbondale High School)*

The '67 Carbondale Terriers came into the Super-Sectional with an impressive 26-2 record. Both of their losses were to the Rangers.
(Carbondale High School)

Coach Cherry dubbed point guard, Kenny Lewis, the engine of
the great '67 Terrier team. *(Carbondale High School)*

L.C. Brasfield ahead of the pack in their first meeting with the Rangers just
before Christmas in Carbondale. *(Carbondale High School)*

Carbondale center, Billy Perkins, was a force to be reckoned with in the post. *(Carbondale High School)*

Hoover shoots a jumper over Lewis in what many called "the game of the decade." *(Benton High School)*

In what many believe was the turning point in the game, Peaches Laster steals
the ball and delivers a thunderous dunk that shook the Arena.
(Carbondale High School)

The final score of the '67 Super-Sectional. It was one of the toughest defeats in
Coach Herrin's coaching career. *(Carbondale High School)*

Carbondale's L.C. Brasfield is carried off the floor after his game winner against Rockford West in the Semi-Final game of the '67 State Tournament. *(Carbondale High School)*

The Terriers accept the 2nd place trophy after being defeated by Pekin in the State Championship. *(Carbondale High School)*

CHAPTER NINE

Danny Johnson

"I want to tell my story as a legacy to my children and my grandchildren. I want them to know my story. I want them to be inspired by it." – Danny Johnson

On Monday, August 3, 2020, I picked up the phone and called Danny Johnson. Danny answered with a quick, "Hello." I explained my intentions about the book and asked him if there was a good time that we could sit down and talk about his experience as a Benton Ranger. Danny said, "My family is in Nashville…how about right now?" I said, "Let's do it." Danny lives just two miles west of our house. By the time I gathered my notebook and questions, I heard a knock on the door. We shook hands and exchanged pleasantries. I knew enough about Danny to know that he would be a fun interview. He was dressed in khaki shorts and a short sleeve shirt and looked like a guy that could whip me in one-on-one despite being two decades older in age. Danny is about 6'2" and he is lean and still very athletic-looking for someone close to seventy years old. As he walked to the couch to sit down, I had the thought of starting a rigorous exercise program that would return me back to my playing weight. I chuckled to myself at the thought, and then refocused my thoughts on the interview.

Danny Johnson's number 15 is now retired, and hangs high in the rafters of Rich Herrin Gymnasium. Johnson was an incredible high school talent. His senior year of '68, he was, without a doubt, the most outstanding high school basketball player in Southern Illinois and possibly the state. Danny was a tremendous athlete that possessed incredible jumping ability and quickness. He could rise up and dunk the ball a number of different ways. He had lightening quick hands and if you put the ball in front of him, it was gone. In '68, Johnson accumulated 156 steals in just twenty-eight games and averaged 5.57 steals per game. Johnson played the game wide open and there has never been a Ranger more astute at stealing a bad pass. Offensively, he was a slasher and he found ways to score. Johnson's points came from fast break lay-ups, offensive rebounds, steals, penetration, and short jump shots. He was also crafty enough to know how to get to the free throw line. Johnson was a fan's delight because he played the game with an energy and intensity that was unmatched. Much of who Danny was as a player, and who he is today, is about where he came from. He had a very difficult childhood and those tough experiences fueled his motivation to succeed. He is the only living member of his immediate family. He is a survivor. Danny Johnson played the game of basketball with what he described as "an edge".

I broke the ice by showing him a picture of his wife, Sherry, in the 1968 Benton yearbook. The image of Sherry is in color, and it shows her sitting by herself on a bench in front of the old high school. The picture is shot through the opening of a maple tree, and it looks to be during the fall season, possibly in September of 1968. She is wearing a red dress, and there looks to be a slight breeze as her hair is suspended above her right shoulder. Her other possession is a plaid purse that sits near her on the bench. She is beautiful. When this picture was taken, she was dating her future husband, Danny Johnson. As with all of the men we have talked about in the book, there is usually a good woman that helps them along the way. Sherry Milligan Johnson was that and more for Danny Johnson.

Danny Johnson: *Sherry saved me.*

I asked Danny how they met and his eyes lit up. He couldn't wait to tell me the story. I just sat back and took it all in as he told possibly the greatest "love at first sight" story that I've ever heard.

Danny Johnson: *I was a junior…and I was in study hall with Coach Phillips. It was two weeks after my mother was buried. In walks this new girl into study hall class. It was Sherry. Coach Phillips walked her over to my table and seated* *her right across from me. I took one look at her, and I'm telling you…it was love at first sight! I couldn't take my eyes off of her! Thank you, Coach Phillips!*

What Danny didn't know in those first moments in study hall was that Sherry would prove to be even more beautiful on the inside. Sherry (Milligan) Johnson was the daughter of a preacher. She grew up with a strong faith in God and told Danny, "If we date, you must go to church with me." Danny went to church, and Sherry gradually tore through the tough exterior that was created by Danny's difficult childhood. Sherry provided Danny with the love and support that he was never shown when he was a boy. He found someone who truly loved him and supported him without any judgment, and he held on tight. Sherry loved Danny, and he adored her.

I first knew of Sherry Johnson when I was in the third grade at Douglas School. She taught fourth grade and I couldn't wait to be in her class. She was pretty and nice. That's just kind of how you think when you're in the fourth grade…you know. Unfortunately, I didn't get to be in her in class in the fourth grade because I transferred to Grant. However, my eighth Grade year, I found myself in her English class at the middle school. Mrs. Johnson was a great teacher because she loved ALL of her students. There were no discipline problems because she killed you with kindness.

As a young man, I was hired at the Benton Middle school as a teacher and coach. Sherry was near retirement and we were now co-workers. I coached everything; baseball, basketball and track. One day, late in the spring, we had a track meet and I had forgotten to get a substitute for my last hour class. Most teachers just don't want to sub when they have a last hour prep period. It just makes for a long day. I felt bad asking anybody, but as I walked through the library I saw Sherry. Before I could even ask, she offered to take my class. That is Sherry Johnson. She would do anything for you. The story is simple but for me, that kind of sums her up.

Danny Johnson: *Sherry is all about family. We have family gatherings all of the time and it is always Sherry that gets us together. One Thanksgiving we went outside because my grandson Kruz was talking about how he was faster than Jo Jo. Jo raced Kruz to the mailbox from the house and the whole family was outside watching this. It was hilarious and that's something we will all remember.*

Today, Danny Johnson is most proud of his family. He loves his two children, Missy and Jo Jo, and he is all about his grandchildren. His eyes light up when he talks about his grandchildren; Dymin, Kruz, Trace, Jerzy, Lively and Rumer.

Danny Johnson was the son of Alfred and Gladys Johnson. His father served in World War II and was wounded in battle. There is an old black and white picture of Alfred taken while he was serving in World War II in the presence of the great comedian Bob Hope. Unfortunately, Alfred was not a good father. He was a heavy drinker and was abusive to Gladys in the presence of the children. As Danny has grown older, he admits that there are times that he tries to justify his father's abusive behavior by believing he could have suffered from PTSD, but he is not sure. In our interview, I could sense that the childhood memories were painful for Danny to recall. He explained that there were times the drama in the family was so chaotic, he and his siblings stayed with his Grandma and Grandpa Carlisle, on his mother's side of the family. Danny had two older sisters; Donna and Carolyn. He had a younger brother named Randy. They were all two years apart in age, with Donna being the oldest.

Gladys, Danny's mother, had a brother named Richard who served time in prison at Menard Correctional Facility in Chester, Illinois. Menard Prison is still in operation today and houses some of the toughest convicts in the State of Illinois. Danny remembered Grandma and Grandpa Carlisle taking him and his siblings to Menard to visit Richard. The family was allowed to visit Uncle Richard, but only behind a thick pane of glass that separated them. The family then trekked their way back to Benton.

Danny Johnson: *I remember one time in high school our class went on a field trip to visit the Menard prison. I think it was a sociology class. My classmates were kind of freaked out, but I had been there before….and as we walked through the prison, I saw my Uncle Richard and yelled, "Hi" to him…The class really didn't know what to think.*

The Johnson family was constantly on the move. Before his freshman year in high school, Danny lived in short stints at several different residences in Benton. The family also lived in faraway cities like in Dayton, Chicago, and even Denver, Colorado. This was all before Danny entered high school. The constant moving was stressful and it didn't provide any type of stability and consistency for Danny and his siblings. He made it a point to tell me that he never had his own room growing up. He never had the luxury of just shutting the door and spending some time alone to get away from the craziness of his life. He certainly didn't have a desk to do his schoolwork, or a wall to decorate with his own personal items. Sometimes the family slept in the same room, and if he was lucky there might be a room for him and his younger brother Randy.

As a boy, he remembers a time when things were so bad that he was taken away and placed in foster care. He coaxed his foster parents to take him home to retrieve some personal items. When he arrived at home, he ran to the family outhouse and locked the door because he wanted to live with his mother. To lure him out of the outhouse a social worker told him they were going to go grocery shopping for some items for his mother. Danny came out of hiding and was taken back to his foster parents, where he received a whipping for running away. It was a tough life for Danny, but this was all he knew.

His father, Alfred, was in and out of his life for most of his childhood, but Danny never really felt any love from his father. He pointed out that the last time Alfred lived permanently with the family was in Chicago. Danny was in the eighth grade. While the family was in Chicago, an incident occurred between his parents that pushed Gladys past the breaking point. In the middle of the night, Gladys quietly shuffled Danny and Randy to the car while Alfred was asleep. Donna and Carolyn, Danny's sisters, were in the care of Grandma and Grandpa Carlisle in Benton. Under the influence of alcohol, Gladys climbed into the driver's seat of the car and headed back to Benton. Benton was six hours south, with an alcohol-impaired Gladys behind the wheel. As the trip wore on, Gladys became tired. Fearing that she would fall asleep, she pulled the car over on the side of the road and sat Danny in the driver's seat. She gave him a quick tutorial of how to drive and then dozed off. There Danny was, in the eighth grade, with no experience behind the wheel, racing south on Interstate 57 in the middle of the night. As time passed, Danny grew tired and pulled the car over on an exit ramp, and they slept that night in the car. When the sun came up in the morning, Gladys hopped in the driver's seat and said, "I'll take it from here." After arriving in Benton, she found a temporary apartment on South McLeansboro Street, near the Boneyard Woods area. This was the last time Alfred lived with the family on any permanent basis. Danny then finished his eigth grade year at Webster Junior High.

Danny Johnson would have been a great coach and teacher. In fact, that is exactly what he was studying to be at Western Kentucky University. This is why I say that: Danny does everything with passion. He is a gifted story teller with a great ability to engage his audience. All great teachers and coaches have this ability to pull you in. Danny spoke with his hands and there were times he would rise to his feet and pace about the room as he told a story. He held nothing back. Everything was fair game and he spoke from his heart. He went to places in our interview that were deeply personal and painful. I just sat there mesmerized by his life story, and the experiences he had to overcome as a young man. I asked him, "Danny, how much of your personal story do you want in the book?"

Danny Johnson: *Put it all in there…I'm not telling my story for anyone to feel sorry for me. That is not my purpose. I want to tell my story as a legacy to my children and my grandchildren. I want them to know my story. I want them to be inspired by it.*

Danny told me a story about his father that got us both laughing a little bit. He started by saying, "Matt, I've got to tell you this story about my dad. If I'm lying, I'm dying." He said, "This is cray-zee."

Danny Johnson: *I had another Uncle named Sam, who was Richard's brother, and he was a character but a great guy. Sam also spent a little time locked up, but he was fun and I think I get a little of my personality from him. He would sometimes come over to our house when I was little. I think we were living in Hill City at the time. He liked to play the guitar and he would sing a little bit. Well he came over one night with his guitar and it was just he and my dad in the room next to me. They got into some kind of argument about something. I was in another room and it began to get loud…and then I hear "Bang-Bang-Bang!" I peeked into the room to see what was going on and my dad had a handgun and he was shooting at Uncle Sam as he was running through the yard. I'm not kidding you! I went to bed and woke up the next morning and my Dad and Sam were at the kitchen table having breakfast together. I'm not lying, it was Crazy!*

The story really lightened the mood. By this time in the conversation, he was just rolling with information. He was animated and was talking a mile a minute and I couldn't keep the pace. I decided it was best for me to put my pen and paper down, and just listen. At this point, I knew I would remember everything he was telling me. He then went on.

Despite the tough upbringing and the constant moving, he explained that he loved his mother. Danny didn't want to live with foster parents. He wouldn't have it; he wanted to live with his mother. Why? Because he knew that she loved him. She looked after Danny the best she could despite her own demons and circumstances. She tried and Danny recognized that. He loved her and he realized that she was trapped in a lifestyle that she didn't want. She didn't want to be abused, she didn't want to have problems with alcohol, but she just did.

Danny Johnson: *I had two pair of blue jeans, and my mother would always keep one pair clean so I could wear them to school. My mother would listen to all my games on the radio. Joe Browning did the games then. I would come home and she would tell me everything that happened in the game. She was proud of me, and she would tell me all of the nice things that they said about me on the radio. She wanted me to know that. My mother never came to watch me play basketball in high school, because she had such low self-esteem. She didn't feel like she belonged in the gym with all of the other parents and people.*

Danny then paused for a moment in deep thought. He was reflecting back and thinking of his mother, he was completely silent. I let the moment go without saying anything, and he looked at me and said something about his mother that was from his heart.

Danny Johnson: *There were times that me and Mom bumped heads, and if it got really bad I would walk down the street to Bill Bettress' house and crawl through his bedroom window and sleep there. The next day it would be Okay. My mother was the only security blanket I had. I loved her. It didn't matter what she did or didn't do. It didn't matter what she said or didn't say. She loved me…and I loved her.*

When Danny was in the seventh grade, he began hanging around the pool hall on East Main Street. The owner of the pool hall was a man by the name of George Shuranko. George offered Danny a part-time job and it was an opportunity to make easy money. The tiny pool hall on East Main attracted some of the best pool players in the country. Minnesota Fats would sometimes grace the doors and the players played all day and into the late hours of the night. There was heavy betting on every game, and these were guys that could toss around some money. Certainly more money than Danny had ever seen in his lifetime. Danny worked off of tips, and he racked balls for big games. He was street wise and the winners usually came thru with generous tips.

Danny Johnson: *There was a time that I went home with three hundred dollars. I was rich! Are you kidding me! I would give more than half of my money to my mom and I would even give some to Randy. Oh, Carolyn, you need a dress, here you go!*

Truth told, besides the relief and food stamps that Gladys received from the government, the pool hall money proved to be very profitable for the family. Danny would even encourage his friend Bill Bettress to come up and work at the old pool hall. Later, Danny took other jobs to earn money, but he could not pry Bettress away from the pool hall. Bettress believed the money was too good. Danny also began playing money games himself. He was shrewd about who he played and most often he came out ahead. Johnson worked at the pool hall on and off from his seventh grade year to the summer of his sophomore year. Thank You, George Sharunko!

We had spent at least two hours talking about his upbringing and his family. By the way, this is the real story of Danny Johnson; basketball is just a part of it. I realized we had not even touched on basketball so I broke in and asked, "Danny, you had a lot of things going on in your life, how did you make time for basketball?"

Danny Johnson: *Bob Gallow was one of my teachers at Hill City Elementary School and he first introduced me to basketball. I would walk over to the court behind Douglas School and sit there and just wait to get into games. I played whenever I could.*

Danny remembered that in the seventh grade, he played for Bruce Jilek. Coach Jilek had tryouts for the seventh grade team and he wrote the players' names that made the team on a chalkboard in the gym. Danny's name was not on the board. Danny was devastated and he went home and cried because basketball was important to him. Coach Jilek then saw him at school the next day and asked, "Why weren't you at practice last night?" Danny was confused and answered, "My name wasn't on the board, so I assumed I didn't make the team." Jilek looked at Danny with surprise and realized that he had accidentally left his name off of the board. Coach Jilek then assured him he was on the team, much to Danny's relief.

As an eighth grader, Johnson played for Sherwood Pace at Webster Junior High. He liked Sherwood because he was "kind to him." As a youngster, Danny noticed people that went out of their way to help him. Help could come by way of a ride home after practice, a meal that was paid for or someone who gave him a job to earn a little extra money. Kind gestures like these went a long way with Johnson. Bruce Taylor's mom occasionally picked Danny up if she saw him walking to and from practice. Bruce and Danny became very close friends in high school, and were teammates on the '67 and '68 teams. With that being said, our conversation turned to people in the community that helped him along the way. He loved talking about those people who showed him kindness and tried to support him.

Danny Johnson: *I didn't play basketball as a freshman. I was racking balls at the pool hall…but Harry Stewart was the guy who encouraged me to play basketball. He saw that I could be a player…and he saw that basketball could help me. He stayed on me about playing and I felt like he really cared for me. Harry is one of those people who saved me. He talked to me as if he cared for me and I trusted him.*

Those people who are longtime residents of Benton, Illinois, remember Battle's Grill. Battle's Grill sat on the Southwest corner of the Benton Public Square. Wayne and Marge Battle were the owners and they loved everything Benton basketball. Battle's Grill was a popular hangout to many of the high school students and the restaurant was lined with giant-sized pictures of all the great Ranger teams. If you were a great player, you were enshrined with an individual picture in the restaurant. As a young boy, I recall going into Battle's and getting a burger and a soda. Ranger pictures everywhere. It was almost like a museum devoted to Ranger basketball. Many of the players admitted in interviews that it was neat to enter the restaurant and see your picture hanging on the wall. Wayne and Marge Battle were big Ranger fans and had reserved seats in the old gym.

Danny Johnson: *Wayne Battle knew my situation…and don't get me wrong. Wayne's heart was in the right place. I was a sophomore and he was trying to help me. He hired me to do some work around the restaurant for some extra money. I liked Wayne and I needed the money. One of my jobs was to clean the* *bathrooms in the restaurant. I was like sixteen or seventeen years old and my teammates are eating in Battle's with their girlfriends…and I'm in the back cleaning the restrooms. I just couldn't do that…and it bothered me. Wayne hadn't thought one thing about it. He didn't understand, so I just didn't work there very long. In fact, Wayne later took me to Western Kentucky to visit the campus before I went off to college. We stayed in a hotel there in Bowling Green, Kentucky. Wayne really cared for me and he is definitely one of those people who helped me.*

It was clear that Danny knew he was different than most of his teammates and many of his classmates. He just didn't have the same family life of many of his peers and it created a burning desire to prove to others that he was just as good or better. I called it a "desire", but Danny called it an "edge". It was clear that what really made Danny Johnson so competitive was his desire to prove people wrong. Yes, he wanted a life better than his upbringing, but most of all, he wanted to fit in and be like everyone else. In grade school, he recalled the shame he felt when his name was mentioned out loud by his teacher because he was late with his book rent. The humiliation he felt by using food stamps and not having the trendy clothes of his classmates.

When he was in eighth grade, Coach Pace gave him a new pair of tennis shoes to wear, but they weren't the Converse shoes all of his teammates were wearing. There was even a man in town who took advantage of Johnson's need for a good pair of shoes. Knowing that Danny would do anything for a pair of black wing-tipped dress shoes, the man sold Danny the shoes knowing they were two sizes too small. The price of the shoes stretched Danny's budget. The shoes rubbed blisters on Danny's feet but he wore them anyway because they represented wealth and prestige. In the end, he realized the man had taken advantage of his poverty. Now that Danny is older, he often wonders why the man didn't just give him the shoes. It's not like he needed the money. He felt small when he was cleaning the bathrooms at Battle's Restaurant. He clearly saw the "haves and the have nots" and he knew which side he was on. All of these experiences were hurtful, but his basketball abilities leveled the playing field and allowed him to feel good about himself. Between the lines, he was something special and being on those great teams provided a positive experience that he so desperately needed.

There were other people in the Benton community who stepped up to help Danny. After politely stepping away from his job at Battle's, he became acquainted with a man by the name of Doyle Culbertson. Mr. Culbertson was the vice- president of the Bank of Benton. He gave Danny an old beat-up truck to drive with the purpose of hauling trash from the taverns in town to the landfill in West City. This was Danny's first vehicle. It wasn't much to look at, but he enjoyed having some wheels. One day, Culbertson took him up town and bought him a black pair of dress pants and a white dress shirt. Life was such a struggle for Johnson that these simple acts of kindness were cherished and never forgotten.

During the summer after his sophomore year, he was hired by Everett and Vera Odum. Everett owned a farm outside of town and he also owned livestock. On the farm, Danny mostly worked on a tractor and disked large areas of land. To his surprise, he loved the work. Johnson enjoyed the peace and solitude of being on that tractor and just thinking about life and dreaming. The experience on the tractor allowed his mind to wander, and most importantly, it gave him a chance to be alone with his thoughts. He then made a point that I'll never forget.

Danny Johnson: *I remember…I would work all morning by myself on the tractor. Everett's wife, Vera, would come out with a large glass of tea and sandwiches for lunch. She fed me. I just thought I was in heaven. See…when you fed me when I was growing up…that meant that you loved me. There were times in my life that I was hungry. I know what hunger pangs feel like and when she brought that food out, she was showing me love. Today, when I feed you…I am telling you that I love you. That is my way of telling you that I love you. I still do it today with my family. I remember when I was young… maybe at Thanksgiving we might have a really nice meal and my Grandpa Carlisle would cry when he gave the blessing. I would think, what is he crying about? Today, when my family is all around the table and I say the blessing… sometimes I get choked up. I get it now. I now know why Grandpa was crying. His family was around him and there was love in the room. It's just about loving people, Matt.*

I was sitting there listening to him tell this story, and I wanted to yell out, "Amen!" Instead, I offered him something to eat, and we both laughed. We were both enjoying the conversation and it seemed each little story was better than the last one. I looked at him and said, "You know Danny, this might be the last chapter of the book." He looked at me with a very serious expression and said, "Why?" I then said, "I'm not going to have any room for any more information when I'm done talking to you." He sat back and just laughed.

Danny quickly changed his tone, and began to tell me about the death of his mother. On Thursday night, January 5, 1967, Danny Johnson's mother took her own life. Johnson told the story, but he sometimes had to pause and search for the right words. It was obvious that it is a memory that is very painful for him to talk about, but he insisted that the story not be sugar-coated. He wanted his grandchildren to know his story and he wanted it told honestly. I listened intently, as he told me about possibly the worst day of his life.

Danny Johnson: *My mother had tried to commit suicide three times before. That night we had a misunderstanding about something...she had been drinking and I remember her saying "You'll be sorry, you'll be sorry." I had heard this before....and I explained to my mom that I had to go to bed and get some sleep. We had a game the next night. The next morning, I went to school and after lunch, me and Kenny Irvin were walking into the building...we were stopped by Coach Herrin. I could tell by the look on Coach Herrin's face...my mom was dead. Coach Herrin and Claude Rhodes took me into a room and told me the news. I immediately went home and did not play in the game that night. My youngest brother, Randy, did not go to school that day and he is the one who found her and made the call for help. My mother was drinking and then overdosed on some pills...it was tough. Here I was playing basketball and everyone knows the story...That was a tough thing!*

Gladys Johnson was thirty-nine years of age. Johnson's father had left years earlier and there was not a guardian at home. With his mom now gone, it was only Danny and his younger brother, Randy, at the apartment. By this time, they were living in an apartment on Joplin Street. Carolyn, Danny's sister who was the closest to his age, then stepped up in a big way. Carolyn loved Danny and Randy, but at the time of her mother's death she was living in Pekin, Illinois, with her husband, Leroy. Knowing that Danny and Randy had moved all of their lives and they were most comfortable in Benton, Carolyn and Leroy moved back to Benton to care for Danny and Randy. It was an act of love by Carolyn that Danny is grateful for to this day. Leroy accepted a job at Menard, supervising "the worst of the worst" in the prison population, but at least they were home.

In 1968, Danny's senior year, his oldest sister, Donna, was stabbed to death in a bar outside of town. The death was unexpected, and Danny missed the first game of the Regional Tournament against Christopher. Think about that. Danny Johnson lost his mother and oldest sister within fourteen months. Life must have been overwhelming to an eighteen-year-old boy trying to make sense of such devastating tragedies. Fortunately, he still had Sherry and there were people in the community who were helpful. It was still a very difficult time for him.

Danny Johnson: *It was extremely tough to go out and play in front of all these people when my family appeared in the paper for all of these things. I didn't want the death of my sister or mother to ever be highlighted. It was just tough.*

Despite his tough upbringing, Danny Johnson continued to fight on. Johnson expressed himself on the basketball floor by playing with a fierce tenacity that drove him to be one of the greatest players in the state in 1967-68.

Sherry (Milligan) Johnson in the fall of '68.
(Benton High School)

Johnson had a turbulent childhood but said, "Sherry saved me."
This is Danny and Sherry at homecoming '68.
(Benton High School)

Danny Johnson's family. (Front L-R Randy, Cousin, Danny / Back- L-R
Carolyn and Gladys) *(Danny Johnson family collection)*

Danny's mother, Gladys.
(Danny Johnson Family Collection)

CHAPTER TEN

Playing With an Edge in '68

*"You certainly didn't want to be that team that lets people down.
We were going to do our part to hold up our end of the bargain."*
– Dick Corn, Ranger Guard

Danny Johnson's childhood story of survival is inspiring. Johnson dealt with his difficulties in a way that great competitors do; with an "Okay! I'll show you!" type of attitude. He lived his life and played the game intrinsically motivated by the events of his life. He was determined to prove his worth by being the best on the floor. On the floor, you were judged by your abilities, and Johnson found a temporary peace when showcasing his talents on Friday and Saturday nights.

Rich Herrin: *Danny Johnson was one of the best players I ever coached…He had tremendous hands…very strong…He could rebound…He could defend. He was a great scorer. He could run and jump…he was quick…a great player.*

In '68, there was no doubt, it was Johnson's team. The Rangers took on his personality and found reasons to play with that edge that so motivated Johnson. The great class of '67 featuring Yunkus and Hoover were gone. In Johnson's mind, their absence was even more reason for this group to step up and prove people wrong.

The '68 Rangers were seven deep most nights. Dick Corn, who played behind Hoover in '67, was the point guard and he was very steady.

He was a good passer and a solid floor general. Corn was respected by his teammates and possessed a great intangible; leadership. He was also the quarterback of the football team.

Coach Herrin: *Dick Corn was a good leader for us. He made things happen and was smart enough to get Johnson the ball. He was a great team player....*

Playing alongside Johnson and Corn in the backcourt was senior Dennis Miller. Miller played hard and was a pesky defender. He averaged eight points a game and was a solid rebounder for his size. Miller had a knack for deflecting passes and was a solid role player. Coming off the bench was junior Doug Collins. There was perhaps no player in the state more in love with the game of basketball than Collins. He played all the time. As a junior, Collins was 6'2" and was developing into a fine shooter. In '68, Doug Collins was just trying to get on the floor and contribute. He was a solid player but he was not yet the Division I prospect he would later become.

In the last two seasons, the Rangers compiled a record of 61-2. But to begin the season in '68, the team lost their first two out of three, and dropped the season opener to Johnston City, 78-76. The spoiled Ranger fans could not believe the team was losing and for the players it felt as if the world was coming to an end. It was not a good start.

Dick Corn: *You certainly didn't want to be that team that lets people down. We were going to do our part to hold up our end of the bargain. Yes, I think it's fair to say that we played with a chip on our shoulder in '68.*

Even though the Rangers started slowly, the team was a basketball fan's delight. They played aggressively by attacking opponents with a trapping 1-2-2 full-court pressure. The guards applied smothering ball pressure, jumped passing lanes and deflected passes that led to easy points. It was Johnson's style of play. He thrived in an up-tempo game in which his athleticism could take over. Dick Corn played the point of the press, with Johnson and Miller on the wings. Corn often angled himself at the point of the press to force the inbounds pass to Johnson's side. Then it was on! Johnson and Corn trapped the first poor soul that caught it and Miller rotated to the middle. Often, Johnson could use his quick hands to just take the ball from the opponent.

The big guys (Taylor, Milton and Tindall) rotated at the two back spots that Herrin learned were so important. The back men, called "bigs", worked simultaneously, moving up if the ball was on their side of the floor, with the opposite big man moving back to guard the goal. The bigs had the responsibility of anticipating passes, but they also had to protect the rim. It was a delicate balance that demanded constant practice.

Coach Herrin: *The first two games we got beat…I kind of felt like it was my fault…We had Yunkus and Adkins…and then Yunkus and Fustin as the back players on our press in '66 & '67. I had not spent enough time teaching Taylor, Tindall and Milton how to play the back of that 1-2-2. We went back to the gym and worked on it though…they got better.*

The Rangers then righted the ship behind the unbelievable play of Danny Johnson. With a record of 1-2, the Rangers traveled to Marion and won 81-74 in overtime. The win gave the Rangers a 1-0 start in conference play and proved to be a huge lift to a team trying to find its identity. Johnson led the Rangers with 26 points and guard Dick Corn chipped in with 17. On December 23, the Herrin Tigers came to town. The Rangers spanked the Tigers by a score of 90-65 in front of a packed house in the Cracker Box. Johnson put on a show by leading all scorers with 34 points. Big Bruce Taylor chipped in with 18.

Dennis Miller: *We knew that we were not a (1-2) team…I believe we had enough confidence in ourselves as a group to turn things around.*

Taylor played a big role in '67 coming off the bench after Fustin suffered a broken jaw. In '68, Bruce Taylor developed into one of the best post players in Southern Illinois and provided the second scoring option in the Ranger offense.

Coach Herrin: *Bruce Taylor was a very good player. He really did a great job for us when Fustin got hurt in '67…He was about 6'4" and he could play facing the basket or with his back to the bucket. He could really score.*

Senior Pat Tindall and Junior Joe Milton rotated time at the other post position. Milton and Tindall played their roles well. The Ranger reserves were Danny Stewart, Laird Wisley, Bob Smith, Larry Williams and Tom

LaBuwi. They were all good workers and provided stiff competition in practice that kept the team sharp.

The 1968 Benton Yearbook features a picture of the team that included four managers; Kirby Williams, Don Mrogenski, Evan Stewart and a young Brad Weathers. A young Rod Herrin is kneeling in the front and he served as the official team mascot. Reserve guard Danny Stewart remembered why being a Benton Ranger was important to him.

Danny Stewart: *When our family moved to town in 1961, I saw the Rangers play in the State Tournament on our black and white television. When we got beat…I almost cried. From that point on…I wanted to be a Benton Ranger.*

After Christmas, it was the Centralia Holiday Tournament. After winning the tournament in '66 and '67, Centralia placed the Rangers in an early morning contest against the Edwardsville Tigers. Edwardsville was a big school and tip-off time was 9:00 a.m. Unfortunately, Dick Corn was sick during the tournament, but he managed to play in all of the games. The Tigers handled the Rangers in a nip and tuck game by a score of 66-62. It was the first loss the Rangers had suffered in the tournament since 1964. Coach Herrin rallied the troops to win the Consolation Championship over the host Orphans, 80-68. In only four tournament games, Johnson scored 109 points for an average of 27.1 points per game. It is the only time in CHT history that the MVP award was given to a player in the consolation bracket. Johnson loved playing at Centralia.

Danny Johnson: *Some of my favorite memories were playing in the Centralia Holiday Tournament. We played against big schools from up North. When you played well at Centralia it validated you as a player.*

In '68, Johnson set the record for steals in a single season with 156 by averaging 5.57 a game. There is a picture in the '68 yearbook of Johnson effortlessly laying the ball in that gives proof to his smooth gate and athleticism. He was lean, yet strong and had springs in his legs. Also, the guy played with an edge. He was relentless. Dick Corn spoke on Johnson's strengths as a player.

Dick Corn: *He had cat-quick hands. He could anticipate a pass and just go get it. We pressed and he got so many buckets off of steals and turnovers. He was a tremendous player.*

After winning the Consolation Championship at Centralia, junior guard Doug Collins was on the verge of quitting the team. Collins didn't play in the first game of the tournament against Edwardsville, nor in the Consolation Championship against Centralia. He was hurt, and he was at his breaking point.

Rich Herrin: *Doug was upset because he didn't get to play at Centralia. He probably should have….I don't know why I didn't play him. I should have…. He left his bag on the bus after we got back from Centralia. He was going to quit. He told Denny Smith and Hugh Frailey and some of the younger guys that he was going to quit…I grabbed his bag off the bus and I knew he might be up town at the Kew Pee Café. I went in and gave him his bag and he said, "Oh, thanks Coach, I must have left it on the bus." Some of his younger teammates he had told earlier about quitting the team were sitting there with him…When I left, they gave him a hard time…They said, "I thought you were going to quit."*

The Rangers opened play in January by defeating the Carbondale Terriers, 79-65. The game was closer than the score indicates and featured the two of the best players in the South Seven Conference; Danny Johnson and Les Taylor. During the game, a funny incident occurred that lived on in Ranger lore. The Rangers called a timeout in the second half and the team hurried to the bench. As the team sat down to get instruction from Coach Herrin, it became very noisy around the Ranger bench, and along with the fact that Coach Herrin was excited, his words were tough to make out. Players that have played for Coach Herrin can relate to this situation. As a player, you are tuned in and you're all ears, but sometimes it just doesn't matter. Johnson remembered the moment, and he enjoyed telling his old stand-by story about playing for Coach Herrin.

Danny Johnson: *Coach Herrin can get excited…sometimes he is just tough to understand. He was pretty animated in the huddle. We just couldn't make out what he was saying. As we walked back out on the floor, Dick Corn came up and asked me, "What did Coach Herrin say?" I told* *him, "Coach Herrin said get Johnson the ball every time down the floor…so he can shoot it."*

In a jam-packed Benton Gymnasium, Johnson scored a career-high 40 points and Taylor scored 32. It was a slugfest, but the Rangers prevailed. After high school, Les Taylor went on to play college basketball at Murray State University.

The Rangers then dropped Harrisburg and defeated Centralia at Trout Gymnasium by a score of 80-69. On January 19th, the West Frankfort Redbirds came to town. The Birds upset the Rangers by a score of 62-58. The team then rebounded to defeat Mt. Vernon the next night at Changnon by a score of 87-73.

Dick Corn: *I remember the win at Mt. Vernon well. After the game we all got on the bus…and they were in the process of building Interstate 57…so we had to take Route 37 home. We were all on the bus and then…we heard this noise like a gun….Coach Herrin said, "Get down, everybody get down!" Our bus got rocked by some Mt. Vernon students. Two weeks later the Mt. Vernon superintendent showed up at our practice and apologized to our team.*

The story speaks to the intensity of the rivalries in the old South Seven. The Rangers had dominated the South Seven since 1966, and the constant success created a bullseye on their back. The Rangers always got the opponents' best effort. When the '68 Rangers pulled one out in the Snake Pit, it was even more reason to rock the bus. Winning is fine, but when you win too much, opponents take exception, and this would be the case for the remainder of Rich Herrin's coaching career at Benton.

After the Mt. Vernon game, the Rangers had a week of practice to gear up for the Quad City Tournament in Carmi. Johnson remembered something that happened in practice leading up to the tournament.

Danny Johnson: *I'll tell you a funny story about something that happened in practice. I could dunk the ball and we had the old fan backboards in the East Gym. Coach Herrin told us that if we ever broke a backboard…we would have to pay for it. Sure enough, we were a few minutes from starting practice and we were warming up and I went up and dunked one and shattered the backboard. Coach Herrin went Crazy! The board shattered and there were pieces of the glass everywhere. I picked up a piece and took it home. I've still got it!*

The Rangers won the Quad City Tournament by defeating Fairfield 81-61. The Rangers then hosted the Marion Wildcats. Bruce Taylor netted 30 points to lead the Rangers in scoring. Taylor developed into one of the craftiest post players in the South Seven Conference.

There is an old belief in Franklin County that when the Rangers and Redbirds meet, you can throw the records out. On February 3, 1968, the Redbirds defeated the Rangers once again behind the strong play of sophomore Tim Ricci. The Birds won, 73-60. The Redbirds proved to be a thorn in the side of the Rangers and complicated the South Seven Conference race. The Rangers needed to win-out to set up a championship game with Mt. Vernon. The Rangers then caught fire and defeated Herrin, Harrisburg, Centralia, and Carbondale. Only Mt. Vernon remained.

Joe Milton: *We had to beat Mt. Vernon to win the conference and I can remember driving to the school for the game and people were lined up waiting in the cold outside for tickets.*

On Saturday, February 24, 1968, the Rangers hosted Nate Hawthorne and the Mt. Vernon Rams. Hawthorne was 6'4" and he was an athlete. Hawthorne went on to play at SIU-C, and played three seasons in the NBA. It was a cold February night, but it was about 90 degrees in the Cracker Box. The Rangers defeated the Rams in a classic by a score of 83-81. Bruce Taylor led all scorers in the game with 24 points. Taylor was nearing the end of his Ranger career, and his individual improvement as a player from the beginning of his junior year was incredible. Ranger fans poured onto the floor after the game. The '68 Rangers had done it; by winning the conference, they left their mark as one of the great teams in Ranger history.

Kirby Williams: *That team really showed its toughness by having to come back and beat Mt. Vernon twice to get a share of the conference. The win at Changnon late in the season was a big win. Changnon is a tough place to play even when you are a lot better team.*

Ranger fans poured into the Cracker Box to see the final home game. The Rangers finished another successful season by defeating the McLeansboro Foxes 75-68, on senior night.

'68 State Tournament Play

After defeating the Foxes, it was on to the Regional Tournament at West Frankfort. The host Redbirds handed the Rangers their only two losses of the season in conference play and they couldn't wait to face the Rangers in the Regional Championship. The Redbirds had to play a tough DuQuoin team led by Alan Crews and Don Stanhouse. The Rangers defeated Christopher in the first game of the Regional, 93-51, without Johnson. He did not play in the game because he was attending his sister Donna's funeral. The Rangers dominated Bluford, 92-61, in the semi-finals but DuQuoin stunned the Redbirds to set up an unlikely Regional championship between Benton and DuQuoin.

In the Regional final, DuQuoin's Alan Crews led all scorers with 26 points and Don Stanhouse chipped in 16 for the Indians, but the Rangers were too much. Danny Johnson and Bruce Taylor went for 22 and 21 respectively, but the real story may have been the play of junior guard, Doug Collins. Collins always had a ball in his hands and it paid off on this February night at Max Morris Gymnasium. The junior came into the game and hit five long jump shots to force DuQuoin to call a timeout. Collins' barrage of long bombs shifted the momentum of the game to the Rangers.

Rich Herrin: *I remember Collins really had a big game that night. He hit four or five jump shots in a row.*

In the end, the Rangers dismantled DuQuoin by a score of 95-72, in a game that many fans thought the Indians could win. The Rangers won the South Seven Championship and were now Regional champions. The team had played with an edge, and found its identity.

With the win, the Rangers advanced to play the Mt. Vernon Rams in the first game of the Harrisburg Sectional. It was a great match-up between the two best teams in the South Seven. The game was close the whole way, but the Rams defeated the Rangers 72-70 in front of a capacity crowd at Davenport Gymnasium. In his final game in a Ranger uniform, Danny Johnson scored 34 points without shooting a free throw, which is a very odd stat line.

Johnson's performance for the '68 Rangers is arguably the greatest single-season performance in Ranger basketball history. Johnson scored 744 points in just 28 games, surpassing Rich Yunkus' single season record of 742 set the year before. The Rangers finished the '68 season with a record of 23-6. Johnson ended his career with a total of 1,035 points in only two years of varsity basketball.

Danny and Sherry's son, Jo Jo Johnson, became the all-time leading scorer in school history while leading the Rangers to a third place finish in the 1992 Class A State Tournament. Jo Jo would finish his career with unbelievable numbers. He scored 2,575 points in his career and broke his father's single season scoring record of 744 points by scoring 950 as a senior. Danny and Jo Jo are the only father-son combination in Ranger history to score 1,000 career points and be selected to the All-State team. Both have their numbers retired at Benton High School.

After graduating from BCHS, Dick Corn attended Monmouth College and majored in education. He also played basketball. Corn is perhaps the most successful coach in the Rich Herrin coaching tree. Corn went on to become one of the greatest high school basketball coaches in Illinois state history. He was hired at Pinckneyville in 1975, and coached the Panthers until 2007. He coached a total of 32 years at Pinckneyville with an eye-popping record of 708-259. Under his guidance, the Panthers won twenty-four Regional titles, seven Sectional titles along with a second place state finish in '88, and a fourth place in '06. The Panthers won State titles in '94 and '01. Corn's teams played hard defensively, and ran a motion offense that emphasized quick ball reversals and basket cuts. Corn created a basketball dynasty at Pinckneyville much the way Herrin did at Benton.

I asked Coach Corn this question; what did you learn from Coach Herrin? I heard him kind of chuckle as if to indicate, "There isn't enough time in the day for me to tell you." He then answered with a very thoughtful reply.

Dick Corn: *As a coach, he demanded that you work hard. If he said that you weren't working hard...that was the worst thing he could say to you as a player. He demanded that you put in extra time as a player. There would be times after practice; especially my junior year when I was just getting some minutes... he would encourage us to play one-on-one or two-on-two after practice. Sometimes he would even play with us. He was also very good at developing personal relationships with his players. He would take us to the annual Kentucky/Indiana All Star game. He was always building personal relationship with his players. You just knew he always had your best interest at heart and the team's best interest. It is most important that your players* *respect you. They don't have to like you. We certainly respected him because we knew he cared about us. There were even times as a young coach that I called Coach Herrin or Ron for advice about a situation I was dealing with at Pinckneyville. We are still very close friends and we talk at least two or three times a week.*

Dick Corn has two daughters; Melissa Corn and Melanie Corn Schweizer. He also has three stepsons; Lane, Mason and Collin Woodside. Coach Corn is now retired from coaching and resides in Pinckneyville, Illinois. He still attends high school basketball games and maintains a very close relationship with Coach Herrin.

After high school, Dennis Miller attended Olney Junior College and played two years of basketball before transfering to Illinois State University. He was on campus when his teammate Doug Collins played for the Redbirds. After graduating from Illinois State University, Dennis returned to Benton and was hired at the Bank of Benton. He is now retired from banking and lives in Marion, Illinois. He married Jackie Stewart Miller, and has one son named Jeff. Jeff would also play for the Rangers in High School. Miller had fond memories of his time spent as a player for Coach Herrin.

Dennis Miller: *If I had to describe Coach Herrin in one word it would be tenacious. He expected all of us to perform to the best of our ability.*

Senior Forward, Bruce Taylor who provided much of the scoring from the post position for the Rangers passed away at the age of thirty-nine, on January 22, 1990. After High School, Bruce played basketball at Union University, in Tennessee. After college, Bruce returned to Benton and worked as a coal miner for Old Ben 26. He married Renee Sandusky Taylor in 1979. They had one daughter, Amy.

Senior Forward, Pat Tindall gave the Rangers valuable minutes at the post position in '68. After graduation, Pat attended Hiawassee Junior College in Tennessee. It was there where he met his wife Cathy and they were married in August 1970. Pat graduated from the ETSU School of Nursing. He later joined the 912th MASH unit and served in Desert Storm. He retired as a Lt. Colonel and he loved his military family. Pat died on September 14, 2019, at the age of sixty-nine. Pat and Cathy had three children; Ben, Valerie and Lora.

Despite the loss of the '67 senior players to graduation, the '68 Rangers created their own identity and provided the community of Benton with yet another championship season. Danny Johnson had one of the greatest individual seasons in school history. The South Seven was loaded with talent in '68, and some believed the team overachieved by winning the Conference Championship. The '68 Rangers kept pace with tradition, yet left their own legacy. Going into '69, the Rangers would be young and inexperienced. The only returning Rangers with varsity experience were Joe Milton and Doug Collins.

Western Kentucky

In some ways, basketball was just starting for Danny Johnson. Following the season, Coach John Oldham of Western Kentucky was very interested in recruiting Danny Johnson and agreed to speak at the Methodist Men's Basketball Banquet. The banquet was held in the spring of '68. Johnson believed Western Kentucky was his best offer and was excited about the prospect of going somewhere and starting over. With only a hundred dollars in his pocket, he was worried about his finances. He knew the money would run out quickly.

Danny Johnson: *By chance, I happened to run into my father who was working in construction at the time. We had a brief conversation and I asked him how he was doing. I hadn't seen him in a long time. I told my father I was going away to school and I asked him if he could give me a little money to help out.… He told me that he would come by the next day with some money.… He never showed up.*

When Johnson showed up on the campus of Western Kentucky in the fall of 1968, it was both good and bad. Johnson explained this to me as I listened intently.

Danny Johnson: *I loved the fact that nobody really knew who I was and where I was from. I wasn't worried about that type of judgment from anyone and that was nice, but I want to tell you something - I missed my baby… Sherry! I wrote her so many letters during that time it was embarrassing! That was one of the first things I did after college…was find those letters and burn them. I didn't want her holding that stuff over my head!*

We both laughed and when Danny was telling the story about missing Sherry, he buried his head in a couch pillow to show his suffering. As a freshman, Sherry attended Leigh Christian College in Cleveland, Tennessee. He missed Sherry and that was his biggest adjustment to life at Western Kentucky. She understood him, and he wanted her there. After their first year apart, Sherry transferred to Western Kentucky, and shortly after, they married.

Danny enjoyed his time at Western Kentucky. As a junior, he played on the greatest Hill Topper team in school history. The '71 Hill Toppers were led by star center, Jim McDaniels. One of the highlights of Johnson's college career occurred on February 22, 1971, in a game against Eastern Kentucky. Johnson hit the game winning jump shot to defeat the Colonels by a score of 94-93 in overtime. The win clinched the OVC regular season championship for the Hill Toppers.

In the first game of the NCAA Tournament, the Hill Toppers defeated Artis Gilmore and the Jacksonville Dolphins, 74-72. With the win, the Hill Toppers finally got their opportunity to play the Kentucky Wildcats. Kentucky was coached by an aging Adolph Rupp, who refused to play Western Kentucky during the regular season in fear of getting beat. The Hill Toppers destroyed their in-state rival 107-83 in the second game of the NCAA Tournament. This is still considered by many to be the greatest win in the storied history of Western Kentucky basketball.

There was perhaps nobody happier about beating Kentucky than center Jim McDaniels. McDaniels was reluctantly recruited by Kentucky, but it was not his desire to break the color barrier at the University of Kentucky. It was known that Coach Rupp was slow to recruit black players, so McDaniels chose Western Kentucky hoping that someday the Hill Toppers might play Kentucky. On that March night in Athens, Georgia, the Hill Toppers played a near perfect game. The win over Kentucky proved to be the final game of Adolph Rupp's coaching career.

The Hill Toppers then defeated Ohio State in Overtime 81-78, to reach the NCAA Final Four. The game was played in the Astrodome in Houston. Johnson recalled the game.

Danny Johnson: *Playing basketball in the Astrodome was like playing in outer space. The place was so big you couldn't hear the ball bounce. The fans were so far away from the floor....the place was just too big. The floor was raised up and there was no shooting background. It was an awful place to play basketball.*

In the semi-final game of the 1971 NCAA Tournament, the Villanova Wildcats defeated the Toppers by a score of 92-89 in overtime. In the third place game, the Hill Toppers met the Kansas Jayhawks and won, 77-75. The '71 Hill Toppers remain the most celebrated basketball team in their school's history. Danny Johnson was part of that amazing run. In fact, he is the only Benton Ranger that has ever played in a NCAA Final Four.

When Johnson finished his career at Western Kentucky in the spring of '72, he was one semester short of graduating. He wanted to teach and coach. But he also needed money, and when his brother-in-law LeRoy informed him of the money he was making in the coal mines back home, he couldn't believe it. Danny and Sherry came back to Benton and Danny found work in the coal mines.

All of his family has passed away. Alfred and Gladys are gone. His sisters Donna and Carolyn have passed, along with younger brother, Randy. Danny Johnson is a survivor. He has not just survived, he has thrived. Today, Johnson is the patriarch of a large family that loves him dearly. He has done the toughest thing a person from a dysfunctional family can do; he broke the cycle. When asked about Coach Herrin, Danny recalled his work ethic.

Danny Johnson: *Coach Herrin worked at it, that's for sure…He lived and breathed it…he was about fundamentals-fundamentals-fundamentals!*

Today, Danny and Sherry Johnson are both retired and reside in Benton, Illinois. Their lives are very much centered on family.

Danny Johnson scored 744 points in '68 breaking Yunkus's single season scoring record set the year before by just two points. He was an amazing talent. *(Danny Johnson family collection)*

Dick Corn played off the bench on the great '67 team and became the floor general on the '68 team. *(Benton High School)*

Big Bruce Taylor filled in nicely after Fustin's injury in '67 and
then became one of the best post players in Southern Illinois as
a senior in '68. *(Benton High School)*

In '68, Dennis Miller was thrust into the Ranger line-up and
became a valuable role player. *(Benton High School)*

After losing all five starters from the previous year, the fighting five of '68 played with a chip on their shoulder. *(L-R-Herrin, Corn, Taylor, Tindall, Johnson, Miller) (Paul Hickman)*

Joe Milton shared minutes with Pat Tindall in the post. Milton getting after it in the old cracker box. *(Benton High School)*

The '68 Rangers played with an edge and kept the winning tradition alive by finishing 23-6 and winning the South Seven. *(Paul Hickman)*

Here is Doug Collins as a junior. Collins came off the bench and had some big games late in the '68 season. *(Benton High School)*

Here is Danny Johnson signing his letter of intent to play for
Western Kentucky University. *(Benton Evening News)*

Johnson's son, Jo Jo, led the Rangers to a 3rd place finish in
the state tournament in '92 and is still the schools leading
scorer with 2575 points. *(Benton High School)*

Johnson's daughter, Missy, was a cheerleader at BCHS. *(Danny Johnson family collection)*

Johnson's grand-daughter Dymin, was a stand-out volleyball player at BCHS. *(Danny Johnson family collection)*

Johnson's grandson Kruse graduated in 2016 and led the Rangers to a 25-6 finish. Johnson is proud of his children and grandchildren and their contributions to Benton Athletics. *(Benton High School)*

CHAPTER ELEVEN

The Bridge to '71

"I fell in love with the game when Coach Herrin came to town. Coach just brought so much pride to our town." – Doug Collins

On Tuesday, October 26th, I had just finished an engaging lecture about the skeletal system to the youth of America when my cell phone rang loudly. I was in my classroom and hurried to my desk to see who could be calling. I expected to see my wife's name or possibly Coach Herrin, since we have been communicating on a regular basis about the book. I wondered if it was my turn to pick up the groceries at Wal-Mart. What could Coach be calling about? I glanced down at my phone and saw the name Doug Collins. Coach Herrin had given me his phone number a week earlier, and I had left Doug a message on his phone about a possible interview for the book. I have to admit, I took a deep breath to gather myself before picking up the phone. It's not every day I talk to Doug Collins. This was the call I had been waiting on! Doug expressed that the best time for both of us to talk at length would be the next day at 4:00 p.m. I was pumped to say the least!

Doug Collins grew up in Benton, Illinois and graduated from Benton High School in 1969. The people of Benton are proud of his accomplishments and have closely followed his life's journey. Any time I bring Doug's name up to someone in Benton, they are quick to point out that they are related to him. In a way, it is true; all of the people in Benton make up his family because he is one of us. Before he was an Illinois State Redbird, an Olympic basketball player or a '76er, he was a Benton Ranger.

After graduating from Benton in '69, he went on to become an All-American at Illinois State, an Olympian and the first pick of the 1973 NBA draft. He was drafted by the Philadelphia '76ers and the great Julius Erving ("Dr. J") was his teammate from 1973-1981. In 1977, the '76ers lost to the Portland Trailblazers in the NBA Championship. Doug earned NBA All-Pro honors for four consecutive seasons. After his playing career came to an end in 1981, he stayed connected to the game of basketball and eventually landed the head coaching job of the Chicago Bulls in 1986. He had the privilege of coaching the greatest player in NBA history, Michael Jordan. Doug would go on to have NBA coaching stints in Detroit, Philadelphia and Washington. He is now an NBA analyst and there is no one that can break down the game of basketball like Doug Collins. He has become Benton's most famous citizen.

Growing up in Benton, I knew about Collins, but had only laid eyes on him a few times in my life. The first time I saw Collins was at summer basketball camp in Sweetwater, Tennessee. It was the summer of '82, before my eighth grade year. The entire camp packed the small gym in Sweetwater to hear him speak about the dedication and work it took to be a great player. As Collins spoke, I hung on every word, but it was what he did that really caught my attention. He probably shot the ball for ten minutes without missing a shot. I watched with amazement as the balled rotated with perfect backspin, splashed through the net, and returned to him like a boomerang. He was a slender 6'6", and curly-headed. He sported a small chain around his neck, and every movement was smooth. Collins had just finished his NBA career with the Philadelphia '76ers. After his shooting exhibition, he picked out two or three of the best varsity basketball players in the camp, and just scorched them in short games of one on one. What really amazed me was his quick first step. At the time, Collins had bad knees, but he was just blowing by these young high school players like they were standing still. It was an education on how good you really had to be to play in the NBA. I was in awe. He was a master of his craft and was by far the best basketball player I had ever seen. The experience of seeing a player so talented made me love the game even more.

The Military Academy in Sweetwater, Tennessee was a grueling five hour ride south in the old yellow school bus. It was the site of our overnight basketball camps when I was a youngster. Later on, the camp was moved to the University of Tennessee Martin. Coach Herrin contacted coaches in the Southern Illinois area and each school would bring 25-30 players from their program. The camp was full of players ranging from junior high to high school. It was a great way to meet players from other towns. TMI was a team camp and it was structured differently than the Rend Lake camp. The coaches divided the players into different teams and developed a game schedule for the week. The games were competitive, and the coaches officiated the games. The gyms were extremely hot and there were times that tempers flared. The conditions of the camp and the schedule made all of us a little tougher, and the pure joy of just having the freedom to play could not be matched. For a kid that loved the game, it was a basketball paradise. The camp lasted a week and if you weren't really in love with the game, then you were ready to go home early. The camp was full of characters and boundaries had to be pushed. One night, a group of campers threw firecrackers out of their dorm windows after curfew. As punishment, the entire camp did push-ups, in what became known as the famous "Midnight push-up night".

The camp went by the name of *Doug Collins Basketball Camp* and each camper received a t-shirt as a souvenir with Collins' picture on the front. My good friend and former Ranger teammate, Brad Wills, told a story that lives on as one of the funniest moments in TMI camp history.

Brad Wills: *I remember one year Scoot* (Scott Sandusky) *and I didn't have a door to our room…it was like camping out for a week. Anyway, I believe Sanford Gray was the president of the Institute…An incident took place and he gathered all of us in the gym to talk to us. It's blazing hot in the gym and he said, "Remember, you guys represent your parents, your schools, and your coaches…and you also represent Jerry Collins." We looked at each other and kind of snickered… He even had a hat on that said Doug Collins basketball camp… He was doing pretty good until he said Jerry Collins…classic*

The coaches divided the players into three levels of play; the Jr. High Level (Junior College), J.V. Level (NCAA) and Varsity Level (NBA). There was no air-conditioning in the dorm rooms and most of us forgot to pack a fan. In fact, conversations about the camp stir up comments like, "It was the hottest place I'd ever been." There was a pool and since there was limited gym space, the junior high group did most of the swimming. I was having the time of my life. Basketball and swimming for a whole week with your buddies; are you kidding me! Again, I was probably thirteen years old at the time. I had never been away from home for any extended period of time, and my parents told me I could go as long as I called and checked in. That first year at TMI basketball camp, I was having so much fun, I forgot I had parents. This was before cell phones, and calling home never crossed my mind. When I arrived home, my parents were torn between giving me a big hug and a good licking.

My last encounter with Doug occurred at the 2008 Annual Methodist Men's Banquet in Benton. Doug was the featured speaker and there were a lot of old Rangers in attendance. At the time, I was the head coach at Benton High School, and I sat next to Doug during the dinner portion of the banquet. Doug is very observant, and as we ate, he was studying all of the people in the room. He would lean over and say things like, "That kid has to be a Labuwi." After being gone from Benton since the fall of 1969, he was able to identify and name most of the people in the room. Doug is an outstanding banquet speaker. Doug speaks from the heart. He is quick to show gratitude to those people in his life that have mentored him and is a wonderful storyteller.

The night before the interview, I called Coach Herrin and told him that I was going to talk to Doug the next day. Coach Herrin then gave me the Doug Collins scouting report. He said, "Let me tell you Biggin'…it will be a great interview…if you don't screw it up….You won't have to say much…He'll do the talking…just make sure you are writing it all down." Coach had to get that little dig in there, which was so natural that I had no reaction to it.

The morning of our interview I had a little extra bounce in my step. After school, I raced home and gathered all of my sources and threw them on the kitchen table. I knew enough about Doug to know that he is all about doing things the right way. Therefore, I tried to anticipate some questions he might ask me as a way of determining my competency level. I studied the BCHS yearbook of 1969. I closely analyzed the '69 Rangers team picture, knowing that it was important to be familiar with his teammates. I turned the pages of the '69 stat book looking for Doug's high-point games, and then searched the back of the book to find his accumulative statistics for '69. They were impressive. I then returned to the '69 yearbook to scan the scores of the games, paying special attention to the results of the Centralia Tournament and the post season tournament. I had prepared my questions the night before, but I really didn't want to follow a script. I preferred that our conversation be natural and relaxed. I looked at my cell phone and it said 3:58. I thought calling right at 4:00 p.m. would send the best signal, so I waited two more minutes. At 4:00

p.m., I picked up my cell phone and called Doug Collins. He immediately picked up.

Doug told me the night before that he would have plenty of time to talk. After we exchanged pleasantries, I explained the purpose of the book and that I wanted to devote several chapters of the book to his basketball life. I also explained that I wanted to gain an insight into his relationship with Coach Herrin. Doug listened intently and expressed his approval.

To begin our conversation, we started with his childhood. I asked him to recall his childhood memories of growing up in Benton. This was Doug's response:

Doug Collins: *Matt, growing up in Benton during that time was incredible. The town had a thriving middle class made up of coal miners, teachers and farmers. Everybody worked hard and watched after each other. Laird Wisely was my best friend growing up. We loved each other, but man did we compete against each other. During my younger years I went to Lincoln school and then when my dad finished his term as sheriff, we moved to 110 South Main Street. I then transferred to Logan School and joined my buddy Laird. We would spend time riding our bikes and playing sports and just doing what kids do. I had an amazing childhood growing up in Benton.*

I then asked about his family. Doug is now sixty-nine years of age, and he is the only living member of his immediate family. He recently returned to Benton for the burial of his mother, Jeri.

Doug Collins: *My dad was the county sheriff and we actually lived in the old jail. My uncle was a deputy. I like to tell people that those days for me were similar to the life of Opie on the Andy Griffith Show. I remember my dad would use the experience at the jail to teach me life lessons. He would teach me right from wrong by saying stuff like, "Doug, this man is in jail because he took something that didn't belong to him." Those teaching moments made me think of the consequences of my actions. Matt, I had good parents and I was a "pleaser". I never wanted to let my parents down and that was just the way I was wired. I'm still like that. I don't want to let you down. My mother's name was Jeri and she was always very supportive. My parents came to my games at the old gym and they sat in the folding chairs opposite the team bench. I had an older sister Linda and a little brother named Jeff.*

During the course of the interview, I found Doug to be one of the most down-to-earth people that I had ever met. The anxiety I felt about talking to the famous Doug Collins vanished immediately. I then shifted the conversation to basketball. One of the first things I noticed about Doug is his passion for life. He speaks with a passion, he coaches with passion and he analyzes basketball games with this same passion. There is perhaps nobody, other than Coach Herrin, that loves the game of basketball as much as Doug Collins. I wanted to know how he fell in love with the game. It was a question I had circled, because I was really curious about his answer.

Doug Collins: *I fell in love with the game when Coach Herrin came to town. Coach just brought so much pride to our town. I remember the '61 team…I was about ten years old and Bobby Orchid was my favorite player. In fact, I wore number 20 throughout my basketball career because my childhood hero Bobby Orchid wore number 20. That is the truth. I do remember a moment that I will never forget. I had developed a good relationship with Bob Tedrow, who was the sports writer for the Benton Evening News. Bob was in a terrible car accident as a young man and was in a wheelchair. He took me to the championship game of the Centralia Tournament in 1965 when we played Thornton. Thornton was ranked number one in the state and we were number two. Matt, the atmosphere in the gym that night was electric. I sat in the balcony. It was a packed house. It was the best high school basketball game I ever saw. I knew I wanted to be part of something like that…it took my breath away.*

When I was growing up, Mike McCarty and his wife took me to some of the away games. Did Coach talk to you about Mike McCarty? Mike McCarty, Chubby Rice, Doc Swinney…. Those were his boys. They had Coach's back … when he had to make a tough decision…that was important.

A funny incident happened at about this point in the interview. I had all these questions circled and I had the mindset that I would get only one shot with him, and I needed to make it count. I was fumbling through my notes, kind of stammering to find the next question and he stopped me and said, "Matt, don't get in a hurry. I know you want to do a good job on this book, so take your time. I've set aside this time for our interview and we can stay on the phone for as long as you need. When we're done talking tonight and you start writing the book…if there is something that you have a question about….just call me…don't hesitate." Doug read me well and I very much appreciated his willingness to answer my questions.

Doug is a master communicator and has probably told his life story hundreds of times, but he didn't cut any corners in our interview. I very much appreciated that. Everything that he said in the interview had profound meaning, there was no fluff. I then shifted the focus of the interview to his playing days at Benton High School.

1969 Rangers

Following the '68 season, All-State Player Danny Johnson graduated, along with solid players like Dick Corn, Bruce Taylor, Dennis Miller and Pat Tindall. The only two Rangers returning that saw action as juniors in '68 was Doug Collins and Joe Milton. Joe Milton started on the '68 team and he was a nice compliment in the post to Collins. Joe grew up in Benton and remembered the first time he saw the Rangers.

Joe Milton: *I can remember in the fourth grade I was at Douglas School in Mrs. Cook's room. She brought in a black and white television and we watched the Rangers play in the State Tournament. It was the '61 team.*

Joe grew up with Doug Collins and remembered competing against Doug as early as grade school.

Joe Milton: *Doug was always a great shooter. I remember playing against him in grade school and he could always shoot the ball.*

The other two seniors on the team were Bob Smith and Laird Wisely. Smith recalled when he first started playing basketball and had good memories about his teammate Laird Wisely.

Bob Smith: *I went to grade school at Logan School. I just really liked playing basketball. Everybody wanted to be a part of the Benton Rangers. Laird was a really fine guy. He always hustled…I was raised kind of poor but Laird didn't treat me any differently. He was a good teammate.*

The '69 Rangers were a young group and it was now their turn to keep the program moving forward. Doug recalled a memory from the end of his junior season when the Mt. Vernon Rams knocked off the Rangers in the first round of the Harrisburg Sectional Tournament.

Doug Collins: *After we got beat by Mt. Vernon in the sectional in '68, I remember Danny Johnson came up to me after the game and he said, "Hey, you're the next guy in line to keep this thing going." That moment meant a lot to me. It was kind of like a passing of the torch.*

Today, the old timers still refer to the sixties as the "glory years" of Benton basketball. In 1969, the BCHS yearbook was still full of black and white pictures and the players were still sporting clean flat-tops. The Rangers were still comfortable in the old Benton gymnasium that many referred to as the "Cracker Box". There was no talk of building a new school and a new gymnasium yet. Life at Benton High School still had the feel of the 1960's. Think about this- Collins was a freshman when the Rangers upset Thornton in the '65 Centralia Tournament behind the play of Jim Adkins. He witnessed the greatness of Rich Yunkus in '66 and '67, and he was Danny Johnson's teammate when he broke the single-season scoring record in '68. Doug had seen all the great players before him, and now it was his turn. Collins would be the last All-State player in the Ranger program in the decade of the 1960's. He represented the last of the "old guard" and served as the bridge to the great '71 team.

Collins had a solid junior season, but his numbers do not hint to the break- out year he would have as a senior in '69. The Rangers opened the season at home against the Meridian Bobcats on December 7, 1968. The Cracker Box was packed full of maroon and white. Collins scored 27 points and was perfect from the free throw line. Benton sophomore and future All-State player Jim Semanski scored ten, and big Joe Milton chipped in with nine. Most importantly, the Rangers won the opener, 76-67, and played well.

Doug Collins: *Matt, the first game I ever started in my high school career was in the '68 Regional Tournament my junior year against Christopher. The reason I started that night is because Danny Johnson was at his sister's funeral and he had to miss the game. I put together some good games in the '68 Regional and hit some big shots against DuQuoin. I was playing with more confidence and it carried into the Sectional...But my coming out party was the first game of the year in '69 against Meridian. Nobody really knew what to expect out of our team... I remember scoring 27 points and going 9-9 from the free throw line.*

Collins told me his stat line over the phone from the '69 opener at Benton. I'm thinking to myself, "Be careful Doug, I have the stat book and I'm going to check your facts." I opened the stat book as he was speaking; there it was: 27 points and 9-9 from the free throw line. Wow, right on the money! Here is my point. Doug Collins would go on to play in 77 collegiate games at Illinois State, 415 games with the '76ers and coached a total of 849 NBA games. He still remembers everything about that season opener in the old Benton Gymnasium in '69. Doug's performance in this first game validated his work in the off season. It was clear that he would be the guy in '69. In fact, he recalled the moment like it was yesterday. The memory is just as vivid as Jordan over Ehlo in the 1989 NBA playoffs. Doug has had so many big experiences, but he has never forgotten where it all started and was quick to point out all of the people that have coached him through life. He credits all his coaches, but is quick to show gratitude to all of his high school teachers at Benton.

Doug Collins: *I had great high school teachers at Benton High School. We had elderly women that didn't marry on the faculty…that devoted their whole lives to teaching young people. I had teachers like Ellen Burkhart and a coach like Rich Herrin. I had unbelievable teachers and coaches that guided me through some pretty difficult times in my life. I had Coach Collie and Coach Robinson in my life at Illinois State. Matt, I am a product of great teachers and coaches.*

In game two the Rangers hosted the DuQuoin Indians and won the game by a score of 94-61. Collins led the team in scoring with 24 points, but it was the inside play of Bob Smith that really sparked the Rangers. Smith scored 23 points and grabbed six rebounds in the Rangers win.

Bob Smith: *One of my favorite memories was one of the first games my senior year. I scored 23 points. It was the only game that I ever scored close to that many points.*

The Rangers then hosted the Marion Wildcats and won in a nail biter by the score of 73-70. The one-two punch of Collins and Milton were too much for the Wildcats. Collins scored a game-high 30 points followed by Milton's 17 points and six rebounds. The next night, the Rangers traveled to Herrin and thumped the Tigers, 83-65. The team was 4-0 overall and 2-0 in South Seven play. It was an unbelievable start for such a young team.

Coach Herrin: *Joe Milton was a good player for us in '68 ...he was definitely a key returning player his senior year. He gave us a post presence.*

The young Rangers then opened the Centralia Holiday Tournament by defeating Princeton 69-66, to move to 5-0. The team was playing well and Collins was leading the charge. As a senior, he played at 6'2¹/²", 155 pounds, and could really shoot the ball. Collins was a student of the game and also knew how to get to the foul line.

In the second game of the tournament, New Trier thumped the Rangers by a score of 88-56. The Rangers were 5-1 entering January.

In our conversation, Doug was quick to praise his teammates. He has stayed in touch with many of his teammates throughout the years.

Doug Collins: *We were a young team my senior year. Joe Milton was senior...he was really big and strong...and he could really run for a big guy. You'll have to do your homework Matt...but Joe may have been in the top five guys in the 100-meter dash in school history at that time. He could fly for a big guy. Bob Smith played inside for us and my buddy Laird Wisely played a guard position... Our other guys that played were like my little brothers. They didn't even have their driver's license yet...that's how young we were. We had Kaspar, Semanski, Lockin, Frailey, Adkins and Denny Smith. I remember driving out to Buckner and picking Semanski up for practice.... Steve Stewart was a freshman...He came up and played on the varsity team after the Centralia Tournament. He ended up getting a big bucket for us in the Regional final at West Frankfort that really helped us win the game.*

Jim Semanski: *Doug kind of took me under his wing.... There were many nights I spent at his house.... There wasn't anyone more dedicated to the game than Doug.... He was the first player to practice and the last player to leave the gym.*

Hugh Frailey was one of the sophomores thrown into the fire in '69. Frailey was left-handed and could shoot it. Hugh grew up in Benton and his father took him to all the games. Frailey's mother taught music at Benton High School for years. He was seven years old when Coach Herrin arrived at Benton and told me that the player he took special note of growing up was Greg Starrick.

Hugh Frailey (Sophomore): *I would get to the gym early with my dad and I would go to the corner of the gym….find Starrick…and glue my eyes to him. I watched every move he made. He was an amazing player to watch at that time.*

When I called Hugh, he mentioned that he just met with Doug about two weeks earlier. Hugh admitted that Collins was his role model as a sophomore.

Hugh Frailey (Sophomore): *If there was a better player in the State of Illinois in '69 than Doug Collins…then I didn't see him. Doug was a straight-"A" student. He was polite to everyone. He was like my big brother. He took care of all of us. He was the hardest worker I had ever seen. When Doug was a senior, he was an extension of Coach Herrin.*

Hugh then recalled a time that he, Doug and Denny Smith went to Carbondale to watch the Holiday Tournament.

Hugh Frailey (Sophomore): *Denny and I were in the back seat together and we were just sophomores. Doug sat in the front seat with Coach Herrin and they talked the whole way down to Carbondale about how we were going to play teams in the conference. They talked defense and offense…. Doug was such a student of the game and he was just so intelligent. Denny and I just sat in the back and listened…It was an education.*

After the loss against New Trier in the Centralia Tournament, the Rangers lost their next four out of five games. One of those losses was to West Frankfort on January 17th, at Max Morris Gymnasium, by the score of 86-76. Collins dominated the game by scoring 37 points but it wasn't enough. Ranger sophomore Rodney Kaspar chipped in 15 points. The Rangers record fell to 6-5. The league was loaded with strength and quickness but Coach Herrin pressed the right buttons to keep the Rangers near the top of the conference race year after year. Collins spoke passionately about Coach Herrin's ability to get the Rangers physically ready for battle in the rugged South Seven Conference.

Doug Collins: *My nephew Robbie* (Williams) *told me a neat story about a conversation he had with Tim Wills. Robbie could not get over the fact that we could compete year in and year out in basketball with the Mt. Vernons, Car-*

bondales and Centralias. He asked Tim, "What did we have that allowed us to do that?" Tim said, "We were expected to compete at that level." Tim's right, we were the Benton Rangers, that's what we do. Coach Herrin's teams were so tough because we played in his image. Coach knew that he had to develop a quicker and stronger athlete to compete in the South seven Conference. He was demanding and that made us tougher. Coach invested his life to basketball, and his love for the game trickled down to all of us. Coach was a stickler with the grades too. If you had a first hour study hall, and then you had last hour athletics, you had a pretty nice set-up to work on your schoolwork. We had to hold up our end of the bargain and make good grades. Making good grades was part of the expectation of being a Benton Ranger.

As the season wore on, the sophomores experienced growing pains as they adjusted to the speed of varsity basketball. The Rangers were young and they were also fighting to hold their own against teams that had superior athleticism.

Denny Smith (Sophomore): *Rich told me, "Get the ball to Collins… Take care of the ball…. And do what I ask you to do and you'll play." He had an idea of how he wanted you to play. He molded you into the player he wanted you to be.*

The '69 team practiced hard and kept grinding. The team had good chemistry and enjoyed each other's company despite the age disparity. The improvement didn't always come with W's. For example, the second time the Rangers played the West Frankfort Redbirds at Benton, the Redbirds escaped with a one-point win. Collins had 35 points in the loss. The Rangers were not about moral victories, but you could see the improvement in the results.

By mid-January, the sophomores were getting more comfortable at the varsity level. Collins continued to score the ball. He scored 40 points in a 91-82 victory over Harrisburg early in the year. Doug was scoring points in bunches and then in early February, he missed four games due to the flu. It was a setback for the Rangers, but other players stepped up to fill the void.

Senior Joe Milton was solid in the post and stepped up his offense to score 24 points in the Rangers' 80-61 victory over Herrin. Rodney Kaspar would chip in with 20 points. Senior guard, Laird Wisely played well at the guard position and was a total disruptor on the defensive end of the floor.

Coach Herrin: *Laird was a great kid. He just played as hard as he could and did everything we asked of him. At times he played the point...sometimes Collins played the point and Laird played the two. Bob Smith was the same way. He was our back-up center and he was a good kid that worked hard.*

The experience the young and talented sophomores were getting at the varsity level would prove to be invaluable. By '71, they must have felt like veterans, but in '69 they were learning the hard way. Nothing was easy in the South Seven, especially if you were young. The young sophomores tested the waters as to what they could do, and couldn't do. They were beginning to understand the importance of strength and quickness and continued to adjust to the speed of the game. There was no better mentor than Collins. He set the tone for the intensity of every drill, in every practice. He was tenacious.

Doug Collins: *My role as a senior was to give everything I had...everyday... I needed to win every sprint and every drill to show the young guys what it took. Our teams back then didn't beat themselves.... We had a toughness about us...you had to beat us.*

On Saturday, February 22, 1969, the Rangers traveled north to play the Mt. Vernon Rams. The Rams were loaded with talent and had punished the Rangers in their first meeting. Nate Hawthorne and Eddie James led the Rams attack and defeated the Rangers 97-73, but the Rams had no answer for Collins. He was clearly the most skilled player on the floor. Collins scored 37 points by hitting long jump shots and finding ways to get to the free-throw line. He played with no fear and exhibited instincts developed by constant play. In one short year, his physical development, skill level, and confidence had noticeably improved. In '69, he had become a player to be reckoned with, and was starting to get noticed by major Division I Universities. This had to be an exciting time in his life. All of his hard work was coming to fruition. I was anxious to ask Doug about the work he did on his own to make himself a player. Here is what he told me.

Doug Collins: *To do something individually you have to have direction. Matt, I'm a self-motivated person. All you have to do is tell me to do something.... You don't have to watch me do it. Sometimes I can be my own worst enemy and be too self- driven. Coach Jilek was my seventh grade basketball* *coach and I remember him telling us things we needed to do on our own ...I did them... My dad put a goal up for me when I was a kid and I played all of the time...but I had to have direction, and I got that from my coaches and teachers. I would work hard, but it's well documented that I was a late developer. I remember one time my sophomore year I was shooting in the gym on my own and Coach Herrin walked over and said something like, "Your shot looks pretty good, but if you don't learn how to run, you won't be able to play." He was trying to get me to realize that if I had no speed I would never get my shot off. I was constantly working on my quickness and speed. My freshman year in high school, I ran the 440 in seventy-five seconds on the old cinder track around the football field. My senior year, I was on the mile relay team and ran the 440 in 52.7 seconds. Coach Herrin had us doing Russian plyometric workouts where we were jumping onto boxes with weighted vests. Matt, you can probably remember this but Coach had everyone run track and if you weren't good enough to run track...he put you in the two-mile run. That is just the way it was. I remember we would run out to Benton Lake with weighted vests on and then spend the rest of the day swimming together.*

'69 State Tournament Play

The young Rangers brought a 13-10 record to the West Frankfort Regional Tournament but the Birds had beaten the Rangers twice and were the top seed in the tournament. On March 4, 1969, the Rangers opened Regional play by defeating Zeigler 74-46. The Rangers then defeated Bluford two nights later in the semi-finals 83-65. Collins led all scorers with 18 points and Joe Milton chipped in 16. The win over Bluford set up the third meeting between the Rangers and the Redbirds. During the sixties, the Rangers had won every Regional Tournament in West Frankfort with the exception of 1964. Even at this, die-hard Ranger fans still feel that Appleton's tip in at the buzzer in the '64 Regional Championship should have counted.

The Regional Championship took place on Friday, March 7th. The Rangers started seniors Doug Collins, Joe Milton, and Laird Wiseley along with sophomores Rodney Kaspar and Hugh Frailey. Off the bench, sophomores Jim Semanski, Denny Smith and Roger Adkins would be ready when called upon. Senior back-up center, Bob Smith, and a young freshman by the name of Steve Stewart would give the Rangers added depth. The Rangers started quickly and led 20-14 at the end of the first quarter.

They then widened their lead to 46-35 at halftime. Collins had 17 points in the first half and sophomore Hugh Frailey chipped in eight points.

The Redbirds were a veteran club with possibly the best sophomore player in the league in Tim Ricci. Today, Tim Ricci is still the all-time leading scorer in Redbird basketball history with 1,708 career points. Bob Brown is close behind with 1,610 career points. Ricci went on to have a fine basketball career at SIU and eventually came back to West Frankfort to coach and teach.

Tim Ricci: *Dale Hutchens and Kenny Griffin were two of the quickest guards in Redbird history. Dave Broy was also an incredible player in '73. We had some great battles with Benton. Benton really brought out the best in our teams at West Frankfort. They raised the bar…so to speak.*

The Rangers won the third quarter by four and had a 66-51 lead going into the fourth quarter. To begin the quarter, it was as if the Redbirds fought to keep their season alive. Senior guards Dale Hutchens and Kenny Griffin came out firing. The Rangers fell into the trap of playing not to get beat, instead of playing to win. They lost their aggressive play on the offensive end of the floor, and the Redbirds held Collins scoreless in the fourth quarter.

Joe Milton: *We had like a 17-point lead on them…and they came back.*

Joe Milton and Roger Adkins each scored two buckets in the fourth quarter, but it was the young freshman, Steve Stewart, that scored a huge bucket late to seal the upset for the Rangers. When the final buzzer sounded, the Rangers escaped with an 81-78 victory.

Joe Milton: *Late in the game…I remember Laird Wisely passed me the ball and I hit a lay-up that gave us enough cushion to win the game. West Frankfort came down and scored but didn't have any timeouts and there was less than five seconds on the clock. After they scored, Doug picked the ball up like he was going to take it out…he knew the situation. Doug just held it and he had this big grin on his face. It was over.*

Winning the Regional Championship had to be satisfying for the Rangers, and especially Collins. All of the great Ranger teams of the sixties played into the Sectional and his team would be no different. The improved play of seniors Joe Milton, Laird Wisely and Bob Smith can't be overlooked. The sophomores were gaining game experience that would be invaluable in earning them a trip to Champaign in two short years. The Rangers were playing their best basketball at the right time, which came to be a trademark of Coach Herrin's Rangers. A high school basketball season can last up to four and a half months. As a coach, you want your players to have that fight in them at the end. Herrin's teams had that toughness, and the players fought hard to keep the season alive. With the win over the Birds, the Rangers advanced to the Eldorado Sectional to face the Mt. Vernon Rams.

In the two previous meetings, the Rams had pounded the Rangers, but had trouble guarding Collins. The Rams of '69 were so athletic, and they had great size. They were an old team that had played together for years and were heavy favorites before the ball was ever tipped. They were led by seniors Nate Hawthorne, and "twin towers", Terry Sledge and Steve Strickland. Eddie James was the only junior starter. The Rams jumped out to a 35-28 lead at the end of the first half. In the third quarter, the Rangers outplayed the Rams and cut Mt. Vernon's lead to three despite a score-less quarter from Collins. Senior Joe Milton, and a host of sophomores provided the offense, as the Rangers inched closer. Doug Collins scored the final 12 points of his Benton Ranger career in a desperate struggle to continue the season but the Rams were too much. Collins finished his final high school game with 25 points, as the Rangers lost by a score of 69-62. The Rams went on to defeat Eldorado 96-80 to win the Sectional Tournament before being defeated by Carbondale in the Super-Sectional by a score of 71-63.

It was the end of the line for the seniors. Joe Milton proved to be a valuable post player for the Rangers in '68 and '69. Joe walked on to the basketball team at Eastern Illinois University and made the team. Joe re-called a neat college memory about Doug Collins.

Joe Milton: *I played against Doug when we were freshman...remember you couldn't play varsity as a freshman in those days and our freshman team at Eastern played Illinois State twice. I remember walking to the student union with Doug after a game and getting a burger.*

Joe had these words when recalling his playing experience under Coach Rich Herrin.

Joe Milton: *Coach worked at it so hard…always talking about basketball. He was always looking for ways to get better. I remember he took some of us to a high school All-Star game in Kentucky. He really wanted you to grow as a player and play at your best…and he was always about getting guys to go to college.*

Today, Joe is retired after selling insurance/financial planning for forty-seven years. He and his wife Karen have three children; Matthew, Monica, and Mark.

Ranger center Bob Smith, worked as a carpenter's apprentice and a coal miner. He retired at age sixty-two from the Taylor Motor Company after nineteen years of service. He and his wife Aren have three children; Misty, Roger and Eric.

Laird Wisely passed away on Wednesday, September 22, 1999 in Barnes Jewish Hospital after a brief illness. These were some words from Laird's obituary: Laird married Cathy Norris Wisely on July 8, 1982. Laird was the founder of Physical Rehab Works and the regional vice president of HealthCare Innovations, and was on the board at HealthCare Innovations. He graduated from Louisiana State University with a bachelor's degree in physical therapy. He was a member of the American Physical Therapy Association and sat on various physical therapy advisory boards. He served as clinical director for several physical therapists and physical therapist assistant schools. In addition to his wife Cathy, he is survived by four daughters; Nikki, Bria, Mallorie and Brittany.

Doug Collins earned All-State honors in '69 by averaging 25.9 points per game. Collins scored 596 points in just twenty-three games. Despite missing four games due to the flu, his '69 season will forever be remembered as one of the greatest single-season performances in Benton basketball history. When Collins reflected on his high school career, he was quick to show his gratitude to Coach Herrin. Their experience together in Benton formed a relationship of love that has lasted a lifetime. Doug spoke about his relationship with Coach Herrin.

Doug Collins: *I'm in the t.v. business…. People want to hear the stories of the athletes… People connect to stories. Matt, relationships are the essence of life. I want to lock arms with people on my team. That is when I'm at my best. I'm big on relationships and I love Coach Herrin. Matt, I wanted to be Coach Herrin. Think about it…. He was tough, fair and honest. I never heard him say a swear word…he is just a good Christian man. I wanted a family like*

Coach Herrin…a wife like Sue. I wanted to be a guidance counselor and teach and coach and give back like Coach Herrin.

Doug now had to decide where he would play college basketball and there were several schools that showed interest. He spoke about his choice to attend Illinois State University.

Doug Collins: *I was being recruited by several Division I schools that included Georgia Tech and Illinois. Coach Herrin guided my decision to be open to Illinois State. His college coach, Coach Jim Collie, was the head coach at Illinois State at the time. It was kind of close to home and I thought it would be a good fit…They offered me a full-ride scholarship. At the time I went to Illinois State, they were not yet considered a Division I School in basketball. We had to play so many Division I Schools on our schedule to be classified Division I School…and eventually that happened.*

Collins was excited about playing college basketball and Benton provided the perfect place to prepare for his journey to Illinois State. Collins remembered that last summer in Benton before leaving for Illinois State that fall.

Doug Collins: *The summer after I graduated high school I was put in charge of opening the gym…. You get up in the morning…head to the gym…. I'm playing, running and lifting and then working in the afternoon… It was baling hay at the Smith Farm or helping my Uncle Roy who was the road commissioner or bagging groceries at Kroger… Then it was back to the gym at night and older guys would come in and we would have great games. It was smoking hot in that gym and then we would head up town to get A&W Root Beer… Then you did it all over again the next day. Great times!*

I think one of the things that truly separated Collins from so many other players was his work ethic. Doug played constantly and was obsessed with improving his athleticism. He wanted to jump higher, be a step quicker and run faster. This takes work that most human beings just won't do. This is not going outside and shooting around for a little while. The Doug Collins workout program involved running, rope jumping and jumping on plyometric boxes. This was work and he did much of it on his own. This was Rod Kaspar's lasting memory of Doug Collins during summer open gyms.

Rod Kaspar (Sophomore): *I remember going in to open gym and seeing Doug Collins on the football field early in the morning running with a weighted vest on. Doug taught all of us about hard work.*

Scott Hall was the point guard on the '74 team and he told me a great story about Collins that made quite a huge impression on him as a young high school player.

Scott Hall: *One summer when I was in high school, I don't remember exactly what year it was- on an extremely hot day I decided to up my training. I pulled out my brother Wiley's weighted Converse high-tops, which his team at Rice University used for training, and went for a run…in the early afternoon…in the hottest part of the day. I wasn't messing around and I had determined to run the two and a half miles out to a school on Petroff Road next door to Old Ben 24 and back home from there. I remember it being a total of five miles. I was about two-plus miles into the run on Petroff Road. It was blazing hot, and all of a sudden I heard footsteps behind me along with some huffing and puffing. It started out faint and grew louder pretty quickly. I didn't look back to see who it was. I thought I was running a decent pace in spite of the weighted shoes but the next thing I knew someone blew past me. It was Doug Collins. I think I heard a faint "Hi Scotty," then I blinked and he was gone. I don't remember if that was before or after the '72 Olympics but I knew at that time that Doug was an Olympian and I remember marveling at this guy who had transformed from a regular kid like me into a super star. Doug, Rich Herrin, my brothers, every Ranger I knew contributed to whatever motivation I had in the sport of basketball. But Doug Collins was in a league all by himself in being an example of hard work and determination to every kid in a Ranger uniform who grew up remembering Doug. The thing I remember most about Doug, and everyone knew it, was that Doug worked longer and harder by a long shot than anyone in Benton had ever seen.*

On to Illinois State!

Doug Collins senior picture in 1969. *(Benton High School)*

This is the old jail today. Collin's bedroom was in the top story
above the entrance. *(Matt Wynn)*

Laird Wisely was a scrappy guard on the '69 team. Laird and Doug were best friends growing up. *(Benton High School)*

In our interview, Doug spoke highly of his teachers at BCHS, including Ellen Burkhart. *(Benton High School)*

Joe Milton provided a solid post presence for the Rangers in '69.
(Benton High School)

The '69 Rangers. *(Benton High School)*

Collins strokes one from the line. *(Benton High School)*

The Rangers battle the Rams at Changnon in '69.
(Benton High School)

Mike McCarty served on the BCHS school board and was a loyal friend and supporter of Rich Herrin. *(Benton High School)*

As a sophomore, Hugh Frailey and his teammates followed Collin's leadership. *(Benton High School)*

Steve Stewart became the first freshman to play varsity
basketball for Coach Herrin.

The '69 team after their Regional championship win over
West Frankfort, 81-78. *(Benton High School)*

CHAPTER TWELVE

Collins Takes Illinois State by Storm

"I loved Illinois State and I'm proud of my alma mater"
– Doug Collins

The summer of '69 flew by quickly and it was now time for college. Doug recalled the day he left Benton for Illinois State. It was a moment he would never forget.

Doug Collins: *I remember leaving Benton and heading to Normal, Illinois with all my belongings jammed into my used Plymouth Fury.... It was a car that my dad had rewarded me with for getting a college scholarship. I didn't know it, Matt ...but when I left that day for Illinois State; my parents were planning on splitting up. I remember pulling up to campus and I saw all of these kids checking into the dorm, and they were all with their parents. I had my little cry in the car.... And then I realized that at that point in time I had to make it. I told myself... I want to be the best student and the best basketball player that I can possibly be. I wanted to create a life for myself.*

When Doug arrived on campus, he bonded well with his roommate Craig Spiers. Spiers and Collins would develop a friendship that lasted a lifetime.

Doug Collins: *I was really blessed to have such a great roommate my freshman year in Craig Spiers. We were both conscientious and we were a lot alike which made my transition easier. You've got to find out what's important to you and the quicker you're able to do that, the better.*

When Doug arrived on campus, he was driven by a real fear that he might fail, especially in the classroom. That first semester Doug followed the rigid schedule of attending his classes and then heading to Horton Field-house to work on his game. After his basketball workouts, he would return to his dorm and study late into the night to prepare for his classes the next day. The thought of skipping a class was not an option. I recently read an article written by Dick Luedke entitled, *Always a Winner, Forever a Champion*, and dated February 2, 2020. The article gives great insight into Doug's academic fears and his intimate relationship with Illinois State Head Coach, Will Robinson. The following stories are some excerpts from the article:

Doug Collins: *I was afraid. I didn't know if I could make it. I didn't know what I could do academically. I was motivated by fear.*

A couple of weeks into his freshman year, Collins took his first two tests, in economics and mathematics.

Doug Collins: *They used to post your test scores with your social security number. My heart was racing a hundred miles an hour trying to find my number and I saw it…and it said "A" next to my number."*

Collins grabbed a notebook and placed it under his number to make sure it all lined up, to make sure he wasn't looking at someone else's "A". The "A" was his. He checked his grade on the other test. Another "A"! The revelation that he had aced his first two college exams gave him a sense of security that he very much needed at that time in his life.

Doug Collins: *I said to myself, "I can do this; I'm going to be okay."*

The future academic All-American was going to be more than okay. He was just as competitive in the classroom as he was on the basketball court. Collins remembered scoring 55 points in a game against Ball State and then racing home to study for the next day's anatomy test.

Doug Collins: *Anatomy was really hard. I remember walking into the class-room. This girl looked at me and said, "I know where you were last night." I said really, where was I? She says, "I saw what you did at the game." And then she said, "Don't look off my paper today because I know you didn't study." She* *was shoe-horning me, pigeon-holing me. So, I looked at her and said, "Don't look off of mine because I'll beat you on this test." A few days later, the teacher handed back our tests face down. With much anticipation, I flipped mine over and then asked the girl who was seated next to me how she did. I got her…. and it was an awesome feeling.*

Collins developed incredible study habits that sprang from an unparalleled self-discipline, especially for a young man away from home for the first time. To say that Collins had a high motor is an understatement, and it made him different, and he knew it. Collins knows himself well; he has a tremendous sense of self-awareness. I got a kick out of Doug in our conversation when he would say things like, "That's just me, that's how I am wired."

When Doug arrived at Illinois State in the fall of 1969, the NCAA did not allow freshmen players to compete at the varsity level. Doug was quick to mention that sitting out of varsity competition that first year allowed him to grow on so many different levels.

Doug Collins: *My first year at Illinois State as a freshman may have been my most enjoyable year. I came in at 6'3 ½", 155 pounds and I needed to mature physically. As a freshman I didn't have to compete for a varsity position and we had a good group of freshman guys. We would play local junior colleges… and we played the first game before the varsity games at home. It was the first time I ever had a black teammate…and I was introduced to a new culture, Matt…. I would go into the inner city of Peoria with some of my teammates and play against black kids. There was just no pressure that first year…. It's not like you're competing for a varsity spot. Academically, my first year was just about getting comfortable in the classroom and just being a college student. My freshman year really allowed me to settle in athletically and academically.*

Collins' dedication and commitment to the game made him a great player at the high school level, and then something happened. It was as if God said, "Okay kid, you've worked really hard, I'm going to give you a few more inches."

Doug Collins: *At the beginning of my sophomore year of high school I was 5'8" tall, I had a doctor's appointment with Dr. Swinney. My mom was 5'3" tall and my dad was 5'10." I remember Doc Swinney looked at me and said, "Doug you're going to grow ten more inches. You don't have any body hair on* *you at all." He was right. My senior year I played at 6'2 ½" and weighed 155 pounds and then at the end of my freshman year of college I was 6'6" and weighed 175 pounds. Those four inches from high school to college changed my life. There is no doubt about that.*

Again, the following excerpts about Doug's relationship with new head coach Will Robinson are from Dick Luedke's article, *Always a Winner, Forever a Champion:*

> At the end of Collins' freshman year, Coach Collie was suffering from multiple sclerosis and could not continue coaching. Illinois State Athletic Director Milt Weisbecker made a courageous move for the times and hired the first black head coach in Division I basketball, Will Robinson. Weisbecker told Collins that Robinson was more than qualified for the job and that his back story was more than inspiring. Robinson was the grandson of a slave and he was born to teenage parents, both of whom died before the age of thirty. He was raised by his grandmother in Steubenville, Ohio, where he finished second in the state high school golf tournament despite not being allowed on the course with white players. Robinson graduated from West Virginia State University, but racial segregation forced him to get his master's degree elsewhere, at the University of Michigan. The color of Robinson's skin then inhibited him from becoming a high school basketball coach, and so he chose to coach for the YMCA in Pittsburgh and Chicago. His success landed him a job at a high school in Detroit where he coached for twenty-seven seasons at two schools in that public league. He won two State Championships in Michigan. The second of those came a week before he was hired to coach the Redbirds of Illinois State. Collins had never had a black coach and Robinson would coach a player with a skin color unlike almost all the players he coached in Detroit. Collins recalled the first time he ever laid eyes on Coach Robinson.

Doug Collins: *I remember going over to Horton Fieldhouse and meeting Coach Robinson for the first time. When I looked into his eyes, I just trusted him immediately. I trusted him with my future.*

No one could have imagined the future in store for Paul Douglas Collins. Not even Collins himself.

Doug Collins: *He was just so wise and I learned so much from him. Coach Robinson instilled in me an insatiable appetite to compete and to never back down and most importantly to have that competitive spirit every day.*

One lesson that Coach Robinson taught Doug was how to handle success. Collins was receiving a lot of attention at the time and Coach Robinson sensed that this important lesson needed to be taught sooner rather than later. Collins had just had one of his best nights scoring 40 points in a one-point loss to Oral Roberts. Collins was the first player to the gym the next day and Coach Robinson was there early waiting on him.

Doug Collins: *Coach Robinson always called me "Champ". That was his name for me. He said, "Hey Champ, your life is changing and I want to show you something."*

Coach Robinson then walked Doug over to a nearby men's room and pointed to a newspaper on the floor opened to an article that documented his outstanding performance the night before. Robinson then said, "You know what that 40 points you scored last night is?" Collins responded, "Coach, I don't." Coach Robinson then said something Doug would never forget; "It's day-old news. You see that it's laying there by the toilet. I hope you know that as hard as it was for you to do that last night, it's going to be harder the next time."

Doug Collins: *He never let me lose sight of the fact that if I wanted to get somewhere; I had to work harder than anyone else. I had to be more committed and I had to listen to him.*

The story reveals an intimate relationship between player and coach that was more like a father and son. Will Robinson was always looking out for Doug by giving him wisdom and truth that he would lean on for the rest of his life. As a father, Collins passed down these same nuggets of wisdom to his son Chris and his daughter Kelly. These were nuggets of wisdom and truth that Doug would carry with him as an NBA player and then shared with grown men who would later play for him. Will Robinson proved to be much more than a basketball coach to Doug Collins; he was his life coach and most importantly a true friend. Collins would often be at Horton Fieldhouse working on his game and he would make it a habit to go talk to Coach Robinson in his office before practice. Doug recalled a time he made one of those visits.

Doug Collins: *I walked into Coach's office, and he had this mirror in his office. He looked at me and asked, "Doug do you think you're handsome?" I said, "No, sir." He said, "I want you to stand in front of that mirror and I want you to tell me if you think you're handsome." I turned and looked in the mirror and said, "No sir, I'm not." Coach Robinson then picked up a basketball and shoved it under my arm. He then said, "You're the most available meal ticket in town as long as you have that basketball under your arm. If you think these girls want to hang out with you because you're handsome, don't lose that ball." He kept things in perspective. I can't tell you all the lessons he taught me.*

Doug had incredible sophomore and junior seasons at Illinois State. Marion native Greg Starrick initially went to Kentucky and then transferred to SIU. He played against Collins for two years when the Redbirds met the Salukis. Starrick gave me some insight into their meetings in college.

Greg Starrick: *When I transferred from Kentucky back to SIU…we had to play Illinois State and Doug Collins…Doug had such good instincts. Our teams had some great battles against each other during that time. Doug Collins was so good…he was un-guardable. He was so smart and had developed an extremely quick first step. He was also a much-improved passer.*

Greg Starrick was an incredible player and he became one of the greatest free throw shooters in college basketball history. In his four year career in college, Greg was 341-376 from the line for .907 shooting percentage. He led the nation in free throw shooting as a senior, shooting 148-160 (.925). He told a funny story about an afternoon game in Horton Fieldhouse against the Redbirds when he missed two in a row.

Greg Starrick: *Old Horton Fieldhouse had windows up-top on the ends and we were playing an afternoon game. The windows had the old fashioned blinds that you could reach up and pull down. The place was packed and full of energy. I got fouled and went to the line to shoot two free throws. An Illinois State fan reached up and flipped the blinds all the way up and there was a glare off the backboard that made it tough to see. I missed both free throws and it was the only time in my career I missed two free throws in a row.*

As Doug's career at Illinois State came to a close, he came to realize how attached he had become to the school. Just four years earlier, he feared failure in the classroom and questioned if he could even contribute to the basketball program. All of his experiences at Illinois State and the '72 Olympics had built his character. Before his college graduation, Collins was number one pick in the 1973 draft by the Philadelphia '76ers. He had made a life for himself.

Doug Collins: *I loved Illinois State and I'm proud of my alma mater. It was a great place to go to school and I came across so many people there that became so important in my life…. I met my best friend Don Frankie at Illinois State and he has been important to my life in so many ways. I also met my wife Kathy. I met Kathy because she was dating a friend of mine who was the quarterback of the football team at Illinois State by the name of Harold Quizer. I would drive her to the road football games to watch H.Q. play. I'm not a rat….believe me. They ended up breaking up and I remember telling H.Q. that he had six months to ask her out…and if he didn't…then I would. He ended up dating someone else and then we just casually went out to get some food on a Sunday night because the dorms weren't serving dinner, and we've been together ever since.*

Just as he did at Benton, he left his mark at Illinois State. In just three seasons of college basketball, Doug scored 2,240 points and remains the all-time leading scorer in Illinois State basketball history. Doug scored over 40 points six times in his college career and netted 57 his senior year against New Orleans. The Court at Illinois State is now named in his honor.

Collins wore 20 in honor of his boyhood idol, Bobby Orchid.
(Rich Herrin family collection)

Collins weaves thru traffic for an easy lay-up.
(Rich Herrin family collection)

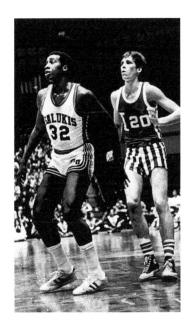

SIU player, Nate Hawthorne and Collins battle for rebounding position in a game at the SIU Arena. *(Ceasar Maragni)*

SIU's Greg Starrick mentioned that Collins was "un-guardable" as a senior. *(SIU)*

Coach Herrin embraces Collins in his final home game at
Illinois State. *(Ceasar Maragni)*

Collins and his family are honored at his final home game in '73.
(Rich Herrin family collection)

Coach Herrin and Coach Will Robinson pose with Doug and Kathy
on their wedding day. *(Rich Herrin family collection)*

Collins with Coach Herrin and Coach Robinson.
(Rich Herrin family collection)

CHAPTER THIRTEEN

The Two Free Throws in the '72 Olympics

"If Doug Collins can walk...he is shooting these free throws."
– Coach Hank Iba

In the spring of 1972, sixty-eight of the nation's best college basketball players were invited to try out for the 1972 USA Olympic Team. Doug Collins was invited. He was the third leading scorer in the nation as a junior and was elated to get the invitation. Once arriving in Colorado Springs, the players were divided into eight different teams and they practiced twice a day and then scrimmaged at night under the watchful eye of US Olympic Head Coach, Hank Iba.

Coach Iba was a college basketball coaching legend at Oklahoma State and he was old school. He did not throw out many compliments and had a somewhat gruff demeanor. Iba was not a fan of fast play and he encouraged a slower game built around sound fundamentals and strong defense. Iba's assistant coaches included a young Johnny Bach and coaching legend Don Haskins of the University of Texas El Paso. Bach served in World War II and marched into Nagasaki after the atomic bomb had been dropped. He was a tough man that eventually played for the Celtics before Red Auerbach came on the scene. Bach went on to have coaching success at Fordham and then after the Olympics in the NBA. Don Haskins burst on the scene after winning the 1966 National Championship by having the moral fortitude to put his best five players on the floor despite their color. UTEP defeated Adolf Rupp's Kentucky Wildcats, who were a college basketball powerhouse. Haskins was a disciplinarian, much like Iba, and he was not afraid to use colorful language to get his point across. After a grueling week of workouts the team attended a banquet in which they were told who made the team. Collins remembered his name being called, and it was at that moment he realized he was an Olympian.

There were twelve players selected to the 1972 USA Olympic basketball team; 6'8" Mike Bantom, 6'9" Jim Brewer, 7'4" Tommy Burleson, 6'6" Doug Collins, 6'1" Kenny Davis, 6'7" Jim Forbes, 6'2" Tom Henderson, 6'8" Bobby Jones, 6'8" Dwight Jones, 6'3" Kevin Joyce, 6'11" Tom McMillan, and 6'6" Ed Ratleff. UCLA center Swen Nater who played well in the tryouts left the team in Hawaii. Unfortunately, Bill Walton chose not to play in the '72 Olympics, citing various reasons. He would have been a difference-maker.

The team trained in Hawaii at a facility on the military base in Pearl Harbor. Doug kind of chuckled when I asked him about the team's training regime to prepare for the Olympics. He was adamant that it consisted of the most grueling practices and conditions that he had ever been placed under. For much of the trip, all twelve players slept in cots in one room. The only reprieve from the torture was an afternoon off that happened to fall on Collins' twenty-first birthday. In the book, *Three Seconds in Munich,* by David A. F. Sweet, Collins commented on the practice sessions in Hawaii.

Doug Collins: *We should have been where there was no sunshine because we were in the gym at least nine hours a day - practiced three times a day. I really don't know how we got through that. It seemed like it would never end. Hot. Mosquitoes. Practices were brutal. I mean they were brutal! Guys just absolutely knocking the crap out of each other!*

The last time the Olympics had been held in Germany was the '36 games of Berlin in what became known as the "Hitler Olympics". Germany was excited about hosting the Olympics and saw it as a chance to show the world how much they had progressed since that time. The athletes were all housed in a newly built Olympic Village in Munich. To send the signal of peace and tranquility to the visiting athletes, security was relaxed. On September 5th and 6th, eight members of the Palestinian terrorist group *Black September* found their way into the village and took nine members of the Israeli Olympic team hostage. After killing two of them initially, they killed the others, along with a West German police officer. The Olympic Games were then put on hold, a memorial service was held for the fallen Israeli athletes, and the games continued.

The United States' basketball history in the Olympics was incredible, almost too incredible for some. In fact, there were those on the Olympic Committee that felt it was time that the USA Basketball team got knocked off their throne. Heading into the 1972 Olympic Games, the United States had won 63 straight games and had won every gold medal game since 1936.

By comparison, the bigger, more experienced Soviets were far from your typical underdog. Led by the inside-outside combination of guard Sergei Belov and forward Alexander Belov, the well-seasoned and well coached Soviets proved to be the stiffest competitor the Americans had ever faced. The Soviets were men. They had played together for years and it was believed they had played approximately 400 games together before they played the Americans for the Gold in '72.

On September 10, 1972, the Gold Medal Game that Coach Iba had predicted was about to take place. It was the young USA team against the more experienced Soviets. The game was frustrating for the Americans because they wanted to run and use their athleticism but that was frowned on by the coaches. Late in the game, with the Americans mounting a comeback and down by one point Collins stole a cross-court pass and attacked the basket to give the USA team the lead. Collins planted to go up for the lay-up when he was undercut by a Soviet player with .03 left in the gold medal game.

To set the scene, it is the middle of the Cold War with the Soviets, and Collins will be going to the line shooting two shots, down by one point. The whole world is watching this basketball game that represented so much more than basketball. There is a strong Cold War atmosphere in the arena, as the two superpowers of the world clash in one of the most controversial endings in Olympic history. Collins is shaken up on the play, as his head rammed into the basket stanchion. Collins rises to his feet with help from his teammates, but he is dazed. In this moment, he is the center of attention. It seems as if the fate of the '72 Olympic gold medal game will depend on his free throws. There is confusion that Collins might be too shaken up to shoot the free throws, but Collins hears Coach Iba say, "If Doug Collins can walk, he is shooting these free throws." Collins told me in our conversation that when he heard Coach Iba utter those words, a bolt of confidence went through his body.

On this day in Benton, Illinois, it was quiet. The whole town sits glued to their black and white t.v.'s, as they too feel the enormity of the moment for their favorite son. There are moments in our lives that we will always remember, but Collins knows that making or missing these free throws will follow him the remainder of his life. The pressure is enormous. Collins takes the ball from the official, bounces it three times and spins it. He nails the first free throw. When he hits that first one to tie it, cheers and screams echo through the streets of Benton, Illinois. He immediately takes the ball and goes through the same routine, knocking the bottom out of the net to give the Americans a one point lead. Both free throws are no-doubters and the gymnasium in Munich, Germany, goes bonkers. Back home, the people of Benton swelled with pride as the game looked to be over.

As I was writing about Doug's Olympic moment, I was curious as to what Coach Herrin remembered about the moment. Where was he? Does he remember who he was with when Doug hit the free throws? I thought this would be really neat to know. I gave Coach Herrin a call and asked, "Hey Coach, where were you at when Collins hit the two big free throws in the '72 Olympics? Can you remember?" I was expecting this really nostalgic answer, and I couldn't wait to hear it. There was a long pause and coach said, "I don't know." I just couldn't accept that answer, because he's got a memory like an elephant. I said, "Come on Coach, think." Then he said, "I guess I was watching it on t.v. like everyone else." This was not the answer I was expecting. He was frustrating me, so I rephrased the question. "Coach what do you remember about Doug's free throws in the '72 Olympics?" There was another long pause, and true to his personality he said, "He made them, didn't he?" I started laughing because that is coach. There was nothing romantic or nostalgic about the moment, he either made the free throws or he didn't. It's as simple as that. Coach became defensive and asked why I was laughing and I said, "Nothing Coach…great answer."

I asked Doug about the two free throws with the entire world watching, and he gave me great insight into how he was able to handle the pressure of the situation.

Doug Collins: *Matt, I'm going to throw out an old military belief that I think holds true. You never rise to the level of your competition; you fall to the* *level of your training. Think about that.... If you are in war and you're getting shot at...and you're not a very good marksman...the fact that you need to be a good marksman in that moment is not going to make you better. Where do you get your confidence? You get your confidence from the work you put in...from your work...I dribbled the ball three times and spun it just like I did thousands of times in the old gym at Benton...you can't cheat the game.... You're going to compete to the level that you are trained. I fell back to my training and it allowed me to handle that situation.*

This is a quote by USA assistant Coach Don Haskins that appeared in David Sweet's book entitled, *Three Seconds in Munich*.

Don Haskins: *I've never seen anything grittier or guttier. I can't believe he swished those two free throws.*

After Collins made both free throws, the Soviets had the ball with the United States clinging to a 50-49 lead. The Soviets had a tough task, as they would have to go the length of the floor with just .03 seconds left and score.

Then it happened, all hell broke loose. These were the last moments of the game as told by Frank Saraceno in an ESPN article entitled "Classic 1972 USA vs. USSR Basketball Game" dated Friday, August 6, 2004:

After the Soviets in-bounded the ball, the referees halted the game with one second remaining. The decision was made to put three seconds back on the clock. At issue was the Soviets' contention that they had signaled for a time-out between Collins' two free throws. The game officials never acknowledged the time out. The validity of whether a time-out was legally signaled for has divided passions on this game for thirty years.

After the Soviets in-bounded the ball a second time, the horn sounded, signaling an apparent American victory. Moments later, the teams were ordered back on the floor because the clock had not been properly reset to show three seconds remaining. Because of this mistake by the scorer's table, the celebrating Americans stood in disbelief when they were told they had not won anything yet. Alexander Belov, who moments earlier had been the goat, became the hero. Rising between Americans Jim Forbes and Kevin Joyce, Belov caught a full-court pass and scored the winning lay-up as time ran out, this time for good. The controversy did not end with the game. Convinced they had been wronged, the U.S. team filed a formal protest with the International Basketball Federation. Later that afternoon, a five-member panel ruled in favor of the Soviets.

After the smoke had cleared and the USA team lost their protest, they were ready to go home. To a man, the players felt that accepting the silver medals would be admitting defeat so they chose not to attend the medals ceremony. Some of the players felt so strongly about the game that they have it in their wills that their family members are to never receive the medal. Today, there is a life-sized picture of Doug Collins that hangs on the east wall of Rich Herrin Gymnasium wearing his Olympic uniform number 5.

There is so much that has been documented about the '72 Olympic team and that final controversial game against the Soviets, but Doug told me a story I had never heard.

Doug Collins: *I remember the first time we met as a team. Coach Iba picked up a piece of chalk and wrote the number 50 on the board and circled it. He told us that we were going to be the best defensive team in the Olympics and we were going to play the Russians in the Gold Medal Game and we were going to hold them under 50 points. Matt, do you know what the score was when I went to the line and hit those last two free throws? We were down 49-48. The free throws put us up 50-49. Unbelievable!*

Collins returned to Illinois State after the Olympics, but he was physically and emotionally drained. The University celebrated his Olympic experience and the next weekend he headed home to Benton. He was given the traditional victory lap around the square as the whole community came out to show their support and appreciation.

Doug was now a famous athlete on the world stage, but he had one more year at Illinois State to finish. He was no longer the unsure kid fearing academic failure. Doug was now toughened by his Olympic experience, confident in his abilities, and sure of his identity. He was making a life for himself.

Doug Collins. *(U.S. Olympic Committee)*

The U.S. basketball team posing for a picture in Olympic Village in Munich.
(Crawford Family U.S. Olympic Archives, U.S. Olympic Committee.)

Coach Hank Iba said, "If Doug can walk... he is shooting these free throws." *(U.S. Olympic Committee)*

Collins hits two free throws under an enormous amount of pressure to give the United States the lead, 50-49, against the Soviet Union. *(Rich Clarkson/ Clarkson Creative.)*

CHAPTER FOURTEEN

"From Benton to the NBA"

"Coach, take a drink of this water and wipe that stuff off your mouth, and know that I'm not going to let you lose the first game that you coach." – Michael Jordan

Our conversation was about ninety minutes old before we got to his NBA career and I realized that a book on Doug Collins would be an interesting project. I was curious about the process of the NBA draft in 1973.

Doug Collins: *Matt, the NBA draft in 1973 was nothing like it is today. I was invited to New York and it certainly wasn't on t.v. I just got a phone call from the Sixers and they said they had drafted me as their first pick in the draft. The year before, the '76ers record was 9-73. They were the worst team in the league.*

I had heard Doug speak at a banquet and he had such great stories about Michael Jordan. I wanted to hear a story about Julius Erving. As a kid, I can't tell you how many times I drove to the basket trying to imitate the moves of Dr. J. The finger rolls, the sweeping reverse lay-ups and the famous dunk from the free throw line inspired me, and it made me fall in love with the creativity of the game of basketball. Don't get me wrong, I could never dunk or do any of the things that "The Doc" could do, but I could imagine, and do creative things on a smaller scale like no-look passes and passing the ball behind my back. I asked Doug for a good Dr. J story and he had one available.

Doug Collins: *The summer I got drafted by the Sixers I was invited to play in an event in the Catskills of New York to honor Maurice Stokes. It was at a place called Kutchers Country Club. The game was held outdoors and there were some big names there. I went to the bathroom and found myself in the bathroom with Wilt Chamberlain. I didn't think he knew who I was but I certainly knew him…but he spoke to me and told me that he thought I would enjoy Philadelphia. I got a picture with him and then during the game…this hush came over the crowd. The game stopped and Dr. J came walking up with this big fro and fur coat on. He was palming a basketball in each hand…he walked up to the goal and dunked both the balls and the people went crazy. I'm thinking…what am I doing here?*

Doug also told me a great story about the first time he met Jerry West.

Doug Collins: *I was excited to meet Jerry West and I knew exactly what I was going to say to him. I shook his hand and said, "Jerry it's nice to meet you…I just want to let you know that I played you every day in my backyard growing up…and you never beat me." We both started laughing.*

Doug played a total of eight seasons (1973-1981) in the NBA with the Philadelphia '76ers and he had the opportunity to play with some of the greatest players of all time. He played with Julius Erving (Dr. J), Darryl Dawkins and George McGinnis, to name a few. In 1977, the Sixers played Bill Walton and the Portland Trailblazers for the NBA Championship, but lost in a close series.

The more I wrote about Collins, the more I wanted to see him play. So, I YouTubed highlights of the '77 series against Portland. What struck me the most was the intensity of the play, and the attacking style from both teams was entertaining to watch. You could hear guys hollering on the floor, and the play was physical to the point of being personal. Guys are just going at each other. Collins was long and lean, with a lightning first step, and quick shot release. Doug was a four-time NBA All-Pro and he was one of the best players on the floor. If you have never seen Collins play, it is worth your while to catch some old highlights on YouTube. He was truly a master of his craft.

After Doug told me the Julius Erving story we had been on the phone for nearly two hours. Our conversation was enlightening, and I gained such an appreciation for his journey and I respected how grateful he was to the people that helped him along the way. We agreed that the way basketball is taught today is different than years ago. Doug said something that made me smile; He said, "I learned the game by station work." I immediately thought about Rend Lake Basketball camp and all those stations. We both agreed that learning the fundamentals of the game through station work was a great way to learn the game.

We both spoke of our love for Coach Herrin and the impact he had on our lives. Doug and I spoke about Coach Herrin's tendency to sometimes look back with regret on decisions he made that might have been hurtful to someone. Doug made a great point when he said, "I told Coach, you can't look back at those things that way. You made those decisions in that moment, and out of the hundreds of decisions you've made that were right, you can't dwell on the two or three that were wrong." Doug asked me some questions about my family, and he knew that my dad was a teacher. I sensed that the phone call was coming to an end, so I asked him a question that he probably gets a lot. Doug, you coached Michael Jordan in Chicago, and know him well, can you give me one good Jordan story?

Doug Collins: *OK, Matt I got one…and this story speaks to who he really is. I got the Bulls job in 1986 and it was my first NBA head coaching job. In our first game of the year…my first game I ever coached in the NBA, we played the Knicks in Madison Square Garden. Hubie Brown is their head coach… they have Cartwright and some other great players…. Matt, I'm a profuse sweater…I am literally sweating through my jacket…. My face is drenched with sweat and I started the game with a piece of gum that I have chewed to a powder…. A white powder and it is all over my mouth. The game is close and late in the game we call a timeout…. I sit down on my stool in front of the guys and I see this black arm reach for me with a cup of water…. It was Michael. Jordan said, "Coach, take a drink of this water and wipe that stuff off your mouth, and know that I'm not going to let you lose the first game that you coach." And he didn't. We won the game and he scored the final points of the game. We then went to Cleveland and won and I'm thinking wow! This guy is special…such a competitor.*

Doug's NBA coaching career is impressive. He was in Chicago for three seasons and guided the Bulls to playoff berths in each of those seasons. In his last year with the Bulls, they lost in the Conference finals. He spent three years in Detroit (1995-1998) and guided two of those teams to the playoffs. He then went to Washington for two years (2001-2003). His last coaching job came with his old team, the Philadelphia '76ers from 2010-2013. Collins ended his NBA coaching career with a record of 442-408 (.521). The numbers are nice, but Doug is most proud of the relationships he has cultivated with his players. He now works as a basketball analyst and puts everything into his preparation just as he did as a player. He knows no other way.

Doug Collins and his wife Kathy now reside in Delaware Valley, Pennsylvania. They have two children. Their son Chris, a former Duke University basketball player, is the head basketball coach at Northwestern University and their daughter Kelly, who played basketball at Lehigh University, is a school teacher in Pennsylvania.

Back in the day, Doug listened to Motown music. Every time he heard the song "What Becomes Of A Broken Heart", it took him back to the pain of the '72 Olympics. Collins lost an NBA Championship to the Portland Trailblazers in '77 and he was on the cusp of turning the Bulls around before he was let go. Doug was close so many times but admits that championships have evaded his grasp. He has always said that if he were to write his autobiography it would be named, *Always a Winner, Never a Champion*. When Doug went to visit his old coach, Will Robinson, one last time in the hospital, Robinson corrected Doug by saying, "Champ, the title should be *Always a Winner, Forever a Champion*." I agree with Coach Robinson.

Collins early in his NBA career in a game against the
St. Louis Spirits at the SIU Arena. *(Ceasar Maragni)*

Doug played a huge part in Philadelphia's run to the
NBA Championship in 1977.

Coach Herrin visits Doug at the Bulls training camp.
(Rich Herrin family collection)

Collins giving a young Michael Jordan some instruction.

Chris Collins was the ball boy at the Bulls games and later played at Duke. He is now the head basketball coach at Northwestern University.

Kelly Collins played college basketball at Lehigh University and is now a school teacher.

Doug with his wife, Kathy. Kathy has been a great mother to
Chris and Kelly and Doug's 1 supporter.

Doug poses with my son, Gehrig, at a ceremony in which the
new Middle School Gymnasium in Benton was named in
his honor. *(Trudee Wynn)*

CHAPTER FIFTEEN

Size and Balance in '71

"I believe Coach Herrin had a vision for our group. He stuck with us and made us better and we had a real special team in '71".
– Rod Kaspar, Ranger Forward

On the morning of September 30, 1970, Rich Herrin walked into the school office to check his mail. The school secretary, Irene Mrogenski, told him that two large boxes were delivered in his name. Herrin quickly grabbed the boxes and hustled them down to the coach's office. It was still football season, but Herrin's mind was consumed with basketball. He ripped into the boxes with the enthusiasm of an eight-year-old boy on Christmas morning. Inside the box came the smell of new clothing. The new basketball uniforms had finally arrived. He reached in the box and quickly grabbed one of the new uniform tops. It was a home white jersey. He held it up in order to scan its appearance. He liked what he saw. The narrow shoulder straps of the sixties had given way to the wide V-neck top of the seventies. The neck and shoulder straps were outlined with two thin maroon stripes. The front of the jersey said "RANGERS" arched around a large number. Herrin then turned the jersey around to look at the back. On the back of the jersey, there were eight small maroon stars that surrounded the number.

Brad Weathers: *You will have to ask Coach Herrin about this…but I think this is right. We had eight guys that were interchangeable. Britton and I were* *like the ninth and tenth guys…we weren't in that group. We got new uniforms in '71 and it was the first time we had stars in the uniform. The eight stars circled the number on the back of the jersey. The eight stars represented the eight guys…the seven seniors and Stewart.*

It was the first time that stars had been incorporated into the basketball uniform, and the star is now a trademark of all Benton athletic uniforms. There are now stars everywhere. There are stars on the cover of the BCHS handbook, signage on the front of the school and the new gated entrance to the football field. The people in Benton took to the stars.

Herrin knew that '71 could be a special year and like most coaches that anticipate a great team, the team received new uniforms. The uniform shorts were also unique. Keeping with the tradition of the sixties, they featured a belt around the waist. The shorts were high cut and both sides featured a circle that resembled a basketball, with Benton spelled out in the middle. The players wore maroon and white tube socks to the knees that fit comfortably into their low-top leather Converse sneakers. The Rangers always looked sharp.

The "Great Eight" included the following seniors; Hugh Frailey, Dave Lockin, Jim Semanski, Denny Smith, Roger Adkins, Rod Kaspar, Rick Thomas and junior Steve Stewart. Seniors Brad Weathers and Danny Britton proved to be key reserves along with juniors Steve Dawson, Jim Davis, Tony Diefenbauch and Brandon Webster. The lone sophomore was Robert Corn.

The team was big and strong across the line-up. Most of the "Great Eight" had played together in junior high and many of them were thrust into the line-up in '69 when they were just sophomores. Semanski, Frailey, Smith, Kaspar and Adkins played key roles as sophomores. They were young players adapting to the speed and the strength of playing against the athletes of the South Seven Conference, but they had now come of age. As young players, they made mistakes, but Herrin believed in this group, and '71 was to be the year that it all paid off. Steve Stewart was just a freshman in '69 when Coach Herrin moved him to the varsity team. In Rich Herrin's twenty-five years at Benton, there were only two freshman brought up to play at the varsity level; Steve Stewart and Billy Smith.

Rod Kaspar: *I believe Coach Herrin had a vision for our group. He stuck with us and made us better and we had a real special team in '71.*

As juniors in 1970, the Rangers finished with a record of 19-10 before falling to Mt. Vernon in the Sectional final, by a score of 70-63. The 1970 team had only two seniors that completed the season; Don Smith and T.J. Learned. The two seniors received little playing time, but give them credit, they stayed. In fact, Don Smith was the only senior that played four years of basketball on the varsity roster in 1969-1970.

Don Smith: *I graduated from Whittington School in '66. We had four rooms in the school and a gymnasium but compared to Benton we just didn't have much. I would lay awake at night when I was in grade school and pray that I could make the team as a freshman. It was like a dream come true when I made the team my freshman year. I could actually remember as a grade school kid, sitting on the stage in the old gym and watching Coach Herrin tape the players' ankles and thinking, "I hope I can be a Benton Ranger someday and have Coach tape my ankles." Some people in the community were jealous of the emphasis that was put on basketball but you know, that's the way it was.*

Smith believes it was his realistic approach to his own abilities and his willingness to work hard that kept him in the program.

Don Smith: *The best players on the team were the juniors and Steve Stewart. As seniors, T.J. and I saw the writing on the wall…and to stay around you had to conform. Our team in 1970 was a year away. We were prepping for a big run the next year…there is no doubt about that.*

Smith told me a great story about what it meant to him to be coached by Rich Herrin.

Don Smith: *One of Coach Herrin's favorite lines he used on all his athletes was, "You've got to compete." He taught all of us to be greater competitors. After I had graduated, we actually had summer track meets. Coach Herrin and his brother Ron organized the meets and we had two or three meets in the summer. I had already graduated from high school and I was running the steeple chase…I was holding my own. As I approached the curve, I saw Coach Herrin out of the corner of my eye. As I ran by he didn't say anything. Usually when I was in high school, he would be up on the curve encouraging me, yelling something to motivate me, but he wasn't. That was the first time that I realized…it was over. There were other times that he barked at me and I* *wanted him to be quiet. But on this day, I missed his voice…I wanted him to yell at me. He didn't…it was over.*

Don Smith stayed in contact with Coach Herrin after graduation and developed a friendship with Coach. After graduation, Don played basketball at Rend Lake College and then later went to Illinois State and earned his degree in education. Don left the Benton area for years but was hired as the head basketball coach at Benton High School in the fall of '97. He guided the Rangers to a Regional Championship in his final season of 2001-2002. Don Smith currently lives with his wife, Sue Ann, in Orlando, Florida. They have two children; Stephanie and Brooke.

Tom Learned, "T.J.", gave back to the program by coaching grade school basketball in the early eighties. He was my sixth grade basketball coach, and I still hold a special place in my heart for T.J. Learned. After high school, T.J. was a devoted Benton Ranger fan and worked in the coal mines for years. T.J. and his wife Lynda (Piercy) Learned were devoted to their three girls; Aleicia, Erin and Kristen. Both Tom and his wife lost their battles with cancer and passed away far too young. They were wonderful people.

Most of the key players on the '71 team had grown up together dreaming of being a Ranger. Denny Smith, Hugh Frailey, Roger Adkins, Rodney Kaspar, Steve Stewart and Brad Weathers were all teammates in junior high. They played well together because they were familiar with each other's tendencies. Everyone could see that this group was going to be special in high school. They all came from good families, and they had grown up in Benton during the "fever" of basketball in the late sixties. They had seen the good teams play, and now it was their turn. The Great Eight gained valuable experience on the 1970 team as juniors, and they were now seniors. They had been a part of two Regional Championships and played in a Sectional final as juniors. Most importantly, they had physically matured and the experience they carried into the '71 season gave them the mentality of battle-tested veterans. This was to be the year of the Benton Rangers.

At first glance, the team's size jumps out at you, but the Rangers were also very skilled at the guard position. The floor general was Denny Smith. Denny played at 5'10", and he ran the show. Smith is still considered one of the great point guards in a long line of accomplished Ranger floor generals. Smith took care of the ball; he just didn't turn it over. He had great court vision and was a tremendous passer. As a senior, Smith was an

82% free throw shooter. If the Rangers spread the floor late and the opposing team had to foul, Smith could put the game away at the free throw line. He made his lay-ups and could be counted on for ten points per game. He was extremely self-aware of his own abilities and his basketball instincts were off the charts. Smith was always hampered with knee problems, but he played through the pain and had a tremendous high school career. Denny was a great interview, and he recalled what it was like growing up in such a basketball-crazy community.

Denny Smith: *We played outside constantly. I lived above Mitchell's Funeral Home when I was real young…I went to Logan School. Later on my family moved to Highland Street and I started going to Grant School. Perry Eisenhower was our coach. That is where I met Steve Stewart. Steve lived on Grayson Street. I also played a ton of basketball at Curt Gunter's house and there were always games at Logan School. Believe me, if you wanted to play, you could find a game. If you were by yourself at Logan and just started shooting….two or three kids would ride up on bicycles and you would have enough for a game. I remember my dad would whistle to call me home…and I knew it was him. I went home to eat. It was like growing up in Mayberry. Everything was so simple and we were all so naïve. Benton was a great place to grow up.*

As a youngster, Denny was a regular at all the Benton home games when he was in grade school and junior high. Smith recalled sitting on the stage of the old gym and watching the great Jerry Hoover play.

Denny Smith: *When I was in junior high, I would go to the home games and sit on the stage and watch the games. The player that I remember the most was Jerry Hoover. He was the player that I wanted to be. He did such a great job of getting the ball where it needed to go…Hoover was tremendous…. Hoover goes to the University of Florida and plays, I mean geez…I sat on the stage and watched all those great teams and they were having fun and winning. It was exciting and I kind of wanted to be a part of that…you know.*

Smith first hurt his knee when he was a sophomore. He admitted that it slowed him a step, but the idea of not playing was never an option.

Denny Smith: *I hurt it my sophomore year…there was a loose ball about half court and I picked it up and dribbled to the corner. Collins was the trailer…I pivoted back toward Collins to pass him the ball and my shoe just* *stuck into the floor. I remember Doug shot it and missed.... Milton tried to tip it in, and play went on for a while before the next whistle. It happened in the corner where Sue Herrin sat and I just grabbed the railing to keep me standing. It was like my knee just exploded from the inside. I remember my knee cap was dislocated and Chuck (Oyler) reached down and moved it. I had it on ice. Rich didn't see it happen. After halftime, Coach Herrin asked if I was ready... Chuck said, "He's ready to go to the hospital. He can't play on this." I tore all of the ligaments and even tore a thigh muscle. My dad and I were the only ones in the hospital room at the time, and my dad said, "The doctor told me you shouldn't play basketball anymore." I didn't really listen to that... Rich then came to the hospital after the game...he cried because he felt like my knee was weak because of the isometric exercises we had done before the season started. He was second guessing himself...but I never did believe that. The knee healed, but not the way it should have. I definitely lost a step of quickness, but I worked on improving my skills to compensate for my injury. I learned to play with it.*

Senior guard Hugh Frailey was also a key piece to the puzzle in '71. Hugh was left-handed and sported a sturdy build, with the Frailey touch of white in his hairline. He played hard and was an above-average rebounder for a guard. He also had a strong basketball IQ, along with a smooth left-handed jump shot. Frailey worked hard to break into the line-up and proved to be a player that was steady under pressure. Hugh always knew he wanted to be a Benton Ranger from a very young age and his moment had arrived.

Hugh Frailey: *My father Kenneth was a building contractor, and my mother Betty was the music teacher at the high school. I had great parents. I went to Lincoln School when I was growing up. My dad took me to most all of the Ranger home games from the time I was four years old. He did not want me running around the gym...so he would sit with me and explain what was going on. My dad played basketball in high school at Benton. I loved to watch the game and I grew up wanting to be a Benton Ranger. I went home and practiced. I would imitate the players...they were my heroes. I wanted to grow up and be a Benton Ranger.*

Frailey was that kid that attended every Ranger game possible. He would ask other families to take him to away games if his dad was not going. He studied the players and loved it when Marion's Greg Starrick came to town. Starrick was Southern Illinois' version of "Pistol Pete" and was Frailey's hero growing up. Frailey was also quick to point out that he remembered the '61 Super-Sectional as one of his greatest memories as a boy.

Hugh Frailey: *I remember the '61 team very well. My dad was able to get us tickets to the Super-Sectional game against Belleville. It was funny how he got the tickets. The Benton tickets had already sold out…Belleville didn't think it would be much of a game. They were twice our size and they had tickets left over. Mike McCarty got us the tickets and me and my dad went. It was like going to the Super Bowl for me…I was excited to be there.*

At the small forward position was junior Steve Stewart. Despite being a junior in '71, he had played regularly with this group as a young player. Stewart could flat out play. He played at 6'3" and was wiry strong. He could do a little bit of everything. He possessed long arms that allowed him to be a force on the offensive boards and was capable of scoring 20 points or more on any given night. Steve Stewart had an incredible career as a Benton Ranger and is still considered one of the greatest players in school history. He would be a part of four Regional Championship teams and score over 1,000 points in his career as a Ranger. When I interviewed Doug Collins about his senior year, he stopped me and gave high praise to Stewart's game.

Doug Collins: *Matt, he was a damn good player…he had such long arms and he could really rebound the ball…. Steve was one of the greatest bank shooters that I've ever seen…. He was really good.*

Rod Kaspar was the first post player off the bench and he brought an energy and toughness that inspired his teammates. Kaspar was a solid defender, a good leaper and a guy you would want on your side. He pestered the opposition with his endless energy, and he owned all loose balls. Kaspar could also score if needed, and was a relentless rebounder. He was capable of putting up solid offensive numbers, and when he was substituted in the game for Lockin or Semanski, the Rangers didn't miss a beat.

Rod Kaspar: *I went to Douglas school and lived on the east side of Benton. My dad ran a sign company. My parents were George and Ruby Kaspar. I had a sister named Linda… I played on the sixth grade team at Douglas School* *and my dad put up a goal in the yard so I could shoot. I grew up in Benton… and I wanted to become a Benton Ranger basketball player.*

Kaspar described the motivation behind his all-out type of play.

Rod Kaspar: *I played at 6'4", 180 pounds and I played full blast. I mixed it up inside and I was a decent leaper. I played hard because I didn't want to disappoint Coach Herrin…and I had to because we played against great competition. I'm where I am at today because of Coach Herrin. He showed me I could do things through hard work. He was like a father, mentor and slave driver, in a good way.*

Senior Roger Adkins was the last of the Adkins brothers to play at Benton High School. Roger's brother Jim played alongside Yunkus in '66. Jim had just graduated from the University of Alabama. When Adkins was in junior high, he was the best young athlete in Southern Illinois.

Hugh Frailey: *Roger was an incredible player in junior high. He could out-run and out-jump everybody and he was averaging 29-30 points a game in the eighth grade. He was extremely talented and he worked very hard in practice. I remember our eighth grade year we all went to the Method-ist Men's banquet. The head basketball coach at the University of Illinois was the speaker. In the middle of his speech, he asked if Roger Adkins was in attendance. He said in front of everyone, "I will be recruiting you." We couldn't believe it.*

Adkins played at 6'2" and he was an athlete. Roger also played football and had suffered from a knee injury that hampered him throughout his basketball career at Benton. Give Roger credit-despite the knee, he played. Roger worked hard in practice and fit in well with the '71 team and con-tributed greatly to its success.

Doug Collins: *Adkins reminded me so much of Kenny Payne who played on the '66 team. He was just so quick and played with great energy…. He was a total disrupter. Very high energy player….*

Brad Weathers was also a senior in '71 and had been part of the group since his grade school years at Lincoln School. Brad was the youngest stu-dent in his class and a late developer, but he loved the game of basketball.

He played the post and weighed about 160 pounds as a senior and had the job of mixing it up with Lockin and Semanski each day in practice.

Brad Weathers: *My parents were Jack and Polly. I went to all the games growing up and we moved back to town just before the fever hit. I went to as many games as possible. If you saw one of the players around town....they were like rock stars. I went to Lincoln School and Denzil Franklin was my basketball coach. I really didn't get to play much on that '71 team. I was a young senior and I remember Rich talking to me about laying out a year. I just didn't want to do that.*

However, to complete the puzzle of '71, there were four players that joined the group as freshman that elevated the team to a State contender. Dave Lockin, Jim Semanski, Rick Thomas and Danny Britton would join the others as freshman and play key roles in the success of the great '71 team.

Dave Lockin had never played basketball before moving to Benton his eighth grade year. He did not play in the eighth grade and admits that nobody would have predicted the lead role he played on such a great Ranger team.

Dave Lockin: *We moved to Benton when I was thirteen years old, from eastern Kentucky. I was in the eighth grade when I came to Benton and I had never played basketball. My dad worked for Inland Steel and my mom was an RN. She worked with Dr. Durham. I had two sisters, Jane and Wanda, and I was the oldest. I went out for the basketball team on a dare from a friend named Roger Davis. We both played football and he talked me into going out for the team. Funny thing, I made the team and he didn't. The first basketball team I played on was my freshman year at Benton High School. Coach Phillips was my freshman coach. All of the other guys in my class moved up and started playing J.V. basketball.*

Lockin admitted that those two years of development at the underclassman level served him well. He was able to work on his game, but it was his rapid growth that made him a factor.

Dave Lockin: *I was about 5'10" at the end of my freshman basketball season. When I started school the next year...I was 6'4". The teachers thought I was a new kid...they didn't recognize me.*

Coach Herrin: *I told our freshman and sophomore coaches to play Lockin as much as possible. I thought he could grow…. Lockin's dad was a good man. He came to see me because Lockin had a "C" in a class…he was a freshman…. His dad wanted him to quit basketball so he could get his grade up. I talked him out of it. But he just wanted what was best for him.*

As a senior in '71, Lockin played at 6'7" and he was well put together, but Lockin's growth spurt as a freshman made him awkward to say the least. He spent much of his time in practice working on his footwork and learning the game.

Dave Lockin: *I had these thunder thighs…and I could leap, but I had no upper body. My sophomore year, Coach Phillips told me that he thought I could be a player. I had to work on my footwork…I had big feet. The coaches worked with me on the tip machine and I had to really work on my ball handling. My sophomore year, I started playing more. It was a year for me to develop. What I really had to do…was learn the game that my teammates were so intuitive with. I just hadn't played as much as they had.*

Senior Jim Semanski also grew to be 6'7", and he was a force to reckon with in the paint. He had a shy disposition, but between the lines he was aggressive and in his element. The statistics suggest that Semanski scored when he needed to, and there were some nights he played the role of a tough defender and rebounder. There was absolutely no ego with Jim Semanski, he just wanted to win games. As an incoming freshman, he made a decision that changed the course of his life forever.

Jim Semanski: *I grew up in Buckner. It was just me and my mom Elizabeth. My eighth grade year…I went to Buckner and we had a good basketball team for our size, but Benton hammered us. A man named Ron Dollins took some interest in me. Where we were living at…I was supposed to go to Christopher High School. By chance, the summer before I was to enter high school…with help from my aunt and uncle from up north…we moved into a house on the edge of Buckner that was twenty feet inside the Benton School District. There was a family that had lived there before us and the kids went to Christopher… so I was given the option of where to go to school. I saw an opportunity at Benton, and I took it. It rubbed some people the wrong way…but that was not my intention.*

Semanski loved the game even from an early age, and he vividly recalled the first point he ever scored in an organized game.

Jim Semanski: *The first game I ever played in was in Valier…I was in the fifth grade. My coach, Frank Furlow, rubbed my stomach before he put me into the game and said, "I think you are ready because I can feel those butterflies." I got fouled and missed my first free throw but then I made my second one. That was the first point I ever scored in a basketball game.*

Lockin and Semanski are without a doubt two of the greatest post players in Ranger basketball history. They quietly went about their business. Semanski realized how fortunate they were to play alongside each other in high school.

Jim Semanski: *Any time you have a second guy in that post position that can play…it takes some pressure off. Dave and I became close friends and we talk two or three times a year.*

Senior Rick Thomas was the back-up point guard to Denny Smith. Thomas played extremely hard and was more than capable. Thomas was dubbed by Benton sports writer Bob Tedrow as the "Logan Flash." Thomas played his junior high basketball at Logan which was a feeder school to Benton High School. Thomas entered the game to spell Smith and the other guards if necessary. He had better than average skills and on other Ranger teams he may have been a starter. Thomas had a sturdy build and he fit in well with the chemistry of the team. Jim Semanski remembered a funny story about Thomas when they were freshman.

Jim Semanski: *Ricky could play. He backed up Denny at the point. I remember our freshman year I had ten points in the first half and he came up to me and said, "Hey, that's enough for you because if you keep scoring…Coach Herrin is going to pull you up to the sophomore team."*

Senior Danny Britton also proved to be a key reserve for the Rangers. In junior high, Britton attended Whittington Grade School and he recalled nothing but good memories about his experience as a Benton Ranger. Danny had a smooth left handed jump shot and was an above-average ball handler.

Danny Britton: *I grew up in Whittington and went to Whittington Grade School. My coach at Wittington was Donald Girten. My dad was a janitor at the school and we lived right across the street from the school. I could see the gym from my house. Bob Johnston was my cousin and he really helped me a lot when I was younger. I remember that Coach Herrin came out to Whittington School when I was in the eighth grade and he asked me to try out for the freshman team. I remember that really meant a lot to me for him to do that. I was left-handed and my strength was shooting the ball. I was more of a point guard. I was just really small. I played a lot my freshman and sophomore years because Coach pulled the other guys up.*

The other juniors on the team were Jim Davis, Steve Dawson, Tony Diefenbach and Brandon Webster. They were all good teammates. They competed in practice and carried out their role of preparing the team for Friday and Saturday nights. To be fair, the Rangers were a top five team in the state and there were basketball teams in the area where this group of reserves could have gotten valuable playing time. They were good players on a great team and they accepted their role well. Sophomore Robert Corn also dressed with the varsity to provide added depth at the guard spot. In fact, Corn would later dress in the State Tournament against Oak Lawn.

In the fall of 1970, the football Rangers lost to the West Frankfort Redbirds in the Turkey Day Game, by a score of 30-20. It was now officially basketball season. After the end of the football season and keeping with tradition, the Ranger basketball players headed to the barber shop to get their haircuts for basketball season. All of the Rangers on the '71 team sported flat-tops and crew cuts; long hair was out of the question and not to be discussed. Dave Lockin and Brad Weathers headed uptown together and entered the three-chair barber Shop. The town barbers all had seats for the games, and they knew all of the players. They loved it when the players came wandering into the shop because they could question the players and get the inside scoop.

On this day, Weathers and Lockin noticed that there were three male wigs neatly placed on three mannequins in the front window. As Lockin was getting his haircut, he fielded questions about the upcoming basketball season and then his mind became fixated on the wigs in the front window. Lockin liked to cut up and Weathers was always game for a good laugh. After paying for their flat-tops, Lockin couldn't help himself, he reached over and took the wig off one of the mannequins in the window and placed it on his head. Weathers broke out in laughter as Lockin adjusted the wig in a nearby mirror. Then, Lockin asked the barbers if he could borrow the wig and bring it back later. They approved. Lockin and Weathers walked out of the barber shop sporting their letterman jackets and strolled around the square. Lockin had the wig on and the boys were drawing attention from the townspeople. Weathers loved the charade and could hardly hold back his laughter. A gentleman who attended the games passed by and wished them luck on the season. Lockin replied, "I don't think I'm playing this year." It was good clean fun and the wig gave them something to laugh about.

Lockin and Weathers then thought of a way to take the wig joke to the next level. On the first day of basketball practice, Lockin (with the wig on) and Weathers entered the gym. Coach Herrin was taping an ankle and was located near the coach's office on the stage. Weathers and Lockin walked up onto the stage and Herrin glanced up and Lockin said, "Coach, I don't think I'm going to play this year." It is likely that Coach Herrin didn't know male wigs even existed, and he did not recognize that Lockin was wearing a wig. He just knew that his hair wasn't cut. Coach Herrin then blew up, "I don't care if you play or not…get your stuff and get out of here if you don't want to play." The joke had gone too far and Weathers began to get nervous and the feeling in the room was now tense. Lockin then reached up and took the wig off of his head and quickly scampered to the locker room to get dressed for practice. It was the first practice of the year and Coach Herrin was ready to go, he was not in the mood for practical jokes.

Practices were tough and the Rangers had just two weeks to get ready for the season opener against the Sparta Bulldogs. The '71 Rangers still looked to run, but they backed off from the full court 1-2-2 pressure that served the teams of the late sixties so well.

Coach Herrin: *We played a variety of defenses with the '71 team. We switched up the defense a great deal. We were just not as quick as some of the teams we had in the past.*

The Rangers had so much basketball success that the Chicago Tribune sent a sports writer down to cover the team for a whole week. The writer was given unlimited access to the players and coaches and he observed practice for three days straight. These were the words of the Tribune writer as he described Coach Herrin during practice:

Chicago Tribune: *Herrin erupts into sporadic volleys of chatter as he puts his crew-cut charges thru a scrimmage. Herrin is dressed in a baggy gray sweatshirt, Bermuda shorts and basketball shoes. He looks and sounds like a marine sergeant with his bulldog face and short hair and the abrupt way he talks.*

Herrin has the same energy he did when he first got the job in '61 and it is obvious that there is no other place he would rather be. He is perfectly at home in the Benton gym teaching and coaching the game that he loves.

Rod Kaspar: *We practiced every day except Sunday. Even on Sunday, we would go into the gym and shoot. He stressed fundamentals and we would work on our offense and then our defense. Practice was hard. He pushed us. Our senior year he told us that we were going to have Tuesdays off. That we weren't going to touch a basketball. So instead of practicing with a ball on Tuesdays he had us come in and we had one-mile relay races. He made it fun. Nobody dreaded going to basketball practice. Everyone worked hard. I was disappointed when I got to college because I didn't have a coach like Coach Herrin.*

As the opener with Sparta crept closer, the Ranger players were excited about the season. They had been battle tested as sophomores and juniors which gave them confidence. The strength of the Rangers came from their balance. The points on a given night could come from any of the Rangers. Most importantly, they enjoyed each other's company and were friends off the floor. Every player on the team was important and they all bought in to the Ranger way of doing things. The players understood that individual honors would only come with team success. The goal of the Rangers to begin the '71 season was to win the State Championship. Denny Smith was quick to express how fortunate he was to play with such great teammates.

Denny Smith: *We always had confidence in each other. When teams started sagging to guard the big men (Lockin and Semanski)…the big men would kick it out. The balance of our team was the strength of our team. We had Hughie, Stewart and Adkins and they were all capable of scoring big on a given night. I remember a time that Steve was hot and Hugh came up and said, "Let's get him the ball until his arm falls off." That's the way we were… Steve would say the same thing if Hugh got hot. We had Kaspar coming off the bench and he played so hard. He was such a spark. Rick Thomas came off* *the bench, along with Adkins…. Brad Weathers and Danny Britton helped us win a game early in the year against Meridian. Our egos never got in the way.*

Hugh Frailey: *We did feel some pressure going into our senior year because the expectations were very high. There were times during the year that if we won a game by less than twenty points people would start to wonder what was wrong with us.*

On Saturday, December 5, 1970, the Sparta Bulldogs came to town to play the highly-touted Runnin' Rangers. The Cracker Box could not hold another human being. The Rangers went thru their rehearsed pre-game warm up in a businesslike manner, and as the adrenaline pumped through their veins, the players elevated a bit higher on their lay-ups. The team then executed a quick three man weave drill that ended with a crisp bounce pass to the lay-up shooter. The starting lineups were announced, and all fans stood in respect for the national anthem. As the anthem was sang, the palms of the players sweated and the butterflies in their stomachs began to churn. The starters received their final instructions from Coach Herrin, and then walked onto the floor in their fresh new uniforms with the infamous eight stars. The Sparta Bulldogs were dressed in their blue and white uniforms and each Sparta player displayed a "deer in headlights" look, as they were initiated to the frightening experience of being the visiting team in the Cracker Box. Finally, the much anticipated '71 season was here.

The fans stood for the tip, which was controlled by the Rangers. In the initial seconds of the game, Hugh Frailey hit a 14-foot jumper to open the '71 season. The game was close until the Rangers exploded in the early minutes of the third quarter to take command of the game and eventually win by a score of 94-79. What can be taken from game one? The big take-away was the balanced attack of the Rangers offense. Five players were in double figures led by big Jim Semanski's 19 points. Stewart chipped in 18 and three other Rangers scored in double figures. Offensively, the story of the game was the individual play of Rusty Cane from Sparta, who exploded for 47 points on 18-27 shooting. The Rangers had no answer for Cane, but one great player could not overcome the balanced attack of the Rangers. Mission accomplished, the Rangers were 1-0.

Another positive from the Sparta game was the effort on the boards. The Rangers won the rebounding battle, 42-20. Herrin believed rebounding was about grit and toughness, and this was a battle he always encouraged his players to win. "Check out…and go get it! Gang, we have to rebound! Rebound! Rebound!" These were common phrases that the players heard each day in practice, as Herrin was relentless in urging his players to go get the ball. The '71 team was not soft, they could mix it up inside and go get it.

The following Saturday, the Rangers traveled south to Meridian High School to play the Bobcats. The team was led by coaching legend Jim Byassee. The '71 Bobcat team gave Byassee his biggest coaching achievement at Meridian by upsetting Thornridge in the 1970 Carbondale Holiday Tournament. Thornridge, led by Quinn Buckner, Boyd Batts, Mike Bonczyk and Greg Rose, went on to win the 1971 State Championship and the 1972 Class AA title. Byassee won 635 games in a brilliant 30-year career and guided the tiny Pulaski County school to a 30-2 record and second place in the first Class A tournament in 1972. On this night, the Rangers were playing one of the greatest Bobcat teams in their school's history. The Rangers knew they would be in for a battle.

I love this game on the Benton schedule, especially in 1971. First of all, I coached three years at Meridian High School, and wouldn't trade that experience for anything in the world. Meridian is a small school that is predominantly black, and they love their basketball. There were many schools in Southern Illinois that backed away from playing the Bobcats in the early seventies, but not the Rangers. Herrin played the Bobcats and didn't think twice about it. He was also responsible for bringing the Cairo Pilots to the Benton Invitational Tournament in 1980. To be the best, you have to beat the best, and Herrin saw the game as a way to make his team better. Herrin did not avoid playing good teams, and he did not avoid playing teams of color. He played them all.

The Rangers exploded to a 23-14 lead by the end of the first quarter, and held a 42-34 advantage at halftime. The Bobcats came storming back and trailed by only four points to start the fourth quarter. As the game neared the end, Semanski, Lockin, Kaspar and Stewart fouled out of the game. With those key Rangers fouled out, the game was in the hands of guards, Denny Smith, Hugh Frailey, Rick Thomas, Danny Britton and the lone remaining post player, Brad Weathers. Weathers recalled those tense moments fifty years ago in Mounds, Illinois.

Brad Weathers: *They were really good…they had Calvin Johnson and the next year in '72 they got second in the state. We had a bunch of guys foul out… the game was pretty close. Coach Herrin called a timeout…me and Britton* *were in the game because we had so much foul trouble. Coach Herrin told me, "Brad, you're back on the press...stand in the key...if you get out of there, I'll kill you." Coach Stewart thought the whole situation was funny...because I was wide-eyed.*

After leading by as many as thirteen points early in the contest, the Rangers found themselves trailing 70-69 with just seventeen seconds left in the game. Reserve guard Danny Britton vividly remembered the last seventeen seconds of the game.

Danny Britton: *We were down one point and they were holding the ball. I got a steal and went in for a lay-up and about broke the backboard. Smith got the rebound and got fouled...he missed the free throw...the ball caromed off the hands of a Meridian player out of bounds. Kaspar received the inbounds pass and was fouled with only two seconds left on the clock...he hit one free throw and that sent the game into overtime. Brad got in the game also and we ended up winning the game in overtime.*

Brad Weathers: *Britton had a lay-up and his adrenaline was pumping so hard he banged it off the glass and it never hit the rim. We settled down though and I got a blocked shot and a rebound. Britton played well...we won the game in overtime.*

The Rangers dominated the overtime period and defeated the Bobcats by a score of 77-71 to hand them their first loss at home in three years. It was a great win on the road against a very good team. The fact that Britton and Weathers were able to contribute to the win lifted the team's spirit and Coach Herrin was especially proud of the win. It was a great team victory and happy bus ride north. The Rangers were now 2-0. Bring on Marion.

The Rangers opened up South Seven play against the Marion Wildcats on Friday, December 18, 1970, at Benton. The Wildcats of 1970-71 struggled and actually finished in the cellar of the conference with a 0-14 record. The Rangers won the ball game by a score of 87-65 and were led in scoring by Dave Lockin. Lockin had 22 points to lead the way, followed by Frailey's 14 points. All of the hard work that Dave Lockin had been putting in was coming to fruition. In '71, he was a different player offensively. He was now a legitimate scoring threat in the post, and now thought of himself as a player that could score, not just defend and rebound. Physically, Lockin looked like a senior. He was now the one bumping other players, rather than being bumped. Again, the Rangers dominated the game in the rebounding department by a margin of 49-23. Rod Kaspar was all over the floor and led the Rangers with 14 rebounds. It is also important to note that Roger Adkins was out due to a knee injury and would not return until after Christmas. Unfortunately, the knee was a constant struggle for Adkins, but he was a team player and supported his teammates from the bench. The Rangers were now 3-0 and 1-0 in conference play.

The next night, the Rangers went to Herrin. In '71, the Rangers traveled in style. The players wore matching collared shirts and ties, with dress slacks. The outfit was topped off by the school-issued blazer, with a patch that said "Benton" on the left chest. It was quite a sight to see all the Rangers enter the opposing gym dressed to the hilt. The dapper look of all those matching sports coats and ties sent a message that said, "We are together…and we are here to win." It was the look that Herrin wanted to exhibit. The players looked like gentleman but it was also psychological warfare on the opponent. The Rangers meant business, and you could tell by their look. It was all part of the plan and it worked well.

The '71 Herrin Tigers were no joke. They were also a veteran team and they had circled this game with the Rangers on their schedule. Herrin jumped out to a 21-11 lead and led 26-21 at halftime. The Rangers missed shots from close range, but continued to battle. In the third quarter, Denny Smith hit a ten-foot jumper to put the Rangers in the lead 32-31. The Rangers stretched the lead to 40-35 late and held on to win 45-43. Benton fans held their breath late in the game as Denny Smith pulled up with a limp in the closing seconds of the game. Coach Herrin made these comments after the game regarding Smith, "I don't think anything serious is wrong, we are keeping our fingers crossed."

On Tuesday, December 22, 1970, the Rangers traveled to Carbondale to play the Terriers at Bowen Gymnasium. It was the final game before Christmas. Winning the Carbondale game would put the Rangers in the driver's seat of the Conference race. The Terriers were coached by Dave Lee, and they were more than capable. In fact, Carbondale finished 8-6 in the conference in '71, which was good enough for fourth place. With just forty-four seconds left in the game, Jim Semanski converted a three point play to break the 45-45 deadlock and give the Rangers the lead for the final time. The victory upped the state's eighth-ranked Rangers to 3-0 in the conference, and 5-0 overall. It was exactly where the team wanted to be before Christmas. Lockin led the Rangers in scoring with 17 points and Jim Semanski chipped in ten points.

After a brief practice on December 23rd, the Rangers spent Christmas Eve and Christmas day with their families. The players enjoyed their two days off, but they were consumed with the anticipation of playing in the Centralia Holiday Tournament. The Centralia Tournament was the ultimate measuring stick. In '71, the Rangers entered the tournament as the number one seed, but it didn't matter, you had to play the games. The players were old enough to remember the two championships in '65 and '66, and they realized that winning the tournament made them legit in the eyes of all basketball fans across the State of Illinois. The Rangers opened the tournament with an afternoon game against the Crimsons, of Jacksonville High School. As the team walked into the gym that morning, every player noticed the full-size replica of the State of Illinois that featured a green light on the geographic location of each of the sixteen schools. The small green lights were sprinkled in every area the state, indicating the broad representation of the tournament. The iconic sign reminded each player that this tournament was special. Win this one, and you are for real! The Rangers defeated Jacksonville 78-58 to move to game two the following day.

Game two was crucial because of the way that the tournament was set up. It was not a true double elimination tournament. If you lost game two in the winner's bracket, you were going home. In the all-important game two, the Rangers faced the Homewood-Flossmoor Vikings. The Vikings came in with the traditional candy-striped basketball trunks and they carried a long history in the tournament. The game was supposed to be close, but the Rangers led 24-10 after the first quarter and never looked back. Most importantly, the game must have been confusing to the opposing coaches that scouted the Rangers. Expecting to see dominant inside play, the Rangers fired away from the outside as Hugh Frailey led a balanced Rangers attack with 18 points. Denny Smith came in with ten points and Rick Thomas came off the bench to hit key jump shots. Everyone knew about the strength and size of Semanski and Lockin, but the outside shooting attack of the Rangers left opposing coaches scratching their heads. Semanski and Lockin scored in double figures and Steve Stewart also played well. Who do you guard? The game against Homewood showcased the guard play of the Rangers and it proved that the Rangers were capable of beating teams from outside, as well as in the paint.

Dave Lockin: *My fondest memory was the travel to and from the Centralia Tournament that year. Coach Herrin drove the short bus. I was terrified because he had one hand on the wheel...he looked back at us more than on the road. We had a boom box and we were listening to Merle Haggard's, "I'm An Okie From Muskogee." Winning the Centralia Tournament just set the tone for the season.*

The win against the Vikings set up a semi-final game against the Champaign Central Maroons and legendary coach Lee Cabutti. The Maroons finished the '71 season at 21-9 and won a Regional Championship. The game was deadlocked at halftime at 31. The Rangers won the second half by 15 points and cruised to a 67-52 victory. It is important to note that to win the Centralia Tournament; you must win two games the final day. Physical conditioning along with a sustained mental focus is critical. The tournament can become a war of attrition. The teams that are in great physical condition and can bring good depth off the bench have the advantage. The '71 Rangers could check all the boxes. In the Champaign Central game, All-State center Dave Lockin led the Rangers in scoring, but what really jumped out was the quality play off the bench. Rod Kaspar came in to score 15 points, Rick Thomas had ten and Danny Britton chipped in with two. Roger Adkins appeared in the game, but saw limited playing time.

The players went to eat between games and relaxed before heading back to the gym for the championship game that night against the Centralia Orphans. The tournament featured sixteen teams from all over the State of Illinois, and the championship game featured two South Seven teams. The game gave proof to the high level of basketball played in the South Seven in the late sixties and early seventies.

As the Rangers listened to their final instructions before taking the floor, they could hear the crowd noise through the thick concrete walls of the locker room located in the corners of Trout Gymnasium. This was it, Benton vs. Centralia for all the marbles. Denny Smith remembered the moment the Rangers took the floor before the championship game.

Denny Smith: *I'll never forget running onto the floor to start the game.... The Centralia fans booed us...it was so loud that you could not hear. Steve Stewart tapped me on the shoulder...I looked back at him and he was saying something with a half grin on his face...I couldn't hear what he was saying because the crowd was so loud...so I read his lips...he said, "I love it."*

The Orphans finished second in the conference in '71 with a record of 11-3 in the South Seven. They featured two of the best players in the league in Rick Meeks and Julius Moss. Meeks and Moss were athletic, yet skilled. Both players could score the ball. To contain the two great players, the Rangers played a triangle and two defense. It worked.

Denny Smith: *Bob Jones was their coach and he did a good job. They had two great players in Meeks and Moss and they had a good inside presence. I remember we played them in the Centralia Tournament and we played a triangle and two defense against them. We guarded Moss and Meeks and I played the point of the triangle. We let Moss and Meeks catch it and then Stewart and Frailey forced them to the middle…toward me. It gave them problems.*

Junior Steve Stewart played his best offensive game of the year and led the Rangers in scoring with 21 points. Stewart's play was incredible, and it was the first game he led the team in scoring. Dave Lockin added 14 points and the "Logan Flash" (Rick Thomas) added ten. Thomas had a tremendous tournament off the bench by scoring in double figures in each game of the tournament. The Rangers defeated the Orphans 64-52. When the final horn sounded, Benton fans flooded the floor to congratulate the players and coaches.

Denny Smith: *Winning the Centralia Holiday Tournament my senior year was my favorite memory. If you won the Centralia Holiday Tournament you were legitimately one of the best teams in the State of Illinois.*

Just minutes after the game, the public address announcer gave the trophy presentation. All of the Rangers stepped forward to touch the gigantic championship trophy; they then hoisted it high in the air toward the Benton fans. The Benton faithful stood and cheered their Rangers. It was a true team effort. After the trophy presentation, the five-man Centralia All-Tournament team was announced. Centralia's Rick Moss was the MVP of the tournament and Julius Meeks also made the five-man team. As the last name was read, the Benton team and their fans realized that the team had done something remarkable. The '71 Rangers had won the Centralia Tournament without placing a player on the five-man All-Tournament team. The players smiled at each other and celebrated the fact that the "sum of their parts was better than the whole". The Ranger fans were seething, but the players and coaches celebrated this strange moment as a testament to their great balance as a team. Most all of the players agreed that winning the Centralia Holiday Tournament was their favorite memory as a Benton Ranger.

Rod Kaspar: *My favorite memory was winning the Centralia Holiday Tournament. I remember that Coach gave us all wrist bands. After the game, kids were coming up to us wanting our wrist bands. We all gave away our wrist bands…I'll never forget that. To me, winning the Centralia Tournament was like winning the State Tournament.*

It is important to note that Denny Smith and Jim Semanski were selected to the Centralia Tournament second team and Steve Stewart was named to the five-man honorable mention list. The Rangers moved to a perfect 9-0. Winning the tournament validated their greatness as a team and fostered the belief that winning a State Championship was not beyond the realm of possibility.

After the tournament, the Rangers were exhausted physically and mentally. The team had a week without games to recharge. The Rangers traveled to Davenport Gymnasium of Friday, January 8, 1971, and thumped the Harrisburg Bulldogs by a score of 78-42. Dave Lockin led the Rangers in scoring with 23 points, followed by Semanski's 11. Roger Adkins played considerable minutes, and played well by scoring eight points and dishing out five assists. This was a good sign for the Rangers.

The following night, the Centralia Orphans came to town with a chip on their shoulder. Coach Bob Jones had the Orphans ready to play, as they raced to a 23-13 lead after one quarter. After the first quarter, the Rangers came out swinging. Centralia led only 52-50 going into the fourth quarter. In the final minutes, the Rangers trailed by a basket and had three chances to tie, but couldn't score. When the final horn sounded, the Orphans celebrated as they avenged their loss in the Centralia Tournament Championship. They had come into the Cracker Box and stolen one. The Rangers were disappointed with the loss, but Rod Kaspar thought of it differently.

Rod Kaspar: *The loss may have helped us in the long run. It made us take a step back and re-evaluate. It may have helped us in a way…it kept us grounded."*

The Rangers were 10-1 and now set their sights on winning the tough South Seven. With the loss, the Rangers state ranking fell to fifth, just in front of ninth-ranked Carbondale. On Friday, January 15, the Rangers defeated the West Frankfort Redbirds by a score of 67-48 at Max Morris Gymnasium. The Rangers played with a chip on their shoulder after the tough loss to Centralia the week before. The following night, the Rangers hosted Mt. Vernon and won easily 75-54, at home.

The Rangers were now 12-1 entering the mid-winter Quad City Tournament in Carmi. The team won three in a row and narrowly escaped in the championship game by defeating Carmi by just three points. The Rangers improved their record to a blistering 15-1 entering the second half of the conference season.

On Friday, January 29, 1971, the Rangers traveled to Marion and defeated the Wildcats by a score of 86-57 to set up a big game against West Frankfort on Saturday night. The Redbirds were really good in '71. They had a group of solid players; Tim Ricci, Gary Warren, Jack Warren and Shane Grotti. The Rangers won the game by the final score of 78-70. Following the game, an excited Rich Herrin had nothing but praise for his team's performance. Dave Lockin scored 25 points and also led the team in rebounding. He had one of the best games of his high school career and the timing was perfect.

Dave Lockin: *Georgia Tech made an arrangement to play at SIU in '71. It was Yunkus' senior year at Georgia Tech and it was also my senior year at Benton. Our team was invited to the SIU game as guests because of Yunkus. I remember SIU won. It was an afternoon game and then we played West Frankfort that night at home. The Georgia Tech team was invited to our game against West Frankfort. Coach Hyder and the Georgia Tech team were there in Benton watching us play. We won…I played well that night, and Georgia Tech began to take an interest. That is how I ended up playing basketball at Georgia Tech.*

The following weekend the Rangers completed a weekend sweep at home, by defeating Herrin and Johnston City. The Rangers defeated Herrin 74-60 and then thumped non-conference foe, Johnston City, 83-49. The Rangers moved to 19-1 and tied Centralia in the Conference race, with a record of 9-1.

The following weekend the Rangers dismantled Harrisburg 92-55 and then traveled back to Centralia to face the Orphans, yet again. The Rangers loved playing at Centralia; it was their home away from home. A win at Trout Gymnasium could seal the deal. Bob Dallas and legendary official Dick Deitz were the officials assigned to the game. Carloads of

Ranger fans packed Trout Gymnasium anxious to see the Rangers put it to the Orphans. Knowing that a South Seven Championship was on the line, the Rangers came out smoking, and took a 19-7 lead after the first quarter. The game was back and forth, but the Rangers held on to win a big one at Trout, 78-69. Centralia's two great players, Meeks and Moss, could not overcome the balanced scoring attack of the Rangers. Lockin led the attack with 18 points, Stewart 16, Kaspar 13, Smith 12, Frailey 12 and Semanski added six. The team now had to win out, to maintain their one-game lead over the Orphans in the conference race.

In the final weekend of the conference season, the Rangers played host to the state ranked Carbondale Terriers and then traveled to Mt. Vernon on Saturday. Nothing was easy. On Friday night, the Rangers defeated the Terriers 68-51, but the game was closer than the score indicates. The Rangers led by only three points entering the fourth quarter, but held on for the victory. The night belonged to point guard, Denny Smith. Smith led the Rangers in assists all year, but on this night, he would score 16 points and go 6-6 from the free throw line to lead all Benton scorers. Frailey chipped in with 13, Lockin and Kaspar 11. Most importantly, Friday night was also senior night. Before the game, all nine seniors were honored for their hard work and dedication. Many of the seniors had played varsity basketball for three seasons. Smith, Frailey…the Ranger fans had grown attached to this group of players. They had seen them grow and mature into the unstoppable machine that they were in '71. Now it was the last time, and the Benton fans stood out of respect for all the memories the seniors had given them. The Benton loyalty echoed through the small gym as the cheerleaders led the cheers. It was a touching moment in the Cracker Box.

On Saturday night, the Rangers completed the sweep by outscoring Mt. Vernon early and rushing to a 77-60 victory. Again, it was balance. Semanski and Frailey led the team with 16 points, Stewart and Lockin 13, and Smith added his usual ten. As the horn sounded, a happy bunch of Rangers rushed to the locker room to celebrate yet another South Seven Championship. Deep in the bowels of Chagnon Gymnasium, the players hugged each other, and the coaches celebrated with the players. They had done it. The Rangers had won the Centralia Tournament championship, and yet another Conference championship. The team had to finish out the season with McLeansboro before shifting their focus to winning a State Championship. This was something a Benton team had never done, but the '71 team had a chance, and they knew it.

For the final regular season game, the Rangers traveled to McLeansboro. The Foxes were always a formidable opponent, but on this night, the Rangers cruised to an 89-62 victory. Lockin led the scoring with 20 points and Stewart came in at 15. Denny Smith set the table with 15 assists. The Rangers finished the season with an overall record of 24-1. Now, it was the new season, the State Tournament.

Again, the community of Benton was all in. There is perhaps no town in the State of Illinois that appreciates good basketball more than Benton, Illinois. In 1971, the gym was always packed and the team was fully covered in the Benton Evening News, the Southern Illinoisan and even the Evansville Courier. The players were the most popular citizens in town, and their every move was tracked by members of the community. Why did Lockin want to walk around the square with the wig on? He knew people would be watching. He knew he would be noticed. The Ranger players were always front and center in the public eye. Jim Semanski told a funny story that reflects the attention the players received from the community.

Jim Semanski: *Coach Herrin had a way of knowing everything that we did. I had a '56 Chevy that we called the Orange Airplane. I ran out of gas on the way to practice and was afraid I was running late. Ron Dollins helped me push start the car and I immediately went to the gym. As I was walking into the gym, I saw Coach Herrin and I started to explain myself…he said, "I already know about it…just get dressed for practice." Before I could get to the gym from the Bottoms in West City someone had already given him the news. We had curfews…you couldn't get anything by him.*

Obviously, that part of the community attention could be annoying, but all of the Rangers agreed that playing in front of the Benton fan base was the thrill of a lifetime. Basketball was important to the players, but the energy created by the fans had a way of transferring to the players, which made playing basketball in Benton a once in a lifetime experience.

Denny Smith: *The community was unbelievable. I remember leaving school at 3:00 on a Friday…and we played that night at home. I would drive by the gym and there are people standing in line back to Chick's Market waiting to get a ticket for the game…. And you know…you're going to be playing in that game. Honestly…I can't put that into words…. It's hard to explain that feeling to somebody.*

State Tournament Play '71

The Rangers opened up Regional play on Monday, March 1, 1971, at Max Morris Gymnasium in West Frankfort. The Rangers thumped the Zeiglar-Royalton Tornadoes by a score of 67-25. The game was over early and there were no injuries. Hugh Frailey led the Rangers with 11 points, followed by Lockin and Weathers with ten. On Wednesday, the Rangers faced off against the Sesser Red Devils. Sesser tried to hold the ball against the much superior Ranger team, and to their credit, the much smaller Devils were only down by twelve going into the final quarter. The cream rose to the top in the final quarter, and the Rangers won by a score of 52-26.

The win against Sesser set up the Regional Championship against the West Frankfort Redbirds. It was a tough match-up for the Rangers, despite winning the two regular season meetings. The Redbirds were very capable. The Rangers always received the Redbirds best effort. The Rangers were up by eleven going into the fourth quarter but the Redbirds did not lie down. Behind the great play of Tim Ricci, who scored a game-high 30 points, the Redbirds fought to stay alive. Gary Warren also played well and chipped in 16 points, but it wasn't enough. On this night, Jim Semanski rose to the occasion, netting a season-high 24 points.

Jim Semanski: *I think one of my greatest memories was beating West Frankfort a third time in the Regional Championship.*

Guard Hugh Frailey hit key jump shots that opened up the Rangers strong inside game. He scored 18 points. Stewart and Lockin also chipped in 14 points. Denny Smith ran the offense to perfection and finished with a game-high ten assists.

Denny Smith: *West Frankfort was a scary team to play in the Regionals. I breathed a sigh of relief when we beat West Frankfort in the Regional championship game. They were scary. They had Gary Warren, Jack Warren, Shane Grotti and Tim Ricci. Jack Warren and I first met at church camp, and we later became very good friends.*

With the win, the Rangers advanced to the Eldorado Sectional to play Joppa. Joppa was a small school and they were an unknown mystery to the Rangers.

Brad Weathers: *After we won the Regional and we were getting ready to play Joppa in the Sectional...I opened the paper and the headline was... "RANGERS WILL WIN"...I thought I was reading it wrong...I thought that prediction was pretty bold and I remember that I didn't want to be jinxed.... And then someone told me that Joppa was also the Rangers.*

On Wednesday, March 10th, the Benton Rangers opened play in the Eldorado sectional against the Joppa Rangers. Long caravans of cars followed the team bus as the Rangers continued their march to Champaign. The Rangers stunned Joppa by jumping out to a 23-6 lead and they never looked back. Every Ranger player, with the exception of sophomore guard Robert Corn, got in the scoring column. The Rangers won 78-44 and were led in scoring by junior Steve Stewart. Four other Rangers were in double figures, while Denny Smith once again led the team in assists.

The Rangers advanced to the Sectional finals to face a hot Harrisburg Bulldog club. The Rangers had no problems with the Bulldogs in their previous two meetings, but the Bulldogs had found themselves, and they were playing better basketball. Harrisburg was coached by Ray Harris and brought a 10-16 record into the contest. At halftime, the Rangers led 27-20. The Rangers then pulled away to win the ball game, 69-56. Sectional Champions!

The Rangers received the Sectional trophy and traveled back to Benton anticipating a large crowd at the square to greet them. The community came out in overwhelming numbers and they lined the square listening for the sirens of the fire truck escort. Local fire trucks met the Rangers near Douglas School, and proudly escorted the team to the square. For the players, the memories of fire truck escorts never leave their mind. The players relished the moment. BCHS teachers came to the square to greet the team. Long-time teacher Ellen Burkhart climbed the steep stairs of the team bus to give a thumbs-up to the team. Burkhart was a well-respected English teacher, and the players were astonished that she even knew basketball was a sport. To some of the players, it was the highlight of the night.

The Rangers moved to 29-1 and were rather surprised to hear that they would be facing Nashville in the Super-Sectional at Carbondale.

Denny Smith: *We were all set to play Centralia in the Super-Sectional... but Nashville beat them and that kind of threw an element of surprise at us.*

On Tuesday, February 16th, the Rangers traveled to the SIU Arena to face the Nashville Hornets. The Nashville team had size and the Hornets brought a 24-3 record into the Carbondale Super-Sectional. As the game progressed, it was clear that the Hornets had no answer for Dave Lockin. The 6'7" center that came out for the freshman team as a dare stuck it to the Hornets. Lockin scored 21 points on 9-12 shooting from the field, and led the Rangers with 12 rebounds. Denny Smith chipped in with 14 points and recorded eight assists. Hugh Frailey added ten points and Stewart did a little bit of everything. They had done it! The Rangers were going to Champaign. Benton fans flooded the Arena floor to celebrate with the team and then hurried home to take part in the victory lap around the square. The town of Benton loved their Rangers! Maybe '71 could be the year.

The Rangers received a lively pep session on Thursday before being chauffeured in separate cars for their three hour trip north to Champaign. On Friday morning, the team ate breakfast before a quick walk-through at an area high school. The Rangers then departed to Assembly Hall for their afternoon match-up against the Spartans of Oak Lawn High School. Oak Lawn is a Chicago-area school with four times the enrollment of Benton High School. It was definitely a David and Goliath match-up, but Oak Lawn's size didn't faze the mental approach of the Rangers. They felt they could play with anybody.

The Spartans were coached by legendary coach Lee Scaduto, who served as the head basketball coach at Oak Lawn for twenty-nine years. The Spartans featured one of the best players in the country in Charles Jerome (C.J.) Kupec. Kupec was 6'9", 200 pounds, built like a Mack truck, and he had skills. After graduating from Oak Lawn, he went to Michigan and played basketball. From there, Kupec played three seasons with the Lakers as a back-up center for Kareem Abdul-Jabbar. Kupec could play, and the focus of the Ranger walk-through centered on devising a way to neutralize him.

Coach Herrin wanted to dress all the players, but the IHSA allowed only ten players on the active roster for the State Tournament.

Brad Weathers: *I didn't dress in the State Tournament. We could only dress ten and Coach was worried about Smith's knee...so he brought up Robert Corn. He was a sophomore and he was a guard. I dressed in the Regional and the Sectional and that was good for me...because I wanted to play.*

To start the game, Hugh Frailey nailed a jump shot that put the Rangers up 2-0. The Ranger fans went crazy with excitement, but Oak Lawn quickly came back and tied the game at two. Oak Lawn was very physical and they pulled away to a 19-13 advantage by the end of the first quarter. Kupec's presence in the paint seemed to bother Semanski and Lockin. He was by far the best post player the Rangers had seen all year. He was physical and big enough to alter shots. Kupec was a problem, and the Rangers sensed it early in the game. The team found themselves trailing by six at halftime. In fact, Lockin's final basket of his high school career came late in the first quarter.

Dave Lockin: *I was disappointed in myself in that game. We played some man and some zone…but I will tell you…C.J. Kupec was really good.*

The Rangers came out and won the third quarter by just one point, but it was Hugh Frailey's hot shooting that kept the Rangers close. In the third quarter, Frailey single handedly kept the Rangers in the game. Hugh scored eight of his seventeen points in the third period and then connected for the first four points of the fourth quarter. He was on fire. The Rangers showed their tenacity by coming back and cutting the score to 53-51 on a basket by Denny Smith. Jim Bocinsky hit a basket for Oak Lawn, but Semanski quickly answered and the Rangers trailed by just two points. Bocinsky hit again, but Smith scored another bucket to cut the Oak Lawn lead to 57-55. On the next possession, Smith was called for a blocking foul on a controversial play on the baseline. It was his fifth foul.

Denny Smith: *Oak Lawn had as many students in their school as we did people in our town. In one class…it was a great accomplishment for us to get to the State Tournament. We certainly didn't feel that way at the time, but looking back you realize getting there was a big deal. Oak Lawn had C.J. Kupec… and he was a player. Hugh had an unbelievable game and I played pretty well.… I fouled out of the game on a blocking call…Rich went crazy…he didn't like the call. Hugh made the All-Tournament team. They were really good.*

Oak Lawn defeated the Rangers that afternoon 71-58, but the team fought and competed like all Rich Herrin teams do. Frailey led the Rangers in scoring with 17 points and Smith chipped in 12. Off the bench, Rod Kaspar scored eight points and Steve Stewart added seven. The locker room was quiet as the Rangers took a moment to reflect on their journey.

The finality of it all was hard for the players to grasp. Benton sportswriter Bob Tedrow may have said it best when he wrote, "The ball just didn't bounce the Rangers' way all afternoon." The Ranger players were disappointed and it is still a game that many of them think about to this day.

Jim Semanski: *I wish we would have played better at the State Tournament. I wish we had that game back.*

Rod Kaspar: *C.J. Kupec was a player. I hate to say it…but we were overmatched. We didn't quit. They were just a better team that day.*

When the team returned home on Sunday, they were met with a brief reception by Benton fans who wanted to express their appreciation for the team's efforts one last time. Both Hugh Frailey and Denny Smith were selected to the All-State Tournament team picked by the Daily Illini. The coaches spoke and heaped praise on the players, especially Roger Adkins for his courage to continue to play despite his knee problems. Then it was over. The experience of playing together as a team has been over for fifty years, but the memories of the journey to the State Tournament live on in all the players of the great '71 team.

I had one last question for all the members of the '71 team. My question was; can you explain the impact that Coach Herrin has had on your life?

Rod Kaspar: *Coach Herrin is like my second father. He taught me how to be a good competitor, good teammate, and even a good father. He could really chew on you and then quickly put his arm around you and you knew it was going to be o.k. He taught us how to be good men. I believe basketball was second. He wanted us to be good people. It was an honor and privilege to play for Coach Herrin.*

After high school, Rod played basketball and graduated from Louisiana College, in Pineville, Louisiana. Rod is now a retired teacher and coach, and he currently lives with his wife Kristie in Wimberley, Texas. He has two daughters; Lindsie and Sara. He also has a son named Sam. He loves spending time with his grandchildren.

Dave Lockin: *Coach Herrin was just always there…he worked so hard…. He was always checking on our grades and encouraging us to do the right things. He had a great influence on my life as well as Coach Phillips.*

After high school, Lockin received a full-ride basketball scholarship to Georgia Tech. He was bothered with knee problems so much that he was not able to continue his basketball career. Lockin has been in the retail automobile business for forty-two years. He is now the fleet manager for the Hennessy Automotive Group, a group of ten dealerships with eleven franchises. Lockin has been with Hennessy for thirty-one years. He currently lives with his wife Jennifer in Atlanta, Georgia. They have two sons; Matthew and Jonathon.

Brad Weathers: *He always took care of me and I was always this kid that just kept hanging around. He would always tell me I was going to get my growth later in life and he was the one that talked to Coach Statham for me about playing at McKendree College. He always contacted people for me when I was looking for a job and even offered to go to a job interview with me. Dick and I always helped Coach with the McKendree Camp. Coach Herrin always enjoyed his job and he is a big reason I went on to teach and coach. He is a friend and father figure.*

After high school, Weathers played basketball at McKendree University and then became one of the greatest basketball coaches in Illinois history. Brad ended his coaching career with an accumulative record of 571-360. He spent 23 years in Carlyle and won the Class A State Championship in 1988-1989. Brad coached eight seasons at Nashville, Illinois and earned a second place finish in the State Tournament in 2013-2014. He and his wife Cindi currently live in Nashville. They have one son, Patrick, and two daughters; Lindsay and Holly.

Danny Britton: *My greatest memory was having the opportunity to play for Coach Herrin. When my son Scott graduated high school he was either going to go to school or go to the military. I told him that in the military he could learn things like hard work, respect, honor. My son stopped me and said, "Dad you didn't go to the military." I said, "No, I didn't but I learned all of those things when I played for Coach Herrin. After high school, I was trying to figure out what to do…I had an appointment with an Army recruiter at 10:00 a.m. but I had a job interview with Old Ben Coal 21 at 9:00 a.m. Jack Webster was the guy from Old Ben that interviewed me. He asked me one question; Danny did you play basketball at Benton High School? I said, "Yes." That was it. I worked at Old Ben Coal Company for 20 years before becoming a prison guard at the Super-Max in Tamms, Illinois. I eventually worked at*

Big Muddy Prison at Rend Lake. Other than my dad...the closest thing I have to a hero would be Coach Herrin. I was just so honored to be a Benton Ranger and I can't say anything negative about my experience.

After high school, Danny worked at Old Ben Coal Mine number 21 for twenty years. He then worked as a prison guard at the Super-Max in Tamms, Illinois before finishing his work at Big Muddy Prison. Danny currently lives with his wife Cindy in Whittington, Illinois. He has one daughter, Billie Jo Cockrum, and one son, Scott.

Hugh Frailey: *He was a great influence...he never quit. He outworked his opponents. I would do anything in the world for him. If you gave 100% on the floor...he would do anything for you. Coach Herrin gave a guy my name and that is how I got into the insurance business.*

After high school, Hugh Frailey went to Southern Illinois University and played college golf. Hugh came back to Benton and worked in banking before becoming a State Farm insurance agent. Hugh currently lives in Benton with his wife Robin. They have three children; Jordan, Drew and Breanne.

Jim Semanski: *Coach is someone that went out of his way to treat me fairly. He checked on our grades and he made us do the right things. He was very much like a father figure.... Ron Herrin was like your favorite uncle. I also enjoyed Coach Phillips and Coach Stewart. Ron Dollins was also a big influence on my life. I remember one time there was donkey basketballgame in the gym as a fundraiser for something. Coach Herrin had the players working the event. I was supposed to be taking money at the door. Coach told me that if someone comes up and they look like they can't pay...walk inside the gym and act like you're watching the game and just let them in. I had some people walk up with no shoes on...very poor...I would walk into the gym and then they would come in and sit and watch. He wanted to let those people in...that always stuck with me.*

After high school, Semanski went to the University of Tennessee Chattanooga then transferred to Louisiana College and then SIU-C. Jim currently lives in Carterville, Illinois with his wife, Karen. They have four children; Joe, Jon, Mary and Carissa. Jim runs his own business called JS Corvette Sales, in Carbondale, Illinois.

Denny Smith: *Coach Herrin was a big influence in my life. I saw Rich help so many people. He helped me by keeping me grounded. He was always there. We had rules and he was on us about making good grades. I think the ball handlers had a different relationship with him. When I was a freshman and sophomore, I just did what I was told...but as a junior and senior we communicated more. You kind of earned that communication. Harry and Moose were also big influences in my life. All of the men that I had as coaches in Benton had a great influence on me...and Rich was kind of the icing on the cake.*

After high school, Denny went to the University of Tennessee Chattanooga but he had knee trouble. Smith came back to Benton and worked in the mines for twenty-two years. Denny currently lives in South Carolina with his wife Marya. He has four children: Amy, Reggie, Cody and Peyton.

The '71 Rangers personified the word team. Each player served an important role and there is no team in Ranger history with greater balance across the line-up than the '71 Rangers. I really enjoyed interviewing the players and learned a great deal about their experience as a Benton Ranger. The players are well into their sixties in age, but they were more than willing to reflect back on the unbelievable ride of '71. As I was nearing the end of my interview with Jim Semanski, he told a story that revealed how special his high school experience at Benton was.

Jim Semanski: *I remember my last day of school at the old school. Everyone was running out of the school all excited...I walked across the street and looked back at that school.... I was sad it was over. Some people don't remember anything about high school. I enjoyed my time at Benton High School.*

Semanski asked me about how the old gym looks. I teach at Benton High School, and I told him it looks much the same. I invited Jim to come up to the high school and we could go in and check it out. This was his response.

Jim Semanski: *I haven't been in the old gym since graduation. I miss that old school. I don't think I can go in there...I can't go in there.*

That is how much it meant to Semanski and I'm sure many of his teammates feel the same way.

Brad Weathers played on the great '71 team and went on to become a great high school coach at Carlyle and Nashville, Illinois. *(Benton High School)*

The "Great Eight" of '71 were responsible for first bringing the stars to the Benton uniforms. *(Ceasar Maragni)*

336

A picture of the 1970 team after winning the Regional Championship.
The '70 Rangers were defeated by Mt. Vernon in the Sectional.
The team was a year away. *(Ceasar Maragni)*

Don Smith was a senior on the '70 team and later coached
at Benton from 1997-2002. *(Benton High School)*

Tom (T.J.) Learned was also a senior on the '70 team and was my 6th grade basketball coach. *(Benton High School)*

This is Denny Smith as a senior. Although Smith struggled with knee problems, Smith established himself as one of the greatest point guards in Ranger history. *(Benton High School)*

As a boy, Hugh Frailey dreamed of playing for the Rangers.
Frailey provided steady scoring and rebounding from the
guard position in '71 (Ceasar Maragni)

Steve Stewart's size and strength from the guard position created match-up
problems for many of the Rangers opponents. (Ceasar Maragni)

Dave Lockin first played basketball as a freshman and developed into an All-State player by the time he was a senior. *(Benton High School)*

All-Stater, Jim Semanski, scored more than a thousand points
in his career and teamed with Lockin to create a
solid inside game. *(Benton High School)*

Rick Thomas came off the bench in '71. Thomas was very skilled and averaged ten points a game in the '70 Centralia Tournament. *(Ceasar Maragni)*

Plagued by a knee problem as a senior, Roger Adkins provided valuable minutes in the post season. *(Ceasar Maragni)*

Jim Semanski battles West Frankfort's All-Time leading scorer,
Tim Ricci, for a rebound in the '71 Regional. *(Ceasar Maragni)*

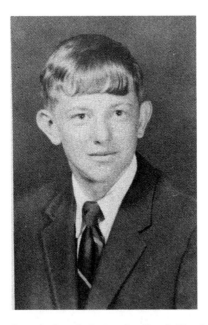

Senior, Danny Britton, loved playing for Coach Herrin and believes
that being a member of the Benton Rangers led to his job
in the coal mines. (Benton High School)

342

The '71 Rangers after their hard-fought victory against the Redbirds in the Regional Championship. *(Ceasar Maragni)*

An excited group of Rangers accept the Regional Championship plaque at West Frankfort. *(Ceasar Maragni)*

The '71 Rangers relax at their hotel before their state quarterfinal match-up against Oak Lawn. L-R Lockin, Adkins, Stewart, Smith, Kaspar, Frailey, Semanski *(Cesar Maragni)*

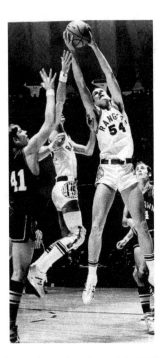

Lockin goes high for a rebound at Assembly Hall. *(Ceasar Maragni)*

Rod Kaspar was a key contributor that said, "Coach Herrin had a vision for our group." Kaspar said, "Herrin was like a second father to me."
(Benton High School)

The great Ranger team of '71. *(Cesaer Maragni)*

CHAPTER SIXTEEN

"Billy"

*"I never remember Billy losing a single wind sprint in
practice in the two years that I coached him."*
– Burton Wills, Junior High Coach

There are over 3.5 million males in the world with the first name of William or Bill. The most common surname in the United States is Smith. Therefore, it is safe to say that the name Bill Smith is one of the most common names in the world. Yet, in the town of Benton, there is only one Billy Smith. From 1971 to 1975, he took the town by storm. Adults in the community adored him and young boys in Benton imitated his every move on the asphalt courts of all the neighborhood grade schools.

In early December of 2020, I called Smith at his home and we agreed to meet for an interview in my classroom at the high school. Billy is quiet and well-liked due to his humble disposition. Much like Danny Johnson, he looks as if he could still play. When he arrived for our interview, he was carrying three scrapbooks that his mother and others had collected over the course of his athletic career. We pilfered through the books and chuckled at the fact that his name was underlined in many of the articles. Feeling a little embarrassed, he quickly told me that this was not his doing. I had to laugh because his modest nature despite all of his accomplishments is one of his most endearing qualities.

Then we both sat down. I explained the purpose of the book and that I wanted to ask him some questions about his childhood and his playing days as a Benton Ranger. He politely nodded in agreement and softly said, "Go ahead."

Billy's first residence was in a small house on Benton Lake. He had loving parents, Tom and Jeanine Smith. He also had two older siblings; Tom and Becky. Billy lit up when he talked about his upbringing and his family. As a boy, Smith attended Grant School and some of his earliest memories about basketball centered on Perry Eisenhower.

Billy Smith: *I remember that as young as third or fourth grade, Perry would make us get in three straight lines and we would pass and there would be one shooter. The lines had to be straight and each group got one shot and then you hustled back to the end of the line. Very regimented. Steve Stewart was my favorite player, because he also went to Grant School.*

As a boy, Billy remembered the success of the Rangers, but only occasionally went to the high school games before beginning junior high. Once in junior high, he made it a point to go to almost all of the home games.

Billy Smith: *We would have to sit in the aisle of the visiting section in the old gym just to see the game, because it was so packed.*

In the sixth grade, the Smith family moved into a home on Route 37 just north of Benton. On their new property, there was an old barn with a spacious loft. In fact, there was so much space, his dad put up a goal. Billy claimed it was a great place to play, even though there was only one light bulb. I could sense that Billy was very close to both of his parents and had a special bond with his father, Tom. Tom Smith was a hard worker and he supported the family by working long hours at the Orient Number 3 Coal Mine. Despite his busy work schedule, he always found time to spend with Billy. Although he wasn't an athlete as a youngster, Tom loved sports and he encouraged Billy to play all sports.

Billy Smith: *My dad was left-handed, but he would let me pitch to him and he would catch me with a right-handed glove. Dad would rebound my shots in the barn loft...I even remember my neighbor, Fred Hunter, would come* *over and we would run pass patterns against each other…my dad would be the quarterback.*

Billy was also very close to his mother, Jeanine. He beamed with pride as he told me how hard she had worked to become a teacher.

Billy Smith: *My mom was a school teacher. She went back to SIU and got her education degree at SIU. She taught school at Washington Grade School and was a first and second grade teacher…and later became principal. She graduated number one in her class at SIU.*

Billy loved all sports and played whatever sport was in season. By the time he was in junior high, Billy realized his special gifts as an athlete. As a junior high player, he had good size and was lightning quick. He was a coach's dream because along with all of his natural ability, he kept his mouth shut and let his play do the talking. Smith was by far the best athlete in most everything that he participated in, but he never drew attention to himself. It was not his way.

He was quick to point out that he learned more about the game of basketball in junior high than any other stage in his development. In junior high, he loved playing for Bob Johnston and Burton Wills. Before Wills and Johnston began coaching together, they spent many weekends in the summer playing fast pitch softball. The two developed a life-long friendship.

Billy Smith: *Bob Johnston and Burton Wills were positive influences, for sure. Burton was as intense as they come and Bob was calm and cool. They balanced each other so well. We learned so much in those two years. I may have gained more in those two years than any period in my development. As a seventh grader, we were undefeated and got beat in the State Championship by Herrin.*

Burton Wills grew up in Benton and graduated from Benton High school in 1957. In high school, he played for Ralph Davison and became a student of the game. After attending SIU and earning a bachelor's degree in education, he accepted a teaching job at Whittington Junior High and served as an assistant coach to his friend, Bob Johnston. They coached together from 1962-1965 at Whittington. They then found themselves together at Benton Junior High in the fall of 1967, with their roles reversed. Wills was the eighth grade coach with Johnston serving as his assistant. Steve Stewart and Tony Diefenbach were key players on Wills' first eighth grade team. In Will's first season, he led the Junior Rangers to a State Tournament title. The Junior Rangers went on to win another State Championship in Wills' last year as Coach in 1972.

Bob Johnston graduated from Benton High School in 1954. Benton was primarily a football school at the time, but newly-hired basketball coach, Ralph Hooker, had the Rangers playing good basketball as well. Hooker was on the verge of turning the program around, but he got sideways with the other coaches and left after only three seasons. Wills described Hooker as more of a basketball coach than a football coach, and Benton was not quite ready to compromise its football power. Hooker then left.

Johnston had a more relaxed demeanor and really knew the game. He took his job as an educator very seriously and was not just a good coach; he was a good teacher. Bob Johnston was a man of few words. He set out with the goal of teaching his young players about the importance of a winning attitude and drilling them with basic fundamentals. As the seventh grade coach in the Benton machine, he fit perfectly and was a great compliment to the fiery Burton Wills.

For the next five seasons, Burton Wills and Bob Johnston ran a tight ship heavy on hard work and fundamentals. They consistently sent players to the high school level that were prepped mentally and physically for the no-nonsense demands of Coach Rich Herrin. It was a marriage that served the program well and cannot be overstated. The culture, discipline, and fundamentals of the Ranger basketball program were now being introduced to players as early as the sixth grade. It was a system, and the system churned out players for the next decade.

Bob Johnston: *There was a little communication between us and Coach Herrin…but not a lot. We were friends. We had to run our programs the way we saw fit. I went to most all of the high school games…home and away.*

Coach Burton Wills and Coach Bob Johnston still live in Benton and I asked both of them about Billy Smith. Bob Johnston was quick to praise Smith.

Bob Johnston: *He was head and shoulders above everyone at the junior high level. He was very intelligent…you didn't have to tell him anything twice. Of course, he also had a lot of talent.*

Burton Wills: *Billy was a tremendous student. He would run wind sprints and never lose. That tells you what kind of competitor he was. I could never remember him ever losing a wind sprint…ever! We would sometimes practice before school. Maybe forty minutes before school started we would get some shooting in. We had just had a game and Billy scored a crazy amount of points…I can't remember how many…I don't think he missed a shot. Billy's father drove him to school and came into the gym and asked to speak with me. Bill's dad, Tom…he was very quiet and he hadn't said anything all year, so we sat down and he said, "We're very happy with your coaching…but don't you think Bill shot the ball a little too much?" I wasn't expecting that question. That is not what you usually get from parents. I remember saying, "Tom, you people are great people and Billy is a great young man, but I will never tell your son not to shoot." That's the kind of people they were.*

As a freshman, Billy volunteered to run in a cross country meet at Olney that was well before his first football game. He asked Coach Ed Miller if he could run in the meet to "see what it was like". Miller quickly agreed in hopes that he might run cross country. The Olney meet was a big one and schools from all over the area attended. Entering the meet, Smith had no cross country training under his belt, but managed to finish in the top twenty. Let's face it, kids don't just run cross country to see what it's like. Billy ran the meet because he loved to compete.

Another great story about Billy occurred his sophomore year and it involved a unicycle.

Billy Smith: *I wanted a motorcycle for Christmas. My parents got me a unicycle instead. I learned to ride it in the basement. When you rode it, you were probably five feet off the ground. After I learned to ride it…I learned how to dribble the basketball while riding it. So I brought it up to the gym…Big Mac tried it many times…He was taking some nasty falls…leaving gouges in the gym floor. Coach Herrin told me to never bring the unicycle to the gym again…he was afraid someone would get hurt.*

Paul Dinkins: *I think Billy was one of Benton's all-time great athletes. He was quick as a cat. He was a great guy and a great teammate. I think Billy was the only athlete in Benton history to earn sixteen varsity letters. You will have to check that…football, basketball, track, and baseball.*

Robert Corn: *Billy Smith was one of the greatest basketball players to ever play at Benton High School. You know that Billy was our leading scorer as a sophomore, the second leading scorer as a junior, and the third leading scorer as a senior and he played within the team. He set aside personal accolades for the betterment of the team. The success of the team was most important to him.*

Billy Smith is perhaps the best multi-sport athlete that Benton High School has ever produced. He was not the type to focus on one sport, he did it all. Smith earned sixteen varsity letters in his high school career and it is still a record at Benton High School. Think about this. Each of Billy's four years, he earned a varsity letter in football, basketball, baseball, and track. In football, he played the quarterback position and was an accomplished baseball pitcher along with being a 22'0" long jumper. In basketball, he was the centerpiece player for three years and earned the honor of being a high school All-American as a senior. Billy Smith was truly the Bo Jackson of Benton High School.

For the next three years, Billy smith would dominate the South Seven in more than just basketball. He was truly amazing!

Billy Smith as a senior. *(Benton High School)*

Smith played football all four seasons and was an All-South
player as a senior. *(Cesar Maragni)*

Steve Stewart and Billy Smith were the only two basketball players
to play at the varsity level as a freshman for Coach
Herrin at Benton. *(Ceasar Maragni)*

In the Spring, Billy ran track and played Baseball for four seasons
at the Varsity level. Smith is still the BCHS record holder in the
triple jump. *(Ceasar Maragni)*

A picture of Billy signing his scholarship to play basketball at Georgia Tech. In the picture is Coach Herrin and his parents; Tom and Jeanine.
(Ceasar Maragni)

A picture of Billy in action as a yellow jacket.
(Billy Smith family collection)

This is a picture of the State Champion Jr. Rangers of 1972 coached by Burton Wills and Bob Johnston. Burton Wills is in the back row left and Bob Johnston is in back row right. *(Paul Hickman)*

CHAPTER SEVENTEEN

Keeping with Tradition in 72

"We had great tradition and sometimes that tradition can win some games for you. We were the Benton Rangers and we expected to win." – Robert Corn, Guard

The sustained success of the great Benton teams of the late sixties and early seventies created a winning attitude that rippled thru the junior high and grade schools. It was like a small snowball rolling down a hill that gets bigger with each revolution. The unprecedented success of the Rangers inspired young boys in Benton to not only play basketball, but play it well. Almost every player on the '72 team attended the Ranger games when they were growing up. During the Yunkus years, David Hurley's parents dropped him off in front of the old gymnasium and he waited in line by himself for hours to get into the game. Hurley's parents did not even attempt to attend the games, knowing that it was virtually impossible to find a seat. Roy and Virginia Dinkins took their son, Paul, to most all of the Ranger home games so he could witness the play of Yunkus, Johnson and Collins. He was hooked. As a first grader, Dennis Andrews' parents had seats at midcourt and he dreamed of one day being a Benton Ranger. Allan Wisely lived across the street from the high school. As a boy, he walked across the street to watch the Adkins brothers play because they were his neighbors. Chris Moore's favorite team growing up was the '67 team with Yunkus and Hoover. Billy Smith started going to the games on a regular basis in junior high and his favorite player was Steve Stewart. In fact, they were now teammates in '72. Kenny Summers grew up in Akin but was well aware of the Ranger mystique. Robert Corn, Tony Diefenbauch, Brandon Webster and Steve Stewart played on the great '71 team that went to State a year earlier.

The players on the '72 team had seen the greatness of the past. A winning culture had been established and the players felt a sense of duty to protect the program's identity. They expected to win with experience or not. It was their turn.

The leader of the '72 team was Steve Stewart. By the beginning of the '72 season, Stewart had established himself as one of the greatest players in Ranger basketball history. He was the only Ranger returning in '72 with varsity experience. In the championship game of the Centralia Tournament in '70, Stewart led the Rangers in scoring. He had three seasons of varsity basketball under his belt. As a senior, he inherited teammates that had no varsity basketball experience. Chris Moore could only speculate on what Stewart must have been thinking when the season began.

Chris Moore: *He had to wonder as a senior in '72…what am I doing playing with these guys?*

But Stewart proved to be the ideal leader for the young Rangers. He accepted his new teammates and did all he could to keep the Ranger machine moving forward.

David Hurley: *We had so much fun with Steve. Everyone had watched the '71 team for the last three years…and then they were all gone. We had no varsity experience except for Steve. Steve kept everything loose…he welcomed all of us in. He was the cornerstone of the team and Rich gave him a lot of rope. He had quick hands, very smart and just saw the floor so well.*

In 1971-72, Ranger fans were introduced to Billy Smith. Billy had cat-like quickness and great basketball instincts, but he was just a freshman. In Coach Herrin's twenty-five-year run at Benton, Smith and Stewart were the only players ever pulled up to the varsity level as freshman. They were both special players and now they were playing together; Stewart in his last year and Smith just coming in. Stewart served as a valuable mentor to Billy, as did junior point guard Robert Corn.

Billy Smith: *Those first two years…Robert Corn kind of took me under his wing. He was confident in himself and a great leader. He was the floor general…he ran the team. Robert made things happen.*

Corn grew up in Macedonia and explained that he lived just feet inside the Benton school district. As a junior, Robert was 6'2" and well put together. Basketball was important to the Corn family. The Corn boys, Dick, Robert and Jerry, grew up under the watchful eye of Bob and Eloise Corn. Bob Corn expected his boys to work hard at home just as Coach Herrin demanded in the gym. The Corn boys stayed busy putting up hay and were actively involved in 4-H. Bob loved athletics and made sure his boys had every opportunity to play. In fact, Bob transferred Robert to Ewing just before his seventh grade season at Akin to play for Coach Norman Carlile at Ewing.

Rich Herrin: *Robert was a tremendous leader…he was hard-nosed and got the job done…always played hard.*

Senior guard Tony Diefenbach played sparingly as a junior but was suddenly thrust into the starting line-up in '72. Diefenbach provided steady play at the guard position.

Billy Smith: *Tony Diefenbach had good physical strength…he could shoot the ball.*

The other senior on the team was a transfer from Christopher by the name of Brandon Webster. Webster was a solid football player that provided the regulars with scrappy competition in practices.

Junior guard David Hurley loved the game and wanted to be a Benton Ranger since his early days of watching Yunkus and Adkins in the Cracker Box. There is a picture of Hurley shooting a textbook jump shot in the yearbook.

Robert Corn: *David was a very good player…he was a good shooter. Everyone knew their roles…and David certainly knew his role.*

Sophomore forward Paul Dinkins was another up and coming talent that was a product of the ripple effect. Affectionately called "Dink" by his teammates, Paul shot the ball left-handed but could use his right hand almost as well as his left. Dinkins played at 6'4" and he was long. He could score the ball and was very sound fundamentally. Paul's teammates described him as one of the nicest guys you would ever meet and a good teammate.

Robert Corn: *Paul and I became good friends. Paul was a very good player… he was quiet but played with toughness…. Paul is one of the nicest guys I've ever been around.*

The inside game centered on junior Chris Moore and sophomore Steve McCommons. Moore was a good defender and rebounder and had the ability to score when needed.

Rich Herrin: *Chris and Mac did a good job for us…they got the job done for us on the boards…played hard…. They were key players for us on those teams in '72-'73.*

For the next three seasons, Steve McCommons provided a tough style of play that his teams so desperately needed. He played at 6'5" and was a fierce competitior. As a sophomore, he was prone to foul trouble as he jostled for position in the paint. "Big Mac" played full throttle and he was a guy you wanted on your team. McCommons was an outstanding football player but he took a liking to basketball in junior high. He played a key role in the post on three solid Ranger teams beginning in '72.

Paul Dinkins: *Big Mac was a dandy. He was a good one to have…he was our enforcer. I remember one time in junior high, Mac got in a fight after school. He had this kid in a headlock and he injured his hand because he was bashing him in the head so hard. When he went home…his mother, who was a sweet lady…but tough herself…was so mad at Steve that she wouldn't take him to the doctor. She made Mac ride his bike to the doctor's office to get treated.*

Junior guard, Allan Wisely, was the younger brother of Laird Wisely, who played with Collins on the '69 team. Wisely loved to play and went to the games as a youngster. Although playing time was tough to come by, Allan battled in practice and accepted his role.

Junior guard Kenny Summers was from Akin and he persevered through his freshman and sophomore seasons with very little playing time. Kenny loved the game and "Fly" never quit. He stood at 5'5" and flew around the court. He was everywhere. In track, Summers became one of the few Ranger pole vaulters to jump 13'6". As a basketball player, Summers had the "no fear" mentality of a pole vaulter. He showed no regard for his own personal safety by diving into the stands for loose balls or setting up to take charges on guys twice his size. He played with a reckless abandon.

Kenny Summers: *I had two of the best parents ever made. My dad poured a concrete pad in our backyard and I played all of the time. I grew up in Akin on a farm and I was expected to work. The only thing my dad struggled with was practice because we lived further away from the school. Basketball was always my number one love. I loved it from day one. I would do anything to play. I had several different coaches at Akin…but mostly Kent Hodge.*

Reserve guard Dennis Andrews contributed by providing stiff competition in practice at the guard spot. Andrews brought a positive attitude along with gritty play. He first began playing basketball at Hill City School and then transferred to Washington School in the fifth and sixth grade. His Uncle, Henry, served as his coach. Andrews was also a solid low hurdler on the track team for Coach Herrin.

Junior Mark Zinzilieta was also on the team but did not play his senior season. Zinzilieta received little playing time but enjoyed the game and put the team first. He was also a standout runner on the track team. As the season crept closer, the players had differing opinions about the expectations of the '72 team.

Paul Dinkins: *The expectation was to win…because of the upbringing we had, we expected to win.*

David Hurley: *I didn't feel there were a lot of expectations for '72. We lost so many players from the '71 team. The better teams in the conference that year were Mt. Vernon, Herrin and Benton.*

Robert Corn: *The expectations were low for '72…. We had one great player in Steve Stewart. It had to be one of Coach Herrin's best coaching jobs. We had great tradition and sometimes that tradition can win some games for you. We were the Benton Rangers and we expected to win.*

The Rangers opened the season at home against the McLeansboro Foxes on December 3, 1971. Benton fans packed the Cracker Box to see their young team. Chris Moore scored the first basket of the season and the Rangers jumped out to a 20-9 first quarter advantage. Behind the play of Marvin Webb and John Irvin, the Foxes stayed close and only trailed 31-27 at halftime. Sophomore Paul Dinkins calmly buried two big charity tosses down the stretch and the Rangers held on to win 68-61. The youngsters played well, but it was a typical first game. There was much to improve, but it was early. David Hurley led the Rangers in scoring with 13 points.

"We played in spurts," Herrin said after the game. On this night, Herrin sported bell-bottom trousers with white dress shoes. Herrin's bulldog face and tight flat-top contrasted greatly with his flashy dress of the early seventies.

The Rangers then traveled to Sparta and defeated the Bulldogs by a score of 64-47. They were 2-0. On December 11th, Jim Byassee and the Meridian Bobcats came to town and defeated the Rangers by a score of 71-66. It was the first time the Bobcats had ever won at the Cracker Box. In 1972, the Meridian Bobcats finished second in the Class A State Tournament. The Bobcats finished 30-2 and were led by All-State guard Calvin Johnson. It was this Meridian team that handed the Rangers their first loss. On this night, Calvin Johnson sent the sold out Ranger crowd home disappointed by scoring a game-high 28 points.

The Rangers then opened the conference season at Marion. The Rangers came away with an easy victory, 71-54. Steve Stewart led the Benton attack by scoring 27 points and grabbing 13 rebounds.

On Friday, December 18th, the Rangers defeated the Herrin Tigers by a score of 70-63. Herrin was led by Gary Rafe, Mike Newbold and a feisty guard by the name of Joe Hosman. Hosman would go on to become one of the greatest coaches in Southern Illinois basketball history. He currently has a career coaching record of (654-335) and is still coaching at Massac County High School, located in Metropolis, Illinois. The Tigers were a year away and considered by many to have a shot at winning the South Seven Conference. It was a quality win for the Rangers.

On Tuesday, December 21, the Carbondale Terriers came to town. The Terriers were a veteran ball club led by Southern Illinois coaching legend David Lee. The Rangers won a tight one behind three key buckets from senior guard Tony Diefenbach and the tenacious rebounding of

Chris Moore. The Rangers were now (5-1) and (3-1) in conference play. It was a good start heading into the Centralia Tournament.

The Rangers opened the Centralia Tournament by defeating New Trier, 73-52. This was Steve Stewart's third Centralia Tournament appearance and it showed. Stewart led the Ranger attack with 31 points and 12 rebounds. Stewart had a history of good performances in the tournament but this one was special. He did it all. The following day the Rangers met the Maroons of Champaign Central. The Rangers had a 57-48 lead with just 2:23 left in the game but the last two minutes proved disastrous. The loss bounced the Rangers out of the tournament. After the game, Herrin commented, "There was not just one thing you could put your finger on, it was just a combination of several things."

After the tournament, the Rangers finished the first loop of conference play by defeating Harrisburg and then Centralia. Sophomore Paul Dinkins had a coming out party by scoring 27 points against the Orphans. With much of the attention of the defense focused on Stewart, Dinkins made the Orphans pay. With the win, the Rangers moved to (7-2) overall and (5-0) in conference play before facing rival West Frankfort. In a crazy game, the Redbirds defeated the Rangers in double-overtime behind the great play of Greg Mitchell, Dave Broy and Jack Warren, by a score of 68-63. After the game, Herrin stated, "This one hurts. We can't afford to lose games like this and expect to win the conference." To end the first loop through conference play, the Rangers nipped the Mt. Vernon Rams at the Snake Pit by a score of 62-61. Junior guard Robert Corn hit four clutch free throws late in the game to seal the win for the Rangers who now led the conference with a 6-1 record at the halfway point.

Robert Corn: *My sophomore year in '71, Denny Smith really took me under his wing and helped in my development as a point guard.*

On Monday, January 20, the Rangers traveled to Fairfield to play the Carmi Bulldogs in the opening game of the Annual Quad City Tournament. The Rangers escaped in double-overtime to win 70-66. David Hurley and Paul Dinkins led the way with 17 points and Steve Stewart chipped in 13. Senior Brandon Webster, who was a charter member of "Harry's Heroes", came in and scored a key basket late in the game. The other charter members of Harry's Heroes stood and pumped their fists as they celebrated Webster's basket on the bench.

Dennis Andrews: *Let's be honest…I sat the bench on those teams. The guys that didn't play a lot went by the name of Harry's* (Coach Stewart's) *Heroes. Brandon Webster was a senior that season and he was a member of the Harry's Heroes squad. He was a good football player that had moved in from Christopher. We were playing someone and we were winning big and Coach Herrin put us in. Brandon got three fouls quickly…then he got his fourth. We hadn't been in the game long. Coach Herrin took Brandon out of the game…Brandon later told a teammate that he couldn't believe Herrin took him out of the game because he was going for five fouls…. A foul was as good as a point… why not five? Fouling was a way to get your name in the paper.*

Another member of Harry's Heroes was guard Kenny "Fly" Summers. Members of the exclusive group cheered on the regulars hoping for wide margins of victory. Two minutes of game time was about as much as a hero could get. Summers explained his mindset when Coach Herrin subbed him in late in games that had already been decided.

Kenny Summers: *I didn't play much…and I was small…but when he put us into the game we would stretch that last two minutes to ten minutes. That was our time…we did anything we could to stop the clock and stay on the floor longer. Some guys fouled on purpose to get in their names in the paper. We pressed on defense and we were always looking for an open shot.*

The following night, the Rangers hammered the McLeansboro Foxes by a score of 85-47. David Hurley led the regulars in scoring with 16 and Paul Dinkins chipped in with 14 points. It was a big night for the Heroes as they received over three minutes of game time. Brandon Webster, Kenny Summers and Mark Zinzilieta ended up in the scoring column. Allan Wisely and Dennis Andrews all had shot attempts, but did not score.

The Rangers advanced to the championship game of the Quad City Tournament to play the Fairfield Mules. The Mules held the ball, and the frustrated Rangers lost at the horn 40-38. Coach Herrin explained his disappointment to sportswriter Bob Tedrow after the game.

Coach Herrin: *Sure we were tired playing three games in a row, but then Fairfield played three games in a row, too.*

Coach Herrin was not a man that made excuses. He held his teams accountable but was careful to never single out an individual player as a reason for a loss. He handled the media well and protected his players by providing only positive comments in the paper. If he couldn't say something positive, he refused to comment. Negative statements were only thrown at the team as a whole. For example, after the Fairfield game he said, "We didn't meet the challenge head on." "We" included everyone; players and coaches.

The Rangers entered the second half of the conference season with a record of (11-4). On Friday, January 28, 1972, the struggling Marion Wildcats came staggering in to the Cracker Box. They provided little resistance for the Rangers. Steve Stewart netted 25 points and hauled in 14 rebounds as the Rangers dominated the blue and gold by a score of 78-62. Robert Corn added 15 points and Chris Moore chipped in 14. The next night the Rangers traveled to West Frankfort seeking payback for an earlier loss at home. A large crowd at Max Morris gymnasium booed as the Rangers circled the floor to begin their pre-game warm-up. Leonard Hopkins scored a game-high 22 points as the Redbirds sent the Rangers home scratching their heads. In the conference race, the Rangers were now tied for first place with the Herrin Tigers with a 7-2 conference record. Coach Herrin made this comment after the game:

Coach Herrin: *The loss really hurts. We've got our backs against the wall now. The thing we have to do right now is beat Herrin Friday night.*

The Rangers did just that. Playing with a chip on their shoulder, and defending their winning culture, the young Rangers stuck it to the Tigers by a score of 69-57. It was a quality road victory and the win thrust the Rangers into the driver's seat of the conference race. Steve Stewart was carrying the club. He was consistently the leading scorer and rebounder in most games. He was playing his best basketball and providing leadership through his play.

Billy Smith: *Steve Stewart led our team in points and rebounds. Steve just had great hands. He was an average jumper, but he had incredible timing and great hands. He was very smooth. He was the last of the great bank shooters.*

The Rangers traveled to Johnston City on February 5, 1972, for a non-conference match-up against the Indians. The Rangers won easily and seniors Steve Stewart and Tony Diefenbach led the scoring for the Rangers.

In the second quarter, Herrin looked down the bench and barked "Billy… give Hurley a breather." The young freshman had been pulled up since the West Frankfort game but this was the first quality minutes Smith played at the varsity level. Billy Smith came into the game and scored a quick bucket and then scored two more field goals in the fourth quarter. It was the beginning of one of the greatest careers in Ranger basketball history. But on this night in Johnston City, the timing of that simple substitution provided the perfect opportunity for him to succeed.

Why did Herrin insert Billy into the varsity line-up at this point in the season? Bringing a freshman to the varsity level is a huge decision. Coach Herrin was the master at placing players in situations where they could succeed. Herrin was very aware of his player's mental make-up and he seemed to have a way of pulling players up at the right time. He could sense if a player lacked confidence. Herrin saw his chance to insert Billy into the line-up and it was a premeditated plan. He slipped Billy in a non-conference game on the road. It was a more relaxed environment than the loud Cracker Box at home. Billy responded. With that decision, Herrin placed Billy in the best possible situation for him to succeed.

Chris Moore: *Billy was so quick. He was quiet and he could be mischievous in a good sort of way. He fit in well with us.*

On February 11th, the Rangers traveled to Davenport Gymnasium to play the Harrisburg Bulldogs. Southern Illinoisan sports writer Merle Jones predicted in his column a day earlier that "The lights would have to go out in Davenport Gymnasium for Harrisburg to defeat Benton." Jones had set the trap. David Hurley recalled that frustrating night in Harrisburg when nothing went right.

David Hurley: *We played a very sloppy first half and we had no energy. Coach Herrin lit into us at halftime and reminded us about how important the game was if we were going to win the conference. Marion and Harrisburg were the worst two teams in the conference that season. We came out in the second half and we were still playing sloppy. I remember Stewart dribbled the ball down the floor and shot an air ball from the top of the key. I was sitting by Coach Herrin on the bench and he grabbed me and told me to go in for Stewart. It was the first time Steve had been taken out all year. He wasn't expecting to come out of the game and I remember tapping him on the shoulder…he gave me a surprised look. I said, "Hey…your dad wants you." So what do I* *do? About two possessions later I shoot an air ball...Rich takes me out but I always kid Steve that I was the guy that got to replace him. It was that kind of night...we just got beat and shouldn't have."*

The Bulldogs won the contest by a score of 62-60. After the game, the Bulldogs and their fans couldn't hide their excitement. It was the biggest win of the year for the Bulldogs and a spontaneous celebration began taking place as Bulldog fans flooded the floor. The Rangers sluggishly walked off the floor in disbelief and wandered down the narrow corridor leading to their locker room.

This was the low point of the season. They had squandered a great opportunity to take a firm hold on the league and now had to win-out with three games remaining to have a chance of winning the conference. The young team's response to the loss would determine their fate. The team responded. Again, the tradition of excellence inspired the players to pick themselves up by their bootstraps and get the job done.

On February 12th, the Rangers welcomed the Centralia Orphans to town. The Rangers had a slow start but fought out of their funk and finished the Orphans off in front of a capacity crowd. By this time, Ranger fans were educated basketball fans and they knew the conference was at stake. Ranger fans were loud and created a tough environment for the visiting Orphans. The Rangers won the ballgame behind balanced scoring from the regulars. It was a much-needed win for a team that willed themselves thru a difficult stretch of play. It was as if they had broken the spell and returned to their former selves. The following Friday the Rangers traveled to Carbondale and won 61-52. Dink led the Rangers with 20 points and Stewart chipped in 15.

The following night, the Rangers hosted the Mt. Vernon Rams. It was senior night. Tony Diefenbach, Brandon Webster and Steve Stewart were honored before the game. Diefenbach had a solid season for the Rangers and the fans stood to show their appreciation after public address announcer B.L. Finley announced his name. Brandon Webster was then introduced. The Heroes encouraged the crowd to come alive and Webster received a nice ovation for his commitment to the program. Then it was Stewart's turn. As Stewart waited for Finley to announce his name, his mind must have been filled with a collage of memories. The fans stood and gave it a little extra knowing this would be the last time they would witness his smooth gait and soft touch off the glass.

When the celebration was over, there was an overwhelming energy among the Ranger faithful that must have been felt by the visiting Rams. But the Rams played tough and forced the game into overtime. The Rangers won the game 71-63. If you were a Ranger fan, you had to be excited about the future of Benton basketball. At the end of the game, there was only one senior on the floor for the Rangers. The future looked bright.

It was over. The young Rangers under the leadership of Steve Stewart and Robert Corn had done it. They were South Seven Champions. The Rangers finished the regular season with a record of 17-6 and won the conference crown by just one game over Herrin. Coach Herrin was jubilant after the game when he met with local reporters. He had to know that he and his coaching staff squeezed everything possible out of the young team. After the game, Coach Herrin had these comments:

Coach Herrin: *The thing that makes it even sweeter is that we weren't supposed to win the conference. It's a great way for seniors like Steve Stewart, Tony Diefenbach and Brandon Webster to end their careers. When these boys look back on their high school playing days they'll always be able to say proudly that their team won the South Seven Conference."*

Next up for the Rangers was the Regional Tournament at Herrin.

The '72 Regional Tournament

In the new class system, Benton had an enrollment slightly above the 750 cut-off line. This placed the Rangers in the Class AA Division which represented the bigger schools. The Rangers now played stiff competition from the start. There were no patsies. To advance to the Regional Championship, the Rangers had to beat Herrin a third time. It would be a tough task.

The Tigers had the Rangers at home and the Herrin faithful came out in droves to see their Tigers put an end to the Rangers season. The game was back and forth and then came to a climactic end. Robert Corn vividly remembered the ending of one of the craziest games in Benton basketball history.

Robert Corn: *It was one of the most draining games I ever played. Steve hit a long jumper to keep our season alive and tie the game in regulation. He then hit another one to tie in the first overtime. The game was tied when I hit the shot.... If I missed that last shot we would have just gone into another overtime. Steve's shots to tie the game were do or die.*

Ranger fans were so charged up after the game that something happened that has never repeated in Ranger history.

David Hurley: *On the way home. The game was such an emotional win... the fans gathered on the square and waited for the team bus. We were given a police escort around the square after winning the first game of the Regional. Maybe the only time that has ever happened.*

The team was sky-high coming off their narrow escape against Herrin. The win advanced them to the Regional finals to play the Murphysboro Red Devils. The Red Devils were coached by Tom Ashman and they were a solid club that was a year away from really being special. In a nip and tuck game, the Rangers defeated the Devils, 72-69, to win the Herrin Regional. Stewart led the young Rangers with 21 points and 11 rebounds. Freshman Billy Smith scored eight points in the final quarter. It was a gritty performance by the young freshman that the team desperately needed. Chris Moore and Steve McCommons were steady as usual in the post.

Junior Robert Corn made huge plays in critical moments of the game. Corn was 11-12 from the free throw line and ended the night with 13 points. Most importantly, Corn did a good job of getting Stewart the ball in scoring situations. The Ranger floor general finished the game with seven assists. Diefenbach chipped in six points and Hurley added two. It was a total team effort. The team came home to an excited fan base and enjoyed their second fire truck escort around the square in just three days.

The Rangers opened Sectional play against the winner of the Harrisburg Regional. As fate would have it, the winner was the West Frankfort Redbirds. The Birds had beaten the Rangers twice in '72, now they had to beat them again. The casual fan might think that the Redbirds would be pleased with the Sectional match-up with the Rangers, but that was just not the case. Many of the Redbird players were thinking, "Oh no, not again." The game would be at West Frankfort in Max Morris Gymnasium. But that didn't matter. The elephant in the room was the history between the two teams. The Rangers had owned the Redbirds in tournament play since Rich Herrin first arrived at Benton, in the fall of 1960. Yes, the Redbirds had beaten the Rangers twice during the season, but the Redbirds knew the history. Rich Herrin's teams seemed to always find a way and it was a huge psychological edge for the Rangers. Dave Broy, Leonard Hopkins, Greg Mitchell and Jack Warren were all key players for the Redbirds in '72. Dave Broy recalled what he felt upon learning of their match up against the Rangers in the first game of the Sectional Tournament in '72.

Dave Broy (WF Guard): *Matt, I can tell you right now that we didn't know if we could beat Benton a third time. We always felt like we were about ten points down to start the game because they had Rich. I'll tell you this… many years after that game, I came to be friends with Coach Herrin. I'll never forget that he named off all of my teammates. He still remembered our team. You know what that told me? Think about how prepared he was for us when that game started…and some thirty years later he remembers the names of my teammates. He was special.*

Over 5,000 fans packed Max Morris Gymnasium to see the two Franklin County heavyweights slug it out. Redbird player Dave Broy had an incredible performance and led all scorers with 28 points. Robert Corn turned in a key defensive effort by holding Leonard Hopkins to just one field goal for the night. Hopkins scored 22 points against the Rangers in their last meeting. The game went down to the wire, but the Rangers found a way again. It was a devastating loss for the Redbirds, who won two out of three meetings for the year.

Steve Stewart fought to keep his season alive and scored a team-high 21 points and pulled down 12 rebounds. Robert Corn had 12 points along with ten assists. Chris Moore turned in a solid performance, adding ten points while grabbing eight rebounds. The Rangers were playing well, winning close games, and peaking at the right time. One more victory, and the young team that many thought would struggle, could advance to the Sweet Sixteen.

With the win, the Rangers advanced to the '72 Sectional Championship to play the Mascoutah Indians guided by legendary coach John Thouvenin. The Indians had size and came into the game with a record of 27-1. In the first half, Mascoutah's size bothered the Rangers and they took a commanding lead of 37-23 by halftime. The Rangers battled back to close within 11 to start the fourth quarter but the Indians were too big and too experienced. In his final game as a Ranger, Steve Stewart scored 12 points and grabbed 8 rebounds. Chris Moore chipped in ten points.

It was a quiet locker room as the Rangers showered and prepared to board the bus for the short trip back to Benton. Coach Herrin made these comments after the game:

Coach Herrin: *This has been a great year and I think the unselfish attitude of all our players has been the key to our success.*

After high school, Tony Diefenbach found work as a coal miner. At the present time, Tony and his wife, Anita, live in Macedonia. They have three sons; Trampas, Destry and Orrie. Trampas was a member of the '92 team that placed third in the State Tournament.

Senior Forward Brandon Webster stayed in the area and worked in the coal mines and was an accomplished electrician. Unfortunately, Webster passed away at only fifty-six years of age.

Steve Stewart went on to play basketball at Louisiana College. He majored in education and became a teacher and coach. Stewart served as the head basketball coach at Murphysboro High School from 1985-1994. He is now retired and lives with his wife Cathy in Benton, Illinois. They have two sons; Greg and Sean.

The '72 Rangers kept the tradition alive by going (20-7), winning the South Seven Conference and a Regional Championship. The team achieved at a high level despite being young and inexperienced and made memories that would last a lifetime. There were players returning that had gained valuable experience and there were good young players anxious to place their mark on the program. Ranger fans were excited and optimistic about the future of Benton basketball.

Robert Corn provided leadership and toughness from the point guard position in the early 70's. *(Ceasar Maragni)*

Steve Stewart was one of the best players in the state and the senior leader of the '72 team. *(Ceasar Maragni)*

Junior, Chris Moore, gave the '72 Rangers solid post play.
(Ceasar Maragni)

Junior guard, David Hurley, provided great play at the
shooting guard position. *(Ceasar Maragni)*

Sophomore gym rat, Paul Dinkins, came up with some big offensive nights in '72. *(Ceasar Maragni)*

Sophomore, Steve McCommons, teamed with Chis Moore in the post. *(Ceasar Maragni)*

Junior guard, Kenny Summers, loved to play the game.
(Ceasar Maragni)

Dennis Andrews went to the games as a youngster and always
dreamed of being a Benton Ranger. *(Ceasar Maragni)*

Coach Herrin provides the '72 team with some encouragement.
(Ceasar Maragni)

The great Billy Smith as a freshman. *(Ceasar Maragni)*

After losing key players to graduation, the '72 Rangers won the
South Seven, captured a Regional Championship and
finished the season 20-7. (Ceasar Maragni)

CHAPTER EIGHTEEN

The Last Year in the Cracker Box

"I loved the old gym. It was the greatest home court advantage a team could have. The benches were on the ends.... I can still smell it." – Paul Dinkins

In 1968, School administrators and the BCHS Board of Education began to discuss the idea of building a new 43-classroom school that would accommodate up to 900 students. The building plan included a multi-purpose gymnasium that could seat 4,000 people. School officials projected that more gym seating could bring in an extra twenty thousand dollars per year. The Cracker Box only seated 1,163 fans and ranked last in the South Seven Conference in gym capacity by more than 1,800 students. Unfortunately, the project was going to be tough to pull off. The projected cost of the build was close to 1.9 million dollars. In 1968, that was big money and the BCHS Board of Education was divided on the building project. In fact, an article from a board member that opposed the building project appeared in the Benton Evening News just days before taxpayers were to vote on the issue.

Coach Herrin was very much for the building of the new school because it included a new state-of-the-art gymnasium for his players. He thought it made perfect sense that a good team should play in a good gymnasium and on December 13, 1968, he let his feelings be known. In a packed house at the Cracker Box, fans rose to their feet ready for the Rangers to take the floor. Herrin gave each one of his player's placards that supported the building of the new school. Most of the signs said something simple like, "VOTE YES" and every townsperson knew what the "yes" meant. The dilemma of whether to build the new school was the talk of the town. The players held the placards high and walked slowly around the gym, clearly indicating to Benton fans that the basketball program was in full support of the construction of the new school. The players supported the idea because they were all in favor of a new gymnasium.

The next day, on Saturday, December 14th, the citizens of Benton poured into six different voting sites to cast their ballots for or against the building of a new school, along with a new gymnasium. When the smoke cleared, there were 1,806 yeas to 1,682 nays. Benton was to have a new school and most importantly for Herrin, a new gymnasium that he would help design. The actual construction of the new school was slow and there were several glitches but it was possible the new school could open in the fall of 1973.

The success of the basketball Rangers had much to do with the building of the new school. Beginning in the fall of 1965, the Rangers were the hottest ticket in town. Because tickets were so tough to come by, some Benton fans gave up on attempting to attend home games. There were parents of players on the opposing teams that were turned away at the door. The situation was embarrassing.

To the team itself, the Cracker Box was an unbelievable home court advantage. The small floor, the restraining line, the permanent railing down the sides were all unique and gave opponents fits, but it was clear that with a greater facility the Rangers could generate more money to put into the coffers. By 1973, Ranger fans were letting go of the nostalgic feel of the Cracker Box and embracing the idea of a bigger and better gymnasium. Times were changing and the Rangers were ready for a new home.

When practice began in late November, the team looked different. The glaring difference was the graduation of Steve Stewart, who was the first Ranger to play four years of varsity basketball. Stewart was gone to Louisiana College. Steady guard Tony Diefenbach was also lost to graduation along with Harry's Hero legend, Brandon Webster.

Seniors Robert Corn and David Hurley were back with a full year of varsity experience under their belts at the guard positions. Senior Chris Moore was also back and would provide quality post play in '73. Steve McCommons was now a junior and was expected to be the Rangers enforcer in the paint. Junior Paul Dinkins had an incredible sophomore season and returned at the small forward position. Billy Smith was now a sophomore and was the most talented underclassman in Southern Illinois. The '73 season looked promising.

Added to the mix of regulars was junior guard Scott Hall. Scott pointed out that he was the product of great coaches as far back as sixth grade and this helped his development as a young player.

Scott Hall: *We lived on 615 Mitchell Street and Bob Gariepy lived right across the street from us. He was a good man and a great fan and he was always very vocal at the games. Gene Alexander was my sixth grade coach. In the seventh grade I played for Bob Johnston and it was like playing for your uncle. He was awesome to play for and he was a good coach. We finished 17-0. My eighth grade year I played for Burton Wills. He was a fantastic coach. I never trained or ran so much in my life. I think one day we literally ran like eighty laps around the gym. We only had one loss our eighth grade year and that was to Herrin in the state championship. It was a devastating loss.*

Scott was the younger brother of Wiley Hall, who was of one of the finest floor generals in Ranger history. As a junior, Wiley was the starting point guard on the great '61 team. Although they were twelve years removed in age, Scott inherited several of the attributes that made his older brother such a great player.

Billy Smith: *Scott had great quickness. He was a good defender…confident in himself and a vocal leader.*

Scott Hall: *Wiley was older than me and I worshipped the ground he walked on…he was more like a parent. One of the very first memories I have of my brother was seeing him on TV when the '61 team went to State. There was a close up picture of him shooting free throws. I also remember being on my tricycle and seeing him walking home from school wearing his letterman's jacket. He would pick me up and just play around with me.*

Hall was not pulled up immediately with classmates Paul Dinkins and Steve McCommons. It was Coach Herrin's plan to give Hall game experience at the underclass level and then bring him up to the big club as a junior. It worked. As a junior, Hall fit in nicely with the '73 Rangers as the first guard off the bench. He proved to be a solid back-up at the point position to Robert Corn.

Scott Hall: *All of my buddies like Dink and McCommons got pulled up as freshmen and sophomores…at first that bothered me a little. I loved playing for Coach Webb as a freshman. He was really young at the time…not much older than us. I also enjoyed Coach Phillips my sophomore year. It worked out for the best.*

Seniors Allan Wisely, Dennis Andrews and Kenny Summers were also back in '73. It was their job to stay positive and put the team first and that is exactly what they did. Being a reserve player can be the most overlooked and underappreciated duty on a team but the Heroes hung in there and pushed the regulars in practice. Their commitment to the team earned the respect of the regulars and they played a crucial role in creating a winning chemistry. Juniors Mark Manis, Jim Armey and Steve Genisio joined the Heroes and they fit in well. Manis was a stand-out football player and mixed it up with Chris Moore and Steve McCommons every day in practice. Again, Coach Herrin had a team of guys that were more like family, just like he wanted it.

'73 Season

The '73 season opened against Sparta on December 2, 1972. It was a packed house at the Cracker Box as Ranger fans got their first glimpse of the '73 Rangers. The Rangers romped the Bulldogs by a score of 97-52 behind 27 points from sophomore Billy Smith. It was a statement game for Smith and it left Benton fans wondering just how good Smith could be the next two seasons. The sky was the limit. Senior David Hurley added 18 points and Junior Paul Dinkins added 15 points. The Rangers were 1-0.

Unfortunately, the first win of the season came with a cost. Senior floor general Robert Corn collided with Paul Dinkins and broke his right hand trying to brace his fall. Coach Herrin wrapped Corn's hand with tape and to Corn's credit, he finished the game. After the game, x-rays revealed that he had broken his hand on the small finger side, near his wrist. As a senior, Corn was a physical specimen and with the flat-top he had the look of a young marine. Corn brought toughness to the team and was the unquestioned leader of the '73 squad.

Robert Corn: *The injury affected me more mentally than physically. It was my right hand…and I got to the point where I wasn't looking to score…but I learned to play with it.*

During my interview with Dinkins, Paul made a point to tell me the psychological warfare that the Rangers unleashed on their opponents that he felt was sometimes overlooked. He believed that this was a contest that the Rangers seldom lost.

Paul Dinkins: *One thing I remember about Benton basketball was we delivered the message that we were there to win before the game ever started. Our team all wore short haircuts even when the long hair was coming back in style in the mid-seventies. It was part of being a Ranger. When the starting lineups were announced, we sprinted off the bench. It sent the message that…we are the Benton Rangers and we are here to win.*

In '73, the Rangers wore maroon turtle necks under a gold blazer that had a patch on the left breast that said, "Benton". The Rangers were always aware of whom they represented and that their presentation projected a message. Coach Herrin used this to the team's advantage. When watching the Rangers enter the gym, it was normal for opponents to think, "They look like they are going to be a tough team to beat." This was the message that Coach Herrin wanted to convey: "We are here, we are ready to play!"

Chris Moore: *I remember in '73 that we went to go see Coach Herrin about not getting our haircuts and he said, "Don't get your haircuts…I'll just play the sophomores." So we all headed uptown to get our short haircuts.*

To begin the game, the Rangers took the floor accompanied by the song, "Sweet Georgia Brown". The opposing teams stared down at the Rangers thinking, "That's cool, and why don't we run out to music?" They looked like the Harlem Globetrotters. It was entertainment and it was marketed to all. After the drills were completed, young boys gathered under the basket to retrieve the players' shots, hoping they would get the chance to make a pass to their hero. It was not only a ballgame, it was a show, and the players were the main actors. Most of the time, they performed well.

Dennis Andrews: *We ran out to "Sweet Georgia Brown" and we would do the split the post thing and Billy and Robert alternated as the passers. Kyle Herrin was our mascot and one night we ran out to start the game…we were ready to do our split the post drill and Kenny Summers turned around and said, "Where's Kyle?" We were looking for him and spotted him on the bench crying. We ran over him…didn't even know it.*

After the opener against Sparta, the Rangers won their next three games and were 4-0 going to Herrin before Christmas. The Rangers were still without Robert Corn. The Tigers were coached by former Ranger Jeff Ferguson and they were the pre-season favorite to win the conference. The Tigers were loaded. Joe Hosman, Mike Newbold and Gary Rafe led the Tigers' attack and they defeated the Rangers 63-53 in front of a standing room only crowd at Herrin. The Tigers were the real deal in '73 and they would run the table in the South Seven to finish a perfect 14-0 in conference play. They are still remembered as one of the greatest teams in Herrin history.

The Rangers were 4-1 heading to the Centralia Tournament. On Thursday, December 28, 1972, the Rangers methodically disposed of Stephen Decatur by a score of 62-51. The game marked the return of senior leader Robert Corn. Corn only shot the ball once, but did go 5-7 from the free throw line. The return of Corn was a booster shot for the team's confidence and morale.

The next day, the Rangers defeated Pinckneyville 60-59 behind 23 points from Paul Dinkins and 15 points from Billy Smith. The Rangers were in control for most of the game but the Panthers didn't quit and pulled within one point late in the game. The Panthers fouled Corn hoping that the injury would affect his free throw shooting, but the senior hit two huge free throws to put the game away. It was a testament to the confidence that Coach Herrin had in Corn to leave him on the floor. But Herrin knew his personnel and he knew Corn could handle the situation. The Rangers were now 6-1 and heading into the semi-final game of the Centralia Tournament. The Rangers were winning, Corn was back and the Ranger fans were excited. Could the Rangers win another Centralia Tournament championship?

Scott Hall: *Robert and I were buddies…I always looked up to him. He was just physically big and strong. He was a great point guard…so steady…in total command of the team. He was always in the action and for a guard he was big enough to be a good rebounder.*

In the semi-finals, the Rangers met the Mt. Vernon Rams. The Rangers came away with a 64-53 victory behind 16 points from Dink and Smith. The story of the game may have been the gritty play of Robert Corn. It was evident that Corn's hand was affecting his willingness to shoot from the field but he was finding other ways to contribute. In the Mt. Vernon game, he led the team with eleven rebounds and dished out nine assists. He was also 7-9 from the foul line and had nine points. Robert Corn was a guy you wanted in your foxhole and his play was inspiring his teammates.

The win over Mt. Vernon set up one of the most exciting championship games in tournament history as the Rangers met the Belleville West Maroons. Belleville had one of the state's best players in Milton Wiley, and truth be told, they were the favorite despite the Rangers' storied success in the tournament. Wiley was a sophomore and many fans awaited the match-up between Billy Smith and Milton Wiley. In a packed house, the Rangers led by only three at halftime. Dinkins and Corn fouled out in regulation, but the Rangers held on to win their fourth tournament title by a score of 64-61.

Billy Smith: *I probably had the most fun as a sophomore. We won the Centralia Tournament and beat Belleville West and they had Milton Wiley. There was no pressure...defensively I could take chances.*

After the game, a jubilant Coach Herrin stated, "Defense is what did it for us." There is nothing like being around Coach after a big win. It is impossible for him to contain his excitement. In the locker room following the game, jubilant Ranger players and coaches gave congratulatory hugs and handshakes. Winning the Centralia Tournament was a big deal and this was a victory that had to be celebrated. Paul Dinkins scored 68 points in the tournament and was the third leading scorer, just ahead of Smith who scored 65, good for fifth, but Herrin was quick to credit all of his players for the role they played in the victory. These were his comments in the January 2, 1973, edition of the Benton Evening news:

Coach Herrin: *Every player did an outstanding job. Chris Moore had a great tournament. Steve McCommons did a good job, especially against Mt. Vernon. David Hurley was best by the way he sagged on the weak side on defense. Paul Dinkins and Billy Smith were our big scorers. Bob Corn, even with his bad hand, did a good job of taking charge and running our game, and then Scotty Hall came off the bench several times and put some new life in our attack.*

Paul Dinkins and Billy Smith were named to the five-man All-Tournament team. Most importantly, the '73 Rangers were building confidence and playing good basketball. In the Benton Evening News, there was a picture of the team taken immediately after their victory. The trophy is front and center. Dinkins and Smith have the game nets draped around their necks with wide grins. To show his excitement, Big Steve McCommons is on one knee with both fists up. Mac is grinning from ear to ear. Corn is front and center with a look of relief on his face. It was the second Championship picture at Centralia for Corn. He had been a reserve on the '71 team. As they pose for the picture, Hurley and Dinkins have their hands grasped together. A young Kyle Herrin kneels in front of his idol Billy Smith. Little does he know that he will win the Tournament as a senior in '83, marking the last time the Rangers would win the prestigious Centralia Tournament. Coach Herrin has been in countless championship pictures, but his wide grin is telling of the excitement he feels after winning his fourth Centralia Championship Trophy. Winning never gets old for Coach Herrin.

After winning the tournament, the Rangers had a letdown. They traveled to Carbondale and the Terriers upset the Rangers, 43-39. David Lee's Terriers slowed the game down and simply outplayed the Rangers. It was an unexpected loss that hurt the Rangers' chances of winning a third straight conference crown. Herrin made a great point to the papers after the game.

Coach Herrin: *I guess this is one of the things you have to expect when you are a winner. Every time we go onto the floor we become a target for anything. Teams just get up a little higher when they play us. But then I would rather be in this position than be a loser all of the time. We'll pay the penalty of being the target if we can be a winner each year.*

After the Carbondale loss, the Rangers fell to 8-2 but both losses were to conference foes. True to most of Herrin's teams after a loss, the Rangers rebounded and won there next three games by defeating Harrisburg, Centralia and West Frankfort.

On Saturday January 20, 1973, the Mt. Vernon Rams came to the Cracker Box with a score to settle. The Rams jumped to a quick 15-8 lead behind the play of Louis Lidell, but the Rangers fought back and won the game by a score of 52-48. It wasn't easy. Robert Corn nailed down the win with two clutch free throws to seal the win with .05 seconds left in the game. The Rangers were now 12-2 overall, and 5-2 in the South Seven. They were back in the race.

The Rangers then traveled to Jacksonville, Illinois for their mid-winter tournament. The Rangers went 2-1 and their only loss was to a tough Edwardsville team. The Rangers were now 14-3 before beginning their second loop through the tough South Seven Conference.

Chris Moore was now a senior and had developed into a quality post player. Moore was solid on the defensive end and always played hard. Kenny Summers remembers a good story about Chris Moore that occurred when they were all sophomores playing for Coach Stewart. Dennis Andrews confirmed the story.

Kenny Summers: *Our sophomore year over Christmas break, we had a couple of days off…we were playing on the sophomore team…he told us not to do anything stupid and get hurt. So…they just put a new parking lot in at Rend Lake College. Smooth asphalt and concrete as far as you could see. Myself, Chis and Dennis Andrews all had go-carts…we decided to take them out to Rend Lake and run them on the new parking lots. So we go out there…it's like the Indy 500, you know…we are going full throttle. Chris wore a scarf… we would get on to him about it…but that was his way. Chris is going full speed…he looks back and his scarf gets caught in the engine and it ripped the scarf off of his neck. He is lucky it didn't kill him, you know. We come back for practice and Chris has this big burn mark wrapped around his neck…and he was having trouble turning his neck. It didn't look good…I mean it wasn't something he could hide. I didn't say anything…but Coach Herrin found out the story somehow. He called us in and told us there would be no go-cart riding the rest of the season.*

Junior center Steve McCommons was a bull in the paint. He was a fierce competitor and enjoyed contact. McCommons never backed down from a challenge and played the role of the enforcer. But it was his work ethic that ultimately won the trust and respect of his teammates.

Scott Hall: *Bobby and Burton worked like heck with Steve, and Mac started as an eighth grader. They really transformed him as a player and I always loved playing with Mac. I loved physically being under his wing…I always felt safe around Mac. I remember about once or twice a year we would go over to Steve's and his mother Lodema would fix us these amazing spaghetti dinners. She was always so good to us. His father Van was very quiet and unassuming.*

David Hurley: *Steve moved to Benton in the seventh grade. He really wanted to learn how to play basketball and I can remember Burton Wills keeping him after practice and making him run. Steve took it. He really wanted to play.*

To begin the second loop through the conference the Rangers defeated Marion and then West Frankfort to set up a meeting with the Herrin Tigers. The Tigers came to Benton and they were undefeated in the conference. In my interview with Billy Smith, he told me that out of all the games he played in his high school career, his favorite memory occurred in this game.

Billy Smith: *My favorite memory was my sophomore year in the old gym. I stole the ball from Joe Hosman at half-court. He came after me and fouled me and I made the lay-up.*

The Rangers fell behind early but rallied to start the second half and actually pulled ahead 44-43 with 3:40 left in the third quarter. From this point on the game was nip and tuck but three Rangers fouled out late in the game: Chris Moore, Steve McCommons and Robert Corn. Herrin guard Joe Hosman hit two big free throws with .27 seconds left in the game to put the Tigers ahead for good. On this night, junior center Gary Rafe was the best player on the floor. Rafe led all scorers with 28 points helping the Tigers stay undefeated in conference play. Chris Moore led the Rangers in scoring with 14 points. The Rangers were just 2-9 from the free throw line, but overall, Coach Herrin took the loss in stride.

Coach Herrin: *If you're ever pleased with a loss then I guess I'm pleased. We played a pretty fine basketball game.*

The Rangers then won their next three games against Harrisburg, Centralia and Carbondale. In the Harrisburg game the Rangers won big, 96-57, and all of Harry's Heroes broke into the scoring column. Seniors Allan Wisley, Kenny Summers and Dennis Andrews scored a combined ten points and got to play the entire fourth quarter of the game. The Heroes were all over the floor knowing that this could be the last minutes of their careers. The regulars cheered in support of their teammates. It was a feel-good night for the Rangers.

At Centralia, the Rangers won the game by a score of 77-49, but Paul Dinkins suffered a severely sprained ankle. The sprain was so severe that Dinkins missed the final three games of the regular season. Again, all of the reserves played and everyone got into the scoring column with the exception of Kenny Summers. On this night in Centralia, sophomore Rob Dunbar scored his first varsity basket. For the next two years, Dunbar would be the centerpiece of the Ranger attack.

The Terriers tried to hold the ball once again but the Rangers built a 29-8 lead entering the fourth quarter and never looked back. Chris Moore led the Rangers in scoring with 14 points.

The win against Carbondale set up the last game of the conference season at Mt. Vernon. The Rangers were now 19-5 and 10-3 in the South Seven Conference. They had beaten the Rams twice and both games had been physical. It was a match-up between two teams that didn't care that much for each other and that is exactly how it played out at Changnon Gymnasium. The Rangers were without 6'5" marksman Paul Dinkins and the game did not have any meaning in the conference standings. But it was 1974 and it was the Rangers against the Rams. It was possibly the greatest rivalry in the conference. The play was physical and the Rangers held a slight 35-32 halftime lead. With the absence of Dinkins, Coach Herrin was worried about foul trouble. Steve McCommons picked up his fourth foul right before the end of the first half.

Scott Hall: *We were at Mt. Vernon. Mac had four fouls at halftime.... We go in at halftime and I can still hear Coach Herrin with that booming voice: "McCommons you have four fouls...don't get another foul." I can still see it... we are just seconds into the second half and Mac shoots one and the guy guarding him turns and boxes him out. The ball is short and bounces off the front right back at Mac...but not long enough for Mac to jump up and get to it. At this point, I just remember everything went in slow motion...as I saw Mac reach over this kid's back and just clobber him.*

Chris Moore and Rams player Ed Sanders had been shoving each other most of the night. The frustration Sanders felt came to a boiling point in the third quarter.

David Hurley: *We were behind and we needed to make something happen. We didn't want to press but we were forced to and they had trouble with it. The game had been really physical. Guys were leaning into each other before free throws were shot and grappling for position. The officials had to warn both teams several times. Dinkins was hurt. Robert Corn drove the baseline and Ram player Ed Sanders elbowed Corn and knocked him unconscious. I just remember seeing Corn laying there and Coach Stewart came off the bench and just immediately walked out onto the floor...he was not happy. Everyone moved away from Robert when Coach Stewart came onto the floor. They had to wake Robert up by giving him smelling salts. It was the first* *time I had ever seen it done. We won the game and had to have a police escort to the bus.*

Ed Sanders was ejected from the game. Sanders scored 25 points in the game and the Rams didn't put up much of a fight after the incident was over. The Rangers nursed a ten-point lead and held on to win a crazy game by the score of 67-59. With the win, the Rangers finished second behind Herrin with an 11-3 conference record and extended their consistent streak of 20-win seasons. On the way home, the seniors ordered the underclassman to sit near the bus windows just in case Ram fans decided to "rock" the bus on the way out of town.

The final game in the old gym was on Friday March 2, 1973. The Rangers played host to the 21-4 Effingham Flaming Hearts, champions of the Mid-Eight Conference. As usual, it was packed and there was a sentimental feel to the game since it was slated to be the final boys' basketball contest to be played at the Cracker Box. Built in 1942, it had been a huge home-court advantage and the home of some of the greatest games to ever be played in Ranger history.

Paul Dinkins: *I loved the old gym. It was the greatest home court advantage a team could have. The benches were on the ends...I can still smell it.*

Despite the fact that the gym was in its final hours, there was no ceremony or special recognition given to the gym's existence. Along with the closing of the gym it was also senior night. It was the last home game for a special senior group; Robert Corn, Chris Moore, David Hurley, Allan Wisely, Kenny Summers and Dennis Andrews. They had carried the torch well.

Robert Corn: *You know I don't remember a ceremony of any kind. I don't know if we knew for sure it would be the last game...depending on the construction of the new school.*

In the final game at the Cracker Box, the Rangers jumped on the Flaming Hearts and led 24-7 at the end of the first quarter. The game was expected to be close but the Rangers played exceptionally well and closed the gym out in style with a 79-63 win over Effingham. Chris Moore led the Rangers with 20 points followed by Steve McCommons'15 points. The real question is this: who scored the last basket in the old gym? The scorebook indicates that it could have been Scott Hall, Allan Wisely or possibly sophomore Rob Dunbar. The Rangers finished the '73 regular season at 21-4. It was another great season.

Despite the 21-4 record, the Rangers were the third seed in the Herrin Regional and were matched up with the Murphysboro Red Devils. The Red Devils had come of age and they were state-ranked under the direction of longtime coach, Tom Ashman.

On Monday, March 5, 1973, Benton fans were jumpy when they heard over the radio that "Billie Smith" was admitted to the hospital. However, the hospital patient was a woman with that name. Ranger fans breathed a sigh of relief and realized that their beloved "Billy" was healthy and ready for the first game of the Regional. Unfortunately Paul Dinkins wasn't. Dink would play but was still hobbled by the ankle sprain he had suffered at Centralia two weeks earlier.

The Rangers were trailing by only two points at halftime but the Red Devils came out in the second half and outscored the Rangers 23-14 in the third quarter and cruised to a 66-60 win. In all fairness to the Rangers, it was an extremely tough draw out of the gate. The Red Devils were a strong team led by Dan Sullivan and Martin Bankhead. It was extremely disappointing to lose in the first game of the Regional after going 21-4 in the regular season. It didn't seem fair.

Robert Corn: *I was just really disappointed after that game. Coach Herrin's teams always won the Regional and I just hated that we didn't get that done.*

Allan Wisely: *I do remember the Murphysboro game. I didn't play that much but Coach put me in at the end of the game. I think everyone recalls their last game.*

After his playing days were over, Robert Corn became close friends with Coach Herrin and he was emotional when he told me about what Coach meant to him.

Robert Corn: *There were four men in my life that have had great influence. My dad, my brother Dick, Coach Gene Bartow and Coach Herrin. Anytime I come back to Benton that is usually my first stop…to see Coach and Sue. Coach taught me that it was okay for my players to see me outside of basketball. Coach Herrin and Sue made their home open to all of us. Coach Herrin came to Puerto Rico and coached with me. He always made it about family.*

After high school, Robert Corn received a scholarship to play basketball at Memphis State University. While at Memphis State, he developed a good relationship with Coach Gene Bartow. He was there for two seasons before transferring to Missouri Southern. After graduating from Missouri Southern he accepted a teaching/coaching job at a small country high school. He then explained how one phone call changed his whole career.

Robert Corn: *I was in my office at Mountain Grove High School and I got a phone call from Gene Bartow who had recruited me at Memphis State. He said, 'Did you get my message I left you?'" His initial message hadn't been delivered. Well, he offered me a graduate assistant job at UAB and I immediately accepted. If he hadn't made that extra phone call that next day, I probably wouldn't have gotten into college coaching.*

Corn eventually landed back at Missouri Southern and coached for twenty-five seasons. Corn became the winningest coach in school history (413-305) before retiring in 2014. He accumulated the third-most wins among coaches in the history of the Mid-America Intercollegiate Athletics Association, one of the top leagues in NCAA Division II. To show their appreciation for Corn, Missouri Southern named their basketball court in his honor. Robert currently lives in Joplin, Missouri with his wife, Cindy. They have two children; Rob and Scott.

David Hurley was grateful that he had the opportunity to play for Coach Herrin. He recalled a vivid memory from his playing days.

David Hurley: *I can just see him banging that white chalk on the wooden floor, scribbling initials on a figure that maybe resembled a free throw lane and key. He didn't always get the initials correct, but we all got the message loud and clear. And there are probably still shoe heel marks in the old gym floor where he frequently slammed his heels to the floor in frustration with his players over the years. That was a classic trademark and an easy sign if you had made a mistake on the floor.*

After high school, David attended the University of Louisiana at Monroe. Today, former Ranger David Hurley is a hospital pharmacist and lives in Benton with his wife Barb. David and Barb have four children. Hurley reflected on how Coach Herrin impacted his life.

David Hurley: *There was no greater positive influence in my life as the friendships formed, memories made, and lessons learned than my experience with Benton Ranger basketball. Coach Rich Herrin cared about each one of us so much more than simply a basketball player, and it showed every day. Yes there were plenty of tense moments and heated direction from Coach, but not a single curse word was used or player embarrassed or threatened. As a player you wanted to work hard, give everything you had, and do your best out of respect for such a great coach, teacher, and Christian as Coach Herrin. He treated us like family. Coach, you have touched so many lives in so many places and in so many ways. We all remember, and always will. Thank you, Sir!*

Chris Moore now lives in Carbondale and is a Podiatrist. After high school, he attended Illinois Wesleyan University and roomed with NBA All-Star Jack Sikma. He transferred to SIU and then went to podiatry school in Chicago. He now lives in Carbondale with his wife Lori. He has three children; Shane, Madison and Patrick. Moore enjoyed growing up in Benton and is appreciative of his time with Coach Herrin.

Chris Moore: *It was just a magical time in Benton at that time. The coal mines were booming and everyone had money. The kids were good. It was a great place to grow up. Coach Herrin taught me to be quick but don't hurry. He took my boy to basketball camp with him at McKendree College and I don't think I paid a dime. I remember one time hecame to a junior high game at DeSoto and watched my son play. He always remembered his players.*

Kenny Summers settled in Akin, Illinois with his wife Sheila, and runs an excavation business. They have two daughters: Selinda and Shannon. Kenny is always on the move and he was a great interview. He has nothing but good memories about his experience as a Benton Ranger and he has great respect for his old coach.

Kenny Summers: *I enjoyed playing for Coach Herrin because he treated me like a person. Everything that came out of his mouth was positive. Coach could chew your butt out…and have a way of making you feel better. It was like… he's right…I'm glad he said that…I needed that.*

Kenny was a 13'6" pole vaulter for Coach Herrin on the track team and he remembered some scary bus rides with Coach Herrin behind the wheel.

Kenny Summers: *He is the only guy I have ever seen that could drive a bus looking backwards. He would turn completely around on the way to track meets and be coaching us before we got off the bus. He would be turned around for four seconds…then quickly look forward for a second or two and then turn back around. It was scary.*

Dennis Andrews and his wife Jennifer live in Raleigh, Illinois. Dennis is a retired banker from Banterra Bank. They have two sons; Aaron and Jonathon. He loved playing for Coach Herrin and enjoyed reflecting on his days as a Ranger.

Dennis Andrews: *He taught us how to be winners and sometimes you have to be a gracious loser to be a good winner. He taught us teamwork…he taught us that you didn't have to be a starter to make a difference. He taught us to play hard and give 120% at whatever we did. I don't think I could have played for a better high school basketball coach. He still knows me today…he remembers me more for track because I ran the low hurdles…and my sons went to his basketball camps.*

Allan Wisely now lives in Centralia with his wife Jean Anne. They have two daughters; Hilary and Jenna.

Allan Wisely: *He put in a lot of time, energy and effort. He was the assistant football coach and the head track coach. He was a motivator. He would kid with you but when it came time to play there was no one more intense. I remember that after some of our practices, he would play three-on-three with us and I always thought that was pretty neat. He was hands-on all the time. Coach Stewart was the same way…he had such a good rapport with all of the players. I also enjoyed playing for Coach Phillips. About five years ago I saw Rich at the Centralia Tournament. He was being honored that night. He remembered me and we talked about my brothers for 15-20 minutes. He doesn't forget you.*

Excitement abounded in Benton during the summer of '73 concerning the new school and particularly the new home of the Runnin' Rangers. The days of cramming into the Cracker Box were over. In '74, the Rangers returned Billy Smith, Paul Dinkins, Steve McCommons, Scott Hall and some exciting young players by the names of Craddock, Tabor and Dunbar. The Rangers had players coming and they would have a new state-of-the-art gymnasium to showcase their talent.

The old "Cracker Box" today. It is now known as the East Gymnasium. *(Matt Wynn)*

Junior point guard, Scott Hall, backed up Robert Corn at the point guard position. *(Ceasar Maragni)*

Paul Dinkins had a great year for the Rangers in '73 and loved playing in the old "Cracker Box." *(Ceasar Maragni)*

Senior, Allan Wisely, respected all of his coaches in high school.
(Ceasar Maragni)

The undisputed leader of the '73 team, Robert Corn, drives baseline. *(Ceasar Maragni)*

Senior, David Hurley in action. *(Ceasar Maragni)*

Junior, Steve McCommons, left his mark as one of the top three
sport athletes in Rangers history. *(Ceasar Maragni)*

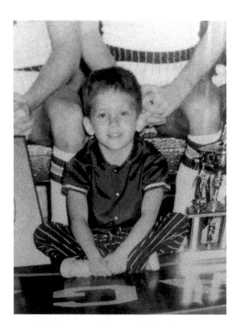

With "Sweet Georgia Brown" blaring, a young Kyle Herrin led
the Rangers onto the floor in '73. *(Ceasar Maragni)*

After winning the Centralia Tournament, David Lee's Carbondale Terriers
slowed the tempo down and defeated the Rangers 43-39 in Carbondale.
Here is a photo of the two great coaches in '73. *(Ceasar Maragni)*

Billy Smith in the Championship game of the '72 Centralia
Tournament. *(Ceasar Maragni)*

The '73 Rangers finished 21-5 but were beaten in the first game of
the Regional by Murphysboro. *(Ceasar Maragni)*

Robert Corn went on to become one of the most successful
coaches in Herrin's coaching tree. Robert Corn coached 25 seasons at
Missouri Southern and accumulated a school record of 413 wins.
The court at Missouri Southern is now named in his honor.
(Missouri Southern University)

CHAPTER NINETEEN

The New Gym and the '74 Rangers

"We have 940 chair-back seats and around 920 have been sold on a season ticket basis." – Coach Rich Herrin

As the 1973-74 school year approached, the construction of the new Benton High School and gymnasium was complete. Benton High School students began the fall of 1973 in a brand new school. But there was perhaps nobody more pleased with the project than head basketball Coach Rich Herrin. The success of the basketball team spurred the need of a new gymnasium, and with a new gymnasium, why not a new school? There was no doubt that Herrin's basketball program was the driving force behind the construction of the new school.

The school featured 43 new spacious classrooms and a large commons area that would also serve as the cafeteria. As girls athletics began to gain momentum, the Cracker Box would now serve as the home of the Rangerettes. The exterior of the school featured a light colored brick, bordered with white concrete pillars. The school was built with the idea that the enrollment might grow to 900 students, which allowed ample space for the 775 students enrolled at Benton High School to begin the '73-'74 school year.

Teachers were excited to move into their new classrooms and the administrators enjoyed their new office space. The basketball Rangers had a new gymnasium and it was built in a manner that was far ahead of its time. In fact, there have been very few structural changes since its original construction. The plan for the gym was well thought out and has stood the test of time. To Herrin, the new gym was like the eighth wonder of the world.

The athletic office was located in the northwest corner of the gym and since Herrin served as the athletic director, he spent much of his time during the school day in this area. The office was divided into two parts; the front was designated for the athletic secretary and a private room in the back served as Coach Herrin's personal office. Herrin used the office to make phone calls to area coaches, talk to players privately, watch film, and create practice plans. Coach Herrin did teach three driver's education classes and managed to include a classroom that was contiguous to the athletic office by a long hallway. The hallway is located underneath the north section of chair seats and is commonly referred to as the Tunnel. Herrin wanted his classroom in close proximity to the athletic office in case of important phone calls.

Coach Herrin: *I did have input into the design of the locker rooms and coaches office areas on the north side of the gym.*

At maximum capacity, the gym could seat 4,100 people. The lower bowl of bleachers surrounding the main court holds approximately 2,000 people. In the upper bowl, there are 940 total reserved chair seats lining both sides of the court. There were also end bleachers in the upper bowl that held up to 1,100 fans. Today, the west end bleachers have been removed in favor of an enclosed weight room. Also, the first row of the original chair seats was removed, allowing fans easier access to the concession areas and rest rooms. In the fall of 1973, the gym instantly became a mecca of high school basketball in Southern Illinois. No team in Southern Illinois desired to play the Rangers, but they did want the experience of playing in the new facility.

It is the same gymnasium that the Rangers play in today, but it is now named Rich Herrin Gymnasium. The "Rich" is currently in pristine shape. In fact, it has been freshly painted and there have been various upgrades to the facilities that have added to its appeal. The original chair seats in the upper bowl were red. Evidently, the chair seats were supposed to be maroon but an error was made and the company in which the chairs were purchased persuaded the school to take them at a bargain price. Therefore, the seats in the upper bowl have been West Frankfort red for more than forty-five years. The maroon banners that designate State qualifying teams and South Seven Conference Championship boards elegantly hang in the east rafters. Large banners hang above center court to honor the five Rangers whose numbers have been retired. A beautiful maroon scoreboard with the signature white stars sits high above center court. There are also smaller scoreboards in two opposite corners of the gym. In my opinion, Rich Herrin Gymnasium is still the greatest high school gymnasium in Southern Illinois.

The main entrance is located on the west end of the gymnasium and as fans enter they are met by a lobby area that displays the Rangers most coveted championship trophies. All of the South Seven Championship balls sit side by side in an awesome display of dominance from 1966 to 1988. The Benton Invitational trophies line the bottom of the trophy case and six Centralia Tournament trophies sit front and center. The program's Regional Championship plaques are displayed side by side above the trophy case and go on as far as the eye can see. The beautiful Sectional trophies of the sixties and seventies line the northwest end of the trophy case. In the west lobby, large pictures of the greatest Ranger teams fill the walls, along with pictures featuring the program's greatest players.

Then there is the floor. Today, the gymnasium has a wood floor and its appearance is eye-catching. When the gym was built in 1973, it is safe to say that possibly no gym in the State of Illinois had more floor area. When the bleachers were pushed in and the Rangers utilized the whole court for practice, there were six baskets and two full cross-court floors running north and south. The main playing floor runs west to east.

In 1973, the original floor was made of a new substance called tartan. The people in Benton called it the "rubber floor". Tartan is very similar to rubber and it comes in many colors. It was marketed as being chemical resistant, very durable if kept up well, and most importantly, it provided a slip-free surface good for cutting and changing directions. The tartan floor was seamless and the maroon and white boundary lines popped against the light tan floor. A special scrubbing machine was used to clean the floor before games to ensure that players would not slip. It was a beautiful look. In 1973, this was the new fad in gym flooring and many schools began phasing out wood floors in favor of the new tartan multi-purpose floor.

Paul Dinkins: *I remember going up and sitting in the chair seats…the bleachers were not yet installed…I just sat there and watched them pour that floor. Just the excitement of having a new gym added to the anticipation of the season.*

People in the community could not wait to see the new gymnasium. Even though the Cracker Box was full every night, there were Benton people that just couldn't get tickets. Some locals quit trying to get tickets, knowing that it was impossible.

Problem solved! The most important advantage of the new gym was that the Rangers would now be accessible to everyone in the community. Entire families could grab a bite to eat on Friday night and then head to the game. For the citizens of Benton, basketball games became the thing to do on those dark winter weekends. With a gym capacity of 4,100, there would be few times fans would have to wait in the cold for tickets. Young boys that dreamed of being a Ranger were not sent home, unable to watch the game; the Rangers could be seen by all. School administration no longer had to hear the complaints of the opposing schools that could not get but a handful of fans into the old Cracker Box.

For the basketball Rangers, it was clear that the home court advantage had changed. In the old Cracker Box, space was so tight. The small floor, the restraining line and the permanent railing down the sidelines were now gone. The days of utilizing size to suffocate opposing teams with a 1-2-2 ball press were history. The tight proximity of players and fans and the lack of privacy in the huddle were all things of the past. The small gym was gone.

But the Rangers soon realized they would have a new home-court advantage; the imposing size of the gym. As opposing teams walked into the gym for the first time, the players were speechless and stunned by the enormity of the gymnasium. The facility itself sent a strong message that the Rangers were for real. There was this feeling that "if they have this, they must be pretty good." And they were right; the '74 Rangers were pretty good.

The team was loaded. They had size, quickness, and returned a great mix of veteran guys and young talent. They were the perfect team to christen the new gymnasium. The vast space of the gym was not going to bother seniors Steve McCommons, Scott Hall and Paul Dinkins. They had been through the rugged battles of the South Seven and a tartan floor surrounded by 4,100 seats was the least of their concerns. Billy Smith and Rob Dunbar were the two most talented juniors in Southern Illinois and sophomores Keith Tabor, Mark Craddock and Russ Mitchell would provide valuable depth off the bench.

Paul Dinkins: *I thought we could be very good.... We were blessed with talent and we had a lot of guys returning.*

The other seniors on the team were Mark Manis, and Steve Genisio. Mark Manis earned All-South honors in football and provided competition in the post against the regulars in practice. Steve Genisio was a scrapper. He is the son of Barnie Genisio, who was the superintendent of Benton High School and a close friend of Coach Herrin. Genisio was a three-sport athlete and as a junior in track, he ran a 4:38 mile and he had fond memories of Benton basketball as a young boy.

Steve Genisio: *Dad and Coach were good friends. I remember riding the team bus when I was little. I got to ride the bus some when Yunkus was there…with the cowboy hats and everything. Coach always had soda and ham sandwiches for the players…he would put me to work handing out the sandwiches, you know.*

The juniors on the team besides Billy Smith and Rob Dunbar were Roger Smith, Bill Chrostoski, Bobby Britton, Jesse King, and Kevin Poole. Jesse King only stood 5'8" tall but he was one of the finest all-around athletes on the team. In track, he excelled in the pole vault and as a short sprint man. In football, he started as a wing back and had great hands. Despite limited playing time, King brought energy and a competitive spirit to every practice. Bobby Britton was a swing player that could shoot the basketball. He had good size and he battled hard in practice. As a junior, Kevin Poole was a better than average shooter that battled for playing time at the guard position. Smith and Chrostoski would also play as seniors on the great '75 team.

Roger Smith was a letterman in track and cross country and could be counted on to work hard each day in practice. Roger remembered his first memory of Coach Rich Herrin.

Roger Smith: *I first got to know Coach Herrin because he played on a fast pitch softball team called Whitlow Signs. I was just in grade school. Coach played first base, Bobby Johnston played shortstop, Burton Wills played third base and Maurice Phillips was the catcher. They would bring a pitcher in from up north that was really good. It was one of the best fast pitch teams in the area. I remember Burton Wills hitting a few long home runs…it was good rural entertainment.*

Roger's older brother, Gordon, graduated in the same class as Rich Yunkus, and his older brother, Don, was one of only two seniors on the 1970 team.

Roger was much like Don; he worked hard in practice, but didn't get a great amount of playing time. Roger admitted that his brother's "team first" attitude paved the way for his opportunity to be a member of the Rangers. Roger was one of the lucky ones; he had a seat at all the Ranger home games as a youngster.

Roger Smith: *My mom and dad had two season tickets that were located six rows up on the very end near the fire escape steps. There was a little gap… like a half seat…next to the fire escape steps…that's where I sat when I was in grade school. Rodney Kaspar's parents sat in front of us…his sister Linda taught me how to keep score. We went to about every game with them.*

Bill Chrostoski didn't play basketball in junior high, but he made the team as a freshman. He was left-handed and he was a much improved player entering his junior season. He was affectionately called "Jack" by his teammates. Chrostoski could always be counted on to work hard.

Bill Chrostoski: *I went to Grant School growing up and Perry Eisenhower was my coach. I went to quite a few games growing up. The gym was always full. I remember guys like Jim Semanski and Tony Diefenbach.*

The sophomore class was an extremely talented class. In 1972, under the guidance of coach Burton Wills, they won the Junior High State Championship. Herrin chose to bring Keith Tabor up at the beginning of his sophomore season. Tabor was a knockdown shooter and is still considered by many to be the greatest catch-and-shoot player in the history of the program. He provided instant offense to the '74 attack. Russ Mitchell was another young prospect that was expected to add depth as a sophomore. He was 6'5" tall and had a soft touch around the basket. The other sophomore was Mark Craddock. He was an extremely steady ball handler and he would grow and mature as a player competing with the likes of Smith, Hall and Tabor in practice.

The players noticed the new facilities immediately. The varsity locker room had all-weather maroon carpet with a grey "B" in the middle of the floor. The lockers were brand new and twice the size of the lockers in the Cracker Box. Most importantly, the new locker room provided a space for the players to hang out. Nobody wanted to hang around any longer than they had to at the old Cracker Box, but this was different. Players would be done with practice and linger around the locker room and talk to their teammates about anything and everything. The coach's office was down the hall and the new locker room provided a sense of privacy that all teams so desperately need. Later on, the Rangers bought a radio cassette player and the players played their favorite tunes. It was their space and the team took care of it. The other noticeable improvement for the players was the shower area. Players now looked forward to a warm shower and a shower room that could hold up to twelve players at a time.

Following the traditional Turkey Day Game, the Ranger players headed uptown to get their traditional short haircuts. Some of the players sported a "buzz" cut which was extremely short to the scalp, yet others went with a flat-top. The day was Saturday, November 24th, and it marked the first practice of the year for the Rangers in their new gymnasium. The players were excited to get started and arrived early to get a little extra shooting.

As the players came out to shoot, their new surroundings gave them a bounce in their step. The bleachers were pushed in and all six goals with their fan-shaped glass backboards were in position. The players delighted in the fact that they were able to spread out and shoot without being interrupted by fourteen other balls being shot at the same goal. The tartan floor was different and many of the players rammed their feet into the floor to test its traction. Some players jumped to test its spring. Coach Herrin was already on the floor dressed for practice and delighted in watching his players' reaction to their new surroundings.

Paul Dinkins: *The floor took a little getting used to…the sound of the ball when it bounced was different.*

On Saturday, December 1, 1973, the eighth wonder of the world opened for the general public as the Rangers hosted the McLeansboro Foxes in the opener. More than 3,000 basketball fans flooded into the gymnasium anxious to see the new home of the Rangers. The first game played in the new gymnasium saw the Ranger sophomores thump the Foxes by a score of 71-48. As the varsity Rangers organized in the Tunnel to take the floor, the players bantered back and forth about who would score the first basket in the new gym.

The cheerleaders formed a narrow tunnel and led the crowd of more than 3,000 in a unified clap. The student section, called the "Bleacher Bums", rocked the lower bowl. The older fans in the chair seats rose in great anticipation to see the Rangers dart from the Tunnel. With adrenaline running thru their young bodies, the '74 Rangers took the floor to a loud roar that echoed through the building. The team sported brand new gold warm-up tops accompanied by snazzy pinstripe bottoms. All of the players had freshly cut flat-tops and all of their movements were sharp. Their presentation had to be intimidating to the visiting Foxes.

That first night in the new gym, the Rangers started: 6'0" senior Scott Hall, 6'2" junior Billy Smith, 6'6" junior Rob Dunbar, 6'5" senior Paul Dinkins and 6'5" senior Steve McCommons. To start the game, official Leroy Newton threw the ball up and Rob Dunbar rose high and tipped the ball to a breaking Scott Hall.

Scott Hall: *We were playing McLeansboro at home and I got an easy lay-up off the tip. I was known for missing open lay-ups and Dinkins always had good imitations of my missed lay-ups. I do remember getting this one down and realizing it was the first varsity bucket in the new gym. They always play the sophomore game before the varsity game and Kevin Williams claimed that he got the first basket in the sophomore game…but we told the sophomores that didn't count…varsity points only.*

The Rangers raced out to a 28-11 lead in the first quarter and never looked back. Smith, McCommons and Hall led the team in scoring with 14 points. In the second quarter, sophomore Keith Tabor entered the game and promptly hit his first jump shot. Tabor went on to score 1,276 points in his Ranger career and this was his first varsity basket.

Paul Dinkins: *As a sophomore Keith was raw…a great shooter…you could see that he had great potential. He was very quick and he had a wiry build. He was a pretty good jumper…there was a lot of talent in that body.*

The Rangers then made the long road trip to Jacksonville, Illinois and won 89-81. The game proved to be Rob Dunbar's coming out party. As a junior, Dunbar was a 6'6' string bean that could play inside or outside. Jacksonville had no answer for him as he scorched the nets for 27 points. Dunbar scored every way imaginable and it was obvious that big Rob was going to be a factor.

Paul Dinkins: *Rob could really handle the ball…he became a dandy. With McCommons clogging the middle, Rob could step out and really shoot it from the perimeter…he had an unorthodox shot…but his movements were so fluid.*

Junior Bill Chrostoski recalled playing with Dunbar on the sophomore team.

Bill Chrostoski: *Rob wanted to play in games more than he wanted to practice… kind of like the rest of us, you know. I remember as a sophomore we practiced as hard as Rob wanted to practice. Then when he got to Rich…he practiced harder. He became a great high school basketball player.*

Roger Smith: *Rob was a very good student…very intelligent. He was also a gifted artist. I had a good relationship with him. Everybody wanted to win. From the end of our junior year into our senior season…he really worked hard. By his senior year, he was a little stronger physically. He loved shooting that fade-away corner jump shot.*

The Rangers then hammered Meridian 88-52 at home. It was now time for the first loop through conference play. In '74, the conference race was wide open. Herrin was considered by many to be the favorite until All-State player Gary Rafe was injured in an automobile accident in November. Rafe was expected to be out most of the season and this made the Tigers vulnerable. But the Tigers still had a great player in 6'3" Bill Green. The Mt. Vernon Rams returned conference star player, Gary Mann, and would contend for the conference and for the first time in years; the Marion Wildcats looked to be a factor behind the play of young Jimmy Orr and veteran Kerry Hudgens.

Paul Dinkins: *Herrin and Mt. Vernon were two tough teams in the conference. We had great battles with Herrin since junior high.*

The Rangers had two pivotal conference games with Marion and Herrin on the weekend right before Christmas. With a record of 3-0, the Rangers loaded the bus and headed to Marion for the conference opener. The Marion game was a battle but the Rangers came out on top by a score of 77-75. Coach Rich Herrin made these comments after the game:

Rich Herrin: *I've said all week that Marion had a really good ball club and I think everyone saw that. I thought that Dinkins and McCommons got us going early…. Smith brought us along early in the fourth quarter.*

Following the big win at Marion, the Rangers played host to the Herrin Tigers. Even with Rafe sidelined, the Rangers expected a tight game. In a thriller, the Rangers won the game 72-66. Billy Smith scored 23 points and Dinkins chipped in 19 as the team improved to 5-0 overall and 2-0 in the conference. It was a great start. Dinkins remembered the excitement of playing at home in front of more than 3,000 Ranger fans that first year in the new gym.

Paul Dinkins: *From what I remember it just seemed packed. We had a great student section on the floor…but you could still hear Bob Gariepy yell, "Three seconds!"*

Entering the tournament undefeated, the Rangers were the number one seed in the 1973 Centralia Holiday Tournament. They were now a novelty in the tournament and fans from other towns would stick around and watch the Rangers based on their past success. The Centralia fans hated the Rangers and the Orphanage booed loudly anytime the Rangers played. Again, the Ranger players loved playing the villain and played some of their best basketball at Trout Gymnasium.

Steve Genisio: *When we walked into the gym…we expected to win. We always looked good too…Coach always had us in good uniforms and warm-ups. We ran out to the song "Sweet Georgia Brown". When we went to other towns, I believe they had respect for us because we won and just how we did things.*

The Rangers opened tournament play against Homewood-Flossmoor in a 1:15 afternoon match-up and defeated the Vikings, 60-38, behind 18 points from Rob Dunbar. Paul Dinkins added 15 points. The win set up a match up with the Wheeling Wildcats in an afternoon contest the next day. What a start! The team was 6-0.

In the Wheeling game, the Rangers eased to a 14-10 first quarter lead. In the second quarter, they extended the lead to a 14-point advantage and it looked as though they would cruise to victory. But then, the game changed. The Rangers were charged with a technical foul and then a bevy of mental errors allowed the Wildcats back in the game. At halftime, Benton led 29-25. In the third quarter, Wheeling tied the game at 40 before Billy Smith hit a jump shot to end the third quarter. The fourth quarter was frustrating. With a minute in a half left in the game, Wheeling took the lead for good and won the game 62-60. Many of the neutral fans in the gym rooted for the underdog Wheeling Wildcats. The disappointing loss bounced the Rangers from the tournament.

Paul Dinkins: *It was an afternoon game. Coach Herrin called a timeout... we were behind...Coach Herrin thought Billy and I were trying to do too much to bring us back...he pointed at us and said, "You two need to quit shooting." Billy and I have talked about it. It was just a frustrating game... we got beat.*

The team was now 6-1 heading into the New Year. On Saturday, January 5, 1974, Coach David Lee and the Carbondale Terriers came to Benton. The Rangers won the ballgame 90-63 behind twenty points from Paul Dinkins and sophomore Keith Tabor.

Senior Paul Dinkins was such a steady player and he quietly put together an outstanding high school career. The lefty was a good rebounder and had developed into one of the top players in Southern Illinois. Dinkins was a tough matchup for opponents and he was just such a great guy to interview. Paul is well-respected by his teammates. Dink loved the game and even looked like a Ranger. He was tall, blonde-headed and very skilled.

Billy Smith: *Dink was smooth...left handed. He was a good athlete and fundamentally very sound. He was a great guy and had a quiet personality.*

Scott Hall: *I remember we would have these mandatory open gyms in the summer and there would be times I didn't want to go.... But Paul loved to play...he never questioned it.*

Paul Dinkins: *I loved the game...but really loved to compete. I liked to run track in the spring as much as I liked to play basketball. I was a hurdler and I liked that one-on-one competition.*

Dinkins would go on to score 1,036 points in his high school career and one thing I learned about "Dink" in our interview was he could be very tough on himself.

Paul Dinkins: *My senior year was a year of frustration personally. I kind of feel like...I let the team down. At the end of my junior year, I sprained my ankle pretty good and I really didn't get over that until the end of track season that spring. Then I came down with mono. Then doctors found an abnormality in my liver. I went thru the whole '73 summer unable to play because of this liver thing. The doctors wouldn't let me play. About the time school* *started, I had a liver biopsy and it just revealed that I had a weird-functioning liver...that this was my normal liver function. I missed the whole summer going into my senior year and I really think that set me back. I would have liked to have had that summer to really work on my game.*

The Rangers then cruised to wins against Harrisburg, Centralia and West Frankfort to set up a big match-up against the Mt. Vernon Rams. The game was at Mt. Vernon and Changon Gymnasium was full of Ranger haters. Throughout the years, Benton at Mt. Vernon was always a wild affair. This game was no different. Despite the great play of Billy Smith late in the game, the Rangers lost a close one 52-51. After the game, another chapter of the rivalry unfolded as the Rangers' team bus was sent home with a shattered windshield. It was life in the South Seven and Coach Rich Herrin welcomed the intense competition. This is what the South Seven Conference was about. It was a conference full of bitter rivalries, but also a league loaded with talent. It was a battle every night. With the loss, the Rangers dropped to 10-2 overall and 6-1 in the conference.

In the Mt. Vernon game, the Rangers were beaten badly on the boards, but Steve McCommons held his own. As a senior, McCommons was 6'5", 235 pounds, and was an imposing presence. In junior high, he was pudgy and un-athletic but then something clicked. He became dedicated to improving his fitness and through much hard work transformed himself into one of the better all-around athletes in Southern Illinois by his senior year. He played with an ornery streak that served the team well and all coaches will tell you that teams need guys like this to win. There is a picture in the '74 yearbook that encapsulates his tenacity as a player. With his head not even visible, McCommons is fighting for a loose ball and just grinding a West Frankfort player into the floor. This was Steve McCommons. McCommons sought contact and his eyes lit up when fighting for loose balls. He was the one player most responsible for giving the '74 team a swagger and toughness. Mac was respected by his teammates and they loved playing under his protection.

Billy Smith: *Steve may have worked harder than anybody to become a player. Mac was always going to box out...he did not back down from anybody.*

Dave Severin, a '76 BCHS graduate, is currently serving his second term in the Illinois State House of Representatives. He was one of McCommons' closest friends. Severin was also a good track athlete that played two years of basketball in high school. After high school, Severin also became close friends with Coach Herrin. He enjoyed telling me about his best friend Steve McCommons.

Dave Severin: *As a player, Steve was tenacious. He had a heart as big as the ocean but he didn't always want you to know it. Steve was always for the underdog. He was always sticking up for people that were being picked on. Steve was a great athlete. In track he high jumped, ran the hurdles and still holds the school record in the discus. He was very competitive. Later in life he developed a strong faith and he was so passionate about whatever he did. He was a man's man.*

McCommons went on to play Division I football at Georgia Tech University and there is a great story that speaks to the toughness of McCommons. During one his college years, he came home for the summer and was playing a two-on-two pick-up basketball game at Rend Lake College when the game got a little too physical. The opposing two players were from Mt. Vernon and words were exchanged. Then some pushing and shoving ensued. McCommons then stopped things and said, "I will fight both of you guys, but only one at a time." As Norman Carlile always said about fearless competitors, "He was not afraid of man, beast or fowl."

Another first in 1974 was the Benton Invitational Tournament. When Rich Herrin started the tournament in 1974, it was an eight-team double-elimination tournament. In 1980, Herrin changed the tournament to a six-team round robin tournament for two reasons. First, he wanted the teams to have the experience of playing two games in one day, which was in line with championship Saturday of the State Tournament. Second, Illinois had a limit of only two tournaments a year and a six-team round robin would provide each team with five games. Coach Herrin wanted to max-out on games. He was a gamer.

In the first round of the BIT, the Rangers defeated the Pinckneyville Panthers, 91-54. Coach Dick Corn was not yet at Pinckneyville. In game two, the Rangers nipped the Okawville Rockets, 57-54, advancing to the first BIT Championship game against the Carmi Bulldogs. The head coach of the Rockets was one of Herrin's former players, Dave Luechtefeld. Luechtefeld had unprecedented success at Okawville, and the Rockets would be a mainstay in the tournament until 2019.

A crowd of over 3,000 basketball crazies poured into the gym for the first-ever BIT Championship game. The Rangers led by nine points at halftime but the Bulldogs fought back behind the great play of senior Mike Williams and junior Mark Winter. In the third quarter, the Rangers missed shots and turned the ball over, allowing Carmi to mount a furious comeback. The Bulldogs took command in the third quarter to win the game 47-41. This was a tough loss and when interviewing the players, this game stood out as the biggest disappointment of the season.

Paul Dinkins: *Losing in the championship game of our first tournament was just disappointing. We shouldn't have lost that game.*

Accompanying Rich Herrin on the Ranger bench in '74 was longtime sophomore coach Maurice Phillips along with junior varsity coach Harry Stewart. They had been part of the basketball coaching staff for years and were well known by the community. Flying under the radar to many in 1973-74 was new freshman coach, Don Webb. Webb rarely sat on the varsity bench on Friday and Saturday nights because he was given the task of driving his car all over Southern Illinois to scout area teams. He was hired at Benton in the fall of 1970 with the following duties; science/PE teacher, freshman basketball coach, freshman football coach and varsity baseball coach. In fact, the 1974 team was his first freshman team.

Don Webb: *I remember the 1974 team well when they were freshman. Billy played up…but he did play one game with us at Harrisburg at the end of the year. Harrisburg had a really good freshman team and Coach Herrin let Billy play that last freshman game of the season. Billy had thirty and we won the game. I had Scott Hall, Steve McCommons and some other really good kids that just didn't end up playing varsity basketball. I had Mark Manis, Steve Neal and some others. My first freshman teams practiced in the gym in the old school. Occasionally, we got to practice in the Cracker Box on Fridays if the varsity was playing on Friday night. We did practice there on Saturday mornings. If there was a home game Friday night we would have to go in on Saturday morning and clean up the mess and then practice.*

Don Webb graduated from Benton High School in 1964. Although he played only one year of basketball, he loved the game and knew that he wanted to coach. Webb went on to have unprecedented success at the freshman level and he fed players to the varsity level that were fundamentally sound and skilled enough to keep the Ranger basketball machine in overdrive. Webb was young and enthusiastic and he was learning the game in a hurry.

Don Webb: *Rich told me exactly what he wanted to do, but he also gave me a lot of freedom. I had the pleasure of having a lot of good players over the years.*

After the BIT, the Rangers were 12-3 overall and had one more loop through the conference. The team won their next six games by defeating Marion, West Frankfort, Herrin, Harrisburg, Centralia and Carbondale. Herrin played the Rangers to 61-52, but it was the only game during the winning streak that was decided by less than ten points.

Offensively, the '74 Rangers were a fun team to watch. On a defensive rebound, the big men would pivot to their outside shoulder and deliver crisp passes to the guards waiting in outlet position and the Rangers were off to the races. By this time, the team had a numbered break and each player ran their lanes ahead of the ball. The fast break forced an up-tempo game on their opponents. Defensively, the Rangers pressed to speed the game up and create a game of more possessions while Coach Herrin continued to give his players freedom within the structure of the team.

Scott Hall: *You know I loved playing defense with Billy. I liked to think of us as the Dynamic Duo on defense. Billy was an amazing player…he could deflect a ball to one of us and just break the other way and we would pass it to him for a lay-up.*

It was a fun style of basketball to watch, and even more fun to play. The '74 team was an offensive juggernaut with the likes of Billy Smith, Rob Dunbar, Paul Dinkins and Keith Tabor, who provided instant offense off the bench. McCommons cleaned up the misses on the offensive glass and Hall and Craddock got the ball to the players who could score. In 1974, the Rangers scored more than 70 points, eighteen times. Paul Dinkins gave me a fun fact about the '74 Rangers that was telling of the teams' offensive production.

Paul Dinkins: *As a team we averaged 72-73 points a game my senior year with no three-point line. We were getting up and down the floor pretty fast. Do you know how many total points our team scored in 1974? We scored 1,974 points…. I thought that was pretty neat.*

With only one conference game remaining, the Rangers were 18-3, facing a home date with the Mt. Vernon Rams. The Rams handed the Rangers their only conference earlier in the season by a score of 52-51. The game was at Mt. Vernon and Rams fans had busted the bus windshield and shouted obscenities at the Rangers as the bus sped away. It was a tough night in Jefferson County, and the Rangers remembered it well. It was payback time.

Ranger fans flooded to the gym knowing what was on the line. No, it wasn't a Conference championship, because the Rangers had secured the conference title with their last win against the Terriers. It was the chance to put it to the Mt. Vernon Rams, and who wouldn't want to see that? At the 8:12 tip off, competitive juices flowed between two teams that didn't like each other. For Mt. Vernon, it was a chance to put a season sweep on the Rangers, which to some Rams fans meant more than a conference championship.

It was senior night and before the game Paul Dinkins, Steve McCommons, Scott Hall, Steve Genisio and Mark Manis were honored. A packed house stood and clapped for the five seniors who had given them so many memories. Dinkins and McCommons had competed at the varsity level since their sophomore year. After the ceremony, there were the introductions of the starting lineups. When their names were called, each Ranger player sprinted at full speed onto the floor with a look of focus and determination. There were no theatrics. It was on. Coach Herrin had some final words for his players before the tip but the players were in their own world. They had taken the loss at Mt. Vernon personally and there were no motivational words needed for this game. The Rangers were ready.

From the tip, the game was all Rangers. Every ball bounced their way and their shots were falling. The Ranger fast break was efficient and was forcing the Rams to play faster than they wanted. It was Ranger basketball at its best. Dinkins and McCommons had 12 at halftime and the Rangers led 40-20. It was over. At the time, the Rams were left scratching their heads. In the second half, Smith and Dunbar took over and the Rangers won easily by a score of 77-59. It was a thrashing.

Paul Dinkins: *My favorite game our senior year was when we beat Mt. Vernon at home late in the year. We really played well.*

The final game of the '74 season took place on Friday, March 1, 1974. The Rangers traveled to Effingham to play the Flaming Hearts. Paul Dinkins finished the regular season with one of his best performances of his career. He was 11-16 from the field and led the Rangers scoring attack with

23 points. Billy was Billy. He scored 18 and was a constant disruption to the Flaming Hearts on the defensive end of the floor. Big Rob Dunbar was really coming into his own in the second half of his junior season. He scored 14 points and grabbed 12 rebounds. It was obvious that Dunbar was really going to be special as a senior. The Rangers defeated the Hearts 70-65 and enjoyed a long, happy bus ride home.

'74 State Tournament Play

Now it was the second season and yet another first in '74. For the first time in school history, the Rangers hosted an IHSA Regional Tournament. The chance to host a post-season tournament was yet another perk that came along with the new, spacious gymnasium. In the past, the Rangers were forced to play all of their post-season tournaments on the road because the Cracker Box was just too small. Now things were different and with the building of the new gym, the IHSA rewarded Benton with its first Regional Tournament in 1974.

The new school, the new gymnasium, the new warm-ups and uniforms, the first Benton Invitational Tournament and now the first Regional Tournament; it was quite a year in '74. The Rangers opened the tournament by pouncing on the Harrisburg Bulldogs early and cruising to victory by a score of 90-55. Senior reserves Mark Manis and Steve Genisio both got in the scorebooks.

In the Regional Championship, the Rangers played the West Frankfort Redbirds. The Redbirds were not a bad club. Their record stood at 11-13 but they had pulled some upsets and were very capable. The Birds were led by All-Conference players Mike Vosbein and Sloan Brown. A sea of red with wishful thinking packed the visitors section hoping for a Redbird victory on Benton's new floor. The Rangers had owned the Redbirds in post-season play since Rich Herrin's arrival to Benton in 1960. All of those times the Rangers had defeated the Redbirds in their own gymnasium, and now the Birds had the opportunity to end the Rangers' season in their brand new gymnasium. It would be a sweet revenge. If it happened, everyone from West Frankfort wanted to say they witnessed it and so the people of West Frankfort made the trip to Benton hoping for a miracle. The Rangers came out tight and only led 27-24 at halftime. The West Frankfort faithful were encouraged, but they had no answer for Rob Dunbar. At halftime, Dunbar had 16 points. A big third quarter by the Rangers sent many of the

Redbird faithful to their cars. They had no intention of watching another Regional Championship plaque being presented to the Rangers at their expense. The final score was 68-48. After the game, fans hung around to witness the Rangers cut down the nets and take team pictures huddled around their Regional Championship plaque. The only drawback about winning at home was there was no victory lap around the square.

It was now Sectional Tournament time, and as usual, basketball fever had taken over the community. A huge team picture above the heading of "GO GET 'EM RANGERS" appeared in the March 11th edition of the Benton Evening News. The Rangers dominated the coffee shop talk and the townspeople followed the Rangers closely by reading Tedrow's articles in the Benton Evening News. Just as it was in the sixties, it was special to be a Ranger in '74.

Roger Smith: *We were spoiled rotten. Everyone in the community treated us like kings. I remember it would be a player's birthday and someone would send a cake and we would eat it after practice. I believe 1974 was the first year of the old Pizza Shack on east Main Street. I remember after one practice… Pizza Bob fed the whole team.*

In the first game of the Sectional, the Rangers faced off against Effingham. It would be the second time in just two weeks that they would meet up with the Flaming Hearts. It was a scary game. The Hearts were a solid team and very capable of ending the Rangers season. This was Coach Herrin's comments after their first meeting:

Coach Herrin: *Effingham has a real fine club. It took a great effort from our kids to win. I thought we played an outstanding game.*

The Sectional was held at Max Morris Gymnasium in West Frankfort. It was a short trip for the Rangers but a pretty good haul for the Hearts. The Rangers jumped out to lead the game by as much as thirteen points in the first half but the Hearts fought hard and came back. At Halftime, the Rangers were up 42-36. Dunbar started the third quarter with three quick field goals and then Smith and Dinkins took over. The scoring trio of Dinkins, Dunbar and Smith were just too much for the Hearts to handle and the Rangers won the contest 74-63. The other game of the West Frankfort Sectional featured Breese Mater Dei and Murphysboro. Breese defeated Murphysboro to set up the championship game against the Rangers.

By the time the Sectional Championship is played, most all of the schools are eliminated, leaving many area fans looking for a good basketball game. In my opinion, there is nothing like the atmosphere and intensity of a Sectional Championship in downstate Illinois. Southern Illinois basketball fans always pack the house to see the two best teams in the area. On Friday night, March 15, 1974, it was no different. Max Morris Gymnasium was rocking as both teams took the floor for a chance to advance to the Sweet Sixteen.

The night didn't start very well for the Rangers. The team bus pulled out for West Frankfort but was caught by a train and was stuck in traffic. If you know anything about Benton, trains can present themselves at the most inopportune times and sometimes throw a wrench in your plans. The bus was delayed more than fifteen minutes causing the Rangers to be late for warm-ups, but it didn't seem to affect the Rangers play. In the first quarter, Benton charged out of the gate and took a commanding lead before Breese fought back to pull within four points at 17-13. In the second quarter the game was back and forth and the Rangers led by one at halftime.

In the second half, it was all Breese Mater Dei. It looked as if the Rangers were played out. There just wasn't anything left in the gas tank and Mater Dei's superior size began to take over. Breese pulled away and won the game 72-51.

Paul Dinkins: *I just remember we got out to a nice lead early…we just couldn't hold it and the bottom fell out.*

Scott Hall: *We really came out in the first quarter hot and had a lead and we decided to hold the ball…. Look, they were really good and very big. We just got beat.*

In tournament play, all it takes is one bad game and it's over. Just like that, the Rangers' season came to an end, but it had been a great year. The team finished 23-4, conference champions, and winners of the first Regional Tournament ever held at Benton High School. Most importantly, the players took away memories that lasted a lifetime.

Paul Dinkins: *What stands out to me was how all of my teammates were like family. Scott Hall and I went to kindergarten together…we grew up together…we hunted together. We all had such a fun bunch of guys and we all had the same mind set…we wanted to win.*

I had the chance to ask Paul Dinkins about how Coach Herrin influenced his life and these were his words:

Paul Dinkins: *Matt, that is such a tough question to answer. I don't know where to start. I think the world of him…love him. When I think back, my parents had the easiest job because we didn't want to get in trouble because of Coach. He was like a parent to all of us. He molded and shaped so many young men. You knew to fly right.*

After high school Paul Dinkins went to Creighton University in Omaha, Nebraska to play for the Blue Jays.

Paul Dinkins: *I had a few offers. Going to Creighton was a great experience…I loved the experience of traveling…. We weren't in the Missouri Valley Conference until my senior year. Before that we were independent. When Larry Bird was a junior at Indiana State, we beat them three times. I had a good floorside seat on the bench for those games. Basketball wise, I wish I would have played at a Division II school where I could have gotten more playing time. I just really struggled to make that transition from a small forward in high school to a guard at the Division I level.*

Today, Paul is a retired high school coach and teacher. He served as a P.E. teacher for thirty-four years in the State of Texas and coached basketball and football. He currently lives with his wife Laquita in Levelland, Texas. They have two children; a son, Jarod, and daughter, Lauren.

On December 7, 2008, the Benton community was stunned when Steve McCommons passed away suddenly. He was only fifty-two years old. Steve had an incredible high school career. Academically, he was a good student and was a key player on three great Ranger basketball teams from 1972-1974. In football, he was an All-South tackle and still holds the BCHS record in the discus with a throw of 163'11". The record has held for forty-seven years. In fact, it is fair to say that McCommons is one of the greatest multi-sport athletes ever at Benton High School.

These were some of the words from Steve's obituary: *After high school, he attended Georgia Tech University on a football scholarship and received a B.S. in chemical engineering. He began his career at Inland Steel Coal Co. and was soon promoted to general manager. Because of his determination and commitment to excellence, he became the youngest mine superintendent* *in Inland history. He worked in Illinois, Pennsylvania and Virginia with Inland and Consolidated Coal. He returned home to Benton in 1996 and earned his master's degree in education from Southern Illinois University Carbondale. He was a teacher, coach and mentor all while at Benton High School. His presence and unique style of teaching will be sorely missed for years to come.*

Steve had a strong faith and was a good son, husband and father. Everyone who met Steve quickly became aware of his intense love of Christ and family. Though large and strong, he quickly became tender when talking about his family or his Savior. He attended Whittington Church, where he served as an elder and Sunday school teacher. Steve was also an ordained minister, who was active in ministry for the last 30 years of his life. Steve had many hobbies including cycling, hunting, fishing and playing with his grandkids. He was a huge supporter of the "rambling wreck" of Georgia Tech. He is missed by many. He married his high school sweetheart, Salinda. They have three children; Erin, Jeremy and Casey.

Personally, Steve McCommons was my fifth grade basketball coach and I had the pleasure of teaching with him at Benton High School. He was a stand-up guy that had such a great moral compass. It was an honor to call Steve my friend. He is still deeply missed today by so many.

I enjoyed the opportunity to visit with former Ranger Scott Hall. Hall gave great insight into the '74 team and my last question to him was this; how did Coach Herrin influence your life? There was a long pause as Hall carefully thought about the proper words to say.

Scott Hall: *Well…nothing but immense respect for the man…a complete privilege to play for him. We respected him and we never questioned him. We took his idiosyncrasies as you would a likeable uncle…we never made fun of him in a mean sort of way. It was always with affection. He was a professing Christian and we knew him as a very moral man. We never used bad language in front of Coach Herrin. It was unthinkable. He really cared about us. My parents went through a divorce when I was in high school. It was a difficult time for me and I think he sensed it. About this time he called me and asked me if I could help him put up a fence behind his house. I worked all day with him on that fence and he never said anything about it but he knew I was going through a rough time. It was his way of making me feel better and I never forgot that. I think basketball and Rich Herrin trickled down to everyone else… the other coaches in the program and even the community.*

After high school, Scott graduated from the College of Charleston in 1978. He earned his degree in psychology. He has been happily married to his wife Ruth for forty-one years and they have three children; Aaron, Jeffrey and Lauren. He is currently a therapeutic placement consultant and has been since 2002. Scott and his wife currently live in Franklin, Tennessee.

Reserve guard Steve Genisio went on to work in the coal mines for eighteen years and then went back to school and earned his degree in education. He just recently retired from Waltonville High School after teaching for seventeen years. He is married to his wife Karla and they have two children; Nathan and Stephanie.

Steve Genisio: *Coach may have had his favorites…but he didn't play favorites. I never heard him curse. I remember he would take me and some of the other better freshman track athletes to some varsity meets…it was just always a good time. Coach Herrin was my driver instructor and I got most of my hours driving to basketball camps and clinics.*

Assistant coach Don Webb went on to serve in the Benton basketball program for twenty-six years. While at Benton High School, Webb not only had great freshman teams, but he also rejuvenated the high school cross country program. One of the highlights of Webb's coaching career was coaching Brent McClain to a State Cross Country Championship in 1982. Late in his career, he rebuilt the girls track program by stringing together a series of successful girls' track teams. He also spoke highly of Coach Herrin and valued the time he had to learn under him as a young coach.

Don Webb: *He was always prepared. Sometimes we would eat lunch together and he would be writing out his practice schedule on a napkin. He was always interested in what defense the other team was going to play. This was always what he questioned me about the most. Also, I think I learned from him that all kids are not the same. You have to treat them fairly…but you can't treat all kids the same. You have to know the kids.*

They say timing is everything, and the '74 Rangers were blessed to come along during a special time in Benton basketball history. The class of '74 was the first graduating class of the new school and they were also the first group to play in the greatest high school gymnasium in Southern Illinois. The '74 team set the table for one of the most amazing years in the storied Ranger tradition…1975!

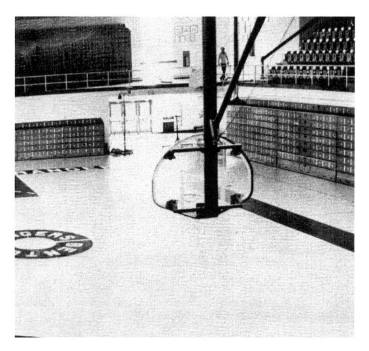

The new school opened in 73-74 and the gym featured a tartan
floor that could seat 4100 fans. *(Ceasar Maragni)*

In '74, Paul Dinkins had developed into one of the finest players
in Southern Illinois. Most importantly, "Dink" was loved by
his teammates. *(Benton High School)*

In 73-74, my dad (Mack Wynn) was in in his first year teaching Biology at Benton High School. My dad loved to fish and hunt and he was an incredible teacher. When he realized I wanted to play basketball, he jumped on board and never missed any of my games. *(Benton High School)*

Who scored the first basket in the New Gymnasium? Scott Hall. Hall shot a lay-up off the tip on opening night against McLeansboro. *(Ceasar Maragni)*

Steve Genisio grew up around the program and
was a senior in 73-74. *(Ceasar Maragni)*

As a boy, Roger Smith went to the games with his parents.
Smith played as a reserve and loved every minute of it.
(Ceasar Maragni)

Bill Chrostoski saw limited action in the post. His greatest
memory was running out of the tunnel in '75 against
Jeff Carling's Centralia Orphans. *(Ceasar Maragni)*

South Seven Champs

The gold warm-up tops and maroon pin-striped bottoms of 73-74
were my personal favorites. What a great look. *(Ceasar Maragni)*

Billy Smith drives to the basket at Changnon Gym in '74.
(Ceasar Maragni)

State Representative, Dave Severin, was a 1976 BCHS graduate. He was best
friends with Steve McCommons and gave valuable insight into his
good friends, Mark Craddock and Keith Tabor. *(Benton High School)*

Steve McCommons battles for a loose ball. *(Ceasar Maragni)*

A young Keith Tabor fights for a loose ball in the
'73 Centralia Tournament. *(Ceasar Maragni)*

An intense Rich Herrin barks instructions from the bench.
(Ceasar Maragni)

Steve McCommons went on to play football at Georgia Tech
and still holds the BCHS record in the discus with a
throw of 163'11. (Ceasar Maragni)

BCHS graduate Don Webb, arrived at Benton in the
fall of 1970 and coached freshmen basketball
for 26 seasons. *(Ceasar Maragni)*

CHAPTER TWENTY

The "Triple Threat" and the Great Team of '75

"As the wins kept increasing - 20, 21, 22…I thought…this is kind of cool." – Pat Golliher

In my first year of coaching the Rangers in 2002-2003, I asked Billy Smith to serve as our volunteer assistant coach. I enjoyed getting to know him and he added so much to our team that season. His son, Shane, was a sophomore and was our future point guard. He developed good relationships with all of the players and they loved his insight of the game. Billy only spoke if he had something valuable to say. He didn't waste words. He was quiet, kind and always pleasant to be around. But don't be fooled. Inside him was a fierce desire to win and if backed into a corner, he would come out swinging.

In our third game of the year, we played the Cairo Pilots in a Saturday afternoon game in the old DuQuoin Tournament. The Pilots were talented and featured some great players; Gary Matthews, Brandon Childs, and Roman Wright to name a few. The Pilots were coached by Larry Baldwin. It was just one of those games. We couldn't do anything right and Cairo couldn't do anything wrong. The Pilots were ahead by more than twenty points and I had taken the starters out. Our team was frustrated and we had to play later that night against a very good Carterville club. There were just a couple of minutes left in the game and Coach Baldwin put Brandon Childs back into the game. Childs was a starter and a tremendous shooter. The game was out of hand and he just shouldn't have been in the game. I later learned that Childs re-entered the game in hopes of getting the tournament's single-game three-point record. Upon entering the game, Childs hit a jump shot from the corner. I was seething. Billy tapped me on the shoulder. I looked at him and he had this mad look on his face and he said, "I would put the starters back in…and tell them to start taking guys out." He wasn't kidding. Smith was quiet but he had a fierce competitive streak that his teammates picked up on when their backs were against the wall. He was the quiet assassin.

As the '75 season inched closer, the town of Benton grew more excited. This could be the year. Billy Smith and Rob Dunbar were returning and they were two of the best players in the State of Illinois. Smith was now a senior and was the unquestioned leader of the team. He could do it all. He could handle it, pass it, and score if need be. He was lightening-quick and had a knack for turning steals and deflections into lay-ups. Most importantly, Smith placed the success of the team above his own personal accolades. Yes, Billy was a great talent, but it was always team first.

Junior Jay Sandusky grew up in the Washington School area and fell in love with the game of basketball from a young age. As a youngster, Sandusky would sneak in the back door of the old gym and sit on the stage and watch the Rangers. He admitted that the '71 team was the first team that really "captivated" him. He was now a member one of the greatest teams in Ranger history and a teammate of "Billy the Kid."

Jay Sandusky: *Billy was always the best player on the floor…he could dominate a game on the offensive end or the defensive end. I always felt that Billy sacrificed a lot of his scoring his senior year because we had Tabor and Dunbar. He always did what was best for the team.*

Junior Pat Golliher came off the bench and gave the Rangers much-needed depth at the post position. Golliher was quick to point out how Billy helped him make the transition to the varsity level.

Pat Golliher: *Billy was like having another coach on the floor…he was so calm. He would come by and just tap you on the leg and say, "Let's go." I looked up to that guy. You know…at Benton we were never allowed to pick on the underclassman…and that's the way it should be. The older guys were expected to lead us…and that's what they did.*

The pecking order was set in '75. Smith was, hands down, the captain and leader of the team. He was now in his fourth year of varsity basketball and he had been through the battles, but it was his personality that was so enduring to his teammates.

Coach Don Webb: *There really wasn't anything he couldn't do. He was a great athlete…he wasn't flashy but very smart. Most importantly he was a nice person. I remember there would be many times during the season that if the freshmen were practicing on Saturday mornings and he didn't have anything to do he would come up to the gym and be at practice. Those were his buddies…even though he was playing up.*

Junior Buck Durham was a blue-collar, no-nonsense post player for the Rangers in '75. Buck was a fierce competitor and picked up the role of enforcer after McCommons graduated in '74. Buck's junior year marked the first time he had been teammates with Billy Smith, but he remembers him well.

Buck Durham: *He was just a very gifted player. Very smart…intelligent… understood the game. He was a hustler…kind of the leader on the team, you know. Everyone respected him.*

Then there was Dunbar. He was now a solid 6'7" and he had transformed himself into one of the greatest post players that Southern Illinois had ever seen. Or was he a post player? In today's game, Dunbar fits the perfect stretch four. He could post up on the block or he could catch it out on the floor and knock down perimeter jump shots. There were nights that Dunbar could just "go off" offensively. But what made Dunbar's game ahead of its time was his ability to handle the ball. Dunbar could take the ball behind his back, between his legs and loved to use the spin move.

Jay Sandusky: *I hadn't seen anything like Dunbar. He was so versatile…he could post up or step out on the floor and shoot it. There wasn't anything he couldn't do. He was such a skilled player for his size.*

As his game evolved, he developed a deadly fade-away with a nice soft touch around the basket. To put it simply, he played like a guard, but was often the tallest player on the floor. Basketball fans that saw him play for the first time were fascinated with his game. Dunbar was not the typical muscle bound, robotic, back to the bucket post player of the seventies. He was smooth and fun to watch.

Billy Smith: *Rob had guard skills and he had a smooth shot. Rob just developed so quickly…there were times I couldn't believe what I was seeing. By the time he was a senior he had matured so much as a player…he was dominating. I think Rob was our MVP my senior year.*

Not only did the Rangers have Smith and Dunbar, but they had the greatest catch-and-shoot player in Ranger history in Keith Tabor. As a junior, Tabor was a tremendous athlete. If he turned sideways, you couldn't see him. He was very slender, but wiry strong and extremely quick.

Dave Severin: *Anything Keith did that involved any kind of eye-hand coordination…he was good at. Shooting pool or hitting a baseball…and especially shooting a basketball. Keith ran the half in junior high at 2:10. He was a 51 quarter guy…that is the kind of athlete he was. I remember one day in track we ran the half mile…and we were busting it. I was giving it everything I had…Keith was just so smooth…not even breaking a sweat. He ran with no effort.*

Billy Smith: *Keith was a great shooter and he could really elevate on his jump shot. He was quick and had great eye-hand coordination. He could get it off so quick.*

Tabor feasted on teams that focused solely on stopping Smith and Dunbar. Opposing teams learned quickly that you simply could not leave him open; he was too great a shooter. As teams began to respect Tabor's shooting ability and guard him closer, it opened driving lanes for Billy Smith and point guard Mark Craddock. At times, the Rangers seemed un-guardable because of the triple threat scoring of Smith, Dunbar and Tabor. The "Triple Threat" was tough to stop. They were just too potent offensively to be shut down on the same night and it made for explosive basketball on the offensive end of the floor.

Coach Herrin: *We had the three big-time scorers in Dunbar, Tabor and Smith and the playmaking ability of Craddock that made it all click. Bucky Durham was the fifth starter and his job was to rebound and play defense and he did that very well.*

The floor general of the team was junior Mark Craddock. Craddock spoke in a slow drawl, but there was nothing slow about his game. Craddock is considered by many old timers as one of the top two or three point guards to ever play at Benton High School. He was known affectionately as "Crock" by his teammates and he was a character.

Roger Smith: *He was a very steady guard. He showed very little emotion and was a "matter of fact" type of guy. Craddock's parents socialized with the Herrins and Mark had known Coach Herrin all of his life. His sophomore year Mark called Coach Herrin "Rich" in practice…Coach Herrin came unglued and stopped practice to tell Mark that he was to address him as "Coach Herrin." In the locker room after practice Mark said, "Man, I've known the guy since I was a kid…I don't see why he got so testy when I called him Rich."*

Craddock was a team-first guy and took great pride in getting the "Triple Threat" (Smith, Dunbar and Tabor) the ball in positions to score. On the floor, he wore eye glasses that were held securely in place with the "old-school" strap that snaked around his head. Crock's basketball IQ was off the charts, and knew where his teammates were on the floor at all times. He also did three things that all point guards must be able to do; he protected the ball, hit his lay-ups and was a tremendous free-throw shooter.

In high school, Mark Craddock and Keith Tabor were close friends, and you often could not see one without the other. In fact, when people talk about them today, they are mentioned together; Craddock and Tabor. Craddock played and practiced hard. He did not mess around, and had the special ability to light Tabor's fire in practice.

Roger Smith: *Tabor liked the games much more than practices. Keith and Mark were always together…very close. Mark really worked hard in practice and he could influence Keith to do the same thing. Keith would react to Mark when he challenged him to play harder.*

The '75 Rangers consisted of four seniors; Billy Smith, Rob Dunbar, Roger Smith and Bill Chrostoski. Roger Smith loved being a part of the team and played his role to the fullest. He played hard every day in practice to prepare the Ranger guards for Friday and Saturday nights and was well-respected by his teammates and coaches. Lefty Bill Chrostoski (Jack) battled hard in practice and gave the Rangers depth off the bench. He loved his experience as a Ranger.

Bill Chrostoski: *Those two team plaques (1973-74 and 1974-75) from my junior and senior year are on my wall…those were good times. It's just hard to believe that so many of those guys are gone. I sometimes think about that when I look at those team pictures.*

Besides Buck Durham, Jay Sandusky, Pat Golliher, Keith Tabor and Mark Craddock, there were five other juniors; Eric Forby, Andy Lampley, Russell Mitchell, Scott Meacham and Craig Beck.

Eric Forby: *I went to Douglas School in grade school. That was such a good time in my life. There was a court behind the school and I would wait for the older guys to get off work and I would get into games. These guys were working and they weren't necessarily basketball players but they loved to play. All of the older guys kind of took care of me and when I was finished I would walk home to eat and I couldn't be late. I lived on Ward Street. A guy by the name of Randy Smith really took care of me. He was just a super guy and he loved the game. He would take me to practice and even pick me up at times. He was a big influence on me when I was a kid. In my opinion, he is one of the greatest Ranger fans we've ever had. He went to all of the games.*

Forby was a quality player and an extremely gifted athlete. Eric Forby still holds the school record in the long jump at 22'8". At 6'3", Forby played above the rim and he often entertained his teammates with powerful dunks before and after practices. As a junior, he was stuck playing behind All-American Billy Smith, but wouldn't have traded that year for anything.

Eric Forby: *I didn't play a great deal on the '75 team because I was kind of Billy's back up. He was incredible. I don't think there was a better athlete than Billy Smith. He could do anything. He was the guy.*

Andy Lampley was a 6'1" jumping jack that just made things happen. In '75, Lampley competed for playing time at the post position with Buck Durham, Russell Mitchell and Pat Golliher. He was a sparkplug that always brought energy and hustle to the game.

Pat Golliher: *Andy was a really good jumper…very physical and a good defender.*

Russell Mitchell provided depth at the post position. Mitchell was a big body that took up space and gave the Rangers size off the bench. In fact, Coach Herrin utilized a rotation system with Durham and Mitchell for the final starting position all season until Durham won the job late in the season.

Bill Chrostoski: *Russ was a good defender and rebounder.*

Scott Meacham was also a junior and he was a fine athlete in his own right. Meacham was a solid football player and a gritty competitor. As a senior, he found success wrestling. Meacham blended nicely with the team and brought energy to each practice. Rounding out the junior class was guard Craig Beck. Beck was also a fine football player that loved to hunt and fish. I remember my father had a great relationship with him and would take Beck duck hunting in the winter. Beck was a team player and busted his butt every day in practice.

After the Centralia Holiday Tournament, Coach Herrin brought up sophomores Rodney Herrin and Joe Durham to complete the roster. Rodney was the oldest of Coach Herrin's three sons and the former Ranger mascot. In practice, Rodney Herrin was competing against veterans like Smith, Tabor and Craddock. What a learning experience. Joe Durham was also brought up to fill a varsity spot and competed hard against the likes of Buck Durham, Pat Golliher, Russell Mitchell, Andy Lampley, and Rob Dunbar. Both of the sophomores were wide-eyed, but they were improving.

With so many players returning, the Rangers were the overwhelming favorite to win the conference. The Centralia Orphans and Mt. Vernon Rams were expected to give the Rangers a run for their money. In the November 30, 1974, edition of the Benton Evening News, the four seniors (Chrostoski, Dunbar, B. Smith and Roger Smith) posed for a picture sporting their fresh flat-tops and new practice gear. They all have wide grins as if to say, "Get ready, this is going to be a great year." And a great year it was!

On December 3, 1974, a large number of Ranger fans raced east on Route 14, anxious to see the season opener against the McLeansboro Foxes. They were not disappointed. The Rangers played well and won the ballgame 76-55. Next up for the Rangers was a Saturday night contest with the Jacksonville Crimsons.

Over the radio, an excited Joe Browning said, "Keith Tabor for two from way downtown!" Tabor was on fire. It was a shooting display for the ages and he was draining shots from every spot imaginable. He scored 31 points and shot a blistering 14-19 from the field. Most of Tabor's shots were beyond 20 feet as he busted up the Jacksonville zone. Rob Dunbar quietly netted 28 and Billy Smith played the role of passer and led the team in assists with 11. The Rangers won the ballgame 92-71. It was an offensive clinic and the kind of game Herrin loves to coach. It was up and down, the ball being scored and the players having fun. This was Ranger basketball. An excited Rich Herrin made this comment after the game:

Rich Herrin: *Early in the ballgame, we looked good…and shot fabulous.*

On Friday, December 13th, the Rangers loaded the team bus and drove an hour south to Meridian High School. The Bobcats were always a formidable opponent and Meridian was a tough place to win. The Rangers looked sharp with their maroon shorts lined with white pinstripes and their matching tops that displayed a slanted Benton in script over the number. All of the players wore high-top maroon Chuck Taylors with striped tube socks to the knees. This was the style in '75. A young Kyle Herrin led the Rangers onto the floor.

In a squeaker, the Rangers won 69-64. The headline in the Benton paper the next day read, "Rangers Stagger To Win Over Hustling Meridian."

Rich Herrin: *I'm very happy we won the ballgame, but very disappointed in our overall play. We could have played with a lot more enthusiasm than we did. We played just hard enough to win…but that won't get you by better clubs.*

Oh, well. When you can play poorly and win, it's always better than playing poorly and losing. The Rangers were now 3-0 and opened South Seven play with games against Marion and Herrin before heading to C-town for the holiday tournament.

On Friday, December 20th, the Marion Wildcats traveled to Benton. The Cats had two great players in Pickens and Orr but it would not be enough. The Rangers jumped out to a ten-point lead to open the first quarter, but the Wildcats fought back to pull within one at halftime. The Rangers then came out in the third quarter and put the game away by outscoring the Wildcats 25-10. The third quarter displayed the explosiveness of the Ranger offense. Dunbar led all-scoring with 24 points and Tabor added 20 with Smith chipping in 14 points. Craddock was steady and Buck Durham was playing his usual blue-collar game in the paint. Although Durham was not counted on to score points, he was a very good rebounder and defender. Buck did not come to Benton until his seventh grade year and hadn't played much basketball before moving to town.

Buck Durham: *I grew up in San Francisco until our family relocated to Marion, Illinois and then we settled in Benton at the beginning of my seventh grade year. My dad was a surgeon and he wanted me to play basketball because Benton was a basketball powerhouse. As a young player, I was kind of spastic. I really didn't know what to do when I got the ball and I was always in a hurry. I made some embarrassing mistakes as a seventh grader. I remember the '71 team...those guys were my heroes.*

The Rangers were now 4-0 and 1-0 in conference play. The next night the Rangers played the Herrin Tigers on the road. Gone were Gary Rafe and Joe Hosman, but the Tigers had Mark Maller. The Rangers won the game 81-68 and moved to 5-0 on the year and 2-0 in the South Seven Conference. It was a happy ride home and Rich Herrin and his coaching staff knew that win or lose, the Centralia Tournament provided the competition the Rangers so desperately needed.

The team entered the tournament as the top seed. All of the fans in the Centralia Tournament were aware of the Benton Rangers. They win and they look good. They play good basketball and they have a passionate coach. Because of their success, the Rangers knew the bullseye was on their backs, and they wouldn't have it any other way. The tournament started with a big win over Ridgewood by a score of 69-32. All of the Rangers saw action. Jay Sandusky, Russ Mitchell and Andy Lampley got into the scoring column for the Rangers.

The following day, December 27th, the Rangers won a nail biter 60-59 over Rich East. The Rangers trailed by six points in the fourth quarter but fought back to tie the game. Tied at 57, Mark Craddock blew by his defender and made a lay-up to put the Rangers up 59-57. It was the only shot that Craddock took all afternoon. Rich East then scored to tie the game at 59. On the next possession, Dunbar was fouled and hit the front end of the bonus to give the Rangers a 60-59 lead with .09 seconds left. In a wild one, the Rangers hung on. It was a great come-from-behind victory and even though it wasn't the team's best performance, they survived. The Rangers advanced in the winner's bracket and had the confidence that they could win it the next day. Confidence, swagger, faith...whatever you want to call it. This was a big part of the Ranger basketball culture.

Pat Golliher: *We thought we had a superior program because we had a superior coach. I thought I was better than you because I played at Benton. I believed that every time I came onto the floor.*

In the semi-final match-up, the Rangers met the Belleville West Maroons. The Maroons had the dynamic duo of Milton Wiley and Rusty Lisch, but the Rangers had the "Triple Threat." The afternoon game in old Trout Gymnasium turned out to be a classic. In a high-scoring game, the Rangers won a wild one, 92-84. Dunbar scored 31 points followed by Smith's 26 and Tabor's 25. It was an incredible display of offense by three great players. The Rangers played three of their best quarters of the year to jump on top by 15 heading into the final quarter and held on to win. This was a monumental win and the question was; would the Rangers have enough that night to win the championship game?

That afternoon the Rangers got a bite to eat and then relaxed at a local motel. A young Rod Herrin remembered the motel stay.

Rod Herrin: *Joe Durham and I were sophomores. Dad put the top eight guys two to a room so they could get some rest and then he put like eight of us in one room. There were like eight guys in one room. Joe and I wrestled for space on the bed and we accidentally put a hole in the wall. When dad walked into the room, Joe tried to hide the hole in the wall by putting a lamp in front of it but that didn't work. Dad saw it...he was really mad, saying stuff like I don't know why I brought some of you guys. What did he expect, you know... putting eight of us in one room?*

Two hours later, the Rangers found out that they would be playing the Centralia Orphans for all the marbles. If you are a basketball fan, it doesn't get any better than this; Benton vs. Centralia in the championship game. It was well after 8:00 p.m. when the game finally began.

Centralia had a colorful young coach by the name of Jeff Carling. Carling thought outside the box and was a showman. He demanded so much attention that the team was dubbed "Carling's Darlings". Carling had an underneath out-of-bounds play where four of his players fell to the floor, and then one player broke to the basket for a lay-up. The Centralia fans welcomed his energy and enthusiasm and he was also winning. He created excitement and gave the Centralia basketball program a boost of energy. Jeff Carling could run for mayor if he could beat the Rangers, and he knew it.

At game time, old Trout was packed, creating an uncomfortably hot and stuffy environment for the spectators. But nobody in the building wanted to be anywhere else. The balcony was full and the gym was filled with the clashing color combination of maroon and red. The scent of popcorn wafted thru the crowd and it was so loud that you could not talk to the person sitting by you. This was what it was all about.

Billy Smith: *I loved playing in the Centralia Tournament. I felt like I played some of my best basketball in the Centralia Tournament.*

The Rangers were booed unmercifully as they ran onto the floor but the players smiled with every step knowing they were hated because they were good. It was respect at its fullest. Carling brought his players onto the floor to rousing shouts and applause from the Centralia faithful. The Centralia student section, dubbed "the Orphanage", was in a frenzy as Coach Carling passed by with his wide-collar shirt and bell-bottomed trousers.

Carling had the attention of the crowd, but Rich Herrin had the best team. In an unforgettable display of perseverance and toughness, the Rangers dug deep and won the ballgame 72-71. Centralia's Demarlyn Chapman scored 29 points leading all scorers. Chapman's performance was incredible, but the Rangers had Smith, Dunbar and Tabor. There were just too many guns for the Orphans to cover. Keith Tabor led the Rangers in scoring with 20 points and Dunbar added 19. Bill Smith chipped in 15 and Mark Craddock had ten points. Craddock had eight points in the final quarter with the game in the balance. Buck Durham, Andy Lampley and Russ Mitchell banged inside and won the rebounding advantage by one.

Buck Durham: *Winning the Centralia Holiday Tournament in '75 was my favorite memory as a Benton Ranger. That tournament was the most fun to play in. It was the most challenging. We had some great battles against Centralia, and they had that flashy coach* (Jeff Carling).

After the game, Benton fans flooded the floor as the Rangers were presented the championship trophy. Most of the Orphan fans raced to the exits, it was a sight they could not watch. When the trophy presentation was over, the All-Tournament team was announced and Rob Dunbar was chosen as the tournament MVP. Billy Smith was selected on the first team and Keith Tabor earned second team honors.

Dunbar's play in the tournament was jaw dropping. He averaged 21 points and eight rebounds per game. Dunbar tipped balls in, filled the lanes on fast breaks, shot over players on the block, buried fade-aways from the short corner and hit perimeter jump shots. He did it all!

Pat Golliher: *Rob was like a Kevin McHale type…not very physical but he was all over the rim. He was a finesse player.*

Another player that really earned his stripes in the tournament was point guard Mark Craddock. Ranger fans felt good any time Craddock had the ball. He was dependable and smart. A great team player.

Dave Severin: *Crock was just so smart…In grade school Mark was like the spelling champion of the entire town in the fourth, fifth and sixth grades. He played with tenacity and he was a great free-throw shooter. He was a very good defender. He was one of the best guards to ever come through the program. He was all about getting Billy and Tabor the ball where they could score. He protected the ball so well…so smart and could really see the floor.*

The Rangers moved to 9-0 after winning the Centralia Tournament for a record fifth time. On top of that, the win in the championship game was Coach Herrin's 300th victory at Benton High School. After winning the tournament, the Rangers defeated Carbondale and Harrisburg to move to 11-0 and set up a rematch with the Orphans. Many older Ranger fans believe the Centralia game to be the greatest game ever played in the Rich. Bill Chrostoski and Roger Smith remembered this night as their greatest memory as a Ranger player.

Bill Chrostoski: *I remember winning the Centralia Holiday Tournament in '75. Then about a week later Centralia came to Benton. Jeff Carling brought his "Darlings" into our place. There were 3,500 plus people in the gym. I remember standing in that Tunnel…hearing that crowd…before we ran out. It was incredible. That's what it was all about…you know.*

Roger Smith: *When we ran out of the Tunnel, I always ran out in front of Billy. The place was packed and the adrenaline was flowing…it was the first time I ever touched the rim. It was in pre-game warm-ups that night. Centralia ran out and Carling would stand at half-court and he would take his players thru these calisthenics…like they would drop on the floor and do* *push-ups. Murphy Hart was kind of the leader of our student section, and he came on to the floor and mimicked the Centralia players' every move. It was hilarious!*

Again, Carling was up to his old tricks. He called Coach Herrin the week of the game and made him a proposition. With the Centralia-Benton game looming, he offered a friendly wager; the losing coach shaves his head. Coach Herrin denied the challenge. He knew better than to get involved in Carling's antics.

Coach Rich Herrin: *Carling really created excitement. He did a lot for Centralia basketball…he was a pretty good basketball coach and his teams played hard.*

Today, the game is still considered to be one of the greatest games in Ranger basketball history. People flocked to see the Rangers and Orphans and now you had the game within the game; Herrin and Carling. Basketball fans braved the weather and stood outside the 4,100-seat gymnasium to get tickets. The place rocked!

A good friend of mine and former Ranger, Ron Brookins, was a freshman when the Orphans came to town. Brookins became a key guard on the '78 team, but on this night, he watched in awe as the "Triple Threat" tangled with "Carling's Darlings."

Ron Brookins: *If I could go back in history and see one sporting event… it would be the Benton Centralia game when I was a freshman. I would want to be sitting right behind the Rangers' bench where I could see and hear everything. Matt, I'm telling you…those guys were good. That '75 team had incredible talent…I actually remember we scored right off the tip…it was an incredible game. The seats were full and people were standing in the corners.*

The Rangers jumped out of the gate quick. The Rich was rocking as the team built a 44-34 lead at halftime, but the Orphans came out hot in the third quarter to outscore the Rangers 19-11. In the closing seconds, Smith and Craddock hit free throws down the stretch to win a close one, 77-74. Tabor shot lights out and scored a game-high 26 points. The Rangers were now 12-0 and All-American guard Billy Smith was the third leading scorer behind Dunbar and Tabor.

Roger Smith: *Bill was the guy that made everything go. In his career, he played every role...ball Handler...leading scorer...second leading scorer. He literally filled every position the team needed. He could do that.*

The practices in '75 were something to behold because of the talent on the floor. They were so competitive. Rich Herrin's practices were designed to push his players and he ran a tight ship.

Pat Golliher: *Matthew, Coach Herrin never cursed...but he would get upset... throw his practice papers down...kick the bleachers. He always got his point across. In practice, he sent me to the showers early twice...he came and got me and told me to get back out there and work harder. He could really motivate me. He still motivates me today when I'm running by myself at the cemetery; I can still hear his voice. When I was at home...I was under my dad's control...but when I left the house, I was under Rich's control. I remember when we would practice after school and we weren't doing something right...I can still hear him say, "Do it again, gang." We didn't take a shower until things were done right.*

    Practices were intense. Coach had a drill where he would roll the ball on the floor and two players would have to go get it. It was intense.

Another way in which Coach Herrin may have been ahead of his time was his emphasis on scouting. The Rangers sent assistant coaches out all the time to scout for upcoming games. Scouting reports were part of each game's preparation and sometimes even film was watched. During this time, viewing film was cutting-edge because filming games was a more complicated process than today. Herrin and his coaching staff didn't leave a rock unturned when preparing for the opposition.

Pat Golliher: *You know, we had a good scouting system, too. We had scout teams that ran the opponent's plays in practice, and they were on the money. We had teams scouted.*

After the Rangers defeated Centralia, they won games against West Frankfort and then Mt. Vernon. The overall record stood at 14-0 and the team was now 7-0 in conference play.

    It was now Benton Invitational Tournament time, and the Rangers looked to avenge the disappointing loss to Carmi in the championship game the year before. The Rangers opened tournament play with an 84-60 win over Paris and then defeated Bob Brown's Eldorado Eagles by a score of 68-62. Eldorado had a strong team with Bill Morris and Mike Duff, but the Rangers held on for the win. On the other side of the bracket, Ron Herrin's Olney Tigers upset second-seeded Alton to set up a Benton-Olney Championship. Brother against brother.

The Rangers finished off the tournament in style by defeating Olney by a score of 85-63. The game proved to be most important for the Tigers; it gave them a chance to feel out the Rangers in case they met in post-season play. And they would. But until then, the Rangers were rolling and gearing up for the second loop of conference play.

The team won their next four by defeating Marion, West Frankfort, Herrin and Harrisburg. In those four games, the team averaged eighty points a contest. They were now 21-0 and the Benton Evening News played on the unbeaten streak by counting each win.

Pat Golliher: *As the wins kept increasing…19, 20, 21…I thought, this is kind of cool.*

The Rangers then traveled to Centralia for their last battle of the season with the Orphans. During the pre-game warm-ups, Coach Carling's wife led the Orphan players in calisthenics and then some funky music blared from the speakers with the intent of distracting the Rangers. In the end, the Rangers broke the Orphans by defeating them a third time, twice on their own floor. The '75 team was mentally tough and knew how to win close games. Late in the game Craddock and Andy Lampley hit pressure-packed free throws to seal the win. They were now 22-0.

Rich Herrin: *Down the stretch we played with great composure.*

On February 21, 1975, the Carbondale Terriers came to town. The Rangers jumped out to a 19-10 first quarter lead and it seemed like things could not be going better. Then it happened! Teammate Roger Smith explains:

Roger Smith: *It happened right in front of me. He came down and was driving the baseline dribbling with his left hand…he then used a whirl dribble and went to spin away from the baseline. When he did…his knee and his body moved but his foot stayed planted. He went down immediately.*

After the play, Dunbar lay motionless on the tartan floor. The gym fell silent. The Ranger players and fans had a sickening feeling as Coach

Herrin attended to Dunbar for what seemed like hours before he was carried off.

Roger Smith: *Coach Herrin called for someone to help him off the floor. Me and Russ Mitchell carried him off the floor that night.*

To this day, Benton fans can still recall the spot on the floor where Dunbar went down and the hush that fell over the gymnasium.

Jay Sandusky: *You could have heard a pin drop in that gym when Dunbar went down. In that moment we went from a great team to a very good team.*

When play resumed, the Rangers muddled through the game and won by a score of 76-47. As fans exited the gym that night, it would have been impossible to determine who won the game. The fans grieved for Dunbar, and without him the journey to the State Tournament would be an uphill climb. The injury was devastating to Rob personally. He was coming into his own as a player, and was getting college attention. The injury to his knee was so severe that he was lost for the season. He was a senior.

Bill Chrostoski: *Rob really had a great opportunity with basketball. If he hadn't of hurt his knee, who knows what he could have done. I just remember that my mom was in the hospital due to her gall bladder and it was at the same time that Rob hurt his knee. After the game, I went to the hospital to see my mom…but then afterward I went to Rob's room to see him.*

The Rangers then pulled together to clinch the conference crown by defeating Mt. Vernon. It was over. The Rangers were 24-0 and finished a perfect 14-0 in South Seven play. It was an incredible season with only one more non-conference game to play, against the Effingham Flaming Hearts.

The Effingham game was played on senior night and Ranger fans came out in droves to send off Billy Smith, Rob Dunbar, Bill Chrostoski and Roger Smith. The four seniors had done more than keep the tradition going; they had raised the bar to unfair heights for the Ranger teams of the late seventies. For some in the crowd, it was the end of an era. Billy Smith was soon to be gone. Many Ranger fans stood and applauded with lumps in their throats as Smith was acknowledged in a pre-game ceremony at center court. Dunbar was then introduced and the Benton faithful gave him a touching round of applause as he stood propped on his crutches to acknowledge the fans. Smith and Chrostoski were then announced and received their just due from the crowd.

After the short ceremony, the ball was tipped and the Rangers played to keep their season perfect. On this night, it was all about staying unbeaten. Everyone on the team knew they had to do more with Dunbar out. Every player took it upon themselves to pick up the slack. Tabor went off for 36 points, followed by Smith's 24 and Buck Durham scored a season-high 18 points. The good news was the Rangers finished the season at 25-0. Perfect!

Rich Herrin: *We were still a pretty good team after Dunbar got hurt. But we didn't have the size, and that hurt us.*

'75 State Tournament Play

The first indication that things were not quite right without Dunbar was the opening game of the Harrisburg Regional, against West Frankfort. The Rangers had beaten West Frankfort by 13 and 14 points in their first two meetings. The team was out of sync and got off to a poor start and trailed by as many as ten points in the second quarter, and six midway through the fourth quarter. In a wild ending, 6'3" junior Buck Durham, scored the winning basket with .35 seconds left on the clock.

Buck Durham: *They were guarding all of our scorers, you know. I'm standing at the free throw line wide open and I get the ball and turn and shoot it. I wasn't a great shooter. I was a defender and a rebounder…blue collar. When I shot that ball I heard Rich yell, "NO! NO!"…and then it swished right in… and he yelled, "YES! YES!"*

After the win, the team was 26-0 but the body language and mood of the players did not match their unprecedented success. The Rangers were worried. They were not the same team without Dunbar, and they knew it. It was as if they could see the end coming. But for now, they were still alive. Coach Herrin had these comments after the close victory over West Frankfort:

Coach Rich Herrin: *They made us play their game early by controlling the tempo. They scrambled for the loose ball and we didn't.*

With the win, the Rangers advanced to play Harrisburg for the Regional Championship. The Bulldogs were capable, and were led by Joe Culbreth and Paul Whitehead. Early in the game, Buck Durham ran into foul trouble but the Rangers survived due to the deadly shooting of Keith Tabor. Tabor scored 36 points and put on an incredible shooting display. He scorched the nets at Davenport Gymnasium to advance the Rangers to the Sectional. Billy Smith had 20 points and all the Rangers did what they had to do to win. The attitude was simple; survive and advance.

The Harrisburg Regional victory set up a game with Olney in the first game of the Sectional Tournament at West Frankfort. The Rangers had won their previous meeting with the Tigers by a score of 85-63 with Dunbar. But that was with Dunbar. The Olney Tigers were coached by Ron Herrin. The Tigers had a good basketball team led by Larry and Terry Bussard who were cousins and they also had strong play from senior Tony Phelps. Most importantly they were playing well and Ron Herrin had them believing they could win. The Tigers were a good basketball team despite the fact that Benton had dismantled them earlier in the year. Basketball seasons are long, and sometimes the chance of defeating the opponent depends on when the game is played. Olney was hot and after the injury to Dunbar, Benton was not.

Tony Phelps: *We had a good team. That same year we beat Jay Shidler and the Lawrenceville Indians at home by three. Shidler was a junior…we held him to 26 and he was averaging something like 34. We were proud of that. Lawrenceville won the Class A State Championship in 1976…so yeah, we had won some big games.*

With Dunbar now out, the Rangers had two great scorers in Billy Smith and Keith Tabor. Ron Herrin felt the time was right to employ a triangle and two defense; guarding Smith and Tabor man-to-man and then playing a triangle-type zone to guard the basket. The gimmick defense is most effective when an opposing team has two dominant scorers at the guard position. Gimmick defenses are sometimes a gamble and they can backfire if they don't work. For Ron Herrin, if the gimmick defense doesn't work then the blame would fall squarely on his shoulders. It was a risk Ron Herrin would take.

Tony Phelps: *I believe Ron was planning on using the triangle and two because I can remember going over it before we ever got into the Regional*

Tournament. We just didn't have a very tough Regional…and I believe Ron was looking ahead in case we played Benton in the sectional. The Rangers embarrassed us in the BIT, but without Dunbar we thought we could win. I would like to say that we could have beaten them with him…but I just don't think we would have. He was so good. We just couldn't stop him…he was big and moved like a guard. Ron had us believing it could work.

On this night in West Frankfort, Ron Herrin's game plan worked and the Rangers grew frustrated by the defense and had trouble scoring. With Dunbar, Ron Herrin would not have employed the defense but with Tabor and Smith both being guards it worked.

Billy Smith: *It was a frustrating game. It was the first time that I had been gimmicked. They played a triangle and two and they guarded me. We just couldn't get anything going. I remember late in the game I took a bad shot and I heard Robert Corn in the stands shout, "No!" because it wasn't a good shot. He was right.*

When the game was over, the Herrin brothers shook hands and Ron was glad to get the victory but he hurt for his brother. Why? Because as Coach Rich Herrin must have said a million times, "He was the greatest big brother a guy could have."

After the game, the Rangers showered and dressed in complete silence. The loss was devastating. It was their only defeat. Some players shed tears and others were completely silent as they tried to make sense of it all. It wasn't supposed to end like this. An emotional Coach Herrin addressed the team after the game and thanked them for their effort and the enjoyable ride they had together. It was difficult for him to speak through his emotion.

For the Rangers, it had been an unbelievable season full of accomplishments; an undefeated regular season, South Seven Champs, Centralia Tournament Champions, Benton Invitational Champions and Regional Champions. But the thing that pained the players and coaches most was the question of what might have been without Dunbar's injury. It was tough to think about and this thought haunted the '75 Rangers for the rest of their lives. What might have been?

After many years of reflection, Jay Sandusky made this point about his junior season:

Jay Sandusky: *Our team was honored a couple of years ago at the Alumni game and I have the '75 team plaque hanging on my wall at home. I was looking at all of the guys in that picture and there were nine players that played some level of college basketball…and Buck played football at Tulane. There was a lot of talent on that team.*

After it was over, the seniors on the '75 team looked back with fond memories of their experience as a Ranger and the opportunity they had to play for Coach Rich Herrin.

Roger Smith: *He set a good example for us as a person. He did go out of his way to help people. If he could…he would always help people out. I love Sue, too. There is always a strong person at home behind the big man. Before the Sectionals my senior year, we had a pep rally. He was going through all of the seniors and talking about each one of us individually. When he got to me, he said, "If I had a fourth son, I would want him to be as good as Roger. I'll never forget that."*

When Roger told me this story, he was emotional. He became great friends with Coach Herrin after his playing days and misses him greatly. After high school, Roger went to Rend Lake College. He then farmed full time with his father. He now owns his own business and Coach Herrin always requested his work. Roger is married to his wife Penni and they have three children; Aubrey, Brett and Bart.

Bill Chrostoski explained to me that being a Benton Ranger was one of the greatest experiences in his life.

Bill Chrostoski: *We had a fun bunch of guys and we all had a common goal. It was a good time in my life and I'm glad I had the chance to experience it. One thing I recall him saying was, "Not all of you are going to eat this ball." He was right, you know. For some of us…it was time for us to start thinking about what we wanted to do with our lives. I realized it was time for me to start thinking about going to college…and that set me on a path to my career.*

After high school, Chrostoski earned his bachelor's degree in microbiology from SIU Carbondale. He currently lives in Troy, Illinois. He worked for thirty-seven years in the public health business. He has two sons; Eric and Philip.

Billy Smith loved playing for Coach Herrin and he lit up when we talked about his coaches.

Billy Smith: *I enjoyed all of my coaches at Benton. Perry Eisenhower, Bob Johnston, Burton Wills, Donnie Webb, Coach Stewart and Coach Phillips… they were all great. Coach Herrin was great…other than my dad, you know. I remember one time he got upset with me. I kind of showed my butt one time when I was a junior. He sat me down and said, "I'm disappointed in you." Wow…that was…that's all he needed to say. I always felt like Coach Herrin was a step ahead of everyone. He was established…he had our respect. When I got to college at Georgia Tech…don't get me wrong, it was a great experience… but I would have loved to come back and played four more years for Coach.*

In the April 20, 1975, edition of the Evansville Courier there is a picture of Billy Smith signing his letter of intent to attend Georgia Tech and play basketball. Coach Herrin is standing behind Billy. Rich Yunkus, Dave Lockin and Steve McCommons all went to Georgia Tech and now Billy would be the fourth Benton athlete in the Georgia Tech pipeline. Smith played Division I basketball and played with and against great players in college. He made many life-long friendships but admitted he had trouble adjusting to a new style of play in college.

Billy Smith: *Dewayne Morrison was our coach at Georgia Tech. He wanted to play slow. I remember one time I got the outlet pass and was pushing the ball up the floor…I heard Coach Morrison trying to tell me to slow down. It was different. After my first year at Georgia Tech, I was looking to transfer to Evansville. They just didn't have a scholarship available. If I would have transferred to Evansville, I would have been in that plane crash. I stuck it out at Georgia Tech. I had some great teammates.*

There is a life-size picture of Billy hanging in Rich Herrin Gymnasium that recognizes his All-American status as a senior. He finished his Ranger career with 1,311 points which ranks him as the eighth leading scorer in school history. Most importantly, he played on four teams with a cumulative record of 91-17. Many people in Benton still believe Smith to be the greatest multi-sport athlete in school history. Today, Billy still holds the school record in the triple jump with a jump of 43'8 ½". In basketball, his number 23 is retired and hangs above center court. As a senior, he was also an All-South football selection. After high school, he worked in the field of information technology and is now retired. Today, Billy Smith lives in Benton with his wife Cathy and they have three children; Lindsay, Drew and Shane.

On Tuesday, December 31, 2019, Rob Dunbar lost a year-long battle with cancer and passed away at his home in Marion, Illinois. Dunbar had recently retired from the Illinois State Police Crime Lab at Carbondale in 2012. Rob is survived by his wife Jennifer and their four children; Alecia, Jeff, Dustin and Kara.

In just two seasons, Rob scored close to 1,000 points in his career and was named the most valuable player of the Centralia Holiday Tournament in 1974. He is still remembered by many as one of the greatest basketball players in Ranger history. In fact, following his death, there was a moment of silence for Rob's passing at a home Ranger basketball game. Rob's death was a blow to the Benton basketball family and sportswriter, Jim Muir, wrote an article honoring the life of Rob Dunbar. In his article, he interviewed Coach Rich Herrin and Dunbar's teammate Billy Smith.

Coach Rich Herrin: *First, I was very saddened to hear the news about Rob. He could do it all with a basketball, he was very talented and could score inside and* outside. *I knew he was good as a junior but as a senior he worked himself into a great player. It was just a shame for him and the team that he tore up his knee. There is not a doubt in my mind that if Dunbar hadn't gotten hurt we would have made it to the Super-Sectional in Carbondale and played East St. Louis. And I think we could have matched up with them."*

Billy Smith (Lifelong friend and teammate): *At 6-feet-7, Rob could just do so many things. He could handle the ball like a guard and could grab a rebound and then take the middle on the fast break. There was no dunking then, but Rob would just take the ball up and drop it in…over his head. He was a great jumper. It was incredible to be his teammate. There were times on the floor when I would watch him make a move under the basket and score and I would just sort of stop and think "wow" – he could just do everything on the basketball court. He's clearly one of the greatest players ever in Benton basketball history.*

The '75 team was an incredible team that Ranger fans still talk about to this day. The amazing play of Billy Smith, Rob Dunbar and Keith Tabor dazzled Ranger fans but left many with this question; how deep in State Tournament play could the Rangers have advanced if Dunbar hadn't been injured? On to '76!

Coach Herrin and Coach Stewart pose for a quick picture following
the annual Soap Game in the fall of '74. *(Ceasar Maragni)*

Billy Smith is possibly the greatest three sport athlete in
school history. Smith went on to play Division 1 basketball
at Georgia Tech University. *(Ceasar Maragni)*

Jay Sandusky appreciated his experience as a Benton Ranger.
Here he is as a junior. *(Ceasar Maragni)*

Pat Golliher provided key minutes off the bench in 74-75.
(Ceasar Maragni)

Buck Durham was the enforcer inside for the Rangers. Durham was blue-collar and an important part of the Rangers success in '75. *(Ceasar Maragni)*

Rob Dunbar was a guard in a big-man's body. Today, Dunbar is remembered as one of the greatest Rangers of all-time. *(Ceasar Maragni)*

Keith Tabor drives to the basket during the 74-75 season.
(Ceasar Maragni)

Mark Craddock was extremely steady at the point guard spot.
Craddock ranks high among Ranger point guards.
(Ceasar Maragni)

Rod Herrin dressed on the great team of '75 as a sophomore.
(Ceasar Maragni)

Rangers and Orphans battle in the '74 Centralia Championship. *(Centralia High School)*

Coach Herrin sports the white shoes in the '74 Centralia Tournament. *(Ceasar Maragni)*

Coach Herrin and the Rangers are presented with the '74 Centralia Tournament Championship Trophy. *(Ceasar Maragni)*

Jeff Carling brought excitement back to Centralia and his flamboyant personality ignited a healthy rivalry between the Rangers and the Orphans in the 70's. *(Ceasar Maragni)*

The "Bleacher Bums" root the Rangers on. *(Ceasar Maragni)*

The 27-1 Rangers of '75. **Front Row-** Meachum, Sandusky, R. Smith, R. Herrin, Beck, K. Herrin **Middle Row-** Lampley, Chrostoski, B. Smith, J. Durham, Forby, Craddock, Tabor. **Back Row-** Webb, Stewart, Mitchell, Dunbar, Golliher, B. Durham, Herrin and Phillips.

CHAPTER TWENTY-ONE

The Rollercoaster Ride of '76

"From the time we were in the seventh grade we had only lost like eight games. We almost lost half that many before the Centralia Tournament in '76." – Jay Sandusky

There is no doubt that there were high expectations for the '76 team despite the fact that All-State players, Billy Smith, and Rob Dunbar were gone. To put it simply, the Rangers returned a group of players that were proven winners. Dating back to the seventh grade, the class of '76 had lost only eight basketball games. They found ways to win. Winning basketball games had been their identity, and Ranger fans had every right to think that this season would be no different.

The Rangers returned three starters from the '75 team that finished 27-1; seniors, Mark Craddock, Keith Tabor and Buck Durham.

"Crock" was now a year older and had been thru the wars of '75. He provided a sense of calm and veteran leadership that proved to be invaluable in '76. Ranger teammate Buck Durham didn't mince words when it came to Craddock.

Buck Durham: *Craddock has to be one of the greatest ball handlers ever. His father really molded him. He would blindfold Mark and have him dribble with either hand when he was a kid. He was just a great guard.*

Craddock's best friend, Keith Tabor, also returned at the shooting guard position. Tabor's shooting ability was incredible, and if he got "hot", he had the ability to take over games. He was such a great shooter that Coach Herrin gave Tabor the green light to launch the ball at his discretion. No shot was a bad shot for Tabor, and the unbridled freedom gave him a sense of confidence which led to shooting performances that left fans in awe. Ranger fans had seen enough of him the past two seasons to have the feeling that every time he shot the ball, it was going in. Teammate Buck Durham saw Tabor's shooting ability firsthand.

Buck Durham: *Tabor could just light it up. He was a great shooter.*

Keith Tabor was a character off the floor as well. Good friend and classmate Dave Severin remembered some fun times with Tabor.

Dave Severin: *Matt, when Tabor got hot…you couldn't stop him. He was a phenomenal bank shooter and I spent many afternoons at Tabor's after school on Lickliter Street. When we were kids…it was the day they handed out report cards. He urged me to come home with him after school so he wouldn't get in so much trouble with his parents. I remember one time we were on the bus and we had a radio playing…the song was "Benny and the Jets"…and when it hit that part of the song we heard Keith belt out, "Daddy and the Band!" He was singing…but not sure of the words. We just laughed and he laughed with us.*

Senior Forward Buck Durham also returned and brought toughness and a competitive attitude that permeated through the team. Although Buck was remembered most as a solid post defender and rebounder, he developed an offensive game that could provide eight to ten points each night as a senior.

Pat Golliher: *Buck was physical…I just always liked Buck's game. He was an enforcer.*

Other returning seniors were Eric Forby, Andy Lampley, Pat Golliher, and Jay Sandusky. It was a talented group of veteran players. Eric Forby was a tremendous leaper and provided the Rangers with versatility at the small forward position. He stood at 6'2" and had a strong lower body defined by muscular legs and hips that gave him great speed and jumping ability. He was a solid rebounder and could handle the ball when called upon. As a junior, Forby played behind Billy Smith, but did see some varsity action.

As a senior, Forby rose to the occasion and played solidly on both ends of the floor.

Buck Durham: *Let me tell you…that was an athlete right there. I don't know if Forby ever got the credit he deserved.*

Andy Lampley also saw limited action as a junior but was expected to take on a larger role in '76. He was a physical specimen that would provide depth in the post. Lampley was only 6'1" but played much bigger. He was a quick jumper and more than willing to mix it up inside.

Senior Pat Golliher also competed for playing time at the post position. He played at 6'5" and was a product of the Ranger basketball program from a young age.

Pat Golliher: *I went to Lincoln School as a kid. I played for Burton Wills and Bob Johnston in junior high. They were my kind of coaches. We were taught to hustle. I remember Coach Wills sent me into the game once…and I walked into the game. He grabbed me and said, "You run into the game." That kind of set the tone.*

The final senior was number 20, Jay Sandusky. Sandusky found playing time hard to come by, but loved the game of basketball and proved to be a valuable member of the team. Jay had a "team first" attitude and an easygoing personality that made him popular with his teammates. He also has a unique perspective on his experience as a Benton Ranger.

Jay Sandusky: *You know they say all the guys that play at Duke are kind of like a family. I think it's like that with all the guys that played for Coach Herrin. It's like a web of guys and Coach Herrin is right there in the middle. We are like family…there is a brotherhood.*

The team also carried seven juniors; Rodney Herrin, Joe Durham, Alan Klochany, Roger Webb, Steve Summers, Bob Boehnlein and Shawn Curry.

As a sophomore, Rod Herrin had dressed on the varsity team but received no quality playing time. But now as a junior, Herrin was the first guard off the bench behind Craddock and Tabor. Rod Herrin played at 5'9"; he was a very smart player and played with an air of confidence that served him well. He had good quickness and was a good jump shooter, but it was his competitive nature that set him apart. Much like his father,

Herrin did not back down from a challenge. In football, he was an All-South defensive back that loved contact.

Joe Durham: *He could blast you in football.*

Rod Herrin grew up in the eye of the Benton Community and there were many Ranger fans that remember him best as the young boy blasting through the paper hoops and leading the Rangers onto the floor.

Rod Herrin: *To me…that was a really big deal. I had my own little warm-up uniform that matched the team's uniforms. The old gym was just packed… it seemed like everyone was there. When the game started…I really didn't have a seat on the bench. I just sat on the ball bag during the games. At the home games, me and some of my buddies would play basketball games in the locker room while the game was going on. I think Dad just wanted us around to be a part of it.*

As a young boy, he explored every nook and cranny of the old Cracker Box while the Rangers practiced. In his free time, he wandered the gym and developed a unique trick that he tried to keep a secret, especially when he was hungry.

Rodney Herrin: *In the lobby of the old gym, there were these mechanical vending machines that sold candy. My arm was so skinny that I could reach up into the machine and get all the candy I wanted.*

Coach Herrin: *Rodriguez would get in that candy machine…I'll tell you that…right now.*

Rod had seen all the great Rangers teams and knew most all of the players. Some boys grow up on the farm and that is where they are comfortable. Rodney Herrin grew up in the gym. In the gym, he was in his element. Ranger point guard Jerry Hoover was the first player that Rod idolized. In '76, Rod's time had finally come. He was now a Ranger player with a chance to contribute to the big club.

Let's face it, sometimes coaches can get under the skin of their players, especially if the coach is your dad. Rod was the oldest of the three Herrin boys and played the role of the guinea pig when it came to playing for his dad. This was something new for Coach Herrin also. He was now coaching his son.

Rod Herrin: *Dad wasn't going to play me unless I earned it. He was a sly motivator. When I was in junior high, he would say stuff like, "So-and-so is pretty good, you're going to have to work hard to beat them out." Nobody was going to beat me out, you know…that's the attitude I had. I played behind "Crock" my junior year. I played a quarter or a little bit more. Mark was really good…he just didn't make many mistakes.*

Joe Durham was another junior that would be heavily counted on in '76. As a sophomore, Joe also dressed on the varsity team and gained valuable experience competing against the likes of Rob Dunbar and Buck Durham every day in practice. Joe played at 6'4" and was a solid mid-range jump shooter. He was a better than average defender and played hard. Much like his teammates, Joe grew up watching Benton basketball from as early as he could remember.

Joe Durham: *In grade school, I went to Logan School and played for Farley Finter. My mom and dad* (Matthew and Evelyn) *had season tickets and we went to every game…home and away. I remember the teams of Yunkus, Burlison and Hoover. One time, Yunkus was playing with a group of guys on the outside courts near Logan School and I was trying to get his autograph. Those guys were your heroes…you know.*

Junior Roger Webb moved to Benton as a freshman from Finley, Illinois. Webb played at 6'3" and he was skilled. He was sneaky around the basket and had a solid mid-range game. Webb was a great leaper and proved to be a huge addition to the program. He vividly remembered the first day his parents brought him to register at Benton High School. He was a freshman.

Roger Webb: *My parents* (Roger and Virginia) *took me to Benton High School for my first day of school. We had just pulled into town. We walked into the office and they were registering me for class and Coach Herrin walked in and said, "Let me take Roger and show him around." He took me straight to the gym. The gym was new and it was incredible. He told me to stay after school and practice with the freshman. And that is what I did. When practice was over…I was ready to go home and I literally didn't know where we lived.*

I hadn't been there yet. We went straight to the high school. Coach Herrin gave me a ride home that day. Years later I found out that Coach Waters (the Finley Coach) knew Coach Waugh at Rend Lake and Coach Waugh told Rich to be looking for me.

Webb admitted that he had a shot to start as a freshman at Finley and plans were made for him to stay, but they fell through. As Roger became more comfortable at Benton, he was thankful for his experience as a Ranger.

Roger Webb: *I went from not knowing anyone in Benton and then how the community turned out to support you. It was great!*

Another junior on the '76 team was Alan Klochany. Klochany was a 6'3" left-handed post player and growing up he attended most of the high school games. He was also good friends with Rod Herrin and remembered the perks that came along with hanging out with the Ranger mascot.

Alan Klochany: *I went to Logan School and my grade school coach was Farley Finter. Since the fourth grade, basketball was really my main sport. I had a goal that was set up near the asphalt at the Catholic church. I went to all the Ranger home games when I was a kid. I remember that I would sneak down into the locker room with Rod (Herrin) during the games and we would play nerf hoop while the Ranger games were going on. I remember watching Dinkins, McCommons and Robert Corn and those teams.*

The next junior was guard Steve Summers. Summers played his junior high basketball at Akin Grade School. He was a very capable player that was the first guard off the bench as a senior in '77. He played his role well.

In the summer of '75, the Rangers received an unexpected surprise when big Bob Boehnlein moved to town. Boehnlein was tall and well proportioned. He resembled a Greek god with his long blonde locks. He was a 6'5" post player. Boehnlein was a key player early, but did not finish the season. Rounding out the team was junior Shawn Curry. Curry was an All-South golfer and liked by all his teammates. He battled hard in practice for playing time at the guard position. This was the '76 Rangers.

On Tuesday, December 2, 1975, the Rangers opened the season with the McLeansboro Foxes at home. It was an enthusiastic Ranger crowd that greeted the team as they ran out of the Tunnel sporting their freshly cut flat-tops. The team was comprised of several independent personalities and they challenged Coach Herrin early in the year about wearing the flat-tops. Students across the country sported long hair, open collared shirts and bell-bottom trousers. The players thought; why can't we? Pat Golliher remembered that the players' resistance to the flat-top rule fell upon deaf ears.

Pat Golliher: *It was the seventies and everyone was wearing their hair out, you know. We were the group that wasn't going to cut our hair. Coach Herrin just said, "I'll find some guys walking the halls…so we got our haircuts." We didn't sit with the girls before the game…you sat as a team. And now…I see why we did all that.*

After warming up, the Rangers headed to their bench for the introduction of the starting line-ups. There were more than 3,000 screaming Ranger fans in attendance. Astute Ranger fans immediately noticed a new uniform style that stayed in circulation for the next twenty seasons. On this night, the Rangers wore their home whites. The uniform top was white with thick shoulder straps bordered in maroon. In the front, the tops were a V-neck style bordered in maroon with an arched inscription that read "Benton" above the number and "Rangers" below the number. The eight stars that originated with the '71 team appeared on the front legs of the uniform trunks. There were four on one leg and four on the other. The trunks were maroon and white with a thick maroon waist band. It was a clean look. It was the image that Coach Herrin wanted to project.

The Foxes played well early and jumped out to a 4-2 advantage. Buck Durham scored the first Ranger bucket of the season off an offensive rebound. From this point on, it was all Rangers. Tabor filled it up. He finished the first half with 22 points as Craddock penetrated to draw the defender and then dished to Tabor. The Bleacher Bums yelled, "Boom!" as Tabor's ball approached the rim. In the second quarter, Rodney Herrin entered the game and scored his first two points of the season. Ranger fans were also excited about the play of senior Eric Forby. Forby finished the night with 20 points. He was exciting to watch as he elevated high in the lane to snatch rebounds at rim level.

Junior Joe Durham was 6-6 from the field and finished with 13 points. The Rangers won the battle on the boards, 46-22. Craddock scored only four points, but was clearly the floor general in total command of his troops.

Pat Golliher: *We weren't as big in '76…but we still thought we were going to do the same thing. Our mindset then was…we are better than you.*

Then, the team lost four straight games. The seniors on the team were not privy to losing games. The losing streak was unexpected and disappointing. It left the team searching for its identity and left Coach Herrin searching for answers. The first loss of the streak was at Jacksonville by a score of 72-64.

Coach Herrin: *Jacksonville had a better ball club than we anticipated. We made the mistakes early and allowed them to control the tempo of the game.*

The Rangers then came home and were defeated by a tough Eldorado Eagles squad led by Mike Duff and Eddie Lane. The final score was 69-62. Coach Herrin was visibly disappointed after the game and had little to say. The Rangers were 1-2.

On Friday, December 19th, the team went to Marion to tangle with the Wildcats in the Conference opener. Marion had two great players in juniors James Orr and Mike Pickens. The Wildcats were much improved and knew the Rangers were ripe. In a back and forth battle, the Rangers lost a tight game by the score of 67-64. As a team, the Rangers were 12-23 from the free throw line. Not good. The team fell to 1-3 overall and 0-1 in conference play.

Coach Herrin: *It's the same story as the last two games…we got beat at the line.*

On Saturday, December 20th, the Herrin Tigers came to town and nipped the Rangers 76-74. In the last ten years of Benton Basketball there had never been such a stretch of losing and the team was feeling the pressure. The group that had lost only eight games since the seventh grade was now 1-4 overall, and 0-2 in South Seven play. The team had been the pre-season favorite to win the conference, but instead found themselves buried in the cellar. What was going on? Coach Herrin sensed the pressure the team was under and tried to put a positive spin on the Rangers' fourth loss of the young season. He made these comments to Bob Tedrow after the game:

Coach Herrin: *I'm as proud of this game…as much as any game I've ever coached. It was a tremendous team effort.*

In all fairness, the team was just not as potent offensively as they were a year ago with Smith, Dunbar and Tabor. Tabor was the only dominant scorer on the club in '76 and this allowed opponents to game plan more effectively. Opposing coaches extended defensive pressure on Tabor and dared the other Rangers to beat them off the dribble. Statistics indicate that Craddock and Forby did what they could to pick up the slack on the offensive end of the floor. But the Rangers would compete. They would scrap. They were blue collar. Opponents still had to beat the Rangers; they were not going to beat themselves.

Following the game, Coach Herrin thought about his team and made a simple adjustment. He decided that Andy Lampley was a player that made things happen, and things needed to happen. He would increase Lampley's playing time in hopes of energizing the team. Lampley was also a blue-collar type competitor and knew only one speed; full throttle. He was also popular with his teammates. The Rangers needed a spark. Why not?

Jay Sandusky: *We got off to a terrible start. It was just a disappointment compared to what we expected of ourselves. From the time we were in the seventh grade…we had only lost like eight games. We almost lost half that many before the Centralia Tournament in '76.*

The final game before Christmas was against the Carbondale Terriers. It was a must-win for the Rangers in terms of climbing back into the conference race. The Terriers were led by Gordy Welch and coached by Doug Woolard. Woolard was a member of the great '67 Terrier team that defeated the Rangers in the Super-Sectional at the SIU Arena. The game was at Benton and the score was back and forth all night. With just .05 seconds left on the clock, Keith Tabor was fouled and went to the line to shoot a one-and-one with the Rangers trailing, 57-56. With ice water in his veins, Tabor calmly splashed both free throws giving the Rangers an early Christmas present and thrusting the team back into the conference race. The Rangers improved to 2-4 overall and 1-2 in conference play. Think about this: If the Rangers would have lost against Carbondale, it would have been the longest losing streak in Herrin's coaching career. The team now turned their focus toward the Centralia Holiday Tournament.

Although the team came into the tournament limping, they were the defending champions. Despite the record, the Rangers still had an air about them. They knew they were a good basketball team and although they had been shaken, it was still possible to right the ship.

The team opened the tournament by defeating Arlington Heights by a score of 58-51. Keith Tabor led the team in scoring with 23 points and Buck Durham chipped in with ten. The win set up an afternoon game the next day against Chicago Marist. The tournament had been good to the Rangers for so many years. Maybe success in the tournament could turn around their fortunes.

On Tuesday, December 30th, the Rangers tangled with the 12-0 Redskins of Marist high school. Marist had size and they were led by Martin Howard and Bob Hearne. The Redskins won the rebounding battle, 38-25. The game was frustrating for the coaches and players. Nothing was going right and it had reached a boiling point for Coach Herrin and Buck Durham. During the game, Buck remembered an exchange of words he had with Coach Herrin.

Buck Durham: *I remember he took me out of the game…and as I was jogging back to the bench he was yelling at me for something…when I got to the bench I yelled back at him to defend myself…his eyes got real big and he turned to watch the game for a second. He then looked at me and said, "Son, you can't talk to me like that!" It was kind of funny.*

After the game, it was a quiet bus ride home as the team reflected on their dismal start to the season. Something had to change.

The Rangers could still win the conference, but it would be a struggle. Herrin was 5-0 and held a firm lead, followed by Mt. Vernon at 3-0. The Rangers were in sixth place just ahead of Carbondale and Harrisburg who were 0-4. Coach Herrin did his best to stay positive, but the future of the season was uncertain. The Rangers were not in a good place.

On January 9, 1976, the Rangers traveled to Davenport Gymnasium to play the last place Harrisburg Bulldogs. They needed a win and the Bulldogs proved to be just what the doctor ordered. The Rangers won the game 85-76 behind 36 points from Keith Tabor. Tabor was firing from the twilight zone and they were going down.

Eric Forby: *There wasn't a better shooter than Keith Tabor.*

Mark Craddock scored 21 points and junior Joe Durham chipped in ten points. Craddock had 12 assists in the game, most of them to his backcourt mate, Keith Tabor. After the game, an upbeat Rich Herrin had these comments for Ranger sports writer, Bob Tedrow.

Coach Rich Herrin: *"We started hustling, going after the ball and we just worked harder than they did. We're not super big and we don't have great talent, but we have good quickness and that is what wins games."*

The following night, the Rangers traveled to Trout Gymnasium to meet the Orphans. Junior forward Matt Duensing led the Orphans with 24 points as Centralia defeated the Rangers by a score of 80-71. It was a disappointing loss because it hurt the Rangers' chances of winning the conference. Again, Tabor led the scoring with 25 points and put up 61 points for the weekend. He was on fire.

On January 16, 1976, the team played host to the West Frankfort Redbirds. At the time, the Redbirds were ahead of the Rangers in the conference standings and they were led by Hugh Bill Moore, Mike Vosbein, Steve Mize and Mickey Garrett. The largest crowd of the year turned out to support their Rangers. The team jumped out to an 8-0 lead and never trailed in the game. Pat Golliher got his first start of the season and Andy Lampley played the finest game of his career by netting 16 points and grabbing 16 rebounds. Lampley was the difference, despite the great offensive night from Hugh Bill Moore to lead all scorers with 17 points. With the win, the Rangers moved to 5-6 overall, and 3-3 in the conference.

The next night the Rangers traveled to Mt. Vernon to play the Rams. The Rams were led by Willie Jones and Larry Davis. The Rangers shot 39% for the game from the field and the Rams were ahead by 16 points with one minute left in the game. The Rangers lost the game 68-58. After the first loop through the South Seven Conference, the Rangers were 5-7 overall and 3-4 in the South Seven play.

Next up was the Benton Invitational Tournament, but around the Herrin home at this time, believe it or not, basketball was not the focus. Sue Herrin was pregnant with the Herrin's only daughter, Kristy.

The Rangers opened the eight-team affair on Tuesday, January 20th, against the Carmi Bulldogs. The game was back and forth. Benton entered the fourth quarter down by a score of 46-44, but baskets by Lampley, Durham and Herrin put the Rangers in the lead 50-46. Carmi then scored five straight points to re-take the lead at 51-50. On the Rangers next possession, Andy Lampley hit a ten foot jumper with 4:08 remaining to put his team back on top 52-51. Bill Walkenbach then scored to put Carmi back ahead, 53-52 to set up a crazy ending. For the next three minutes, neither team could score but with under a minute left in the game, Lampley came up with a big steal. The Rangers then milked the clock and Tabor hit the final jump shot in the closing seconds to win the all-important first game of the tournament. The Rangers defeated the Bulldogs, 54-53.

On Wednesday night, January 21st, the consolation bracket of the tournament was being played and Coach Herrin was at the gym overseeing the games. He knew that the birth of their first daughter was close and it was on his mind as he watched the games that night. Sue Herrin was at home and did not attend the games. When Coach Herrin arrived at home, it was time to have a baby. Sue recalled what she remembered about the night Kristy was born.

Sue Herrin: *Whenever I found out I was pregnant, I was a little stunned. Rich and I decided that we should let the boys know but we wanted to keep it in the family. So we broke the news to the boys over dinner one night… and they took it pretty well. We told them that we wanted to keep the news quiet and in the family. They agreed. Shortly after our talk, Kyle called one of his friends and spread the news. Most of the people were rooting for a girl. I think Rich was wanting a girl because we just didn't have girls in the family. Everyone in the family wanted a girl except Kyle…he wanted a little brother. I was thrilled to death that it was a girl. Half of the town gave me little girl's clothes…. We sure had a lot of fun with Kristy. She was so good.*

Sue Herrin: *Kristy was born right in the middle of the Benton Invitational Tournament. I didn't go to the game that night because I wasn't feeling up to it. I kept waiting for Rich to get home and I was having some labor pains. When he got home he told me that my doctor was out of town. I just started crying. We called Wanda Lockin, who was Dr. Durham's nurse and she was very helpful. She assured me that Dr. Durham would deliver the baby…he was willing to do it. A few days after she was born, the Benton cheerleaders came over and gave me a trophy full of flowers and made over Kristy. Rich went to Knight's Furniture and bought a rocking chair. It had been a long time since we had a baby.*

Kristy Herrin was born in the early morning hours of Thursday, January 22nd. She was healthy and the Herrin family was thrilled. The people of Benton rooted for a girl, and when Kristy and Sue came home from the hospital, they were showered with baby gifts from friends in the Benton community.

It had been an eventful week for the Herrin family, and it wasn't over yet. On Friday night, the Rangers faced off with the Pinckneyville Panthers in the semi-final game of the BIT. In his first year as head coach of the Pinckneyville Panthers was former Ranger, Dick Corn. Corn had played on the great Benton teams of '67 and '68. Thursday night would be the first of many games that Rich Herrin would coach against his former player Dick Corn.

The gym was packed and the Ranger fans were hoping for a turning point to what had been a roller-coaster season. The game was close, going right down to the wire. With .37 seconds left to play in the game, the Panthers clung to a one point lead, 66-65. The Rangers had two chances to score but couldn't convert. The final score was Pinckneyville 67, Benton 65. It was a disappointing loss for the Rangers as they were unable to defend their BIT Championship of '75.

The next night, the Rangers defeated the Carbondale Terriers by a score of 67-56 to take third place in their own tournament. It wasn't what they wanted, but it was a win. The victory over the Terriers put the Rangers at 6-8 overall and 3-4 in South Seven Conference play. At this point in the season, the Rangers still had not found themselves and they were hoping that the final loop through the South Seven would bring better basketball.

On January 30th, Pickens and Orr came to town in a key South Seven match-up. It was do or die. They had to get it going. Unfortunately, they would have to play the Marion Wildcats without leading scorer Keith Tabor, who was suspended for the weekend games. In his absence, the team rallied to defeat the Wildcats 75-63 behind 28 points from Mark Craddock. Crock would not let the Rangers lose and he got help from junior guard Rod Herrin, who netted 12 points in Tabor's absence. The Rangers had a win streak of two. The Rangers then traveled to West Frankfort and defeated the Redbirds by a score of 59-50. Big Pat Golliher scored the final bucket of the third quarter to give the Rangers the lead for good, 42-41. The Rangers never looked back.

Eric Forby: *Pat was a great jumper…always played hard.*

Again, the Rangers were without Keith Tabor, but each player stepped up their game to compensate for his absence. Buck Durham led the team in scoring with 13 points. Eric Forby and Mark Craddock each scored ten points. The Rangers were now above .500 at 8-8 overall and 5-4 in league play. In fact, there was so much parity in the South Seven in '76, the win positioned the Rangers with an outside chance to come back and win the league. Herrin and Mt. Vernon had lost key games making the conference race wide open. Could the Rangers do it?

On Friday, February 6th, the team traveled to Herrin to play the Tigers. Benton's leading scorer, Keith Tabor, was back. The two wins without Tabor had changed the team. The Rangers pulled together without their leading scorer and there seemed to be a greater sense of unity and purpose among the players. It was definitely the high point of what was a very rocky season.

In the Herrin game, the box score indicated that Rod Herrin played sparingly. In '76, Herrin was one of the top juniors in Southern Illinois but was stuck behind two of the greatest guards to ever play at Benton; Craddock and Tabor. In '76, the sophomore game played before the varsity game. Juniors were not allowed to play in the sophomore games and there were only a handful of junior varsity games. Rod Herrin, along with his junior teammates, were caught in between and they desperately needed game experience.

Rod Herrin: *I just wasn't getting a lot of game experience. Craddock and Tabor were really good...I got that. But I was just playing a little more than a quarter in the varsity games. I remember a time that I got to play very little in the varsity game, and I was frustrated and vented to mom about it. Mom would sympathize with me...you know.*

Sue Herrin: *Of course, I wasn't at any of the practices...but I have to admit that I took the boys' side most of the time. I have to give Rich credit...he treated the boys pretty fair.*

Coach Herrin: *I didn't want to make the mistake of bringing Rod up too quickly...Rod and Kyle both had great guards in the class ahead of them.*

The Rangers trailed by three heading into the fourth quarter behind the stellar play of Tiger Keith Clark. Tabor was 10-15 from the field and scored 24 points. Nobody wanted the win more than Keith Tabor, especially after the team had won two big games in his absence. Mark Craddock came up big by scoring 18 points. He was now the calm floor general that could score. The Rangers trailed 60-53 in the fourth quarter but then mounted a furious comeback to overtake the Tigers and win the ballgame 69-65. In fact, with 14 seconds left to play, Joe Durham, canned two pressure free throws to put the Rangers ahead by two. It was a quality win on the road, something the team desperately needed. Herrin fell to 8-3 in league play and was still sitting in first place, but the Rangers were making a move at 6-4. Could they do it?

The Rangers were idle on Saturday night and did not return to action until February 13th, at Harrisburg. They were now a different team and this is what winning does; it breeds confidence. There was now a swagger about the team that didn't exist before Christmas and Benton fans were now jumping on the proverbial band wagon.

Keith Tabor was licking his chops as the bus pulled up to Davenport Gymnasium. Davenport Gymnasium served as Keith's launching pad. He loved shooting at Davenport. On this night, Tabor poured in 26 points on 10-17 shooting and Eric Forby had a big night by scoring 15 points in the Rangers' 71-65 victory. Jerry Johnson scored a game high 30 for the Bulldogs, but it wasn't enough. The team moved to 11-8 overall and 7-4 in the conference.

Herrin was idle on this night and stood at 8-4. The Rangers were only one game in the win column from first place. They began the season in the cellar. The team had won five in a row and playing basketball was fun again, but they had no time to relax. On Saturday night, Jeff Carling's Centralia Orphans were coming to town for a key conference game.

In the previous meeting at Centralia, leading by nine points, Coach Jeff Carling called a timeout with one second left on the clock. The timeout served the purpose of basking in the glory of defeating the rival Rangers. The Orphan fans loved it. All of the Rangers remembered the moment, and there was little need for a motivational speech from Coach Herrin before tip-off. The Rangers were ready, and most importantly, they were now capable. They were playing good basketball.

On February 14th, 1976, the Benton Gym was full of maroon and white, as the Rangers looked to make their move toward an improbable South Seven Conference Championship. In a game for the ages, the team exploded offensively to defeat the Orphans by a score of 88-76. Tabor went off. He scored 31 points but it was the play of Eric Forby, Mark Craddock and Buck Durham that led the Rangers to victory. Forby had 16 points in the first half and displayed his athleticism on several occasions by rising high in the air to block a shot or grab a rebound. Today, Eric Forby lives on in Ranger lore, especially in the sport of track. He told a funny story about an incident that happened his senior season in track that I couldn't leave out of the book.

Eric Forby: *My senior year…I know he* (Coach Herrin) *wanted to get me to State in the long jump. I usually placed in the top two at most all of the track meets. I did get the school record at Olney by jumping 22'8". I remember Rod Shurtz's dad being there. That year Centralia was supposed to have the district track meet. They had cinder and I think Rich* (Coach Herrin) *was worried about the facilities…he wanted all of us to have a shot to advance… so he complained and actually got the meet moved to Mt. Vernon. Nobody else could probably do that at the time, but he did. I had a couple of jumps and I scratched. I was over-striding to the board. I probably could have jumped off my right leg and advanced…but nothing was working that day. I scratched four times and didn't advance in the long jump. He was so mad at me…he stayed away from me. Back then you didn't want to do wrong by your coach. I hated it. Later in the meet I qualified in a couple of sprint races and he finally came around but he never forgot it. Coach Herrin called me "popgun" and I'm not sure why. Every time I saw him after that he would bring that up.*

On February, 20th, the Rangers traveled to Bowen Gymnasium to face the Terriers a third time. Again, it was Forby's play that lifted the Rangers to a narrow 57-55 victory. With the win, the Rangers moved into first place in the conference with a 9-4 mark. With one game to play, Herrin and Marion sat at 8-5 in second place. Many counted the Rangers out early but the players did not. Herrin continued coaching hard and the Rangers kept grinding. A win over Mt. Vernon on senior night could salvage what would have been a lost season. Most importantly, it would give the Rangers another South Seven Conference Championship. And this one would be sweet. Coming back from the dead and just stealing it!

As the seven seniors were introduced prior to tip-off, the fans rose to their feet to bid farewell to ; Mark Craddock, Keith Tabor, Jay Sandusky, Buck Durham, Eric Forby, Pat Golliher and Andy Lampley.

A strong second quarter propelled the Rangers to a 68-57 victory, and yet another South Seven title. Fans poured onto the floor to celebrate the improbable run. Mark Craddock led the Rangers with 21 points and was 11-11 from the free throw line. Eric Forby scored 17, Keith Tabor made 16 and Buck Durham finished with 14 points. This was the Rangers eighth straight victory, and it placed them at a respectable 14-8 overall record, and a 10-4 finish in the conference.

In the last regular season game of the '76 season, the Rangers traveled to Effingham to play the Flaming Hearts. The Rangers dominated the game and won easily by a score of 90-68. Jay Sandusky, Roger Webb and Alan Klochany got into the scoring column. It was a happy bus ride home as the team finished the regular season at 15-8. It was a great recovery from the 1-4 start before Christmas. All was well with the Benton Rangers.

'76 State Tournament Play

On March 3rd, 1976, the Rangers traveled to West Frankfort to face the Harrisburg Bulldogs for the Regional opener. Leading up to the game, the players were loose and had productive practices. The Rangers had won nine straight games and were playing their best basketball of the year and all indications were that this night would be no different. The Rangers were in their home white uniforms and had defeated the Bulldogs twice during the regular season. Both games were relatively close. Entering the game, Bob Pavelonis' Bulldogs were 10-15, but they had some impressive wins in league play. The Bulldogs were capable. The Dogs were dressed in their purple away uniforms.

Led by the play of forward Steve Crabb, the Bulldogs jumped on the Rangers early and led by as many as fourteen points in the first half. The Rangers played lethargic. The energy was not there, especially on the defensive end of the floor. The Bulldogs raced to a 25-16 first quarter lead before the Rangers woke up in the second quarter and outscored the Bulldogs 24-12, to take a 40-37 lead into halftime.

In the third quarter, the Bulldogs played their best offensive quarter of the year by netting 28 points, led by seniors Jerry Johnson and John Alexander. The Bulldogs led the game 65-61 entering the fourth quarter, but the Rangers fought hard to keep their season alive. In the end, the Bulldogs offensive onslaught was too much for the Rangers. The Dogs won a crazy one 90-86 to end the Rangers season much too early. It was over. Are you kidding me?

It was a game that all of the Rangers wish they had back. All it takes is one or two bad quarters in tournament play and you're going home. That is exactly what happened. After nine straight wins, the season came to an abrupt end. It was only the third time since Herrin's arrival in 1960 that the Rangers were eliminated in Regional play.

There is a saying among basketball coaches; "Basketball players can be like bird-dogs…sometimes they point and sometimes they don't." On this night, the Rangers didn't point, and it cost them. Junior Joe Durham remembered that tough night in West Frankfort.

Joe Durham: *I think we had beat Harrisburg twice. We played sluggishly… not much energy.*

After years of reflection, Jay Sandusky spoke honestly about the season that could have been.

Jay Sandusky: *I think when I look back on the '76 season…it is a testament to how ridiculously successful Coach Herrin was at Benton. We won fifteen games and won the South Seven Conference…but I feel like we underachieved.*

Unfortunately, several key members of the '76 team have passed away far too early, but there were four of the seven seniors that still look back on their experience as a Benton Ranger as one of the best times of their lives.

Jay Sandusky is now a retired teacher of thirty-three years from Parker High School in Parker, Arizona. He coached high school basketball for twelve seasons. He currently lives in Tipton, Iowa with his wife Kerri. They have one son, Mike. Jay was such a great interview and he told me about his favorite memory as a Ranger.

Jay Sandusky: *The pick-up games we played in the summer during open gyms were the most competitive games I've ever played. We won a lot of games in the summer because of how hard we worked. You couldn't help but improve when you played in those games in the summer. Older guys would come in and we were just playing against studs. I remember one time…I was actually guarding Doug Collins in an open gym and he yelled, "Ball!" Whenever he yelled ball, whoever had it just passed it to him. He made a jab step and went past me and I felt a breeze…it was unbelievable.*

Jay admitted that Coach Herrin had a great influence on his life and he was fortunate to play for not only a good coach, but an even better man.

Jay Sandusky: *He was such a basketball-lifer. I think my take-away from Coach was that he genuinely wanted you to be not only a better player…but* *a better person. He wanted you to do well. He had a way of making guys feel like they were the most important part of the team. He was a Christian man.*

Buck Durham had an outstanding high school career at Benton High School. Buck was a strong student and was voted by the BCHS faculty as an outstanding senior in '76. As a senior, he was selected as an All-South defensive end and was a starter on the great Ranger basketball team of 1975 that finished at 27-1. He also ran track and got the most out of his athletic ability because of his hard work and ever-present competitive nature.

After high school, Buck Durham spent his freshman year at Tulane playing football and then transferred to Missouri Rolla. As a senior at Missouri Rolla, he played on a football team that finished 10-0. He earned his engineering degree and then completed his master's degree in structural engineering. Buck worked for the Tennessee Valley Authority and then later relocated to the Huntsville, Alabama area. He is currently self-employed and has one daughter, Madeline Claire. He had this to say about Coach Herrin:

Buck Durham: *I never really wanted a "that-a-boy" more from any of my coaches than him. There was this overwhelming desire to please him. I was honored to be a part of his regiment, so to speak...one of his soldiers. There is no question that Rich Herrin was the impetus. He was like a father figure. I wrote him a letter and I told him that.*

Eric Forby served as a teacher and coach at EMGE Middle School in Belleville, Illinois. He also served as the athletic director and dean of students. He is now retired and married to his wife Amy and they have two boys; Jake and Zach. Eric enjoyed his time as a Ranger and told me how his playing experience at Benton helped him receive his teaching job.

Eric Forby: *It was a great ride. I loved all of the coaches and I think my greatest memory was just the journey. You know, the guy that hired me at Belleville for my teaching job was a fan of the Benton Rangers. His name was Jack Ackerman. I mean there were a lot of guys going after this job at Belleville and I got it. I believe my association with Coach Herrin and the fact that I played a Benton helped me get that job. I really do.*

After years of reflection, Forby had this to say about Coach Herrin.

Eric Forby: *We had disagreements…I remember he sat me out to start my senior year because I didn't come in as much in the summer for open gyms because I was working. But he really did take care of his players. Coach taught us the fundamentals of the game. I did go to Rend Lake College and played basketball after high school.*

Pat Golliher lives in Benton with his wife, Connie. He is now retired but worked for fifteen years as a coal miner at Old Ben 25 and twenty-six years in the Department of Corrections. He has three children; Preston, Stacy and Jayme. Much like Forby, Pat believes that playing basketball at Benton provided opportunities in his life.

Pat Golliher: *That little ball has opened up a lot of doors in my life. Between my freshman and sophomore years at Rend Lake College, I picked up a job at Old Ben 25 in the mines. Someone recognized me and said, "Oh, you are one of Rich's boys." And they treated me differently…they took care of me. It was pretty cool.*

Dave Severin married his high school sweetheart Peni (Edwards) Severin. They have one son, Travis. Today, Severin owns a popular screen printing store in Benton by the name of All-Stars and Stitches. He also serves as a Republican member of the Illinois House of Representatives, representing the 117th District. Dave did not play basketball his junior and senior seasons, but he ran track for Coach Herrin in the spring. He is a 1976 BCHS graduate and later developed a close friendship with Coach Rich Herrin.

Dave Severin: *I was sitting in the back of Don Webb's class my freshman year and this little girl who was an office worker shows up with a note. Coach Webb says, "Severin!" I thought I was in trouble but I went to the front of the class and got that note. I looked at it and it was from Coach Herrin. The note told me to be at freshman basketball practice that day…so I went. He put me on the freshman basketball team. In my mind…that simple note solidified that I was okay. I never forgot that.*

The floor general, Mark Craddock, lost his battle with cancer and passed away on Wednesday, July 4, 2012, at his home. He was only fifty-four years old. Mark was the son of Joe and Judy (Moore) Craddock. Mark formerly owned and operated Craddock's Baseball Cards in Benton and M & M Pressure Washing. Keith Tabor's father, Everett, officiated Mark's funeral service. Crock was loved by his teammates. Upon his death, Jim Muir wrote an article honoring Mark's life and several teammates and coaches had much to say about Mark Craddock. These were the words from Muir's article:

Coach Rich Herrin: *He could pass it and he took care of the basketball; he could shoot free throws and he could also shoot free throws under pressure, and he was totally unselfish. When the game was on the line and the other team was pressing, he wanted the basketball. Mark did everything you would want a point guard to do. He loved the game and he was a fierce competitor. When you look back at that 1974-75 team Craddock was the hub of the wheel…he kept it all going.*

Rob Dunbar ('75 teammate): *It's very sad…and it's way too early. He was the ultimate teammate. Mark knew his role and he never, ever complained. He just went out game after game and did his job and did it well. Mark was the glue that held everything together. Coach Herrin had a game plan every time we stepped on the floor, and it was Mark's job to make sure that we executed that game plan. On top of that, he normally got the job of guarding the other team's best player. Mark was always under control and he helped keep everybody else under control. I don't think there is any doubt that without him, we wouldn't have been able to accomplish what we did that year.*

Billy Smith ('75 teammate): *When you look back, it was always Mark that was in control all the time. He was fundamentally as sound as any high school player you will ever see. He wasn't flashy; you didn't notice him on the court, but he always did everything right. He didn't get the credit he deserved for the success we had that year. We probably frustrated him because he was always under control and sometimes the rest of us weren't. We've all lost a great teammate, but we've also lost a true friend. He will be missed.*

Andy Lampley attended Akin Grade School and was a key player in turning around the fortunes of the '76 Rangers. In high school, he was an explosive three-sport athlete; football, basketball and track. Because of his attitude and work ethic, he was popular with his teammates. After high school, Andy found work in the coal mines. Unfortunately, in the early morning hours of September 14, 1992, he died in a fatal car accident on the Akin blacktop. He was only thirty-three years old. At the time of his death, Andy had two children; Travis and Taylor.

As an impressionable sophomore, former Ranger Ron Brookins had nothing but kind words to say about Andy.

Ron Brookins: *I was a sophomore when he was a senior. As a player, he was a blue-collar type guy. He played inside and he was very athletic. As a person, he was just such a great guy. He would talk to anyone. He never talked down to the underclassman. He was a guy you could depend on. Very humble…no arrogance.*

There is perhaps nobody in Benton basketball history that could shoot the ball like Keith Tabor. Keith was a member of the "Triple Threat of '75 and was named to the All-South team in '76. In his three years of varsity action, Keith scored a whopping 1,276 points. He still ranks ninth on the Rangers' all-time scoring list. Most of Keith's points were high-arching, long-range bombs that splashed thru the bottom of the net. It is scary to think about how many points he could have had if he had played with the three-point line.

After high school, Tabor owned Tabor's Pest Control for many years and also worked at Southern Illinois Surgical Appliance in West Frankfort. On Sunday, January 28, 1996, Keith passed away at Franklin County Hospital. He was only thirty-eight years old. He was survived by his wife, Roberta Tabor, of Benton. They had three children; Nick, Jason and Amy.

Teammate Billy Smith remembered his good friend and teammate.

Billy Smith: *Keith was a pure shooter, good balance, good elevation, and perfect form. Offensively, he was always a threat to score. And could score from long range, mid-range, or finish at the basket. Defensively, he had good quickness and great anticipation and often turned defense into offensive opportunities. He approached the game with complete confidence. He was not physically imposing, probably 5'10" and thin as a rail, but he was fearless on the court. At those critical moments in the game, Keith wanted the ball and was willing to take the big shot. Keith played to win. It could be darts or cards or basketball. It didn't matter what the activity was, he was in it to win. His competitiveness, fearlessness and confidence in his own ability made him a great teammate. Away from the basketball court or the baseball field or whatever sport we were playing, Keith was easygoing, fun loving, and a bit mischievous. He was a good friend that we lost too soon.*

Coach Herrin before the beginning of the 75-76 season.
(Caesar Maragni)

Kristy Herrin was born during the '76 season. Here is a picture
of Kristy and Coach in the early 80's. *(Ceasar Maragni)*

Coach Herrin poses with the big three in '76; L-R Mark Craddock,
Buck Durham and Keith Tabor. *(Ceasar Maragni)*

Andy Lampley brought energy and toughness to
the '76 team. *(Ceasar Maragni)*

Eric Forby still holds the BCHS record in the long jump (22'8)
and was a key player on the '76 team. *(Ceasar Maragni)*

Rod Herrin and Coach Herrin in the winter of '76. Rod Herrin
played behind Mark Craddock as a junior. *(Ceasar Maragni)*

Joe Durham played a key role inside for the Rangers in '76.
(Ceasar Maragni)

The Rangers started cold then came back to win the South Seven only to get
eliminated in the first game of the Regional against Harrisburg.
(**Front Row-** Klochany, Lampley, J. Durham, Golliher, Webb,
B. Durham, Forby. **Back Row-** Stewart, Tabor, Craddock,
Sandusky, Curry, R. Herrin, Summers, Herrin. *(Ceasar Maragni)*

CHAPTER TWENTY-TWO

Fun To Be a Ranger Fan in '77

"We really had to fight for our wins." – Rod Herrin

I spent the summer days of '76 at my Grandpa Wynn's on West Main Street. My mom was working as a secretary at the County Treasurer's office and my dad had taken a summer job at Rend Lake. God blessed me with two loving parents and it made for a great childhood. I was too young to attend open gyms or basketball camps, so I took my ball and walked through Biff West's carport and shot for hours at the Catholic church. I was annoyed that there wasn't a net but it was the only goal within walking distance. That summer, my parents took me to my first St. Louis Cardinal game and I do remember that the Cardinals played the Astros. Jim Kaat pitched that night and an aging Lou Brock played the outfield.

When school started in the fall of '76, I found myself in Mrs. Betsy Watson's class. I was in the second grade and attended Douglas School. I took a purple pouch full of marbles to school each day that carried steelies, loggies, pee wees, cat eyes and clearies. Douglas School was known for marbles, not basketball, although the basketball pep sessions were spirited. I remember standing with my classmates and whirling our hands in a circle to make the noise of a deadly tornado. Unfortunately, Douglas was in the cellar with Washington when it came to grade school athletics. I never wore the maroon and gold uniforms at Douglas, but I was proud to be a Tornado. As fall turned to winter, I begged my parents to take me to the Rangers games. I was eight years old. Rod Herrin was my favorite player.

There were only two teams in Coach Herrin's twenty-five year run at Benton that returned no starters, the Rangers teams of 1968 and 1977. In fact, there were only two players returning that had any varsity experience; Rod Herrin and Joe Durham. The inexperience of the '77 team made the team a mystery but the team soon won over the approval of their fans. Everybody pulls for the underdog, especially when the underdog will fight, battle, scrap and not back down from the opponent. This was the '77 Rangers.

The team was led by seven seniors; Rod Herrin, Joe Durham, Roger Webb, Alan Klochany, Steve Summers, Jerry Bell and Randy Phillips. Other members of the team were juniors Rod Shurtz, Ron Brookins, Doug Dunbar, Scott Dunbar, Brad Gesell, Scott Page, Mike Kovarik, Dave Fairchilds and Frank Kolisek. Also dressing as sophomores were Carl Shurtz (Rod's younger brother), Jerry Dawson and Terry Dawson.

Although the Rangers didn't have a superstar, they had a group of players that had more going for them than the eye could see. They were all good friends off the floor and played with a sense of urgency that Ranger fans came to admire. Most all of the players had cycled through the program and had improved along the way. The Rangers were also very smart.

Rod Shurtz: *That was a smart outfit right there. Look at what some of those guys did after high school. That Class of '77 was a pretty intelligent crew across the board.*

Senior Steve Summers was the first guard off the bench in '77. He grew up in Akin and fell in love with basketball as early as the second grade. He attended the Ranger games as far back as the Yunkus days and idolized Danny Johnson and Doug Collins. Steve was a steady ball handler and a knockdown shooter.

Steve Summers: *We played so hard…and we weren't very big. Our freshman year, we were one of the biggest freshman teams in the conference…but we just didn't grow much after that. Playing under Coach Herrin…we knew the fundamentals…if you didn't play hard, you just didn't play.*

The seniors had grown up together and knew each other's tendencies. Because there were only two juniors (Herrin and Durham) that logged varsity minutes, the senior-heavy group only had one year to get it right. They knew it. Most importantly, they played like it. The team was smart, undersized and extremely competitive. They were led by the tenacious play of 5'9", 158-pound guard, Rod Herrin. Teammates, Ron Brookins and Rod Shurtz had this to say about the play of Rod Herrin. Brookins was the second guard off the bench behind Summers in '77:

Ron Brookins: *Matt, very competitive…pound per pound, Rod was as tough as they get. Rod got everything out of his ability. He carried the lunch pail to work every day. I thought Rod handled being a coach's son very well. Let me tell you…he got no preferential treatment from Coach Herrin. He was a very good shooter and he could get to the rim for his size.*

Rod Shurtz: *The guy was a fiery competitor in practice and games. Rod wanted to win…he battled you every day in practice and he would challenge you. He would fight you. You've got to remember that as a sophomore, he played against Billy, Crock and Tabor every day in practice and he was the coach's son…he put it out there. He wanted to prove to people that he could play…and he did. If there was a loose ball…you weren't going to take it from him. You wanted Rod Herrin in your foxhole when you went to battle.*

Teammate and good friend, Randy Phillips, recalled intense battles with Rod growing up that sometimes resulted in injury.

Randy Phillips: *Rod Herrin and I were good friends…we had some interesting practices when we were younger. We went at each other…we were both competing for playing time.*

Rod also had to deal with the pressure of being Coach Herrin's son and it was definitely something that I wanted to address in our interview. I asked Rod, "What was it like playing for your dad?"

Rod Herrin: *Dad was fair. He was intense…I was really hard on myself and I think dad knew that about me. He wasn't on me all the time. Dad made it fun. We would have the players over to the house for pizza parties and for years he would take us to the Kentucky-Indiana All-Star games. I don't know if a lot of coaches engage kids like that today. He loved being around the players. I have to say…it was very reasonable playing for dad.*

Teammate and good friend, Alan Klochany, made this comment about the father-son relationship as he witnessed it:

Alan Klochany: *If you walked in the gym and you didn't know that Rod was Coach's son...then watched practice...you wouldn't have figured it out. Coach was demanding...he was tough on all of us. He made it hard...he pushed us. But I would do it again. Coach played the best players. He* (Rod) *didn't get any special treatment.*

A coach has to make some tough decisions. Who makes the team? Who plays? Who dresses in the State tournament? Who makes the All-Tournament team? Who plays in the All-Star games? Holding players accountable to the rules and punishing players if they are broken can be a challenging part of the job. All of these decisions can be subjective to some and rub people the wrong way. Then, there were also people in the community that believed too much emphasis was placed on basketball or resented Coach Herrin's success. Whatever the case, coaching in a small community can be messy even if you are winning.

There were many times that Sue Herrin had to bite her lip as the crowd around her made un-flattering comments about her husband. Most of the time, it was the visiting crowd, but not always. Being a coach's wife, Sue knew criticism came with the territory, but it was still tough to take.

Coach Herrin was always in the public eye of the Benton community and there were also times that Rod and his brothers were within earshot of ugly criticism directed at their dad. People had their opinions and not everyone was a supporter. Being a teacher and coach, Coach Herrin had close contact with the BCHS student body. In fact, he served as the school's driver's education teacher and many students knew him only as a teacher. This meant that he knew all of his son's classmates. Let's face it, kids can be cruel. Sometimes situations arose in which the Herrin boys felt it necessary to defend their dad. And believe me, they did. The boys always had his back.

Rod Herrin: *When I was in high school...I got in a fight uptown because I was defending my dad. A kid was saying some stuff about Dad. I came home and I looked like I had been in a fight...Dad asked me about it. I told him that I was defending him. He said, "You can't defend me, you'll be fighting all the time." He acted a little mad...but deep down...I could tell he kind of liked it.*

Another strong leader on the team was Joe Durham. As a junior, Joe logged important minutes. Joe's teammates were quick to give him high praise.

Rod Shurtz: *Besides being by far the best singer and dancer in the locker room…Joe could play. We had a little eight track tape player in the locker room and Joe would dance and sing a little. Joe would just battle you…and he had a sweet mid-range jumper.*

Ron Brookins: *You know Joe and I were pretty good friends. We did a little hunting together. Joe was like the Swiss army knife of our team. He was so versatile. He could play the two, three or four position. I like Joe a lot. He was one of our leaders in '77. He and Rod Herrin were the most outspoken on that team.*

Alan Klochany: *Joe was a good shooter. He was solid fundamentally…he walked on at Saint Louis University and made the team. He could play.*

In the first game of the season, the Rangers traveled to McLeansboro to play the Foxes. There was much talk about the Foxes of '77. Four of the five starters were transfer students and the community of McLeansboro anticipated a great season. Transferring in from Mt. Vernon were brothers Terry and Dennis Friedman. From Marion was guard Dale Brewer and from Decatur, forward Brian Aaron. The fifth starter was Larry Karcher. The Foxes were a lanky 6'2" across the line-up and were the favorites.

When the Rangers took the floor on November 30, 1976, they started seniors Rodney Herrin, Joe Durham, Roger Webb, Alan Klochany and junior Rod Shurtz. The Shurtz family had moved to Benton from nearby Waltonville, Illinois. Rod had three younger brothers that also played basketball for the Rangers; Carl, Steve and Jeff. Rod and I are great friends, and he spoke of his family's big move to Benton in the fall of '74.

Rod Shurtz: *My dad was an electrician that worked in Oakville, near Nashville and mom was an elementary teacher at Woodlawn. We lived in Waltonville…a lot of great memories there. We loved Waltonville and that is where I learned how to work. I believe mom and dad wanted to give all of us (Rod, Carl, Steve and Jeff) more opportunities and not in just athletics…but in other areas like music. My brother and I played an instrument. Me and my brothers always attended Coach Herrin's Junior Pro Basketball camp in the summer at Rend Lake. Unbeknownst to me, I believe my dad had formed a friendship with Coach Herrin. We looked at moving to Pinckneyville, Nashville, Mt. Vernon and even Centralia…but in the fall of '74 we moved to Benton. I remember we drove through Benton one day and saw kids in the backyard playing, we saw kids playing pick-up games on the playgrounds…the* *coal mines were booming...farming was part of the community. People had four-wheel pickup trucks, bass boats, shotguns...you name it. The town was very active at that time and so we came to Benton. Benton turned out to be a great place for all of us.*

The Rangers came out strong against the Foxes and flew around the floor applying full-court pressure. It was apparent from the start that the Rangers had good quickness at the guard spots with Shurtz and Herrin. Rod Herrin enjoyed playing alongside Shurtz for more than one reason.

Rod Herrin: *He was really good fundamentally. He was a very good ball handler and was a lot like Crock...he just didn't make many mistakes. We were pretty interchangeable...but when Rod* (Shurtz) *played the point...Dad would move me to the two. I enjoyed playing the two because I had more of an opportunity to score.*

The Rangers led 24-17 with 4:26 left in the first half but the Foxes rallied to go on a 13-2 run, to lead 30-26 at halftime. Mcleansboro increased their lead to 50-42 by the end of the third quarter. In the final eight minutes, the '77 Rangers showed their makeup by battling back from a ten-point deficit to tie the game on a basket by Joe Durham just before the final horn that sent the game into overtime. In the overtime period, Joe Durham and Alan Klochany teamed up to score the final six points of the game giving the team their first win of the year. The winning score was 68-64 in overtime.

Rod Herrin: *We really had to fight for our wins.*

True to their personality, the young Rangers never quit. The team got steady inside play from Durham, Klochany and Dawson. The quick and aggressive guard play of Shurtz and Herrin was exciting to watch. The leading scorer of the night for the Rangers was 6'3" senior Roger Webb. Webb scored 18 points to lead a very balanced Ranger attack. One of Webb's teammates commented on how nicely Roger fit into the blue collar mix of '77.

Ron Brookins: *Roger could jump. Roger was blue-collar...very intense... hard-working. Do anything you ask. He and Rod Herrin had a lot in common. Roger was kind of quiet and he was a great teammate.*

Joe Durham: *Roger transferred in our freshman year. Roger was a solid player. He was fundamentally sound. He played hard and smart. He was very good around the basket.*

Alan Klochany: *He was about my height. We were pretty similar players. He was a good jumper and we alternated a lot at the post position. He was a very good player.*

Roger was a great leaper and could dunk the ball with ease. He would often dunk after practice. All of Roger's teammates commented on Webb's jumping ability. In fact, Rod Herrin spoke of a time their junior year when Webb went up and accidentally shattered a backboard on one of the side goals in the new gym. Rod said, "Dad scared him to death, threatening that he was going to pay for it, but he never did." The Rangers were really not about dunking the ball. There was never a rule against it, but you better not miss it. One miss and you were in deep trouble. Webb knew it.

Roger Webb: *In '77 it was the first year they brought the dunk back to the game. I just remember that David Fairchild went up to try and dunk it at West Frankfort and the ball slid off the rim and went up into the stands. The coaches went crazy. Later in the year I had a wide open lay-up and I could have dunked it…but Fairchild's missed dunk popped into my head and I just laid it in high off the glass.*

Another positive about the opening game was the play of sophomore, Jerry Dawson. Jerry and his twin brother, Terry, were both 6'6" and were still developing as players. But, you can't teach height. Dawson led the young Rangers in rebounding (12) and had two big baskets late to spark the Ranger comeback.

Rod Herrin: *Dad worked with them quite a bit. They were our size.*

On December 10, 1976, the Rangers played host to the Jacksonville Crimsons. Many Ranger fans that didn't travel to McLeansboro poured into the Rich. The team didn't disappoint. The Rangers took control of the game early by outscoring the Crimsons 18-7 in the second quarter to win the game 61-56. Again, Roger Webb led the team in scoring with 24 points and Rod Herrin chipped in 14 points. Senior Steve Summers came off the bench in the third quarter and hit two big jump shots to spark the team.

Rod Shurtz: *Steve was just so steady. He was a good player. He could handle the ball…a very good shooter and could guard you.*

Jerry Bell: *We called Steve "Radar". Good shooter. If he could set and square his shoulders…he was lights out.*

Ron Brookins: *Steve was a very good eighth grade player…he was a really good perimeter shooter and role player…and just a real quiet guy… great guy.*

The Rangers were 2-0 and moving in the right direction. In game three of the season, the team traveled to Eldorado. The Eagles were led by All-State player Mike Duff and his partner in crime, Eddie Lane. In '77, Duff was considered the best player in the Southern Illinois area and Lane wasn't far behind. Roger Webb remembered Duff well.

Roger Webb: *There was a rumor going around during the summer before my junior year that Mike Duff was going to move to Benton. His dad was a doctor and he was going to be working at the Franklin County Hospital. There was no truth to it…but you always had to be on top of your game at Benton because anything could happen.*

With Duff and Lane, the Eagles were heavy favorites. On this night, it was the lefty Alan Klochany, that came up big for the Rangers. In the second quarter, Klochany took the ball right at Duff and scored six consecutive points giving the Rangers a 33-25 advantage at halftime.

In the third quarter, with Eldorado holding a 43-38 advantage, it was more Klochany. He scored seven quick points to pull the Rangers back into the game before fouling out at the end of the third quarter. The Ranger guards loved playing with Klochany.

Rod Shurtz: *He was such a smart guy. That was a smart outfit right there. Look at what some of those guys did after high school. That Class of '77 was a pretty intelligent crew across the board. Al had a quiet game. You might look at the stats after the game and think Al had eight…and then go…oh, eighteen.*

Rod Herrin: *He was left-handed…pretty steady. He was hard-nosed and physical for his size. He had good skills and was a smart player.*

Ron Brookins: *Alan had a smooth left hand…very quiet guy and so smart. Look at that '77 team…there are some pretty intelligent guys on that team now.*

With .19 seconds left in the game, Rod Herrin hit two free throws giving the Rangers a two point lead. The Eagles came down the floor and got the ball to Duff. Duff attacked the rim but was blocked by Dawson. After the block, Duff recovered the ball and hit a short jumper just before regulation to tie the game at 68. A packed house at Eldorado let loose with a roar as Duff's shot found the bottom of the net.

To start the overtime period, Dawson scored on a lob pass from Herrin to put the Rangers up two, 70-68. Eldorado tied the game and then Rodney Herrin scored on a nifty give-and-go play from Shurtz to put the Rangers up two again. In the meantime, the Eagles missed two front ends of a one-in-one. With the Rangers trying to hold the ball, the Eagles fouled junior Rod Shurtz. These were the two biggest free throws of Rod's young varsity career but he calmly went to the line and dropped them both.

Ron Brookins: *Rod* (Shurtz) *just never got rattled.*

Duff came down and scored to pull the Eagles to within two points, but then after a Benton turnover, Duff's final shot rolled off the rim, giving the Rangers a huge win. An excited Rich Herrin shook hands with Eldorado coach Bob Brown and then broke into a jog to get to the locker room. He congratulated each player as they entered the locker room. It was a big one. The Rangers were excited and it was a happy locker room. Realistically, 2-1 after the first three would have been acceptable but a 3-0 start was something to celebrate. As the Rangers showered, they rehashed the victory, and Duff had to be in their discussion. Duff scored 37 points and was the best player on the floor. The Rangers had no answer. Duff's teammate, Eddie Lane, chipped in 18 in the losing effort. The Rangers slayed the Eagles with a balanced offensive attack; Durham had 16, Klochany and Herrin with 15, Dawson added 12 and Shurtz and Webb with eight.

It was a great team win over two of the greatest individual players (Duff and Lane) in the area and the Rangers knew it. They had snuck into Eldorado and stole one. The young and feisty Rangers were 3-0.

Roger Webb: *We had a big win at Eldorado that year. We won by two and Eldorado only lost three games all year. They had Mike Duff and Eddie Lane.*

Rod Shurtz: *I do remember hitting some free throws late with like 14-15 seconds left and then we got a stop at the end to beat them. Eldorado had Duff and Lane...that was a great win for our crew.*

On December 17th, the Marion Wildcats rolled into Benton for the conference opener. James Orr and Mike Pickens ripped the nets for 53 points and spanked the Rangers by a score of 84-67. Orr and Pickens were amazing players for the Wildcats in the seventies and their names are often mentioned behind the great Greg Starrick when it comes to the Wildcats' most celebrated players. Rodney Herrin led the Rangers with 20 points and Steve Summers and Joe Durham both scored ten points each.

The following night the Rangers traveled to Herrin and returned to their winning ways by defeating the Tigers, 68-58. Junior Rod Shurtz led the Ranger scoring attack for the first time all year with sixteen points. Rod explained to me in our interview that it was plain to see what his role was in '77.

Rod Shurtz: *I was fortunate enough to be the point guard on that crew. We lost all of our starters from the year before. I remember looking around and thinking that on any given night we had four guys that could score on that team. We had Rod, Alan Klochany, Roger Webb and Joe Durham. Nobody had to tell me my role. I could figure it out. My job in '77 was to handle the ball, hit free throws and play good defense. That was a good solid Ranger basketball team. We had good depth inside with Dawson coming off the bench... Steve Summers and Brook would come in to spell the guards. Defensively, I just thought we were very aggressive...we had some quickness. One of those teams.*

Ron Brookins: *Rod didn't look to score as much as a junior...but he could score.*

Alan Klochany: *Rod had quickness and he could shoot it. He was a good floor general.*

With the win over Herrin, the Rangers improved to 4-1 and 1-1 in conference play. Next up was the Carbondale Terriers. The game took place on Tuesday, December 21st, and it was the type of game that needed to be quickly forgotten. The Terriers were loaded and led by Gordon Welch and Johnny Fayne. Welch scored 27 points as Doug Woolard's team beat the

Rangers by a score of 77-55. Fayne scored 14. The Rangers fell to 4-2 and 1-2 in the tough South Seven Conference.

The Rangers had almost a week off before they had to play their opener in the Centralia Tournament. Over the course of the next week, the Rangers practiced hard because they knew no other way.

Steve Summers: *Coach Herrin pushed us so hard in practice that it made the games easier.*

It was also a team that liked each other. The players were friends off the floor and they all played hard and had good attitudes. Coach Herrin loved this team because they played so much in his image. They were hard-nosed and very competitive.

Randy Phillips: *We didn't have any superstars on the '77 team…but we had some scrappy guys that would compete and we got everything out of our ability.*

Ron Brookins: *Alan, Joe and Rod played together through grade school and junior high and they hung out a lot. They had been together a long time and they knew each other well.*

In the opening game of the Centralia Tournament, Rod Herrin exploded for 22 points to lead the Rangers to victory over the Hillcrest Hawks. Rod Shurtz chipped in with 15 points and Jerry Dawson came through with another quality game by scoring 13 off the bench. Alan Klochany played steady and added 12. Shurtz made it a point in our interview to stress the impact that Jerry Dawson had on the success of team.

Rod Shurtz: *Jerry came off the bench a few times and really sparked us. He gave us size that we needed and he had a nice touch around the basket. He could do some things. He was a threat.*

The win advanced the Rangers to game two in the championship bracket against the Evanston Wildkits. On this afternoon, the Rangers went cold, shooting 16-52 from the field for a dismal 30%. Despite the poor shooting, the Rangers and Wildkits were tied at halftime at 21, but Evanston won the third quarter by ten points and cruised to a 52-37 win. The Rangers had an opportunity to advance, it just wasn't their day. Roger

Webb led the team with 13 points followed by ten from Rod Herrin. The team fell to 5-3 overall and 1-2 in conference play.

On January 7, 1977, the Rangers resumed play by traveling to Harrisburg. It was the first time the two teams had met since the Dogs knocked off the Rangers in the first game of the Regional in '76. Benton's group of seniors remembered the game well and the competitive juices flowed as the ball was tipped. The Bulldogs came out hot and led 20-19 after the first quarter of play. The Rangers then took command of the game behind 20 points from Roger Webb. Rod Shurtz scored 11 points.

The next night the Rangers played Jeff Carling's Centralia Orphans. The Rangers jumped out to an early lead as Roger Webb fired long baseball passes to a streaking Rod Herrin for lay-ups.

Roger Webb: *Coach Herrin worked with me on throwing a long baseball pass and not allowing the ball to curve. I would take the ball out and throw a baseball pass to Rod Herrin streaking down the floor.*

The Orphans battled back to take the lead late in the game 63-62 and had their best free throw shooter, Matt Duensing on the line. Duensing was fouled by Rod Herrin, and it was his fifth foul. With the Rangers trailing by one and Duensing at the line, it did not look good. Duensing eyed the basket to shoot the front end of the one-and-one. He missed it. Jerry Dawson rose high with both hands to retrieve the carom off the rim and fired the ball to Steve Summers. Summers then whipped a quarter-court pass to Shurtz who dribbled twice and then fired in the game-winning jump shot. Shurtz's jump shot put the Rangers on top 64-63 before the Orphans turned the ball over. The Orphans fouled Klochany and he hit one free throw. The Rangers hung on to win, 65-63, against the hated Orphans. During this time period, it was Mt. Vernon and Centralia that seemed to bring the best out of the Rangers.

Ron Brookins: *It wasn't West Frankfort for me, Matt. The games I loved playing the most were with Mt. Vernon and Centralia.*

Rodney Herrin led the Rangers with 18 points followed by Jerry Dawson who chipped in 15 and pulled down nine rebounds. The big sophomore was helping the Rangers more than expected.

Joe Durham: *He was our only real size. I know I threw a lot of lobs to him.*

On Friday, January 14, 1977, the Rangers traveled to West Frankfort to play the Redbirds. The Rangers came out ready to play and jumped on the Birds to take a 20-11 lead at the end of the first quarter. Durham had ten points in the period and scored another eight in the second quarter to lead the Rangers into halftime with a 42-27 lead. The teams played even in the third quarter before the Rangers cruised to an 85-65 win. Joe Durham had his best offensive game of the year by scoring 28 points. With the win, the young Rangers moved to 8-3 overall and 4-2 in league play.

The next night, the Mt. Vernon Rams came calling. The Rams and Rangers had a passionate rivalry in the seventies. The teams just didn't like each other. The Rams nearly killed Robert Corn in '73 and several times the team bus had been rocked on its way out of Mt. Vernon. The fans sensed this and came out in droves to see their Rangers put it to the Rams. The Rangers did not disappoint. The '77 Rams were loaded; Willie Davis, Perry Pipes, Doug Creel, Scott Wagner and Jerry Wilson. It would be a dog fight.

The Rangers took a five-point lead by halftime and played a strong second half to win the game, 70-62. Seniors Rod Herrin, Alan Klochany and Joe Durham led the way in the scoring department. The win moved the Rangers to sole possession of third place in the conference with a record of 5-2. Carbondale was unbeaten and Marion had only lost one. The Rangers were in the hunt.

The young Rangers stood at 9-3 entering the Benton Invitational Tournament. The BIT was not as revered as the Centralia Tournament, but it was gaining popularity. Good crowds showed up to see the great Benton, Carbondale and Olney teams of the late seventies. The double elimination format made every game crucial. In my interview with Rod Herrin, I asked him about his favorite memory as a Ranger - a common question I asked all the players.

Rod Herrin: *That's a good question. The whole process really...I loved playing in the Benton Invitational Tournament.*

The Rangers opened the '77 BIT with Breese Mater Dei, and in a low scoring affair; the Knights defeated the Rangers 43-38. That one hurt. It is usually not until game two of the BIT that any type of resistance is thrown at the Rangers. A disappointed Ranger team had to forget about it and move on. Rich Herrin put it bluntly after the game.

Coach Herrin: *Nobody is going to feel sorry for us…I'll tell you that much.*

The next opponent for the Rangers was the Alton Redbirds. After a tough tournament opener for Rod Herrin, he came back with a 24-point performance to lead the Rangers past the Redbirds by a score of 69-55. The win advanced the Rangers to the Consolation Championship against the leader of the South Seven Conference, the Carbondale Terriers. Think about that. That is how strong the teams were in the BIT in '77. The Rangers had to be thinking; how could this happen?

Sometimes in the game of basketball there are certain teams that present tough match-ups. For the Benton Rangers in '77, it was the Carbondale Terriers. The Rangers struggled with the Terriers and this time it wasn't Welch or Fayne, it was Jon Hertz and Calvin Cowsan. The Rangers' emphasis on the defensive end of the floor was Gordon Welch and they held him to ten points, far below his average. This left Cowsan and Hertz open and they made the Rangers pay. The Terriers defeated the Rangers by a score of 79-58. Led by Dave Furr, the Olney Tigers won the '77 BIT by defeating Breese Mater Dei, 53-50. On a bright note, Rod Herrin was selected to the five-man All-Tournament team. The Rangers finished the tournament 1-2 and fell to 10-5 on the year.

The Rangers now faced the second loop through the conference. Holding a 5-2 record in South Seven Conference play, the team was doing more than holding their own. They were having a good season. At this point, the question was: Could they defend their South Seven Championship in '76? That was the goal - win the conference.

From this point on, each conference game was critical. The Rangers' second loop opener was a tough match-up on the road with Marion. It was Pickens and Orr again. The team traveled to Marion on the night of January 28th knowing that it was a must win. The Rangers knew it was impossible for Carbondale to lose three of their remaining seven games in conference play. The Rangers had to win.

The feisty Rangers battled. Roger Webb came out hot and carried the Rangers in the first half by scoring ten points. Webb was quite a player and played his best basketball in big moments.

Rod Shurtz: *An athlete…he was our high jumper in track…good runner and jumper. Several times he led our team in scoring. He could score…rebound…and often it was Roger that had to guard guys like Mike Duff. He would challenge you too…a very good competitor and teammate.*

The game was chippy and Coach Herrin was whistled for a technical foul as he argued a call in the first half. There was a second technical foul on the Ranger bench in the third quarter. Then, with 2:17 left to play, Marion player Tony Jones scored a basket and got fouled. Rod Herrin questioned the call and was popped with a technical foul. Sue Herrin remembered the moment.

Sue Herrin: *I was a nervous wreck when the boys played. Rod was very competitive. He always wanted to be the best at whatever he did. He had an explosive manner about him that kept me on the edge of my seat. I remember he had a little "meltdown" in Marion. Of course, we had family there and it was a real close game and I think Rich had gotten a technical. Rodney was standing up on the bench yelling. I realized in that moment…that I was watching exactly what I feared the most.*

The Wildcats defeated the Rangers 79-66 in a wild one. James Orr led all scorers with 26 points and Monty Boatright and Mike Pickens each added 18 points. The Rangers were led by Roger Webb's 17 points. The loss hurt the Rangers' chances of winning the conference. It was a quiet locker room as Coach Herrin encouraged the players to put the game behind them and continue fighting. Coach Herrin had been in these situations before and knew that the team had to pick itself up off the mat and keep battling. There is perhaps no one that can inspire his players to do this quite like Rich Herrin. You can look at the records. Playing in the tough South Seven Conference, the Rangers had never lost five in a row since he had been there. That is amazing. Herrin had a gift when it came to moving his team past tough defeats. With the loss, the Rangers moved to 10-6 overall and 5-3 in the conference.

The next night, the Redbirds came to town. The Birds were having a tough year and were in the cellar of the conference, but they were capable. West Frankfort was led by Rex Hewlett and Greg Smith. Rod Herrin was 10-16 from the floor and 4-4 from the line, as he led the Rangers to a 78-67 win over the Redbirds. Rod's buddy, Joe Durham, described what he remembered about Rod as a player.

Joe Durham: *Rod was a fierce competitor…a sniper…an assassin. He was 5'9" but he played a lot bigger. He was a vicious competitor…kind of like his dad. He was a good shooter and good leader.*

Shurtz had seven assists for the night and eight points. Shurtz and Herrin played well together.

Ron Brookins: *He complimented Rod Herrin so well at the guard spot in '77. Rod* (Shurtz) *was a very calming influence.*

The win improved the Rangers to 11-6 overall and a solid 6-3 in conference play. The Rangers then won the next two games over Herrin and Harrisburg before heading to Centralia. The Rangers had stung the Orphans 65-63 in their previous meeting and this one promised to be a dandy.

A few days before the Centralia game, the flamboyant Jeff Carling was up to his old tricks again. He agreed to shave his head completely bald if the students could raise a set amount of money for a fundraiser aimed at fighting cancer. What do you know? The students did it. Before 1,200 screaming students, Carling went through with his promise in a school assembly. Carling told the student body he would go ahead with the wager because, "My wife said I could do it."

Jeff Carling: *With tournament time approaching, we felt we had to do something different to create interest with the students as well as the community, and maybe inspire the team. We always seem to play better with involvement from the community and the student body.*

The Orphanage immediately lit into the Rangers as they took the floor. They mocked their short haircuts and shouted at the Ranger players as they warmed up. It was the late seventies, and the Centralia players looked the part. They looked like most teenagers in 1977; long hair, and some even with facial hair. The Rangers were clean shaven and sported their signature flat-tops. Steve Summers said he wouldn't have had it any other way.

Steve Summers: *We always had the short flat-tops...that meant something. There were only two reasons you had a flat-top in '77; you were either in the military or you played for the Benton Rangers. We also had the jackets and briefcases for our uniforms. I remember Coach Herrin saying we were going to look the best when we get off the bus...when we play...and when we get back on the bus. And we did.*

The Rangers did everything first class...right down to the shoes. Coach Herrin was always working an angle to get his players free tennis shoes.

502

Alan Klochany: *I remember we all got two pairs of high-top Chuck Taylors...and we didn't have to pay for them. I would cut mine in the summer and wear them as low-tops.*

So, it was the clean-shaven Rangers of Rich Herrin vs. the shaggy-looking Orphans of Jeff Carling. The game took place on February 12, 1977, in front of a packed house at Trout Gymnasium. As the Orphanage affectionately chanted, "Ko-Jak! Ko-Jak!", Jeff Carling gave final instructions to his players before the tip. When both teams walked onto the floor, the visible difference between the two great programs was on display. Centralia was modern, hip and totally represented the time period. The Rangers were buttoned down, formal and business-like.

The game was a classic. Neither team would let the other pull away. The crowd was loud and the balcony at Trout was jammed. The place rocked and it was just a regular season conference game. This was the old South Seven. Electric!

The Orphans raced to a 14-12 lead after the first quarter. At halftime, the game was tied at 31. Rod Herrin and Jerry Dawson had eight points in the half to lead the Rangers. In the second half, the two teams played to a tie. The Rangers then forced overtime on Joe Durham's put-back on Webb's missed free throw. A three-point play by high-scoring Rodney Thomas with 1:30 to play gave the Orphans a 68-67 win. After the game, there was some controversy about the discrepancy in fouls. The Rangers were whistled for 24 fouls against only 17 for the pressing Orphans. Centralia fans wildly celebrated the win and heckled the Rangers as they walked off the floor.

Coach Herrin was disappointed with the outcome, but proud of his team's effort. They had battled to the end. I believe sometimes it is these types of teams that can go under-appreciated. Sure, the '75 Rangers were great to watch, but the teams that have to get everything out of their ability to win games are fun to pull for. With the loss, the Rangers fell to 13-8 overall, and 8-4 in league play. They were out of contention to win the South Seven.

On February 18, 1977, the Rangers played the Terriers yet again. The game was at Benton. Maybe the third time would be a charm, or maybe not. Again, the Terriers dismantled the Rangers led by Gordon Welch's 19 points. Roger Webb led the way for the Rangers by scoring 18 points, but it wasn't enough. The Terriers won the game, 69-56.

The next night, the Rangers traveled to Mt. Vernon. Ranger fans drove north anticipating a slug-fest and that is just what they got. Historically, Ranger fans are always treated with more entertainment than just the ball game at old Changon Gymnasium. The old timers mark their calendars and wouldn't miss it.

At halftime, the game was tied at 29, but an incident that occurred in the second half encapsulated the Benton-Mt. Vernon rivalry.

Rod Shurtz: *Jerry Wilson always inbounded the ball for Mt. Vernon and he was the trailer. I decided I was going to wait back and step in front of him and see if I could get a charge as he ran up the floor. Jerry was a great all-around player, and we became great friends because we played two years together at Missouri Southern. Wilson threw the ball in and I stepped in front of him… he just plows me over…no call…then he just looks down at me and stomps my chest. I still hurt to this day! No call! I remember as I got up off the floor, Coach Herrin was barking at the officials and the Rams fans in the balcony were just going crazy. They loved it! When I speak about that play with Jerry today…he just laughs…and says that I am the guy that invented the flop.*

Jerry Wilson led all scorers with 21, and Mac Thomas chipped in with 20 points. The Rams won the battle by a score of 74-65. It was the Rangers' third consecutive loss and the low point of what was still a very good season.

The Rangers had one final home game against the Effingham Flaming Hearts. A respectable crowd was on hand to show their appreciation to the seven seniors. You have to wonder what was going through the mind of Rodney Herrin as he prepared to play his final game at Benton. He had seen every game since 1965. The gym was his babysitter. Basketball had been his life. This night would be his last home game at Benton. Wow!

All seven of the seniors were introduced and the fans applauded their effort and commitment to the program. Senior Jerry Bell remembered how important it was for him to be a member of the Benton Rangers that year in '77.

Jerry Bell: *My mom and dad went to every home game. We were originally from Marion and moved to Benton in 1969. Dad went to the games in Marion…he saw Starrick and Thompson. He was well informed about the Benton Rangers. The old gym was jammed with people when I was a kid and my favorite player was Denny Smith. He was a great ball handler and he had great* *court vision. I went to Lincoln School and I was the team manager until my sophomore season and Coach Phillips kept me on the team. I went to all the morning open gyms in the summers…did my dad's chores in the afternoon… and then went back up to the gym at night and played. It was important to me. I wanted to be a Benton Ranger.*

Senior Randy Phillips told me that he went to most all of the games growing up and he recalled one of the greatest rewards he ever got in his life came at Rend Lake Basketball Camp.

Randy Phillips: *I went to Douglas School and then Webster Junior High. My mom and Dad had tickets in the old gym and then when the new gym was built they had tickets at center court…two rows up. They had seats in front of Bob Gariepy so when he got loud…they were in the middle of it. I remember at Rend Lake Basketball Camp Coach Herrin told me that for me to play I would have to always give a little bit more…hustle a little more. I was probably in the eighth grade and when I got home I told my dad what Coach said. My dad said, "He's probably right." I remember that on awards day, I got the Hustle Award. He must have seen that after he talked to me and that award meant everything to me. From that point on I hustled more…gave a little more.*

The Rangers were in their home whites and the Flaming Hearts wore their dark red road uniforms. The Hearts were a formidable opponent and the Rangers would have to play well to get the victory. There were no easy ones on the schedule in '77.

As the end of the first quarter approached, the game was stopped and the officials then ordered the teams to their benches. PA announcer, John D. Aiken, announced to the 3,100 fans in attendance that there had been a bomb threat and the game would be suspended. The fans were asked to evacuate the building in an orderly manner while local police inspected the gymnasium for anything suspicious. It was a rather funny sight to observe the reaction of many of the older, more die-hard Benton fans. They exited the building in complete frustration that the game was suspended and totally oblivious to their own safety. Their thoughts focused only on the fact that they could not watch their beloved Rangers play.

The Rangers and the Hearts walked thru the BCHS commons to the East gymnasium and waited it out. This was the story of the bomb threat according to the Saturday, February 26th edition of the Benton Evening News:

Benton Evening News: *The call was reported taken at 8:43 p.m. in the coach's office under the north grandstand. Brett Martin, 10, of 611 Smith Street, told officials he answered the phone. The youngster who received the message said the call was terminated immediately after the threat was made.*

The delay was only twelve minutes, which strikes me kind of funny, especially in the world we live in today. If this would have happened today, Effingham would have been sent home and the FBI would have come in, but not in '77. There was basketball to play and after twelve minutes of solid searching, it was deemed safe enough to bring the basketball crazies back into the gym and resume play.

As play resumed, the Rangers took a 46-43 lead into halftime. Roger Webb played like a man possessed as he poured in 19 points by halftime. Webb scored from every area on the floor as the Ranger guards continued to feed Webb's hot hand. With 4:06 left in the game, Rod Herrin hit a 15-foot jump shot to put the Rangers on top, 72-71. With the game tied at 78 with only 1:33 to play, it was Herrin again. The Ranger spark plug drove the lane and hit a lay-up and drew the foul. Herrin hit the free throw giving the Rangers an 81-78 lead. Herrin and Webb scored the final two Ranger baskets to give the Rangers an exciting 85-80 victory. Despite the bomb threat, Webb scored a career-high 31 points on senior night.

Roger Webb: *My favorite memory was the bomb threat game against Effingham. I remember they cleared the gym and both teams went to the girls' gym. We won the game and I scored 31 points that night. Thanks to the guards for getting me the ball.*

The bomb threat did not sit well with BCHS Principal, Chuck Oyler. He was not amused. Chuck Oyler had stints as the BCHS football coach and wrestling coach and was now the acting principal. Oyler was an ex-marine that served in Korea. He could be an intimidating figure. Mr. Oyler was my principal and he had a presence. You always knew if he was in the room. He was about 6'3" tall and wore a tight military flat-top. He was firm but fair and he did not put up with nonsense. The bomb threat was nonsense. Rod Shurtz told a great story that involved Mr. Oyler a few days after the bomb threat.

Rod Shurtz: *I happened to be in the coach's office a few days after the bomb threat…. Mr. Oyler came down to the coach's office and there was that phone* *that the bomb threat call was received on. The phone was used by a lot of the underclassman to call their parents to come get them after practice. He just reached down and pulled that phone cord out of the wall and said, "Well, that will be the last time we have a bomb threat."*

'77 State Tournament Play

It was now Regional Tournament time and the Rangers were the top seed of the West Frankfort Regional but they were limping. Coming into the tournament, the Rangers had lost three out of their last four games. There was concern. The Redbirds were capable, especially at home.

The Rangers opened tournament play on Tuesday, March 1, 1977. The '77 Redbirds entered the game at 4-18 under the direction of head coach Harold Hood. The Redbirds had recently played Marion well and if guards Rex Hewlett and Greg Smith got hot, the Rangers could be in for a long night. The pressure was definitely on the Rangers. They had manhandled West Frankfort since junior high and this was not the game to lose. They couldn't lose.

On the other hand, it had been a long season for the Redbirds. Sometimes in post-season play, advancing in tournament play depends on how much fight the players have to continue the season. If the Rangers could strike the first blow, it might be over. Coach Herrin and the Rangers knew it would be important to get out to a good start and take the fight out of the Redbirds. The Rangers jumped out to a 20-10 lead in the first quarter and never looked back. Rod Herrin led the Ranger attack with 19 points, and sophomore Jerry Dawson added 14. The Rangers won the game by a score of 68-52. The win moved the Rangers into the Regional Championship against the Mt. Vernon Rams.

In the previous two games, the Rangers had split with the Rams, and this would be the tie breaker. Both teams won at home. On this night, it was Joe Durham that stepped up to lead the Rangers' attack. Early in the game, Durham dropped a series of mid-range jump shots pushing the Rangers to a 20-15 first quarter lead. In the second quarter, Jerry Dawson came alive by scoring four baskets in the paint to lead the Rangers into halftime clinging to a 36-34 advantage. In the second half, Mt. Vernon's Jerry Wilson was unstoppable, but Alan Klochany stepped up to score eight quick points to keep the Rangers ahead. The Rangers led 54-48 at the end of the third quarter.

The final quarter was a fight. Mt. Vernon would not go away. Mac Thomas had a big quarter and Wilson continued to hurt the Rangers. In the final minute, with the Rangers ahead, they went into the four to score. The offense is designed to hold the ball unless there is a lay-up opportunity. The Rams chose to foul junior Rod Shurtz. Late in the game, Shurtz calmly sank 3-4 free throws to send the Rams home. It was over. The Rangers won the Regional Championship by a score of 69-66. Joe Durham led the team in scoring with 21 points and nine rebounds. Joe came up big when it mattered most.

Joe Durham: *Winning the Regional at West Frankfort against Mt. Vernon was my favorite memory. Mt. Vernon was always tough. We played really well and seemed to play good at West Frankfort.*

Junior Rod Shurtz hit key free throws down the stretch in several of the Rangers victories. He did a solid job of running the show for the Rangers and enjoyed competing against the Rams.

Rod Shurtz: *I always wanted to get them. Mt. Vernon had Scott Waggoner, Doug Creel, Mac Thomas and Jerry Wilson. I'm good friends with those guys today. That was a really big win for us when we beat Mt. Vernon for the Regional Championship.*

The team was presented with the Regional Championship plaque and a team picture was taken on the floor after the game. All of the Rangers sported wide grins as they held up one finger, to represent their number one finish.

Jerry Bell: *My favorite memory is when we beat Mt. Vernon in the Regional Championship at West Frankfort.*

After the picture, the Rangers walked down the steps from the floor into the old locker room located in the underbelly of Max Morris Gymnasium. They celebrated together. These are the times that make it worth it. The special moments with the guys you sacrificed with is what it's all about. The Rangers soaked it in! They high-fived, hugged, shook hands and congratulated each other on a great win. Coach Herrin then addressed the team about the game and congratulated the team on their hard work. By this time, think of how many times Coach Herrin had celebrated post game victories in this very locker room. The Rangers owned Max Morris Gymnasium.

The team then boarded the bus and drove north on Highway 37 back to Benton. As the team drove up South Main Street, the bus was stopped by the fire department. Waiting on the square were droves of Ranger fans ready to celebrate. Just as the great teams of Yunkus, Johnson and Collins did, the scrappy, undersized, overachieving '77 Rangers were about to get their lap around the square. On this cold March night, the '77 team was celebrated.

The Rangers were now playing with house money. There were many that felt they would not survive the Regional. The Regional was pressure-packed. To ensure their place in history the Rangers had to beat West Frankfort and win the Regional Championship. Why? Because that is what the Rangers do. The team had lost in the Regional only three times since Herrin's arrival.

In the Sectional, the Rangers traveled to Olney to play Ron Herrin's Tigers. The Sectional presented a different type of pressure on Rich and Rod Herrin. Let's face it, Rich loved his brother, but he didn't want his brother winning the game. In Rod's case, who wants to lose to their uncle? The brother vs. brother match-up created an anxiety that nobody else in the locker room really could have understood.

The first game of the Sectional Tournament was played on Wednesday, March 9, 1977, at Olney Gymnasium. It is now called Ron Herrin Gymnasium. Many Ranger fans made the trip, and of course the Olney fans came out to watch their Tigers. At tip-off, the gymnasium was a sea of maroon and orange. The Tigers were led by Tim Knox, Dave Furr, Darnall Jones and point guard Curt Berger. They were 22-4 and winners of the Benton Invitational Tournament. They were a solid team.

The Rangers started the game well and led 16-10 after a basket by Roger Webb early in the second quarter. Then Olney's Dave Furr picked up his third personal foul of the first half and was forced to go to the bench at the 6:40 mark of the second period. Sophomore Darnall Jones then came into the game for Furr and played well. The Rangers could not capitalize on Furr's early foul trouble. The Tigers took the lead on a pair of free throws from Tim Knox before pulling away to a 31-25 advantage at halftime.

In the third period, the Rangers trailed by as many as ten points before mounting a comeback in the final minutes of the quarter. Two baskets by Webb and a jump shot by Shurtz cut the Tiger lead to 45-41 to end the final quarter. In the fourth quarter, the Tigers methodically pulled away to win the game by a score of 65-53.

Ron Brookins: *When we got beat by Olney at the end of the season. I remember how tough it was for Rod Herrin after that game. I just remember thinking…Wow! This is their last game together* (Coach and Rod)…. *That's got to be tough.*

Today, Rod Herrin is an orthopedic surgeon in Springfield, Illinois. He admitted that he was somewhat inspired by his experience as a Ranger when choosing his career path.

Rod Herrin: *You know one of my best friends, Alan Klochany is a doctor… he went to Saint Louis University. I really liked science in high school. At first, I was interested in being an engineer and I actually went to Missouri Rolla for about a year and a half. I wanted to play basketball…then I thought about being in family practice…kind of like Dr. Swinney. Then one thing led to another and I really started thinking about sports medicine. You know I saw a lot of dad's players have career ending injuries…traumatic injuries…and I thought it would be neat to be able to help someone return to their sport. I remember Atkins, Denny Smith and even Rob Dunbar. We just know so much more about repairing the knee than we did at that time. Seeing those guys go through those injuries definitely played into my decision to be an orthopedic surgeon. I have probably done close to 1,000 ACL reconstructions since I began.*

After high school, Rod first attended Missouri Rolla and then transferred to McKendree College. He did play basketball at McKendree College. He is now in his thirtieth year as an orthopedic surgeon. He has three children; Jake, Kate and Rachel.

Today, Joe Durham lives in Mechanicsville, Virginia with his wife Catherin. They have two children; Connor and Paige. After high school, Joe attended St. Louis University and walked onto the basketball team. Joe is now a physical therapist and is close to retirement.

I asked Joe about the influence that Coach Herrin made on his life and these were his words:

Joe Durham: *Discipline…we got the crew-cuts every year. He had a system. We ran the same things offensively and defensively from the junior high up. All of the summer basketball camps…Coach gave us every opportunity to succeed.*

After high school, Roger Webb played basketball at Rend Lake College. He has always farmed and now works as a food supervisor at Shawnee Prison. He is married to his wife Cindy and they live in West Frankfort. They have three children: Jonathon, Megan, and Emily. He has three stepchildren: Morgan, Dominic and Anna Beth. Roger enjoyed all of his coaches at Benton High School.

Roger Webb: *I enjoyed all my coaches at Benton. I remember coach Phillips would work with me before school individually. We had a lot of coaches that wanted us to succeed. I was honored that I had the opportunity to play for Coach Herrin. He wanted us to play the right way and be gentlemen off the floor.*

Steve Summers (Radar) now lives in Kansas City, Missouri with his wife Gloria. They have two children; Larry and Julie. After high school, Steve played one year of college basketball at Graceland College. For the past twenty-five years he has been very active in the real estate investment business. Steve has fond memories of Coach Herrin and the lessons he learned during his time as a Ranger.

Steve Summers: *I remember Coach told us once that "the harder you work the luckier you are." I believe that is true in all walks of life. We create our own luck by how hard we work no matter what line of work we are in.*

After high school, Alan Klochany attended medical school at St. Louis University. He became a doctor and is now retired from his practice in Charlotte, North Carolina. Klochany actually held the high jump record at Benton for a short time with a jump of 6'3". He has now been married for thirty-six years to his wife Suzanne and they have three children: Ryan, Jordan and Katie. Klochany has great memories of his playing days and his experience to play for Coach Herrin.

Alan Klochany: *My favorite memories of that time were the friendships that were created. You know...I was always surrounded by good people. Everyone I played with was a quality person and the whole experience was a great way to grow up. You need role models growing up. Coach was like a second father figure...and if you take away sleep time...I was around Coach Herrin about as much as my parents. I also believe he instilled leadership qualities in all of us. Throughout my career in medicine, I've been placed in leadership roles, and I think Coach had something to do with that.*

Randy Phillips now lives in the Giant City area with his wife, Becky. They have two children; Lindsay and Amber. He has worked for more than twenty years for Stiles Office Solutions in Carbondale, Illinois. In our interview, Randy told me that his favorite sport growing up was baseball, but he loved his time as a Benton Ranger and playing for Coach Herrin.

Randy Phillips: *The thing about Coach was you might go into practice with a negative attitude but he had a way of bringing out a different side of you. We always left practice on a positive note. I saw him one day a few years ago at Coleman Rhodes Furniture in West Frankfort. He was coaching at Morthland College. He saw me and hollered at me across the store. I went over to talk to him and he said, "You got any eligibility left, big guy?" He knew everybody. Always spoke and had time for you. You have to respect a guy like that.*

Jerry Bell currently lives in Benton with his wife, Cathy. They have two children; Caitlin and Courtney. After high school, Jerry worked for the Department of Corrections for close to ten years before serving twenty-one years with the Department of Natural Resources. He is now retired. Jerry had this to say about Coach Herrin:

Jerry Bell: *Me personally, Coach Herrin helped me become a man. His coaching was not only about the game of basketball. It was about the game of life. Coach Herrin took care of me. He made sure I had good practice gear and tennis shoes. He gave me a part time job at the concession stand to put some money in my pockets. He was a compassionate man. He taught me to play 110% all of the time. If he was able to see a spark in you...he could light your fire.*

The scrappy Rangers had a great season finishing with an overall record of 16-10 and 8-6 in the South Seven Conference. They were the first team I vaguely remember. It was an honor to interview this group for the book.

This is the old Douglas School entrance stone. It is now a historical landmark at the park. Today, Douglas School no longer stands.
(Matt Wynn family collection)

This is my 2ⁿᵈ grade picture at Douglas School. I was eight years old. I begged my parents to go to the Rangers Games. *(Matt Wynn family collection)*

The scrappy '77 Rangers. **Bottom Row-** Fairchilds, Heard, Page, Dunbar, Kovarick **Middle Row-** Kolisek, J. Dawson, Webb, Durham, Klochany, T. Dawson, Gesell **Back Row-** Herrin, R. Herrin, Bell, Shurtz, Phillips, Brookins, Shurtz, Summers. *(Ceasar Maragni)*

Rod Shurtz took care of the ball and was dependable from the free throw line late in games. Rod drives to the basket in '77. *(Ceasar Maragni)*

Steve Summers was the first guard off the bench in '77.
(Ceasar Maragni)

Ron Brookins saw limited action as a junior in '77.
(Ceasar Maragni)

Joe Durham called Rod Herrin "an assassin." Herrin was a knockdown shooter
and a fiery competitor. After biding his time behind Craddock
in '76, Rod was clearly the leader in '77. *(Ceasar Maragni)*

Randy Phillips was a reserve guard off the bench for the
Rangers in '77. *(Ceasar Maragni)*

Alan Klochany provided quality post play in '77.
(Ceasar Maragni)

Coach Herrin poses with the big four inside; Dawson, Klochany,
Durham and Webb before the beginning of the '77 season.

Roger Webb had serious hops. Webb was a key player on both ends of the floor for the Rangers in '77. *(Ceasar Maragni)*

Jerry Dawson goes high to snatch a rebound at Carbondale. *(Ceasar Maragni)*

Jerry Bell was a reserve guard for the Rangers in '77.
(Caesar Maragni)

CHAPTER TWENTY-THREE

True Grit in '78

"He was putting our class together when we were in the sixth Grade." –Doug Dunbar

Think back to your childhood. What was your first memory? Doctors believe that most people begin developing long term memories at age seven. Sure, there are some moments that we may remember before this time, but not many.

With that being said, I was a little behind the norm when it came to recalling my first memories. Life first came into focus for me in the fall of 1977. I was eight years old and just beginning the third grade at Douglas School. Douglas School was one of the five elementary schools (grades 1-6) in Benton. The school was located on the east side of town and many of the students came from hardworking, blue-collar families. The old two-story school building was a majestic site and bigger than life to my third-grade eyes.

I was in Mrs. Betty Hutchens class and my classroom was located upstairs. It was the place where I met my life-long best friend, Michael Yarberry. We were sports junkies and we also shared in organizing most of the games and activities that took place at recess. There were games of all kinds; kick and catch, nerf football and kickball, to name a few. It was also a long-standing tradition at Douglas that every student play marbles. Each day, I took my marble bag and placed it in the cloak room so I could pick them up before recess. I can shut my eyes and still recall the faint voices of my classmates at recess accompanied by the squeaking sounds of the old swing sets.

I also loved baseball. I remember witnessing Reggie Jackson hit three homeruns on three pitches to beat the Dodgers in the '77 World Series. It was the most amazing thing I had ever seen in the sports world to that point. And then in February of '78, Leon Spinks upset Muhammad Ali to win the heavyweight boxing title. My dad loved the heavyweight fights. On this night, we watched the fight together and rooted for the underdog Spinks. I also remember the great winter storms of 1977-78 that canceled school for nearly two weeks. All kids like snow days. I remember Walter Cronkite delivered the news and Jimmy Carter was our president. As an eight-year-old boy, these were some of my earliest memories.

But the one thing I remember the most about the winter of '77-'78, was watching the Benton Rangers. My dad, Mack, was the biology teacher at Benton High School and for a few extra bucks, he worked the pass gate at all the home basketball games.

I remember getting to the games early and wandering around the gym. I became acquainted with the coaches and I can still remember that it was a big deal when Coach Herrin spoke to me. All of the coaches and players were my heroes.

I have to say with certainty that it was the '78 team that first inspired me to be a Benton Ranger. These were my guys. The seniors were Rod Shurtz, Ron Brookins, Doug Dunbar, Brad Gesell, Frank Kolisek, and David Fairchilds. The juniors were Carl Shurtz, Dave Jones, Jim Ward, Rob Hammond, Jerry Dawson, Terry Dawson, Mike Garret, Jeff Shew, Sid Page and Bart Oyler. This was the first team I really remember.

There were many in Southern Illinois that gave the '78 Rangers little chance of finishing in the top half of the conference due to their lack of varsity experience.

Rod Shurtz: *Merle Jones was the long-time Sports editor of the Southern Illinoisan and he wrote an article at the start of the season that talked about our winning history. Then he basically went on to say that our team just didn't stand much of a chance. He doubted us.*

On Tuesday, November 29, 1977, I jumped in my dad's red truck and we headed to the home opener against the McLeansboro Foxes. On the way to the game, we turned the radio on and heard the following comments from Coach Herrin about the '78 team. At this point, Herrin held a 428-133 career record and was considered the top high school basketball coach in Southern Illinois and possibly the state.

Coach Herrin: *It's a rebuilding year, in a sense. We lost four starters and one top reserve, but that turnover occurs every year. We're not rebuilding for next year but for this year. We will start point guard Rod Shurtz and Jerry Dawson in the pivot. The other spots will be a game-time decision.*

At the conclusion of the sophomore game, I stood and clapped with more than 3,000 fans as the Rangers darted from the Tunnel and snaked into the magic circle. I studied every player and their movements. I noticed the red, white and blue warm-up balls, used only for pre-game drills, and watched as the players ran through a regimented series of drills that left me mesmerized.

As I positioned myself behind the bench, the buzzer rang and the starters began to take their warm-ups off. It was the first indication as to who would start the game. In the first game of the '78 season, the Rangers started Rod Shurtz, Ron Brookins, Rob Hammond, Jim Ward and Jerry Dawson. The top reserves were Doug Dunbar, Carl Shurtz and Dave Jones. Rob Hammond still remembers the moment he finally saw his name etched into the starting line-up.

Rob Hammond: *I remember my junior year showing up to the first game of the year and we really didn't know who was going to start. I saw my name on the board and naturally there were some nerves. As the year went on there was a rotation and then eventually I was coming in off the bench.*

The Foxes were coached by Dave Lee and he returned experienced players that were very physical. The Foxes had already beaten Elverado, 76-39, and were led by 6'4" junior forward Kent Anselment. It was a game that could go either way for the young Rangers.

I watched the game and hung on every play. I noticed how the players ran the floor, boxed out, dove for loose balls and made the extra pass. I was learning the game by watching. Most importantly, I was watching the game being played the right way. I was getting an education. When there was a break in play, I gladly handed the players their towels and peeked over their shoulder to hear Coach Herrin in the huddle. This was my way of being a part of it. I was now that kid. I was the kid being sucked in by the powerful eye of this basketball hurricane. I knew one thing. I wanted to be a Benton Ranger. I was eight years old.

For the Rangers, it was a typical opening game that featured first-game jitters and icy field goal shooting. The Rangers shot 20-49 from the field and were whistled for 25 fouls but they redeemed themselves by shooting 15-19 from the free throw line. The Foxes kept it close late in the game but with the game tied at 52, the Foxes made the mistake of fouling senior Rod Shurtz. Shurtz connected on both of his free throws to put the Rangers ahead for good. The Foxes didn't score on the next possession and junior Jerry Dawson was fouled and hit one free throw with .12 seconds left to give the Rangers a 55-52 victory.

After the game, the Rangers turned the eight-track cassette player on loud and lingered around the locker room and rehashed the victory. They were 1-0.

Dave Jones: *The locker room was our kingdom. We even got a stereo put in there. I think Shurtz had a lot to do with that. That's where we hung out.*

Rod Shurtz was the senior point guard and the only returning starter on the team. When Shurtz came on the scene in '77, Rodney Herrin was moved to the two spot to give him more opportunities to score. In '78, Shurtz would not have that luxury. As a senior, Shurtz was again the floor general, but now he would also have to take on more of a scoring responsibility.

In the first game, Shurtz led the team in scoring with 20 points and Jerry Dawson added 12. As a boy, Rod Shurtz and his brothers grew up on a large piece of property in Waltonville, Illinois, surrounded by two of the greatest bluegill ponds in Southern Illinois. From an early age, basketball was the sport that he most loved.

Rod Shurtz: *When I first started playing basketball, my dad poured a concrete pad and put a goal up for us. When he put that goal up, that was the start of things for us. Besides doing the chores that were laid out each day…that's what we did. We played all of the time. In the winter we would shovel off the pad and play. If the ball got really cold it would lose its bounce and we would go inside and warm it up and then go back out and play.*

Rod also had the unique experience of playing alongside younger brother Carl. Carl was now a junior and would play a key role off the bench. Carl

Shurtz brought hustle and energy and gave the Rangers key minutes at the back-up point guard position.

Carl Shurtz: *The transition to Benton was pretty easy for me. We moved during the summer and I went to open gyms and I was able to meet people before school started. I was an eighth grader when we moved over and I played for Norman Carlile. It was a good move for us.*

In game two, Doug Dunbar was inserted into the starting line-up and Ron Brookins came off the bench. In my opinion, Ron Brookins is one of the greatest competitors to ever come through the program. He did not sulk or pout about Herrin's decision to bring him off the bench. But he did have a response. He scored twenty points on 10-13 shooting from the field and flew around the floor leading the Rangers to a tough 64-60 win. Doug Dunbar also played well and scored 14 points in his first varsity start. It was a coming out party for Brookins and Dunbar. Jerry Dawson scored 13 points and Rod Shurtz chipped in ten points. The Rangers were 2-0. Coach Herrin had these comments after the game:

Coach Herrin: *Our pressure shook them up later in the ballgame, with Dunbar and Brookins putting it in the hole.*

Brookins grew up in Ewing, Illinois, a small country community about five miles north of Benton. All of the students that attend Ewing Grade School feed into Benton High School. As a junior, he was the second guard off the bench. He loved the game of basketball and you could see it through his fiery play. He was affectionately called "Brook" by his teammates. As a freshman, Brookins sat in amazement as he watched the great '75 team dominate opponents. He dreamed of playing for the Rangers and now he would have his chance. He would have one year of quality playing time to get it right. This was it.

Ron Brookins: *I don't ever remember not being in love with basketball. When I was a kid, it was a big deal to be able to watch the State Tournament on t.v. I listened to the Rangers on the radio…there is just something special about listening to those games on the radio. Benton made it easy to love basketball. I remember going to a couple of Sectional Tournaments as a kid at Eldorado…that was a big deal. My favorite player was Billy Smith. You have to understand…I watched Billy when I was in junior high and then when he* *was a senior, I was a freshman. I remember in 1972 sitting in my Aunt Edith's living room with my cousin Gary Rose as Collins shot the free throws in the '72 Olympics. Matt, I'll never forget my cousin saying, "Come on Doug, put us on the map!" I'll never forget that. When we lost that game, we were devastated.*

Brookins had moxie and played the game with an unbridled passion that seemed to rub off on his teammates. He was a nasty competitor that hated getting beat. He pounced on loose balls and could get under the opponents skin by dishing out rough box-outs from the guard position. Opponents didn't like Brookins, but his teammates appreciated his tenacious play.

Rod Shurtz: *Here was a guy that was a good friend. Ron was one of those guys you wanted on your side. He played with confidence and he was adamant about winning. Ronnie took things personally. He could score and handle the ball. I remember one time in starting lineups…I sprinted out you know…and then Ron was announced. He came out and he was so excited that when he gave me a high-five he jammed my right thumb and that thing swelled on me. Ron was just so excited to play…always.*

Dave Jones: *Ronnie was just a good ole country boy…salt of the earth…hard worker.*

Brad Gesell: *Ronnie was quick and very scrappy. He wasn't scared of anybody…he was a great teammate.*

Rob Hammond: *Hard-nosed. He would do anything to win. Brook was very competitive and a great teammate.*

Doug Dunbar: *I played with Brook after high school. He was a good hard-nosed basketball player…scrapper…good shooter…good defensive player and he was like the rest of us…he did not want to lose.*

On Friday, December 9, 1977, the Rangers hosted Eddie Lane and the Eldorado Eagles. Lane was a tough match-up for the Rangers and he scored the last two field goals of the first half to give the Eagles a 35-31 advantage at halftime. The Eagles built a 43-37 lead, but the Rangers came storming back due to their ball-hawking defense to regain the lead at 51-49 at the end of three periods. Junior Carl Shurtz backed up his brother at the point guard position giving the Rangers great defensive play. He also scored eleven points and was 5-5 from the free throw line.

Carl Shurtz: *I remember he put me in a lot when we went four corners so we had four guards in the game. I think that was the most enjoyable year for me as a player.*

The Rangers simply wore down the Eagles. In the fourth quarter, Eddie Lane fouled out of the game at the 1:36 mark. Lane scored a game-high 33 points, but it wasn't enough to beat the balanced attack of the Rangers. The Rangers won the ballgame by a score of 74-66. Rod Shurtz led the Rangers' scoring attack with 15 points and hit key field goals and free throws down the stretch to seal the win. Doug Dunbar added 13 points and Jerry Dawson chipped in with ten.

Four days after the Rangers defeated the Eagles, tragedy struck. On Tuesday, December 13th, the Evansville Aces were leaving Evansville for a game at Middle Tennessee State. Eldorado's own Mike Duff and Kevin Kingston, along with Greg Smith (West Frankfort), were on board when the team plane crashed killing all 29 passengers. The headline in the Evansville Courier on Wednesday read, "The Night it Rained Tears." It was a miserable week for all of Southern Illinois as people grieved for the families of the 29 lives taken far too soon.

On Friday, December 16th, the Rangers traveled to Marion to play the Wildcats. It was the all-important South Seven opener. Sitting at 3-0 and playing with confidence, the Rangers pounced on the Wildcats early. They rushed out to a 10-0 lead and never looked back. The balanced scoring attack of the Rangers encapsulated the team. Everyone had to do their part. Rod Shurtz led the team in scoring with 17 points, followed by Ron Brookins with 15. Doug Dunbar and Jerry Dawson added 14 points. Jones, C. Shurtz, Ward and Hammond all did their part. It was a feel-good night in Marion. Everyone played well and the Rangers were rolling.

The next night the Rangers hosted the Herrin Tigers. The Tigers, behind the shooting of forward Von LaQuatte and guard Brad Payne built a 30-20 advantage by the end of the first half. Guard Ron Brookins, who was still fighting for a starting position, scored 25 points on 12-20 shooting from the field but it was his defensive play that most impressed Coach Herrin.

Coach Herrin: *He had seven steals and did a heck of a job for us.*

The Rangers moved to 4-1 overall and 1-1 in the South Seven, with Johnny Fayne and the Carbondale Terriers looming. The Terriers were the pre-season favorite to win the conference. Doug Woolard's club also featured 6'5" standout Charles Pugh.

In a Tuesday night match-up, the Terriers came into Benton unbeaten. The game was a good old-fashioned South Seven slugfest. Carbondale was good. Fayne popped corner jumpers and led the Terriers to a 32-30 half-time lead. The Rangers fell behind by ten points in the second half but battled back to cut the Terrier lead to 57-55 after a Dunbar free throw. Defensively, the Rangers applied full court pressure the entire second half and forced 22 Terrier turnovers. They also won the battle on the boards, 39-36. Dave Jones, Jim Ward, and Doug "Dunny" Dunbar battled on the boards to keep the Rangers in striking distance.

Rod Shurtz: *Dunny was just shifty. Here he was 6'0" tall…he had to be our leading rebounder. He could read the carom of the ball so well.*

Despite the great effort from the Rangers, the Terriers won the game by a score of 61-57. Despite the loss, it was a great team effort that did not go unnoticed.

Coach Herrin: *Give Dunbar, Jones and Ward credit for their work on the boards. They flat got out there and battled. If we never win another ball game, but get that kind of effort, I won't be disappointed.*

The Terriers were loaded; Craig Bardo, Johnny Fayne, William Mathis, Charles Pugh and Randy Gibson. The Rangers came close. They did not beat themselves. Although the team improved, the record fell to 4-2 overall and 1-2 in league play.

After the Carbondale game, the Rangers had seven days off. The team practiced early in the mornings over Christmas break and then took Christmas Eve and Christmas Day off. Keeping with tradition, the team prepared for the always-tough Centralia Holiday Tournament. By this time, the players had seen the tournament when they were kids and every player understood the importance of a good showing in the tournament. The players also understood that they were the keepers of the flame and it was their job to carry on the great Ranger mystique that they brought to the tournament.

Rod Shurtz: *One of the biggest things that really inspired me to play was going to the Centralia Holiday Tournament with Mom and Dad. Dad would always take three days off and take us to the tournament and we would stay all day and just watch games. You got to see some of the best teams in the state play. I think my dad said it…. "Some years the Centralia Tournament was better than the State Tournament." I believe that. I always dreamed of playing in that tournament. I remember watching the Rangers when they would roll into town. They had the flat-tops with the blazers and the way they carried themselves. People were impressed by that. The way they warmed up…it was all business-like. All business…when I got to Benton I wanted to play for Coach Herrin.*

The '78 team entered the tournament at 4-2 and was not recognized as one of the higher seeds in the tournament. But the Rangers had all of the intangibles. The team was fundamentally sound, unselfish, quick and very smart. They featured a balanced attack of competitors that hated to lose. Did the team have a Rich Yunkus or Danny Johnson? Absolutely not. And because of this, most basketball fans predicted the Rangers would be eliminated early.

Ranger fans were excited about the tournament and showed up in force to see the opener against Peoria Woodruff. The Rangers found themselves ahead by three entering the second half and then the wheels came off. The third quarter saw Woodruff storm back to take a 57-51 lead entering the fourth quarter. The Rangers mounted a comeback in the fourth quarter behind the play of veteran guard Rod Shurtz. Shurtz was the only Ranger in the line-up with playing experience in the tournament. He led a balanced Rangers scoring attack with 18 points and calmly handled the ball despite trapping pressure from the Woodruff guards.

Brookins also chipped in with 15 points and Dave Jones scored nine. It was a great win. Nothing was going to be easy for this group of Rangers. Ranger fans liked what they saw. They had confidence that every time they paid for a ticket, the Rangers would give them their money's worth.

The next day the Running Rangers played Belleville West. West was a good club and was expected to win but the feisty Rangers held a 17-13 advantage at the end of the first quarter. The Rangers extended the lead to 37-31 at halftime behind the play of reserve post player Brad Gesell. Gesell was the perfect example of the '78 team's persona. Gesell played at 6'3" and maximized his ability through his work ethic. He usually received spot playing time, but not on this afternoon. This was his moment. He was undersized compared to West's post players but he battled for rebounds and scored six crucial points in the second quarter to inspire the team. Gesell attended Ewing Grade School with teammate Ron Brookins and they are still very close friends today.

Brad Gesell: *I went to school at Ewing and I probably have some pictures of me playing basketball as young as the fourth grade. I never saw the Rangers play much growing up. No, that was big time. My dad wanted me to work… it helped the family go. Coach Herrin kept me but I didn't come into the gym in the summer as much as the other guys because I was always working. There was a lot of competition for spots but I played a little as a senior.*

Ron Brookins: *Brad worked a lot for his dad growing up. I always had the impression it was hard for him to get basketball time growing up because he was always working. Brad and I are really good friends. Brad played the five and he was only about 6'2½". We had a lot of guys in that position. I'll tell you about Brad, Matt…he came every day and worked hard in practice and never complained. I loved playing with him at Ewing in junior high and he really gave us quality minutes in the Centralia Tournament as a senior. He is a fun-loving guy that would do anything for you…a great teammate and friend.*

In the second half, Belleville made a run but the Rangers kept pace behind the hot shooting of Rod Shurtz. Gesell scored six more points in the fourth quarter and Shurtz put the game away by hitting several key jump shots late in the game. The Rangers won the game by a score of 68-62.

Shurtz had another big day. He seemed to play his best basketball when the game was on the line. Over the course of his career, Shurtz made a habit of hitting pressure free throws late in games to seal close victories. His play in the first two games of the '77 Centralia Tournament clearly established him as one of the better guards in the tournament.

Dave Jones: *Rod was our leader on that team. He was really the floor general. He was a great leader on and off the floor.*

Dave Fairchilds: *Rod was the floor general…everything went through him. You wanted Rod on the free throw line late along with Brookins.*

Doug Dunbar: *Without Shurtz…I mean Rod was a great ball handler and he reminded me a lot of Craddock. He had a great sense of control and we were not the same team when he was not in the game. Shurtzy was as good as any of them* (point guards) *that have ever come through.*

With the win, the Rangers moved to the semi-final game the following day against the Evanston Wildkits. The Wildkits were the top-seed in the tournament. Despite winning their opening two games, they had not played well. Evanston is located near Chicago, Illinois and has an enrollment twice the size of the Benton. The Rangers were clearly the underdog entering the game against Evanston. Because of this, something unusual happened. Most of the crowd rooted for the Rangers. The game was a clear David vs. Goliath affair and the crowd understood the matchup. Still bruised by narrow defeats and the success of the Rangers in the tournament, only the Centralia Orphan fans rooted against the Rangers.

Against Evanston, the Rangers came roaring out of the gate to take a 25-18 halftime advantage. Playing with added confidence, Brad Gesell scored six points in the second quarter to widen the lead. The Rangers led by as many as eight points in the final period, but a basket by Latodd Johnson and three more Johnson free throws trimmed the margin to 50-47, with 4:23 to play. The Kits battled back and held a one-point advantage with .40 seconds left before Doug Dunbar hit two free throws to put Benton ahead, 54-53. On the next possession, LaTodd Johnson hit a short jump shot and later added a free throw to give the Kits a narrow 56-54 win. Doug Dunbar led the Rangers scoring attack with 14 points followed by Ron Brookins, who added ten.

The Rangers played well, but the loss was disappointing. It was a missed opportunity. At this time, Benton basketball was so successful that there were just no moral victories. The Rangers were expected to win. The players that came before the '78 team had set the bar extremely high. There were standards to meet and traditions to carry on.

Following the game, the Rangers put their feet up in a motel for a couple of hours and returned to Trout Gymnasium that evening to play the Orphans for the third-place game. Yes, the Orphans. And they would be expected to win.

The Rangers took the floor to a mixed sound of boos and cheers. The Orphanage booed the Rangers unmercifully while the Rangers fans did their best to drown out the boos with cheers. It was high school basketball at its best; the Rangers vs. the Orphans.

Playing two games in one day can make the final game into a battle of attrition. Both teams were physically and emotionally spent, but the Rangers had less time between games and it showed. The Orphans controlled the first half and led 36-33. When the third quarter began, it looked as though the Orphans were going to pull away, but the Rangers mounted a furious 14-2 comeback to take the lead 51-50 entering the fourth quarter. The Rangers then pulled out to a 69-58 lead with only 4:32 remaining, but they were exhausted. The gas tank was on empty. Cheered on by a capacity crowd, Centralia came back to win the game 78-76.

The unseeded Rangers finished 2-2 in the tournament, but they played outstanding basketball to earn a solid fourth place finish. Their two losses were by two points each.

The loss dropped the Rangers to 6-4 overall. All of the Rangers played well but fans began to take notice of the tenacious play of Jones and Ward in the post. They battled and fought for rebounds against some of the best big men in the state. Brookins and Dunbar were coming into their own at the guard spot. Carl Shurtz and Rob Hammond gave the Rangers huge minutes off the bench on the final day. Reserve post player Brad Gesell undoubtedly played the best basketball of his career, and then there was senior Rod Shurtz. Shurtz had an outstanding tournament but was snubbed when it came to making the All-Tournament team.

Rod Shurtz: *We go into the Centralia Tournament and we won the first two games. Then got beat by Evanston and Centralia. I had a good tournament, but I didn't get selected to the All-Tournament team. Our next practice, I was in the training room and Coach Stewart said, "Hey Shurtzy, come here. I want to talk to you for a minute." He said, "You had a very good Centralia Tournament. You played well at both ends of the floor. I wanted to tell you that. Then he looked at me and said, "Sometimes life is like a s*** sandwich, you just hope to get some crumbs sometimes." That meant a lot to me. That is one of the only times he ever spoke to me privately like that. I have to give Coach Stewart a lot of credit for what we achieved. He knew the game. Coach Stewart had a calming effect and there were times when Coach Herrin would be going a mile a minute in a real crucial situation...and he could calmly say "Look, here is what needs to be done."*

After the tournament, the Rangers had a whole week of practice before hosting the Harrisburg Bulldogs on Friday, January 6, 1978. Typically, it was these long lulls between games that Coach Herrin did something that post player Jim Ward, fondly remembered.

Jim Ward: *There were times in practice when Coach Herrin would walk around with this gallon jug of Vitamin C tablets and he would hand them out to us. You probably couldn't do that today.*

Harrisburg was winless in the conference and entered the game with a record of 2-6. The Rangers jumped out to a 14-4 advantage early in the first quarter and then fell apart over the next two and one-half quarters, allowing Harrisburg to take a 46-43 lead into the fourth quarter. But the Rangers exploded for thirty points in the final eight minutes to win going away by a score of 73-66. Rod Shurtz paced the fourth quarter blitz with nine points and reserve David Fairchilds added six points in the quarter.

Fairchilds played at an athletic 6'5" and came off the bench to spark the Rangers' victory over the Bulldogs by scoring a career high 11 points. Much like Gesell, Fairchilds was a spot-time player but on this night he played like a man possessed. Fairchilds was a fun interview.

David Fairchilds: *I moved to Benton in the summer of '74. My dad was in the military and we were in Hawaii, where my dad was stationed when he retired. My brother* (Jonathon) *and I played organized sports since kindergarten. One of the reasons my dad chose Benton is because Benton had such a good basketball program. Football was my love but I ran track also. If you played basketball, Coach had a rule that you had to run track. I hurdled and high jumped. We lived in West City.*

Fairchilds was a good leaper and he was one of the few players on the team that could jump up and dunk the ball. He preferred to jump off of one leg and when he had his steps right, he could throw the ball down with power. In a junior varsity game a year earlier at West Frankfort, Fairchilds had a break-away and he was all by himself. This was it; his chance to dunk the ball in a game. It was also one of his favorite memories as a Ranger.

Dave Fairchilds: *Dunking came back my junior year. One thing I respected about Coach Herrin was that if you came through the program he tried to keep you. My junior year we had eight juniors. Coach rotated us…four would play* *in the varsity game and four in the JV game. On this night in West Frankfort I was playing in the JV game before the varsity game. It was near the end of the game and we were ahead and the varsity team was coming up the stairs to get ready to run out. I tipped the ball and Carl Shurtz came up with it. I was going to shoot a lay-up and then I heard Carl say, "Dunk it." I went up and banged it off the back of the rim. Rod Shurtz has exaggerated it...he said the ball hit a little girl in the stands. But I don't think that happened. Coach Herrin didn't say anything about it that night, but the next morning we had practice. I heard some rumblings that he was not happy with it. When I got to practice Coach called me over. He said, "I want to see you do what you did last night again." I grabbed a ball and dunked it...and he realized I could do it. But he was just letting me know that he knew about it.*

Carl Shurtz: *Dave was one of those guys that could dunk it. He used to do it all the time in practice. I think I was the one that passed it to him and I remember saying, "Dunk it, Diamond!" When he missed it, Coach Stewart just had his head in hands and then he claimed it hit a girl in the stands and there was going to be a lawsuit.*

With the win, the Rangers improved to 7-4 and 2-2 in league play. The next night the Rangers traveled to Centralia to meet the Orphans again. It was all Orphans in the first half as they raced to a 35-23 lead. In the third quarter, the Rangers outscored the Orphans 23-12 to trail by only one entering the fourth quarter. It was a very tough Centralia team led by Anthony Murray, Rueben McClain, John Wiegel and Tony Worlds. The Orphans pulled away from the Rangers late to win 69-60. Brookins led the Rangers with fifteen on 6-9 shooting from the field. Junior Dave Jones added 13 points and led the team in rebounding with nine.

Although Ward was sick and did not play in the second half of the Centralia game, he and Jones were making their presence felt with their gritty play in the post. At this point in the year, Ward and Jones were earning more playing time and finding themselves on the floor together for extended minutes. They played the game with a reckless abandon. Ward endeared himself to Ranger fans by stepping in front of penetrating guards and drawing charges and Jones had taken over the role of the enforcer. They were tough players. Jones guarded the opposing team's best big man while Ward took on more of a scoring role. The play of Jones and Ward in the post and the feisty play of Shurtz, Brookins and Dunbar from the guard spots gave the team a blue-collar identity.

Doug Dunbar: *I don't know if Dave or Jim thought they were going to be thrust into those positions as a junior. Scott Dunbar and Terry (Dawson) didn't finish with us. Dave and Jim accepted it and you have to give them credit, they hung in there and played their butts off. They competed. They didn't want to get beat.*

Dave Jones and Jim Ward looked more like middle-linebackers than they did post players. Both players were limited in some areas but they complimented each other so well in the post. Together, they became a force to be reckoned with in the South Seven.

Dave Jones: *We (Ward) spent every day in the summer up there playing. We worked really worked hard to play on that team. Jim and I were workhorses and we weren't afraid to get in a little scrabble. Rod, Ronnie and Doug did most of the shooting and Jim and I guarded and rebounded. That was Coach's way.*

While many of his teammates chose to walk across the street to Chick's Market before school and load up on doughnuts, Dave Jones was dedicated to making himself stronger. In 1978, the benefits of lifting weights were not clearly known. Some fitness gurus saw weightlifting as a good thing, and some did not. Jones did.

Dave Jones: *I would come in before school and workout upstairs on an old universal weightlifting machine that the school had purchased.*

As a junior, Dave Jones played at a solid 6'3" and weighed 190 pounds. Jones had strong biceps to go along with a very strong lower half that gave him an uncanny leaping ability for his muscle-bound frame. Today, teammates affectionately call him "Big Team".

Dave Jones: *I really don't know for sure why some of those guys call me that. I showed up at the reunion and that was the first thing some of those guys called me. I don't know…you will have to ask them…but I do know that if someone ever challenged us…I was front and center.*

Rod Shurtz: *Big Team had that Southern Drawl. Team was confident in his abilities and he was a knocker…banger…raw…strong. He would muscle you inside.*

Jim Ward: *Dave was strong as can be…he worked so hard. He had a nice touch at the free throw line. I don't think Dave lost a tip all year…maybe to Russell Cross of Chicago Manley. Dave could really jump.*

Although Jones was an All-South football selection and the gridiron was clearly his ticket to a college education, he desired to play basketball for the Rangers. It was a pull that he could not resist.

Dave Jones: *My best memories about Benton basketball were seeing the teams growing up…the discipline…the work ethic that Coach demanded. I wanted to be a part of that type of program. I went to grade school at Lincoln School until the sixth grade, but we moved to Louisiana and I didn't come back to Benton until after my eighth grade year. My dad promised me that he would get me back to Benton and me and my dad moved back just before my freshman year. My mom came a little later. I grew up watching the Rangers in the old gym. Everybody wanted to be a Ranger. We lived right by the Lockins on Main Street. The building of Rend Lake was pretty much my dad's vision. The lake…the golf course…you name it. My dad hired Doug Collins one summer to help dig the lake. I just thought that was the coolest thing.*

Jones was in the know on all of the Ranger players growing up because of the special relationship his grandpa had with the basketball program.

Dave Jones: *Homer Jones was my grandpa and every one in Southern Illinois knew him. He was the guy that cut all the flat-tops for all of the players. He knew everything that happened in town.*

Jones' good friend and teammate in the post, Jim Ward, was also a standout football player that loved playing the game of basketball. Ward explained his basketball journey.

Jim Ward: *I went to Lincoln School and I grew up with Rob Hammond. We were on the same team in grade school. Coach Herrin would kid me and say… that's why I never could get a double-double…because there were never enough offensive rebound opportunities because Rob made so many shots.*

When Ward was in the eighth grade, he remembered Coach Carlile made an innocent comment that made quite the impression.

Jim Ward: *I think it was our eighth-grade year, we were up on the stage and Norman Carlile said that I reminded him of Steve McCommons. That was big…you have to remember, we saw some great teams growing up. I'll never forget that.*

Jim Ward lost both of his parents at a very young age. He lost his father while he was in high school and lost his mother when he was attending college at Western Illinois. It had to be a very difficult time in his life, and I could tell in the interview that his relationship with his Coaches and his teammates helped to fill the void left by his father's absence.

Jim Ward: *Between my freshman and sophomore years in high school my dad passed away. Coach Herrin and Coach Stewart both just kind of took me in. Coach Herrin had me tag along to some basketball clinics in the driver's ed. car. One time we were going to Pinckneyville and me, Randy and Rod (the Herrin brothers) were in the backseat…and Kyle was laying across us in the backseat. Kyle had a basketball, and he was throwing it against the window. Rod hit a button and the window came down…the ball just flies out of the car. I'm thinking…oh boy. I remember Coach Herrin just stopped the car and turned around without saying a word and we went back and Kyle got the ball. I was waiting for him to explode but he never got upset. I remember that…it was so much like a family.*

Ward's teammates remembered him as a stand-up teammate and a tremendous worker.

Dave Jones: *Jim was one of the hardest workers I've ever been around. He didn't have a great amount of natural basketball talent but he got everything out of his ability. Jim was probably a little better offensive player than I was. I usually guarded the best post player.*

With the loss to Centralia, the Rangers fell to 7-5 overall and 2-3 in South Seven Conference play. The team's goal was to win the conference but it didn't look good with just two wins in five conference games.

The following weekend, the Rangers defeated the West Frankfort Redbirds at home, 64-55, and then won a thriller at Mt. Vernon, 62-60. Many of the players believed that the Mt. Vernon win served as the turning point of the season. The game was full of drama and then it came to an even more dramatic ending.

Changnon Gymnasium was packed to the gills to see the Rams and the Rangers. Historically, this was a game that Ranger fans circled on the schedule. The game was always entertaining but the teams disliked each other so much that the game became only part of the entertainment. As always, the play was physical and the game was back and forth. With the Rangers trailing 60-58, Doug Dunbar missed a jump shot to tie the game, but then came up with a steal and assist to Hammond for a bucket to tie the game at 60.

On the next possession, Mac Thomas was called for a charge by steamrolling Dave Jones on a drive to the basket with just .05 seconds left on the clock. Jones had a one-and-one opportunity from the free-throw line with the game tied at 60.

Dave Jones: *I stepped into the lane and drew a charge and that put me on the on the line. I wasn't a great free-throw shooter…50 to 60% at best.*

The Mt. Vernon student section taunted Jones as he strutted to the other end of the floor to shoot the biggest free throws of his short varsity career to this point. Jones stepped to the line and received the ball from the official. He held the ball momentarily and then wiped the sweat from his brow. He eyed the bucket as the Mt. Vernon fans did everything in their power to disrupt his rhythm. Despite being a very average free-throw shooter, Jones had a stubborn confidence that welcomed the moment. Jones then reached into his giant bag of confidence and calmly knocked the bottom out of it. It was the first shot of a one-and-one attempt, and you could see the pressure leave his body after the ball splashed through the net. Ranger fans went crazy! With the Rangers up 61-60 and only .05 seconds remaining, Jones was playing with house money. Jones shot the second one and the ball caromed off the inside of the front rim and then hit the glass and fell in. After Jones hit both free throws, the Rams could not get a shot off before the horn. "Team" had done it. And with that, Jones pointed to the Rams student section to taunt his doubters. For the Rangers, the scene was chaotic yet beautiful at the same time. After the game, bedlam ensued.

Dave Jones: *I hooted and hollered after I hit the free throws…and this just made the Mt. Vernon fans irate. It was standing room only that night. I'll never forget Coach Herrin running off the floor in a dead sprint.*

Carl Shurtz: *It was tense after the game…scary, really. Big Dave was point-ing into the crowd and the Rams fans didn't like it.*

Rod Shurtz: *It was always a dog fight when went to Mt. Vernon. Big Team hit a couple of free throws late and Ronnie and I were back. When the game was over and we were running off the floor…we were getting hit by coins. Big Team was taunting the Mt. Vernon student section as we ran into the locker room. Everybody was excited.*

The Rangers fought their way through the unruly Mt. Vernon crowd and found themselves together at last. As an athlete, this is why you put in the hours. Are you kidding? For the team to go into Changnon and steal one was the ultimate. Jones' dramatic free throws and the dangerous journey to the locker room was the icing on the cake. Or was it? Rod Shurtz explains.

Rod Shurtz: *The windows in the locker rooms could be opened from the outside and a guy yells some obscenities and then reaches through the window and waved a gun at us. We all ran and got in the showers. It was a great win. It was an excited locker room.*

Jim Ward: *Someone yelled, "Gun!"…and Coach Herrin had every one of us on the floor.*

A happy group of Rangers safely exited Mt. Vernon. The players grouped up and talked about the night's events as they ate their traditional ham sandwiches and guzzled down their soda. On the bus radio, the hit song, "We are the Champions", by Queen, blared and the players sang along. It was a perfect night. A night the players would always remember.

With the big win, the Rangers improved to 9-5 overall and a respect-able 4-3 in conference play. The Rangers then turned their focus to the Benton Invitational Tournament.

The Rangers opened tournament play by defeating the Pinckneyville Panthers by a score of 63-57. Ron Brookins led the Rangers scoring attack by scoring 16 points and Doug Dunbar chipped in 14.

With the win, the Rangers advanced in tournament play to face off with the Olney Tigers. From 1975 to 1979, it is fair to say that the Olney Tigers owned the Rangers. Ron Herrin had great teams in the late seven-ties and eliminated the Rangers from post-season play in 1975 and 1977.

Again, the Tigers were loaded. The Tigers were led by Darnall Jones, Tony Jennings, Gary Bussard, Jim Jenkins and Tim Jennings.

The game was a typical back and forth battle between brothers, Rich and Ron. The Rangers trailed 72-71 with less than .15 seconds left in the game when Brookins passed the ball inside to Fairchilds but the ball caromed off his hands out of bounds. The Rangers had to foul and Jim Jenkins iced the game by hitting the final two free throws. Darnall Jones had a game high 24 points to lead the Tigers and Jim Jenkins added 21.

In the final period of the game, the Tigers went to a zone but Rob Hammond almost single-handedly brought the Rangers back. He hit six long jumpers to force Olney to change to a man to man defense. Hammond's performance was a foreshadowing of the shooting display he would barrage teams with as a senior in '79. Who was the better shooter? Hammond or Tabor? It is a discussion that Ranger fans still have to this day.

Rod Shurtz: *We faced a zone quite a bit in '78 and I just remember I loved being able to pass to Brook and Dunny. And I loved when we brought Robbie Hammond off the bench. Robbie Hammond could really shoot the ball.*

The Tigers defeated the Rangers 74-71. The loss moved the Rangers into the third place game against the Carmi Bulldogs.

On January 21, 1978, Rod Shurtz hit a jump shot at the horn to give the Rangers a 64-62 victory and a third-place finish in their own tournament. Shurtz ended the game with 12 points but it was Doug Dunbar who led the Benton scoring attack with 22 points. The Bulldogs were led by Steve Stone's 32 points. Stone would be an All-Tournament selection on the five-man team. Carbondale defeated Olney 74-63 in the title game to win the BIT in '78. With the win, the Rangers moved to 11-6 overall, with one more loop through the South Seven remaining.

In the January 20, 1978, edition of the Benton Evening News, there is a picture of Tom Whittington getting his hair cut. At the time, he served as the seventh-grade basketball coach at Webster Junior High in Benton. He had made a deal with his players that if they went undefeated, he would get his hair cut short. Sure enough, the seventh-grade Rangers finished the season at 22-0 and Whittington is pictured making good on his promise. The point is this; good players were coming. The lower levels were stocked full of players which made the early eighties look promising. The future of Benton basketball looked bright.

To begin the final loop of South Seven play, the Rangers hosted the Marion Wildcats. Marion came into the game struggling and the Rangers took advantage. The Rangers won the ballgame by a score of 78-59 behind 35 points from Doug Dunbar. Dunbar shot 16-25 from the field and had been a consistent scorer for the Rangers all year. In fact, Doug Dunbar had very little playing time as a junior but led the Rangers in scoring in '78. Dunbar was a jack of all trades. He could score, rebound, handle the ball and had a knack for coming up with big plays in key moments. Dunbar was the cousin of the great Rob Dunbar. Doug became a huge key to the success of the '78 Rangers and had been groomed for this moment.

Doug Dunbar: *I grew up playing basketball in Kent Tabor's backyard. Everett Tabor poured a concrete slab and they had a nice outdoor court. Kent, Keith, Rob (Dunbar) and Mark (Craddock) would all be there. I was a little bit younger and tagged along. We also played on the outdoor courts at Logan School. We would go up to the old gym in the summer when I was a kid… Doug Collins would be up there. I went to Douglas School and Gene Alexander was my Coach. The courts were always available…you always had the opportunity to play.*

Dunbar told me in his interview that the reason he graduated with the Class of '78 had everything to do with basketball.

Doug Dunbar: *I've got a good story about Coach Herrin. Coach Herrin reached out to all the sixth-grade coaches at the various grade schools and he would have the best one or two sixth grade players from each grade school report to the junior high practices. The Dawson twins and myself were very young for our class. Coach approached our parents about possibly being held back…to grow and mature. So that is what happened…we had to sit out a year. By being held back it placed us in Scott Dunbar's class and he could have been really good….and he had size. It didn't work out…but he was putting our class together when we were in the sixth grade. Rod (Shurtz) and his brothers came in from Waltonville when Rod was a freshman. Coach knew where he wanted to go…and he knew how to get there. Coach Herrin was involved with every kid in the program from the time they picked up a basketball. He went to grade school games…he's putting those teams together six or seven years before they got to the high school. I knew somebody cared.*

Doug was affectionately called "Dunny" by his teammates. Dunny had earned the respect of his teammates through his play. He played hard and fit in nicely with the feisty mentality of the '78 team. Dunbar's teammates expressed what he brought to the young Rangers.

Ron Brookins: *When Doug got hot…he was hot. Dunny could shoot the dang basketball now. Dunny gave us a legitimate offensive threat every night. I think teams prepared for Dunny and Rod more than the rest of us. He had a good basketball sense about him. Doug was not a bad defensive player either. If Doug got off early…we were in good shape. He just improved so much. I played with him at Rend Lake. He made us better.*

Rod Shurtz: *He was a great bank shooter and I think that was because he was a great pool player. If you wanted to put money on something…Dunny would play you. He could get in there and finagle and get rebounds.*

David Fairchilds: *He was a sharpshooter…several of our plays were designed to get Doug in good position to shoot. He was a very good catch-and-shoot player.*

After trouncing the Wildcats, the Rangers traveled six miles south to meet the Redbirds. They had defeated the Redbirds earlier in the season but on this night it was all Redbirds. The Rangers laid an egg. The Rangers were sluggish and out of sync. Dunbar led the team in scoring with 12 but nobody really played well. The loss dropped the Rangers to 12-7 overall and 5-4 in league play. Most importantly, the loss put pressure on the Rangers to win out with games like Centralia, Mt. Vernon and Carbondale still left on the schedule. It would be an uphill battle from here to win the conference.

The following weekend the Rangers traveled to Herrin. Herrin was near the top of the conference and coached by Benton native Jeff Ferguson. The Tigers had already defeated the Rangers at Benton earlier in the season. The Rangers jumped out to a 10-4 advantage and the Herrin Tigers called timeout. On the next possession, Herrin scored to make it 10-6 Benton. Then, things got crazy.

Rod Shurtz: *We jumped out to a 10-6 lead and Coach Herrin called a timeout. I remember Brook came up to me as we were walking to the bench and said, "What are we doing." Coach said we're going to go four to score. We could run it, too. I think that game turned the corner for us.*

Patience, plus the ability to dribble, pass and make pressure free throws are pre-requisites for a successful four-corner offense. Only a lay-up off the glass is allowed. The '78 team could run it. It is fair to say that the '78 Rangers executed the four corner offense as well or better than any team Herrin coached at Benton.

As the game unfolded, Coach Herrin looked like a genius. The Rangers made all the right decisions and deflated the Tigers by scoring on a series of backdoor cuts. It was a clinic. The four-corner offense worked and the Rangers stole one at Herrin to put them back in the conference race. As Fairchilds watched the game plan work from the bench, he was not surprised.

Dave Fairchilds: *Coach was a phenomenal strategist. He knew how to get the best out of each person. He was always really good at utilizing his talent to get the match-ups we needed.*

Doug Dunbar led the team in scoring with 18 points and Rod Shurtz addedten for the victorious Rangers. The win improved the Rangers to 13-7 overall and 6-4 in League play. Ron Brookins recalled that night in Herrin like it was yesterday.

Ron Brookins: *I think Rich thought we had an advantage at the guard spot against them. I think he felt like we could handle it well enough…and all three of us* (Shurtz Dunbar, Brookins) *were good free throw shooters. I had a turnover late in the game and blocked a shot at the end of the game…and then it was over. The win gave us confidence and it made other teams prepare for us differently.*

On Friday, February 10th, the Rangers traveled to Davenport Gymnasium for their final game with the Bulldogs. The Rangers exploded out of the gates to gain a 24-6 first quarter advantage and held on to win by a score of 62-50.

The next night the Rangers hosted the Orphans in their final meeting of the year. A packed house came out to see if the Rangers could stay in the hunt for a conference title. Centralia had beaten the Rangers both times and played for the sweep. Again, the Rangers dominated in the opening quarter to lead 21-11. The Orphans then cut the Rangers lead in the second quarter to 32-27. Dave Jones was an animal on the glass and was having his way inside the paint. Jones ended the game with a career high 16 points. Rod Shurtz also had 16 points followed by Dunbar's 14. The Rangers were starting to believe. They were playing good basketball and had momentum. Near the end of the game, longtime Ranger fan Bob Gariepy led the Ranger faithful with a "Give me an R-A-N-G-E-R-S" Cheer. It was that kind of night.

Rod Shurtz was having a nice year at the point guard position considering the scoring burden that he also had to carry. I asked him about his relationship with Coach Herrin as a point guard. How was that? What was the communication like?

Rod Shurtz: *You always had to be on your toes. He made it clear that if I was the point guard I had to know not only my spot but everybody else's spot. We had plays but they were directed at pulling the strengths out of each of us. Coach Herrin always stressed to me that I had back responsibility also…I remember hitting a lay-up and then ducking my head and running full speed back to the defensive end of the floor and if I wasn't there…I was in trouble. I think that happened once and I may have started to question if that was my job…he made it clear in his own way that was my job. The first time I questioned him was the last time I questioned him.*

Shurtz still believes that one of Coach Herrin's greatest gifts was his ability to motivate his players. He explained to me that Coach Herrin was very good at knowing what buttons to push and when to push them.

Rod Shurtz: *One time in practice he thought I didn't go hard enough after a loose ball and he stopped practice and chewed on me and then rolled the ball on the floor and made me go after it. I went after the ball as hard as I could and popped off the floor and zinged a chest pass to him that went through his hands and hit him in the chest. I thought…oh boy, here we go! He just got excited and said, "Gosh dang it, that's the way you've got to compete!" Coach would challenge you physically and mentally to get a reaction out of you. He might call you out in front of everybody…it could be embarrassing…but he was challenging you.*

With one weekend left in South Seven play, the Rangers had to beat Carbondale and Mt. Vernon to win the league. Carbondale was really good and they had already beaten the Rangers at home. On Friday, February 17th, the Rangers traveled to Bowen Gymnasium to play the Terriers. In the first half, Dunbar struggled to score and the Rangers were down by seven at halftime. Play was sluggish and it seemed the Rangers were playing tight. In the third quarter, Dunbar scored 13 of his game-high 21 points to lead the Rangers over a stunned Terrier team.

Dave Jones: *Doug could shoot it. I mean he could really go on streaks.*

Once the Rangers took the lead, they decided to hold the ball and play keep-away from the talented Terriers. With the conference championship in the balance, this is how Brookins remembered the last few minutes of that crucial conference game at Carbondale.

Ron Brookins: *Carbondale was really good and they had beaten us at home. Late in the game we were up and holding the ball and they were in a half-court trap and they just quit chasing us. I couldn't believe it…they quit.*

Jim Ward also remembered the Carbondale game in '78 as one of his best memories as a Ranger.

Jim Ward: *A game that sticks out is when I was a junior and we had to go to Carbondale and win to have a chance to win the South Seven…and we did.*

The Rangers defeated the Terriers by a score of 66-55. The next night the Rangers would have to defeat the Mt. Vernon Rams to get a share of the conference. The Rangers controlled their own destiny after a 2-3 start in the conference. If the Rangers could beat the Rams, it would be a comeback similar to the one in '76.

The game was at home and the energy in the building that night was incredible. Ranger fans knew exactly what was on the line. Rod Shurtz remembered the moment well.

Rod Shurtz: *When we played Mt. Vernon late in the year to win the conference…you just couldn't ask for a better atmosphere. The fans created a tunnel before we ran out that snaked around the west end of the floor. I remember Robbie Williams's mom* (Linda) *leading the charge. That night was special.*

To add to the drama of the game, it was also senior night. The crowd rose as the senior players and their parents were introduced. Shurtz, Brookins, Dunbar, Fairchilds, Gesell and Kolisek were all honored for their effort and dedication to the program. Win or lose, they had carried on the winning Ranger tradition.

When the game finally started it was plain to see that the Rams were a solid basketball team. They were led by Doug Creel, Mac Thomas and Scott Wagner. Nothing was easy. The Rangers would have to play. In a classic Rangers-Rams battle, the Rangers were simply too much. The Rangers were stingy on the defensive end allowing just 52 points. While the Rams focused their defensive emphasis on Brookins and Dunbar, Rod Shurtz scored a game-high 22 points from the point guard position. In the end, the Rangers defeated the Rams 57-52. With the win, the Rangers captured a share of the South Seven Championship with Carbondale, and it was their ninth conference championship in the last 13 seasons. It was a sweet win, and who better to beat than the Rams?

Ron Brookins: *When we played Doug Creel and those guys...it was personal. It was for them, too. Today, Doug is one of my good friends. But that's the way it was back then.*

Rod Shurtz: *You know my thing growing up was never about West Frankfort. It was about Mt. Vernon and Centralia.*

With the win, the Rangers moved to 17-8 overall and 10-4 to win a share of the conference title. The Rangers had won their last 11 out of 14 games and were playing great basketball.

In the final regular season game of the year, the Rangers bused north to play the Effingham Flaming Hearts. The Hearts had an outstanding young player by the name of Mitch Arnold. The last game of the year against the Hearts was always competitive and on this night it was all Hearts. The Hearts defeated the Rangers 79-62. The Rangers ended the regular season with a respectable 17-9 record.

The Rangers were the number one seed in their own Regional Tournament and began post season play with a match-up against the dangerous Harrisburg Bulldogs. It was only two years ago that the Bulldogs bounced the Rangers out of postseason play by defeating them in the first game of the Regional Tournament by a score of 90-86. The Rangers held a slight two-point advantage at halftime before pulling away to win the game, 69-52. Jim Ward led a balanced scoring attack for the Rangers with 14 points, followed by Brookins with 13, and Jones with 12.

The win placed the Rangers in the Regional Championship to face the Mt. Vernon Rams yet again. It was the second time the two heavyweights would meet in two weeks. The Rangers had won both meetings and understood that it was difficult to beat any team three times, especially the talented Rams.

The Rich hosted its largest crowd of the season. More than 3,700 fans poured into the gymnasium to watch what promised to be a game for the ages. In the first quarter, the Rangers jumped out to a 17-13 lead and then the Rams pulled to within one at halftime. Jamie Doggan had 12 points at halftime to lead the Rams attack. By the end of the third quarter, the Rangers held a slim 49-47 lead. Dunbar was playing great basketball when it mattered most. He had 20 points to lead the Rangers going into the fourth quarter. The two teams fought valiantly to keep their seasons alive and then something ironic happened at the end of the game. Dave Jones, who had hit the all-important free throws at Mt. Vernon to seal the win, was fouled again with .31 seconds left with the Rangers clinging to a 59-58 lead. Surely, Jones couldn't do it again. Jones calmly went to the line and hit both free throws yet again to seal it for the Rangers. It was the nineteenth win for the scrappy Rangers and the Regional Championship solidified the team's place in Ranger history.

The three senior guards, Shurtz, Brookins and Dunbar, rose to the occasion. Dunny led the team in scoring with 22 points. Rod Shurtz scored 14 points and dished out nine assists. Ron Brookins had ten points and added five assists. The others also played big in the win. Jones and Ward mixed it up inside with Jones coming through in the clutch yet again. Jerry Dawson, Rob Hammond, Dave Fairchilds and Carl Shurtz played well off the bench. It was a great win.

The Sectional Tournament was to be held at Max Morris Gymnasium in West Frankfort. The Rangers were to meet the Olney Tigers yet again. All of the Ranger fans attending the first game of the Sectional with Olney were asked to wear maroon in support of their underdog Rangers. Olney was a good basketball team and they were hot. They had won nine straight entering the game but the scrappy Rangers were also playing well. In the last few years, Olney had been the Rangers' nemesis.

On Wednesday, March 8, 1978, basketball fans packed Max Morris Gymnasium to see the highly anticipated game between the Rangers and the Tigers. The gymnasium overflowed with the awkward colors of orange and maroon. In the first quarter, Olney jumped out to a 21-16 lead behind seven points from Tony Jennings. In the second quarter, both teams slugged it out and the Rangers outscored the Tigers by only one. The score at halftime was 42-38, in favor of Olney. It was clear that the Rangers had a match-up problem with junior Darnall Jones. Jones was a crafty player that could score all over the floor and he had good size. The Rangers had no answer for Darnall.

In the third quarter, Ron Brookins must have placed himself in this position a million times as a kid and now it was real. He was taking over the Sectional game by draining shots all over the floor. Brookins had six long field goals in the third quarter to give him 23 points going into the fourth quarter. Most importantly, he had shot the Rangers to a 56-50 lead going into the fourth quarter. The Tigers had no answer for Brookins. Shurtz remembers Brookins' performance well but he also remembers the Tigers being at the free throw line too many times for his liking. For the game, Benton was 3-7 from the line, compared to Olney's 27-34. Wow!

Rod Shurtz: *Brook had a great game. They shot a lot of free throws in that game and we didn't. I remember Brook coming up to me as they were shooting two free throws and he said, 'Those guys have been shooting free throws all night.' That was a tough one.*

In the fourth quarter, the Tigers made a surge behind the play of Jones and Gary Bussard to take a 68-64 lead with only 1:25 to play. Brookins then scored again to pull the Rangers to within two, 66-68. On the next possession, Jones was fouled and he made one of two free throws to give the Tigers the win, 69-66. Unfortunately, the Tigers' win overshadowed a great individual performance from Rangers guard Ron Brookins. Brookins finished his high school career with a 29 point effort.

After the game, you could hear a pin drop in the Ranger locker room. The place where Coach Herrin had won so many big games was now a place of calm and reflection. Coach Herrin gathered the '78 team one last time and thanked them for their hard work. He was emotional. In the moment, he had to be proud of the scrappy team that played so hard and possibly overachieved to win the conference. It was a fun bunch that had played in their coach's image; passionate, tough and competitive. It was a difficult team to let go of, but the memories they made together would last a lifetime.

After high school, point guard Rod Shurtz went on to play college basketball at Missouri Southern and majored in English education. Shurtz would go on to coach basketball, cross country and track at the high school level. He coached at St. Elmo, Centralia and finished his career at Benton High School. In the spring of 1990, Shurtz was hired as the head coach of the Benton Rangers. He led the 1992 team to a third-place finish behind the school's all-time leading scorer, Jo Jo Johnson. Later on, Rod served as my assistant basketball coach when I was hired as the head basketball coach in the spring of 2002. Shurtz was instrumental in the building of the Benton Future Rangers Program that still serves Benton grade school students today. Rod is now retired and he spends much of his time serving Immanuel Baptist Church in many different capacities. Rod and his wife Tonya live in Benton and they have three children; Seiger, Sayler and Macy.

Rod loved playing for the Benton Rangers and was quick to point out the impact Coach Herrin made on his life.

Rod Shurtz: *He always expected you to give your very best. We were always put in positions to do that. The gym was open…it was always about working hard and doing things the right way. My relationship with Coach Herrin grew these past couple of years. When I was at Benton coaching, Coach was at SIU rebuilding that program. We started developing a friend relationship. I started working some of his camps. In the last two or three years we have really gotten closer. He gave me the greatest compliment I've ever received. He didn't tell me I was a great ball handler or a great shooter, he said, "Shurtzy you played hard. You were a hard worker." That was the ultimate compliment coming from him. I miss that guy.*

Ron Brookins went on to play two years of basketball at Rend Lake College and then transferred to SIU-C to earn his bachelor's degree in math education. Upon graduating from SIU-C, he was hired at McEachern High School in Marietta, Georgia. Brookins later became the head basketball coach at Harrison High school also located in Marietta, Georgia. Ron later earned his master's degree in administration and became the principal of Marietta High School. He currently lives in North Georgia with his wife Susan and they have three children; Tyler, Whitney and Chandler.

Ron loved playing high school basketball and some of his greatest memories were playing for the Benton Rangers.

Ron Brookins: *Matt…some of my favorite memories were playing at home and running out of that Tunnel…being able to wear that Benton uniform. I wanted to wear that uniform.*

Brookins also loved playing for Coach Herrin and expressed his gratitude toward Coach Herrin for giving him every opportunity possible to play.

Ron Brookins: *Where Rich made the impact on me was...he loved the game...he loved people...and you knew it. He held you accountable. He doubted me as a player at times but looking back...he is going to play the guys that can play, work hard and do the right things. He saw that in people. He was a tireless worker and was so passionate about the game. I trusted that he would reward you if you kept working and did the right things. Rich gave everybody the same opportunity to play. He fought to have a freshman, sophomore and J.V. team. He opened the gyms in the summer to all of us. The camps in the summer...my mom and dad didn't have the money when I was a kid to send both me and my brother to basketball camp at Rend Lake. It was thirty-five dollars. He made sure me and my brother went to camp. He removed all of the obstacles and excuses and gave us every opportunity to play. That showed me he cared about people.*

Brad Gesell is currently the co-owner of Gesell Pump Service. He and his brother have grown the business and they are very successful. Brad currently lives in Benton with his wife Susan and they have two children; Samantha and Harrison.

Brad said this about his playing experience for Coach Herrin and the Benton Rangers.

Brad Gesell: *Coming from a small school...being on the basketball team made me feel like I was part of something big. The flat-tops and just the way we did things. People knew who you were in town. People recognized you. Coach Herrin taught you to be competitive and he taught you that you had to pay the price. You had to sacrifice. It's the same way in life...you have to sacrifice and make good choices. He held us accountable. He molded young men. There are a lot of guys that played for him that have went on and done great things.*

After High School, Doug Dunbar also went to Rend Lake College and played two years of junior college basketball. He played at Rend Lake with teammate Ron Brookins. He then worked in the coal mines until landing a job as a golf pro at the age of twenty-eight. He managed several golf courses in the Southern Illinois area before moving to Columbus, Ohio. Doug now lives in Columbus, Ohio near his daughter Sascha.

Doug was a fun interview and he admits that he enjoyed his Ranger experience and learned many life lessons playing for Coach Herrin.

Doug Dunbar: *The thing that I learned most from Coach Herrin is that whatever you put into something…is what you're going to get out of it. The time he spent up there at the gym. He was like a second father to a lot of us.*

Reserve post player Dave Fairchilds lives in Abiline, Texas with his wife Serina. They have three children; Lee, Kyle and Mason. After high school, Dave joined the Air Force and retired in 2006. He still works at the Air Force Base.

Fairchilds was able to look back at his experience as a Ranger with many fond memories and he also enjoyed his experience playing under Coach Herrin.

Dave Fairchilds: *He was willing to trust you. He was a man of his word. When I was in the game I never questioned myself because Coach wouldn't have me in the game if I didn't deserve to be in the game. He gave me confidence as a player. He inspired you to always give your best.*

The team that Coach Herrin had so carefully put together as early as sixth grade was now gone, but Dave Jones, Jim Ward, Carl Shurtz, Jerry Dawson and sharpshooter Rob Hammond would return. A talented group of sophomores would help out and the Running Rangers could be counted on to stay competitive. On to '79!

Coach Herrin makes his point in an early season practice in 77-78.
(Ceasar Maragni)

The Clean-cut Rangers of '78 just before the start of the season. **Bottom Row-** Jones, Hammond, Brookins, Kolisek, T. Dawson **Middle Row-** Vanhorn, C. Shurtz, Gesell, R. Shurtz, J. Dawson, Herrin **Top Row-** Shew, Fairchild, Page, Chady, Ward, Dunbar. *(Cesaer Maragni)*

The leader of the '78 team was point guard Rod Shurtz. Shurtz would later go on to coach the Rangers to a 3rd place state finish in 1992. *(Benton High School)*

Doug Dunbar (Dunny) had a tremendous senior season by leading the team in scoring. Dunbar was also an uncanny rebounder for a guard. *(Ceasar Maragni)*

Rob Hammond provided a deadly shot off the bench in '78.
(Ceasar Maragni)

Dave Jones hit two big free throws at Mt. Vernon to give the
Rangers a huge win on the road. Jones played the role of the
enforcer for the next two seasons. *(Ceasar Maragni)*

Brad Gesell gave the Rangers quality play off the bench all year in '78. Gesell had an outstanding Centralia Tournament in '77. *(Ceasar Maragni)*

Jim Ward was blue collar inside. There was perhaps no Ranger better at drawing charges. (Ceasar Maragni)

Fairchilds and Shurtz were involved in a memorable missed dunk at West Frankfort Both were good players that provided quality play off the bench for the Rangers in '78. *(Ceasar Maragni)*

Ron Brookins played sparingly as a junior but was a stand-out guard on the '78 team. Brookins was a solid outside shooter and a tenacious competitor. A guy you wanted on your side. (Ceasar Maragni)

An excited group of Rangers celebrate their Regional Championship win over Mt. Vernon. The team finished 19-9 and captured a South Seven Championship. *(Caesar Maragni)*

CHAPTER TWENTY-FOUR

"Scrappy Play and Long Bombs in '79"

He would take a pass from me…and as soon as he shot it,
I would say, "Boom baby!" – Carl Shurtz

On the night of December 8, 1978, the Rangers were defeated by the Pinckneyville Panthers, 48-41. The game was at Pinckneyville. The McLeansboro Foxes defeated the Rangers in the opener at McLeansboro, 53-44. The Rangers were 0-2 and not playing well. On the way home from Pinckneyville, the bus ride was quiet. On this December night, the players were in deep thought as they stared into the darkness out of the bus windows. They were soul-searching.

Senior Rob Hammond scored only four points for the night and there was nobody on the bus more frustrated with the team's loss. When the bus pulled up on the west side of Rich Herrin Gymnasium, the players filed off the bus. Hammond went straight home, grabbed his basketball and went to his room.

Rob Hammond: *When I was a kid, I started doing something that really helped me. I would lie on my back in my room and I would put the ball above my face and shoot at the ceiling. I got to sit and watch the rotation of the ball off my fingers, and I would try to barely nick the ceiling…it made a sound when I hit it perfect. I must have done that a million times. I did that all through high school, too.*

Hammond knew he needed to score for the team to win. Juniors Curtis Smith and Steve Shurtz would provide some offensive help, but the bulk of the scoring fell on the shoulders of Rob Hammond. And he was capable. Hammond had textbook shooting mechanics which he credited to playing in the era before the three-point line.

Rob Hammond: *I played all the time and obviously that's big…but there was not a three-point line when I played, so I never remember getting the ball below my waist and slinging it from my hip. I think the three-point line can get young kids into bad habits.*

Rob Hammond was now a senior. He had received limited playing time off the bench as a junior and he had one year to get it right. As a youngster, Hammond came through the Ranger system and remembered going to all of the games growing up.

Rob Hammond: *I went to the Rangers games all the time when I was a kid. I sat on the west end of the stage so I could get a better look at the players when they walked out of the locker room. They would walk out and be spinning the ball on their finger and stuff…I thought that was so cool and I knew right then that I wanted to play for the Benton Rangers. I remember Fustin wearing the head gear after he got hit in the jaw. My sister graduated in the class of '71…so I got to go to Champaign and watch them play at state. We played Oak Lawn and they had C.J. Kupec.*

In the paint, the Rangers returned seniors Dave Jones, Jim Ward and Jerry Dawson. Jones and Ward were seasoned and provided gritty play that permeated through the team. Jerry Dawson would give the Rangers size and experience off the bench. Senior Carl Shurtz also returned at the point guard position. Jeff Shew and Bart Oyler were the senior reserves. Shew was athletic and a very good track athlete. Oyler was the son of Principal Chuck Oyler and was coming off a very good football season.

    The incoming juniors were a talented bunch of athletes that turned out to be solid basketball players. The ten juniors on the team were; Jerry Corn, Jim Labuwi, Kent Yancik, Steve Shurtz, Curtis Smith, Steve Rusher, Dallas Carlisle, Brad Aaron, Rod Potts and Randy Herrin. As juniors, Smith, Shurtz and Labuwi would see most of the action.

    In the first two games, the Rangers were averaging a dismal 42.5 points per game. It was clear that this team had to find ways to score.

Hammond would have to shoot it well and the team needed everyone to chip in. The offense had to get it going.

On December 16, 1978, the Metropolis Trojans came to town. They were led by 6'6" Sikeston transfer, Dave Stevers. The Rangers played without the services of 6'3" senior Jim Ward, who missed the contest due to a mild concussion. The plan was for Jeff Shew to fill Ward's spot, but he suffered a scratch to the eye that left him out of service. Junior post player Kent Yancik filled in as the first post player off the bench. Yancik didn't remember the Metropolis game, but the rugged practices against Jones, Ward and Labuwi was something he never forgot.

Kent Yancik: *That's what I remember. Those guys just beat the crap out of me in practice. And you know Coach gave me very little shelter. You had to man up. Practices were hard with those guys but they were important because they made me a better player.*

Metropolis jumped to a 22-16 lead after the first quarter and led 41-34 at halftime. In the first quarter, Yancik scored his first two varsity points of his career. The good news was the Ranger offense showed signs of coming alive. Curtis Smith had 11 points at the half, followed by Hammond with ten. The offense looked much better, but the Rangers had no answer for Stevers, who led all scorers with 13 at the break.

In the second half, Rob Hammond tickled the twine from deep. He finished the night with 25 points. Hammond's shot was back but the Rangers once again lost. It was only the second time in Coach Herrin's nineteen years at Benton that he had a team start at 0-3. The spoiled Ranger fans were getting impatient. The team needed a win but there were no patsies on the schedule. The next weekend, the Marion Wildcats were coming to town for the South Seven opener.

In the fall, the Rangers had a 6-4 football team and nine players on the basketball team went out for football. Only two players in the top eight didn't play football: Steve Shurtz and Rob Hammond. Shurtz was an All-Conference cross country runner and Hammond was an All-South golfer.

Coach Stewart guided the Rangers to a 6-4 football season, but the long wait for the Turkey Day Game took its toll. Many of the players felt that the 0-3 start was because they were still getting in basketball condition. There is perhaps no other sport as demanding as playing basketball at a high level. A basketball player must be well-conditioned and adept in a variety of basketball skill sets.

Dave Jones: *We didn't start the season so well because four out of our five starters played football. We just weren't in basketball shape.*

While the Rangers were off to a tough start, I was having some basketball trouble of my own. As the 1978-79 school year started, I was forced against my will to attend Grant School. Up to this point, I had attended Douglas School. At Grant, I was in the fourth grade and everything was new. I missed my friends at Douglas, especially my best pal, Michael Yarberry. They didn't even play marbles at Grant. On the first day of school, I was reprimanded by Principal Bill Hedges for talking at lunch. I couldn't believe it. At Douglas, we were allowed to talk and even throw some food if you didn't get caught. Grant was button-down. My first impression of the school was it was way too strict, but I learned to adapt.

Of the five grade schools in town, Grant had the players. We were called the Grant Green Gorillas. Now, that was cool. I liked our nickname. The school colors were green and white. I liked our colors too because I was a big Celtic fan. Mr. Gene Alexander was the sixth-grade basketball coach. He is now affectionately known by all in Benton as "Mr. A". He is eighty-five years old. But when I was a fourth grader, he was in his fifties, and I thought that he was the next coming of John Wooden. Every boy in the fifth and sixth grade was on the team but there were only two uniforms available for fourth graders trying out for the sixth-grade team. Naturally, I wanted a uniform.

My good friend Wade Durham was clearly the best player in our class and was placed on the team. No try-out. This left only one uniform. The war for the last remaining uniform would be with my cousin, Tom Malkovich. Tom was also one of my best friends, but you can throw that out of the window. I needed that uniform.

To determine who would be on the team, Mr. A had us play one-on-one to three points at recess. Again, it was a different time and Mr. A probably couldn't pull this off today, but that short game was my tryout for the team. Even Tom would agree that we were both bad players but as soon as Mr. A announced the game, I began to think about strategy. Tom was left-handed and slightly stronger than me at the time. I knew I had to keep him from backing me into the post.

A coin flip decided who received first ball, and of course I lost the flip. Losing the flip was huge because it forced me to get a defensive stop. Tom literally backed me underneath the goal three consecutive times, and hit three left handed hook shots. I had no answer. Worse than that, I got man-handled. Tom won 3-2. I was too young and dumb to make any kind of adjustment. I was devastated. It was over. No basketball for me this year! I remember thinking to myself; I shoot every day after school and get beat in a game to three and I'm done for the year. It didn't seem right. I returned to class completely crushed and took my seat in the back of Mrs. Ruth Ann Auten's class. I buried my head into my hands and rested my face flat on the desk so my classmates could not see me sobbing. Basketball was my love and this loss was a setback for my plans to one day play for the Celtics in the Boston Garden.

Mr. A then peeked his head into Mrs. Auten's room and called me out in the hallway. He recognized my pain, and led me to a closet that had a trunk full of old Grant uniforms. He picked up a white uniform top and held it up to my chest and said, "That should fit." I couldn't believe it! Was I hearing this right? I was now on the team. Who cares if I cried to get the uniform? Our game was close, I did score twice. I thought of everything to justify why I should be on the team. It all made sense. I'm in.

My tears dried up quickly after getting the uniform. When I came back into the classroom, I flashed the uniform at Tom, who appeared to be a little irked at my good fortune. The team picture of the 1978-79 Grant Green Gorillas is a classic. Most of my teammates in the picture are sporting the coveted green uniform jersey, while I am in the dead center of the picture in my tattered number 35 white tank top. I treasured that white uniform even though I looked to be standing only in my under-wear. Oh well, I guess I was just lucky to have a uniform! In that same picture is Randy House, who was a sixth grader. House was a player in the sixth grade, and he would be my college roommate at SIU my fresh-man year. Most importantly, he would be a lifelong friend. I do not have enough room in this book for the life and times of Randy House, but it might be my second book.

Enough about me, let's get back to the Rangers. On Friday, De-cember 22nd, the Marion Wildcats rolled into town. Marion was led by Jeff Hutchinson and Tony Jones. The Rangers were 0-3. They needed a win.

Carl Shurtz: *Marion was pretty good our senior year. They had Tony Jones. We hadn't won a game and Coach said he wasn't going to Coach us that night…and so we just started running and going. I think when he said that it gave us a sense of freedom that we were missing. We got ahead by 10 or 15 points.*

The Rangers came out smoking and led at halftime by a score of 47-33. Hammond was on fire! After his 25 against Metropolis, he was shooting the ball with complete confidence.

Rob Hammond: *You know…as a shooter…I just always had confidence… probably because I shot the ball all the time. Don't get me wrong…there were times that I would struggle…but I would correct it. Coach Herrin also helped me in that area because he always wanted me to shoot the ball.*

The Rangers outscored the Wildcats and won the game by a score of 84-80. Ranger fans shook the building as Hammond poured in a game high 32 points. Big Jim Ward was back from the concussion and he pitched in 14 points. With only .08 seconds remaining in the game, Ward grabbed a missed Ranger free throw and stuck it back in to push a fragile two point lead to four. Ward's rebound bucket sealed the win. Marion's Tony "Too Tall" Jones led the Wildcats with 26 points. It was a solid win that moved the Rangers to 1-3 overall and 1-0 in the conference.

Jim Ward: *Marion was the turnaround game for us.*

The next night, the Rangers traveled to Herrin to meet the Tigers. The Tigers were were led by Irv Lukens and Craig Baumgarte. The Rangers had some momentum and Coach Herrin came into the ballgame with the strategy of giving much of the defensive attention to Lukens and Baumgarte. It seemed like the right defensive game plan but that's why they play the game. The player of the game turned out to be Tiger guard, Gil Tope. Tope found himself open all night and he made the Rangers pay. There is an old saying among basketball coaches for players that find themselves wide open; "There is a reason they're open." On this night, Tope took the shots and hit them. He finished with a game-high 24 points and the Rangers were badly beaten, 66-49. It was the third game of the young season that the Rangers were held under fifty points.

With a 1-4 overall record, the Rangers entered the Centralia Tournament as the sixteenth seed and opened with a tough Chicago Manley team. Manley featured perhaps the greatest player in the state in '79, Russell Cross. The Rangers were still capable of surprising the field at Centralia. They had done it so many times. Benton had won the tournament a record five times and had the respect of all the teams in the field. Chicago

Manley came into the tournament with a 5-1 record and featured size and athleticism. They were the number one seed in the tournament.

In the first quarter, the Rangers stayed close but then Manley blew the game open in the second quarter and held a 46-32 advantage at the break. Hammond recalled a funny story about the first half of the Manley game.

Rob Hammond: *I remember it was just like Hoosiers. Manley was extremely athletic and we called a timeout and talked about slowing the game down and making so many passes before we shot the ball. The very first time I got it…I'm in the corner wide open…and I shot and made it. I remember Coach Herrin just looking at me…he then took me out. I'll never forget that.*

In the second half, Manley widened the lead but the Rangers played hard. In fact, the team took pride in their gritty play by making the number one team work to win their first game.

Jim Ward: *We played them as well as anybody.*

Chicago Manley defeated the Rangers by a score of 72-54. Coach Herrin spun the loss to his players as an opportunity to advance in the consolation bracket. As he had done so many times in his career, he was able to motivate his team to come back and compete on day two.

The Rangers were 1-5 overall. The loss to Manley placed them in the consolation bracket against Peoria Woodruff. The game was in the morning and it was attended by very few. Many of the Ranger fans chose to tune in on the radio. The Woodruff game was a crazy affair for Jim Ward. The game was back and forth and it came down to the wire. Woodruff was forced to foul, and Ward missed five consecutive free throws and two were the front end of one-and-ones. It was a nightmare for Ward. It was now in his head. The basketball gods then took Ward from goat to hero. With only .08 seconds left in the game, and behind by one point, Ward hit the game-winning jumper from the elbow to give the Rangers the win. It was much needed. After the game, the players were more relieved than excited. It was win number two and a chance to win another one. Hammond led the Rangers in scoring with 18 points followed by Jim Ward with ten.

In the semi-finals of the Consolation Tournament, the Rangers played the Arlington Huskies. It was a 9:00 a.m. start and the Rangers played sluggishly. The Huskies bounced the Rangers from the tournament by a score of 44-38.

Rich Herrin: *It was a frustrating game. We just have to come back next weekend and play well against Harrisburg.*

On Friday, January 12th, the Rangers traveled to Davenport Gymnasium to face off with the Harrisburg Bulldogs. The team had been idle for almost two weeks but Coach Herrin used the extra practices to improve the team's physical conditioning, tweak offensive sets and fine tune the defense. When the Rangers took the floor against the Bulldogs they were a better basketball team. They never trailed in the contest and put together their most balanced offensive attack of the season. At halftime, the Rangers led the Bulldogs by a score of 40-18 before cruising to a 70-44 victory. The victory thrust the team back into the conference race at 2-1. There was hope. Despite sitting at 3-6 overall, the Rangers focused their attention on the conference race. The win at Harrisburg was a reward for two weeks of rigorous practice.

It was a feel-good win. The Rangers emptied their bench and senior Jeff Shew, came off the bench to score five points. Shew had sandy blonde hair and stood at 6'4". He had a slender build with arms and legs all over the place. Shew could do something that many of his teammates couldn't; he could dunk the ball. He was also one of the top 440 runners in Southern Illinois.

Jeff Shew: *I went to Grant School, and my grade school coach was Perry Eisenhower. He scared me to death but he had a mindset like Coach Herrin. He was all about discipline. We didn't have basements and computers back then. I grew up on East Taylor Street and we played outside all day…backyard football and basketball…you name it.*

On this night, Jerry Corn scored his first two varsity points against the Bulldogs. Junior Randy Herrin also saw action. Randy was the second son of Sue and Rich Herrin. In 1978-79, he was a junior. Much like his cousin Jim Herrin (Ron's son), Randy didn't see playing time in his future and decided not to play as a senior.

Randy Herrin: *You know, Matt…Rodney and Kyle went on and earned basketball scholarships. I just never got to play that much. I was old for my class and I matured early…and then everyone else in my class got their growth spurts. I sat the bench quite a bit. I didn't go out for the team my senior year. I was busy. I ran cross country and I was in student council. I didn't want to* *sit on the bench another year. I don't think Dad was thrilled about me not playing…but he never once made me feel bad about that. He was not mad or upset about it.*

Randy went on to tell me a funny story. H.M. Aiken was a retired BCHS biology teacher and was a big Ranger fan. In fact, Aiken worked the concession stand for years at the old Cracker Box. H.M. knew the Herrin family well and he thought he knew the boys. The incident took place after Randy graduated high school and Mr. Aiken was getting up in age.

Randy Herrin: *I had graduated from high school. I think I was at Rend Lake…I was standing near the coach's office with Carl Skinion. We were just standing there watching Dad's practice. H. M. Aiken walks up…the old biology teacher. He said, "Hey Kyle, how you doing?" He thought I was Kyle. I didn't want to correct him…so I just went with it. I said, "Hey Mr. Aiken." Then he said, "How's Randy doing?" I said something like, "Pretty good." Then he said, "You know Randy is a really good kid, he just never was the player his brothers were, was he?" I could hear Skin-man start laughing. I think I said something like, "I don't know…he had a pretty good jump shot." When he left, we both started cracking up. From that point on, if anyone gets us mixed up…I correct them.*

Although basketball was not his central focus, Randy was thankful for all of the experiences that basketball provided him growing up.

Randy Herrin: *We were always going to the gym in the summertime with Dad. It was exciting for our family. When we were very young, all of our vacations centered around basketball. His success as a coach made our childhood even more exhilarating. There were times it was like something out of a movie. The elation that came along with winning those Super-Sectionals and going to State was incredible. The years that we advanced to the State Tournament were really special. Of course, we never could win that first game and I do think that was something that Dad was always disappointed with. I think that bothered him. When the season was over I remember it would be sad for a few days.*

After the Rangers much-needed win at Harrisburg, the Centralia Orphans came to town. As usual, Ranger fans packed the gym hoping for an upset. Centralia was really good. They were now coached by Jim Roberts and were led by stand-out guard Tony Worlds. What a great basketball name and he had game. Roberts looked more like a science teacher and did not have the charisma of Jeff Carling, but he could coach. The Rangers had momentum and they wanted to keep it going.

In the first quarter, the Rangers opened up an offensive barrage on the Orphans and led by a score of 42-34. The Orphans tried to chip away at the lead, but the Rangers led at halftime, 53-44. The offense was firing on all cylinders. Hammond was raining long range jumpers. Dave Jones, Jim Ward, Jerry Dawson and Jim Labuwi were controlling the glass and doing the dirty work.

Junior Jim Labuwi played at 6'5" and weighed 222 pounds. He was hard-nosed and welcomed contact. He fit in well with Jones and Ward and gave the Rangers quality minutes off the bench. It was clear that Labuwi would slide into the role of the enforcer as a senior. For his size, Labuwi was agile and had a nose for the ball. He was a very good rebounder and came up with big baskets in key situations.

In the second half, the Rangers continued to play well. Carl Shurtz had his best offensive game of the year. Shurtz was a senior and he sported a full head of blonde hair and played at 5'11" and 160 pounds. Defensively, he played with a reckless abandon. He flew around the floor looking for steals by overplaying passing lanes and could apply intense pressure on the ball if needed. Offensively, he could knock down the short jumper, but he was most valuable as the floor general. Carl Shurtz had a sick sense of where his teammates were on the floor, especially Hammond. Against Centralia, Shurtz drove gaps to draw the defense and then dished the ball to Hammond who was prepared to catch and shoot. Hammond finished the game with 28 points and most of his bombs were set up by Carl Shurtz. There is perhaps no guard tandem in Benton history that understood each other more than Shurtz and Hammond. It was a beautiful thing to watch.

Carl Shurtz: *That was my job. I loved feeding him the ball. He would take a pass from me and as soon as he shot it…I would say "Boom baby"…trying to get his confidence going. When Rob was on…he could shoot with the best of them. He could fill it up.*

Kent Yancik: *I just remember Carl and Rob played together so well.*

Jim Ward and Kent Yancik were quick to point out how important the play of Carl Shurtz was to the '79 team.

The Rangers won a wild one at home by defeating the Orphans, 88-83. In the final minute of the game, Orphans guard Tony Worlds drove the lane but Jim Ward slid in front of him to draw the charge. Ward was perfectly set and flopped backward to get the call. It was World's fifth foul of the game. It was classic Jim Ward. Ward picked himself up off the floor and tugged his glasses back into place and hustled to the other end.

Carl Shurtz: *He could draw a charge better than anybody in the game.*

There was no celebrating. No emotion. Ward was doing his job. When the buzzer sounded, the Rangers entered the locker room, showered, rehashed the game and cranked up the music. It was a big win that moved the Rangers to 4-6 and 3-1 in the conference. They were only one game behind the Carbondale Terriers.

Jim Ward: *One of my favorite memories was just the time in the locker room…the camaraderie.*

On Friday, January 19th, the team traveled to West Frankfort. The Birds were under the direction of new head coach Tim Ricci. Ricci is still the all-time leading scorer in West Frankfort history and Redbird fans were excited when Ricci returned to West Frankfort to coach at his alma mater. In the pre-season votes from the coaches, the Redbirds were picked last in the league but they were off to a great start. The Redbirds were big and physical. Eric Shostrum, Joby Wilson, Keith Griffth, and Jeff Cima were long and strong. The Redbirds favored a more deliberate pace. The Rangers wanted to run.

From the tip, the Redbirds controlled the pace of the game. The Rangers jumped out to a 12-8 lead, but then the Redbirds came back and took the lead at halftime by a score of 17-16. It didn't look good for the Rangers. With 6:15 left to play in the game, Frankfort's Jeff Cima tipped in an offensive rebound to give the Redbirds a 31-26 lead. From this point on, the Rangers made a surge led by Carl Shurtz, Steve Shurtz and Rob Hammond. The Benton guards opened fire from the outside, scoring ten points but still found themselves down, 35-33. At the 2:21 mark, Griffth missed the front end of a one-and-one and then Carl Shurtz hit a twisting jumper in the lane to give the Rangers a 39-35 lead. Frankfort then lost their composure late in the game and turned the ball over several times.

The Rangers won the ballgame 47-40. It wasn't pretty, but it was a win. Herrin had these comments after the game:

Rich Herrin: *At halftime, Harry* (assistant coach Harry Stewart) *told our guards to step up maybe three feet. Our shots were coming from too far out in the first half. In the second half, we stayed organized and moved more and were patient enough to get better shots.*

The following night, the Mt. Vernon Rams came to town. The Rangers were now 5-6 overall and 4-1 in conference play. Most importantly, they had found themselves. They were finding ways to win and their basketball legs were back. They were playing with confidence.

In the first period, the Rangers took a 12-10 lead. In the second quarter, the Rangers used a suffocating full-court press to force seven Rams turnovers to take a 31-18 halftime lead. In the second half, the Rangers built an eighteen-point lead and cruised to a 65-58 victory. The team was unbeaten in 1979, 5-0. The Rangers were now 6-6 and 5-1 in the conference. Coach Herrin had a knack of correcting tough starts. Randy Herrin always thought his dad's true character showed the most when things weren't going well.

Randy Herrin: *You know they say a great measure of someone's character is how they handle disappointment. How you act when things go bad. I remember seeing Bobby Knight...who is a great coach...throw that chair. My dad would never do that. He would get excited...kick the bleachers...get animated because he was passionate about the game...but he always was in control of his character.*

On January 26, 1979, the team opened play in the sixth annual Benton Invitational Tournament. Could the Rangers keep it going? They were hot. The Rangers opened tournament play with Breese Mater Dei. For some odd reason the BIT is synonymous with wintery weather. In '79, it was no different. Snow fell across Southern Illinois all week which plagued attendance.

The Rangers cruised to a 78-60 victory over Mater Dei in game one. Rob Hammond scored 27 points and Jim Ward chipped in with 14. With the win, they advanced to meet the Olney Tigers. Beginning in '75, the Tigers had been the Rangers' nemesis. In '79, the Tigers were loaded again and featured stand-out players Tony Jennings and Darnall Jones.

When the Rangers and Tigers took the floor, only the die-hards could make it to the game because of the weather. It was a great game. The Tigers were just too much but the Rangers played well. The Tigers won the game, 67-65, and advanced to play Carbondale in the tournament championship. Carbondale featured Johnny Fayne. Fayne was a senior and a tremendous talent. The match-up of Darnall Jones and Johnny Fayne in the '79 BIT Championship was a classic battle. In a game for the ages, the Terriers defeated the Tigers by a score of 87-76.

That same night, the Rangers were defeated by the Carmi Bulldogs, 57-46, in the third place game. The tournament proved to be a disappointment for the Rangers. The team fell to 7-8 but they still had a chance to win the conference, where they were 5-1.

On Friday, February 2nd, the Rangers traveled to Marion. In their first meeting, the Rangers ambushed the Wildcats by a score of 84-80. A huge Marion crowd was in attendance along with a large contingent of Rangers fans. The large Marion pep band played and the place was rocking. The Wildcats took advantage of the loud gym to take a 20-14 lead at the end of the first period. The Wildcats played with a chip on their shoulder and stunned the Rangers in the first half by taking a ten-point halftime lead. The Rangers won the second half, but it wasn't enough. Tony Jones scored a game-high 25 points. The Rangers were led by Hammond with 16 points. There were few bright spots. It was a game to forget.

The next night, the Redbirds came to town. Coach Ricci's plan was to contain Rob Hammond which allowed Jones and Ward to go to work. Despite the size and physical play of the Redbirds, it was the inside play of the Rangers that dominated the game.

Rich Herrin: *We don't count on any one person. Hammond is our leading scorer, but we've got others that can put it in the hole.*

The Rangers trailed 9-6 at the end of the first quarter and then exploded for 26 points in the second quarter. Big Jim Labuwi scored ten points in the quarter and Dawson and Ward each scored a basket.

Jerry Dawson was now a senior and had been a mainstay in the post position since his sophomore year in '77. Coach Herrin spotted Jerry and Terry Dawson in grade school and saw their potential. Jerry proved to be a valuable player for the Rangers because of his size. Dawson also developed a nice touch around the basket.

Jerry Dawson: *I remember Coach Herrin would come by Grant School and watch Terry and I play at recess. He worked a lot with me and my brother on being able to shoot with both hands around the basket.*

In the third quarter, the Rangers extended the lead to 48-38 and ended up winning the game 69-60. Curtis Smith led the Rangers with 14 points. Smith was starting to become more comfortable at the varsity level. Senior guard Matt Florian ripped the Rangers for 23 points and Keith Griffth added 13 for the Redbirds, but it wasn't enough. With the win, the Rangers moved to 8-9 overall and a respectable 6-2 in the conference race. West Frankfort coach, Tim Ricci, had these words after the game.

Tim Ricci: *Hammond is averaging 20 points a game and we held him to eight, but their other guys did a good job. Their bench and depth really helped.*

It was a great win because it was a team effort offensively but Carl Shurtz admitted that Hammond's ability to shoot the ball was the key to their offense.

Carl Shurtz: *When Hambone had 20 or better…we were pretty tough to beat. He was a pure shooter. A great guy. We went as Rob went.*

On Tuesday, February 6th, the Rangers traveled to Bowen Gymnasium to play the Carbondale Terriers. It was a make-up game that had been cancelled earlier in the year due to the weather. The Terriers were in first place in the conference and featured two of the league's best players in Craig Bardo and Johnny Fayne. It would be a great test for the Rangers. If they could win, they had a legitimate shot at the conference title.

Carbondale started the game hot. In the first quarter, Mack Ackerman provided the scoring punch and led the Terriers to an early 16-9 advantage. The Rangers then came alive as Hammond and Labuwi scored three baskets each. Carbondale held a slim 31-27 halftime lead. At the 7:43 mark, Hammond hit a long jumper to put the Rangers up 42-41. Then only two minutes later, Jim Labuwi scored to put the Rangers on top, 46-45. From this point on, it was all Carbondale. Craig Bardo came alive to spark the Terriers to a narrow 54-49 victory. The Terriers moved to 23-1 for the season and 9-0 in the South Seven Conference.

Just three days later, the Herrin Tigers came to town. The Tigers had won the earlier meeting but the Rangers were now a better team. The

Rangers came out smoking and held a 48-35 advantage with just .37 seconds left in the third quarter. Then something happened. The Ranger offense shut down and for the next seven and a half minutes they were held scoreless. The most frustrating part of the scoring drought was that the Rangers were plagued by turnovers. Herrin was led by Irv Lukens with 25 points and his bucket at the 1:16 mark tied the game at 48. With just .52 seconds left in the contest, Rob Hammond scored to put the Rangers on top, 50-48. The Rangers fouled Gil Tope on the next possession and he hit one free throw to pull the Tigers to within one, 50-49. With time running out, the Tigers chose to foul Curtis Smith. Wrong guy! Smith calmly went to the line and hit the first shot, but then missed the second. Herrin was unable to get a shot off to tie and the Rangers escaped with a 51-49 victory.

The Rangers had Saturday night off. Of course, Herrin traveled to Olney to watch his brother's team play. It was common to see Ron at a Benton game if his team was not playing. They were brothers in the truest sense and they followed each other's progress. They bounced ideas off of each other and spent long hours on the phone talking basketball.

On February 16th, the Harrisburg Bulldogs came to Benton. The night served as a coming out party for junior Curtis Smith. Smith made a believer out of Coach Herrin, who was not sure Smith could play as a junior. Now, he was not only playing, he was leading the team in scoring on some nights. Smith drove the right baseline and dropped a series of mid-range jump shots. The Bulldogs had no answer. The Rangers won the game 64-48 and improved to 10-10 overall and 8-3 in the conference. Smith's teammates remember his maturation as a player.

Dave Jones: *Curtis had a quiet personality…exceptional athlete…tough. He had great eye-hand coordination. He could score and was a great all-around player.*

Carl Shurtz: *Curtis could score. He was coming into his own.*

The hard-nosed play of Ward and Jones cannot be overstated. Jones was acting as the enforcer by rebounding and guarding the best opposing post player. Ward was scoring and sliding in front of quick guards to draw charges. Most importantly, they were giving Yancik and Labuwi an education in tenacity and toughness. Jones and Ward always played hard and their intense approach to games and practices inspired the younger players. Very rarely did Ward and Jones lose the war on the boards despite being undersized. Coach Herrin loved their gritty play and praised their effort at every opportunity.

Rob Hammond: *Ward and Jones both played so hard. They rebounded like animals. They were both great teammates.*

The following night, the Rangers traveled to Centralia for a match-up against the Orphans. Not only did the Orphans have Tony Worlds, they also had John Weigel and Mike Murray. The game was incredible. The Rangers played well in a tough environment but Tony Worlds hit a 17 foot jumper just before the final horn to give the Orphans a 62-60 victory.

Rich Herrin: *It was just as good as winning. They just got the shot down when it counted.*

In the long run, Coach Herrin knew that the Centralia game would battle-harden the team come tournament time. Dave Jones led the Rangers by scoring 15 points and Carl Shurtz added 13 in the contest.

On February 23rd, Craig Bardo and Jonny Fayne combined for 43 points to defeat the Rangers in a nip and tuck battle that went down to the wire. The Terriers hit important free throws down the stretch to seal a 66-61 victory over the Rangers. With the loss, the team moved to 10-12 overall and 8-5 in conference action. Again, it was budding star, Curtis Smith, who led the team in scoring with 19 points. Teammate Steve Shurtz added 13 points.

Steve Shurtz was the third of four brothers that played for the Rangers. Steve proved to be very dependable and versatile throughout his career. Shurtz was blonde-headed like his brother Carl and played at 5'10". Steve was a good shooter and could also play the point if needed. He was a tough competitor. As a junior, Steve played steady and was pesky on the defensive side of the ball.

The following night, the team traveled to the Snake Pit to play the Mt. Vernon Rams. But there was a problem. Hammond was in a shooting slump. In the last four games, Hammond had only 24 points and was held scoreless at home against Harrisburg. There was no doubt that Curtis Smith was contributing more on the offensive end, but Hammond had to get back on track and everyone knew it.

Dave Jones: *Rob was our scorer. He was like the golden boy...He was real quiet...great guy...friendly...just like he is today. Now...he could flat-out shoot the ball.*

Jerry Dawson: *He* (Hammond) *could knock the eyes out of it.*

The Rangers got off to a good start by taking an 18-12 lead after one. Most importantly, Hammond hit his first three shots. He was back. The Rams cut into the lead in the second quarter, but the Rangers held a 31-26 advantage at halftime. The game was back and forth but it was nothing like the Jones free throws of a year ago. It was a clean game and the Rangers pulled away to win 65-61. It was a quality win on the road. Hammond led all scorers with 18 points, followed by Curtis Smith with 17 points. The Rangers improved to 11-12 overall and finished with a respectable 9-5 record in the conference.

The Rangers had one home game left against the Effingham Flaming Hearts. Effingham was loaded and entered the game at 21-2. The Hearts were touted as one of the best teams in the state. They had a tremendous player by the name of Mitch Arnold. Arnold played at 6'5" and he was a tremendous scorer who also had uncanny jumping ability. He was possibly the greatest scorer in the state in '79.

As the Rangers ran out of the Tunnel, the fans rose to their feet, recognizing that this was the senior's last home game. In a short pre-game ceremony, all of the seniors were recognized along with their parents. The game was an incredible display of offense from both teams. It was a shootout. Arnold and Hammond were dueling like Ali and Frazier.

As a senior, Rob Hammond played at 6'0", 160 pounds. He had a quick release and could heat up fast. Hammond was in the zone, raining deep jump shots from every spot imaginable. The Rangers won the game 86-81 in double overtime. Hammond remembered the night well.

Rob Hammond: *That night they played me, man...and I can remember shooting over one of their guards. I liked to catch and take a couple of dribbles left and that last hard dribble got me into my shot.*

Mitch Arnold finished the game with 44 points on 18-29 shooting from the field and he was 8-9 from the free throw line. He was incredible. Think about playing that kind of game and losing. Hammond scored a career high 36 points and was 14-25 from the field and 8-8 from the foul line.

Jim Ward: *Rob had 36 and Mitch Arnold had 44. It was unbelievable. Jim Ford had just moved to Benton and he told me after the game that from that point on...he was a Ranger fan.*

It is important to note that Rob Hammond's mindset as a shooter was to always take a good shot. He was not a "gunslinger". He let the game come to him and avoided forcing shots. Hammond played the game the right way and every shot he took was within the offense.

Rob Hammond: *He told me one time, "Hambone...you're the only guy I ever had to get onto for not shooting the ball enough."*

'79 State Tournament Play

With the win, the Rangers improved to 12-12 entering the Regional Tournament. The only losing season in Rich Herrin's tenure up to this point was the '63-'64 season. The team finished 11-14. To finish above .500 for the season, the Rangers had to win the Regional Tournament. It wouldn't be easy.

The 1979 Regional took place at Davenport Gymnasium, in Harrisburg. The Rangers opened against the Mt. Vernon Rams. They had defeated the Rams twice but both games were narrow victories. There would be no easy games in tournament play. They would have to fight their way through a tough field of Southern Illinois teams for a shot at the state tournament.

On Wednesday, March 7th, the Rangers and Rams battled to keep their seasons alive. It was a game of runs. In the first quarter, the Rams seemed uninterested and the Rangers jumped out to a 12-4 lead. In the second quarter, the Rams came out fighting and pulled ahead to take a 22-20 halftime lead. In the third quarter, the Rangers took command of the game by outscoring the Rams 23-8 to take a 43-30 lead. The Rangers then methodically put the Rams to sleep and won the game, 57-46. Hammond led all scorers with 18 points and Curtis Smith chipped in with 13 points. The Rangers now seemed to have a one-two scoring punch with Hammond and Smith that was missing earlier in the season. The win capped off a three-game sweep of the '79 Rams. Most importantly, the Rangers improved to 13-12 overall to advance to the Regional Championship against the host Bulldogs.

Entering the game, Harrisburg head coach, Gene Haile, suspended double figure scorer Ken Henshaw who received a technical foul in the previous game. Coach Haile had a rule that if one of his players receives a "T", they must sit the next contest. True to his word, Henshaw did not play. Despite a scary fourth quarter surge, the Rangers won the game, 52-49. They had done it. They had won the Regional and were guaranteed an overall record above .500. It was Coach Herrin's sixteenth Regional Championship in 19 seasons at Benton.

The players celebrated the victory and then boarded the bus anxious to see fans waiting on the square to greet them. I'm a little biased, but there is perhaps no town in Illinois that knows how to celebrate good basketball like Benton. As the Rangers were met with a police and firetruck escort into town they had the satisfaction of knowing that they fought their way back to respectability. It was a good season, but it was not over. Now the question was; could the Rangers make an improbable run to the State Tournament?

The players were optimistic about their chances to win the Sectional Tournament for two reasons. First, it was at home. The Rangers played their best basketball of the season on their homecourt and they were excited about using the crowd as their sixth man. Secondly, they were matched up against the Effingham Flaming Hearts. Of course, the Hearts were very good, and they had a great player in Mitch Arnold, but the Rangers had already beaten the Hearts. They knew for sure it was possible.

The much anticipated game with the Hearts did not take place until Wednesday. If you were a Ranger fan, the days leading up to a big game were exhilarating. The game was the talk of the town. The businesses on the square were window-painted to support the team and then there was the fight for tickets. For the players, it is a surreal experience. For the players, the practices leading up to the Effingham game were crisp and filled with enthusiasm. The players proudly wore their Ranger jackets all over town and were recognized by all. Everyone was in anticipation. It was a magical time to be a Ranger.

Many Benton people argue about the largest crowd ever in the Rich. Rob Hammond became very close personal friends with Coach Herrin after his playing days were over. He made these comments in our interview.

Rob Hammond: *Coach Herrin told me that the Effingham game was the largest crowd we ever had for a game at Benton. Every bleacher seat was made into a reserved seat. That had never been done before...it was standing room only.*

It was a shocker to me and I was there. Like many fans, I thought the great battles with McLeansboro in the early eighties, or even the '75 match-up with Carling's Darlings had the greatest crowds. Not true. The game with the most attendance in Benton History according to Coach Herrin is the Benton-Effingham game of the '79 Sectional.

I went to the game that night and sat with my parents in the red seats. The gym was electric when the Rangers took the floor and then the Benton crowd erupted into a chorus of boos as Mitch Arnold and the Flaming Hearts took the floor. As a kid, these moments were powerful. I had been to all the home games and any game I could get a ride to on the road. If I wasn't at the game, I listened to the voice of the Rangers, Ron Head, on the radio. I was invested. Rob Hammond was my favorite player because of his outside shooting prowess. Watching Rob Hammond shoot the ball inspired me to play even more on my own.

When the ten players walked out to start the game, there were over 4,000 people watching every move they made. I studied Mitch Arnold and watched the way he moved without the ball and then slashed to the goal when the opportunity presented itself. I watched as Jim Ward checked out inside and the way Carl Shurtz orchestrated the offense. I watched intently. My dream was to be on the floor in this type of game someday. I wondered what it was like to play in front of so many fans. What was it like to be called out for the starting line-up or even run out of the tunnel? What was it like to get a firetruck escort around the square? I did know one thing as I sat there that night; I wanted to be a Ranger someday.

Then the game started. I did not eat or drink soda. I wasn't going to the bathroom. I did not want a ring-pop from the concession stand. I wanted to watch the game without any distractions. I was transfixed by the intensity of it all. Everything started as well as it could for the Rangers. The one-two punch of Hammond and Smith were on target. Jones and Ward dominated the boards and Carl Shurtz ran the show flawlessly. After the first period, the Rangers led 18-16.

Rob Hammond: *I just remember we were playing really well. Dave Jones got a basket and then got fouled early in the game and got a three-point play. We were in control of the game.*

In the second quarter, the Rangers exploded for 27 points as Hammond splashed long jump shots from deep. Bone was on! It looked as if the Rangers had the Hearts' number. Almost like a psychological advantage due to their double-overtime win just two weeks earlier. Things were clicking and the Ranger fans stood and cheered as the team headed to the locker room with a 45-36 halftime lead. At halftime, Hammond had 18 points and Dave Jones chipped in with seven. Big Team always came up big when the lights shined the brightest, and it was no different on this night. During the halftime intermission, Ranger fans discussed the game with the fans around them. There was a buzz in the gym. You could feel it.

Early in the third quarter, Hammond hit another jump shot. He had 20. It was the last two points of his basketball career. At the 5:12 mark in the third quarter, the Rangers were ahead by a score of 51-42 and the unthinkable happened.

Rob Hammond: *We were on offense. I was to the right side of the key and we shot the ball and missed…they grabbed the rebound and threw an outlet pass. I turned to my left and my knee bent back and I fell to the floor. I tried to get up…and then just fell back on the floor.*

As I watched from the red seats, I thought he would get up. I had never really seen a bad injury before. When play stopped, you could hear a pin drop in that gym. I mean it was completely silent. Coach Herrin came onto the floor and bent over Hammond in anguish. Doc Durham (Buck's dad) was in attendance and quickly came to the scene. Coach Herrin had given Hammond a towel. In deep frustration, Hammond buried his face into the towel to hide his emotions. Doc Durham gently examined the Rob's knee as Ranger fans held their breath. That is all I could see. In the moment, you could see a quiet conversation taking place between Durham and Coach Herrin.

Rob Hammond: *When Doc Durham came out…I remember he said to Coach Herrin, "He's messed it up." I remember Coach Herrin just looked down. They had me in the tunnel trying to run on it but I couldn't put any weight on it…so I couldn't stop. I blew my ACL and was in the hospital for twelve days.*

The game was delayed for six or seven minutes. Teammates helped Hammond hobble off the floor. As the game resumed, Hammond was in the

Tunnel testing his knee. Could he run on the knee? With every step, excruciating pain shot through his knee. He had torn his ACL and every time he attempted to stop his knee shifted with pain. It was over.

Jim Ward: *That game is surreal when I think about it today. I remember when Rob went down and we just kind of looked at each other as if to say, "Who is going to do this now?"*

When play resumed, the team was shaken. The dynamics were thrown off and the Rangers were looking for an emergency go-to guy that they really didn't have. Curtis Smith was not afraid and Steve Shurtz along with Jones and Ward tried to step up and score, but it wasn't the same. The Rangers were up nine points with 5:12 remaining in the third quarter when Hammond left the game. With coach Herrin trying to prevent foul trouble for his regulars, he placed Jerry Corn into the game. As a junior, Corn had been used very little and he vividly remembered that moment.

Jerry Corn: *I didn't play a whole lot in '79 on the varsity team. I played in the J.V. game before the varsity game. When Rob left the game with the knee injury, Coach Herrin put me in the game. I probably played more in that Sectional game than I did all year long. It took me a while to settle down. The place was packed and I was nervous as a cat.*

When the fourth quarter started, the Rangers were down two and fighting to stay alive. Give the Rangers credit, they continued to battle. At the 3:54 mark, Mitch Arnold fouled out of the game and the Rangers began to rally. In fact, a tip in by Dave Jones at the 1:15 mark pulled the Rangers to within two points. The real hero of the game was the Hearts' Dale Grupe. When Arnold exited the game it was Grupe that hit key baskets to push the Hearts past the Rangers. The final score was Effingham, 74; Benton, 68. It was a tough pill to swallow. A disappointed Rich Herrin had these comments in the March 15th edition of the Benton Evening News.

Rich Herrin: *The injury just frustrated us. Everybody was stunned. It hurt us mentally more than we realized. I feel if he had stayed in the game…with the way he was playing…and the way the whole team was playing with such intensity, that we would have won without a doubt.*

Dave Jones feels the same way and he still struggles with the game and thinks back to what could have been.

Dave Jones: *We would have beaten Effingham that night in the Sectional if he hadn't blown his ACL. We had the game in control when he got injured and they came back and beat us. I believe we would have won that Sectional.*

For Coach Herrin, it was another injury or sickness at an inopportune time to a great player. In '58 it was Stan Luechtefeld, Yunkus in '67, Dunbar in '75 and now Hammond in '79. He had to feel snake-bit.

The '79 Rangers finished 14-13 with a respectable 9-5 record in the conference. They also won a Regional Championship. It was a successful season on the floor, but it doesn't compare to the lifelong friendship and memories created along the way.

Rob Hammond's knee eventually recovered but he was never able to play college basketball. However, he was a Division I athlete.

Rob Hammond: *At the time, SIU was talking to me and they were actually at the Effingham game. I probably could have played somewhere. But I did get to play four years of golf at SIU. My college roommate at SIU was Darnall Jones.*

Again, Hammond became great friends with Coach Herrin after his playing days at Benton. They had a special relationship and Rob looked to him much like a second father. Rob and his wife, Gay, live in Benton and they have three children; Bryson, Alecia and Brad. He is currently the president of US Bank in Benton.

Rob Hammond: *The thing I missed the most about high school was not being able to be around Coach anymore. Other than my dad he probably had the greatest influence on my life. He was such a good person. He was about working hard and being fair. He always wanted us to play aggressively but never dirty.*

Point guard Carl Shurtz recalled how special it was to play basketball at Benton.

Carl Shurtz: *The atmosphere…that big crowd and that big gym. Just running out onto the floor…the starting line-ups…it's amazing how many people wanted to watch a basketball game back then. It was special.*

Shurtz also took a moment to recall what he learned the most from playing for Coach Herrin. Today, Carl lives in Benton and has two children: Natasha and Nathan.

Carl Shurtz: *Coach Herrin was a head of his time. He was so dedicated. We played so much and to get better you had to play. I think he was doing that before other schools were. He was a good man too. Hard work pays off in life. I carried that with me. Another thing I remember him teaching us about was Lombardi Time. If you got to practice right on time you were twenty minutes late. Always be where you're supposed to be at least 20 minutes early. That always stuck with me and I do that to this day.*

Dave Jones was a great interview for the book and he was very grateful for his opportunity to play Benton basketball. After high school, Jones was intrigued by the discipline and structure of the military.

Dave Jones: *I was going to go to Illinois State to play football and the phone rang one night and it was Bill Parcells. He was coaching football at the Air Force Academy...so I went. He left when I got there and the rest is history for him. I spent eight years flying in the Air Force and served in Operation Desert Storm. I am currently a captain and fly commercial planes. The Air Force was tough academically, but I got through it.*

Jones admits that Coach Herrin left a lasting impact on his life after high school. Dave lives with his wife, Lisa, in the Dallas area and they have five children; Joshua, Sara, Matthew, Jonathon and Joseph.

Dave Jones: *I had the opportunity to take on the responsibility of running a junior golf league in Texas that has raised more than 350 million dollars in scholarships. Many of the principles I learned playing for Coach Herrin helped me so much in this endeavor. I was able to help send kids to college through the game of golf just like Coach Herrin did with basketball. All five of my children played college golf.*

Dave Jones: *The biggest thing that I learned from Coach Herrin was work ethic and doing things the right way. I've done some really challenging things when I served in the military. Coach taught me that the little things matter, and it helped me get thru my military experience. Coach Herrin also had a* *moral compass. I respected him for the type of man he was with his family. He meant a lot to me and I wrote him a letter…and he wrote me back.*

After high school, Jim Ward has been working as the Director of operations with McDonalds since 1984. Jim lives in Benton with his wife Leigh Ann and they have three children; Daulton, Ashtyn and Jennifer. He was grateful to have the opportunity to play for Coach Herrin.

Jim Ward: *When you are sixteen or seventeen years old…you don't think about that question but looking back on it…his Christianity really shined through to us. I had Coach Herrin at his best. He was always fair. I remember him telling me one time, "You made me play you." I would run thru a brick wall for him. I remember these three words in his obituary, beloved former players. I thought to myself how many guys feel the same way about him as I do? He was always there. He touched my life in so many ways.*

After high school, Jerry Dawson began working at McAfoos Tractor Sales. He worked there for seventeen years. He then took over his dad's pawn shop in town and has been there for twenty-five years. Jerry has a quiet personality and enjoyed his experience as a player under Coach Herrin. Jerry currently lives in Benton with his wife Sarah and they have one boy, Jeremy.

Jerry Dawson: *He was Mr. Basketball. He lived the game every day. The main thing I remember was the positive attitudes of all the coaches. I was around Coach Herrin for three years every day and I always enjoyed going to practice. He was somebody that if you had a problem, he would talk to you. He always had the answer for everything.*

Jeff Shew started as a volunteer fireman at Benton right out of high school and ended up serving forty-one years for the Benton Fire Department. Jeff is currently retired and lives with his wife Liz and they have two children: Daulton and Katie. Jeff enjoyed his time with Coach Herrin ad respected him greatly.

Jeff Shew: *He knew the game. He could teach the game. We went in before school and shot free throws all of the time. The physical conditioning was demanding. He was just down to the basics. The discipline…the training…you take that mindset wherever you go.*

As a new decade of Ranger basketball would begin, the gang of 1980 led by upcoming star Curtis Smith promised to be a fun team to watch. There was also a strong freshman and sophomore class coming. The future of Benton basketball looked bright for years to come.

Watching Rob Hammond shoot the ball was inspiring.
Hammond was lights out in '79. *(Ceasar Maragni)*

Coach Harry Stewart led the football Rangers to a solid 6-4 record
in the old South Seven in the fall of '78. *(Ceasar Maragni)*

I am 35 in the middle. Tom Malkovich is in the back row next to Mr. A.
It was Malkovich who whipped me in 1 on 1 for what we thought
was the final spot on the team. *(Matt Wynn family collection)*

Carl Shurtz ran the '79 team well and had a sick sense of getting
Hammond the ball at the right time. *(Ceasar Maragni)*

Ward loved the comradery of his teammates. Jim was a key player on the '79 team. Ward was a solid rebounder and could score the ball. *(Ceasar Maragni)*

Jeff Shew and Rodney Potts were key reserves on the '79 team. *(Ceasar Maragni)*

Randy Herrin also played as a reserve on the '79 team.
(Ceasar Maragni)

Kent Yancik developed his game in '79 practicing against the
likes of Dawson, Ward and Jones. (Ceasar Maragni)

Dave Jones grew up watching the Rangers and remembered seeing Doug Collins. Jones wanted to be a part of something special. Although Jones went to the Air Force to play football, he was a key player in the success of the Ranger teams in 78 and 79. *(Ceasar Maragni)*

Steve Shurtz in action against the Terriers in '79. *(Ceasar Maragni)*

Curtis Smith helped Rob Hammond carry the scoring load in '79.
Herrin called Smith a "self-made player." As a boy, Smith played constantly
on the courts of Douglas School. *(Ceasar Maragni)*

The '79 Rangers after their Regional Championship victory at Harrisburg.
Front Row- Labuwi, S. Shurtz, Jones, Ward, Hammond, C. Shurtz, Smith,
J. Williams **Back Row-** J. Dawson, Yancik, Herrin, Corn, Oyler, Shew,
Stewart, Knight, Phillips. *(Ceasar Maragni)*

Jerry Corn saw action in the sectional when Hammond
went down. *(Ceasar Maragni)*

Rob Hammond goes down with a knee injury in the 3rd quarter of the Benton
Sectional against Effingham. The injury changed the game.
(Ceasar Maragni)

591

CHAPTER TWENTY-FIVE

Rangers drop to Class A in '80

We were one of the small teams in Southern Illinois…but the
big teams didn't want to play us. – Kent Yancik

In the fall of 1979, I was entering the fifth grade at the newly-opened
Benton Middle School. The Middle School had been under construction for close to two years, but it was finally ready to open its doors to
all incoming fifth to eighth grade students living in the Benton School
District. The school featured a fifth and sixth grade wing on the west side
and a junior high area on the east side. A giant library with all the bells
and whistles separated the two areas. A state-of-the-art gymnasium with a
tartan-rubber floor would be the new basketball home of the Junior High
Rangers. Inside, the school was modern and contained a multitude of
brand new classrooms. A giant asphalt playground with four sturdy basketball goals is located in front of the school. The cafeteria area is nestled
between the gymnasium and the spacious band and art classrooms.

As an incoming fifth grade student, I liked the new school immediately. First off, there were lockers. It took me only 600 tries and two weeks
to work the combination to correctly open my new locker. However small
it was, it felt good to have your own designated space in this giant house
of education. Mrs. Karen Montoya was my fifth-grade teacher and I liked
her immediately. Also, I had the opportunity to meet the other kids in my
class…the Class of '87. In the old system we were all separated into the

neighborhood schools, but the middle school allowed us to all be in one place. Everything was new and it was exciting.

The middle school system was the trend in education at this time. It made perfect sense. Entire grade levels in one building allowed teachers to coordinate a more consistent curriculum. Rules set forth by the administration were consistent and applied to all students and the fact that everyone was in one place was just easier. Coordinating bus routes among five different grade schools was a thing of the past. Gone were days when Logan grade school students had to bus to Washington School to eat lunch. The whole middle school system was thought to be more efficient and the people of Benton were for the change. It all made sense.

As a fifth-grade student, the educational benefits of the middle school were the last thing on my radar. The first time I noticed a chink in the armor of this revolutionary middle school system was when it came time for basketball season. Winter was approaching and the Rangers were getting ready to begin the season and I'm thinking, "What team am I on this year?" What was going to happen with the fifth and sixth graders who wanted to play basketball? Benton didn't have five grade schools any more. Was there going to be just one Benton fifth and sixth grade team? It was a legitimate question that Coach Herrin had to address.

Coach Herrin: *Bringing everybody to the Middle School made sense…but it made it a lot tougher on our basketball program…I'll tell you that right now."*

Tim Wills was a sophomore on the 1980 team and is the oldest son of former junior high coach Burton Wills. Tim remembers his dad had this to say when the middle school first opened.

Tim Wills: *I can distinctly remember my dad saying that the opening of the middle school was going to hurt Benton basketball. He went through the numbers with me and explained how there would be less kids playing basketball… and he was right. Mark Kerley is a great example. He matured late and he struggled to play as a fifth and sixth grader. If there had been one Benton team, he may not have had a team to play on…but he played at Douglas in the fifth and sixth grade and he was on the team. It kept him involved and then look what happened. Mark developed into a very good high school player. There is no way we go to the Super-Sectional my senior year without Mark Kerley.*

I did play basketball that year. Coach Herrin divided all of the fifth and sixth grade boys that wanted to play basketball into six different teams. My coach was Steve McCommons and I absolutely loved it. But over time, the middle school format did not prove to be as effective as the old system of five separate grade schools when it came to developing basketball players. Tim Wills explains.

Tim Wills: *The coaches were teachers in the grade schools that cared about the kids and worked with the kids. It wasn't a parent that was strictly interested in their own child. We were so far ahead of the game at that time because if you remember…parents couldn't even attend the grade school games. The only people in the gym were the coaches, scorekeepers, officials and cheerleaders… that was it. We weren't able to look up into the stands at our dads…it was a great system. I don't think that there is any doubt that the varsity coaches that came after Coach Herrin probably paid the price for the new middle school system.*

In 1980, the Rangers returned a group of nine seniors; Curtis Smith, Steve Shurtz, Kent Yancik, Jim Labuwi, Jerry Corn, Brad Aaron, Rodney Potts, Steve Rusher and Dallas Carlisle. There were only two juniors; Mike Malcom, and Danny Lynch. Coach Herrin also brought up three sophomores; Tim Wills, Robbie Williams and Mark Kerley.

Toward the end of the '79 season, Curtis Smith established himself as the second scorer on the team behind Rob Hammond. Smith was a 6'1" guard/forward that went about his business in a quiet manner. He could really play. It was clear that Curtis Smith would be the go-to guy for the Rangers in '80. As a young player, Coach Herrin admitted that he wasn't convinced that he could contribute, but Smith changed his mind.

Coach Herrin: *I'll tell you something about Curtis. Curtis made himself a player. He played all the time and kept working…he turned out to be a great player and an even better person.*

Jerry Corn: *Curtis was a self-made player. I remember watching Benton Junior High play when I was in the eighth grade at Akin and I don't even remember Curtis. As a freshman, I remember playing with him…thinking, this guy can play. He was the ultimate gym rat. Always there way before practice shooting…and then stayed late to shoot.*

Smith won Herrin over by playing every day. He loved the game and endeared himself to his teammates by having a tough competitive nature that was often masked by his quiet demeanor. His teammates also loved his easygoing and humble personality. Curtis Smith was not a player that drew attention to himself. It wasn't his way.

Tim Wills: *Curtis was quiet but he was tough. Curtis, Mike Garret, Dave Jones…these were guys I wouldn't want to get in an alley fight with. I remember playing against Curtis in practice and if you relaxed…you got burned. He never took a play off. Some guys will let you relax a little bit…not Curtis. He was always going to the offensive glass. I think that is why he was such a great scorer. He was a fun guy to play with. Curtis didn't say much…he had a very strong confidence in himself without having to blow his own horn.*

Teammate Steve Rusher attended Douglas School with Curtis and they became good friends. He recalled fond memories of those early days growing up with Curtis on the east side of Benton.

Steve Rusher:*Me and Curtis would walk to the high school together when we were kids and watch the BIT. We watched the great Eldorado teams of Duff, Lane and Barry Smith. Olney had Larry and Gary Bussard. We used to have a big open field in front of my mom and dad's house and we would play baseball…break for lunch…go back out and play and break for supper. I loved that guy. As a player, Curtis was a pure shooter, a hustler and was always humble.*

I remember watching Curtis Smith play and I have this visual memory of him as a player. I can see him driving right baseline off the dribble, and then quickly rising up and hitting a baseline jumper. He didn't need much space to shoot it and I never saw him get his shot blocked.

Tim Wills: *He had that jump shot that he shot over his head and he would lean back making it virtually impossible to block.*

The point guard position in 1980 was shared by Steve Shurtz and Jerry Corn. Steve Shurtz played at 5'10" and sported a thick head of blonde hair. One of the trademarks of the '80 team was their toughness. Shurtz fit in well.

Tim Wills: *Steve was the point guard most of the time. He and Jerry were interchangeable. Steve was quick and a very good defender. The best stories of Steve's toughness were in cross country. He would literally run himself into complete exhaustion. He had a good sense of the game and was really hard-nosed. As a player, he had an ornery streak in him that served him well. He wasn't afraid to mix it up.*

Jerry Corn was the younger brother of Robert and Dick Corn and admitted that his brothers had a great influence on him growing up. He remembered attending his brothers' games in the old Cracker Box.

Jerry Corn: *You always look up to your big brothers… I don't remember Dick's games as much but I do remember Robert's games. I remember being with Mom and Dad at Mt. Vernon when Ed Sanders knocked Robert out. I was just a little guy and it turned into a scary moment for me. Mom and Dad had season tickets in the old gym. It would be zero outside and about 150 degrees in the gym. The place was packed and I had to sit on my mom and dad's lap when I was little.*

Corn played sparingly as a junior but did log important minutes in the sectional game against Effingham. Corn was a good athlete and much would be expected from him as a senior.

Tim Wills: *Jerry was a tremendous athlete. He was quick and strong. He was a great competitor.*

Kent Yancik: *Jerry was pretty savvy and knew the game. I always felt like I just played in the moment… I didn't think like a coach.*

In the paint, Jim Labuwi, Kent Yancik, Brad Aaron and Dallas Carlisle rotated at the two post positions. Labuwi and Yancik were the starters and Brad Aaron and Dallas Carlisle came off the bench.

As a senior, Labuwi played at an athletic 6'5", 235 pounds. For his size, he was light on his feet and his offensive footwork around the basket had improved greatly. He was a force to be reckoned with on both ends of the floor.

Kent Yancik: *Jim was a competitor. I remember him being such a good re-bounder and he could score a little bit. He could just move guys out of the way. I can say for a fact that he took a lot of pressure off of me.*

Senior Kent Yancik played sparingly as a junior but was much improved after competing each day in practice with Jones and Ward in '79. Yancik was a classic back-to-the-basket player that was extremely intelligent and had a soft touch around the basket. He had the ability to step out and knock shots down in the short corner and the elbow area. Yancik was tall and rangy enough to alter shots on the defensive end of the floor. He became a quality player and just what the Rangers needed to compliment Labuwi inside.

Jerry Corn: *Jim was probably 6'5"…and then you had Yancik at 6'4"…and just long. They gave us a presence inside.*

Kent Yancik is a classic victim of the basketball trap of the Ranger program. The trap is this; there were so many good players at Benton that some guys just got one year of varsity basketball. This was Yancik. Had Yancik been at another school, he probably would have started as a junior. It was extremely hard to play two years at Benton. As a youngster growing up in Benton, Yancik found himself pulled in by the excitement of Benton Basketball.

Kent Yancik: *I went to Grant School and Mr. A was my basketball coach. The 1975 team was my favorite team growing up, with Tabor and Dunbar. I just remember how packed it was…the lines for tickets. Basketball was the attraction in the town and the games were community events. I never really thought I was all that athletic but there was a system. The whole system and the atmosphere was something big that I wanted to be a part of.*

Backing up Labuwi and Yancik was Brad Aaron and Dallas Carlisle. Aaron and Carlisle gave the Rangers size off the bench. Most importantly, they could play. Brad Aaron played at 6'1", 180 pounds and was an athlete.

Steve Rusher: *Brad had a unicycle and would ride it to school when we went to Douglas together. Brad was a heck of a runner in grade school…and in high school he played football and became a very good pole vaulter.*

Tim Wills: *Brad and Jerry were possibly the two best natural athletes on the team. Brad was strong and could really run. He had a really strong upper body…he would come in at the post position for us. He was a key contributor for us. He was an outstanding pole vaulter in track. Dallas was a little like Curtis in that he started playing late. Dallas had good size and strength and there were some times that he really helped us.*

Steve Rusher and Rodney Potts were the reserves at the guard position. It was their job to play as hard as they could each day in practice to prepare the regulars. They did just that and they both loved playing for Coach Herrin. Steve Rusher grew up in Benton and attended the games growing up.

Steve Rusher: *Playing basketball for the Rangers was something that I had a great sense of pride in. Just being an athlete from Benton and being a part of that was really special. I went to Douglas School with Curtis Smith, Brad Aaron and Dallas Carlisle. Paul Lawrence was our sixth-grade basketball coach. I spent a lot of time playing pick-up games at Douglas School with Randy Smith. He was a little older and he always had red shoestring liquorish with him.*

Randy Smith still lives on the east side of Benton. Smith is a BCHS graduate of '72 and a lifelong Ranger fan. Although he didn't play basketball in high school, he loved the game and sat behind the bench to watch Coach Herrin's every move. Smith served as a mentor to Eric Forby and was an ever-present figure on the old Douglas School courts in the sixties and seventies. Smith is now sixty-seven years old, but he is still a huge Rangers fan.

Randy Smith: *You know, I remember when it got dark out…we would pull our cars up and turn the lights on so we could see and we would keep playing. In the winter, we would shovel the court off and play in freezing weather.*

Senior Rodney Potts enjoyed everything about his playing experience and admitted that he was pulled in by the success of the basketball program at a very young age.

Rodney Potts: *I'm still proud to say that I went to Benton High School and played for Rich Herrin. I went to Washington School and my sixth-grade coach was Gene Miller. I did go to the games…because it was the Benton Rangers. I was hanging out with my buddies of course, but I would sit and watch. I* *do remember Billy Smith and when I was smaller I just knew him as a great player but then later I realized what a great person he was. Coach Herrin molded him, and obviously his parents. He was a great player…but he didn't have to tell you he was.*

The juniors were Mike Malcom and Danny Lynch. Malcolm was an undersized post player that competed every day in practice against the seniors. As a junior, he played sparingly but provided great hustle and leadership on the '81 team. Danny Lynch was a solid football player and battled hard in practice.

Tim Wills, Robbie Williams and Mark Kerley were sophomores on the team. Williams and Kerley gained valuable experience practicing against the upperclassmen. Their time was coming.

Tim Wills' time had come. Although he was just a sophomore, Coach Herrin thrust Wills into the role of sixth man and he provided great guard play off the bench for the '79-'80 Rangers. He would play alongside guys that were two years older.

Tim Wills: *Back then, you didn't even make eye contact with any of the upper-classmen. There was a pecking order…so I just kept my head down and kept to myself. I remember I had a study hall class my freshmen year in the library and they would sit us three to a table. So this is like the first day of school and I got assigned to a table with Dave Jones and Dennis West. They were both seniors and were about twice my size. At first, I thought, oh boy, here we go. Dave could have broken me in half and Dennis was about as big as Dave and had a beard. Actually, it worked out real well, they kind of took me in and back then* (Big Team) *Dave Jones was bigger than life to me. They were good to me.*

Wills also gave credit to the upperclassmen on the team for making his transition to varsity basketball an easy one.

Tim Wills: *That year was really different…I was playing with guys that were two years ahead of me and the games really mattered. It was intimidating. I give the older guys a lot of credit…if there was any animosity about me playing as a sophomore, I didn't know it. They accepted me and I really didn't have to deal with that issue.*

Even though the season was young, Ranger fans were excited about the post-season. The enrollment cut-off line between Class A and Class AA basketball was set at 750 students. It was the first time in school history that the enrollment at Benton had fallen under 750 students. Because of this, the '79-'80 Rangers dropped down to compete in the small school Class A State Tournament. All of the other schools in the South Seven were still in Class AA. The Rangers fans were excited about the change because they felt the Rangers could make some noise in Class A. The possibility of winning a Class A State Championship was real. With the return of a talented senior class led by Curtis Smith, it could happen.

Jerry Corn: *We were excited. It was the first year that we were going to be Class A. As sophomores under Coach Phillips we were undefeated in both football and basketball. We felt like we were going to have a good year.*

On Friday, November 30, 1979, the Rangers hosted the McLeansboro Foxes in the opener. The Rangers started this line-up: Steve Shurtz, Jerry Corn, Curtis Smith, Jim Labuwi and Kent Yancik. Yancik was impressive. The Ranger pivot man turned and shot the ball with his arms extended high and released the ball at the top of his jump. Yancik had a soft touch. He was deadly within a range of fifteen feet. Affectionately called "Yank" by teammates, he was also a very intelligent player with a nose for the ball. Yank could read the carom off the rim and go get it as well as anyone in the league. Yancik was likeable, but most importantly, he was dependable.

Tim Wills: *Kent was talented. He was tall, lanky and very intelligent. He was a good defender and you always knew what you were going to get out of Kent each night. Kent could really play and was just so consistent.*

Steve Shurtz and Jerry Corn shared the point guard position and captained the Ranger offense. In the second quarter, Tim Wills hit a perimeter jumper for the first two points of his varsity career. He would go on to score 985 career points. Dallas Carlisle came off the bench to score 12 points, and senior Steve Rusher scored three points. The Rangers won the game by a score of 72-49. They were 1-0.

In game two, the Rangers slipped by the Pinckneyville Panthers by a score of 71-68. The Rangers were led in scoring by Kent Yancik with 22 points and Steve Shurtz added 19. On a positive note, the Rangers were finding ways to score without relying too much on Curtis Smith. Yancik raised eyebrows with his play in the post and the team looked to have more offensive weapons than they had anticipated. Jerry Corn scored ten points in the contest. There is a classic picture in the December 1st edition of the Benton Evening News that is telling about Corn as a player. Corn is high in the air with his arms outstretched anticipating a pass. The picture exhibits his athleticism and his tenacity as a player. Jerry Corn always played 110%.

Kent Yancik: *He was a competitor and always gave it his all.*

On Friday, December 7th, the Rangers defeated the Metropolis Trojans by a score of 73-53. After scoring just fourteen points in the first two games, Jim Labuwi exploded for a career-high 28 points to lead all scorers in the game. Labuwi scored every way possible. It was a clinic in the post and a boost of confidence for the big senior. The Rangers were 3-0.

Tim Wills: *Jim was just so big and strong...very athletic and quick feet for his size. He was kind of our enforcer on the team...and I think he enjoyed that role. We don't have near the team we had that year without him. He was a load.*

In game four, the Rangers traveled to Marion and passed their first test in the South Seven by defeating the Wildcats by a score of 92-65. Curtis Smith came into the game shooting just over 30% from the field, but he broke out for 28 points to lead the Rangers' scoring attack. He was joined in double figures by Jim Labuwi with 16 pointsThe Rangers were now 4-0 overall and 1-0 in the South Seven Conference.

In the final game before Christmas of '79, the Rangers hosted the Herrin Tigers. Again, it was Curtis Smith. Smith shot the lights out and led all scorers with 25 points. Yancik and Labuwi controlled the paint. The Rangers won the battle on the boards 43-22, with Yancik leading the way with 11 rebounds. Senior Gil Tope led the Tigers with 18 points, but it wasn't enough. The Rangers were scoring points and playing well. To this point, the bench play was excellent. Wills, Aaron and Carlisle were contributing. The Rangers were 5-0 and it was the best start since the great team of '75. Could the Rangers go to Centralia and win? Ranger fans were optimistic.

On December 27, 1979, the Rangers opened tournament play with the Edwardsville Tigers. The 6-0 Rangers struggled to a 56-49 victory by shooting 42% from the field and just 55% from the foul line. Again, Curtis Smith led all scorers with 18 points followed by Steve Shurtz with ten points. Smith was playing good basketball and had clearly emerged as the Rangers' main scoring threat. Yancik remembers what it was like playing with Curtis Smith.

Kent Yancik: *Curtis was awesome! He played so hard…and he wasn't flashy. He was our go-to guy. He always took the big shots. He was a great shooter…a great guy.*

The win over Edwardsville set up an afternoon match-up the following day with the Homewood-Flossmoor Vikings. The Vikings took the floor in their traditional thick, red-striped bottoms. The Vikings employed a tenacious zone defense against the Rangers that bothered everyone but Curtis Smith, who scored a game-high 30 points. The Rangers were down 12 starting the fourth quarter, but Smith single-handedly brought the Rangers back to within three, at 53-50. The Rangers then went cold and Homewood pulled away to a 61-52 win. Homewood's Tom Bramschrieber led the Vikings in scoring with 18 points. It was the first loss of the season and the Rangers fell to 6-1 overall and 2-0 in Conference play. Despite the loss, the Rangers had to be pleased with their fast start. Coach Herrin did show concern in his remarks a few days after the tournament.

Coach Herrin: *I think we're a better basketball team than what we showed at Centralia. It's a good start but we have work to do…that's all there is to it.*

The Rangers had a week off before their next big test in conference play. The Terriers were coming to town and they were led by Craig Bardo, Mark Ackerman and Mike Armour. The Terriers were loaded. They were the pre-season favorite to win the league. Entering the game, the Rangers were 6-1 and feeling good about themselves after a solid week of practice. During this week of practice, the team spent long hours in the gym without the anxiety of thinking about an upcoming game. The players had a brief time to relax. Coach Herrin even brought out the jug of Vitamin C during the middle of the week. It was a needed break.

On Saturday, January 5th, the Terriers came to town with the lead in the South Seven on the line. Ranger fans packed the gym hoping for a Ranger upset. The Terriers employed a full-court pressure defense that forced ten Benton turnovers and gave them a 17-11 lead at the end of the first quarter. The momentum then shifted to the Rangers as Smith and Yancik put on an offensive show. After the Terriers widened the lead to eight to start the second quarter, the Rangers went on a 9-2 run that pulled them within one point with 4:40 left in the half. Curtis Smith popped a 16-foot jumper with 1:18 left in the half to put the Rangers on top, 28-27. The Terriers scored the last four points of the half to take a 31-28 lead into halftime. In the third quarter, the Rangers went cold and the Terriers surged ahead. Craig Bardo scored eight straight points and Mark Ackerman scored baskets to extend the Carbondale lead to 53-42 at the end of the third quarter. The Terriers were able to hold on and win the game by a score of 74-63. Carbondale shot the ball at a 59% clip for the game and won the rebounding war, 30-24. Curtis Smith scored 25 points to lead the Rangers and Kent Yancik chipped in with 18 points. Mark Ackerman led the Terriers with 24 points and Craig Bardo had 24. With the loss, the Rangers fell to 6-2 overall and 2-1 in the league.

On Friday, January 11th, the Harrisburg Bulldogs traveled to Benton. The Bulldogs were struggling but were led by Randy DeMario and Rick Buchanon. The Rangers came out sluggish and fell behind 20-17 early in the second quarter. Smith and Yancik then took over and the Rangers built a 37-33 by halftime. It was all Benton in the second half, as the Rangers extended the lead and then cruised to 82-62 win. Curtis Smith scored 27 points and Kent Yancik came in with 21 to lead the Rangers' offensive attack. Smith was establishing himself as one of the area's top guards and was playing with unbelievable confidence. Yancik was doing his thing in the post and had become the Rangers' most reliable offensive weapon after Smith. Sophomore Tim Wills came off the bench to score 12 points. It was a feel-good night for the Rangers. The win improved the Rangers record to 7-2 overall and 3-1 in conference play. They were now in a tie for second in the league with the Centralia Orphans. To break the tie, the Rangers traveled to Centralia the next night.

When the Rangers pulled into Centralia the following night, they felt good about their chances. The players loved playing at Trout Gymnasium. On this night, Centralia head coach Jim Roberts was in the hospital complaining of severe headaches, and the Orphans were under the direction of assistant coach J.J. Dematti.

In the first quarter, the Orphans jumped out to a 17-4 lead before the Rangers cut the lead to 19-12 by the end of the quarter. Coach Herrin was assessed with a technical foul for protesting an official's call but it may have been a ploy to wake his team up. It looked to be working. The Rangers pulled to within 33-29 at halftime before Yancik was whistled for a technical for protesting an official's call. The Orphans pushed their lead to 49-42 entering the fourth quarter. The Rangers then made one last surge, but it wasn't enough. The Orphans won the game, 78-73. Centralia's Reuben McClain scored a game-high 24 points and J.R. Johnson added 19 to lead the Orphans offensive attack. Steve Shurtz played well and kept the Rangers in the game late with key baskets and led the scoring attack with 20 points. The team fell to 7-3 overall and 3-2 in conference play.

The Rangers then had two important games with the West Frankfort Redbirds and the Mt. Vernon Rams before the Benton Invitational Tournament. It was clear that the team needed to win both games to stay in the hunt for a conference championship. On January 18th, the West Frankfort Redbirds came to town under the direction of young head coach Tim Ricci. Entering the game, the Redbirds were 8-2 overall and 4-1 in the South Seven. Coach Ricci had the Birds playing and Frankfort fans flooded the Rich in hope of seeing their beloved Redbirds knock off the Rangers. The Redbirds were led by Keith Harpool, Keith Griffth, Matt Florian, Randy Lewis and Greg Cima. In attendance on this night was Doug Collins. Collins was playing for the '76ers but was sidelined with a foot injury and was at the game to watch his nephew, Robbie Williams, in the sophomore game.

The Rangers were ready to play and jumped on the Redbirds to lead 16-9 after first quarter play. They then extended the lead to 34-24 at halftime. The Rangers won the game 70-65 with the bench scoring 25 points. Both Tim Wills and Jim Labuwi led the way with 17 points. Brad Aaron came in and provided a spark by scoring eight points. All of his baskets came in key moments of the game. Keith Harpool led the Redbirds' attack with 20 points, followed by Keith Griffth's 16 points. With the win, the team pulled into a tie for third place in the conference with the Redbirds.

The following night the Rangers traveled to Mt. Vernon to play the Rams. The Rams were struggling for wins in the conference. It didn't matter. The bullseye was always on the Rangers back at Changon. The game promised to be a thriller. The Mt. Vernon colors of black and orange were everywhere and the Rams' student section openly shouted insults at the Benton players. It was typical. What a great rivalry. In the first quarter, the Rams built a 16-10 advantage, but the Rangers came back to tie the score at 31 at the half. In the third quarter, the Rams outscored the Rangers by six. The Rams were led by the great play of the Piper brothers and rugged inside play from Ben Dogan. In the fourth quarter, seniors Kent Yancik,

Curtis Smith and Jim Labuwi led the Rangers to a gritty 58-57 win in the Snake Pit. Tim Wills had two key buckets late and the Rangers stole one on the road. In the locker room, Coach Herrin was grinning from ear to ear. It was his type of win; a close game in a hostile environment. He had done it before but these types of wins never get old. Coach Herrin had these comments after the big win at Mt. Vernon:

Coach Herrin: *It was a great win…we showed some guts, and the win keeps us in the South Seven race.*

With BIT play starting on Monday, the team had a shoot-around on Sunday afternoon to prepare for Okawville on Monday night. In a move that many today considered to be genius, Rich Herrin changed the format of the BIT Tournament to a five-game round robin format. He invited the best Class A teams in Southern Illinois and kept the Class AA Olney Tigers (Coached by his brother Ron). The teams in this first round robin tournament of its kind would be: Benton, Olney, Pinckneyville, Okawville, Cairo and Edwardsville. Edwardsville was also a Class AA school from the St. Louis area.

The six teams would play five games in just a week. The tournament would provide the teams with more games, but it would also battle-harden teams for post-season play. Herrin organized the schedule of the tournament to emulate the final week of the State Tournament. At that time, the Super-Sectional was on Tuesday, and the quarterfinal game was played on Friday. If a team won in the quarterfinal game, they played two games on Saturday for the state championship. The final week of the State Tournament was a grind, both physically and emotionally.

So with that in mind, Coach Herrin set up a five game schedule on Monday, Wednesday, and Friday, and two games on Saturday. It was a grueling schedule. Teams that played well in the tournament used it as a springboard for the second half of the season, but if a team struggled, it could bury them. The tournament was the first of its kind. Because of its success, round robin tournaments began to pop up all over the state. Longtime voice of the Benton Rangers, Jim Muir, dubbed the BIT acronym as the "Best Illinois Tournament". Today, the tournament is a major event in the Benton Community and a week that all of the townspeople and businesses welcome. The BIT is still thriving.

In the spring of 1979, Coach Herrin was in the process of assembling the tournament. He wanted to invite the very best Class A schools in the area. One of his first calls was to Cairo head coach, Bill Chumbler.

Bill Chumbler: *I remember when Coach Herrin called me and invited us to the Benton Invitational Tournament. He said he wanted to invite the best Class A teams in Southern Illinois for a five-game round robin tournament. I believe it was us, Okawville, Pinckneyville, Edwardsville, Benton and Olney. He wanted to play the best teams and I don't think color ever entered his mind. I have a great amount of respect for him.*

Coach Chumbler knew that playing in the Benton Invitational Tournament was a good thing for his players.

Bill Chumbler: *First of all, we wanted to play against the best competition, but I think people had a perception about Cairo that we were a bunch of thugs and that wasn't true…I wanted to showcase these kids. They were good kids and people needed to see that. Also, I wanted to get my kids college exposure. I wanted the college coaches to see those kids and make up their own minds if they wanted them. We had to play in good tournaments for our kids to get seen and Benton was one of them…along with Eldorado for years and then the Carbondale Tournament.*

Chumbler was a great player at Mississippi State and then transferred to Murray State and became captain of a racer team that won the Ohio Valley Conference in 1968. He had a great love for the game of basketball and he always knew he wanted to coach. Chumbler's first high school coaching job was at Century High School in 1969 and was then hired by Cairo in the summer of '73. Chumbler was a tough man that understood the racial problems of the world around him.

Bill Chumbler: *When I first got to Cairo there was racial tension. Jesse Jackson marched in Cairo. I got the job in the summer of '73…Coach Chandler was let go and when I got there we only had nine games scheduled. They were all on the road. Nobody would come into Cairo and play so I picked up six more games. So, we had fifteen games, all on the road. I told the kids, "It's not your fault, it's the way it is right now and we're going to have to do a little extra." We're going to have to act right, clean up and display the utmost sportsmanship with the officials. One punch and everything we worked for could be ruined. People would say, "That's Cairo." I think that attitude is a shame. Our kids have proven that they deserve better than that. My first ten years at Cairo…we didn't have one player technical. I always had great kids.*

Chumbler knew that building relationships with his players was going to be the most important part of his job. Upon getting the job, he focused on getting to know his players.

Bill Chumbler: *Back then, Meridian owned Cairo. They were the best team in the Deep South. I was told in the interview that all I needed to do was beat Meridian. When I got the job our superintendent wouldn't let us practice in the gym…so I was young enough to play. I played college basketball at Murry State and at that time I was young enough to still play. I grabbed my tennis shoes and talked my assistant coach into going to Pyramid Courts in the projects of Cairo. The kids were playing there. When I got out…there were dice games going on and older guys had open coolers of beer on the other side of the courts…and then there were guys playing and a group sitting out watching the game. I pulled up in my car and got out and there were a couple of guys that pointed at me and began talking to each other…they approached me and said, "Are you Coach Chumbler?" I said, "Yes, do you mind if I play with you guys?" I went and grabbed my tennis shoes and played that day and I went back every day…and I started to meet my players. My superintendent didn't like me doing it and he called me in on it. That's what I had to deal with back then. I had fifty-six kids at our first tryout.*

For all intents and purposes, Bill Chumbler was the real-life version of television's "White Shadow." Chumbler knew the BIT would be a challenge and the travel would be tough on his players. Cairo was a full hour bus trip north on the interstate. He also knew that he wasn't going to get many calls from the officials. But he immediately accepted Coach Herrin's invitation to the tournament and Cairo remained in the tournament until 2009.

It is important to know that when Coach Herrin made this call to Coach Chumbler, he knew that Cairo was really good. He also knew they wouldn't bring many fans. It was clear that he wanted to play the best teams. Gate money was not the first thing on his mind. Herrin always wanted to play the best teams; therefore his players were expected to beat the best. Coach Herrin played all-comers and that type of courage filtered to his players. He didn't schedule teams to get wins. It wasn't his way. In my opinion, it was this "anywhere-anytime" mindset that he infused into his players that set the stage for his unbelievable run at Benton.

The Rangers opened the Benton Invitational Tournament on Monday night against the Okawville Rockets. They did not look sharp. The team shot 47% from the foul line and missed four front ends of one-and-one chances in the game. The Rangers played poorly throughout the game as they trailed 19-17 after one period and 31-25 at intermission. Okawville's Mike Blumhorst hit two free throws with .22 seconds left on the clock to give the Rockets a 56-53 lead. Steve Shurtz then hit an off-balance 15-foot jump shot to pull the Rangers to within one at 56-55. The Rangers then fouled Kevin Obermeier. Obermeier missed the front end of the one-and-one and the Rangers rebounded, but Steve Shurtz's 20-foot jumper bounced off the rim giving the Rockets a huge win on opening night. With the loss, the team fell to 9-4 and were 0-1 in the tournament.

In the next game, the Rangers matched up against the state ranked Cairo Pilots. It was the first ever meeting between the two teams and Cairo came into the game as the overwhelming favorite. The game was a 9:00 p.m. tip-off and a large crowd came out to see if the Rangers could contain the fast-break style of the Pilots. As the game drew closer, the players dressed for the game and the locker room was more quiet than usual. Kent Yancik remembered the moments before playing the highly-touted Pilots in the BIT.

Kent Yancik: *The Cairo game I remember. We had been somewhere to watch them play…I think I was with Curtis and Steve, and we had our Ranger jackets on. They saw us with our Ranger jackets on and started to talk to us a little bit, "You guys aren't nothing," stuff like that. There were only three of us…so we didn't say much back and then that led into the game. We played with a little more fire in that game. Everybody was mentally ready for that game.*

When the Pilots took the floor, they were met with boos from the Benton student section. The anticipation of the game was incredible. Cairo had one of the best players in the state in Anthony Webster. Webster was 6'7" tall and he was long. He could score around the basket and had a knack for altering shots on the defensive end of the floor. He was just a junior.

Bill Chumbler: *The story on Anthony Webster was…I first met him at the park. He was young and maybe 6'4" at the time. I noticed him and asked somebody who he was…they said his name was Anthony Webster. I asked him where he played basketball at…and he told me that he didn't play. He said he was from Kansas City and he was in Cairo visiting his dad. His dad was a guy by the name of "Switch" Wilson. I asked Anthony why he didn't play and* *he told me that there were players everywhere in Kansas City and he wasn't one of the better ones. I said, "You should come to Cairo and play." He said, "I would like that, could you call my mom and talk to her about it?" So I did. When I called her she was concerned about him moving to Cairo for various reasons and then I kind of forgot about it. School started and he wasn't here… and then one night I get a knock on my door, and it was Anthony. He said, "Coach, I'm ready to go." I said, "Welcome to Cairo, Anthony."*

The Pilots came into the game with a 15-1 record. They were expected to win. The Rangers trailed by as many as ten points early in the contest before they regrouped and ended the first half trailing 30-27. A tip in by Jim Labuwi and a fast break lay-up by Shurtz gave the Rangers their first lead at 31-30. Benton then finished the quarter in strong fashion and led 46-43 at the end of third quarter play. A jumper by Curtis Smith and three free throws from Steve Shurtz put the Rangers up 51-45 with 6:55 left to play in the game. The Rangers built a 65-57 lead with just 1:39 left but the Pilots battled back and cut the lead to 65-61. Curtis Smith then hit two pressure free throws to extend the lead with just .24 seconds left. It looked like it was over, especially with no three point line but Taurice Mallory scored two consecutive baskets and pulled the Pilots within two points, 67-65 with only .08 seconds remaining. Then, things got crazy. It was Benton's basketball on the sideline and Chumbler recalled the moment.

Bill Chumbler: *We were behind and Benton was taking the ball out of bounds near our bench. The official was holding the ball and he never would give the ball to the Benton player taking it out of bounds…he held it…I was yelling for our kids to foul. I was assuming the official would give the kid the ball but he continued to hold it. In that case if a team commits a foul while the official still has the ball it is a technical foul. If the Benton kid would have had the ball it would have been a one-and-one…and that is what we wanted. The official held the ball and called a technical. So, I was livid.*

The Rangers won the game by a score of 70-67, but Chumbler was fuming. As Chumbler and Herrin approached each other to shake hands, they engaged in a heated discussion. Fans from Cairo and Benton saw the awkward exchange and poured onto the floor. Bedlam then ensued.

Jerry Corn: *The biggest thing I remember at the game was the handshake at the end of the game. It looked like Coach Chumbler knocked Coach Herrin's hand away when they went to shake hands. People started coming out on the floor and Coach Herrin looked at us and said, "Get to the locker room." I went to the Tunnel and I was hollering at my teammates to come on. Coach Herrin then came through and pushed me back into the coach's office. He thought I was saying, "Bring it on." I remember Big Mac (Steve McCommons) was at that game and he came out onto the floor to help be the peacekeeper. It was a great win for us.*

I did ask Chumbler about the exchange and this was what he recalled from that moment that happened forty-one years ago.

Bill Chumbler: *After the game, we went to shake hands and I looked at him and said, "You (expletive) cheated us." Rich pulled his hand back and said, "I don't shake hands with somebody that uses that kind of language." Then I said something like, "You don't shake a lot of hands then." And that was it. It was in the heat of the moment and we were both trying to win the game. We left it right there and we became great friends.*

With the win, the Rangers improved to 10-4 overall and were now back in contention to win the tournament.

Kent Yancik: *We broke the Cairo defense down all night and it was a great Rich Herrin type of win.*

On Friday night, the Rangers defeated the Edwardsville Tigers by a score of 75-66. With the Ranger big men in foul trouble, Brad Aaron entered the game and scored nine points to spark the win. Curtis Smith led all scorers in the game with 18 points and Labuwi added 15. Jim Labuwi was having an incredible tournament. In the Cairo game, he led the Ranger scoring attack with 22 points. If the Rangers could win-out on Saturday, they could at least share for the tournament title.

On Saturday, January 26th, the players woke up early and got a full breakfast. In just twelve hours the team had to play two games that would determine their fate in the tournament. It would be nice to win that first tournament in the new format. The first game of the day was a 12:00 p.m. tip-off against the Olney Tigers. The Tigers entered the game winless in the tournament. The Rangers were huge favorites.

The Rangers started slow and struggled to score. Despite being 0-2, the Tigers came in ready to play. Olney guard Warren Wendling was having a day. Wendling splashed long jumpers and had 14 points at halftime. The Tigers held a stunning 33-14 lead at halftime. This was not supposed to happen. The Rangers laid an egg. It would be tough to come back from being down 19 points, but Coach Herrin set the goal of cutting the Olney lead in half to start of the fourth quarter. It didn't happen. The Tigers led 45-30 at the end of three quarters and Olney milked the clock to win the game by a score of 52-40.

Rodney Potts: *When we got beat in the afternoon session on Saturday by Olney...that cost us the BIT title. We just didn't play well.*

In the night-cap, the Rangers defeated the Pinckneyville Panthers by a score of 63-53. Kent Yancik led the Rangers' scoring attack with 21 points followed by Jim Labuwi's 17 points. With a tournament record of 3-2, the Rangers finished in a four-way tie for first place with Cairo, Okawville and Pinckneyville. This odd four-way tie raised some concern about the tournament, but there has never been a four-way tie for first place since. The tournament still remains one the greatest mid-winter basketball tournaments in the State of Illinois. With the win, the Rangers improved to 12-5 overall.

After the tournament, the Rangers took Sunday and Monday off to rest their legs. The team spent the rest of the week preparing for the second loop through the South Seven Conference. On Friday, February 1st, the team returned to conference play by hosting the Marion Wildcats. The Rangers jumped out to a fast start and led by as many as ten points and held an 18-11 advantage at the end of the first quarter. In the second quarter, Steve Shurtz supplied most of the Ranger offense by scoring eight points to push the lead to 28-21 lead at halftime. By the end of the third quarter, Curtis Smith scored ten of his game-high 23 points to extend the lead to 45-30. The Rangers then cruised to a 65-46 victory.

The following night the team traveled to West Frankfort to play the Redbirds. The Rangers sputtered early but were able to defeat the Redbirds by a score of 50-42. Steve Shurtz scored 16 of his game-high 20 points in the fourth quarter to lead the Rangers offense.

Steve Rusher: *Shurtzy was a scrapper and a good shooter.*

Kent Yancik chipped in 17 points. Keith Griffth led the Redbirds in scoring with ten points. With the weekend sweep, the Rangers improved to 14-5 overall and 7-2 in Conference play. At this point, the Rangers were one game out of first place, trailing only Carbondale and Centralia.

The following weekend, the eighth-ranked Rangers traveled to Herrin. A win at Herrin could pull the team closer to a South Seven title. In their earlier meeting in Benton, the Rangers had trounced the Tigers 71-53.

As expected, the Tigers came ready to play and jumped out to a 20-11 first quarter lead. The Rangers battled back in the second quarter to cut the Herrin lead to 35-33 by halftime. In the third quarter, the Rangers fought hard and tied the score at 38. The fourth quarter was full of exciting back and forth play and it looked as though the Rangers were going to escape with the win. With a three-point lead and less than ten seconds to play, Gil Tope hit a 16-foot jump shot with .09 seconds left to cut the Benton lead to 62-61. Coach Herrin then called timeout to set up an inbounds play, but the timeout allowed the Tigers' trapping full-court defense to set up. On the inbounds play, Herrin guard Gil Tope came up with a steal and passed the ball to reserve guard Scott Warren. Warren rose up and buried an eight-foot jump shot with only .03 seconds left. The Rangers inbounded the ball to Tim Wills and he misfired on a desperation heave to end the game. The Tigers defeated the Rangers by a score of 63-62. The Herrin crowd erupted and Tigers fans spilled onto the floor to congratulate their team.

Rodney Potts: *We took a tough loss to Herrin late in the year that really hurt our chances of winning the conference.*

With the loss, the Rangers fell to 14-6 overall and 7-3 in conference play. The Rangers were now two games behind Centralia and Carbondale in the loss column. The loss would make it extremely difficult to get a share of the conference crown. It was a tough one.

Here was the good news; the Rangers had an off night on Saturday. Coach Herrin used the extra time to prepare for Harrisburg and Centralia the following weekend. As usual, practices were demanding. There was no substitute for hard work. Guard Rodney Potts still remembers the intensity of Coach Herrin's practices.

Rodney Potts: *Practices could get a little intense. They were always full-speed and if you had a good practice Coach would mix up some Gatorade…but only* *if you had a good practice. During that time you were preparing for two games each week. We were in the South Seven Conference playing with schools that were bigger than us but everyone was afraid to play Benton because Coach taught us the fundamentals and we were so well prepared. When Coach would get excited, one word flowed into another…but you knew what he meant. He worked with us and he taught us about basketball but he was teaching us about life at the same time.*

On Friday, February 15th, the Rangers traveled to Harrisburg and won handily, 64-53. Kent Yancik led the scoring attack with 20 points followed by Curtis Smith with 18. The next night, the Rangers dismantled the first-place Centralia Orphans by a score of 84-73. It was a solid win. The seniors led the way with a balanced scoring attack; Smith, 22; Yancik, 21; Labuwi, 16; and Shurtz with 13. Centralia's Reuben McClain led all scorers with 31 points, but it wasn't enough. The Centralia win was the best the team had played since the Cairo game. The week of practice definitely helped. The Rangers improved to 16-6 overall and 9-3 in conference play.

After another productive week of practice, the Rangers traveled to Bowen Gymnasium for a Friday night match-up against the Terriers. The Terriers were ahead of the Rangers in the conference race and had thrashed the Rangers earlier in Benton. Basketball seasons are long and teams have their highs and lows. This was not the time to play the Rangers. The team was sharp. The extended practice time helped the Rangers re-group. On the offensive end, the team's execution could not be better. Their passes were crisp, cuts were sharp, and their timing was perfect. On the defensive end, the Rangers played scrappy and seemed locked in. The team was winning and they were playing with enthusiasm. The Terriers, on the other hand, were not. They had just been upset by Mt. Vernon. They were in a late-season funk. The Terriers were ripe, and the Rangers knew it.

The Rangers held a 36-34 lead at halftime. In the second half, the Rangers fought to stay in the game. The Terriers fought just as hard. With the game tied at 66, and just .10 seconds left, Carbondale ran a weave and got the ball to Billy Anderson who misfired on 16-foot jump shot. Kent Yancik went high and snatched the rebound, but was fouled just before the horn sounded. The foul sent Yancik to the line with a one-and-one attempt. There was no time left on the clock and the game was tied. For the game, Yancik was 0-4 from the line. Tim Wills remembered that tense moment in Carbondale.

Tim Wills: *At Carbondale, Kent gets fouled with no time left on the clock. If he hits one it's over. Carbondale called a time-out to ice Kent and we came back to the bench and all of the sudden Coach Herrin just starts going off on Brad Aaron for no reason. Kent then went to the line and hit the free throw. After the game, Coach Herrin apologized to Brad and told us that he didn't want anybody talking to Yancik during the time-out.*

Coach Herrin's ploy to divert attention away from Yancik worked and the Rangers pulled out of Carbondale with a huge win. When Yancik's free throw went down, a contingent of Ranger fans that made the trip celebrated. The win pulled the Rangers into a second-place conference tie with the Terriers. The Orphans had already won the conference by finishing 12-2. It was still a great win for the Rangers and a happy bus ride back to Benton.

On Saturday, February 23rd, the Rangers finished the season with a home game against the Mt. Vernon Rams. Ranger fans packed the Rich one last time to pay tribute to the nine seniors. Keeping with tradition, a short celebration honored the sacrifice and dedication of the players and their parents. All nine seniors and their parents were introduced before the game to a thundering applause.

This was also a special night for Rich Herrin. If the Rangers could win, Herrin would have 400 wins at Benton in just 20 seasons. At Okawville, he posted a 95-17 record in just four years. Overall, Herrin had a total of 494 wins entering the game. He was just six wins away from 500.

From the opening tip, the Rangers controlled the game. Curtis Smith dropped shots and Steve Shurtz and Kent Yancik played solid. Labuwi, Corn, Carlisle and Aaron contributed to the 69-57 win over the struggling Rams. The Rangers finished the regular season at 18-6 overall and 11-3 in Conference play. Coach Herrin won number 400 at Benton. All were happy. The players hung around the locker room after the game to savor the victory. The Rangers now looked forward to competing in the Class A State Tournament for the first time in school history. Most importantly, they had a good team. The town was beyond excited.

'80 State Tournament Play

The team opened post-season play with the Woodlawn Cardinals in the Norris City Regional. When the Rangers took the floor a sea of fans dressed in maroon jammed the lower bowl of seats. Woodlawn was no match for the Rangers. All twelve Benton players that dressed got in the scoring column. The Rangers won easily by a score of 79-58.

On Wednesday, February 27th, the Rangers played the Wayne City Indians. Wayne City tried to hold the ball, but the Rangers raced to a commanding 27-13 lead at halftime. In the third quarter, the Indians fought back to cut the Ranger lead to 35-26 heading into the fourth quarter. The Rangers then outscored the Indians by nine points in the final quarter to win a very ho-hum game, 56-38. With the win, the Rangers advanced to meet David Lee's McLeansboro Foxes in the Regional Championship. In the Regional Championship, it was too much Yancik. Kent Yancik scored a career-high 28 points to send the Rangers to the Eldorado Sectional. The Rangers won by a score of 78-57.

As the team bus entered town, the victorious Rangers were met with the traditional fire truck escort. Benton fans cheered as the bus slowly circled the town square and made its way back down East Main to the high school. It all seemed too easy. There were no Centralias or Carbondales. Where were the Mt. Vernons? Up to this point, Class A competition seemed like a cake walk. Next up for the Rangers was Ridgeway. Say what? Who is Ridgeway? It was too good to be true. Of all the great teams, the 1980 Rangers looked to have a chance. This could be the season.

On Tuesday, March 4th, the Rangers opened the Eldorado Sectional playing Ridgeway. In the first quarter, Curtis Smith scored all twelve of Benton's points to put the team in front 12-4. The Rangers took a 25-13 lead into halftime. Ridgeway played hard but trailed 35-22 at the end of the third period. The Rangers cruised to a 53-35 win. The win advanced the Rangers to the Sectional final against the Zeigler-Royalton Tornadoes. Again, it all seemed too easy.

On Friday, March 7th, up to 1,500 Benton fans made the trip to Eldorado for the Sectional Championship. The Tornadoes were led by big Jim Mitchell. For the Tornadoes, it was the Super Bowl. Ziegler is a very small town just minutes from Benton, and a win over the mighty Rangers would be an event the Zeigler-Royalton players would remember for a lifetime.

The Rangers came out tight in the first ten minutes of play and found themselves behind 17-14 early in the second quarter. The team then caught fire and outscored the Tornadoes 11-2 in a two minute stretch to take a six-point lead. Jim Mitchell kept the Tornadoes in the game by scoring a game-high 25 points. Ahead 45-38 with 3:55 to play in the third quarter, the Rangers went to work. Steve Shurtz and Tim Wills hit consecutive baskets to extend the lead to 13 points with 1:30 left in the quarter. Then another surge of Ranger baskets pushed the lead to 59-40 after three quarters. It was over. The Rangers then cruised to an easy 74-50 Sectional title. In fact, the game remains the widest margin of victory in a Sectional Championship in Rangers basketball history.

It was an excited locker room at Duff Kingston Gymnasium. The players celebrated. Sectional titles were special. Coach Herrin congratulated the team and talked about the schedule of events leading to the Super-Sectional on Tuesday, with Okawville. The team showered and looked forward to another firetruck escort around the square. Another new tradition had also developed. When the team won a Sectional, a small contingent of fans met at the gym for an informal reception. Players would speak and Coach Herrin always addressed the crowd. Kent Yancik remembers the little traditions well.

Kent Yancik: *Basketball was such an important piece of culture in our town and in Southern Illinois for that matter. One thing that stands out to me is the parades at the square as the team came back into town and the impromptu gatherings at the gym after the parade.*

There is a picture in the March 8th edition of the Benton Evening News of Kent Yancik holding the Sectional trophy high in the air with his warm-up top draped over the hardware. He has a wide grin as he acknowledges the fans awaiting the team's arrival at the gym. The team gathered at center court and the bleachers were pulled out on the south side to allow for fan seating. Coach Herrin addressed the small crowd and then several of the players spoke.

Behind the players, a giant banner was taped to the north bleacher that read, "Congratulations Coach Herrin on Win # 500!" The Sectional Championship win was also Coach Herrin's 500th career win. He had twenty-four seasons of high school coaching under his belt and was just forty-seven years old. He had gotten to 500 wins quickly and there was talent coming. In the impromptu gathering at the gym, the fans acknowledged Herrin's milestone. It was a great night to be a Ranger.

Again, the town of Benton was basketball crazy. Maybe this would be the year the team could bring back the trophy. The Rangers opponent in the Carbondale Super-Sectional was the Okawville Rockets. The Rockets were not a flashy team. They weren't as athletic as a Centralia or a Carbondale. The Rockets were very well-coached and fundamentally sound. But the Rangers matched up well. It was anybody's game. Jerry Corn remembers the match-up.

Jerry Corn: *They had a good inside player by the name of Moeller. He could also step out on the floor and shoot it and he gave us problems. At the guard spot they had Rennegarbe and he was just a fantastic guard. We matched up with them pretty well.*

Tim Wills was just a sophomore. He was wide-eyed and also remembered the Rockets well.

Tim Wills: *Gary Moeller was a really good player. Rennegarbe was a sophomore and he was really good. Both of those guys were very skilled and then they had two wing guys that were really good also. Okawville was well-coached and fundamentally sound.*

Southern Illinois basketball fans poured into the SIU Arena on Tuesday, March 11th, to see the Class A Carbondale Super Sectional game between the Benton Rangers and the Okawville Rockets. The colors of maroon and white clashed with the blue and orange of Okawville. At the end of the first quarter, the score was tied at 14. Both teams were adjusting to the enormity of the Arena and the spacious shooting background that can be the ruin of good shooters. Steve Shurtz led the Rangers with eight first quarter points. In the second quarter, the Rockets played well as Moeller worked his magic in the post. Curtis Smith struggled to find his shooting rhythm early and the Rockets took a 33-28 lead into halftime.

Ranger fans then began to realize that this wasn't Ridgeway or Woodlawn. The Rockets were very good. Rangers fans expected their team to be in command of the game at this point but instead found themselves down five. The Rockets were no joke. This was the first time the Rangers had been challenged in post-season play. No, please, not the Okawville Rockets!

Coach Herrin's defensive strategy against the Rockets was to play a triangle and two on Moeller and either one of the wings. Moeller was always guarded but the Rangers spontaneously switched off on the wings so there would not be a pattern. Coach Herrin felt that Obermeir and

Blumhorst were similar players, but Tim Wills remembers the frustration of the triangle and two strategy.

Tim Wills: *I just remember being in the doghouse in that game because we played a triangle and two defense on Gary Moeller and either one of the wings. I would come down on defense and pick up one of the wing players and the other guy would hit a jump shot. I always chose the wrong guy.*

In the third quarter, Curtis Smith began to find his stroke. He scored eight points and led the Rangers offense. At the end of three quarters, the Rockets led the Rangers by a score of 45-42. In the final period, Okawville led by as many as seven points before the Rangers made one last charge. Corn hit two free throws to cut the lead to 53-48 at the 4:44 mark. Steve Shurtz hit a lay-up 25 seconds later to pull the Rangers to within three points with 4:19 left. At the 4:00 minute mark, Yancik hit a jumper to pull the Rangers to within one point, 53-52.

From that point on, the game went back and forth. With .13 seconds left in the game, Gary Moeller hit a ten-foot jumper to put the Rockets up 58-56. Coach Herrin then called timeout.

Jerry Corn: *We called a timeout and Coach Herrin drew something up to get Curtis the ball. Well, they were all over Curtis… When Curtis received the ball in the corner he was double-teamed and so he passed it to me at the free-throw line. I thought it was going in when I shot it, but it bounced around a little while and by the time Yancik got it and stuck it back in…the final horn had sounded.*

Kent Yancik: *I can see the whole last minute of that game in my mind. I can still see that ball coming off the rim. We tried to get the ball to Curtis but they knew where it was going. Jerry took the shot and I remember I got the rebound after the horn had sounded.*

When the final horn sounded, the Rockets won the game by a score of 58-56. Gary Moeller scored a game-high 24 points and ripped the hearts out of the large contingent of Rangers fans. In his final Ranger game, Kent Yancik scored 20 points and Curtis Smith chipped in with 12 points. It was a gut-wrenching loss for Rangers fans. Coach Dave Luechefeld's Rockets went on to place third in the State Tournament. It was over.

In the locker room, the Rangers gathered one last time. An emotional Coach Herrin addressed the team and thanked them for their effort. The Rangers then showered and dressed in silence before boarding the bus back to Benton.

Kent Yancik: *I don't ever remember a quieter bus ride home.*

Although the Rangers didn't advance to the State Tournament, they created memories that lasted a lifetime. They all enjoyed their experience as a Benton Ranger.

Rodney Potts currently lives in Carterville and works as an engineer and has two children; Sydney and Bryson. He is proud that he had the opportunity to play basketball at Benton and admits that Coach Herrin had a great influence on his life.

Rodney Potts: *I only got spot time as a player…but a lot of us that were on the bench knew that if we played at another school we might have had the opportunity to play. Coach Herrin taught us life lessons about being prepared, understanding why you're doing something, and doing things with integrity. And it didn't stop when I graduated high school. Coach was very involved in me getting my official's license and even encouraged me to do games at the college level. He even gave me some games to officiate when he was coaching at Morthland College. I use exactly what he taught me in my engineering job. He invested time in me all the way up until the time he passed. He has definitely been one of the greatest influences of my life.*

Jerry Corn spent thirty-two years as a teacher, coach and administrator. Jerry spent up to seventeen years teaching and coaching at the Benton Middle School. He recalled the influence that Coach Herrin had on his life.

Jerry Corn: *Coach influenced so many people to go into coaching. I really didn't know what I wanted to do and I tried to get a job in the coal mines, but I couldn't get on. The mines were not in great shape at the time and there were few jobs available. My brother Robert was at UAB and he said, "Why don't you come down here and get your degree to coach and teach?" So that is what I did. I lived with Robert for a semester or two and worked as the team manager at UAB. I roomed with Bruce Baker for one year.*

Today, Kent Yancik is the senior director of Lead Frame Products. He and his wife Darlene live in Tempe, Arizona and have two boys; Justin and Andrew. Kent admitted that he passed on many of the life lessons he learned from Coach Herrin to his own children.

Kent Yancik: *My take-away from Coach Herrin was hard work, obviously. He was very process oriented. He was about trusting the process and doing things the right way and living with the results even if the results were not what you wanted. My son is a pitcher and I've used this with him. Maybe a pitch isn't working on a certain day…I will ask him, "Are you doing everything the right way? Just keep trusting that process." I use it today in my work life.*

Steve Rusher now works as a draftsman for Traylor Brothers in Evansville, Indiana. He is married to his wife Tara and they have two children; Rachel Lane and Luke.

Steve Rusher: *He used to get on to us pretty good in practice and he would say that if he ever quit getting on us then that was a bad sign. Coach was a competitor and believed that hard work would always pay off. He always got the best out of you.*

Curtis Smith married his high school sweetheart, Linda (Erwin) Smith. They have two daughters; Amber and Kelsey. Unfortunately, Curtis Smith passed away Sunday night, June 24, 2018. He was just fifty-six years of age. He is also survived by his parents; James and Virginia.

Curtis is missed by all that knew him. Curtis stayed in the Benton area and worked for the Department of Corrections. He was a humble Christian man and was everyone's friend. I am proud that he was my friend. He had a way of touching the lives of all those that knew him. Curtis earned All-State honors as a player in 1980 and was loved by his teammates. After high school, Curtis' true passion was coaching basketball and loved teaching the game. More than that, he loved his players. He was named the SIJHSAA Coach of the Year in 2015.

He was inducted into the Rend Lake College Hall of Fame in 2004, and still holds numerous basketball records. Teammate Tim Wills is now the athletic director at Rend Lake College, and he learned several things about Curtis' college career when preparing to speak on his behalf at his RLC Hall of Fame Induction Ceremony.

Tim Wills: *You know, Matt...I was looking at his college numbers and he played two years at Rend Lake and two years at Missouri Baptist. I think he had a thousand points at both places.*

Legendary Cairo basketball Coach, Bill Chumbler, coached the Cairo Pilots from 1972-1993. The school had never won 20 games in a season when he arrived. He won 16 Regional titles and averaged more than 21 wins during his 21-year stint. His 1981 and 1991 teams finished third in the state and he coached the Illinois All-Star team in 1993. His career record is 780-290. He was inducted into the Illinois Hall of Fame in 1992 for his coaching achievements. He is now retired and spends much of his time with family and is a big bass fisherman.

Something else happened in 1980 that took the town by surprise. After the Rangers lost to Okawville in the Super-Sectional, the Benton Rangerettes won the first and only state basketball championship in BCHS history. The team finished (25-6) and upset (23-2) Sidell (Jamaica), 52-42, to win the Class A State Championship. The Rangerettes were coached by Sally Niemeyer and they were loaded. The Rangerettes were led in scoring by the great Cheri Nagreski. Coach Niemeyer would go on to coach for seventeen years at Benton High School and was the first true trailblazer for girls' athletics at Benton High School.

As for the boys, the Rangers graduated nine seniors in the class of '80 but good basketball would continue. With three solid seniors and a talented incoming sophomore and junior class, the '81 team promised to be a fun team to watch. On to '81.

The Middle School concept was new and there were many advantages but it did not help the basketball program. Today, the Benton Middle School campus is responsible for all children Kindergarten thru the 8th grade.
(Matt Wynn Family Collection)

Tim Wills in the winter of '79. As a sophomore, Wills was the first guard off the bench for the 79-80 team. *(Ceasar Maragni)*

The 1980 Rangers. (Ceasar Maragni)

This picture represents Jerry Corn perfectly.
Jerry was high energy and played with great
intensity. *(Ceasar Maragni)*

All-Stater, Curtis Smith, drives the right baseline. Smith was quiet and humble but a fierce competitor. *(Ceasar Maragni)*

Steve Rusher was a reserve guard on the 79-80 team. Rusher grew up by Douglas School and went to the games as a kid. *(Ceasar Maragni)*

Randy Smith was a loyal Ranger fan. Smith could be seen behind the team bench with a scorebook and a pocket full of licorice. *(Matt Wynn family collection)*

Steve Shurtz played a key role at the guard spot for the '80 Rangers. *(Ceasar Maragni)*

Jim Labuwi was the enforcer on the '80 team. Labuwi was athletic and provided the team with rebounding and scoring in the paint. *(Ceasar Maragni)*

After getting spot time as a junior, Kent Yancik became one of the best post players in Southern Illinois as a senior. In the picture, Yancik goes up strong against Rocket strong man Gary Moeller. *(Ceasar Maragni)*

The Cairo Pilots entered the Benton Invitational Tournament in 1980 and
provided the BIT with memorable moments. This is a picture of
Coach Bill Chumbler with the '81 Pilots that got 3rd in state.
Coach Chumbler is on the far right standing and Anthony Webster
is 34 in the picture. *(Bill Chumbler family collection)*

Here is Coach Herrin after winning 400 against Mt. Vernon
in the last home game of the '80 season. *(Ceasar Maragni)*

Bill Chumbler was inducted into the IHSA Hall of Fame for his body of work at Cairo. Rich Herrin made the recommendation. Here is Chumbler again posing with the great '81 Pilots. *(Bill Chumbler family collection)*

CHAPTER TWENTY-SIX

Close Games in '81

"We just had trouble finishing games." – Tim Wills

On this Friday, I quickly jumped out of the car and ran up the concrete ramp to enter the Rend Lake College Basketball Camp. Camp started in ten minutes and I had to see what team I was on. It was close to 100 degrees outside but as soon as I entered the gym the air-conditioning quickly cooled my body. I ran down the stairs to check the board. I was a Celtic! Yes! I checked the other names on my team and decided that we could hold our own when it came time to scrimmage. I grabbed a basketball from the rack and shot around until camp started. Then the whistle blew, I racked my ball and hustled to center court. There were probably 40-50 kids in my fifth & sixth grade morning session. The campers came from all over; Benton, Pinckneyville, Sesser, Mt. Vernon, West Frankfort, Thompsonville, etc.

Coach Herrin led us in a defensive stance and reaction drill and we were then divided into groups and placed at stations where we were instructed by area coaches on the different skill sets of the game. In my opinion, basketball is the most difficult sport to teach because it involves so many skills. The coaches were high energy and really worked at teaching us the game. The camp was not designed to make money. There were two three-hour sessions and the camps taught the game of basketball through station work. The instruction was invaluable to young players. I was exposed to important basketball terminology that I would later hear from my junior high coaches. The coaches emphasized the importance of always being in an athletic position and catching the ball in a triple threat position. Even basic basketball movements such as pivoting and jump stopping were drilled. We were also exposed to complex basketball reads like back door cuts, curling or fading around a screen and even slipping a screen. There were stations that covered the proper way to set down screens, back screens and the execution of the screen and roll. Full-court drills like the five-man weave involving multiple players were taught, and you had to be watching in line so you didn't goof up the drill. Other important elements of the game such as ball handling, defensive slides, passing, lay-up shooting and rebounding were all covered. A popular drill called "square the corners" combined ball handling and shooting. There was even a station where campers watched old 18 mm films of NBA and ABA players teaching the proper way to shoot a jump shot. There were six goals, so there were six stations. Each group rotated to a different station on the whistle. We were only allowed to scrimmage after the fundamental stations had been covered. The camp moved at a fast pace and there was absolutely no standing around. I loved it. I was learning all the little nuances of the game that I loved.

To get an encouraging "that-a-boy" from one of the coaches was often the highlight of my three hours. On the last day of camp, free-throw and jump-shot competitions were held, along with three-on-three and one-on-one competitions. At Rend Lake Basketball Camp was the first time I ever received a trophy. In '80, I won the 1-on-1 competition and it became my goal each year at camp. Awards were always given the last day of camp and a picture was taken for the newspaper. Each camper received the standard grey t-shirt with red lettering that said, "Rend Lake Basketball Camp".

As we were getting ready for our awards ceremony on the final Friday of camp, Jack Sikma came walking down the steps in his Seattle Super Sonics warm-up. I couldn't believe it. I had seen Doug Collins before but never Sikma, only on t.v. Are you kidding me? I couldn't believe it. He was tall and had thin blonde hair. As he spoke to us, his green and gold Seattle warm-ups popped. He then showed us his famous inside pivot move. By learning these little intricacies of the game at a young age, the camps developed my basketball IQ and gave me a true understanding of the game. The Benton Rangers could think the game, and by the time I was in high school, I felt equipped with enough basketball sense to play the game the right way. As I got older, Coach Herrin took us to overnight camps as far as Sweet Water, Tennessee and Martin, Tennessee. These were team camps and it was common to play up to nine games a day. Honestly, these experiences at basketball camps provided some of my fondest memories. Growing up in Benton, opportunities to play basketball were always available and encouraged. This was my second summer at Rend Lake Basketball Camp. I was going to be in the sixth grade.

When school started in the fall of 1980, I was in Mr. Johnston's sixth grade class. Yes, Coach Bob Johnston, the former seventh grade basketball coach that helped Burton Wills win state championships at the junior high level. Mr. Johnston was no-nonsense and he was an outstanding teacher. I will just say this; there was no problem with classroom management. Mr. Johnston had us under control. He was very structured and conscientious about following the curriculum and we came to enjoy the structure. He did such a good job that no one dared give him a hard time. He had our respect.

There was an educational experiment underway at the middle school called open classrooms. The idea was there would only be filing cabinets and partial partitions that separated each classroom. I have no idea why the open classroom concept was attempted but needless to say, it didn't work. There were no permanent walls that separated the classrooms. As you can imagine, noise from other classrooms were a distraction and every teacher was conscious of keeping noise to an absolute minimum. It was not a very healthy learning environment and was eventually changed.

In the sixth grade wing, Mr. Finter's classroom butted up to Mr. Johnston's class. Mr. Finter was very sports-minded. He was always designing tournaments that encouraged his students to compete. During the football season, he divided his students into two teams and he would be the all-time quarterback. He was fun, and different.

Because of the open classroom concept, I could pretty much hear everything that was going on in Mr. Finter's class. One afternoon, Mr. Johnston had our complete attention as we were going over our spelling words. All of the sudden, Mr. Finter's class became noisy. Finter's students began talking loudly and I could hear desks moving. I heard Mr. Finter say that he would be the official and to make sure to keep the noise down. I thought, "What in the heck could they possibly be doing?" Then, I heard all of these muffled noises and out of nowhere a small orange nerf ball flew over the filing cabinets into our classroom. Mr. Johnston had a frustrated look on his face and said, "Matt, can you throw that back to them?"

Yes, Mr. Finter's class was playing a competitive game of nerf basketball. What was I doing? Spelling words. It just didn't seem fair. It was one of those moments you never forget when you're a kid and I have to laugh about it today. When I'm in a teacher in-service and we are discussing the best ways to effectively teach our students, I can't help but smile when I think of that nerf ball flying into our room and interrupting our spelling lesson. We all came out okay. Those were the days!

As for the '80-'81 Benton Rangers, they were a fun team to watch despite their 13-15 record. As usual, I went to all the games. In fact, I never remember a basketball season that produced so many close games. The Rangers played 28 games and 22 of those games were within ten points. It was a great season for the fan that wanted to see close games, but it was a frustrating season for fans that thought the team should win every game.

There were only three seniors on the '80-'81 team; Mike Malcolm, Billy Moore and Dave Bolen. Mike Malcolm did not always live in Benton, but the successful basketball program played a part in his move to Benton.

Mike Malcolm: *My family lived in St. Louis and then we moved to Marion. My dad got a job at Inland Coal Mine in Sesser, Illinois. My dad didn't know Coach Herrin but he knew Sue because they went to school together. He knew Coach through Sue and knew that he was a good basketball coach, so we came to Benton. When we came to Benton we moved into a relative's house near Grant School. When we finally moved to Benton it was between my sixth and seventh grade years. I grew from 5'0", 165 pounds to 5'7", 165 pounds in just six months. I didn't gain one pound. In St. Louis I played street hockey and soccer and then in Marion I did play basketball in a league but when we first moved to Benton one of my friends, Carl Hunt, got me involved in basketball. I played for Coach Whittington and Coach Carlile in junior high.*

Even though Malcolm arrived late to Benton, he attended the high school games and remembers watching the great teams of the late seventies.

Mike Malcolm: *When I was in junior high, me and my buddies would sit up in the bleachers above the hospitality room and keep stats for the BIT. We got to see players like Mike Duff from Eldorado, Craig Bardo and Johnny Fayne from Carbondale. When I was in junior high, Benton had great guard play.*

There was Ron Brookins and Rod Shurtz, Robbie Hammond and guys like Craddock and Tabor. All of that left a big impression on me.

Malcom played at 6'1", 180 pounds, and would have to play the power forward position. He was an undersized post player that played with tremendous grit and toughness. Malcom recalled a moment after the '80 season when Coach Herrin sat down with him and defined his role in '81.

Mike Malcolm: *After my junior season, Coach Herrin called me down to his office. We had just lost all of our seniors and we only had three seniors in my class. He told me, "Next year I need you. I need you for leadership purposes. I need you to play good defense…rebound and control the paint." That was my job.*

Another senior in '81 was Billy Moore. Billy was a 5'10", 155 pound guard with good quickness. Moore was now fully recovered from injuries he had received in a car wreck in November of his sophomore year.

Coach Herrin: *Billy is a versatile athlete with outstanding quickness. He is short of playing experience but has the qualities to make a contribution to the team.*

The other senior on the team was Dave Bolen. Bolen played at 6'1", 168 pounds, and was out for basketball for the first time in his high school career. Bolen was fun-loving and kept things light. He worked hard and fit in well with the team.

Coach Herrin: *He shows flashes of promise but lacks game experience.*

The junior class was loaded and it was the future. The juniors were; Tim Wills, Robbie Williams, Clark Dixon, Adam Furlow, Mark Kerley, Kevin Bickings, Ed Hungate, Dale Baker, Mike Crider and Ted Czuprynski.

Tim Wills was the only returning player that had varsity experience. Wills played a key sixth-man role for the 1980 "Sweet Sixteen" team. Wills provided steady play and much-needed leadership to a young club. He also had a good Farley Finter story.

Tim Wills: *I went to Logan Grade School and my sixth-Grade coach was Farley Finter. We would practice basketball at recess…and after school outside. We were in our school clothes. Farley had this book with plays in it that the New*

York Knicks would run. It was really neat how he did it. He gave each of us a Knick player's name...and he would run these plays with us and we thought it was great. We were playing like we were the New York Knicks.

Wills was a gym rat and grew up under the watchful eye of his father Burton Wills. He loved the game and believes that it was his dad's discipline that made him an effective coach. He told me a funny story.

Tim Wills: *My dad was tough and disciplined. My younger brother* (Brad) *did appraisal work for years and he was at this guy's house once and he introduced himself. The guy said, "What was your last name again?" My brother said, "Wills." Then the guy said, "Who is your dad?" My brother said, "Burton Wills." The guy shook his hand and said, "I've got respect for you...because you grew up hard."*

Tim told me that he was blessed with two great parents and that his father had a tremendous impact on his development as a player.

Tim Wills: *My dad had a ton of influence on me as a player. When he was coaching at Webster Junior High...I was going to grade school at Logan, which was adjoined to Webster. When I was finished with school I would walk through the junior high and go to my dad's practices. I remember playing one-on-one with the managers. My mom told me that I learned to add and subtract by reading the scoreboard of Dad's games and then trying to figure up how many points we were ahead. We were ahead almost all the time...because Dad's teams didn't lose much. I was fully immersed into basketball as a kid.*

Tim admitted that Billy Smith was his favorite player growing up.

Tim Wills: *Billy Smith was my hero. I wanted to be Billy Smith. He was a great student, great athlete and a great person.*

Coach Herrin had these words in the December 2nd edition of the Benton Evening News about Tim Wills before the start of the season.

Coach Herrin: *Tim is a complete player who could develop into one of the finest backcourt performers in Benton history. He can handle the ball and pass and also plays defense with abandon.*

The point guard job for the '81 Rangers belonged to junior Robbie Williams. Williams played at 5'10", and 142 pounds. He was extremely quick and very driven. He was not afraid to vocally push his teammates to work harder. Williams was a show-time passer that enjoyed a good assist more than scoring a basket. He dribbled the ball so low, it was a blur. The ball looked to be an extension of his hand. He enjoyed making plays that ignited the crowd and he brought an authentic emotion to the game that was different than all the guards that played before him. Defensively, he had quick hands and could pick opposing players clean in the open floor. Williams was a great point guard and was possibly the most entertaining guard in Ranger basketball history.

Williams lit up when recalling his youth and vividly remembered seeing Coach Herrin at his grade school games.

Rob Williams: *In the first and second grade I went to Logan School and Tim Wills and I had Mrs. Herrin for a teacher. Tim and I would sometimes slide over to the junior high because Tim's dad was coaching and we would shoot after school. In the third grade, I went to Grant School and got a uniform. Mr. A was our coach. I had a great experience at Grant…I played all sports. The competitions between the grade schools were big. Tim stayed at Logan. I can still remember those grade school games in Webster Junior High, and I can still see Coach* (Herrin) *sitting in the top row of the bleachers watching our games. Don't think we didn't know he was there, either. We always knew when Coach was in the gym and that gave us a little more juice. I can still see him up there.*

Robbie was a regular at all the high school games and has a great respect for all the Rangers that came before him.

Rob Williams: *We all thought so highly of the program because of Coach Herrin. I remember watching those games and just imagining myself being out there. I don't remember many games in the old gym. I do remember when the games were over…I would go down to the scorer's table just to get my hands on the game ball…the Rawlings RSS ball. I remember the Billy Smith and Robbie Dunbar teams. Billy was like the Swiss army knife of basketball…he could do it all. I remember when Rob Dunbar hurt his knee against Carbondale… remember it like it was yesterday. Tabor had to be the greatest shooter to ever play at Benton…he was incredible. Craddock was the first true point guard I remember watching. I liked watching Rod Shurtz play. He had a swagger and* *a cool factor that I really liked. I like to be a little spicy as a player and Rod had that…he was also a good leader and had some quickness. I loved watching Rod Herrin. He was feisty and tough. I was there when Robbie Hammond hurt his knee…he had to be the second best shooter to play at Benton. I remember Ronnie Brookins and the Sectional game against Olney. It was an unbelievable high school game.*

A huge influence on Robbie's life was his uncle, Doug Collins. Robbie was quick to point out in our interview what a great influence Doug had on his life both on and off the court.

Rob Williams: *Doug was like everything to me…he was my uncle, my dad, my brother, my friend and my hero. I've had so many opportunities by just being around him. I've been to the Spectrum several times with just him… to go to a '76ers practice. I saw Julius Erving and George McGinnis…it was unreal. His life experiences and the contacts that he has are unbelievable. Don't get me wrong, I loved growing up in Benton and I wouldn't trade it for anything…but being around Doug allowed me to see that there was a bigger world out there. We are as close today as we've ever been.*

This is what Coach Herrin had to say about Robbie Williams coming into the '80-'81 season.

Coach Herrin: *Robbie is super-quick…he is an outstanding passer, and he can also shoot it. Robbie just needs some varsity experience.*

At the small forward position was Clark Dixon. Dixon played at a lean 6'1" and was possibly the best athlete on the team. As a senior, Dixon placed ninth in the IHSA Golf Tournament in the fall and was starter on the basketball team that went to state and then advanced to the state track competition in the high jump in the spring. Dixon credits a hard decision by his parents to hold him back in the sixth grade for helping his success in the classroom and as an athlete.

Clark Dixon: *I went to Douglas School in the sixth Grade and my parents decided to hold me back a year. I was the youngest student in my class and it was a good decision by my parents because it allowed me to gain confidence academically…and then of course it helped athletically because I was able to* *grow and mature physically. Paul Lawrence was my coach in the sixth grade… the year I was held back…I wasn't allowed to play basketball.*

Clark also took a special interest in the basketball program because of his uncle and former Ranger, Steve McCommons.

Clark Dixon: *I started playing like a lot of kids back then. My dad put up a goal in the back yard. My hero was my uncle Steve* (McCommons). *He would sometimes take me to basketball camps and he took me into the locker room the night the gun was waved thru the window. I was real small…but he involved me in his basketball world a little bit.*

Clark Dixon was quick to point out that he had a very unique relationship with Coach Herrin. They were neighbors.

Clark Dixon: *It didn't hurt that I lived across the street from Coach Herrin. There were times Coach would say, "Come on Clark…we're going to the gym." Kyle and I were close in age.*

Clark often went over to Coach Herrin's house to play with the Herrin boys and he remembered the kindness of Sue Herrin.

Clark Dixon: *I also grew up across the street from one of the greatest ladies in the world…Sue Herrin. When I was little, I was different looking because of my cleft palate. Some people treated me differently and I could pick up on it too. She treated me as if I was her fourth son. She treated me like anyone else. She is the best.*

Clark often went to the gym with Coach Herrin and Kyle and would sometimes sneak down to the locker room. Clark told me a funny story involving Coach Herrin that ended up being a memorable life lesson.

Clark Dixon: *One time I was in the locker room with Kyle and the players were getting their ankles taped. There were always some empty tape rolls laying around the athletic table. But I took a full roll of tape home with me. When I got home, my mom asked me where I got the tape. She knew. My mom never asked me a question that she already didn't know the answer to. It told her that I took it from the gym. Mom used this to teach me a lesson. She took me by the arm and marched me over to Coach Herrin's house. I was terrified. She* *knocked on the door and I had to explain to Coach Herrin that I stole his tape. It made such an impression on me that I can vividly remember the moment even today. Coach Herrin handled it with grace and gave me a little scolding. My mom handled it with grace and gave me a lot of scolding. That was forty years ago.*

As a boy, Clark remembered going to the Rangers games in the old Cracker Box.

Clark Dixon: *My first recollection of the old Cracker Box gym was the dents in the floor. The team's bench was on the end in front of the stage...and there were literally dents in the wood floor where Coach kicked his feet. I remember running around in that old gym and it was so loud...so loud! I would not have wanted to be a visiting player in that gym. It was so hot in there too... even though it was the middle of the winter.*

Coach Herrin had these words about Clark Dixon before the '80-'81 season.

Coach Herrin: *Clark is a tremendous athlete. He has great quickness and leaping ability and is improving all the time as a player.*

Joining Mike Malcom in the paint was 6'3", 165 pound junior Mark Kerley. Kerley's father, Bill, had played on the great team of '61. Kerley admitted that he was a project.

Mark Kerley: *It all started in the eighth grade after basketball season. Me and Bryan Knight sat on the end of the bench. I remember Coach Carlile told me that it would be different in high school. It would be better. I made a lot of progress between my eighth grade and freshman year. I was a starter on the freshman team with Coach Webb.*

Kerley was a tremendous shooter and had a knack of getting to the foul line. He was pushed hard by his teammates and coaches. There was a need in the class for a big man and Kerley was the answer. He vividly remembered a day in practice he was pushed to the limit.

Mark Kerley: *I remember the yellow box. Coach made me step up on the yellow box on my tip-toes. One day in practice we did workouts with weighted vests. We all had to wear these weighted vests and Coach was really getting on* *me pretty good for slacking…he would say, "Suck it up." When the workout was over we all handed coach our weighted vests. He was collecting all of them and then I handed him mine…and his arm collapsed. All of the other players had one five-pound weight in their vests….and I had three. Coach Herrin said something like, "Sorry about that, big guy…I didn't know…" I thought…Yeah, right.*

Kerley credits all of those open gym hours he played in the summer for his rapid improvement.

Mark Kerley: *I mowed yards in the summer. I would get up every morning and go in and play in open gym…leave open gym and then go mow yards until early afternoon…and then come back and play at night. We played on Monday and Thursday nights at Benton and on Wednesdays at Rend Lake College.*

Mark also remembered going to all the Rangers games growing up.

Mark Kerley: *I went to Grant School and I played for Mr. A. Every Friday and Saturday nights my family went to the games. I remember Billy Smith and Steve McCommons.*

Coach Herrin worked long hours to develop Mark Kerley in the off-season and it paid off in a big way. These were Coach Herrin's comments about Mark entering his junior season:

Coach Herrin: *He has the talent…he just needs the experience. Mark has worked hard and he will help us.*

Coming off the bench and playing a key role for the Rangers the next two seasons was 6'3" Adam Furlow. Furlow played extremely hard and was loved by his teammates for his willingness to do anything to help the team win.

Tim Wills: *Pressure didn't bother Adam and he could shoot it. I think he had the same level of confidence as everyone else.*

Juniors Dale Baker and Kevin Bickings would be the back-up guards and provided quality competition for the regulars in practice.

Coach Herrin: *Bickings and Baker are good competitors and will give us hustle off the bench.*

Ed Hungate played at 6'1", 182 pounds, and came off the bench to provide depth in the post. Hungate was a tremendous football player, and the son of assistant Benton football coach Ken Hungate. Ed would go on to play football at the University of Illinois.

Coach Herrin: *Eddie's a very physical player who could see varsity action and give us some needed rebounding help.*

Juniors, Mike Crider and Ted Czuprynski rounded out the team and saw junior varsity action. They were both good teammates and competed hard in practice. This was the '81 team.

How good were the young Rangers going to be? That was the question. Yancik, Smith, Labuwi, Corn and Steve Shurtz were gone from the year before. One thing was sure, the juniors were going to get the game experience they needed and there was a good freshman class on the way. It looked as though the young Rangers were a year away, but they would battle.

It was clear when the Rangers took the floor against the McLeansboro Foxes in the opener that the leadership of the team would center on guards Tim Wills and Robbie Williams. On offense, the ball was in their hands 90% of the time. They were clearly the engines of the young team but they were not clear about what to expect before the year began.

Tim Wills: *We thought we were going to be better than our final record (13-15). We had three seniors on that team with me, Robbie, Clark and Mark. Adam Furlow also played a little bit our junior year. In no way did we think we were going to be below .500 and not win a regional. We just had trouble finishing games. We lost a lot of close games in '81. There were times that we needed a basket and we just didn't have a go-to guy to get us that basket.*

Rob Williams: *I remember running out for warm-ups thinking…this is varsity basketball…here we go. I really never had a feeling of how we were going to be. Tim was the only guy that had any varsity experience. I was just trying to figure it out, learn and win at the same time. I always wondered what Coach thought when we took the floor in '81. Did he see the big picture? He kept those thoughts close to the vest. I always wondered.*

At McLeansboro, The Rangers won the opener 74-70 in overtime. Tim Wills led the Rangers in scoring with 27 points followed by Mark Kerley's 16 points. Rob Williams chipped in 14 points. Williams had a glowing debut by handing out nine assists, and many of those went to much-improved post player, Mark Kerley. Kerley's 16 points were a good sign. The Rangers needed some points from the paint. Wills played steady and shot the lights out from the outside.

After the opener, the Rangers fought to a 4-2 record entering the Centralia Holiday Tournament. The Rangers had also beaten Metropolis, Okawville and Herrin. Their only two losses were to Pinckneyville and Marion. Every game was close and the young Rangers were fun to watch because of their underdog appeal.

In the Centralia Tournament, the Rangers were defeated in the first game by Homewood-Flossmoor by a score of 70-50. The team then came back the next day to defeat Rich East by a score of 54-40. Wills and Williams combined for 33 points to lead the Rangers' scoring attack. Unfortunately, the Rangers were ousted by Chicago Marist, 68-60. The young Rangers were 5-4 overall and 4-2 in South Seven play.

A big positive from the Centralia Tournament was the play of 6'3" reserve forward Adam Furlow. Furlow played well at both ends of the floor and was earning the confidence of Rich Herrin. The bright lights of the Centralia Tournament did not bother Furlow. He hit key baskets and battled hard on the boards. It was a sign of good things to come because he would play a huge role in the team's success for the next two seasons.

In the next five games, the Rangers were only able to win one game. The Rangers suffered narrow defeats to Carbondale, Centralia, West Frankfort and Mt. Vernon. Their only win was a 65-58 victory over the Harrisburg Bulldogs. The West Frankfort loss was a back-breaker. Keith Griffth's 15-foot jumper with time running out propelled West Frankfort to a 57-55 victory over the Rangers. Griffth led all scorers with 30 points for the night. The Rangers then lost another heart-breaker to the Mt. Vernon Rams by a score of 55-53. It was the first time the Rams had ever won in Benton's new gymnasium. The Rangers were 6-8 overall and 2-5 in conference play. There seemed to be a persistent problem.

Tim Wills: *We had trouble finishing games in '80-'81.*

This was the low point of the year for the Rangers. They had lost four out of five heading into the BIT. It was not going to get any easier. They had to find ways to win and the team knew that the stiff competition in the tournament would make them a better club.

The young Rangers battled through a grueling week of basketball to end the tournament at 2-3. Although the Rangers were competitive, they suffered losses to Cairo, Edwardsville, and Pinckneyville. All of the losses were within six points. The team was improving, but it wasn't showing up in the win column. The Rangers defeated Okawville and Olney for their only two wins of the tournament. Edwardsville won the 1981 BIT by finishing a perfect 5-0. The '81 Rangers were now 8-11 overall with one loop to go through the South Seven.

The high point of the season began on January 30, 1981, with an 80-64 win at Marion. The Wildcats had defeated the Rangers in their first meeting, but not this time. Mark Kerley led the Rangers in scoring with 18 points and Robbie Williams chipped in 15 points. It was a sign that the tough competition was paying off. The next night, the Rangers hosted the West Frankfort Redbirds. Still seething from the buzzer beater by Keith Griffth, the Rangers played tight. They were behind 41-28 entering the fourth quarter but the Rangers made a furious comeback to tie the score at 46. The Redbirds turned the ball over with seconds remaining and Coach Herrin called a quick timeout. After the timeout, Williams pushed the ball up the floor and passed to Clark Dixon on the right wing. Dixon's shot caromed off the front of the rim and Mike Malcolm tipped the ball in just before the horn to give the Rangers a thrilling 48-46 victory.

Mike Malcolm: *It bounced off the front of the rim and I just went up and tipped it in.*

Coach Herrin: *It was the best comeback I've ever been a part of…coming from that far back that quickly.*

Malcolm only scored four points for the night, but he was definitely playing out the role that Coach Herrin had defined for him the previous spring. All of Malcolm's teammates agreed that if anybody deserved that tip-in, it was Malcolm. Mike Malcolm was not the leading scorer of the team, but he had endeared himself to his teammates by his willingness to place the team's success above his own accolades. Malcolm was an unselfish senior surrounded by a group of talented juniors that were just a year away. You could just see it. Winning basketball was coming and

Malcolm's team-first attitude helped his young teammates grow in their abilities throughout the trials of the '81 season.

Rob Williams: *Malc was a lunch-pail guy…You always knew what you were going to get out of Mike Malcom. He always gave everything he had. I looked up to Malc because he was a year older. He was a great teammate…a tough guy and he gave us a little football mentality.*

Tim Wills: *Mike Malcom was a 6'1" post player who did a really good job for us. He played hard inside.*

Clark Dixon: *Mike was blue-collar. He had good hands and he was very strong. He was a good teammate and he contributed offensively more than he realized. There were several times that we ran plays through him.*

In my interview with Mike, he told me about a conversation that he had later in his life with Coach Herrin. I wanted to share it because it was very telling of the kind of teammate Malcolm must have been and it also revealed his feelings about his old coach.

Mike Malcom: *I hadn't seen Coach Herrin since I graduated from high school. My son was going to basketball camp at McKendree College one summer and I had to send the check to Carterville, Illinois. I assumed that was where he lived. So I sent the check. A couple days later I get a call on the phone and it was a Carterville number. At first I thought, I bet I filled out the application wrong…then I picked it up. Coach says, "Hey…hey…is this Mike Malcom?" I said, "Yeah, Coach." He said, "Is this the Mike Malcom that played for me?" I said, "Yeah, Coach." I bet we talked for close to an hour…and he brought up all kinds of things that I had forgot about. In our conversation he said, "I probably abused you a little bit…you always had to guard the best post player." I said, "Coach, you sat me down and told me what my job was…when I guarded a great player like Anthony Webster, I knew I wasn't going to shut him down, but it was my job to stop him from getting his 20 points a game. If I could hold him to 15 or something like that it would give us a chance. I took great pride in that role. I try to tell my son, "Hey, not everybody can be the scorer…it takes role players to have a great team. When I took my son to camp…I talked to Coach and got a picture with him and he got to meet my son. I love that guy.*

Malcolm had also befriended Mark Kerley. He had taken the junior under his wing and he was not resentful when Mark was the one scoring the points in the paint.

Mark Kerley: *Mike was a big boy…we always got along well together.*

The Rangers then defeated Herrin and Harrisburg to run their record to 12-11 overall and 6-5 in league play. The Rangers had won four straight conference games. In the Harrisburg game, Tim Wills scored 29 points and the Rangers won the game 106-78. It was an offensive explosion for a team that averaged just less than 60 points a game.

The Rangers then dropped their last three conference games of the year to Centralia, Carbondale and Mt. Vernon. It was a disappointing end to the regular season. In the last regular season game, the Mt Vernon Rams blew the Rangers away in the Snake Pit by a score of 81-48. The Rangers finished the season 12-14 overall and 6-8 in conference play. To avoid finishing less than .500, the team had to win the Regional Tournament.

Here is the good news; because of their enrollment, the Rangers competed in the Class A State Tournament for the second year in a row. On Wednesday, February 25, 1981, the Rangers opened Regional play with the Bluford Trojans. The Rangers won the game 77-55 to advance to the Regional semi-finals to play the West Frankfort Redbirds. Clark Dixon led the team in scoring with 15 points followed by senior Billy Moore. Senior Dave Bolen also got in on the fun and scored five points in the last four minutes of the game.

Mike Malcolm: *Billy was a good player. He was a good ball handler and he had a nice outside shot.*

Clark Dixon gave me some insight into the forward thinking of Coach Herrin in '81. He believed Herrin was coaching his heart out in the present, but also planning for the future.

Clark Dixon: *There were times as a junior that I would practice with the varsity after school and then jump into coach's station wagon and go play a j.v. game. I remember he would tell me in those car rides to step up and be a leader. He wanted me to take control of those games. He would challenge me to step up and be more of a leader. Coach Herrin made me step my game up. He expected more of me than I expected of myself.*

A sea of maroon flooded Max Morris Gymnasium to see if their Rangers could take two out of three from the Redbirds. The teams had split 1-1 and both games came down to the final possession. In a nail-biter, the Redbirds defeated the Rangers in overtime by a score of 61-60. Redbird fans flooded the floor to celebrate their first regional victory over the Rangers since Herrin arrived at Benton. Jeff Moore led the Redbirds in scoring with 14 points and Keith Griffth added ten points. You would have thought the Redbirds won the Super Bowl as they celebrated the semi-final victory after the game.

The dejected Rangers walked slowly across the floor to their locker room. There had been so many Ranger championships celebrated in this very locker room, but not tonight. It was over. The Rangers sat quietly and waited for Coach Herrin. Redbird fans could be heard celebrating through the thick concrete walls. It was a terrible feeling. And even worse, it was the first Ranger team to finish below the .500 mark since the 1963-64 team finished 11-14. Rob Williams vividly remembered that moment.

Rob Williams: *The thing that motivated me going into my senior year was our loss in the Regional Tournament against West Frankfort. We had a big lead and we choked. I'll never forget walking down those steps and turning right and going into the locker room after we got beat. That was all I needed to motivate me for my senior season. It was the most disappointing loss I had in high school. I was devastated.*

Although the varsity season was over, there was one basketball tournament left to play: the Murphysboro Sophomore Tournament. The Sophomore Tournament was always late in the year, and it gave the sophomores the opportunity to play some extra games. The competition was always good. Coach Herrin made the trip to Murphysboro to see his sophomore Rangers play. As he sat in the bleachers and thought about the future, a freshman Ranger by the name of Bruce Baker was dominating the tournament. He was a special player and Herrin knew it. He thought about bringing Baker up to the varsity level as a freshman but decided against it. As he watched Baker play, he knew that this was the player he would build his team around for the next three years. As for the talented junior class, they now had a full year of varsity basketball under their belts and they would now pick up Baker. Much was to be expected of the '82 Rangers and they would not disappoint.

Senior, Mike Malcolm is now retired after serving as a major in the Department of Corrections. He has three children; Blaine, Linzie and Leighton. He loved playing for the Rangers and said this about Coach Herrin:

Mike Malcolm: *Coach Herrin was a great basketball coach…but he was a great molder of young people. Look at all the players who have gone on to do great things with their lives…well, I attribute Coach Herrin as a big part of that. Coach Herrin was one of those guys that if he said something he meant it. There is a saying, I say what I mean, and I mean what I say. That was who he was…it didn't matter if you were the first player or the fifteenth player.*

On to the great team of '82!

God blessed me with two great parents that sent me to every basketball camp possible and never missed a game. The reason I had such a great childhood is because of my dad (Mack) and mom (Juva). Here we are in the winter of '81. I was 12. *(Matt Wynn family collection)*

Coach Herrin giving instruction at Rend Lake Basketball Camp. *(Ceasar Maragni)*

Coach Herrin with Rend Lake Coach, Jim Waugh, at basketball camp. Coach
Waugh coached many Rangers while at Rend Lake and was
truly a gentleman. *(Ceasar Maragni)*

A great picture of the senior leader of the Rangers in '81, Mike Malcolm.
Malcolm played hard and accepted the role of rebounder and defender.
(Ceasar Maragni)

Tim Wills takes it to the hoop in the dramatic comeback against the Redbirds. *(Ceasar Maragni)*

Rob Williams with a tear drop over the Terrier defenders. Williams was a great player that could bring the crowd to its feet with no-look passes and nifty ball-handling skills. *(Ceasar Maragni)*

Clark Dixon trapped in the corner at Changnon Gymnasium.
Dixon was a fierce competitor that gave the Rangers lock-down
defensive play and clutch scoring. *(Ceasar Maragni)*

Senior, Billy Moore, gave the Rangers quality minutes off
the bench in '81. *(Ceasar Maragni)*

The Machine. Mark Kerley found his way in the post and
became a scoring machine in 81-82. *(Ceasar Maragni)*

Coach Herrin signals for one of his players to enter the game.
(Southern Illinoisan Library)

Dave Bolen was a senior on the '81 team. *(Ceasar Maragni)*

A great picture of the '81 Rangers. **Front Row-** Scott, Williams, Bickings, Baker, Crider, Summers **Row 2-** Hungate, Bolen, Kerley, Malcolm **Row 3-** Allen, Dixon, Furlow, Herrin, Czuprinski, Moore, Wills.
(Ceasar Maragni)

CHAPTER TWENTY-SEVEN

Winning with Style in '82

"Our senior year was the culmination of a lot of work that came to fruition. It was the best year I ever had playing basketball." – Rob Williams

In the fall of 1981, I was now in the seventh grade. It was a big move. The junior high wing of the Benton Middle School was located behind the library that was nestled in the center of the school. The locker area was more spacious than that of the fifth and sixth grade area. P.E. was now mandatory and we were expected to shower after class, which made for some interesting stories. What was really exciting for me about junior high, was the basketball. Tom Whittington was my seventh-grade coach, and he was a good one. I didn't know it at the time, but he was a key player on the '61 team. Coach Whittington stressed discipline and fundamentals.

In our first seventh grade game of the year, we played the West Frankfort Redbirds. The game was at West Frankfort. Physically, our team was small and weak compared to the Redbirds. Unfortunately, the Birds were strong and quick. Many of their players were already physically mature. Their arms bulged with young muscle and many players had armpit hair. Not a good sign. The Birds pushed us around and blew past us off the dribble. It was a frustrating night to say the least. The Redbirds defeated us that night by a score of 33-8. I'll never forget looking at the scoreboard after the game and thinking; what is wrong with us? I had grown up watching the Rangers win and then we do this. Are we really this bad? Coach Whittington was frustrated too, but he quickly embraced the fact that we were a work in progress. He never quit coaching us and we improved as the year continued.

Something else happened in the fall of '81 that was a complete game changer. My grandpa, Gwen Wynn, along with my parents, surprised me with one of the greatest gifts of my childhood. A new basketball goal complete with an asphalt playing surface. I'll never forget that cold, rainy day. Grandpa was the Benton Township Supervisor and he always wore a suit with black wing tip shoes. We were big buddies. On this day, he sported a black overcoat with a checkered hat. When he arrived, he motioned me to come outside. I hustled outside and saw two men placing a heavy black pole into the ground. It was a new basketball goal. I was ecstatic. My dad made a regulation-size wooden backboard that bolted to the pole. The backboard was painted white with a bright orange square in the center. It looked very official. Dad then fastened the orange rim to the backboard and then ran the new white nylon net thru the eyelets of the rim. The goal looked beautiful. Despite the drizzle and cold, the black asphalt was poured and smoothed out. It was a state-of-the-art playing surface. To me, it looked like the Boston Gardens.

I then grabbed my indoor/outdoor MacGregor ball and lost myself in shooting the basketball. I shot constantly. I invited my friends over and we played all the time. My house became the place where all of my friends gathered. That basketball goal contributed a lot of great memories to my childhood. I wish I had a dollar for every shot I took on that goal. My dad eventually put lights up on both sides of the goal, allowing me to play at night. Before I got my driver's license, I spent much of my time on this court playing the game I loved. In the winter, I shoveled the snow off the asphalt and played. As I shot the ball, the songs of Midnight Star and Earth, Wind & Fire blared through the neighborhood from my jam box. Those were the days. I am convinced that this court gave me the opportunity to improve my game to the point that I was able to play in college.

I was now playing junior high basketball. I had a brand new court. But the thing I remember most about my seventh grade year was watching the '81-'82 Rangers. They were electric. The team had personality and they played the game with excitement and flair.

The guard play was incredible. In my opinion, Robbie Williams and Tim Wills rank as one of the best guard tandems in Benton basketball history. They had a telepathic sense between them and they complimented each other so well. They had grown up together and had competed against each other from an early age. Being a seventh grader, I remember times in open gym when Robbie and Tim guarded each other, and it would get heated. The intense competition between the two challenged each of them to improve their game. By the time they were seniors, they were two of the best guards in the State of Illinois. Despite the healthy competition on the floor, they are still the best of friends and have great respect for each other.

Tim Wills: *Robbie and I are related and were good friends. We were both competitors. We never came to blows…but we competed hard against each other in open gyms. The things he did better than me forced me to work on those things…and the things I did better than him forced him work on those things. Today, the whole competition thing is over except for golf. Robbie was a great passer and ball handler…super quick…and he had great court vision. He was a true point guard. My senior year, we played a two-guard front and it probably put me in a position to handle the ball more and it helped me. It was a lot of fun playing off of Robbie.*

Rob Williams: *To me…Tim was the best…but I wanted to be good too. When it came to competition, we both wanted to beat each other. Coach fostered that competition also. There were a lot of times he matched us up against each other. We didn't want to lose. The competition allowed us to see our strengths and weaknesses. We were both bad losers. Tim and I are very different people. Tim is more likely to think before he says something and is a little more reserved than me. I'm more emotional but when it came to basketball we were a lot alike. We both played to win…even if it was a test at school…we competed. To me…Tim was the best. We had our battles, of course we did… we had success together and hard times. He was my guy.*

Adding to the great guard play of '82 was junior Kyle Herrin. Kyle was no longer the Rangers mascot. It was now his time to make his mark on the program that he had dreamed of being a part of for so long. It must have been an incredible experience to lead the Rangers onto the floor in the mid-seventies. Kyle did recall some fun moments as the Rangers mascot.

Kyle Herrin: *I was blessed to be able to do that…most kids are not able to experience that. I remember one time at Marion I went out to shoot at halftime and made like 13 shots in a row and the crowd starting cheering for me. Back in in '72 or '73…I went to the back of the bus and Chris Moore* *told me a scary story about rats infiltrating Benton High School and I went to the front of the bus crying and dad told me that it wasn't true. One time we were coming back from Mt. Vernon and we all hunched down in the car because they would throw rocks at you if they knew you were from Benton. My grandpa (Homer) sat straight up in the car and didn't hunch down with the rest of us...like nothing was happening. I was in the locker room at Mt. Vernon when they waved the gun inside. It was an awesome thing to get to do. I had my own little uniform...I still have it today.*

Kyle attended Grant School and his sixth-grade coach was Gene Alexander (Mr. A). He recalls having his favorite teams and players when he was younger.

Kyle Herrin: *My favorite team growing up was probably the '75 team with Dunbar and Billy Smith. It was probably the first team that I really watched closely...and remember. I remember really being down when Dunbar hurt his knee. Billy Smith was probably my favorite player. He was just so good at everything he did...and he was a nice guy too.*

Physically, Kyle was bigger than Rod and Randy. He was very steady at the point guard position and played like a coach's son. He understood the game well. It was as if he was a play ahead of everyone else on the floor. Again, Benton had players, and playing time was always a battle. Kyle admitted that it was tough to come off the bench as a junior, but he understood what he had to do.

Kyle Herrin: *I played behind Rob and Tim and I think I would have had the opportunity to play more at another school.... But that is what happens when you are in a really good program with a lot of good players. That was a great team and there is no doubt that Rob and Tim were the engines of that team. There were times as a junior, I played in the j.v. game and then would play in the varsity game... I have to admit it was frustrating at times. Rob and Tim were both great players and I consider them to be great friends...but I just wanted to play.*

In '82, the Rangers also returned seniors Clark Dixon, Mark Kerley, Adam Furlow. Dixon and Kerley were returning starters and Furlow was a key reserve on the '81 team.

Besides Kyle Herrin, the juniors were Cameron Skobel, Brad Piazza, Brian Thomasson, Mike Kolisek, Jim McMahon, Steve Bigham and David Spencer. Skobel was a tremendous athlete that would get spot minutes late in the season. Brad Piazza quarterbacked the Rangers to a South Seven football championship and Brian Thomason was also a solid football player. Mike Kolisek was a standout golfer and Bigham, McMahon and Spencer competed hard every day against the regulars.

The only sophomore on the team was Bruce Baker. Baker was a player. As a sophomore, he played at 6'7" and had tremendous hands. He caught everything that was passed to him and was extremely driven for someone who was only a sophomore. Baker was also a great shooter. He could step out of the post and hit perimeter shots if left open. Baker had great instincts and was an offensive machine. He had an uncanny knack for getting to the foul line. He was a tenacious rebounder and the thing about Baker that stood out to me was this; he loved the game. I always got the impression when I watched Bruce Baker play that he was having fun. Most importantly, he played hard and played to win. He was a special player but as a sophomore, he had to prove himself to Wills and Williams.

Clark Dixon: *Tim and Rob were our leaders. There was a core group of guys that we put on the floor our junior and senior year that had played with each other since grade school. We were all competitive about being as good as we could possibly be. Just watching Tim and Rob want to get better made me want to get better. They loved the game…I wanted to be better tomorrow than I was today because of their love of the game…it was contagious to all of us.*

Bruce Baker: *They treated me like a guy that had to prove himself. It didn't matter what you had done up to that point. All the trophies and the accolades you had didn't matter. I was starting from scratch with those guys…that's all there was to it. Robbie was a great leader and Tim was the same way.*

Bruce Baker wasn't from Benton. He moved to Benton in the sixth grade from Centralia.

Bruce Baker: *My dad worked as a railroader in Centralia and he got an interview to be a coal miner. Dad got the job and we moved to Benton. He started to work at the coal mines and he didn't like it at all. We were already in Benton and me and my brother had made some friends so we decided to stay.*

He continued to work in Centralia so sometimes that was tough on him when we would go to Centralia and win. I moved to Benton in the sixth grade and my first coach was Perry Eisenhower. I fell in love with basketball in Centralia. Basketball was huge in Centralia.

In the sixth grade, Baker attended Lincoln Elementary School and played for Perry Eisenhower. As soon as Baker moved to Benton, he began going to the high school games. He looked up to Coach Herrin and began to figure out what it meant to be a Benton Ranger.

Bruce Baker: *I did go to the Benton games. We always went to the Holiday Tournament in Centralia. Rod Shurtz, Dave Jones, Jim Ward…I looked up to those guys. I remember the warm-ups and it was a dream come true to be able to play for the Rangers.*

There was one noticeable difference to the look of the Benton Rangers entering the 1982 season. Gone were the flat-tops. In fact, the Rangers all agreed to get perms. It was a totally different look than ever before and it was a sign that Coach Herrin was changing with the times. It was a popular hairstyle trend in the early eighties. Clark Dixon had a good word when it came to Coach Herrin's approval of the new hairstyle.

Clark Dixon: *I've often speculated how the flat-tops came to an end. It could have been that Sue nixed it. Everyone was wearing their hair that way at the time and Coach Herrin just went with it. I always said that mine was natural…everybody else had to buy product.*

Rangers fans were looking forward to not just a winning season, but a championship season. Yes, possibly a state championship. The team returned four starters and with the addition of Baker, Kyle Herrin and Adam Furlow off the bench it was possible. The Rangers were going to be a force to reckoned with in '82. Rob Williams made this point about the history of his class regarding basketball:

Rob Williams: *The first time I thought we might be okay is when we won the Benton Freshman Tournament. Tim played with us. We were always a little better than .500…but we had never really been that good all the way through.*

On Tuesday, December 1, 1981, the Rangers opened the season at home against the McLeansboro Foxes. The Foxes were coached by Dave Lee and they were a year away from the glory years of '82-'83 and '83-'84. Darin Lee, Stacy Sturm, Rod Irvin, Tracy Sturm, Scott Craven and Curt Reed Jr. were just some of the young Foxes on the roster. For the next two years the Foxes would be a thorn in the Rangers side, but not in '82. It was still a mystery as to who would fill the one open starting position for the Rangers. Baker was not sure if he would start the first game of the year, but he remembered that moment when he first saw his name in the starting line-up.

Bruce Baker: *A guy that really mentored me was Coach Stewart. He told me as a freshman that if I would work hard that I would be out there playing varsity basketball as a sophomore. He really encouraged me. I remember one time I said, "It would be an honor to play as a sophomore." I remember him saying, "You better be out there starting." He really wanted me to start as a sophomore. Before the first game my sophomore year Coach Herrin put the starters on the board, and I was one of them…Coach Stewart looked at me and winked. I really worked hard over the summer for that. All of my coaches put that confidence in me. Coach Carlile, Coach Whittington, and Coach Stewart had all prepared me for that moment.*

Getting the starting nod from Coach Herrin on such a great team was not something Baker took lightly. He reflected back on his feelings in that moment.

Bruce Baker: *I just remember thinking…this is an elite team. I can't take this for granted. I remember thinking that I was ready and I had to be. I didn't want to let those four guys down…and I didn't want to let myself down. I also knew that if Coach put me out there…then he thought I was ready. I wouldn't be out there if he didn't think I could do it. That gave me confidence.*

The Rangers routed the Foxes 68-46. Rob Williams led the team in scoring with 18 points. Unfortunately, Tim Wills was sidelined with a sprained ankle early in the first quarter and was unable to finish the game. Coach Herrin had these comments after the game:

Coach Herrin: *It was a little worse than we thought. It was still puffy this morning and we decided to have x-rays taken. I hope it's just a sprain.*

The inside play of Kerley and Baker is what stood out. They each scored 14 points and combined for 15 rebounds. Baker remembers a funny play that happened in the game that speaks to his ongoing process of being accepted by the senior guards.

Bruce Baker: *I remember Robbie threading the needle and throwing me a no-look pass in my first game and I didn't have my hands ready…and it went out of bounds. I remember him saying something to Tim loud enough where I could hear it like, "I don't know if he is ready to play up here…maybe he needs to be sitting up in the stands with the sophomores." I remember thinking… this is serious stuff.*

As a sophomore, Baker had the luxury of playing with great guards, but it is important not to miss that the improved play of Mark Kerley eased the pressure on Baker on both ends of the floor. Kerley shot the ball with tremendous confidence, and teams had to be aware of where he was at all times. He was always a threat to score. Often times, Kerley drew the opposing team's toughest post defender, allowing Baker to have his way with a weaker defender. There were times that Kerley guarded the best opposing post player to keep Baker out of foul trouble. Baker admitted that he learned little intricacies about post play from Kerley that he carried into his college career at UAB.

Bruce Baker: *Mark knew he where he was going when he caught the ball. I remember he would say, "Get 'em on your hip." He would say, "If they are leaning on you…they are tired." He had really good instincts and a nice soft touch around the basket. He loved to use the backboard. The backboard was his friend. He was an offensive machine.*

Another positive from game one was the play off the bench of Kyle Herrin. With Wills' injury, Herrin was thrown into the fire early and played well. Herrin scored six points, dished out two assists and grabbed six rebounds in Will's place.

Clark Dixon remembers well what Kerley meant to the team and he marveled at his offensive ability in the paint.

Clark Dixon: *Mark Kerley was slow and not a great jumper…but he had great footwork in the post. He would just mess guys up. Mark understood his skill set and he loved the game. I think a lot of the opponents underestimated his abil-*

ity…and he would just burn them. Mark would abuse people in the post…and I remember Rob and Tim would just laugh as they were running to the other end.

On Friday, December 4th, the Pinckneyville Panthers came to town. The team was without the services of Tim Wills, who still had a tender ankle. The Rangers jumped out to a 32-25 halftime lead and then outscored the Panthers 20-9 in the third quarter to win the game 68-46. The player of the game was sophomore, Bruce Baker. The Rangers were 2-0.

I have to say this about the '82 team…. This is a weird statement, but it is true: the '82 team executed the pre-game warm-up better than any team I ever saw. The warm-up uniforms were sweet. There was a name flap on the back and the pinstripe warm-up bottoms were a cool look. All of the players were skilled and displayed a presence when they warmed up. Williams and Wills alternated popping to the free throw line to deliver Globetrotter-style passes to the scissor cutters for lay-ups. I remember the tight magic circle with the two red, white and blue warm-up balls. It was a show.

Rob Williams: *I tell my wife today, nothing compared to coming out of that locker room to "Sweet Georgia Brown". She just kind of looks at me like, "really…" Bob Gariepy yelling, "Three seconds!"…. Skin-man and Kenny Irvin. I can still see it today…and I knew where everyone sat when I ran out. It was kind of utopia there.*

The Rangers then won the next three games convincingly. They defeated the West Frankfort Redbirds 55-48 and then handled the Metropolis Trojans, 69-53. On Friday, December 18th, the Rangers defeated the Carbondale Terriers at home by a score of 60-48. Baker led a balanced scoring attack with 15 points. It was clear that he had won the respect of the veteran guards by his tenacious play.

Rob Williams: *Bruce gave us an element that we never had before. I trusted Bruce. I certainly don't remember Bruce walking in like he was going to take over. In fact, I remember the opposite. I thought he was a wide-eyed sophomore. I felt Bruce earned it with us in the summer. Nothing made me feel better than when a guy showed appreciation that I passed him the ball. He truly appreciated getting the ball. We knew he fit in. I have a tremendous amount of respect for Bake.*

Tim Wills: *Bruce was a really good player. Here is the thing about Bruce… he was so self-confident and a lot of times you see guys like that and they don't play hard all of the time. Bruce played hard every possession. Bruce played hard on both ends of the floor. He wanted to win like the rest of us. There was an unspoken agreement with me, Robbie and Bruce. He might say this, too. We were seniors and Bruce was our leading scorer until he got hurt…and he was just a sophomore. It was kind of like, "You're really good…and we know you're really good…but we're not ready to turn the team over to you." I will say this; I averaged fewer points as a senior than as a junior. I knew where the ball needed to go. Winning was the goal.*

Just as the guards were gaining respect for Baker, Baker admits that he had the utmost respect for All-State guards Rob Williams and Tim Wills.

Bruce Baker: *Robbie could do things with the ball that I had never seen before. Robbie pushed me to be a better ball handler. He would do two ball drills and these little ball handling drills. He would throw that no-look pass all the time…and I had to be ready. He was extremely quick. He was a vocal leader. Tim is in line as one of the greatest people I've ever met and he would do whatever it took to win. He would pat me on the seat at times and give me encouragement. He was also a knockdown shooter.*

The Rangers were 5-0 overall and 2-0 in the conference. They were also winning games with Tim Wills not playing at 100%. It is obvious by his point totals that the ankle was still hurting when he returned to play the last four games before Christmas. Wills finished his career with 985 points and this injury-ridden string of games before Christmas probably cost him the chance of scoring 1,000. Tim would never say that because he is team guy first, but I thought it was worth noting.

The Rangers had one game remaining before Christmas break against the Centralia Orphans. The game was played at Centralia on Friday, December 22, 1981.

Bruce Baker scored 27 points, but Centralia's John Willis scored 30 to lead the Orphans to a 77-76 victory. With the loss, the Rangers fell to 5-1 and 2-1 in conference play. Clark Dixon had his most productive offensive night of the year by scoring 15 points and handing out five assists. Dixon is one of the finest all-around athletes to ever come through Benton High School. When Clark was a senior, he went to State in three different sports; golf, basketball and track. He was well respected by his teammates, and played a great role in the success of the '82 team.

Rob Williams: *The thing that stands out about Clark is that he was probably the best athlete on our team. Clark had a mean streak that I loved...Clark's going to fight with you. He was so athletic. Clark was hard on himself. He always worked hard and he always drew a tough defensive match-up. I had total trust in Clark as a teammate.*

Bruce Baker: *There wasn't anyone I ever played with that was leaner than Clark. I remember asking him, "Clark, do you eat?" Clark was a good floor leader. He had so much tact about it too. If Robbie got on to me...he would come up and say, "He just wants to win, don't take it personal." And sometimes I needed to hear that. He was like having another coach on the floor...a super good guy.*

After the loss to Centralia, the Rangers prepared for the Centralia Holiday Tournament. It was a welcome break for Tim Wills. He needed time without a game to rest the ankle. The Rangers were off to a good start. Could they win the Centralia Tournament?

The team opened the tournament with Edwardsville and big Paul Schaefer. Schaefer was good. He scored 31 points and led all scorers, but young Bruce Baker almost matched him with 28 points and led the Rangers to an 83-66 victory. Baker was an offensive machine. Both Wills and Williams dished out eight assists. The guards were getting Baker the ball where he needed it and he was scoring. Mark Kerley had a quiet 13 points and Tim Wills scored ten. The ability of the guards to get Baker the ball at the right time was uncanny.

Clark Dixon: *Bruce made a difference. He just had these big ole meat hooks for hands. As a sophomore, Bruce knew who the leaders of the team were. He always wanted the ball...and he was always looking to please Tim and Robbie so he could get it. Bruce needed to score for us. There is no doubt that he had to prove himself to Rob and Tim.*

With the win, the Rangers advanced to meet the Arlington Huskies. The Huskies won the game by a score of 60-47. The Rangers didn't play well. Mark Kerley was the only Ranger player in double figures with ten. The Rangers fell to 6-2 overall.

The Rangers resumed play on Tuesday, January 5th, at Okawville. Okawville was no joke. The Rockets had two of the best players in the state in Paul Jansen and Greg Rennegarbe. Jansen was big and strong and was a great scorer inside fifteen feet. Rennegarbe ran the show. He had great quickness allowing him to dribble, penetrate gaps, and literally breakdown a defense. On this night, Mark Kerley led the Rangers in scoring with 25 points and Baker added 23. Williams and Wills were sacrificing their points by making the extra pass into the post. Why? Because Kerley and Baker were scoring. It was a beautiful balance of team play between the guards and the bigs. The Rangers moved to 7-2.

With the Benton Invitational Tournament looming, the Rangers caught fire and won four straight conference games. The streak began with an 85-63 win over the Harrisburg Bulldogs. With the opposing defense focused on the seniors, Bruce Baker scored 25 points to lead all scorers. The team then defeated the Herrin Tigers by a score of 72-58. In the losing effort, Ron Reed scored 13 points to lead the Tigers' offensive attack. Reed was an outstanding guard that became a very successful high school basketball coach at Effingham St. Anthony. Again, Baker led a balanced scoring attack with 20 points, followed by Mark Kerley with 19 points. Clark Dixon scored 12 points and remembered the game well. He marveled at Coach Herrin's ability to motivate all of the different personalities on a basketball team.

Clark Dixon: *Coach Herrin never treated us the same way. He knew how to push people's buttons. He always wanted me to expect more of myself. He did not want any of us to accept mediocrity. Yes...he could be gruff, but he was so much more than that. He cared about his players. At Herrin, I picked up my fourth foul right before the halftime buzzer sounded. Coach Herrin met me at the center circle and we chatted all the way to the locker room. Believe me...it was a one-way conversation. This lasted the entire half. As we came back out for the second half, he leaned over and said, "You're starting the second half. I played the 2nd half without fouling out and when he took me out, he walked down to the end of the bench and said, "That was a good second half." He could also build you up.*

The Rangers then defeated the Marion Wildcats at home by a score of 73-50. The next night, they traveled to Mt. Vernon and thumped the Rams by a score of 64-45. The Rams were a year away from being very good. They were led by juniors Steve McCoy, Eric Hawthorne and

Kevin Riggan. Rob Williams led the team in scoring with 15 and Baker chipped in with 14 points. With the win, the Rangers improved to 11-2 overall and 6-1 in conference play and jumped to fourth place in the Class A State Rankings. Coach Herrin had these words after the win at Mt. Vernon.

Coach Herrin: *Our defense was really tough. While we didn't shoot the ball too well, our defense enabled us to overcome it.*

The Rangers now faced the grueling week of the Benton Invitational Tournament. The team opened the tournament with the Okawville Rockets and struggled to get it going early in the game but battled back and escaped with a 55-54 win. Big Paul Jansen led the Rockets scoring attack with 19 points and Baker matched him with 19 points for the Rangers.

On Wednesday night, the Rangers defeated the Cairo Pilots by a score of 66-59 and then met the Edwardsville Tigers led by Paul Schaefer. In a game that went down to the wire, the Tigers defeated the Rangers 41-40. It was a devastating defeat. The Rangers then won their last two games of the tournament against Olney and Pinckneyville to win the BIT with a final record of 4-1.

In the Saturday night game against Pinckneyville there was a play that I will always remember. Robbie Williams raced to save a ball from going out of bounds in front of the Rangers' bench. He retrieved the ball with both feet in bounds and as he was slowly falling out of bounds, he looked down the floor and then slung a full-court behind-the-back pass to a racing Tim Wills who scored a lay-up. It is not a play that you typically see in high school basketball. The play also said something. Williams never hesitated throwing the pass and it speaks to the trust that Coach Herrin had in his abilities. The pass led Wills perfectly to the goal and the crowd oohed and aahed as the play happened, and then reached the crescendo when Wills hit the lay-up. Wills' reaction after he hit the lay-up was priceless. Nothing! There was no celebrating. Wills had played with Williams forever. It was just Robbie making a play. That single play personified Williams and Wills; Williams with the flashy pass and Wills finishing the play with the fundamental lay-up. Williams was appreciative of the freedom that Coach Herrin gave him on the floor.

Rob Williams: *I had to prove to Coach that I could do it. He didn't micro-manage the game. Coach didn't micro-manage offense. He was far ahead of his time. Every player expresses himself in different ways and he allowed us to do that. Coach had this innate ability to get the most out of a guy. Again, I played with emotion, and I thought that if I could make an exciting play…it would bring emotion from the crowd. It was my way of bringing that to the team. Coach would sometimes talk to me about a shot I might take and rightly so…but I'm a little stubborn and he gave in a little and allowed me to play with that flair. He didn't take that away from me.*

Teammate and close friend, Clark Dixon, remembered what it was like being the teammate of Wills and Williams.

Clark Dixon: *It's hard for me to talk about Robbie without mentioning Tim. He and Tim were both good ball handlers…but they were different. Robbie was flashy…he took the ball behind his back and he was good at that. Tim was just solid. He was not as flashy…but he just didn't make many mistakes. They thought about basketball on a different level than the rest of us. They could see things before it happened…they had a great sense of the game.*

Kyle Herrin: *They helped me a lot because they pushed me. They were both very good players. Rob had this knack of stealing the ball from me when I was younger…but it was good because it helped make me a better ball handler. They made me a better player. All of those guys were great to play with; Bruce, Adam, Mark, and Clark.*

Rob Williams, Tim Wills and Bruce Baker were selected to the BIT All-Tournament team. With the final two wins of the tournament, the Rangers improved to 15-3 overall.

Then it happened. In a practice following the BIT, Bruce Baker got hurt.

Bruce Baker: *It was at the end of practice…I went up and landed on Jim McMahon's shoe and just turned that ankle and broke it. My doctor said I was done…but I stayed in shape.*

Tim Wills: *I just remember there was a long pass down the floor and Bruce was running after it and he had to jump stop for it and he rolled his ankle. It was after the week of the BIT and we just thought that he sprained it.*

We eventually got him off the floor and finished practice. Bruce went to the hospital to get it x-rayed. After practice, Robbie and I were shooting around and I remember Coach Herrin came out of the coach's office crying. I knew immediately why. The hospital had called and told Coach Herrin that Baker had broken his ankle. I know what was going on in his mind. Not again…because he knew we had a really good chance to be good if we could stay healthy.

At the time, Baker was the team's leading scorer. There is no doubt that it was a setback. How did Baker's injury affect the dynamics of the team? Every player now had to score more. Teams now placed their best post defender on Mark Kerley. Every player had to make a concerted effort to grab a few more rebounds in Baker's absence.

After Baker's injury had time to soak in, the Rangers had to adopt the next-man-up mentality. Here was the big question; who would take his spot? Coach Herrin went with 6'3" senior Adam Furlow. Furlow had been effective off the bench and was a solid player.

Tim Wills: *Adam was our first post player off the bench…but when Baker went down…he moved into the starting line-up. I don't think we lost a game when Adam came in and replaced Bruce. He did more than adequate…and that is a testament to Adam's ability.*

Rob Williams loved Furlow's game and also admitted he was the key to some great wins down the stretch for the Rangers.

Rob Williams: *Adam was one of my best buddies in high school. Adam was a great free-throw shooter…and we trusted him to hit free throws late in games. Adam was fearless. He got put into a tough spot when Bruce went down and he played great. We had a little guard-around play and he would fake the hand-off to me and Tim and rise up and shoot it. He had that kind of confidence in himself. Tons of respect for Adam.*

Clark Dixon: *Adam was a hardworking player that made the most of his ability. He was a great teammate and he made a huge contribution when Bruce went down. He had to figure out where he fit in…and he did. He always played hard.*

Baker's injury also had an effect on Kyle Herrin's playing time. Although Herrin did not receive the press of Wills and Williams in '82, he was more than capable. Herrin had played well all year off the bench and would now be asked to play more. There were times he would sub-in for a big man, and the Rangers would go with a smaller line-up. Kyle was thrust into the sixth-man role and it was something that he embraced. Kyle's teammates remember what he added to the '82 team.

Clark Dixon: *Think of what it must have been like to be Kyle Herrin. The coach's son and then having to play behind Tim and Rob. Think of the pressure that he must have felt...but Kyle found his own way...and ended up helping us in so many ways. I never worried about Kyle because he got to go home to Sue.*

Tim Wills and Robbie Williams also had high praise for what Herrin brought to the club.

Tim Wills: *Kyle was hard-nosed. Probably at any other time period he would have started as a junior. Kyle would come into the game for me or Robbie... but there were times he would take a big guy out and we would play with three guards.*

Rob Williams: *We were bad losers. We were all like that...Clark and his bony elbows...Kyle was like that too. The greatest thing was this; we had to earn it. Nothing was given to us.*

After the BIT, the new-look Rangers had one more loop through the South Seven before Regional play. The Rangers first defeated the Redbirds by a score of 57-49. Adam Furlow stepped up in Baker's absence to lead the team in scoring with 14 points. The Rangers then went on the road and defeated the Carbondale Terriers 78-68 behind 22 points from Mark Kerley. Furlow and Williams both scored 20 and Tim Wills chipped in with 14 points. With the win, the team improved to 17-3 and 8-1 in conference play.

The Rangers then dismantled helpless Harrisburg by a score of 71-43. Again, Furlow scored 15 points and was playing the best basketball of his high school career. Kyle Herrin had seven points off the bench and the team was finding ways to win without Bruce Baker.

The Rangers then defeated Centralia, Marion and Herrin to set up their final game of the season against Mt. Vernon. A win over Mt. Vernon would secure the South Seven Conference Championship. Rangers fans filled Benton's gymnasium. It was senior night. A large crowd stood and applauded the five seniors and their parents in a short ceremony before the game. Clark Dixon remembered the night well.

Clark Dixon: *I felt sorry for Mt. Vernon that night…they didn't have a chance. That game was over in a hurry.*

Tim Wills scored 21 points and led the Rangers to an easy 70-56 victory over their Jefferson County rivals. Mark Kerley scored 18 points and Rob Williams chipped in with 17 points. Adam Furlow continued his great play and added ten points. With the win, the Rangers improved to 22-3. They had not lost a game since Baker left the line-up. Wow!

In a late February edition of the Benton Evening News, a picture in the sports section shows the Rangers hoisting their South Seven Conference Championship board into place in the east rafters of the gymnasium. It was now the third year in a row that the team would compete in the "small school" State Tournament. They had a chance.

'82 State Tournament Play

In the first game of the Norris City Regional, the Rangers played the McLeansboro Foxes. At halftime, the Foxes led the by a score of 15-14. Coach David Lee favored a slower tempo in order to disrupt the Rangers fast pace. In the second half, the Rangers pulled away, forcing the Foxes to play faster, and won the game by a score of 51-40. The win set up a rematch with the West Frankfort Redbirds. The Birds had come from behind to end the Rangers' season just a year ago. The Rangers wanted revenge.

In what was expected to be a closer game, the Rangers jumped on the Redbirds and led at halftime by a score of 33-13.

Coach Herrin: *I don't think we could have played any better. We got loose balls and hit the lay-ins. Our defense was awfully tough also.*

In the fourth quarter, Rangers fans held their breath as Tim Wills went to the bench after jamming two fingers fighting for a rebound. Again, Kerley led the Rangers in scoring with 19 points followed by 15 from Rob Williams. Furlow chipped in with ten points. The Regional Championship win over West Frankfort was extra special for Rob Williams. He was still bitter about the Regional loss a year ago and there is picture of Williams in mid-air offering a high-five to Tim Wills after the victory. The team bus was met at the square by over two hundred excited fans craving a run to the State Tournament.

Rob Williams has fond memories of his days playing at Benton. He later received a full-ride basketball scholarship to Northern Iowa but admitted that nothing compared to his experience as a Benton Ranger.

Rob Williams: *How we played. How we prepared. How we looked. You were playing for Coach, your teammates, and your community. You had such pride in the program. The gyms were packed even on the road in the South Seven. When they played "Sweet Georgia Brown" and you busted out of that locker room…you thought you were pretty darn good.*

On Wednesday, March 3, 1982, the Rangers tangled with the Eldorado Eagles in the first game of the West Frankfort Sectional. The game was back and forth. At the end of the third quarter, Robbie Williams canned a 45-foot shot to extend the Ranger lead to 35-31.

Coach Herrin: *Robbie's basket was a big one for us.*

With only 1:17 left in the game, Clark Dixon calmly sank two pressure free throws to extend the lead to six points. The Rangers never looked back and won the game by a score of 61-50. With the win, the team moved to 25-3 and advanced to the Sectional Championship to play the Cairo Pilots.

On Friday, March 5, 1982, the Rangers loaded the bus early and headed to Max Morris Gymnasium to face the Pilots. They had soundly beaten the Pilots in the BIT, but not on this night. The Pilots were led by Selma Snow, Armone Matthews and Michael Ayers. The game was highly anticipated and Benton fans covered Max Morris Gymnasium. The colors of maroon and white blanketed the "Max". Before the game, the Rangers were shooting around and an incident took place that Clark Dixon remembers to this day.

Clark Dixon: *We were at West Frankfort early for the Sectional and we were shooting around and I clanked one off the rim. Chumbler happened to be walking by about that time and said, "I hope we see a lot of that tonight." In my mind. I was like, go away, Bill.*

Clark Dixon: *When the game started…they came out in a triangle and two on Robbie and Tim. They left me open…and I was able to hit a couple of shots to pull them out of it.*

Dixon hit three jump shots early in the game and forced Chumbler to rethink his defensive strategy. It was possibly the three biggest shots that Clark Dixon hit in his high school career and his teammates recalled Dixon's clutch shooting.

Tim Wills: *Cairo put a triangle-two defense on Robbie…and I remember Clark hit two or three big jump shots. I don't think Coach Chumbler was committed enough to the defense to stay in it after Clark hit those shots. He changed defenses and that opened things up for the rest of us. Who knows what would have happened in that game if he doesn't hit those jump shots. They could have stayed in that defense and we could have gotten beat. Who knows?*

Rob Williams: *Clark hit two or three big jump shots in the soft spot of the triangle and that pulled Cairo out of it. If he doesn't hit those shots…who knows… you play tighter. I was so happy for Clark that night. A lot of respect for Clark.*

Entering the fourth quarter, the Rangers had a 14-point lead, but the Pilots didn't quit. The Pilots slapped a full-court press on to speed the game up and force turnovers but the Rangers handled it well. In the second half, Selma Snow scored 22 of his game high 28 points in an unforgettable shooting display. I was in the seventh grade and I was there that night. I can still see Snow hitting corner jump shots and keeping the Pilots in the game but it wasn't enough. The Rangers won the game 79-68 behind 24 points from senior Mark Kerley. The Rangers lingered around the gym afterwards and took pictures and then went into the locker room to celebrate. They congratulated each other and then prepared for another firetruck escort around the square. Rob Williams still remembers how special those moments with his teammates really were.

With the win, the Rangers advanced to the Carbondale Super-Sectional to play the Okawville Rockets. Earlier in the season, they had defeated the Rockets both times but the games had been close. Bruce Baker was itching to play and he had been in a cast for weeks.

Bruce Baker: *My uncle Jim* (Muir) *found a saw and we cut that cast off and I played on it in the Super-Sectional. The doctor called the house and he was mad but I had to play in that game.*

On Tuesday night, March 9th, the Rangers traveled to the SIU Arena to meet the Rockets. Bruce Baker was back but was not 100%. The Arena was packed with fans from both towns along with many fans from across Southern Illinois that wanted to see a great game. And that is just what they got; a great game.

In the first quarter, the Rangers and Rockets played to a 14-14 tie. The Rangers then took a 33-32 lead into the locker room at halftime. In the second half, the Rockets came out and took a three-point lead to end of the third quarter. As expected, the game went down to the wire. I was at the game and my stomach was in knots. Okawville had knocked off the Rangers in the 1980 Super-Sectional and I thought it was going to happen again. The players recalled those tense moments in the final seconds of the 1982 Super-Sectional.

Rob Williams: *I remember the final play like it was yesterday. We missed a free throw and they threw an outlet pass and I went for the steal and didn't get it...so I'm trailing the play. They throw the ball to Schwankhaus on the baseline and Bake challenged him and they called a foul. I thought we lost. I was thinking every negative thought in my mind.*

Bruce Baker: *When he got the ball he was driving and going hard to the basket and I was doing everything I could not to foul him and not to hurt my ankle at the same time and I bumped him. I looked like Chester from Gunsmoke because I was gimping so bad. I thought I lost the game for us but he missed them both.*

Tim Wills recalled the situation and those nervous moments after Todd Schwankhaus was fouled.

Tim Wills: *We burned more timeouts than one to ice him. I do remember the Benton fans ran to the opposite end of the floor...where he was shooting...to wave their hands and give him a hard time. I thought Jim Labuwi was one of them. We are up one point. If he hits one...we're going into overtime and if he hits them both we get beat. If he misses both of them...we win.*

Wills remembers the drama that unfolded as Schwankhaus went to the line with the weight of the world on his shoulders.

Tim Wills: *His first shot was all over the rim and it just bounced out…and then you could just see it. He missed the second one and of course, we're elated. You're not thinking about his feelings in that moment. After watching my son play, I still have feelings for that guy. That had to be tough.*

When Schwankhaus missed the free throws, there was no time on the clock. The game was over. Benton won the game 69-68. Coach Dave Luechtefeld immediately consoled Schwankhaus and the celebration began. In all fairness to Schwankhaus, he is one of the reasons the Rockets played so well. He played a great game and scored 11 points to pick up some of his struggling teammates. I will say this; a game is never decided by one play. There were a ton of possessions that could have changed the game to the Rockets favor. Clark Dixon was ready to blame himself for the loss if Schwankhaus would have made both free throws.

Clark Dixon: *The one thing I remember about playing in the SIU Arena was sitting there watching him shoot those free throws. I remember that I had missed one earlier in the game and I was thinking, "If you would have hit that one we wouldn't be here right now."*

When it was over and the players returned to the locker room, Clark Dixon had a thought that he just couldn't get out of his head.

Clark Dixon: *My first thought was that we are actually going to Champaign. In my yearbook, Robbie intentionally put "We are going to the bighouse next year." He put that thought in our head and I think he wrote that in all of his teammates yearbooks. That was the expectation for our senior year. We all bought into that.*

The Rangers returned home and received yet another firetruck escort around the square. After the victory lap, fans came to the gym for an impromptu reception celebrating the victory. Rangers fans were already scheming to get tickets to the State Tournament. It was a magical time that Rich Herrin had lived many times, but was excited to get another crack at a State trophy.

Tim Wills shared a funny memory about the day of the Super-Sectional. Backtracking to the day of the Super-Sectional, the players were in school. Channel 3 T.V. called Coach Herrin to request interviews with the players that would air that evening to preview the game. Coach Herrin told the players to meet in the gym during lunch.

Tim Wills: *We all met down in the gym…but Mark was a no-show. Evidently he went up town to get something to eat and got caught in traffic and he came in late. The t.v. people recognized him and they got their cameras back out and did a quick interview with him. They asked him several questions but when asked about the outcome of the game he said, "I think I can shoot it well enough for us to get by." And the funny thing is…he did. That is exactly what happened. He shot the ball well and we barely won.*

With a hobbled Bruce Baker, Mark Kerley picked up the slack and scored 22 points to lead the Rangers in scoring. He scored 25 points in the Sectional final. All of that work in the gym had paid off and Mark Kerley developed into one of the better players in Southern Illinois.

Tim Wills: *Mark was always our best shooter. He had a soft touch and really good hands. As a freshman and sophomore, Mark couldn't gain any weight. He drank protein shakes; you name it…but he just couldn't gain weight. Coach Herrin worked Mark on his quickness and jumping ability…and I give Mark credit…he improved his athleticism.*

Rob Williams: *Mark made a big improvement between his junior and senior years. We were hard on Mark because Mark was our only big guy. We needed him and we pushed him. We were hard on him in a good way because we needed him to be good. Coach pushed Mark pretty hard too. I love Mark to death. Sue Kerley was the one that did our hair. Mark could really shoot it and he gave us another guy that could score.*

Mark admitted that he was lucky to have the opportunity to play with Tim and Rob and recalled his memories of playing with Williams and Wills.

Mark Kerley: *Robbie was a really good guard. Some of the passes he got to me…I don't know how he did it. Tim Wills could shoot the lights out of it.*

The Rangers received a tough draw in the 1982 Class A State Tournament. It was Coach Herrin's fourth Elite Eight appearance at Benton and

676

they would have to play the number one team in the state, the Lawrenceville Indians. The Indians entered the game undefeated and had two great players; Marty Simmons and Doug Novsek.

Marty Simmons was considered to be the best basketball player in the state in 1982. Simmons could score inside or out. He was a tenacious competitor with a basketball IQ that was off the charts. Entering the tournament, he was the most talked-about player in the State of Illinois.

Doug Novsek was a tremendous shooter. Novsek's father, Joe, played professional football for the Oakland Raiders. Novsek played at 6'5" tall and could shoot the ball like Keith Tabor. The Indians were extremely disciplined under the direction of legendary coach Ron Felling. The Rangers were possibly the second-best team in the state. The noon quarter-final game between the Indians and the Rangers was believed by many to be the State championship. Clark Dixon recalled the hype that led up to the game.

Clark Dixon: *I remember some crazy sportswriter from Evansville put us ahead of them. We had played 30 games and had never been beaten by a Class A School. It was a tough draw for us and basically the State championship was played in the quarter-final game of the tournament that year.*

On Thursday, March 12th, the Benton student body met for a pep session to send the players off. The band played and several of the players addressed their classmates. Coach Herrin thanked the students for their support and promised the team would play hard and give their best effort. After the pep session, the players were led to the west side of the gymnasium and piled in separate cars to assure a comfortable ride to Champaign. The cars were donated by local car dealers.

Once arriving in Champaign, the Rangers grabbed a quick bite to eat and then went back to the hotel for some much-needed rest. It was hard for the players to think about anything else but the game. This is what they had worked for since they were in grade school and the sheer anticipation of the game consumed every thought and interrupted the sleep of some of the players.

The next morning, the team ate breakfast together as a team and Coach Herrin went over some last minute details about the game plan. The Rangers were well aware of Lawrenceville's personal. The team bus then departed for Assembly Hall. As the team pulled up, they couldn't wait to take the floor. In their childhood, the players had memories of watching the State Tournament on t.v. or even attending some of the games as a fan.

It was now their moment to play at this great basketball mecca. Game time was at 12:00. It was number one Lawrenceville vs. number four Benton.

One of the most important factors in winning a big game is a team's confidence level. The Rangers knew that Lawrenceville was a great team, but they also thought they could win. In fact, this was a characteristic of all Herrin-coached teams. The players always felt they were going to win. Tim Wills explains.

Tim Wills: *The Lawrenceville Game…in '82. Oh…we felt like we were better than they were. We knew about Marty and we knew about Doug. For such a small town, they were loaded. That was just a really good team and a really tough draw for us. That year, they were the best team in the tournament…but I think we were in the top four…with Monmouth and Herscher. Lawrenceville was undefeated going into that game…but we still thought we were better than they were. Matt, we had no business beating Carbondale and some of the teams we beat…but I think we always thought we could…and I believe that confidence came from Coach Herrin. Coach Herrin had such a way of instilling confidence in us. Robbie Williams said we were not as good as we thought we were…and there is a lot of truth to that.*

It was the largest crowd for a tournament game up to that point. Benton playing Lawrenceville was a big deal. Both towns had to be empty.

The Indians could not come into a game with more confidence. They entered the 1982 quarter-final game at 31-0. The fear of taking the Rangers lightly worried Lawrenceville coach Ron Felling. Felling knew the game wouldn't be easy, and he badgered his players all week about how Benton was the best team in the state. The Lawrenceville players grew tired of hearing about the Benton Rangers. Needless to say, at 12:00, the Indians were ready to play.

Lawrenceville Guard, Doug Novsek: *We were a very confident team. We had the goal of going undefeated and we never thought anybody could beat us…but we thought Benton could beat us. They were really fast on tape with Robbie and Tim and they had a good team. They had gotten our attention.*

Benton's defensive game plan against the Lawrenceville was different. The Rangers started in a triangle and two defense and focused their attention on stopping Simmons and Novsek.

Early in the game, the Rangers battled the Indians to an 8-8 tie and then the Indians took the lead by five on a tip-in by Tim Leighty with just .16 seconds left in the first quarter. Doug Novsek was feeling it and hit two bombs and a free throw in the quarter. The athletic and pesky Clark Dixon drew the defensive assignment on Novsek to start the game.

Clark Dixon: *I remember guarding Doug Novsek. I would start in one corner and then he would run me though a series of screens…. He was 6'5" and he didn't need much time to shoot it. I remember running through picks all afternoon.*

As a team, the Rangers struggled shooting in the wide expanse of Assembly Hall. In my playing career, I experienced this dilemma several times. When there is less space behind the goal, it seems like the goal is closer and the ability to perceive distance from the rim is easier. It's hard to explain. I also thought long nets made the rim seem bigger. It was a psychological element that all shooters battle. In the first quarter, the Rangers were 4-13 from the field and it proved to be an omen of things to come.

Tim Wills: *I was 1-11 from the floor…and Clark was 1-10. I struggled shooting in Assembly Hall. I think a lot of it was all the space behind the baskets. I wish we could have gotten a shoot-around before the game. I fouled out in the fourth quarter…and I let my shooting affect the rest of my game. It was a tough day. That game still bothers me when I think about it.*

The poor shooting on the offensive end combined with the Rangers' inability to stop the Indians with the triangle and two defense put the Rangers in a 35-24 hole by halftime.

Tim Wills: *We stuck a triangle and two defense on Doug and Marty…but Marty was just too much in the post and they ran Doug off of a billion screens and he was 6'5" tall so we had trouble bothering his shot.*

Simmons played like a bull in a china closet. He was 6'6" and physical with a soft touch from anywhere on the floor.

Mark Kerley: *The thing I remember most about that game was Marty Simmons. He was just so big and tough to move around.*

Clark Dixon recalled something that makes sense to anyone that is familiar with Assembly Hall.

Clark Dixon: *It was the quietest game I've ever been in. I don't remember hearing the crowd when I played…it's like the sound went over us.*

I thought Dixon's comment was interesting because several players expressed that they had trouble hearing the ball bounce. Again, the space of the facility made for a different playing environment.

To begin the third quarter, five consecutive points from Ernie Hoh put the Indians on top by 16 with just 7:09 left in the third quarter. The Indians were in total command of the game. It was clear that it was not to be. Rob Williams finally got the Rangers on the scoreboard with a 17-foot jumper from the corner to give to cut the lead to 14 at the 6:24 mark. The two teams then traded baskets for the next three minutes but then the Indians stretched their lead to 20 points.

Lawrenceville maintained their torrid shooting pace in the final period as they quickly widened the gap to 26 in the first two minutes of the period. Toward the end of the game, both teams substituted and the Indians cruised to a 75-62 victory.

If there was a bright spot, it was the play of Rob Williams. In the losing effort, Williams dished out six assists and had 18 points. He was also chosen as a member of the All-Tournament team.

Tim Wills: *Robbie played well…I just had a bad game.*

Rob Williams: *There is just not much good I remember from the Lawrenceville game. I thought we played a little scared of them. I was so disappointed we had to play them. It was a tough draw for us. They were very good and they were very disciplined. Only two guys really shot the ball; Simmons and Novsek.*

In the game, Doug Novsek scored a game-high 25 points and Marty Simmons scored 23 and grabbed 16 rebounds. It was a dominating performance by the Indians and they went on to win the 1982 Class A State Tournament by defeating Monmouth, 67-53. The Indians finished the 1982 season with a record of 34-0. The next year, the Indians won the Class A State Championship again with another 34-0 record. They were led by senior Marty Simmons. Coach Ron Felling went on to win Four state Championships. He later became an assistant coach for Bob Knight at the University of Indiana. In just two years, the Indians were a perfect 68-0.

After the game, emotion filled the locker room as Coach Herrin addressed the players. The players sat silently and reflected on their basketball career and struggled to grasp the reality that it was over.

Clark Dixon: *The immediate thought I had when I took my jersey off was… it was the last time I would ever play basketball as a Benton Ranger.*

Tim Wills: *There were a lot of tears in the locker room. Our goal was to win the State Championship…that locker room brought home the reality that we weren't going to win it.*

It has now been close to forty years since the Rangers lost to Lawrenceville in the State Tournament. After years of reflecting on the game, the players wish they could play the game over with a healthy Bruce Baker.

Rob Williams: *If Bake hadn't of gotten hurt…we might have beaten Lawrenceville.*

Tim Wills: *If we played Lawrenceville ten times, we might have beaten them once…maybe twice with Baker healthy. Bruce was not Bruce…he was still coming off of his ankle injury. Robbie and I have talked about it before and he always says, "I wish we had the chance to play them with Baker healthy."*

Bruce Baker: *I would have loved to have had a crack at them at 100%. I think I could have held my own. I was hobbling and give them credit…they got the jump on us.*

After the loss, the Rangers stayed and watched the remainder of the tournament. It was really the last time the group would be together. As they watched the 1982 tournament play out, they found themselves filled with the feeling of what might have been if they had beaten Lawrenceville. Spring was approaching and it would be time for another track season. Then, it was deciding what to do with their lives. What college to attend? Many of the '82 Rangers left Benton but one thing is for sure, their memories as a Benton Ranger carried with them the rest of their lives.

When the team came home on Sunday afternoon, they were greeted with an emotional reception from the Rangers faithful. The sirens sounded as the team bus approached the square. The players stuck their heads out of the narrow bus windows and waved to the crowd. The bus then circled the square and headed to the high school for a short reception in the gym.

Clark Dixon: *There was a reception at the high school and you realized that it was a big deal to a lot of people. My grandparents were there…I spoke, but no one could understand a thing I said because I was crying.*

Rob Williams: *After we lost at Champaign, we went into the gym and there was a pep session. I just cried. We couldn't talk. You know who bailed us out? Sue Herrin. She grabbed the microphone and said a few words. It killed us.*

Despite the Lawrenceville loss, Wills, Williams and Dixon have nothing but great memories about their senior season.

Tim Wills: *My senior year was my favorite year even though the expectations were really high.*

Rob Williams: *Our senior year was the culmination of a lot of work that came to fruition. We were good enough to win. It was the best year I ever had playing basketball.*

Clark Dixon: *The whole two years combined was a learning process of a group of guys that were scared and unsure of themselves in '81…to a team that had a high level of confidence in ourselves.*

Mark Kerley: *It was the whole experience…the fire trucks meeting us on the square. It was all very special.*

The '82 Rangers were fun interviews. I sensed in their voices that playing basketball at Benton High School was very special. They spoke with enthusiasm and gave great insight. All of the players spoke highly of Coach Herrin and the impact he made on their lives.

After high school, Rob Williams attended Northern Iowa on a basketball scholarship. He now works as a State Farm agent and lives in

Galesburg. He and his wife Kris have three children; Garret, Madison and Casey. Rob took away many life lessons after playing for Coach Herrin.

Rob Williams: *Preparation, hard work, discipline and a big one for me is self-confidence. Life is tough and you got to be able to pick yourself up when you fall. You have to be a competitor. My Uncle Doug loved Coach to death. Doug never came to Benton without visiting Coach Herrin. Doug and I had this conversation…and Doug said, "He saved our lives." He took us from a small coal mining town and put us on a stage where we had opportunities. He put us in position for many opportunities. Coach was a true ambassador and character of basketball…and we're losing those guys.*

Tim Wills is married to his wife Kelly and they have two children; Jordan and Mason. Tim went on to play college basketball at SIU-E for the late Coach Larry Graham, and then served as a graduate assistant at SIU-C for Coach Herrin. Tim was then hired as the head basketball coach and athletic director at Rend Lake College. He was quick to point out that Coach Herrin had a great impact on his life.

Tim Wills: *The one thing Coach instilled in all of us was work ethic. He was always the hardest work in practice. He was always up moving around, teaching us, demonstrating something or even motivating us. He was never one to sit down and yell…he was always active. He did the same thing in games… working the sidelines and pulling up his socks…kicking the bleacher. You can't demand work out of someone and not work yourself. He was always working. How many hours did he spend in that gym in the summer? You know another thing Coach did was this…he coached us really hard during the season, but he let us play with freedom in the summer. That was so important. He let us learn the game by allowing us to play. He didn't coach us in the summer…and we had a lot of guys go on to play in college and I think this is a big reason. They knew how to play and they understood the intricacies of the game that you can only learn by playing it. Also, coach really did care for his players. He drove to Alton, Illinois to be at my wedding. He didn't have to do that. He understood that it wasn't about the wins in the end…it was about the relationships you build. I think he understood that even more as he got older.*

After high school, Clark Dixon went to Southern Illinois University and played golf. He also walked on the basketball team for one year and high jumped on the Saluki track team. Clark graduated from dental school and works as a dentist in West Frankfort, Illinois. Clark lives in Benton with his wife Alicia and they have one daughter, Sara. Clark knew Coach Herrin as both his neighbor and basketball coach.

Clark Dixon: *I knew Coach Herrin as my coach and my neighbor. I got to see him interact with the kids in the neighborhood. I remember him pulling us through the snow on a car door in the winter. Rich and Sue have always been great friends with my parents. He and Sue treated me like one of the family. I also knew him as my coach. He was always pushing me and challenging me to be more than I thought I could be.*

Mark Kerley and his wife Melissa live in Benton, Illinois. After high school, Mark received a basketball scholarship to Hannibal Junior College in Hannibal, Missouri. Mark has now worked for twenty-six years at Continental Tire in Mt. Vernon and has three children; Hunter, Courtney and Matthew. His contribution to the '82 team cannot be overstated. With the guidance of Coach Herrin, Mark improved through much hard work to become one of the better post players in Benton basketball history.

Mark Kerley: *Coach Herrin taught us how to be a better person, along with being a good basketball player. He taught us to do things right.*

On to '83!

This was my 7th grade coach, Tom Whittington. Coach Whittington never quit on us and we improved. He is one of the best coaches I ever had. (*Benton High School*)

This was the asphalt court at my house on the Poor Farm. I wish I had a dollar for every shot I put up on this court. (*Matt Wynn family collection*)

Tim Wills as a senior. Wills was such a fundamentally sound
player and a great compliment to his running
mate- Rob Williams. *(Benton High School)*

Rob Williams was an absolute wizard with the ball. Wiliams had crazy handles
and a flashy game that ignited Rangers fans. *(Ceasar Maragni)*

Kyle Herrin was an all-state player as a senior. As a junior, he gave the Rangers valuable minutes off the bench. *(Ceasar Maragni)*

Clark Dixon was a fiery competitor. Dixon hit a huge jump shot in the Sectional against Cairo to pull the Pilots out of a triangle and two. *(Benton High School)*

Bruce Baker as a sophomore. Baker was an unbelievable talent that played on three Ranger teams that advanced to the State Tournament.
(Ceasar Maragni)

Mark Kerley was an offensive juggernaut that teamed with Baker in '82. Kerley shot over, ducked under and pivoted around taller more athletic players to lead the Rangers in scoring. *(Ceasar Maragni)*

When Baker went down with an injury, Adam Furlow stepped up and the Rangers did not lose until the State Tournament. *(Ceasar Maragni)*

Coach Herrin can be seen thru the perms instructing the '82 Rangers. *(Ceasar Maragni)*

The Herrin family in '82. **Front Row-** Coach, Sue and Kristy
Back Row- Randy, Rod and Kyle. *(Rich Herrin family collection)*

Coach Herrin talks it over with his former player Dick Corn in the BIT. Corn
won 708 games at Pinckneyville and won two state Championships. *(Southern
Illinoisan)*

The '82 Rangers hoist their South Seven Championship board
in late February. *(Ceasar Maragni)*

Jim Muir helped Baker play in '82 and then later became the
Voice of the Rangers. *(Benton High School)*

Herrin talks it over with the officials in the '82 Super-Sectional against the Okawville Rockets. *(Ceasar Maragni)*

Coach Herrin shows his frustration in the quarterfinal game of the '82 state tournament. *(The Southern Illinoisan)*

Rob Williams signs to play at Northern Iowa in the spring of '82.
(Ceasar Maragni)

The '82 Rangers. **Front Row-** Powenski, Skobel, Bigham, Kolisek, Scott
Row Two- Piazza, Dixon, Spencer, Wills, Furlow, Herrin, Williams
Top Row- Webb, Herrin, Kerley, Baker, Thomason, McMahon,
Smith, Stewart *(Benton High School)*

CHAPTER TWENTY-EIGHT

The Rangers Re-load in '83

"Everyone knew their roles on that team." – Kyle Herrin

On July 23, 1982, I was playing tackle football in our backyard with a group of my buddies when I saw my dad's red truck make the curve into our driveway. He shouted for me to come into the house, so I put the game on hold and ran inside. I raced into the house and my dad said, "Hey…I need to talk to you a minute." With that first line, I immediately thought I was in trouble. Did I forget to feed the dogs? Did I not take out the trash? He then sat me down and told and said, "Grandpa passed away." I was stunned. It was my first experience with death. I went to my room and had a good cry. My grandpa was a powerful influence on my childhood. He was always there. It was my Grandpa Gwen Wynn that put the goal up for me and took me to the football field to watch the Rangers practice. He attended all of my Little League games. Most importantly, he spent time with me. We had a very close bond. In my eyes, he was the best.

In my dad's formidable years, my grandpa came down with a life-threatening case of tuberculosis and was quarantined to a St. Louis hospital for more than a year. Grandma Molly and my dad visited him, but could only wave from the window. While my Grandpa was in the hospital, he did a lot of soul searching. There were many lonely days in the sanitarium and he frequently thought about death. As time went on, my grandpa turned to God. He read his Bible and began to grow in his faith.

My grandpa eventually recovered and returned home a different man. He became a Sunday school teacher at First Baptist Church and was a deeply devoted member of the congregation. The thing that I remember the most about Grandpa Wynn was his soft personality. He was patient, loving and kind to everyone. This was the grandpa that I remember.

On a more positive note, another thing I remember about my eighth-grade year was the improvement of our basketball team. My seventh-grade year, West Frankfort defeated us by a score of 33-8. It was an embarrassing defeat that stuck in my craw. Our seventh-grade team improved as the year went on but we finished with an overall record well below .500. It was a tough season.

During the summer, our team played all of the time. We had open gyms at the middle school and most all of us went to the Rend Lake camps. We also had the opportunity to attend an overnight camp at Sweetwater, Tennessee. The summer of '82 was all basketball. Don Fotheringham, a teammate, came over to the house and we spent hours playing one-on-one army. There was no fooling around. We played hard. At night, we turned the lights on and played well into the evening hours. There were many times that we played past midnight and the echo of the ball bouncing against the asphalt was the only sound reverberating through the old poor farm neighborhood.

Besides playing constantly, my teammates and I were growing and maturing. Our team looked different. We were all a few inches taller and much stronger. Our eighth grade coach was Norman Carlile. Carlile was a basketball junkie and was always scheming of ways to beat the opponent. He loved the game of basketball and made the gym available for us to improve. Norman Carlile and Tom Whittington were instrumental in keeping the Ranger machine running. In fact, their role in developing the great players of the late seventies and early eighties cannot be overstated. The combination of hard work, growth and good coaching made our basketball team a force to be reckoned with in the eighth grade.

In our first game of the year, we defeated the West Frankfort Purple Dragons easily at home. Yes, the same team that beat us 33-8 in our first game as seventh graders. Our biggest win came in the Junior High Sectional against the Carbondale Leopards. The game was played at the Benton High School Gymnasium. The Leopards had beaten us twice during the regular season. They were a pressing team and their athleticism overwhelmed us into turnovers and sloppy play. Coach Carlile put us in a sagging man-to-man defense with one rule; no lay-ups. We beat the

Leopards that night by a score of 60-33 and advanced to the Class L State Tournament. Our eighth-grade team finished the year by winning more than 20 games and placing fourth in state. The system was working!

At the high school level, the system was also working. The Rangers lost five key seniors from the '82 team; Mark Kerley, Tim Wills, Rob Williams, Clark Dixon and Adam Furlow. In '83, the Rangers returned junior Bruce Baker, who was possibly the best player in Southern Illinois, and point guard Kyle Herrin. Herrin played a key role as the first guard off the bench in '82. Then the Rangers caught a break. In the late summer of '82, Charlie and Sue Peters moved their family of five athletic boys from Anna-Jonesboro to Benton, Illinois. It was a game changer for the Rangers.

Mark Peters: *On the day we moved to Benton we found a rental home and my Dad said, "Go down to Huck's and grab a newspaper." So, when I get the paper…it was the Southern Illinoisan and on the upper left corner of the front page of the paper was a picture of Ronald Reagan and a headline…on the right corner of the paper was a headline that says, "Peters brings his basketball to Benton." We tried to move quietly but we just couldn't believe it.*

As a junior, Mark was voted the MVP of his football, basketball and baseball teams at Anna-Jonesboro. He enjoyed his coaches there and admitted that it was an extremely tough decision for his parents to move the family to Benton.

Mark Peters: *My parents moved us to Benton because they felt like we had more opportunities. They moved for us. My mom continued to work in Anna, and it was tough for her…it was an unpopular decision…but we loved Anna and the people…It was just parents loving their kids…even though they knew it was going to bother people.*

In his junior season, Peters was recruited by Mississippi State to play basketball and baseball. He stood at 6'5" and was skilled for his size. He could handle the ball like a guard and was an athlete in every sense; strong, a good jumper and quick. Peters quickly won his teammates over with his fun-loving personality and willingness to work hard. He was also a great student. Mark remembered his love for basketball from a young age.

Mark Peters: *I was pretty sure that I was going to be a Boston Celtic when I was in the third grade. I played all sports growing up…it just depended on the season.*

As a junior, Mark's varsity basketball coach at Anna-Jonesboro was Don Smith. Don Smith was one of only two seniors that played on the Rangers team of 1970. The summer before the move took place, he attended several basketball camps and became acquainted with the Rangers players.

Mark Peters: *In the summertime I went to invitation-only type basketball camps. I met Bruce and Kyle and some of the Benton players at these camps. My coach at Anna was Don Smith who was a Benton guy and he encouraged me to meet some of the Benton players…and so I did. So I knew some of those guys before coming over.*

As a junior, Peters had another experience that also made a big impression.

Mark Peters: *I remember my junior year…I went to one of the Benton Invitational games and it just blew me away. The gym was packed and the crowd was electric. The intensity of the games…and watching players that were college-prepped and ready to go. I remember leaving…thinking…I would give anything to be a part of that.*

At the small forward position in '83 was junior Daren Carlile. Daren is the son of former Benton Junior High Coach, Norman Carlile. Carlile does not remember a time in his life without basketball. His father not only coached at the junior high, but also kept the official book for the varsity Rangers. Growing up, he attended all of the high school games.

Daren Carlile: *When I was really young…I remember going to the old gym. It was really cool…and completely packed full of people. I ran around with Kyle and Jeff Johnston. I do remember Billy Smith playing…he just really stood out to me. He was just so good. I remember when Dunbar hurt his knee…we were riding high and were ranked second in the state.*

Daren admitted that his father played a huge role in his love for the game of basketball.

Daren Carlile: *My dad has forgotten more basketball than I will ever know. He had the most influence on me as a player. My dad is eighty-two years old, and he can still evaluate players today. He just knows so much about the game.*

Carlile stood at a sturdy 6'3" tall and he was a tremendous pole player. He was big enough and strong enough to guard a skilled post player. From the guard position, he was a strong rebounder, skilled ball handler, and big enough to see over pressure and strong enough to step through traps. He played at a steady pace and could rarely be forced to get in a hurry. He could hit a mid-range jump shot if the opportunity presented itself. With Baker, Peters and Herrin doing most of the scoring, Daren quietly did his job. He was a perfect fit.

Kyle Herrin: *Matt, I can't tell you how many hours we spent playing one-on-one. Our parents were best friends and we were always together. Daren was really smart and knew his role and played it so well. He was such a hard worker and a great friend.*

Daren recalled some of those great one-on-one battles with Kyle Herrin and remembered one in particular.

Daren Carlile: *Kyle was a competitor…he hated to lose. He and I played hundreds of games of one-on-one, and he beat me more times than I beat him. It killed him if I beat him. I'm an easygoing guy…so it didn't bother me as much when I lost to Kyle…because I knew he was a very good player. One time on the west end of the gym…I beat him. Kyle got mad and took the ball and kicked it like a soccer ball into the chair seats. Right as he was kicking the ball into the chair seats, Coach Herrin walked out of the coach's office…and saw it. Coach got so mad at both of us. The one time that I beat him out of a hundred…we get in trouble.*

The opportunity to play one-on-one in a gym with your teammate was always there. Carlile believes that gym availability and the opportunities to play was a real reason for the Rangers' success.

Daren Carlile: *You know…before you called…that was something that I wanted to talk about. I was around Coach Herrin as early as I can remem-*

ber. I was so lucky to have gone through when I did…we had great teams. Think about this Matt…we had the gym open every morning from 7:30-11:30 am…Monday thru Friday. Yeah…we may have played for a couple of hours and then played a game of wiffle ball…but we were bonding as a team. The gym was open on Monday and Thursday nights and we played at Rend Lake on Wednesday nights. You know, I remember in the spring…some guys were running track…some weren't. I can't tell you how many times Robbie Williams or Tim Wills would say, "Daren, can you call your dad?" We would go to the middle school and play if there was something going on in the gym. Coach Herrin issued every basketball player a ball with a number on it and we put it in our lockers. He didn't want you to come to the gym and not be able to practice because you didn't have a ball. We had the camps in the summer. The availability was unreal. We had unlimited access to play basketball and that was really important.

Playing alongside Kyle Herrin at the off-guard position was senior Cameron Skobel. Skobel had thin red hair and stood at 5'10", and 140 pounds soaking wet. He was lightning-quick and darted around the floor with endless energy. Defensively, he jumped passing lanes and gave up his body for loose balls along with guarding the opponent's best offensive guard. Offensively, he could sometimes play thirty-two minutes without scoring, but the team was not the same when he wasn't in the game. Like Carlile, he was very self-aware of what he could and couldn't do and tended to always make the safe decision on the offensive end of the floor. Skobel was not looked upon to score and embraced his role as a defensive stopper. Skobel's 110% effort inspired his teammates and made the Rangers a tough team to beat. He seemed to be in every play.

Skobel was not your prototype two guard. He did something that is almost impossible to do in the game of basketball; he made the transition from playing inside in junior high to a guard in high school.

Cameron Skobel: *You know what opposition I played in junior high basketball? I was the center. I was 5'10" and played with my back to the basket. I was the leading scorer in junior high and the low scorer when I graduated. That's a hell of a transition. I had a hard time moving from the post to the guard spot. Inside eight to ten feet I could shoot the ball, but outside of that I wasn't a good shooter. Coach Herrin sat me down for a heart-to-heart when I was a freshman. He talked to me just like a father talks to his son. We were by ourselves and there were no distractions. He said, "Here's what I need you* *to do. Practice your shot as much as possible…some will go in and some won't. Right now, you may be the fastest kid in the school…and that is exactly what I'm going to use you for. You are going to be a defensive stopper." And that is exactly what happened. My senior year, I averaged more steals than points. I worked at it and a big reason I was able to make that adjustment to the guard spot was from his guidance. He knew what he was going to do with me when I was a freshman. He could tell you how to get there. He complimented me too in the papers…he appreciated my effort.*

Skobel excelled on the football field and was one of the Rangers top sprinters on the track team.

Cameron Skobel: *I ran the 330 hurdles, the 4 x 100, and the mile relay in track. In football I was a defensive halfback and flanker on offense. I was also the kick-off and punt returner.*

The other seniors on the '83 team were Mike Kolisek, David Spencer, Steve Bigham and Jim McMahon. They were all capable players and provided the regulars with plenty of competition in practices.

Jim McMahon: *I was telling someone the other day…I got to play against one of the top five teams in the state my junior and senior year every day in practice.*

Mike Kolisek was a stand-out golfer in the fall and was good friends with Kyle Herrin in high school. Many people have tried to impersonate Coach Herrin, but there may be no better impersonator that Mike Kolisek.

Mike Kolisek: *I went to the games as early as six years old and Kyle (Herrin) was sitting on the ball bag watching the games. I remember seeing Paul Dinkins, Chris Moore, Hugh Frailey, Rick Thomas. Probably the best team I saw growing up was Tabor, Dunbar, Craddock and Smith. I was there when Dunbar hurt his knee that night.*

Rounding out the team were juniors Jay Bradshaw, Alan Shell, Jeff Johnston, Troy Hewlett, Keith Ray and Brian Eubanks. Bradshaw, Hewlett and Shell received spot playing time early in the year. As a junior, Jeff Johnston played junior varsity basketball and was being groomed for the point guard position as a senior. He was the son of former seventh-grade coach Bob Johnston. Johnston attended Ewing Grade School but remembered being at some of his dad's practices in old Webster Gymnasium.

Jeff Johnston: *When my dad was coaching with Burton Wills at the junior high, I remember sitting on the medicine kit and watching the games. One time I had an earache, but I wouldn't leave because I wanted to watch the game. Another time…I was pretty small…I jumped off the old Webster school stage and busted my chin on the stage and I ran down to the old locker room steps and cried because I didn't want to let the bigger guys see me cry.*

Johnston also remembered attending the Benton games as a youngster and recalled why he chose jersey number 23 in junior high.

Jeff Johnston: *The '74-'75 team was the first team that really caught my eye. I would cut out newspaper clippings from the newspaper and post them all over my room. My room was a running bulletin board of the season. They had a place in the program where you could keep score and I always kept the score. I was always a Billy Smith fan. Later when I started playing…I chose number 23 because of Billy Smith. I remember being extremely upset when Rob Dunbar tore his knee up.*

The only sophomore on the '83 team was Randy House. One thing I do remember about the '82-'83 season was watching the sophomore games before the varsity games. Physically, House was a man among boys in the sophomore games and I loved to watch him maneuver around the basket. He was a red-headed lefty and stood at 6'2" with wide shoulders and a narrow waist and was clearly the best sophomore player in the area. He had great instincts along with a strong basketball IQ.

Randy House: *Coach Stewart was the greatest coach ever. He said, "I don't care who shoots as long as Randy touches the ball first. Our sophomore year, we were okay. Coach Stewart gave me a lot of freedom and I was putting up some points. It was a fun year.*

It was obvious House was going to be a great player. But the question was; should Coach Herrin move him up?

Randy House: *Dude…we were good. It really didn't bother me much at the time that I wasn't playing varsity. Who was I better than? That was a really*

702

strong team in '83. In my opinion, I was more of a post player…young…not ready. Playing at the sophomore level was good for me…it really gave me some confidence.

In the fall, many of the basketball players chose to run cross country to stay in shape for basketball. Although Peters was a stand-out football player at Anna-Jonesboro High School, he chose not to play football to pursue a full-ride basketball scholarship. So, Peters ran cross country with the rest of the basketball players in the fall of '82.

Kyle Herrin: *Mark was pretty straight-laced…and he and his family had just moved to town. We were running cross country in this race called the Franklin County Fun Run. We had like twenty-five cross country guys. I told Bruce, Daren and Mark that we should just cut off the middle mile…it was in the woods at the park…and then we'll just hide out and jump back into the race and run the final mile. Little did I know that Coach Webb was at the mile and a half mark. So that is what we did. We stopped…and then got back in the race with one mile to go. We came across the finish line like we were wore out and my dad came straight to me and said, "Where were you?" Then he told me that he knew we didn't come through at the mile and a half mark. Dad was really mad at all of us. I felt bad for Mark….he hadn't been at Benton ten days and I already had him in trouble.*

Tim Wills and Rob Williams had been the starting guards the past two seasons. They were gone. Kyle Herrin and Cameron Skobel would now fill their shoes. It did not take long for the team to realize that Kyle Herrin would be the leader of the '83 Rangers.

Bruce Baker: *The guards in '83 with Kyle and Cameron were so different than Robbie and Tim. They were just different players. Kyle worked so hard over the summer and he was just so steady. Cameron just kept getting better also. I remember that Cameron would tell the other team things like, "We're going to win this game." He was very confident.*

As a senior, Kyle Herrin stood at 5'10" and it was clear that he was physically stronger and more filled out. Herrin was a tenacious competitor that, much like his father, hated to lose. At the point guard position, he just didn't make many mistakes. He rarely turned the ball over and he had a personality that his teammates gravitated to. Herrin did not care about point totals; it was always about winning the game. Herrin played like the coach's son that he was, and developed into one of the finest playmakers in Benton basketball history. Cameron Skobel had high praise for his back-court mate.

Cameron Skobel: *The first thing that comes to mind about Kyle is that he played with a chip on his shoulder. He wanted people to know that he was playing because of his skill and not his last name. And he was. He worked hard…he was a competitor. He was the ultimate professional on the floor… the director. I remember Coach Herrin might holler out a play and Kyle would change it if he thought it was best. He ran the team the way his dad wanted him to…but he might change something if he saw something might work better. He was a great guy to play with.*

Baker had nothing but respect for Herrin and acknowledged what a great leader Kyle became for the team at the point guard position.

Bruce Baker: *Here is a guy that steps in and is our leader immediately. It was amazing…Kyle was our leader from day one. Kyle played with an unbelievable amount of confidence. He knew what he was and what he wanted to do. I can remember looking at him in the locker room and the sweat would just be dripping off of his nose. Kyle was a sweater like me. He played so hard. He was a gamer.*

Jeff Johnston: *That team was always Kyle's team. Kyle was a hard-nosed competitor. He was the kind of guy you wanted on your team…he didn't want to lose. I remember times in open gym and if you were on his team and you weren't running the floor…he would be mad enough to fight you. He was a good leader.*

Mark Peters: *Kyle was the team captain…he was our point guard and was a good leader. He had incredible talent and he was the best ball handler I ever played with in high school. I enjoyed playing with Kyle as much as anybody. He would pass it and you better be awake. That's the kind of guy you want to play with. I visited Kyle several times at Tennessee Martin when he played there in college and we became good friends.*

Although Skobel didn't score much, he earned the respect of his teammates through his effort and tenacious play on the floor.

Daren Carlile: *Cameron was an athlete above anything else. He was a good football player and he could really run. His best attribute in basketball was his defense. He was fearless. Cameron was not a fighter…but you could just look at him and know…that dude would fight anybody anywhere. He was a great teammate.*

Kyle Herrin: *At 5'10"…Cameron could run all day. He was just a real talented athlete. Hard-nosed…always worked hard…and he wanted to win. He wasn't just about Cameron, you know. He was our shut-down guy and he always guarded the best opposing guard. That also kept me out of foul trouble and freed me up to handle the ball. He was just another great teammate.*

Mark Peters: *"Skob" was just sneaky fast…quick and unpredictable. You just never knew what he was going to do. He was kind of like our Dennis Rodman…he played a great role for us.*

During the early fall of '82, I got a call from Coach Herrin. He said, "Hey big guy, can you come up to the middle school and play…we need another guy to play cross-court. I told Coach, "Be right there." I grabbed my tennis shoes and my mom quickly chauffeured me to the middle school gym. I was in the eighth grade and beyond excited to get the call. When I walked into the gym there were nine high school guys shooting around. One of them I had never seen; it was Mark Peters. I knew Mark had moved in, but had never seen him up close. The thing that first struck me about Mark was his size and strength and the way he carried it. He was not awkward and looked to be about as tall as Baker. We chose teams and it was clear that my job was to just be happy that I was there. That is what I did. Coach Herrin watched us play and I just remember the fierce competition between Peters and Baker. After we played our first game to seven, I then realized how hard Mark played. They were the two alpha males and there was just one ball. I wondered how that dynamic might play out. Were they going to be able to play together?

Bruce Baker: *He made me raise my game to a new level. Even though your teammates…you want to always make sure that you're doing your part and playing with that edge. The timing was perfect. We had met at a basketball camp. I remember thinking, I'm going to have to bump my game up with this guy and make sure I was doing my job. He could really box you out. The* *front of my thighs still hurt because of his bony butt boxing me out. He could rebound and his game was very polished. He had great instincts...and knew where the ball was coming off. Mark told me, "What I want to do here at Benton is match your drive. I'll play as hard as you play." And he did that. Mark was a gym rat.*

Mark Peters: *I played against Bruce in some summer camps. We liked each other...and we competed hard against each other...neither one of us wanted to take a back seat to the other. Bruce was the high scorer on that team even as a junior. He was the backbone of that team...even more than me.*

Baker and Peters played hard against each other but they grew to respect one another and became good friends off the floor. Peters remembers Baker being a ton of fun off the floor.

Mark Peters: *I remember one time in high school...I was sick and didn't go to school. I was at home by myself. Bake had this hot rod car...and I hear over this loudspeaker, "We have the house surrounded...come out with your hands up!" I look outside the window and its Bake. He just got this new loud-speaker...and he was standing by his car laughing his butt off.*

As the season approached, once again, anticipation grew high in the community about the basketball team. And rightly so.

Daren Carlile: *We were excited when Mark Peters moved to town. We knew Bruce was as good as anybody. I was super excited to play with Kyle. We never got to play with each other because he was a year ahead of me. Kyle was just smart...competitive...hard-nosed and he hated to get beat. He was not a good loser. Skobel was just an intense defender...fast hands. He was our defensive stopper and he embraced that role. Bruce and Mark were just so good...I didn't have to score...so I rebounded and just did my thing. Everybody knew their roles.*

The Rangers opened play at Mcleansboro on Tuesday, November 30, 1982. Brian Sloan, the son of Chicago Bulls player and McLeansboro native, Jerry Sloan had just moved in from Glenbard North High School. He stood at a solid 6'8". For the next two seasons, Sloan and Baker was the most anticipated match-up in Southern Illinois.

The Foxes were led by Coach Dave Lee. Lee's son, Darin, was the point guard. Darin Lee was the floor general and was one of the best guards in Southern Illinois. Senior Curt Reed, Jr. was a force on both ends of the floor and then there were the Sturm brothers; Tracy and Stacy. Tracy was a 6'2" slasher and Stacy was a 6'3" back-to-the-bucket post player. Big Kevin Kirsch was a senior and Rod Irvin was the first player off the bench. The Foxes were loaded.

As the players boarded the bus, Mark Peters found a seat by the window and reflected on his journey to Benton. He was about to play his first game as a Benton Ranger, and he was nerved up to say the least.

Mark Peters: *I felt a lot of pressure when we first moved to Benton. It was like…I can't be bad! I can't not start…you know. I can't have an off-night. A lot of things went through my head. I remember the first game with McLeansboro better than I do the BIT game with them…because that was my first game.*

The old gym at McLeansboro overflowed as the varsity game approached. The Rangers were in their maroon away uniforms with the traditional eight stars on the front panels of the shorts. The Foxes were in their home whites trimmed in green. On this night, the Foxes were without the services of starting point guard Darin Lee, who was out with an injury. Rod Irvin started in his place. In the first quarter, Mark Peters scored seven points to lead the Rangers to a 13-10 lead. The Rangers led at halftime by a score of 25-22. The play was physical and intense. The packed crowd hung on every play. It was high school basketball at its best.

In the third quarter, the Rangers spread the lead to 36-29. Sloan and Baker battled each other for position in the post. Baker had 15 points heading into the final period. Kyle Herrin took over the game late and sealed the win by scoring eight points in the final quarter to lead the Rangers to an easy 54-40 victory. There was perhaps nobody more relieved with the win than Mark Peters.

Mark Peters: *I remember the relief I felt to win that first game against McLeansboro.*

Junior Daren Carlile also remembers the McLeansboro game for a different reason.

Daren Carlile: *I remember the first game really well because it was my first varsity game. You couldn't have squeezed another person into that old gym at McLeansboro. There were high expectations for that team, especially when Brian Sloan moved in. They were just getting used to playing with him… we handled them pretty good. I just remember having a ton of respect for those guys. They had Sloan and then Darin Lee, Curt Reed, Scott Craven, the Sturm brothers…they were a good team.*

On Friday, December 3rd, the Rangers defeated Pinckneyville, 75-57, and then defeated Mt. Vernon at home by a score of 71-53. In the Pinckneyville game, Baker went off for 32 points. Kyle Herrin remembers what Baker brought to the team.

Kyle Herrin: *Bruce played up with us in junior high and I knew right off the bat that he was going to be a player. He was hard-nosed. He played hard and he wanted to win. Bruce played up with us when he was a freshman on the sophomore team and we were 22-0. We played for Coach Stewart, and he would be like, "Ok, let's play hard on both ends of the floor!" There wasn't much that Coach Stewart needed to say. A lot of our success that year was because of Bruce. Bruce was like a receiver in football…he always wanted the ball. He was such a competitor. There were times when we clashed and even came to blows, but we knew that we needed each other to get to where we wanted to go. I think he would say the same thing. We squared off one time in summer open gym…Rod Shurtz was running it…. Bruce was swinging down at me and I was swinging up at him. But we were both competitors and we both wanted to win. At the end of the day, I have nothing but the utmost respect for his abilities as a player. We would not have been able to achieve what we did without him…he was a great teammate.*

On Sunday, December 5th, the Benton Community gathered at the gymnasium to honor Coach Herrin's career at Benton High School. Earlier that year, the BCHS school board voted in favor of naming the new gymnasium in his honor. The school board members were; Mark Kern, David Hurley, Bill Kerley, Bill B. Smith, Roger Edwards, Kenneth Price and Bill Uhles. The vote was unanimous. Community members and fans filled the south side of the gym for the presentation. All of the current players sat in the bottom row of the bleachers. Coach Herrin and his family sat in chairs on the gym floor facing the crowd. A souvenir booklet was sold featuring pictures of Coach Herrin's greatest moments. Illinois Sate Representative

James Rea presented a proclamation declaring December 5th to be Rich Herrin day throughout the state. The president of the BCHS board and former player, Bill Kerley, made a special presentation and Benton Mayor LeLand Brown presented Coach with a key to the city. Ron Herrin and Dick Corn also spoke on Herrin's behalf. The dedication of the gym was presented by Frank "Doc" Hunsaker, who was Herrin's high school coach at Bridgeport. At the time, Rich Herrin was fifty years old. He had a career of 549-191 and was approaching 500 wins at Benton High School. The new gym was now named "Rich Herrin Gymnasium".

Sitting at 2-0 and playing in the newly dedicated Rich Herrin Gymnasium, The Rangers prepared for their toughest test of the year against the Mt. Vernon Rams. Mt. Vernon was a strong team in '83. They featured 6'2" jumping jack Eric Hawthorne along with inside player Kevin Riggan. Steve McCoy and Darren Hacker were solid at the guard spot.

Daren Carlile: *I think we beat Mt. Vernon three out of four times that year. Mt. Vernon was a powerhouse. I remember my dad went to see Mt. Vernon play before we played them. When he came home he said, "I don't know if you guys can beat them."*

The game was played at Benton and Daren Carlile remembers an incident that happened in the game.

Daren Carlile: *So we hadn't played them yet…in the days leading up to our first game at home with them Coach Herrin talked to us about what to expect. He told us that they were going to steal the ball from time to time and they like to dunk it off the steal. This kind of gets them going. Don't get upset if that happens. So I'm dribbling down the right side of the floor and I made a crosscourt pass…Hawthorne steals the ball and goes down and just tomahawk-dunks one. So immediately… Coach Herrin subs in for me and chews me pretty good. "Gosh dang it, Carlile!" So I am thinking…I thought we weren't supposed to get upset if they dunked. I'm not upset…but Coach was…it was funny.*

Cameron Skobel recalled an incident that happened in the first of four meetings with the Rams.

Cameron Skobel: *We played a triangle and two on Darren Hacker and Eric Hawthorne. I guarded Hacker. We were good friends. Mark Peters guarded*

Hawthorne. Coach Herrin told me that when Hacker didn't have the ball that I could guard everyone. I stole the ball from Hawthorne and I was laying on the ground and he was kind of in mid-air and it looked like he was going to stomp on me...Mark Peters kind of pushed him away. I remember Mark got us in a huddle and said, "We're not going to play this game." We went on to win the game by 18 points.

The following night, the Rangers escaped with a 74-71 win at home against the Massac County Patriots. Again, Baker led the team with 26 points followed by Mark Peters with 17. Kyle Herrin and Daren Carlile led the team with seven assists. Baker and Herrin were leading the team but the play of Mark Peters and Daren Carlile cannot be overstated. Both players were finding their place on the team and excelling in their roles. Cameron Skobel was doing his thing on the defensive end of the floor and led the team with four steals. Skobel laughed as he remembered pinning Daren Carlile with his nickname.

Cameron Skobel: *Better known as "Ooze." You know I gave him that nickname. If you didn't know...there were times that Darin didn't move very fast. We were in practice and I said something like... Hey "Ooze" could you slide over here a little faster? Coach Herrin heard it, and that was all it took...it stuck. He and Mark Peters were a lot alike. They were businesslike...quiet. They could both handle the ball and shoot it. Darin and Mark were both very confident in their ability. They were great guys to have on your team. If it came to pushing and shoving...they always had your back.*

Then on Friday, December 17th, the Rangers pounded the Redbirds by a score of 62-41 at Max Morris Gymnasium. Bruce Baker led the way with 26 points and Cameron Skobel chipped in with ten points. The win moved the Rangers to 5-0 overall and 2-0 in South Seven Conference play.

On Tuesday, December 21st, the Rangers traveled to Bowen Gymnasium to play the Carbondale Terriers. It was their last game before heading to the Centralia Tournament. The Terriers were solid and featured Avery Henry, Darron Rushing, Mike Altekruse, Tom Stein and Joe Hamilton. The Rangers jumped out to a 16-12 advantage before Carbondale captured the lead, 30-29, at the half. Behind the play of Bruce Baker, the Rangers took a 43-40 advantage after three quarters of play. The game went back and forth. With under .30 seconds to play, the Rangers led 56-55 and needed one defensive stop to escape C-town with the win. The Terriers worked the ball to Mike Altekruse, who hit an 18-foot jumper with just .06 seconds remaining to defeat the Rangers. The Carbondale win created a crazy five-way tie for first place in the conference before the new year. With the loss, the Rangers moved to 5-1 overall and 2-1 in Conference play.

The Rangers headed into the Centralia Tournament with a legitimate shot to win. After six games, the Rangers were confident despite the loss at Carbondale. They knew they were a good basketball team. The Rangers opened tournament play with a convincing 53-39 win over Champaign Centennial. Baker, Herrin and Peters led the Rangers in scoring. The win advanced the Rangers to a match-up with the Arlington Cardinals. The Cardinals had two great players in Rick Elkins and Chris Berg. The Rangers never trailed in the contest and won game two by a score of 55-49. Kyle Herrin played the angles and pumped bounce passes into the post for easy scores all afternoon. Herrin finished the game with a whopping 12 assists. He also scored 14 points. Herrin ran the team flawlessly and relished his moment in the Centralia Tournament. Kyle was clearly one of the best guards in the tournament and the team was firing on all cylinders. Once again, Bruce Baker led the Rangers in scoring with 22 points and Mark Peters chipped in with 14 points. Daren Carlile led the team in rebounding with seven and Cameron Skobel raced around Trout Gymnasium disrupting the Cardinals offense.

The Rangers were now heading for the semi-finals against the Madison Trojans. On Wednesday, December 29, 1982, fans caravaned behind the team bus in hopes that the Rangers could win a sixth tournament championship. Many Benton fans planned on staying all day knowing that the Rangers were guaranteed the third-place game that night if they lost in the afternoon. Anticipating the games, old timers carpooled to the tournament fully engaged in conversation about the team the entire trip.

At halftime, Benton led Madison by a score of 27-22. In the third quarter, the Rangers blew the game open with the formula of Herrin to Baker. Herrin recorded 12 assists and Baker led all scorers with 28 points. Mark Peters also scored 18 points in the 63-44 romp over Madison. Benton fans quickly exited Trout Gymnasium and headed to Jerry's Bigger Jigger to eat and kill time before the evening session. The team celebrated their victory and ate together at a down-town diner. After the meal, the team lodged in a local motel to put their feet up before departing for the championship game.

On the other side of the championship bracket was the Mt. Vernon Rams. The Rangers had already beaten the Rams handily at home by a score of 71-53. This game would be different. The championship match-up speaks to how competitive the South Seven was during this time. There were 16 teams at the Centralia Tournament from all across the state, but it was Benton and Mt. Vernon in the final game. In the early eighties, the South Seven remained as one of the most rugged leagues in the state.

The crowd buzzed as the two teams took the floor for the 1982 championship game of the Centralia Holiday Tournament. The balcony overflowed with fans and a sea of orange and maroon blanketed the gym. The Rangers ran out to loud boos from the Mt. Vernon faithful with the Centralia fans joining in. The Benton faithful then overcame the jeering and chanted, "RANGERS! RANGERS!" It was on!

I was in attendance at the game and it was one of the greatest high school basketball games I ever saw growing up. The Rangers wore their home whites lined in maroon and the Rams wore their road black out-lined in orange and white. The gym shook during the introduction of the starting line-ups. The standing room only crowd then stood silently for the national anthem and then it was game time. As the ten players took the floor, there was an intensity to the moment that was hard to put into words. I remember thinking, wow! So many great players on the floor at the same time, I knew it was going to be a good one.

At the end of one, the Rams led 14-12. Both teams were in the feel-ing-out phase and it was obvious after the first eight minutes that the game was going to be close. In the second quarter, the Rangers took a 28-27 lead into halftime. The crowd hung on every play. I was with a bunch of my buddies tucked underneath the balcony and we had to peek around a support beam to see the game.

In the third quarter, the Rangers extended the lead to 41-37 with only one period to play. To open the final quarter, the Rams got hot and got clutch baskets from Steve McCoy and Eric Hawthorne. Before Hawthorne hit an eighteen-foot jumper from the left wing, I heard a Mt. Vernon fan yell, "Shoot it Popsicle"! When he hit that shot, that place went bananas and Coach Herrin called a quick time out. After the time out, the Rangers regrouped and battled back.

There is a saying in athletics; "The cream rises to the top." Bruce Baker scored ten of his 23 points in the fourth quarter and popped a 15-foot jumper from the free-throw line to put the Rangers up 56-55 with just .37 seconds left to play. The Rams then missed a shot and Baker was fouled on the rebound with only .08 seconds remaining. Under immense pressure, the junior quickly grabbed the ball from the official and with all the confidence in the world banged home the first free throw of a one-in-one. He then hit the second free throw to put the Rangers up 58-55. Coach Herrin instructed his team not to foul and the Rams scored an easy lay-in and quickly fouled Kyle Herrin with only .02 seconds on the clock. With the score 58-57 and .02 seconds left, Kyle Herrin knocked in both free throws to put the Rangers ahead by three. Mt. Vernon threw a long baseball pass to the other end and scored to make the final score 60-59 Rangers. You could not have written the script any better; Kyle Herrin at the line to nail down his dad's sixth Centralia Tournament championship. Rangers fans flooded the floor to congratulate the players and coaches. That game. That scene. I wanted to be on that floor someday.

There is a picture in the 1983 yearbook of Mark Peters standing with both hands high in the air that says it all. Winning the Centralia Tournament was special and the transfer from Anna-Jonesboro certainly did his part. After the tournament, the All-Tournament team was announced. For the first time in history, three players from the same team were voted on the All-Tournament team; Bruce Baker, Mark Peters and Kyle Herrin. Bruce Baker was chosen as MVP of the tournament by leading all scorers with 94 points in four games for an average of 23.4 points. It is also important to acknowledge the play of Carlile and Skobel in the championship game. Carlile scored nine points and grabbed five rebounds. Skobel scored eight points and hit two pressure free throws late in the game.

When reflecting on his high school career, Kyle Herrin pointed out that defeating Mt. Vernon in the 1982 Centralia Holiday Tournament was one of his favorite memories.

Kyle Herrin: *I would have to say that the Mt. Vernon game in the Centralia Holiday Tournament Championship my senior year was a big one. It was Dad's last tournament championship and his sixth overall. I think he still has the most championships in tournament history. Mt. Vernon was really good. They had Hawthorne, Riggan and a bunch of good players.*

Later in college, Bruce Baker met up with Mt. Vernon's Kevin Riggan. Riggan wanted to know how the Rangers did it. Baker was quick to give credit to Coach Herrin.

Bruce Baker: *He came to my apartment one night when we were in college and he said, "How did you guys do it?" What was it about Benton?" I told him* *that it was the way that we were led. Coach Herrin was a winner and losing was just not part of our vocabulary.*

With the win, the Rangers improved to 9-1 overall. Winning the Centralia Tournament moved the Rangers to eighth in the Class 2A state rankings. The team bus pulled around square late on that Wednesday evening to be greeted by hundreds of fans that understood the magnitude of winning the Centralia Tournament. The players hung out the bus windows and waved. It was a perfect day.

The Rangers returned to practice to prepare for a string of five games before opening play in the annual Benton Invitational Tournament. Just as the sixties and seventies, Herrin's practices challenged his players both mentally and physically.

Mark Peters: *We practiced like we played. During the season there wasn't a bunch of bull going on outside of basketball…and if there was…there were guys on the team that policed that.*

Playing with great confidence, The Rangers won five in a row and four league games to remain in first place in the South Seven. The Rangers defeated Okawville, Centralia, Harrisburg, Herrin and Marion. The winning along with the productive practices gave the team a feeling of invincibility. All of the players believed they were going to win every game. The attitude was simple; we are the Benton Rangers and we win.

Mark Peters: *I just knew we were going to win every night and I was completely shocked the four times that we got beat. Coach Herrin knew how to win. He could take about any group of guys and win with them…his records speak to that. Having Coach Herrin and practicing the way we did…the way we prepared…somebody was going to get their butt kicked and most of the time it wasn't us.*

Randy House: *I never went into a game in my high school career thinking we were going to lose a game because he gave us the attitude that we were better than everybody else. Coach made us carry ourselves better than everyone else…the haircuts…the uniforms…our warm-up routines…the briefcases we kept our uniforms in…who did that back then? Coach applied that pressure subliminally to all of us…and then we had all of the great teams* *that came before us in the sixties and seventiess. There was pressure to keep that going.*

The big story about the '83 Benton Invitational was the addition of the McLeansboro Foxes. The Edwardsville Tigers left but the young and talented Foxes stepped in to fill the void. For the next thirty-eight years the Foxes brought competitive teams to the BIT that had a unique style of play. Former coach Dave Lee explained how the Foxes got the opportunity to participate in one of the greatest mid-winter tournaments in the State of Illinois.

David Lee: *We were in a tournament at Harrisburg and Rich called us about coming over to the BIT. I didn't really know if we could compete over there… we were a small school and you know how that is…sometimes you have talent and sometimes you don't. Rich talked me into coming over and it was one of the best decisions I ever made when I was at McLeansboro.*

Heading into the grueling week of the Benton Invitational Tournament, the Rangers were 14-1 overall and 6-1 in conference play. In the first game of the BIT, the Rangers defeated the Pinckneyville Panthers by a score of 71-41. Bruce Baker led the Ranger attack with 21 points followed by Mark Peters with 17. Kyle Herrin added ten points and dished out nine assists. Jeff Johnston, David Spencer, Jay Bradshaw, Mike Kolisek and Troy Hewlett all got in the scoring column.

Cameron Skobel: *The BIT my senior year was the greatest week of basketball that I ever played. I loved playing Pinckneyville. Coach Corn coached the way Coach Herrin did and they had a friendly rivalry. It had a lot to do with the fans too. A lot of the fans came to watch Coach Herrin and us. They came out of respect for him…they liked his passion for the game and his players.*

Junior Troy Hewlett saw spot action at the guard spot in '83 and was the team character. Hewlett was affectionately called "Shide" by his teammates for his streaky shooting. Hewlett could get Baker going and the two of them together could be a riot. The practice after the Pinckneyville game, an incident happened involving Hewlett and Coach Herrin which lives on in Ranger lore.

Jeff Johnston: *I think it was after practice. We were all kind of goofing around...throwing up some half court shots...Coach Herrin came out and said something like, "Why don't you guys shoot game shots?" Troy ran over to the bleachers...I think they were pushed in at the time...and sat down on the bench and slung one up. I don't think Coach Herrin found it very funny...but we did.*

In game two of the BIT, the Rangers ripped the Cairo Pilots by a score of 81-61. Baker scored 32 and Mark Peters chipped in with 21. Cairo's Selma Snow and Michael Ayers led the Pilots attack with 18 points each.

On Friday, January 21st, the Rangers played the Okawville Rockets. In the first game of the new year played at the SIU Arena, the Rangers won easily 50-35. Coach Dave Luechtefeld had his team ready and the game went to the wire. Mark Peters' basket tied the game at 58 with under a minute to play. After a Rocket turnover, the Rangers had the ball with just seconds left. Kyle Herrin swished a runner as time expired to give the Rangers a 60-58 victory at the horn. Ranger fans chanted, "Ky-le! Ky-le!" An excited Herrin pumped his fist and led his teammates into the locker room. Hewlett had four big points off the bench. Paul Jansen led the Rockets in scoring with 22 points. The Rangers were now 17-1 and 3-0 in the BIT.

Bruce Baker: *Kyle was the best shooter off the run that I've ever seen.*

Later that night, Darren Lee banged home a 16-foot jumper to beat the Olney Tigers to keep the Foxes unbeaten (3-0) in the tournament. The tournament was shaping up to be a Saturday night championship game between the Rangers and the Foxes.

On Saturday, the Rangers had a 12:30 tip-off with the Olney Tigers. The Tigers played tough but the Rangers pulled away to win the game 68-60. Mark Peters led the team with 22 points, but the story of the game was the play of reserve guard Troy Hewlett. In an attempt to rest legs for the showdown with the Foxes, Coach Herrin inserted Hewlett into the game and he responded. Shide scored nine points off the bench to contribute to the victory. The Foxes also won that afternoon to set up one of the classic championship games in BIT history.

A packed house was on hand to watch McLeansboro and Benton battle it out for the championship of the '83 BIT. Both teams came into the game unbeaten in tournament play and McLeansboro was a different team than the Rangers had faced in late November. Darren Lee was in the line-up and Brian Sloan was now comfortable with his new team.

David Lee: *My son was on that team…then Brian Sloan moved in from Glenbard North High School…Curt Reed, the Sturm brothers, Scott Craven and Kevin Kirsch. We had some great athletes.*

The game began at 9:12 p.m. and for the next two hours fans were entertained with one of the greatest games ever played in the BIT. The Rangers won the tip and Baker scored the first points of the contest. PA announcer John D. Aiken enthusiastically announced Br-u-u-u-u-ce Baker, much to the delight of the Rangers fans. It must be a sound that Baker can still hear today. The gym shook. After the first half, the Rangers took a 26-20 lead into halftime intermission.

After halftime, the Rangers came out sluggish and a Brian Sloan basket gave the Foxes their first lead at 41-40. The Foxes pushed their lead to 47-42 to end the third quarter. Senior Kyle Herrin then took over and scored the first nine points of the period as the Rangers regained the lead 51-49 with 5:14 left in the game.

David Lee: *I remember Darin had trouble with Kyle Herrin…he was a great player. I'll never forget walking into that gym at Benton and looking at that crowd…I still think that is the most people I've ever seen in that gym.*

The two great teams battled back and forth for the next four minutes of the game. Sloan picked up his fifth foul with .59 seconds left in the game and his team up by one. Before fouling out, the 6'8" junior scored 21 points. Mark Peters hit both ends of a one-and-one to give the Rangers a 58-57 lead. On the next possession, Tracy Sturm hit a 15-foot jumper with just .38 seconds left to give the Foxes a 59-58 lead. The Rangers then turned the ball over but the Foxes returned the favor to give the ball back to Benton. The Rangers used their final timeout in regulation to design a play to get Herrin the ball hoping for a duplication of his heroics of Friday night. Herrin's jump shot rimmed off, but Mark Peters rose high to rebound the ball and was fouled on his shot by Kevin Kirsch. It was Kirsch's fifth personal foul. Under immense pressure and his team down by one point, Peters missed the first one. McLeansboro fans did everything they could to distract Peters on his second attempt, but he dropped it to send the game into overtime.

Tied at 59, the game went into overtime: advantage Benton, especially with Sloan and Kirsch fouled out of the game. Unfortunately, the Rangers seemed spent to start the overtime period. Darren Lee scored the first five points of the overtime and the Rangers just couldn't recover. A sea of fans dressed in green flooded the floor as the final horn sounded. The Foxes defeated the Rangers 66-63 in overtime. It was a tough defeat for the Rangers. Bruce Baker, Kyle Herrin and Mark Peters were selected to the BIT All-Tournament team. With the loss, the Rangers fell to 18-2.

Daren Carlile: *We probably overlooked them a little bit when we played them in the BIT.*

Kyle Herrin scored 16 points in the game and almost willed his team to victory in the second half. Kyle played for his dad. I was curious to ask him about his experience playing for his dad. He told me a funny story that I could relate to because I'm sure there were many times my son felt like this when I was coaching him individually.

Kyle Herrin: *Fortunately, all of my teams were pretty good. It wasn't the practice times that were the toughest. Dad didn't get on me all the time because I knew what to do…it was the alone time that was sometimes tough. Like going up to the gym on a Sunday afternoon and shooting. I remember one Sunday he was getting on me about something, and I said something back to him…he could be demanding. He said something else and I took the ball and whizzed it at him overhand and hit him and I took off running. And he took off after me. He was chasing me and I realized that this was never going to end until he caught me so I stopped at the water fountain and he kicked me. It's kind of funny to think about today but it wasn't funny at the time. Overall, it was really great playing for Dad…he didn't have a lot to get on to me about and we had good teams. It went so fast…it was a blur.*

Being a coach's son, Kyle was with his dad all of the time. He was the Ranger mascot. As a youngster, he rode the buses to the games and even tagged along to the track meets in the spring.

Kyle Herrin: *One time when I was little we went to a track meet in Olney and my dad always drove the bus. We had like thirty guys on the track team and the meet was coming to an end and he had me go into the school and order 30 cheeseburgers from Dairy Queen for the track team. So I called Dairy*

Queen and told them who I was and that I needed 30 cheeseburgers and orders of fries. The guy from Dairy Queen said, "Do you want singles, doubles or triples?" It kind of caught me off guard and I was under pressure to answer on the phone and I said, "triples." Well, we get there and Dad goes in and gets the burgers and comes back to the bus and says, "Gosh Dang it, Kyle! You ordered triples and they are like $1.50 more for each burger." And I remember the track guys all started cheering because it was more food for them.

On Friday, January 29, 1982, the Rangers traveled to Mt. Vernon to play the Rams at Changnon Gymnasium. It was the third meeting between the two teams and the Rams finally defeated the Rangers behind 23 points from Eric Hawthorne. The final score was 64-60. The loss knocked the Rangers out of first place in the conference but the following night, the Rangers recovered to beat West Frankfort at home, by a score of 76-50. The Rangers were now 19-3 overall and 7-2 in conference play.

On Friday, February 4th, the Rangers played host to the Carbondale Terriers. The Terriers handed the Rangers their first loss of the year just before Christmas and it was a crucial conference game for both teams. The halftime score was knotted at 28 as Bruce Baker and Joe Hamilton dueled in the post. Baker had 14 points at halftime with Hamilton answering with ten. In the second half, Hamilton used his hips and explosive jumping ability to rip the nets for 26 points and lead the Terriers to a 57-54 win. After the fast start, the team had lost three out of their last four. The team seemed to have peaked over Christmas and was searching for a second wind.

The following night, the Rangers traveled to Trout Gymnasium to tangle with the struggling Orphans. The Orphans jumped out to a 34-21 lead by halftime and led the game by one point heading into the fourth quarter. Kyle Herrin scored 12 points in the final eight minutes of the contest to put away the Orphans by a score of 52-46. The Rangers improved to 20-4 overall and 8-3 in conference play. It was a much-needed win for the players, and it was a happy bus ride.

The next weekend, the Rangers blew away Harrisburg and Herrin to set up the final home game of the year against the Marion Wildcats. With a record of 1-12 in conference play, the Wildcats were struggling. It was senior night at Rich Herrin Gymnasium and the fans stood and applauded each senior as they greeted their parents at half-court. The national anthem was played by the BCHS band, and the crowd rose as one army for the introduction of the starting line-ups. After the line-ups, the starters ripped off their button down warm-ups and rubbed their sweaty hands with rosin. Kyle Herrin organized the starters into a small huddle to encourage his teammates and then the fighting five took the floor. The teams shook hands before the tip and each Ranger player pointed at their defensive assignment. Daren Carlile rubbed the bottom of his shoes and took his place around the center circle.

The game was no contest. The Rangers were ahead 64-48 with just three minutes remaining in the game. Bruce Baker scored a game-high 25 points and pulled down six rebounds while Kyle Herrin scored 14 points and added eight assists. Late in the game, Mike Kolisek and Dave Spencer scored baskets and sophomore Randy House scored his first two points in a varsity basketball game. The Rangers won the game by a score of 69-56. The team finished the regular season with an overall record of 23-4. It was an incredible year and the team now turned its attention to one last run to the State Tournament.

'83 State Tournament Play

The Rangers opened Regional play at Trout Gymnasium against the Salem Wildcats. In '83, the team returned to the 2A Tournament with the large schools. Salem head coach Jim Corona did everything possible to slow the Rangers down. The Wildcats elected to hold the ball and the two teams were tied at eight after one quarter. In the second quarter, the Rangers outscored the Wildcats 10-1 to take an 18-9 lead at halftime.

In the second half it was much the same. The Rangers won an ugly game by a score of 32-25. Give the Wildcats credit; the game was closer than expected. Joey Combs led the 10-13 Wildcats in scoring with ten points. Baker led the Rangers with 15 points and Peters had nine. With the win, the Rangers advanced to the Regional Championship against the Mt. Vernon Rams. It would be their fourth and final meeting of the year.

The game started at 7:00 p.m. and fans from Benton and Mt. Vernon filed in early and took their seats on opposite sides of the gym. This was the big one. Once again, a packed lower bowl and full balcony viewed the action. The two teams played to a 30-30 tie at halftime. Baker and Hawthorne led their teams in scoring as the game went back and forth. In the third quarter, the Rangers widened the lead to seven on a three-point play by Baker with .10 seconds left in the quarter. After Baker's free throw,

Mt. Vernon rushed to inbound the ball, but Cameron Skobel stole the pass and fed a streaking Kyle Herrin who laid the ball in before the third quarter buzzer sounded. The Rangers faithful went bananas! The basket changed the momentum of the game and the Rangers held on to win the game by a score of 52-50. Daren Carlile grabbed 13 rebounds and Bruce Baker scored a game-high 22 points. After the game, the Rangers posed for a team picture at center court with a look of relief written all over their faces. The battles against the Rams were over. Done!

With the win, the Rangers improved to 25-4 and advanced to the first game of the Salem Sectional. Waiting on them was the Effingham Flaming Hearts. The Hearts and Rangers no longer played during the regular season but there was history between the two clubs. It was the Hearts that had eliminated Rob Hammond's Rangers from the '79 Sectional and now they would meet again.

The old gymnasium at Salem was a unique structure. The gym had a lower bowl around the floor and then bleacher seating in the upper concourse on two sides and one end. The gym could hold a large crowd and Benton fans dressed in maroon filled the old Salem field house. The Rangers were the favorites and wasted no time taking control of the game by jumping out to an 8-2 lead before Effingham called a quick time-out. I was at the game and it was fun to watch because the game was never in doubt. The dynamic scoring duo of Bruce Baker and Mark Peters led the Rangers by combining for 37 points. The Rangers won by a score of 59-46 but the game was not as close as the score indicates.

On that same Friday, the Rangers boarded the bus to Salem for the Sectional Championship against Belleville-Althoff. Althoff was no joke. They were a large metro-school that played a tough schedule. It was anybody's game. The Crusaders had three quality players in Bill Meyer, David McFarland, and Larry Gleason. The Rangers had their big three of Kyle Herrin, Bruce Baker and Mark Peters. The crowd buzzed as both teams went thru their 15-minute warm-up period. As the Althoff starters were announced, the Rangers fans turned around and faced away from the floor. Knowing that Kyle Herrin was the coach's son, the Althoff fans rode him relentlessly the entire game. Herrin was a competitor and the razzing from the fans fueled his competitive juices. Kyle Herrin played the best game of his high school career. Althoff pressed the Rangers, but Herrin blew through the press and made the Crusaders pay. On this night, he was a one-man press release.

Kyle Herrin: *They had a good pressing team and I was down in my back. My back was hurting going into that game. But I remember that I was able to break their pressure.*

Daren Carlile: *The more intense and tight the game was…the better he was. He could take his game to another level.*

Another headline of the Althoff game was the play of Mark Peters. Peters scored ten points in the third quarter and 19 for the game. It was one of the best performances of the year when it mattered most. It is a credit to Mark and his ability to transition into an elite program and fit in so well with his teammates. Peters worked hard and let his play speak for itself. The move to Benton was a good experience not only for him but also the team.

Daren Carlile: *First off, Mark is a great guy. He was smart…athletic…a really good player. He knew the game and he could play inside or outside. He wanted to win…just a very complete player…the total package.*

With his team ahead by only three points with 1:31 left in the game, Daren Carlile went to the foul line to shoot two big fourth quarter free throws. He had missed two free throws earlier in the game and admitted he was not the best foul shooter.

Daren Carlile: *For some reason I met eyes with Jim Muir before the official handed me the ball and he said, "You can do it." I didn't hear him…but I read his lips. I'll never forget that.*

Carlile hit both free throws to extend the Rangers lead to 58-53 with just over a minute left in the game. Althoff missed a shot on the next possession and was now forced to foul. With the clock winding down, Kyle Herrin kept the ball in his hands and forced the Crusaders to foul him. Herrin nailed six free throws in the waning minutes of the game to seal the Sectional Championship. It was over. The Rangers defeated Althoff by a score of 65-59. It was a tremendous win and the team seemed to be getting their second wind. An excited Rich Herrin had these thoughts after the game:

Coach Herrin: *It was a great victory for us…and it means that we are one of the best sixteen teams in the State of Illinois.*

Following the game, Kyle Herrin displayed his competitive fire when the team was presented with the Sectional plaque.

Daren Carlile: *Against Belleville-Althoff in the sectional final the Althoff fans were just giving it to Kyle. They were on him. Kyle played a great game and when we won the Sectional…he took that Sectional Plaque and took two steps to the left and held it in front of the Althoff fans. The Althoff fans threw cups at him and he was blocking the cups with the plaque. As the year went on…Kyle just got better and better.*

There is a picture in the '83 yearbook that gives evidence to this moment. With the Benton crowd behind him, Herrin is grinning from ear to ear as he holds the plaque high in the air toward the Althoff hecklers. The Rangers moved to 27-4. Most importantly, they were still alive and advanced to Tuesday's Super-Sectional at the SIU Arena.

After the game, Benton fans flooded onto the floor and celebrated the victory with the team. Team pictures were taken and the players lingered on the floor in their uniforms talking to the fans. The players then showered and boarded the bus in anticipation of the traditional hero's welcome. The bus traveled down I-57 South and took exit 71 and then met the local fire department in West City. The sound of sirens alerted the fans at the square that the team was close. The fire trucks laid on the horns and red lights flashed as the team crept up West Main toward hundreds of fans awaiting their arrival at the square. The players hung out of the bus windows waving to their family and friends. It was the same as in '61. The bus then stopped in front of the courthouse as the fans cheered, "RANGERS, RANGERS"!

The bus then slowly made its way to Rich Herrin Gymnasium for a brief reception. Fans hurried from the square and took a seat in the south bleachers as the players and coaches addressed the Benton crazies. In the spirit of fun, teammates urged Mike Kolisek to do his best Coach Herrin impersonation.

Mike Kolisek: *I do remember when we won the Sectional and we had the reception in the gym…they asked me to do an impersonation of Coach. I did it…I don't think Coach and Sue were too thrilled.*

From the gym, the players went home and talked about the game with their parents and went to bed. They had three days to prepare for the East St. Louis Lincoln Tigers in the Carbondale Super-Sectional. It was an exciting time to be a Ranger.

The Tigers were a pressing team with great athletic ability, but the Rangers had a chance. They were playing their best basketball of the season. On Tuesday, a pep session was held at the end of the school day. The band played the school loyalty song and the team thanked the student body for their support and urged everyone to come to the game. Then it was time.

Later that evening the Rangers traveled to the SIU Arena to play the Tigers of East St. Louis. The Tigers were led by All-Stater Mark Dale, Antonio Rhodes, Roderic Horne, Calvin Phifer and Baron Wilson.

The Arena was packed full of Southern Illinois fans wanting to see the Rangers upset the metro-area Tigers. Benton fans were everywhere. In the first quarter, Mark Peters scored five points but the Tigers led 12-11 after one. I attended the game that night and there was one play I will never forget. In the second quarter, Cameron Skobel gambled to steal a pass in front of the Benton bench and lunged into the arms of Coach Herrin.

Cameron Skobel: *The play happened right on the sideline. He would tell me, "If you can get a finger on it…go after it. Even if you just knock it out of bounds…you will disrupt their offense." So I went for a steal and didn't get it and leaped into Coach Herrin…he kind of spun and flung me back into play. He just helped me get back after it. My dad talked to me about that play and said that it almost looked rehearsed.*

The crowd chuckled at the play, but it was telling of the fire in which they both competed; player and coach. Skobel gave high praise to his former coach.

Cameron Skobel: *I mean this in a good way. There were times that he was hard to understand but by his body actions and his hand gestures we knew exactly what he was talking about. I don't care what anyone says…the man could motivate kids to play ball. Part of his persona was kicking the bleacher and yelling. He was so passionate about what he was doing…you couldn't take that out of him. That man knew all of his players' strengths and weaknesses. He knew how to get the very best out of each one of us. It was the way he treated his players that was the key to his motivation. He was hard on us out of love for us and the game. He wanted us to do right. He didn't want us* *to smoke…he didn't want us to drink…he didn't even want us to chew. He wanted us to do the right things.*

At halftime, the Tigers led the Rangers 20-19. In the third quarter, the Tigers extended the lead behind the play of Antonio Rhodes. Mark Peters kept the Rangers to within three points by leading the team in scoring with 13 points going into the final quarter. With five minutes left in the game, the Tigers extended the lead to ten and it looked like the season was over but the Rangers came thundering back to cut the Tigers lead to one point. In the end, the Rangers just did not have enough. When the final horn sounded, the small contingent of East St. Louis fans rushed the floor to celebrate their 53-49 victory over the Rangers. The loss was devastating. Following the game, Coach Herrin made these comments to the Benton Evening News:

Coach Herrin: *We had a great season. We had a bunch of good players this year and maybe they were even better gentlemen then they were players.*

The players walked slowly to the locker room in the underbelly of the Arena. The players sat in disbelief and cried knowing that this was it. It was over. For the seniors, the finality of the moment was too much. Many of the players buried their heads into their maroon towels and wept.

Coach Herrin has been in these locker rooms before, but this one had to be tough. Yes, the season was over but it was the last game with his son, Kyle. Kyle Herrin had developed into one of the finest point guards in Rangers history and Coach Herrin saw many of his own qualities in his youngest son. Coach Herrin had taken him to the gym as a young boy and rarely missed any of his games. Kyle played the game with a tenacity and toughness that made his dad proud. Reflecting on his playing days, Kyle was thankful he had the opportunity to play for his dad.

Kyle Herrin: *The first thing that jumps out at me was he was going to make you work hard. He was honest…he never cussed. There are some players that may not have liked him but they respected him. He really did care about people and wanted us all to be good people. He set an example for us. He wanted to win but he went about it the right way to get those wins. He wanted to win games but it was not always the most important thing. I was very close to Dad because I was with him a lot growing up. I want to add something, too. Dad went to almost all of my home games at Tennessee Martin. I can't believe how* *many games he was at. He would race down right after practice and get there before the game started. He hardly missed any home games of mine in college. He was a good dad, too.*

After high school, Herrin went on to play basketball at the University of Tennessee Martin. Today, Kyle is a claims adjuster with Country Financial. He lives with his wife Tina in Carterville, Illinois and they have five children; Mackenzie, Mallory, Hunter, Britton, and Reece.

Mark Peters accepted a full-ride basketball scholarship to Mississippi State University. Today, Mark and his wife Janice live in Lake Charles, Louisiana and they have three children; Christopher, Bradley and Nicole. Mark's parents have now passed away, but his mother, Sue, was an active member of Immanuel Baptist Church in Benton and I knew her well. She was very influential in Mark's life.

Mark Peters: *Every morning I have a quiet time and I have these books that my mom has given me and they are devotional with her thoughts underneath them. She gave these books to all of the kids. I start my day by reading some of my mother's spiritual reflections...it is one of the greatest treasures that I have.*

Today, Mark is the Site Executive Director at Lotte Chemical USA Co-operation. Peters was quick to point out that he learned a great deal in his one season under Coach Herrin. Much of what he learned is still applicable in his worklife.

Mark Peters: *Absolute hard work. Nobody is going to give you anything. If you want something...you have to work for it. You have to care and bring it every day. You couldn't work hard enough for Coach Herrin...he always felt like you had another gear. Playing hard covers up a multitude of sins. I expect that out of my employees today. I want them to care and bring it every day.*

The human floor burn, Cameron Skobel, loved his time as a Benton Ranger and had this to say about his playing experience under Coach Herrin:

Cameron Skobel: *There were a lot of different things he taught us. Work ethic...I got a lot of my work ethic from my dad. My dad was a hard worker... but Coach Herrin reinforced that. Coach Herrin would say, "You got to be hard-nosed...you can't give up." That served me well in the military. You're a* *team and you take up for your teammates. That kind of grit bleeds over into everything you do.*

After high school, Cameron earned an electrical engineering degree and then decided to join the military. Today, he works as an electrician for Amtrak in St. Louis. Cameron and his wife Tina live in the St. Louis area and have three children; Tim, Brittany and Chris.

Today, Mike Kolisek owns his own company, K-Medical Device Distributions. He lives in Fishers, Indiana with his wife, Cristine. They have three children; Kelsie, Madi and Kennedi.

Mike Kolisek: *You always gave 100%. I was talking to my mom about this the other day…besides my mom and dad…he was a father figure. He drove me to some of my practices before I had my license. He taught us how to respect other people. He was a prankster too…he took a group of us to Six Flags…and took all of our wallets. He just laughed about it. I keep my wallet in my front pocket to this day because of that.*

Reserve post player Jim McMahon had this to say about playing for Coach Rich Herrin.

Jim McMahon: *He taught us how to be a good basketball player…but most importantly he taught us how to be decent people. He knew the game…but he wanted us to be decent citizens. He wanted that for all of us…from the guys that played to the guys that didn't play as much.*

The 1983 Rangers finished the season with a record of 27-5. By advancing to the Sweet Sixteen, the Rangers were the first team to advance to the State Tournament back-to-back years in two different classes. It is also important to note that East St. Louis Lincoln was forced to forfeit their win against the Rangers for playing an illegal player. The player was too old. The loss of Herrin, Peters, Skobel, Kolisek, McMahon, Bigham and Spencer would be tough but the future looked promising with the return of Bruce Baker and Daren Carlile.

This was my Grandpa, Gwen Wynn. Grandpa was an amazing guy that always had time for me. *(Matt Wynn family collection)*

This is a picture of me in the 8th grade. While I was in the 8th grade, the High School Rangers were rolling. *(Matt Wynn family collection)*

When Mark Peters moved to Benton in '83, all eyes were on the Rangers. *(Ceasar Maragni)*

Daren "ooze" Carlile as a junior. Carlile was a big guard that played a key role on the 83 & 84 teams. *(Ceasar Maragni)*

Kyle Herrin took the leadership reigns immediately in '83. Herrin was one of the best point guards in the state. *(Benton High School)*

Cameron Skobel provided energy and was a defensive juggernaut.
(Ceasar Maragni)

Mike Kolisek was a reserve guard on the '83 team.
(Ceasar Maragni)

Jim McMahon was a reserve post player on the '83 team.
(Ceasar Maragni)

Jeff Johnston was a junior in '83.
(Ceasar Maragni)

Randy House had possibly the greatest sophomore year a player could have but House saw limited action in '83. *(Ceasar Maragni)*

Baker climbing the ladder to pull down a defensive rebound.
(Joe Jines- Southern Illinoisan)

Brian Sloan from McLeansboro was a thorn in the
Rangers side in 83 & 84.

The Benton community gathered on Sunday, December 5th, 1982, to honor Coach Herrin. It was on this day that the Benton Gymnasium was officially named "Rich Herrin Gymnasium." *(Ceasar Maragni)*

Coach Herrin receives an award from school board member, Bill Kerley. Kerley played for Herrin in '61. *(Ceasar Maragni)*

Rich Herrin Gymnasium. *(Benton High School)*

Mark Peters celebrates the '82 Centralia Championship while
Daren Carlile passes to a teammate. *(Ceasar Maragni)*

Here are the mighty Rangers after their 6th Centralia Tournament
Championship in '82. A Tournament record at the time. *(Ceasar Maragni)*

Troy Hewlett (Shide) gave the Rangers great minutes off the bench in '83.
(Ceasar Maragni)

The great team of '83. **Front-** Johnston, Doxie, Kolisek, Browning
Row Two- Smith, Payne, Hewlett, Herrin **Row Three-** Rea, Spencer, Herrin,
Bigham **Row Three-** Carlile, Shell, Eubanks, Bradshaw **Row Four-** McMahon
and Skobel **Row Five-** Peters and Baker. *(Ceasar Maragni)*

After being taunted the entire game by the Althoff fans, Kyle Herrin shows the
Crusader fans the Sectional Championship plaque. *(Ceasar Maragni)*

Coach Herrin and the players celebrate the Sectional Championship
at a short post-game reception. *(Ceasar Maragni)*

CHAPTER TWENTY-NINE

An Elite Team in '84

"I never went into a game at Benton thinking we were going to get beat. I think a lot of that was Coach Herrin...the way he carried himself and the confidence we had." – Bruce Baker

In the fall of '83, I was now a freshman in high school. My first day of high school is a little blurry but in one of my classes I met two people that would be lifelong friends. After lunch, I headed upstairs to Coach Stewart's health class. Coach Stewart was nearing the end of his career but was still the sophomore basketball coach. I walked into class early and took a seat near the back of the room and studied everybody that came thru the door. Will any of my close friends be in here? Are there going to be any good-looking girls? Will there be seniors in this class? All of these funny thoughts were going through my mind.

Okay. It looked like a lot of upperclassmen that I didn't know. Then a towering figure with long hair walked in and sat next to me. He looked intimidating, like someone that would stick you in a trash can before school. In this situation, you have two choices; avoid contact or turn and make friends. I chose to get in good with the guy. I looked over at him and our eyes met and he then pulled a switch blade out of his pocket. I thought I was going to wet my pants. He then laughed and said his name was Devory Eubanks. Fortunately, Devory and I hit it off and he turned out to be a blast and a good blanket of protection.

Just seconds before the tardy bell, Coach Stewart lumbered into class and took his seat at the teacher's desk. There were about twenty students in the room. He sipped his coffee and looked at all of us without saying a word. The room was quiet as we studied his every move. This was the effect he wanted. Coach was an intimidating figure that had been at the high school for twenty-five years or more at this point and had many of our parents in class. He then began to call roll. He gruffly said, "BUNTIN!" I heard this soft voice on the other side of the room say, "Here!" I looked over to see who answered and noticed a girl that I had never seen before. She was very good-looking, but I thought there was no chance. At the time, I had a severe case of acne, and a sweating problem that I couldn't shake. I'll just put it like this, I wasn't on anybody's radar. Coach Stewart took a long time taking attendance. After calling a student's name, he would say; "Who are your parents?" He called each of us by our last names and then issued us a textbook.

The Buntin girl in Coach Stewart's class that was so good-looking and nice ended up being my best friend and my future wife. Even Coach Stewart picked up on the fact that I was crazy about her by saying, "Wynn...I think you are sweet on Buntin." Her name is now Trudee Buntin Wynn and we have two children; Bailey and Gehrig. Besides accepting Jesus as my personal Savior, marrying Trudee Buntin was the best decision I've made in my life and that health class is where it all started.

About fifteen minutes into class, the door opened and a new student strolled in with a pass. Coach Stewart asked him a question and he politely smiled and nodded. He didn't say a word. The young man then took a seat about three rows in front of me. I studied him closely and came to the conclusion that he was an athlete. He was dressed in athletic clothing and was slim and muscular. He sported a buzz haircut and had a foreign look. The new student's name was Kai Nurnberger. Nurnberger was a German exchange student that arrived in Benton just days before school started in the fall of '83. Kai was a senior and spoke very little English but had a fun and inviting demeanor. Kai could play.

Kai Nurnberger: *One of our federation coaches in Germany was always trying to send players over to the United States for a year and then they would come home and play for the national team. There was this guy in Effingham* (Chuck Klein) *that was responsible for bringing German players to Southern Illinois thru the Rotary Club. That is how Jens Kujawa and Eve Blab came to the United States. It developed late with me...they asked me in June if I* *would want to come to the U.S. and play for a year and I said I would, but I didn't get a call about coming over until about a week before school started. They asked Olney first, but they said no...from Ron it went to Rich. My dad drove me to the airport and I traveled to Iceland, then Chicago and then St. Louis. I spoke very little English and I was told to look for the man in the red pants. The man in the red pants was Dave Waggoner from Benton. So if the man in the red pants was a hijacker or something...I would have gone with him. I did not intend to stay. I was going to stay one year and then go back.*

The first time I played pick-up with Kai, I noticed something unique about his game. He was faster with the ball than without the ball. When Kai had the ball in the middle of the floor on a fast break, he could blow by you off the dribble. It was almost as if the ball served as a jet-pack of energy. He was so explosive. Kai admitted that the game of basketball was played differently in the United States than it was in his homeland of Germany.

Kai Nurnberger: *The European game was more technical. There were more skills taught. In the United States there was more emphasis on strength and athleticism. The game was more deliberate in Germany and much quicker here. If I had to play super-deliberate like some teams and hold the ball for 7:55 and then get one shot...I would quit.*

Although soccer is the main sport in all of Europe, Nurnberger grew up playing basketball and was greatly influenced by his parents' love for the game.

Kai Nurnberger: *There were hotspots in Germany where basketball was popular. My parents were very involved in basketball when I was growing up. My father was a better tactician and he began teaching the game in his early twenties. In Germany, basketball was played as a recreational sport...there were clubs. Each town had their own teams and they would play against each other. There were adult leagues and my mom played basketball until her late thirties.*

Kai's first impression of the United States and Benton, Illinois was good. He liked it.

Kai Nurnberger: *I lived with some great families. The Davis family took me in. It was a change. The first time I played in open gym at Benton...Russell*

Davis took me to the gym because I didn't have my license. It was one of those open gym nights. There were all kinds of people there. I didn't know anyone. It was fun because we just played…no coaches. In Germany we were always being instructed in the gym… but it was neat to just play. I remember that there were some players that could really play and some were not as good… but I didn't know anybody. The language was different… but I liked it. Basketball is basketball… you just go play.

Daren Carlile: *Put yourself in Kai's shoes. He struggled with the language when he first came over and he had a coach that was hard to understand. It was hard for us to understand Coach at times. I recognized his talent right off the bat.*

It was obvious that Nurnberger was talented enough to help the team, but that same summer the Rangers caught another break when Jay Schafer moved to town.

Jay Schafer: *My freshman year at Marion was tough. Our freshmen practiced every morning at 6:00 a.m. and the sun wasn't even up…it was still dark out. I had P.E. third period and then varsity practice after school. The varsity team didn't want some 6'5" freshman in their practices and those guys were so much older…I didn't know any of them. I just remember the summer after my freshman year…I just told my dad that I was miserable. My dad had to live less than 21 miles from his job with CIPS and I remember sitting at the table with a map and we drew a circle with a protractor from Dad's work and went shopping for schools. We went by Herrin, West Frankfort and Carterville and since it was the summer there was no one there. So Dad said, Let's drive up to Benton. We pulled up to the west side doors and they were having a summer basketball tournament. I went inside and was in the lobby area talking to an older kid. He asked me what I was doing, and I told him, "We are going to move…and I'm shopping schools. The older kid left me standing there and ran up the stairs to the upper deck and got coach Webb. He came down and said, "Why don't you play?" The competition on the floor was fierce with Baker and Jason Carson from Pinckneyville. My dad came inside and I played a little bit. When I was done playing, I told my dad, "This is the obvious choice." That same day we went to Huck's and grabbed a paper and looked for a place to rent. We found that little place on Industrial Park Road…and I remember going out back and doves were flying around the field behind the house…that was enough for me. I believe that was a Wednesday. All that happened in one* *day. It took us two days and three pick-up loads and we were moved in by Saturday.*

Schafer was just what the team needed. As a sophomore, he was 6'7" and was a shot-blocking machine. As a sophomore, Schafer had the role of blocking shots and rebounding. Baker, House and Nurnberger took care of the scoring.

Daren Carlile: *Jay had good size to start with…he was long. He also played with more confidence as the year went along. He was like me…he didn't have to score much on that team.*

Randy House: *Schaf moved in the summer of '83…he came from a tough program at Marion and came in with a bunch of guys that knew how to play. He fit his role well. He was a good shot blocker and rebounder as a sophomore…and that's what we needed him to do.*

Kai Nurnberger: *The shot blocker in the middle…he was young and raw… he had great timing and had a knack of knowing when to jump and when to keep his feet. I could make a mistake on defense and he could guard the goal and make up for it.*

Bruce Baker: *He was an unbelievable shot blocker.*

Schafer was tall from a young age and grew up playing in the Marion Youth League.

Jay Schafer: *So the story goes that Steve Bond and a guy named Bob Jackson at Longfellow School saw me at the water fountain getting a drink. Steve asked, "Are you signed up to play youth basketball yet?" They thought I was a second grader, but I was only in kindergarten. Steve tells the story that I was already 6'0" tall. They let me play with the third and fourth graders when I was in the second grade. I couldn't get a standard size ball to the rim…I was that weak. By the eighth grade, my group had come around and we were pretty good. We ended up losing in the state tournament to DuQuoin and Monte Kuhnert.*

After moving to Benton, it didn't take Schafer long to figure out that the '83-'84 team was something special.

Jay Schafer: *I played there the rest of the summer and I was really excited about getting to play with kids my own age because I had always played up. In one of our first meetings they were handing out camp information to the sophomores and they skipped over me. I asked for the information and Coach Stewart said, "Rich told us that you're playing with him." Then Kai comes in... and when we started practicing for real, I remember thinking...I've moved up in the world here. You could just tell in practice that this was a good team.*

Another new face on the '84 team was sixth man David Peters. David was the younger brother of Mark Peters and was now a sophomore. Physically, Peters was strong and had tremendous jumping ability and wasn't intimidated by playing with older players, something he credits to his older brother Mark.

David Peters: *Mark is someone that I looked up to my entire life from being a man to being an athlete. He was always the best player on all of his teams growing up. Mark and I spent hours together playing basketball. When Mark was in the fifth grade he was a pitcher and he could throw hard for his age. I was in the first grade and real small. I would go out and warm him up between innings and some of the fans were worried I was going to get hurt...but that is how you learned. Mark is a big reason that I became an athlete.*

As a sophomore, Peters had a healthy respect for all of the juniors and seniors on the team.

David Peters: *My sophomore year I played with the guys that Mark played with...I idolized those guys. I just knew that we were going to be very good. Rich did a great job of making it clear that everyone had a role to play. Not everyone was going to be the scorer. I knew my role immediately. There were times that he would give me a ride home from practice and talk to me about how I could help the team. It was a dream come true.*

The centerpiece player of the '84 team was senior Bruce Baker. Baker was an incredible talent that could score from inside and outside, and was considered to be the top player in Southern Illinois. I loved watching Baker play. As a senior, he played at 6'8" and had incredible hands. He just caught everything. Baker was an intelligent player but what stood out was how hard he played. He was relentless. I asked Bruce this question: "What motivated you to play so hard?"

Bruce Baker: *I think it came from Benton. I watched Coach Herrin's teams play and I would see him take out a player that had just scored two or three baskets in a row and then I figured it out. I knew in my heart that he wasn't playing hard on both ends of the floor. I had that bob that kept my determination and made up for my lack of quickness. You have to know where the ball is coming off. I studied the players to see who missed shots short. I loved the game...you have to love the game and you have to play it the right way.*

Randy House: *Bruce could score...but Bruce played hard every play. He always played hard. He was always in the gym. He was a step slow and not a great jumper, but he made himself a player and a great shooter. All that guy wanted to do was win.... He never took a day off.*

Daren Carlile: *Bruce was Bruce. I don't know if I played with anybody that had a greater set of hands. You could pass it to Bruce at his feet and he would come up with it. He wanted to win. Off the court, he was hilarious and a lot of fun. He could somehow wallow it in. I enjoyed playing with him.*

Jay Schafer: *Bruce did more with less than anybody I ever played with. He could just get great position by using his body. He was a stretch four before that ever became a thing because he could step out and shoot it.*

Many of Baker's teammates remember him being a blast off the floor. He had a great sense of humor and loved to laugh.

David Peters: *Bruce was one of the funniest guys to be around and had a great laugh. Bruce wouldn't drive anywhere without his car stereo turned up full blast and he liked to squeal those tires. He was funny in a good way...he didn't party all of the time. Sometimes after games, Bruce would come over to our house and watch the Three Stooges and just laugh. My mom would make cherry pies for us and we would sit there and watch the Stooges. I remember one day in open gym I got in a fight with Bruce...we were swinging at each other and then two hours later we were cruising town in his car listening to the Gap Band. That was Bruce.*

Baker played three seasons of varsity basketball and each year, there was a new set of guards. In '84, Nurnberger was the Rangers' point guard and totally new to the Benton program.

Bruce Baker: *Kai was a character. I have to grin when I think of Kai. When he first got to Benton I remember thinking…how are we going to be able to mold him into the team? He didn't speak much English. The guy was unbelievable. He was so strong. It didn't take us long to realize that we had a winner with him. It didn't take long for him to get that Benton attitude either.*

Playing alongside Nurnberger at the guard spot was senior Daren Carlile. As a junior, Carlile had an outstanding season and was now thrust into more of a leadership role.

Randy House: *Daren had good size, good strength and he was just always enjoyable to be around. Good teammate…didn't force shots but wasn't afraid to take a shot when he was open. He was a good rebounder. Everybody knew their roles and kind of stayed in their own lanes.*

David Peters:*Daren was good friends with Mark. I idolized Daren. Daren was just a good dude…a nice guy. He was a good rebounder and defender and good leader on the floor.*

Kai Nurnberger: *A really good athlete. He was a good teammate. We practiced quite a bit together in the fall. He was a leader on the floor.*

After one of the greatest sophomore seasons a player can have, Randy House was now the second scoring option behind Baker. House could do a little bit of everything. He had a great feel for the game and played with a truckload of confidence which rubbed off on his teammates. He was very crafty around the basket and was developing a strong perimeter game. Randy explained his development as a player.

Randy House: *I went to Grant School and my coach was Mr. A. I started going to the Rangers games when I was eight or nine years old. My dad* (Ron House) *was a teacher at the junior high for a couple of years in the early seventies and he had Billy Smith, Rob Dunbar and a bunch of the players in class. We probably went for Dad as much as for me. I can't say that I ever really dreamed about being a Benton Ranger. I lived two doors down* *from Billy Smith out in the country. I had a goal, and there was not a lot of people to play with, so I played a lot. I definitely could have played more. I did the shoveling the snow off the court thing…there wasn't much to do. I did go to the Rend Lake camps in the summer for three or four years… but I wasn't a big camp goer. I played my seventh and eighth grade years…but I wasn't the guy. I can think of three or four guys in junior high that were better players than I was. The summer between my freshman and sophomore year, my dad dropped me off at the gym at 6:45 every morning before he went to work. I was there before Mark Craddock got there to open the gym. I grew four to five inches and gained 20 to 30 pounds doing nothing…and I was stronger than everybody as my sophomore year began. I was kind of a "bull in the china shop" type of player. I played inside as a sophomore and I think that experience really helped me later on at SIU. That is really when I learned how to take someone out on the floor and then blow around them… and that's when I learned how to play in the post. I loved the game of basketball…it was a team sport. The game rewards you for how hard you play… and I did play hard. Playing hard can sometimes hide some deficiencies you might have as a player. I liked that.*

Bruce Baker: *Randy was just one of the strongest guys I ever played with. He just played with so much grit.*

Daren Carlile: *Randy was good from Grant School. It's not like Randy was looking for confidence but he just tore it up his sophomore year. That sophomore year really helped his confidence level. Along with Bruce, I had total trust in Randy taking big shots for us.*

As the team got to know one another, Randy House and Kai Nurnberger became close friends. In fact, House and Nurnberger later teamed up to play at Southern Illinois University and both scored more than 1,000 points in their careers. I had a front row seat for most of their games at SIU and in my opinion, Randy and Kai deserve to be inducted into the SIU-C Hall of Fame. Kai and Randy still remain very close friends today.

Kai Nurnberger: *When he was younge, he had that enforcer mentality… chiseled. Do anything to win. For a 6'4" guy…how he could get rebounds and score around the basket was amazing. He had those short, stubby, shotgun-shell fingers and could tip the ball in.*

Randy House: *Kai was one of a kind. An Olympian…I mean what do you say? He was as good a point guard as we could have asked for. He hit 90% of his free throws and never turned the ball over…and could score.*

Senior Jeff Johnston played all summer long at the point guard position and it was his job until Nurnberger came to town, but there is perhaps nobody that could have handled the situation better than Johnston.

Jeff Johnston: *It was difficult…I mean there wasn't any doubt who should have been playing. He played Division I basketball and was an Olympian. The hard part for me was I suffered a knee injury in football and it was bothering me…and I was just trying to figure out the role I was going to have. We had a good summer. The rumor at first was that Kai was a forward…and then the first time I saw him playing with some guys I figured it out…he wasn't a forward. The thing I remember about Kai was that he was very strong. Kai had an adjustment to make when he came over also and that took him a little while.*

Although it was difficult, Johnston came to practice every day and worked hard and didn't pout. Jeff Johnston found his role as the second guard off the bench and appeared in 27 of the 31 games played in the '84 season.

Daren Carlile: *Jeff was a total pro about that situation. Jeff went to all the camps with us…and had grown up in the program. He couldn't have handled that whole situation any better. On the other side of things, Kai wasn't cocky at all…he made it easy for all of us to like him.*

There were two other seniors that saw limited action off the bench in '84; Jay Bradshaw and Troy Hewlett. Bradshaw played in twenty-five games as a senior and on any other team in the South he may have started. He stood at 6'5" and was a solid rebounder and post player off the bench. Troy "Shide" Hewlett was back for another year and saw limited action off the bench.

The other juniors on the team were Alan Shell, Chris Head, Jim Odum, Steve Rich, Matt Sullivan and Jeff Thompson. The two sophomores were David Peters and Tony Shell.

The '83-'84 Rangers opened the season with the McLeansboro Foxes in game two of the Southern Illinois Tip-off Classic at the SIU Arena.

Randy House: *Coach Herrin always had an angle. Just like playing that first game of the season at the SIU Arena in the Tip-Off Classic against McLeans-boro. He wanted us to play on that floor in case we made it to the Super-Sectional. And that is exactly what happened. He was way ahead of his time when it came to stuff like that.*

The Foxes were loaded with a very talented senior class led by Brian Sloan. In front of a packed SIU Arena, the Rangers came out flat. The Foxes pumped the ball inside to Sloan and he delivered by scoring a game-high 30 points. Daren Carlile led the Rangers with 15 points but the Foxes won the game 61-55.

The Rangers then ripped off four wins in a row by defeating Pinck-neyville, Massac County, Mt. Vernon and West Frankfort to run their overall record to 4-1 and 2-0 in the conference. In game two against Pinckneyville, Randy House remembered a key decision Herrin had to make for the team to move forward.

Randy House: *Coach Herrin started the season playing me inside and Bruce outside. After the Pinckneyville game, he moved me outside and Bruce back inside.*

It was now time for the Centralia Holiday Tournament. Led by Bruce Baker's 21 points, the Rangers defeated Chicago Marist by a score of 61-48 to advance to the quarter-final game against Larry Graham's Madison Trojans. In a disappointing game, the Trojans bounced the Rangers from the tournament by a score of 45-42 behind Mike Young's ten-foot jumper with :04 seconds left on the clock. With the loss, the Rangers fell to 5-2 overall. It is perhaps the most talented Rangers team to be sent home so early from the tournament, but in all fairness the team was still learning how to play with each other. Assistant Coach Ron Smith was hired at Benton in the fall of 1982 and later followed Coach Herrin to SIU-C. He made these comments about the team's early struggles:

Ron Smith: *Kai had to adjust his game because the travelling rule in the U.S. was called differently than in Germany. We just got better as that year went on.*

After the Centralia Tournament, the Rangers dropped their next two against Carbondale and Centralia to fall to 5-4 overall and 2-2 in conference play.

Jeff Johnston: *We lost a game to Centralia early in the year and we shouldn't have. We lost a game to Madison early and then the McLeansboro game. We had just picked up Schaf from Marion and then Kai. It took us a while to get things rolling…we played our best basketball after the BIT.*

After the loss to Centralia, the Rangers defeated Harrisburg, Herrin and Marion in convincing fashion to run their record to 8-4 overall and 5-2 in league play. The team was beginning to find themselves and play better basketball. Next on the slate was the Benton Invitational Tournament.

The Rangers won their first four games of the tournament by defeating Pinckneyville, Cairo, Okawville and Olney to set up the championship game against the McLeansboro Foxes on Saturday night. Bruce Baker had already committed to play at the University of Alabama Birmingham and he had been the story of the tournament. Baker was a prolific scorer and Rangers fans always felt at ease when he had the basketball in his hands. In the Wednesday night game against Cairo, he scored a career-high 43 points and then came back Saturday morning and busted up Olney for 25. Without a doubt, Baker was the most outstanding player in the tournament.

Coach Herrin: *Bruce was one of the top ten players in the entire state when he was a senior. He is a hard worker and a dedicated player.*

Coach David Lee: *Baker was so solid. He was one of those types of players, Matt…he was a little slow…couldn't jump, but he could do so many things to beat you. He was a great player.*

Rich Herrin Gymnasium was packed to the gills on Saturday night to watch the two heavyweights battle it out. The Foxes had nipped the Rangers earlier in the season and the game is still remembered by many as one of the greatest games ever played in Benton basketball history. People stood in the corners of the gymnasium and young fans were perched on the end railing with their feet dangling over the sides. It was a sight to behold.

The Foxes entered the game at 19-0. Jeff Johnston had a different memory about that cold January night in '84.

Jeff Johnston: *The thing I remember most about that game was driving to the game and trying to find a parking place. It was amazing the amount of people that were in the gym that night. When we played McLeansboro there was just a different feel to that game. It was different than playing Carbondale or Centralia. All five of their starters played college basketball.*

Foxes head coach David Lee explained to me how amazing it was to coach in that game. There is perhaps no other coach in Southern Illinois that shared more history with Coach Herrin than David Lee and Lee vividly remembered the great battle on that January night.

Coach David Lee: *I was a senior on the McLeansboro team Rich's first year at Benton. I kind of had my way as a player…and I remember he jumped up off the bench and started yelling and he scared me to death. He was one of the first coaches to ever get off the bench. I have nothing but respect for Coach Herrin. He was the top coach in Southern Illinois. He was such a high-caliber person…he was a Christian man, and he had such high standards. He was the Chief. I remember walking into the gym that night and seeing all those people. It was the most people I had ever seen in that gym.*

After a hard-fought first half, the Foxes led 20-19. The tempo of the game favored the Foxes and Randy House explained the intensity of such a deliberate game.

Randy House: *I just remember the crowd and intensity of that game for thirty-two minutes was incredible. Every possession mattered.*

Baker had 13 points and continued his dominating play on the offensive end of the floor. At halftime, Coach Herrin elected to go to a triangle and two defense.

Daren Carlile: *I guarded Sloan and he had ten and got most of his points late. Randy guarded Tracy Sturm and did a good job on him. Kai played the point of the triangle and Bruce and Schafer played the blocks.*

At first, Benton's triangle and two defense seemed to be working and Lee knew he had to make some sort of adjustment. The game was getting away from him.

Coach David Lee: *We were behind something like 39-32. They played that triangle and two on us and guarded Sloan and Sturm and it was bothering us.*

With the game in the balance, Lee called a timeout early in the fourth quarter to make his adjustment. In the timeout, Lee turned to long range sniper, Bryan Cross, to bust up the triangle. Cross was a junior reserve guard that could really shoot the ball. This was the perfect situation to use Cross. Cross remembers his instructions from Lee that night.

Bryan Cross: *Coach Lee told me to shoot it if I was open. Benton just had the one guy on the top of the triangle...and Jeff Morris was with me at the top. That was my role on that team as the sixth man...was to shoot it. That's what good coaches do...they put their players in a position to succeed.*

With the game in the balance, Bryan Cross knocked down jumper after jumper to give the Foxes a hard fought 48-45 victory over the Rangers. McLeansboro fans dressed in green flooded the floor when the final buzzer sounded to celebrate one of the greatest wins in McLeansboro basketball history. Bryan Cross will never forget that crazy night in Benton. It still remains one of his favorite memories.

Bryan Cross: *There was an unbelievable crowd there that night. Standing room only. My grandma was there and she was in a tight seating position and had to hang her feet off the balcony. Individually, that was a great moment. A guy the other day was putting my tires on and said something about that game. Benton had great teams. They were in the South Seven Conference at that time. I had nothing but respect for the Rangers and Coach Herrin.*

As for the Rangers, it was a devastating loss.

Randy House: *We should have beaten them. We matched up well with them at each position.*

Daren Carlile: *When the game was over, I do remember Coach Herrin said, "This one is on me.... I should have flipped the triangle." He didn't do that a lot. I respected him for saying that.*

With the win, the Foxes won the tournament by finishing with a perfect 5-0 record. McLeansboro went on to win the Class A State Championship in 1984 by finishing the season with a perfect 35-0 record. Bruce Baker finished the game with 29 points to lead all scorers and set a new BIT scoring record with 136 points in just five games. Baker, Nurnberger and House were selected on the '84 BIT All-Tournament team.

After the loss to McLeansboro, the Rangers blasted Mt. Vernon by a score of 102-62. Baker led the Rangers in scoring with 33 points and reserve post player Jay Bradshaw added ten points along with David Peters. The Rangers then traveled to West Frankfort and dismantled the Redbirds by a score of 84-62. With the wins, the Rangers improved to 14-5 overall and 7-2 in the conference. Baker scored a game-high 38 points to lead the team in scoring. Baker was clearly the best player in Southern Illinois.

Kai Nurnberger: *He was a really good player...a hard worker. He was savvy around the basket...he knew how to find the tiniest creases in the defense and score.*

Jeff Johnston: *He was so good at positioning his body and Bruce always wanted the ball. He didn't shoot the ball every time he caught it but he wanted the ball and usually good things happened when he had it.*

On February 10, 1984, the Rangers traveled to Bowen Gymnasium to play the Carbondale Terriers. The Terriers had beaten the Rangers earlier in the season by a score of 43-32. The Terriers were led by Glen Martin, Mike Altekruse, Ronnie Tate, Joe Hamilton and Avery Henry. At this point in the season, they were in first place in the conference race and considered to be the best team in Southern Illinois. They were solid. Basketball around the Southern Illinois area was very good in '84.

Randy House: *Carbondale was really good along with McLeansboro. We were playing in the South Seven Conference and it was pretty good. We were just trying to compete.*

The Rangers jumped out to a 36-31 lead at halftime and then played even with the Terriers to remain in the lead 52-47 entering the fourth quarter. At the time, Carbondale was undefeated. Randy House vividly remembered Coach Herrin's thought process late in the game.

Randy House: *I'm not a big fan of losing games...and it was at halftime. Coach Herrin comes in with a "team vote" type manner and says, "Do you* *want to beat them now or in the Sectionals?" We lost the game that night but we almost won the game anyway. In the second half, I played more loose than I had all year. They were undefeated when we played them. Coach Herrin was working an angle. He knew that if we played Carbondale in the Sectional and they were undefeated, the pressure would be on them. If we win the game at Carbondale…it turns into a revenge game for them.*

The Terriers defeated the Rangers 69-67 and remained unbeaten but had to carry the heavy burden of being undefeated. Junior Randy House led the team in scoring with 21 and Bruce Baker chipped in 18 points. Daren Carlile scored 14 points.

To end the regular season, the Rangers ripped off five straight victories to finish the regular season at 19-6 overall and 11-3 in South Seven play. The South Seven had been so competitive the last two seasons that the team finished second despite winning 27 games in '83 and 24 games in '84.

The Rangers were now playing their best basketball of the season. The players understood their roles and Nurnberger and Schafer were now well adjusted to their new teammates. Sophomore David Peters settled into the sixth man role and was providing great play off the bench. The team looked to be ready for an exciting run to the State Tournament.

David Peters: *That team had such good comaraderie. We just all went out and got our heads shaved on a whim. It sounds funny but it never entered my mind that we might get beat. We knew every time we played we were going to win.*

'84 State Tournament Play

Due to their enrollment, the '84 Rangers competed in the Class AA State Tournament. With a weekend of practice, the Rangers now embarked on defeating Harrisburg in the first game of the Mt. Vernon Regional Tournament. The Rangers were the number one seed.

The Rangers won the opener by defeating the Bulldogs by a score of 82-60. Daren Carlile and Randy House led the team in scoring with 18 points followed by Kai Nurnberger's 14.

Bruce Baker: *Daren and Randy were just so strong and had good size. Daren played the game the right way and he played a great role on our team. Daren knew what he had to do for us to win.*

One of the keys to the Rangers' success late in the year was the improved play of Kai Nurnberger. He was now much more comfortable with his role on the team and his new surroundings in the United States.

Ron Smith: *Kai did not have many adjustments to make in the classroom because he was a very smart guy. School wasn't an issue with him.*

Daren Carlile: *Kai adjusted and played with confidence. Later in the year he was running the show and we were better.*

In the championship game, the Rangers nipped the Centralia Orphans by a score of 71-62. Baker scored a game high 33 points to lead the Rangers' scoring attack. Ben Willis led the Orphans with 17 points. The team moved to 21-7 overall and received the traditional fire truck escort around the square. The win set up a game for the ages in the first round of the Benton Sectional Tournament against the Carbondale Terriers. In fact, the headline on the sports page of the Benton Evening News article read, "Benton, Carbondale - One Mo' Time!"

There was much anticipation to the Tuesday match-up between the Rangers and Terriers. Carbondale came into the game at 27-0 and had beaten the Rangers twice. The pressure was definitely on the Terriers just the way Coach Herrin wanted it. The Rangers knew they could win the game despite their two losses and the game would be played in their home gym. And even better, they would play the role of the underdog. Jeff Johnston recalled the history between the Rangers and the Terriers.

Jeff Johnston: *Those games against Carbondale were so fast...so intense. Our class never beat Carbondale all through high school. I do remember thinking after they beat us badly in the sophomore tournament that we would eventually beat them. We didn't have Bruce in the sophomore tournament and I remember having that thought. We never had the thought that...oh there is no way we can beat them. And we did. I never went into a game hoping we would win...I thought we would win.*

I arrived at the game early and had been traveling with the team all year filming the games. Filming the games was my ticket to be able to travel with the team. I remember taking my tripod and camera above the chair seats on the north side of the gym and waiting for the game to start. Basketball fans from all over the area came to see what promised to be a game for the ages.

Kai Nurnberger: *I was surprised to go to a gym and have 3,000 people there to watch 17-year-olds play basketball. In Germany, you might have a hundred people and the gyms were more like the East Gym. Much smaller…that was a crazy, crazy thing. I played on the Junior National team, and we played in front of 1,500 to 2,000 people. I had some experience playing in front of larger crowds. I couldn't believe such a little town had a gym that size. Kind of crazy and fun.*

In my opinion, it was the greatest game I ever witnessed in Rich Herrin Gymnasium. Carbondale and Benton were loaded with Division I players and Doug Woolard and Rich Herrin were two of the great coaches in the State of Illinois. Daren Carlile had a good feeling about the game.

Daren Carlile: *I had been very lucky to have the opportunity to play in some big games. We had the McLeansboro games and the Centralia Tournament Championship against Mt. Vernon. The Carbondale games…we had been in some big games. The crowd didn't bother us…but there is no doubt that it was a great atmosphere that night. That night during the starting line-ups…I just had this feeling that we were going to beat them. We were really starting to come together and peaking at the right time.*

Bruce Baker had this to say before the Rangers tangled with the Terriers in the first game of the Sectional:

Bruce Baker: *I remember the thing that Coach Herrin told us about that game…he said we have one thing going for us…they are going to come in overconfident because they had beaten us twice. We knew that we could beat them if we just played our game. We were close the first two times and just lost in the end. We were right there.*

756

When the Rangers took the floor, the gym shook with excitement. In the first quarter, 6'3" center Joe Hamilton rose high in the lane and dropped three mid-range jump shots to lead the Terriers to a 14-12 lead. In the second quarter, Baker scored a basket and the P.A. announcer said, "BRU-UUUUCE! Baker!" Chills went down my spine. At halftime, the Terriers led by a score of 31-28. It was anybody's game. Sophomore Jay Schafer recalled the game as being very physical.

Jay Schafer: *It was actually the first game of the Sectional but it was the Sectional Championship. We knew it was going to be a battle. I broke my nose for the first time in the second quarter. At halftime, I was kind of out of it and one of the coaches said, "maybe we need to take him to the hospital." I remember Coach Herrin said, "they're just going to tell him he can't play." About that time he reached around me and tried to straighten my nose. He said, "That looks a little better." I was kind of out of it...you know.*

I do remember a play in the third quarter that will always be etched into my memory. There was a loose ball near mid-court and Kai flashed through the middle to scoop it up and jetted in for a left-handed lay-up. The play spoke to Nurnberger's athletic ability and skill. He was extremely quick and strong and although he was right-handed, he made the left-hand lay-up look easy. When Nurnberger laid the ball off the glass, the fans went crazy and the play shifted the momentum back to the Rangers.

With just .07 seconds left in regulation, Glen Martin was fouled by Daren Carlile, which sent him to the line for a chance to win the game. The game was tied at 55. Coach Herrin called two timeouts to ice Martin. Martin missed the front end of the one-and-one and the game went into overtime. To begin overtime, the Rangers had the momentum and it started well for the Rangers.

Daren Carlile: *I just remember on the first possession of the overtime period, Schaf scored on a three-point play and we never looked back. For him to take that shot in that kind of game as a sophomore...was impressive.*

Rich Herrin: *Schafer's three-point play was a big one.*

The Rangers pulled away from the Terriers and won the game by a score of 68-58. It was Bruce Baker's birthday and he went on to have a game-high

19 points in the contest. After many years of reflection, Baker had these thoughts about the game:

Bruce Baker: *They just didn't play us the same way in that game…I thought they took us lightly.*

Jeff Johnston: *We got them in the Sectional…the one time we beat them. After we beat Carbondale in the Sectional there were fans lingering around in the gym waiting for us to come out.*

There was much excitement following the game. The fans reacted as if the Rangers had won the State Championship but it was only the first game of the Sectional. The team had to re-focus for the Sectional Championship on Friday against Charleston or Taylorville. The task of re-focusing the players' attention fell to Coach Herrin and these were his words to the Benton Evening News following the Carbondale victory:

Rich Herrin: *It was an awfully sweet victory. It was one of the sweetest we've had here in a long time. But the biggest thing is that we have to be careful about overconfidence and we can't let Charleston or Taylorville slip up on us.*

On Wednesday night, Taylorville defeated Charleston to meet Benton in the Sectional Championship on Friday night. Taylorville had a German exchange student of their own by the name of Jens Kujawa. He was 7'0" and well put together.

The Taylorville game was scary. The game was a slower tempo and the Rangers fell behind 27-20 at halftime. Kujawa only had two points but his presence in the lane altered shots and he was a force to be reckoned with on the boards. Jeff Scroggins led Taylorville in scoring at halftime with 11 points. Baker led Benton with eight points. It was now Coach Herrin's turn to make an adjustment.

Bruce Baker: *Kujawa's size was a problem and he was the biggest guy that we played against that year. Coach Herrin was smart enough to pull me out of the lane and let me shoot it from the outside so he* (Kujawa) *had to come out and guard me. That opened up driving lanes for our team. Coach Herrin also switched defenses in that game constantly and I think it messed them up.*

The Rangers won a tight contest by a score of 52-49 to win the Sectional Championship. Rangers fans poured onto the floor to celebrate the win. The student body celebrated the victory with the team and Bruce Baker felt like the entire school was part of the team.

Bruce Baker: *Playing basketball in Benton was unbelievable. Our classmates and students in the school were great. Guys like Mike Osborne and Jeff Killion would come to the games with my name on their shirts and support all of us. The student body was like an extension of the team…we were all on the same team, you know. When I look back on it…the greatest times of my life were at Benton.*

With the win, the Rangers advanced to the Carbondale Super-Sectional to play the Collinsville Kahoks. On Tuesday, March 20th, the Rangers led a caravan of Benton fans to Carbondale to meet the 15-13 Kahoks. The Rangers controlled the game from the start and held a 51-34 lead at the start of the fourth quarter. They defeated the Kahoks by a score of 60-52 to advance to the State Tournament. With the win, the Rangers moved to 24-6 for the season.

Bruce Baker lead the Rangers in scoring with 26 points and Randy House chipped in with ten. In the loss, Michael Hunter scored 25 points for the Kahoks. When the Rangers came back to Benton, they were met in West City and received a fire truck escort around the square. Fans lined the streets and waved to the players and then a quick reception was held at the gym.

On Wednesday, the Rangers practiced after school in preparation for their quarter-final match-up against the Evanston Wildkits. Again, it was a tough draw. The Kits were unbeaten (30-0) and ranked second in the state. After watching film on Evanston, the players believed they could win the game despite their gaudy 30-0 record. Again, this was a trait of most of Coach Herrin's teams; they believed they could win.

Bruce Baker: *I never went into a game at Benton thinking we were going to get beat. I think a lot of that was Coach Herrin…the way he carried himself and the confidence we had.*

A pep session was held Thursday afternoon to send the team off to Champaign and then a scramble for tickets ensued. Many fans slept in the gym the night before the tickets went on sale to guarantee a quality seat for the game. School was impossible. Everyone was talking about the game and it was decided that school would be called off on that Friday to give all students the opportunity to attend the game. Later that afternoon, the Rangers caravaned to Champaign in separate cars just as they had done in the past.

Jeff Johnston: *Coach Herrin was pretty smart. The first thing I noticed was that we were in one hotel…and the cheerleaders were in a different hotel. We saw some film on Evanston. We thought we had a shot at them.*

Daren Carlile: *I remember we saw them on film and Coach Herrin said, "I think we can play with them…in fact, I think we can beat them."*

The tip-off against Evanston was set for Friday, March 20th, at 12:15. The Rangers were dressed in their home whites and Evanston was in their dark blue uniforms. The head coach of the Evanston Wildkits was former Centralia stand-out, Herb Williams. The centerpiece of the Wildkit attack was senior Everett Stephens. Stephens was one of the top guards in the state and had already signed a scholarship to Purdue University. He was a long 6'2" and extremely athletic.

Randy House: *He wasn't very big. Lightning-quick and had great lateral quickness. He was long and very athletic.*

McLeansboro coach David Lee remembers exactly where he was when the Rangers were ready to tip-off with the Wildkits.

Coach David Lee: *We had already won the State Championship in Class A the week before. When Benton played, I went home early and watched the game by myself on television. I rooted for Benton because I wanted both of the State Championship teams to be from Southern Illinois.*

To begin the game, the Wildkits surged ahead and took a 14-6 lead, but the Rangers settled down and fought back to tie the game at 18 with just under three minutes to play in the half. Kai Nurnberger then hit a 20-foot jumper to give the Rangers their first lead of the game at 20-18. Baker and Stephens then traded baskets and with just .04 seconds left in the first half, and Nurnberger hit a true jump shot just inside the half line to give the Rangers a 26-25 lead at the break.

Kai Nurnberger: *That was just something…it was a jump shot just inside half court. I was so surprised when I made it I ran the wrong direction to the locker room.*

Daren Carlile: *In the first quarter of the game we weren't sure and were behind a little but Kai hit a half-court shot just before halftime to give us some momentum.*

The team hustled off the floor pumping their fists. The halftime buzzer-beater shifted the momentum in favor of the Rangers. Ron Head was the voice of the Rangers at the time and he rose out of his seat on press row throwing his fists in the air. The Ranger faithful were excited. Yes, the Wildkits were a solid basketball team, but it was clear that the Rangers had a real shot to advance.

Jay Schafer: *I thought we were better than them and I was really surprised that they didn't have more of a dominating inside game for a school their size. At halftime, Rich just starts yelling at me, "You have got to defend and rebound, or we can't win this game!" Coach Webb then came over and said, "Hey, you've got 13 rebounds…you're doing fine…he is just trying to get you fired up. Just keep playing hard."*

In the second half, the Rangers picked up where they left off. They had a strong third quarter and were on the verge of putting the game away a couple of times but couldn't seem to put the nail in the coffin. The Rangers led 43-40 after three periods. In the fourth quarter, Rangers fans were on the edge of their seats. Benton held a lead of 61-55 in the final quarter when Stephens took command of the game. The Rangers turned the ball over on three consecutive plays resulting in baskets by All-State guard Everett Stephens. Evanston tied the game at 61 and then after another Benton turnover, the Kits chose to milk the clock for one shot, but failed to connect. Daren Carlile remembered that it was the German exchange student that stepped up before the overtime period to offer some words of encouragement.

Daren Carlile: *We were kind of shell-shocked when we started the overtime and I'll never forget…Kai got us together and said, "Overtime is our time." He was the leader of our team in that moment.*

In the overtime, Benton's Randy House scored the only Ranger points, and two Benton baskets that might have gone in were swatted away by Stephens. The Rangers lost a heartbreaker by the score of 65-63. Rangers fans sat in disbelief and some even cried.

David Peters: *It was such a shock when we got beat. We had cheerleaders crying...think about that.*

After the loss, the team slowly walked to the locker room to meet for the final time. Bruce Baker scored 25 points in the loss. A disappointed Rich Herrin addressed his team and admitted that it was one of the toughest losses he ever experienced.

Jeff Johnston: *I don't remember what was said after the game. I was in my own little world. I just remember thinking...it's over.*

Coach David Lee: *It just made me sick when they got beat.*

The players have now had plenty of time to reflect on the game and they all agree that they missed an opportunity. Bruce Baker tipped his hat to Stephens.

Bruce Baker: *I have that game on DVD and every time I watch it...it looks like we're going to win it. We had them beat. I saw Herb Williams in college, and he told me the Benton win in the State Tournament was the biggest win of his high school coaching career. I give Everett Stephens a lot of credit...he just took over the game.*

Daren Carlile: *We outplayed them in the second half. We were up six with 1:40 to play. We don't lose those games. We tightened up. I turned the ball over and then then we had a couple of turnovers after that and the game went into overtime. When we lost that game...we were just sick.*

Jay Schafer: *When I watch that game today on tape...up five with about 1:20 left in the game...I still think we are going to win.*

Kai Nurnberger: *That is normally a win. There was no one play that cost us that game. I made a turnover late, Daren made a turnover late. Our team could have played with anybody that year.*

Randy House: *Honestly…we were probably the second-best team in the state that year in Class AA. We were better than Evanston. We led the whole game…we had them. We played not to lose instead of playing to win. Daren had an unfortunate turnover…but if you look at the tape…I turned the ball over on the next possession and then Kai turned it over. We tightened up.*

Jeff Johnston: *There wasn't one mistake that cost us that game…there was a series of mistakes. It just wasn't meant to be.*

Growing up in Benton, I still believe the '84 team was the best team I ever saw play. I was too young to see the teams of the sixties and even the great '75 team. The team didn't win the Centralia Tournament or the BIT or the South Seven Conference. Think about that. But in the end they had a six-point lead on the number one Class 2A team in the State of Illinois. They were right there. Randy House believes it is one of the greatest teams in Benton history and I have to agree.

Randy House: *Looking back…it was one of the best teams in Benton basketball history and we picked up two dudes in the summer. It is not like we all had played together since the third grade…it was a hodge-podge.*

Bruce Baker went on to play college basketball at the University of Alabama Birmingham for Coach Gene Bartow. Baker finished his career with 1,710 career points and is the second leading scorer in Benton history behind Jo Jo Johnson. In my opinion, Bruce Baker's number 55 must be retired. Baker was the centerpiece on two Elite eight basketball teams and one team that made the Sweet Sixteen.

Bruce now lives in Morris, Alabama. After earning a bachelor's degree in education from the University of Alabama Birmingham, Bruce worked as an elementary teacher for many years at Arthur Elementary School and taught night classes that gave special needs children the opportunity to get their degree. He also worked for a division of Homeland Security in the Florida Keys. In 2013, Baker's leg became infected and had to be amputated. It has been an adjustment but Baker assured me he is fighting to get back in the game.

Bruce Baker: *When I lost my leg in 2013 it was from an old ACL tear that went bad. It was my left leg and it was amputated above the knee. I'm working* *at it and I keep trying because that is what I've been taught. Those are lessons I learned in basketball...to never give up.*

Baker remembered getting a special call after his amputation surgery from Coach Herrin that meant a lot to him. He came alive when talking about Coach Herrin and is thankful he had the opportunity to play for him.

Bruce Baker: *After my amputation surgery, I got a call from Coach Herrin and he told me that he knew this was a big hit...but keep getting after it. He told me that he was proud of all my accomplishments as a player and a person and that meant a lot to me. He just gave me some kind words because that is the kind of man he was. I remember after the State Tournament my senior year he gave me a ribbon off of his coat and I still have it. I don't know where all my trophies are...but I still have that ribbon because he gave it to me. Coach Bartow told me one time that Coach Herrin could coach on any level. He said, "When you have a gym that is named after you and you are still alive...you can coach." As a player it was phenomenal to be able to play for Coach Herrin. I learned something from him every day. The knowledge he had about the game. He forgot more about basketball than I'll ever know. He had the ability to motivate people and the players liked him. He took Kai and Schafer in a short amount of time and molded them into our program.*

Jeff Johnston is now a teacher and coach at Christopher High School. He lives in Ewing with his wife Jan. They have two children; Jared and Jenna.

Jeff Johnston: *He had a way of motivating you to go harder than you thought you could go. It started in the introduction of the starting line-up...we sprinted out. He had a way of getting the most out of all of his players.*

Daren "ooze" Carlile lives in Littleton, Colorado with his wife Shelley. He works as a dentist. He loved his experience as a Benton Ranger under Coach Herrin.

Daren Carlile: *Mental toughness. You know everybody talks about Coach Herrin as a basketball coach. Coach was a Christian man and he wore that on his sleeve. Sure, he wanted to win...but I truly believe he wanted the best for all of us. He took a lot of pride in preparing boys to become men. When he was hard on us...he was preparing us for life. I felt that even when I played for him.*

Kai Nurnberger now lives with his wife Michelle in Hebron, Kentucky and they have two children; Sean and Kailie. He works for Kroger. After high school, Kai played college basketball at Southern Illinois University and then played professionally for fifteen years in Germany. In 1992, Kai was a member of the German Olympic team that played the Dream Team, which included Jordan, Bird, Magic etc.

Kai Nurnberger: *It was a neat experience. We had Detlef Schrempf and he knew a lot of those guys. We were ahead 2-0...we should have just pulled the plug.*

Kai had the unique experience of playing for Coach Herrin at Benton and then in college at SIU. Kai loved his playing experience for Coach Herrin.

Kai Nurnberger: *You got to have fun at it. He wasn't defensive-minded. He was an offensive coach...and I liked that. He wanted it to be fun for us and he let us express ourselves on the floor. He gave us freedom.*

The Rangers finished the '84 season with a 24-7 record and are still looked upon today as one of the great teams in Ranger history. With the strong nucleus of Randy House, Jay Schafer and David Peters returning, the Rangers look forward to another great year in '85. On to '85!

My wife and I dated in high school. We met in Coach Harry Stewart's Health class when we were freshmen. *(Benton High School)*

This is a picture of Trudee and I in college at SIU.
(Matt Wynn family collection)

Kai Nurnberger was a foreign exchange student that landed in Benton for the 83-84 school year. Nurnberger was accepted immediately and went on to play at SIU and then later professionally in Germany. He played in the '92 Olympics against the dream team. *(Ceasar Maragni)*

Daren Carlile was a force on the boards and a versatile defender in '84. Carlile also made two clutch free throws against Belleville Althoff to seal the Sectional Campionship. *(Ceasar Maragni)*

Jay Schafer was a transfer student from Marion that gave the '84 team a shot blocking presence. Schafer went on to become an All-State player. *(Ceasar Maragni)*

Randy House was thrust into the line-up on '84 and he was ready. House was a tenacious rebounder and could score. *(Ceasar Maragni)*

David Peters was a solid guard off the bench in '84.
(Ceasar Maragni)

Jay Bradshaw gave the Rangers depth inside in '84.
(Ceasar Maragni)

The Rangers after the big sectional win against Carbondale. **Front Row-**
Johnston, Bradshaw, Schafer, Nurnberger, Baker, House, Carlile, Peters, Webb
Back Row- Smith, Shell, Head, Thompson, Sullivan, Rich, Herrin, Hewlett,
Odum, Stewart. *(Ceasar Maragni)*

Baker against Collinsville in the '84 Super.
(Southern Illinois)

Carlile, Baker and Peters go high for a rebound.
(Southern Illinoisan)

Jeff Johnston drives and kicks in '84.
(Benton High School)

Baker had mitts for hands and he could score the ball like nobody
I had ever seen. Bruce is one of the greatest players in
Rangers basketball history. *(Ceasar Maragni)*

Carbondale coach, Doug Woolard, was one of best coaches in Southern Illinois.
Woolard's Terriers were tough in '84. *(Carbondale High School)*

772

Joe Hamilton was the man in the paint for the Terriers in '84.
Big Joe had a smooth turn- around jumper. *(Carbondale High School)*

The engine of the great Terriers of '84 was Glenn Martin.
(Carbondale High School)

Stephen Bardo played at Illinois and added depth to the great
Terrier team of '84.

Mike Altekruse was a great three-sport athlete and key member
of the great Terrier team of '84. *(Carbondale High School)*

The '84 Terriers. *(Carbondale High School)*

A picture taken on the night the Rangers upset the Terriers in the '84 Sectional.
A packed house at the "Rich." My favorite game growing up.
(Benton High School)

Carlile and Nurnberger get together late in the
Carbondale game. *(Southern Illinoisan)*

Coach Ron Smith during the '84 season.
(Benton High School)

776

Carlile and the Rangers celebrate the '84 Sectional Championship. *(Southern Illinoisan)*

Schafer goes high to block a shot against Collinsville in the Super-Sectional. *(Southern Illinoisan)*

The '84 Rangers being sent off to Champaign.
(Southern Illinoisan)

Baker to the hoop against the great Everett Stephens of Evanston. *(Southern Illinoisan)*

Coach Herrin and Coach Stewart in the '84 quarterfinal game against Evanston. *(Southern Illinoisan)*

The Benton Cheerleaders mourn the loss to Evanston in the State Tournament. It was all over. *(Southern Illinoisan)*

Coach Herrin talks to the Benton fans at the end of the '84 season. *(Southern Illinoisan)*

CHAPTER THIRTY

Coach Herrin's Final Drive in '85

"My dad was on Coach Herrin's first team at Benton…and I was on his last." – Chris Head

Kyle Herrin barked, "Wynnie…check it up." With the game tied 6-6, Herrin inbounded the ball to Tony Shell. Shell took two hard dribbles left-baseline and rose high off the floor to shoot. As the ball was in flight, Shell said, "Next." The ball hit the bottom of the net and Tony flashed a wide grin, sending my team off the floor in disgust. With very little being said, both teams headed to the west gym entrance to take in wafts of air being sucked in by the noisy attic fans. It was nine in the morning, and it had to be 90 degrees-plus…but it didn't matter. This is where we all wanted to be.

It was the summer of '84, and I was entering my sophomore year of high school. Kyle Herrin was now playing college basketball at the University of Tennessee Martin and was home for the summer. He was the man in charge of opening the gym. I was 6'1", 135 pounds, and doing everything I could to guard Herrin who was bigger, stronger and more experienced. This was the value of open gym.

For the past two decades, open gym hours were from 7:00 a.m. to 11:00 a.m., Monday through Friday. We also played on Monday and Thursday nights at 6:00 p.m. On a typical morning, the older players divided us into three teams of five or six with a play two-sit one rotation. The cross-court games were played to seven and with the older guys always on the west end of the floor. The younger players played on the east end of the floor.

My seventh-grade summer, Tim Wills was a senior and the older guys needed one more player to make ten. Wills looked over at the east end of the floor and said, "Matt, we need one more...lets go." I was pumped. In a small way, it was like getting called up to the big leagues. My only assignment was to guard a bad upper-classman and just hold my own on the offensive end. Unfortunately, the guy I was supposed to be guarding scored the first two points of the game. After the second bucket went through the net, Wills tucked the ball under his arm and slowly walked to the other end of the floor. Before he checked the ball, he looked at me and said, "Hey, if you're not going guard anybody...I'll go down there and get somebody that will." He called me out right there and it motivated me. A big part of becoming a Benton Ranger was earning the respect from the guys that came before you. The Tim Wills story encapsulates why the open gyms were so valuable. It was the older players' responsibility to make sure that the games were competitive and it became a rite of passage. As a young player, you were accountable not only to your coaches but also the older players. There was a pecking order.

In the summer of '84, I was now a west-end guy. Open gyms provided all of us with the opportunity to play. The constant play allowed me to discover who I really was as a player. It exposed my strengths and weaknesses and developed an intrinsic will to compete without coaches barking instructions. So, what did I learn when Kyle Herrin guarded me? I learned that his size and strength bothered me. I had to get stronger and quicker. I had to improve my athleticism. Yes, I could shoot the ball, but my ball handling skills needed work. Could I bring the ball up the floor against the defensive pressure of the Cairo Pilots? These were the type of questions I had to ask myself. As a player, there is always someone better. I had a lot of work to do and improvement came by playing against great competition.

Senior guard Chris Head is the son of Ron Head, who played on the '61 team. Chris grew up watching the Rangers and loved the open gym concept.

Chris Head: *Open gym was always competitive. All the guys that graduated would come back and play against the younger guys. It was so tough to play in that hot gym in the summer...but it was fun. It was so hot that it became a competition to see who could wring the most sweat out of their shirts.*

Tim Wills' younger brother, Brad, was entering his junior season. We were teammates and good friends. As a junior, Brad stood at 5'9" and was a solid ball handler and fiery competitor. Wills loved the open gym format.

Brad Wills: *The open gyms were the most fun I had playing basketball. I just wanted to play. Those night open gyms when guys would come in from all over to play were great. I may not have been as good as some of those older guys but I was always trying to get better and we were playing against good competition. I loved the open gyms.*

As Brad mentioned, the night open gyms were special. Carloads of players from surrounding towns traveled to Benton. As a basketball player, there is nothing like playing against fresh meat. It's hard to explain. As a player, I wanted to leave a lasting impression on that kid that drove in from McLeansboro or Mt. Vernon. Everyone played for respect. The competitive juices came alive in the night games. It was intense but fun. On Monday and Thursday nights, Benton was the place to be if you were a good high school basketball player in Southern Illinois.

After the morning games, guys made doughnut runs to fuel up for the traditional wiffle ball game. Home plate was in the northwest corner of the gym near the coach's office. We played with a taped up wiffle ball using baseball rules. Everyone tried to hit left-handed to take advantage of the short porch in right field. A ball smashed into the red seats was a homerun. A homerun to left field was a shot because it had to be hit on a line to avoid the ceiling and rafters on the east side of the gym. A good wiffle ball game was a chance for us to bond outside the realm of basketball. I can still see Carl "Skin-Man" Skinion sliding head first to score a run while wearing his full-body sweat suit. The sweat suit and the rubber surface created ideal conditions for an effortless slide across the plate. Any time Skin-Man slid in under the tag, the gym erupted into laughter. It's funny, I must have played in hundreds of basketball games in the summer and don't remember any of them, but I vividly remember the great slides of Carl Skinion.

Another golden moment in wiffle ball history was the "Shide" Conspiracy in the summer of '83. Rod Shurtz was running the gym and umpiring the daily wiffle ball games. Shurtz came up with the genius plan that any close play would go against Troy Hewlett's (Shide's) team. Hewlett was very accomplished in throwing out rants of profanity and the scheme was designed to provoke Hewlett into a swearing fit. Shurtz would even delay the call until the gym was quiet and then look at Hewlett and signal the runner "out" with a dramatic gesture. Hewlett seethed with anger and protested each call loudly. And then he finally blew. Shide came to bat with runners in scoring position. He smacked a groundball to shortstop and beat out the throw to first base by a half-step. A highly animated Rod Shurtz jogged down the line and then punched Hewlett "out". It was simply too much for Hewlett to take. Shide then unleashed a long list of profanities that sent the gym into a crying laughter. In a crazy way, the wiffle ball games, the doughnut runs, along with the cross-court games, created a bond among all of the players. When you play together, eat together and laugh together and you have talent; you win together. And it's fun!

In the summer of '84, I started dating my wife and although I wasn't driving, we managed to spend a lot of time together. After open gyms, I played pitcher's hand wiffle ball for baseball cards with Michael Yarberry, Billy Wolf, Scott Ezell and John Launius. I had a blast playing Colt league baseball for Merv Spillman and I was a huge New York Mets fan. Looking back, these were some of the greatest times of my life.

In the fall of '84, I chose to play football rather than run cross country. Mistake! I thought I was going to be the quarterback. I led many of my teams to great comeback wins at recess at Douglas School. I had a feel for the nerf football and often scrambled out of tough situations like my favorite player, Roger Staubach. I was a terrible football player. The regulation football was twice as big as the nerf football and my scrambling ability didn't seem to work with real pads on. I couldn't generate enough speed to hit anybody and I wasn't very mean.

With football now over, there was just one more week until official basketball practice was to begin. I was approaching the magic number sixteen. I was in Coach Herrin's driver's education class and one day he pulled me aside and said, "Hey...I'm going to bring you...and Launius and Vanhorn up to practice and dress with the varsity. You've got to get quicker and stronger, big guy." He then put a death clamp on my hand and said, "Need to get tougher too...I could probably whip you right now." He laughed and sent me back to my seat.

I have to chuckle when I think of Coach Herrin as my driver's ed teacher. The drivers ed gig fit him perfectly. Coach didn't want to be cooped up in the classroom. He didn't want to get a book out or sit behind a desk. Coach liked action. Many of his students gained their driving hours by chauffeuring him around town to run errands or road-tripping to basketball clinics. There are so many stories about his driving escapades, but this one perfectly summed up his approach to teaching Drivers Education:

Daren Carlile: *Coach Herrin was our driver's education teacher, right. Kyle and I were big buddies. Kyle had literally been driving since he was like ten years old. Coach Herrin would drive as fast as he could, and Kyle was a mini-Coach Herrin behind the wheel. I passed the classroom part of the drivers ed Course and then you had to drive. I think Coach Herrin figured that I had the same amount of driving experience as Kyle...so he says, "Hey big guy, I need you to drive me and the coaches to Norris City to scout a game." I think it was Coach Phillips, Coach Webb, my dad...all the coaches. I had very little driving experience. On top of that...I had to drive the 15-passenger school van at night to Norris City with all the coaches in the vehicle. I was very unsure of myself but I did make it. Is that not classic Coach Herrin? Think about the liability there. None of the other coaches thought twice about it.*

His approach to driver's education sometimes showed itself in the way he coached the game of basketball. I'll never forget one practice in college, we were working on getting through ball screens and a player asked him, "Coach do you want us to go over the top of the screen...or slide underneath the screen?" Coach gave a sharp response, "You've just got to get through the screen...find a way and get through it!" His response was basically...figure it out. How do you learn how to drive? You drive the car.

Randy House: *He taught rebounding the same way he taught getting over a screen. You just have to do it.*

With the big three of House, Peters, and Schafer back, '84-'85 promised to be a solid season. Coach Herrin had this to say about the big three before the season started:

Coach Herrin: *Randy is probably the best Class AA player we've got in the South this year. He can play both inside and out. He is a real physical player and plays with great confidence. David is the type of player who exhibits great confidence wherever he plays. He is a physical player and a good perimeter* *shooter. Jay has great anticipation and even though he is 6'7" he plays much bigger than he is. He just may be the best intimidator we've ever had here… and he plays well with his back to the goal.*

As a youngster, House knew of the Rangers and enjoyed playing basketball on his own.

Randy House: *I went to Grant School and my coach was Mr. A. I started going to the Rangers games when I was eight or nine years old. My dad (Ron House) was a teacher at the junior high for a couple of years in the early seventies and he had Billy Smith, Rob Dunbar and a bunch of the players in class. We probably went for Dad as much as for me. I can't say that I ever really dreamed about being a Benton Ranger. I lived two doors down from Billy Smith out in the country. I had a goal, and there was not a lot of people to play with, so I played a lot. I definitely could have played more. I did the shoveling the snow off the court thing…there wasn't much to do. I did go to the Rend Lake camps in the summer for three or four years…but I wasn't a big camp-goer.*

Chris Head: *Randy was my best friend. We don't do much together now but I know if I ever needed something I could call him. In high school we hunted together, and we were in many of the same classes. We had a good rivalry growing up…he went to Grant and I went to Logan and then we grew to be great friends in junior high. Randy was a hard worker.*

David Peters: *Randy and I became really good friends…especially his senior year. Anytime it snowed, Randy and I cut doughnuts in the student parking lot and one time our cars got out of control and we about slid into each other and totaled both of our cars. Randy was a pure athlete…he could have been a great baseball player or football player.*

At the point guard position in '85 was David Peters. Peters was an unbelievable three-sport athlete; football, basketball and baseball. Peters played an important role on the '84 team and was now depended on to be the Rangers' point guard. He was a junior.

David Peters: *Much like the year before, we didn't think anyone could beat us. I remember that I moved to the point guard position that year and as a freshman I played inside. It was an adjustment.*

Randy House: *Dave was a baseball player…a good football player…and a tremendous athlete. He was a big guard that could pass and shoot. When Dave came into the game we didn't lose anything. He wasn't scared of the moment because he grew up with his older brother beating him up. He wasn't going to get pushed around…he wasn't scared.*

Jay Schafer: *Pete was just so unusually strong for a point guard. He just held people off and could get to the rim…and he could jump. Kai was more of an artist and Dave would just overpower you…that transition from Kai to Dave at the point was pretty seamless.*

Schafer was now a year older and more seasoned at the post. As a sophomore, he was expected to rebound and block shots but he was now expected to score.

Jay Schafer: *I remember having some 30-point games as a junior and I had a good year in terms of blocking shots. There were some times Randy would let guys go defensively and have me clean it up. Coach Herrin would always say how important it was that I could alter shots. I might block a certain number of shots but alter twice as many.*

Joining the big three in the starting lineup was Jeff Thompson and Tony Shell. In '84-'85, Jeff Thompson was the tallest player in the South at 6'9". He received very little playing time on the great '84 team but was expected to contribute greatly as a senior. Thompson was a step slow but had a deft shooting touch from fifteen feet.

Coach Herrin: *Jeff has made great strides since last year. He always could shoot the ball but he has to play with more confidence.*

At the small forward position was Tony Shell. Tony gave us a second southpaw in the starting line-up. I grew up playing baseball and basketball with Tony and I can honestly say that the most frightened I had ever been in my childhood was when Tony was forty feet away from me with a baseball. Tony was all arms and legs and could throw a baseball through a brick wall but sometimes didn't know where it was going. Shell was a 6'3" jumping jack that did a little bit of everything on the floor. He could rebound, score and was a great fast break finisher that could dunk the ball with ease. He was an athlete.

Coach Herrin: *Tony is playing with much more intensity this year. He may end up as being one of the top players in the area. Tony has excellent jumping ability and good quickness.*

Jay Schafer: *Tony Shell could really jump and run.*

Jeff Shurtz: *Me and Tony grew up together. Tony was just…a good guy…a good-hearted person. He was always kind of shy and quiet and at our last class reunion they were trying to get some of us to karaoke the song "You Dropped A Bomb On Me." That's what we listened to back in the day. We couldn't get Tony to do it. He was just a great teammate and friend.*

The first post player off the bench was 6'4" junior Scott Webb. Webb was a great high hurdle runner in track and such a good teammate.

Coach Herrin: *Scott has made great progress. He is a fine athlete and will see a lot of playing time.*

The top two backcourt reserves were juniors Brad Wills and Jeff Shurtz.

Coach Herrin: *Both Jeff and Brad have super quickness and are fundamentally sound. When we play Wills and Shurtz with Peters, Shell and Schafer, we will have a quick pressing lineup.*

Jeff and Brad had older brothers that played in the program and Benton Ranger basketball had been a part of their lives as long as they could remember.

Brad Wills: *Because my dad coached at the junior high, I don't remember a time in my life that I didn't know Coach Herrin. My favorite player growing up was Billy Smith. When I was about four years old I made my parents address me as Billy Smith or I got mad. After Billy, there was Keith, Curtis, Robbie and Tim…but my initial guy was Billy Smith.*

Jeff Shurtz: *Just growing up around my brothers…I was quite a bit younger but you look up to your brothers. Basketball was in our blood. That's what we did and that's what we were going to do. I remember going to all of their games when they were in high school and I even went to Steve and Carl's games when they played at Rend Lake. There were times Mom and Dad would take me* *and we would make the Seven-hour drive to see Rod play at Missouri Southern. I was in awe of Billy Smith, Rob Dunbar and Mark Craddock. I just remember being really excited and interested in the game at that time. I was one of those kids that wanted to talk to those guys and they would acknowledge you…you know. I was there when Dunbar hurt his knee…and Keith Tabor was one of my idols too.*

Jeff Shurtz: *Me and Brad had a good time together. Brad was a hard-nosed guy…very competitive. He just grew up that way. I always enjoyed playing with him.*

Senior Chris Head was a top reserve guard that battled for playing time. Head had been around the Benton Ranger basketball program as long as he could remember.

Chris Head: *I remember watching games in the old gym. My grandparents had seats in the front row and I would sit on their laps and watch the game. I re-created the games using a clothes basket… "Steve Stewart for two!" I would play the games out. I remember when Rob Dunbar and Robbie Hammond hurt their knees. Then you had the old BIT…the great guard combination of Tim Wills and Robbie Williams was so much fun to watch.*

Coach Herrin: *Chris can shoot it and could give us some important minutes.*

Junior Freddie Gibson was the son of the new BCHS football coach, Fred Gibson. Gibson went on to play football at SIU and started at the quarterback position. He was smart, tough and fast and set records at SIU for career rushing and passing yards. Gibson provided great competition in practice against the regulars. He was a great teammate.

Coach Herrin: *Freddie is a physically talented player that just needs some playing time.*

The other three seniors on the team were Jim Odom, Steve Rich and Mark Melcher. Odom and Rich played four years of basketball in high school but Melcher was in his first season. Melcher was a good teammate that provided the regulars with good competition. Odom and Rich had been in the program for years.

Jim Odom: *Mr. A got me into the game from a young age. I still call him on his birthday. You know I didn't get to go to a lot of the high school games growing up because my mom was a single working mom. The grade school programs were so good back then. Farley Finter, Mr. A, Perry Eisenhower…those guys were great coaches. I was a little heavy and was the manager in junior high and then lost some weight and went out for basketball in high school. I think my motivation to continue to play came from Coach Herrin's program. It was the thing to do at the time…and he taught the game in such a way that it caught on.*

Steve Rich: *I don't recall ever missing a game growing up. We lived on McCann Street. Some of my favorite players were Keith Tabor, Mark Craddock and the Shurtz brothers. It didn't matter who you were…the best player or the fifteenth guy on the team…people knew who you were. The gym was packed and it was just a very special time and it was so much fun to be a part of.*

In '84-'85, I was a sophomore and dressed with classmates John Launius and Brian Vanhorn. Launius was a 6'3" center/forward with a very soft touch and Brian Vanhorn was a 5'10" point guard with lightening quickness. They were both great teammates. At the time, I was 6'1", 135 pounds and I was in love with the game of basketball.

Senior Bryan Cross brought his pack of Foxes into Franklin County to face the Rangers in the opener. The previous year, Cross scored 20 points in a dramatic Foxes upset of the Rangers in the '84 BIT and it looked as if it could happen again. With just seconds left in the game and the Rangers up by one, Jeff Shurtz rose high in the lane to snatch a missed free throw and was then fouled immediately. The junior guard calmly canned two big free throws to give the Rangers an exciting 48-44 win over the Foxes. Bryan Cross led all scorers with 17 points and Randy House led the Rangers with 16 points.

In game two, the Rangers lost 62-61, due to a costly turnover late in the game. The inside duo of Red Epplin and Jason Carson combined for 38 points to drop the Rangers to 1-1 for the season. The next night, Jeff Thompson scored 23 points to lead the team past the Massac County Patriots to improve the Rangers to 2-1 before entering South Seven Conference action. The team was heavy on size and still searching for their identity. With the luxury of having the twin towers of Schafer and Thompson inside, House was moved out on the floor and expected to score.

Jay Schafer: *Randy had to take on more of a scoring role and I do remember that I was expected to score more also.*

In game four, the Rangers traveled south to play the Marion Wildcats under the direction of their new head coach, Larry Jenkins. The game was played on December 14th and the game was big in the eyes of the people of Marion. The Wildcats had struggled for the past two seasons and the people of Marion were anxious for better basketball. Another source of excitement was the possibility of sticking it to the Rangers and Marion transfer Jay Schafer. Just a year earlier, Schafer had left Marion for greener pastures at Benton. Marion knew it.

Marion slowed the game down to a snail's pace. Marion's go-to player was 6'1" guard Steve Lacy. Lacy was an incredible football player and a solid basketball player. Lacy still remains one of the greatest all-around athletes in Marion history. The Wildcats led 18-14 at halftime. The crowd of Marion fans was energetic, and the student section came alive with each Wildcat basket. The place was loud. We could not get it going. House was score-less through three quarters. The Wildcats held on to win the game 35-34. Marion fans flooded the floor and jeered the Rangers players as they walked to the locker room. The Cats had beaten Herrin and Schafer and they were soaking it in. I was one of the first players in the locker room after the game and I was still learning Coach Herrin. It was my first season with him. We all took a seat in the locker room and nobody said a word. Through the silence, sound penetrated through the concrete block locker room and I could faintly hear the Marion fans celebrating. Coach Herrin then flung the door open and slid down the wall and cried. I had never seen this. Up to this point, Whittington, Carlile, Webb and Stewart had never cried in front of me. The thing I noticed most was this; Coach was not grandstanding. These were tears of defeat and anger. This was my take-away from that locker room: Coach Herrin hated to get beat. He was a competitor.

The team was 2-2 and not playing well but practice rolled on and we made a nice run before hitting the Centralia Tournament. Was it because Coach Herrin cried in the locker room? No. It was because losing wasn't acceptable. Not at Benton. Herrin picked up the pace in practice and tweaked the offense in the attempt to turn things around. It worked. Herrin believed that good practices meant good play.

Randy House: *We practiced hard. I don't remember running a lot of line tappers...we got our running and conditioning in with the ball. We very rarely* *scrimmaged…it was more like a controlled scrimmage. About three possessions and then there would be a break. You might start with half-court offense and then we would have to get back and play defense and then he would reward you with taking the break. Half-court offense was my favorite.*

On Friday, December 21, 1984, the team ripped Mt. Vernon by a score of 75-32. The team was firing on all cylinders. Jay Schafer led the scoring attack with 19 points and Jeff Thompson chipped in with 14. To end the first half, Coach Herrin called timeout and sat up the old pop-out play to attack full-court pressure. Unfortunately, Peters threw a pass to House before he stepped out of bounds. There was about thirty seconds left in the first half. As soon as we turned the ball over, Coach Herrin left the bench and went into the locker room. He was gone. We finished the first half without our head coach. I thought about checking into the game and then thought I better not. When the horn sounded we all sprinted into the locker room and again he was in tears. This time it was tears of embarrassment. My takeaway from the incident was two things; he wanted things done right and he was passionate. It mattered to him that we did things the right way. Late in the game, Coach Herrin put me in the game and I hit a wide open 15-foot jumper from the corner. It was my first varsity points as a Benton Ranger. I finished the night with four points.

In the first game of the Centralia Tournament, we pounded Union County, Kentucky by a score of 76-53. Jeff Thompson led the Rangers in scoring with 14 points and House chipped in with 11.

The following day, we defeated Homewood-Flossmoor by a score of 53-49. Dick Seidel led the Vikings in scoring with a game-high 19 points. Seidel was a player and the big redhead went on to play college basketball at Davidson University. Jeff Shurtz recalled an incident that occurred in the Homewood game that he would never forget.

Jeff Shurtz: *Anytime we went to Centralia, everybody was rooting against you. It was a hostile environment and I enjoyed playing there. I knocked the ball out of this kids hand and they called a foul on me…but it was clean. The ball rolled over to some chair seats on the floor and it went right in front of my dad. The Master (Dad) put his foot on top of the ball. After the official reported the foul and was on the other side of the floor….he put his hands up so dad would pass him the ball…my dad just looked at him. The official had to run across the floor and pick up the ball under my dad's foot. He was taking up for me a little bit…I just remembered that really fired me up.*

The next morning, we were defeated in the semi-final match-up against Chicago Carver. Carver had unbelievable talent. NBA legend Tim Hardaway played the point and Tulsa-bound "Dr. Dunk" Wade Jenkins played inside. Jenkins led the team in scoring with 20 points and Carver won an exciting game by a score of 53-46. Schafer led the way by scoring 14 points. He was having a stellar tournament on both ends of the floor. Shurtz remembered a funny incident from the loss against Carver.

Jeff Shurtz: *One of the funniest memories I have about Coach Herrin happened in the Centralia Tournament. I threw a pass and I saw a guy coming to steal it so I threw it into the stands so it wouldn't get stolen. He took me out of the game and said, "Shurtzy, you can't shoot it, dribble it or pass it." Two or three minutes went by and he said, "Get in there for Webb." Webb messed up and here I go back into the game. I still laugh about that.*

Later that same night, the Rangers defeated the Centralia Orphans in the third place game by a score of 70-57. Centralia had three very talented seniors; Ben Willis and Mike Maines. Future Saluki Rick Shipley was just a sophomore. Once again, the Rangers were led in scoring by Jay Schafer who scored a game-high 22 points. With the win, the Rangers improved to 6-3 overall and 1-1 in South Seven play. Jay Schafer was the only Benton player chosen to the CHT All-Tournament team.

After years of waiting, Brad Wills logged his first minutes in the Centralia Tournament. Wills had seen his brother play in the tournament and admits that getting the chance to play against that competition was special.

Brad Wills: *Overall, to be able to play in the Centralia Tournament…that was special. We played against guys like Tim Hardaway, Rodell Davis, Joe Griffin and Wade Jenkins. Those were talented players but we were expected to beat them. It was just another game. Coach Herrin instilled that kind of confidence in us. Guys like Coach Herrin and my dad…they wanted to play the best.*

We won the next five conference games by defeating West Frankfort, Carbondale, Centralia, Harrisburg and Herrin before heading into the Benton Invitational Tournament. The team was playing well and stood at 11-3 overall and 6-1 in the conference. After the first loop through the conference, we were in first place with only one loss.

Our team cake-walked through the first four games of the BIT Tournament to set up a much-anticipated game against the McLeansboro Foxes on a Saturday night. One thing is for sure, Bryan Cross loved shooting the ball in Rich Herrin Gymnasium. In a nail-biter, the Foxes did it again. They had now beaten us three years in a row and this one stung. Cross led all scorers with 18 points and Stacy Sturm chipped in with ten. Schafer led us in scoring with ten points. Schafer, House and Peters were selected on the ten-man BIT All-Tournament team.

After the loss to the McLeansboro Foxes, we went on to win the final seven games in conference play to win the South Seven with a record of 13-1. In our final conference game of the season tragedy struck. Plagued by untimely injuries throughout his career, Rich Herrin and the '85 Rangers suffered a setback in their final conference victory at Herrin.

David Peters: *I was coming down the floor on a fast break and jump stopped to make a pass and my knee cap dislocated. I was taken in an ambulance to the hospital and when I got home it was after midnight…and I remember all of these people being at the house. Rich was there, Ron Smith was there… Coach Herrin called Doug Collins and he spoke to me on the phone that night to offer me some encouragement…telling me that I could recover from the injury. Looking back on it, that was pretty amazing.*

Teammate Jeff Shurtz remembered that losing Peters was definitely a setback.

Jeff Shurtz: *Dave was just a super athlete. He had so much talent. It was a tough injury for us.*

Even with the tragic injury to Peters, the season had been successful. It was a great accomplishment to finish 13-1 in the South Seven. It was the first time in three seasons the we had won the conference. Brad Wills recalled the season this way.

Brad Wills: *My junior year, the thing that sticks out to me was we weren't one of the best teams in Benton History…but we were a solid team. We were still the program in Southern Illinois…at that time. As a high school program we were at an elite level…and we certainly weren't the reason for that. Our team was a part of the program that had already been built by the guys that came before us. It was the consistency of Coach Herrin. He was ahead of his* *time in so many ways…the way he organized practices…open gyms…sum-mer camps…and playing at a faster tempo. He was so competitive and he was always trying to get better and wasn't afraid to be innovative and change something in order to improve. As success does, it builds on itself. The old system with the grade schools competing against each other was a great system and the timing of that was significant.*

In our final game at Cahokia, the Comanches defeated us by a score of 49-44 behind 12 points from Tim Goodwin. It was our first game with-out Peters but the Comanches were a solid team. With the loss, the Rang-ers finished the regular season with a record of 22-5 and were South Seven Champions. Could they make a run?

'85 State Tournament Play

In the first game of the Harrisburg Regional, we played the Mount Cara-mel Golden Aces. It was a beat-down. After jumping out to a 24-0 lead after the first quarter, we cruised to a 91-27 victory to advance to the Regional Championship on Friday night against the Mt. Vernon Rams. In the game against the Aces, Randy House drove the middle of the lane and tomahawk-dunked the ball in traffic. It was a play that brought me off the bench. I hadn't seen a dunk in years!

On Friday, March 8th, our team faced the Rams for the third time. The Rams were young and we had handled them easily in the first two meetings. We started the game well and led 40-20 at the end of the first half. Late in the game, Coach Herrin put the reserves in the ball game and something happened that will forever be remembered in Ranger lore. I was actually in the game at the time. Senior Jim Odum was a reserve post player and one of the hardest workers on the team. He accidentally scored in the wrong basket. When the ball went through the net, everyone kind of froze for a minute and then came the laughter. I have to admit, I felt for the guy.

After the game, we all dressed and boarded the bus and prepared for the traditional fire truck around the square. It was my first one. I remem-ber thinking to myself about how neat it was to actually be on the bus. For so many years I was that kid standing on the sidewalk cheering… now…I'm on the bus. Despite scoring ten varsity points as a sophomore, I hung my head out of the window and got a small taste of what it was like for all those guys I cheered for growing up. After the fire truck escort the bus went back to the gym for an informal reception. Our team stood at half-court and after Coach Herrin addressed the crowd, the seniors were introduced and encouraged to speak. Then it was time for Odum to speak. What is a guy going to say that scored in the wrong basket? In that moment, he handled the situation perfectly.

Jim Odom: *We had a reception at the gym following the game and the seniors got the opportunity to speak to the crowd. I was introduced as the guy that made the basket in the wrong goal and everybody got a kick out of it.... So when I took the microphone I kind of paused to get everyone's attention and said, "I want to thank Coach Herrin because...he taught me everything that I know." Everybody started laughing...it was a fun moment.*

Although Jim Odum didn't play a lot of varsity minutes, Jim loved his experience of playing for the Benton Rangers.

Jim Odom: *The treatment we received from the community was amazing. I was able to make a relationship with a season ticket-holder by the name of Everett Odum. Basketball was a unifying force in our community and being a part of something so well recognized in the state was very special.*

Senior Steve Rich played four years of high school basketball and loved every minute of it.

Steve Rich: *Everything about being on the team was special...the locker room...the bus rides...certain songs can give me flashbacks to those times.*

With the win, we advanced to the Benton Sectional to play the Carbondale Terriers. We had beaten the Terriers in our first two meetings but that was with Peters. Our team was very capable but anytime a regular player is taken out of the mix it changes the dynamics of the team. Tony Shell and Scott Webb had performed well and so had Shurtz and Wills, but now everybody had to do more.

The Carbondale team was led by senior Ronnie Tate. Tate was extremely strong and quick and one of the better players in the conference. The Terriers also featured junior phenom, Stephen Bardo. Bardo played college basketball at the University of Illinois and led the Fighting Illini to the Final Four in '89 as a junior. Today, he is one of the best college basketball analysts in the country. Bardo and Tate were surrounded by great teammates; Stacy Corthen, Clayton Greer, Brent Beggs and William Cobb. It was just a year ago that we had ended Carbondale's perfect season and the Terriers were looking for revenge.

Brad Wills: *I just remember that Bardo grew like crazy and ended up being 6'6" and became the leader of that team.*

With the game against Carbondale approaching, the discussion in Benton circles focused on Peters. Would he play? Coach Herrin had this to say about Peters' injury:

Coach Herrin: *I thought Saturday there was a good chance that Dave could return in 8-10 days but there is still considerable swelling in his injured right knee. I still don't think there is ligament damage but he still may not play anymore this season.*

Doug Woolard had to prepare his Terriers for a Rangers team with or without Peters and we had to do the same. It would be a game-time decision.

On Friday night, March 12, 1985, the Benton Rangers and Carbondale Terriers battled for the right to move to Friday's Sectional Championship. The home crowd went crazy as we took the floor but all eyes zeroed in on David Peters. Was he healthy? Would he play? How is he moving? Wearing a heavy knee brace, it was obvious that Peters was hurting and his mobility was limited, but he did play.

David Peters: *I played later on that season…but it was painful to play and I had very limited mobility.*

From the tip, it didn't look good. Our team lacked energy and the Terriers took an early 20-13 lead and held a 36-32 halftime advantage. Tony Shell had one of his best offensive nights of the season. With much of the defensive pressure centered on House and Schafer, Shell found himself open and was dropping mid-range jumpers when it mattered most. To begin the fourth quarter, we were ahead 49-48 but then the bottom dropped out. A myriad of missed free throws, turnovers and missed shots plagued the Rangers and the Terriers avenged their '84 loss by winning the game by a score of 70-60. The Terriers went on to win the Benton Sectional but lost in the Super-Sectional to Cahokia.

Peters did what he could and scored just five points for the night. Scott Webb came off the bench to score ten points and Schafer and House each chipped in with 14 points. For the seniors, it was their final game. An emotional Coach Herrin addressed the team afterwards and had these words for the Benton Evening News following the defeat:

Rich Herrin: *Carbondale has a pretty good basketball team. Give them credit...tonight they outplayed us.*

After the conclusion of the season, the Annual Methodist Men's Basketball Banquet was held to honor the team. The organizer of the banquet, Bill Dixon, was never an athlete but he was a man that was well-organized and committed to his work in the educational department at Southern Illinois University. Dixon was adamant about things being done the right way. He lived in Benton with his wife Judy and two children; Valerie and Clark. The Dixons attended the Methodist Church and became lifelong friends with Rich and Sue Herrin. The friendship of Bill Dixon and Rich Herrin transcended the fact that Dixon was never an athlete.

Bill Dixon: *Coach would say, "Be ready in fifteen minutes...I'm going to McLeansboro to scout and you can go with me...and I went. I went out of friendship. Our families vacationed together and we became neighbors in 1968. Matt, I have to say...I had little interest in athletics until I met Coach Herrin. The relationship with Rich and Sue came about as friends.*

The banquet is a very formal affair. The players were expected to dress in suits and ties and the cheerleaders wore dresses. Banquet organizers took pride in bringing in speakers from across the country to address the team. Each year, one player is chosen to receive the annual Charles D. Hill Award that emphasizes sportsmanship and team play. In 1985, the recipient of the Charles D. Hill Award was Randy House. House was in the process of deciding where he would play college basketball. San Diego State and SIU-C showed the most interest. Randy had this to say about his thoughts about playing in college:

Randy House: *Between my junior and senior year...we went to Blue-Chip Basketball Camp in Georgetown, Kentucky. At the end of camp each player got an evaluation and my evaluation said major college...I thought...huh. It just helped my confidence level.*

Just days after the banquet, House signed a letter of intent to play Division I basketball for the SIU Salukis. House wanted to stay close to home and liked the thought of playing with good friend Kai Nurnberger. There is a great picture in one of the April editions of the Benton Evening News of House with the pen in his left hand, his parents Ron and Diana at his side and Coach Herrin in the background. They are all smiles. Herrin is still the head coach of the Benton Rangers, but the signing of House at SIU would prove to be a godsend to Herrin. He just didn't know it yet. House was proud of his high school basketball career and said this about his playing experience under Coach Herrin:

Randy House: *I think one thing I'm proud of is that in my four years at Benton High School we won a total of 103 games and that may be the most in any four-year span in the history of the program. I can't necessarily compare Coach to anyone else because he is the only guy I ever played for. But he's got to be pretty good. He was ahead of his time with his summer program and giving kids the opportunity to play. Those expectations that we had at Benton…he set those expectations. He was a great offensive coach and he allowed his players to play with great freedom. When our team at Rend Lake won the Junior College National Championship it solidified to me that Coach Herrin's way works. Everything that I did I took from him. We played hard…we had great comaraderie…we had good kids. His way works.*

As a senior, Randy was chosen as a member of the '85 Class AA All-State team. House went on to have a fairy tale college career and played a key role in rebuilding the SIU basketball program. House went on to score over 1,000 points in his college career and is still considered one of the greatest basketball players in Saluki history. Today, Randy is the owner of RKH Insurance, among other things. He lives in West Frankfort with his wife, Debbie, and they have two children; Rorrie and Ryley.

Reserve players Chris Head, Steve Rich and Jim Odom recall what they learned in their experience for playing for Coach Herrin.

Chris Head: *You know…My dad was on Coach Herrin's first team at Benton… and I was on his last. You know I had the utmost respect for Coach Herrin. He was a good person and he always treated us like human beings. To get respect you have to show respect.*

Chris now lives in Benton with his wife Tammy and they have two sons; Justin and Dakota. Chris now works at Benton High School and is in charge of the building and grounds. He has been involved with the Benton baseball program for the last twenty-seven years and is responsible for maintaining the six baseball fields at Benton Community Park among other duties.

Steve Rich: *Coach helped me in so many ways. I wouldn't be where I'm at without Coach Herrin. I was hired on the athletic staff at SIU my senior year. Coach Herrin and Fred Huff had a lot to do with that. Then I interviewed at Murray State for the Assistant Athletic Director's job…I was just twenty-two years old and probably over my head. Steve Newton was the basketball coach at Murray at the time and he had a lot of influence on who would be hired. Coach Newton told me, "I just got off the phone with Coach Herrin. We are going to hire you…his word is good enough for me." Fast forward a few years and I interviewed for a similar position at Eastern Illinois and again the basketball coach…Rick Samuels was the coach… Samuels talked to Coach Herrin and I was hired. Matt…he always looked out for me.*

Today, Steve Rich lives in Charleston, Illinois and is now Assistant Vice President of University Advancement at Eastern Illinois University. He has worked at Eastern Illinois University for the past twenty-seven years. Steve and his wife Cindy have two boys; Bryn and Brock.

Jim Odom: *Coach Herrin was good at motivating players. I remember having shin splints one time and he said, "Well Jimmy O…you can play or go home." He always showed respect the right way…he was fair. I remember him poking me in the chest with those fingers so hard that it hurt. Coach taught you how to be a competitor. Nobody knew more about the game than Coach. Having a winning spirit is important. Basketball teaches you how to be a teammate and play a role on a team. There were just so many things we learned.*

Today, Jim is a lawyer and lives in Sparta with his wife, Margaret. They have four children; Alice, Clara, Samuel and Daniel.

After high school, David Peters went on to sign a full-ride football scholarship to SIU-C as a punter. In fact, Peters and teammate Freddie Gibson played football at SIU during the same time period I was playing basketball at Southern. One day during pre-season conditioning on the track of old McAndrew Stadium, SIU Assistant Basketball Coach, Rodney Watson, led us in 400 intervals. These were killers. The sun was beating down and it was hot. Nobody wanted to do them. We had to make a certain time with each 400 or there were consequences. The SIU football team was in full pads practicing in the middle of the field. I remember finishing one of the intervals and barely making my time. I was panting like a dying dog with my hands on my knees. I heard this voice say, "Hey." I looked up and it was Pete. Pete was leaning up against the kicking net laughing at me. He said, "Wrong sport, dude." I laugh every time I think about it.

Today, David Peters works as an architect with his wife Tina. They own a company called Autograph Home Entertainment. The company specializes in creating and installing custom home theaters. They live in St. Louis. Pete loved Coach.

David Peters: *Besides my dad…Rich Herrin made more of an impact on my life than any other male figure. He taught me that no matter how hard you thought you were playing…you always have more in you. And he was right… you know. He was at my dad's funeral…my mom's funeral…he would pick us up for practice and take us home. I remember one time he told me, "I was really hard on you. You had a lot of talent and I didn't want you to cruise…I wanted to push you." The feeling I had playing for Rich Herrin was incredible. My last football game at SIU was in South Carolina…something like 28,000 people in the stadium…it didn't compare to running out of that tunnel at Benton and hearing that crowd…and Rich created that atmosphere.*

As a senior, Jay Schafer was selected to the Class AA All-State team in 1986. After high school, he signed a full-ride basketball scholarship at Southern Illinois University and became teammates with House and Kai. I later joined them in the fall of '87. At SIU, Schafer was a valuable post player off the bench that won the respect of his teammates by playing hard every day in practice. Jay is now a lawyer with his wife Michelle, at Schafer Law. They have two children; Cole and Montana.

Jay Schafer: *There are several kinds of coaches out there…but the coaches that could win were the ones that could x and o and three minutes into the game make adjustments on the fly. He also had the players that could fix things on the fly.*

After high school, Tony Shell played basketball at Freed-Hardeman University in Henderson, Tennessee where he earned a degree in computer science. In the summer of 2021, Tony passed away but he is survived by his wife Sandra and their four children; Stephen, Spencer, Emily and Lauren. Along with being a great athlete, Tony truly was a great teammate and friend to all of us.

Today, Brad Wills works as a financial planner for Alliance Investment Group in Carbondale, Illinois. Brad and I remain good friends and our sons played basketball together in high school. Brad's son, Austin, received a full-ride basketball scholarship to Trevecca Nazarene University in Nashville, Tennessee. Brad and his wife Sandra live in Benton and have two children; Austin and Mia. Wills had this to say about what he learned from Coach Herrin:

Brad Wills: *I think it would be his pursuit of excellence. He worked so hard and we expected good outcomes. The bar was high. It wasn't ever like... "I hope we win tonight". It was expected.*

Jeff Shurtz remains as one of the top all-around athletes in Benton history. In the spring of '86, Jeff won the Class AA State Championship in the pole vault with a jump of 15'3". Earlier that fall, he placed tenth in the IHSA State Golf Tournament. Today, Shurtz is an asbestos removal supervisor at SIU-C and has held this position for twenty-plus years. Jeff lives in Benton with his wife Natalie and they have two children; Georgie and Stricker.

Jeff Shurtz: *Coach taught us how to work hard. I learned discipline and always had the upmost respect for him.*

With six seniors returning, the future looked bright for the Rangers. In the Spring of '85, the basketball players ran track and life seemed normal; just another year. But this wasn't the case. Hoops drama beyond the city limits of Benton played out and it threatened to disrupt the ebb and flow of Rangers basketball. Things might never be the same.

Tony Shell was a junior in '85. Shell was a slasher on the offensive end and a solid rebounder. *(Ceasar Maragni)*

Chris Head's father Ron was on Coach Herrin's first team at Benton. As a senior in '85, Chris was on Coach's last team. *(Ceasar Maragni)*

Brad Wills was a scrappy junior that gave the Rangers depth at the guard position in '85. *(Ceasar Maragni)*

Randy House as a senior. It was House's team in '85.
(McCutchen, Southern Illinoisan)

Point guard, David Peters in '85.
(Ceasar Maragni)

Jay Schafer with the mid-lane jump hook.
(Dalzell, Southern Illinoisan)

Finally! As a sophomore, I dressed with the '85 Rangers.
(Ceasar Maragni)

Big Jeff Thompson as a senior in '85.
(Ceasar Maragni)

Jeff Shurtz did all the little things that make a winner. Shurtz pounced on loose balls and was a shutdown defender. *(Ceasar Maragni)*

Scott Webb was a solid inside player in 85 & 86.
(Ceasar Maragni)

The twin towers of Jay Schafer and Jeff Thompson made for
a strong inside game in '85. *(Ceasar Maragni)*

Reserve guard, Steve Rich in '85.
(Ceasar Maragni)

Jimmy O in '85. Odum was a reserve post player.
(Ceasar Maragni)

The '85 Rangers. **Front Row-** Thompson, House Schafer **Row Two-** Wynn, Smith, Rich, Van Horn, Wills **Row Three-** Shurtz, Melcher, Gibson, Gibson, Shell, S. Webb, D. Webb, Odum, Launius, Head, Herrin, Peters. *(Ceasar Maragni)*

CHAPTER THIRTY-ONE

A New Challenge

"Don't go Rich….don't do it." – BCHS Principal - Chuck Oyler

In the spring of '85, Allen Van Winkle knew that the gig was up. It was over. Van Winkle had just finished his fourth season as the SIU Men's basketball coach, compiling a record of 49-62, but the lack of success on the floor was only part of the story; there were allegations of cheating. It was found that center Kenny Perry was receiving money from SIU booster Roy White. The question was whether Van Winkle knew about the payments. White said that Van Winkle knew about the payments, but Van Winkle denied having any knowledge of payments made to Perry. It was a mess. Under pressure, Allen Van Winkle resigned as head coach of the basketball Salukis on April 9, 1985. A Division I coaching job in Southern Illinois was now open and naturally there was speculation that Rich Herrin would be interested.

Herrin had created a dominant high school program at Benton and the thought of coaching Division I Basketball was intriguing. What interested Herrin the most was the challenge of it all. The job would require high level recruiting, travel and trusted assistant coaches. Even though Southern Illinois is a small media market, the job would require a certain amount of public relations work. If Herrin were to even get the job, his family would have to move from their comfortable home in Benton, Illinois. There were a lot of things to think about.

Dr. Dean Stuck was now in charge of SIU intercollegiate athletics as appointed by the school's president, Albert Somit. Dr. Stuck was not a basketball guy. He was a former high school football coach in Iowa. Dean Stuck had a reputation of cleaning messes. Just years earlier, he was appointed to fix some problems that were occurring in SIU's Zoology department. The problems went away. So, when Lew Hartzog left as SIU's athletic director in the spring of '85, Stuck was placed in charge and it was now his job to clean up SIU Basketball. Stuck did not waste time. The SIU head basketball job was posted shortly after Van Winkle's resignation.

Herrin talked with his wife, Sue, about applying. The job was going to be a challenge. There was dissention on the '84-'85 Saluki team and not much talent returning. It was definitely a rebuild to say the least. The Salukis had not been to the NCAA Tournament since 1977 and money was tight in the athletic department. Legendary SIU Broadcaster Mike Reis explained the state of the basketball program in the spring of '85.

Mike Reis: *Southern was in a mess in the mid-eighties. They were about to drop a couple of sports after. They were operating on a small staff and I say that because I didn't work internally then…I was just covering the games. So many things were going wrong…including poor basketball attendance. Southern doesn't profit if basketball isn't profitable…and it wasn't then. So they were looking at everything at that time. They had cut scholarships in half in every sport except basketball, women's basketball and football. Baseball, for example, went from 15 to seven. So that's the way it was trending…and I certainly got the vibe from the people I talked to that two things could happen; dropping football or dropping to Division II in all the sports.*

Despite all of the negatives, Herrin wanted the job. He had created a basketball dynasty at Benton High School and was confident that he could turn around what looked to be a dead-end program. The challenge was so great that he could not resist. On April 20, 1985, Rich Herrin wrote his letter of application to Dr. Dean Stuck. He was fifty-two years of age. In the application, he included his accomplishments, family information and several references. Herrin made up his mind; it was now or never.

Mike Reis: *When I first heard he was interested…I called him. We were talking about something else and then all of the sudden he says, "Maybe you've heard but I'm interested in the SIU job." I said, "Well…that's why I'm calling,*

I heard that…and I wanted to hear it from you." He said, "Well I don't know if you think I should get it…or whether I would be good enough…or if you would help me…but I sure hope you don't hurt me." I knew he wanted it bad. He wanted it so bad he could taste it.

There was one thing for certain; Herrin had local support. He was a Southern Illinois icon and even people in the area not privy to basketball knew of him.

Mike Reis: *I did feel that he answered a question that Southern has always faced…and that is trying to get consistent support outside of the Jackson and Williamson County area. When Southern's attendance is good and the interest at Southern is at its best…it is when people from Union, Franklin, Jefferson and Saline County are interested. I thought that could help…and there certainly were positives for that…I knew he would rally people around the flag pole. Could he do the job? I don't recall having strong feelings either way. I don't recall saying, "There is just no way that will work" and I don't recall saying, "He is just the perfect choice." So…my concern was for him personally and the career decision he was making…but secondarily…could he do the job? There was nothing to prove that…but there was every bit of evidence to prove he was a successful high school coach. Was he giving up too much?*

When the application deadline arrived there were a total of 69 applicants for the position. Overall, the field of applicants was considered weak at best. It was understood in coaching circles that the SIU job could be career suicide.

Dr. Dean Stuck: *We were required to have a committee when we hired someone, so we created a committee of five people. I did make it clear to the committee that I wanted their recommendation…but I would present to the president who I wanted.*

Under the guidance of Dr. Stuck, the committee studied the 69 applications and thinned the field to just ten. Instead of inviting the top ten finalists to interview on campus, Stuck secured hotel rooms in St. Louis.

Dr. Dean Stuck: *We didn't want that many coaches tramping around campus.*

Each of the ten applicants was interviewed by the committee. Dr. Stuck and the committee then chose the three finalists for the job. Herrin was one of the three. The other two finalists for the job were Bradley assistant Tony Barone and Steve Cottrell from Western Carolina.

Dr. Dean Stuck: *We brought the three finalists on campus to interview with the president and other administrators. Rich Herrin was one of the finalists. I did not know him at all before the interviews…although I was aware of him. The SIU President was impressed with Steve Cottrell. The Committee wanted Tony Barone…I wanted Rich Herrin. We just got put on probation for cheating. I felt like Herrin was as honest as the day was long. I went to the President of the University with my recommendation…and we must have discussed this for better than an hour. He was concerned that Herrin had no college experience…but I argued for him until the president finally looked at me and said, "Oh hell…go hire him."*

Dr. Dean Stuck went with his gut feeling and on May 13, 1985, Herrin was officially named the SIU head basketball coach. Both Herrin and Stuck addressed the local media in a press conference held on the SIU campus.

Rich Herrin: *This has been one of my goals…that I'd like to be the basketball coach at a Division I school. It's just a great honor, a great challenge and I think I can do the job. I think I can give Southern Illinois something they can be proud of.*

Dr. Dean Stuck: *He knows how to win. Certainly he's come from a winning program. He will be a good ambassador for Southern Illinois University. And he has demonstrated to us that he is committed to the academic program.*

Just a day after Herrin accepted the SIU job, he took time to reflect on his wonderful years in Benton. He sat alone in the Benton athletic office. He had been so busy getting the SIU job that there was little time to think about leaving Benton. The reality of leaving Benton began to hit home. It was difficult for him to come to grips with the fact that he was leaving the place in his heart that he would forever consider his home. It was a great run; the players, the victories, and the unwavering support of the community dominated his thoughts.

As he reminisced, BCHS Principal Chuck Oyler quietly entered his office with a cup of coffee in his hand. Oyler took a seat in front of Herrin's desk and looked him in the eyes and said, "Don't go Rich…don't do it." Herrin buried his head in his hands and cried. Close friend and BCHS assistant coach Ron Smith vividly remembered when Herrin was hired at SIU.

Ron Smith: *I was aware of what was going on with his interviews for the SIU job. I learned of him getting the job late one night. Early the next morning we met at the gym and he asked, "Are you interested in the Benton job or would you like to come with me?" I told him that I would like to go with him…and I joined him that August as a part-time assistant and then became a full-time assistant at SIU my third year. It was such an unusual hire in college basketball…to hire a high school coach. Coach saw it as another challenge. He was incredibly confident and I think he knew he could coach at that level. He had a swagger.*

SIU (1985-1998)

In the early summer of '85, the Herrin family moved from the home they had built in Benton to Carterville, Illinois. Carterville sits just minutes from the SIU campus in Carbondale, Illinois and serves as a satellite community to many SIU employees. Herrin signed a five-year contract with SIU that paid him less than what he was making at Benton High School. He wanted the job. The move was an adjustment for Kristy and Sue more than the boys. Rod, Randy and Kyle had moved out of the house. At the time, Kyle was the starting point guard at the University of Tennessee Martin. Kristy Herrin recalled those early years at SIU.

Kristy Herrin: *At Benton I remember that I would run and play and just be completely sweating after the games…but there were times that I would sit and watch games that were close, and really be into it. When dad got the job at SIU, mom didn't just let me run in the Arena. I sat with her. I watched a lot of games there. I knew which games to pay attention to.*

After winning 521 games in just twenty-five seasons at Benton, he was now 0-0 at SIU and there were doubters about his ability to win at the college level. There were seven local players on Herrin's first team at SIU

('85-'86). One of the local players was junior, Doug Novsek, from Law-renceville, Illinois. Novsek had crossed paths with Herrin in the '82 State Tournament when he lit the Rangers up in the quarter-final game.

Doug Novsek: *Everyone doubted him and we even doubted him at times... but he had so much enthusiasm and so much confidence on how to get it done. He loved being there...he got me back to loving the game.*

Although the team did not have great talent or athleticism, they battled. In Herrin's first college game, Chicago State came into the SIU Arena and jumped on the Salukis early to take a 27-8 lead.

Rich Herrin: *After the first three weeks of practice last fall, I didn't know for sure if we could win a game.... And when I called time out in our first game of the season against Chicago State...looked up at the scoreboard down 27-8...I said to myself, I don't know how you got into this mess, but you've got to find a way to get out of it.*

Despite the large halftime deficit, the young Salukis fought back. Herrin's troops came back to win the game on a shot by Saluki Hall-of-Famer Steve Middleton. Pandemonium then broke out among the 2,000 Saluki fans that stayed to the end. The win against Chicago State served as a prelude to what was to come for the next thirteen seasons. They were going to play an up-tempo brand of basketball that would appeal to the fans. It was a great start. Mike Reis said that Herrin's first year was one of the most enjoyable seasons he ever covered.

Mike Reis: *They were great guys...and there were no expectations. They played their butts off and Herrin coached his butt off. It was an enjoyable year.*

On Herrin's first team at SIU were two of his former Benton players; Kai Nurnberger and Randy House. Nurnberger was going to be a sophomore at Southern but didn't have a good experience as a freshman and chose to leave the team. He had plans of going back to Germany...until Herrin got the job.

Kai Nurnberger: *Without Coach Herrin...I wouldn't have played at South-ern. I had left Southern and I was ineligible. When Coach Herrin got the job, he explained that he couldn't give me a scholarship until I got eligible but if* *you can get eligible…I'll give you your scholarship back and you'll play. And that is what happened. My parents paid for my education the year I sat out and he put me back on scholarship when I became academically eligible. I'm grateful for that.*

Nurnberger scored 1,348 points in his SIU career and ranks seventh in career assists with a total of 371. He was an offensive juggernaut and a key player in the rebuilding stages of the program. Kai was a deadly free throw shooter with the game in the balance. Nurnberger nailed down so many clutch free throws in his career that he was dubbed "Cool Hand Kai" by Southern Illinois sports writers. He netted 287 free throws in just 328 attempts to finish with a career free throw percentage of .875 for his SIU career. In a game late in his career, he was intentionally fouled with the game on the line. Kai quickly turned to the opponent and said, "Thanks…appreciate it." And then calmly went to the line and stroked the two free throws.

After graduating from SIU in '89, Kai returned to Germany and played on the 1992 German Olympic team that played against Michael Jordan and the Dream Team. Nurnberger played professional basketball in Germany for the next fifteen seasons and is undoubtedly the most decorated international player in the history of SIU basketball. As of today, Kai Nurnberger is yet to be inducted into the SIU Hall of Fame. I played with seven Hall-of-Famers…Kai is one of them.

The team Herrin inherited that first season lacked size and athleticism. He knew that recruiting would be the key. He had to bring in some players. A great surprise to Herrin in that first season was the play of Randy House. House was an undersized post player that had a knack of scoring around the rim and became a fan favorite due to his tenacious play in the paint. House finished his SIU career with 1,121 points and is definitely in the conversation when it comes to the Hall of Fame.

Randy and I were teammates in high school and at SIU. He stood at a sturdy 6'4" and played with great self-confidence. He never allowed himself to be psychologically overwhelmed. He had such a swagger and trust in his abilities that he took on the nickname "Rambo" because of his fiery play against bigger and taller opponents. The nickname fit and House became a cult hero to Saluki fans across the area.

Randy was my college roommate my first year at SIU and that is when I really got to know him. During the '87-'88 season, the Bradley Braves came to the Arena. They had the great Hersey Hawkins. Hawkins ended up having a successful career in the NBA with the Philadelphia '76ers. In a game late in the season, Hawkins put up 49 on us by hitting shot after shot from every angle imaginable. It was a clinic. In the final play of the game, he punched a thunderous dunk over the top of House just seconds before the final horn. Hawkins' dunk was a nice exclamation point to an incredible individual performance. The Braves won the game. With House being my roommate, I had to give him a hard time about getting dunked on. House was always slow to praise opponents no matter how good they were. On the way back to the dorms I said, "Man… Hawkins can play…huh?" House paused for a moment, looked at me, and said; "He's not bad." I just burst out in laughter. He even flashed me a smile…but that was all the respect he was going to give him.

Another great House moment was the Rex Chapman story. In June of '88, Rick Shipley, Erik Griffin, myself and Randy were watching the NBA draft on TV in the dorm. It was Phoenix's turn to pick. David Stern says, "With the eighth pick in this year's NBA draft, the Charlotte Hornets select Rex Chapman from the University of Kentucky." The room fell silent for a moment as we took it in and then House said; "I can't believe that…I'm better than he is!" And he wasn't joking. We laughed about it, but it was this stubborn belief in his abilities that served as the engine to his incredible college career at SIU.

But know this: behind the image of his bravado and machismo was a guy that would do anything for you. House was an incredible teammate. A foxhole guy. More importantly, he is a loyal friend. I don't see Randy all of the time, but if I was stranded in a desert and had one phone call, I might call him. When I coached at Benton from '03-'09, Randy helped on a volunteer basis and the kids loved him. He was then hired as the head basketball coach at Rend Lake College. In 2013, Coach House and his Rend Lake Warriors won the 2013 NJCAA Division II National Championship by defeating the Moraine Valley Cyclones by a score of 87-69. House recruited players from all over the Midwest but he was able to get them to play together because they knew he would do anything for them. That is Randy House.

Randy House: *I signed with SIU a couple of weeks before he got the job…he would tell you that he didn't think I was good enough to play…but you can't always measure what is inside a person.*

In what proved to be a great decision, Herrin also chose to hire Benton assistant coach Ron Smith to fill the part-time assistant's job. The two full-time assistant coaches in '85-'86 were Steve Carroll and Herman Williams. Smith related well with the players, but it was his unwavering loyalty to Herrin that was so crucial during those first three seasons. Smith later became a solid international recruiter, landing players like Emeka Okenwa, Marcello Da Silva and Mirko Pavlovich. He was also instrumental in the signing of Tyrone Bell and Saluki Hall-of-Famer, Ashraf Amaya. In the early years, it is evident that Herrin made an effort to surround himself with players and coaches that he could trust.

In Herrin's first season, the team was 8-20. Years later, Herrin claimed it might have been his best coaching job. House had this to say about that first SIU team he played on in '85:

Randy House: *Well, if you look at what we were playing…the Valley has changed a little bit. There are no West Texas States…there is no Tulsa's…there is no Creighton's…there is none of any of those on the schedule. Plus…if you look at our non-conferences back then…they included what?…the Missouris and Purdues…the Nebraskas and Arkansas at Arkansas with Nolan Richardson…should we have won any games?*

In Herrin's first two seasons, the team went 8-20 (in '85-'86) and then improved to 12-16 (in '86-'87). Sharpshooter Doug Novsek made two points about what impressed him most about Herrin in those first two rebuilding years.

Doug Novsek: *One of the first things I noticed was he was realistic about what he was getting into. We suffered a lot of losses…but we were better that second year. We went into Illinois State and won on the road. I never saw him despondent. He didn't overanalyze things. When the game was over…he went to the next game. Secondly…he knew how he wanted to play the game. He wasn't going to play slow to try and win games. He wanted to play fast. He was going to establish that…whether we won or lost.*

Herrin's ability to pick himself up after a tough loss is something that Mike Reis noticed and respected.

Mike Reis: *He had a tremendous desire to work…even when things didn't go well. He could pout with the best of them…but when he was coaching*

Southern…and he may have had to learn this…he learned how to shake it off and get back up.

After Herrin's second season at Southern, he had to make one of the toughest decisions of his coaching career.

Mike Reis: *When he changed his staff, Matt…that was extremely painful for him.*

In the spring of '87, Herrin let go assistant coaches Herman Williams and Steve Carroll. Any time assistant coaches are fired, there is a risk that the players they recruited could grow unhappy and leave also. Herrin was worried about Steve Middleton. Would he leave? Middleton had a close relationship with the coaches that were let go and was one of the best players in the Missouri Valley Conference. Middleton was an offensive machine and his uncanny ability to score the ball made SIU dangerous. Steve decided to stay for his senior year ('87-'88) and teamed with point guard, Kai Nurnberger, in what proved to be one of the greatest offensive guard tandems in Saluki history.

Herrin then landed two recruits that may have saved the program. Mike Reis believes that SIU basketball started to turn the corner when Rick Shipley and Sterling Mahan signed.

Mike Reis: *In his first two years we won 8 and 12 and we were back to the question of…could he win at the college level? Could he pick up the recruiting quick enough? But two things happened; he changed the staff and he got Ship and Sterl. When those two committed…that made them an NCAA Tournament contender. He got two guys in that could help him in recruiting* (Bobby McCollum and Scott Howard) *and he probably learned recruiting more and the assistants learned how to use him to recruit. I think they used him to close deals…especially with parents.*

In the spring of '87, Herrin hired Bobby McCollum and Scott Howard as his full-time assistants. McCollum was a crackerjack recruiter that landed Freddie McSwain, Kelvan Lawrence and Tony Harvey. Howard only lasted one season. When Scott Howard chose to leave, Herrin promoted Ron Smith to the full-time assistant's position. To fill Smith's part-time position, Herrin chose a young, enthusiastic coach by the name of Rodney Watson. Watson was from Paris, Illinois. He did his student teaching for Ron Herrin in 1982 at Olney High School. He later coached at Coulterville and had a State qualifying team at Madison High School before being hired at Division II Nebraska-Omaha. Watson knew the game well and was a tireless worker that proved to be a solid coach on the floor, along with organizing summer basketball camps and handling the public relations events that came with Saluki basketball. Watson later became a full-time assistant and played a key role in the program moving to the next level.

In the spring of '87, I joined the team as a red-shirt walk-on. Yes… a red-shirt walk-on. It was the bottom of the depth chart but I was just glad to be there. I was 6'1", 160 pounds. I knew it would take time. In fact, I really didn't know if I would ever play meaningful minutes as a Saluki. But that was my goal; contribute to a Division I basketball team. I spent much of '87-'88 focused on improving my strength and quickness. Fortunately, the three-point shot was introduced to the college game shortly before I arrived. This was my ticket. But I had to gain enough athleticism to play on the defensive end of the floor. I knew that…and for the next two years, this was my focus. I wanted to play…not just sit.

Every day in practice, I guarded Middleton and Nurnberger. They were two of the best guards in the Valley and that experience was crucial to my development. I dressed home games only and didn't travel my first year ('87-'88). There is a picture of me in the '87-'88 SIU media guide that I chuckle at every time I see it. I look like I'm twelve years old. My jersey is wrinkled and clearly too big for my narrow shoulders. Along with Nurnberger and House, my high school teammate, Jay Schafer, signed with SIU in the spring of '86. All of those guys were on scholarship. But I had fun. I loved the coaches and I liked my teammates. I roomed with Randy House on the third floor of Abbot Hall, in Thompson Point. My high school sweetheart, Trudee Buntin, lived just down the road at Boyer Hall.

Over the course of the next five years, I developed close relationships with Rick Shipley, Sterling Mahan and Erik Griffin. They became three of my best friends throughout my journey at SIU. Our coaches recruited good people first and that made my basketball experience that much better. Coming from Benton, it was the first time in my life that I had close friends that were black. The diversity of campus life was amazing. When I walked thru the SIU Student Center for the first time, students were shoulder to shoulder and I must have heard three different languages. I loved my experience at SIU. I realized for the first time that the world was much bigger than Benton, Illinois. My experience at Southern opened my eyes to so many things.

One of the first guys I met on campus was Sterling Mahan. We were in a pre-season scrimmage game in the fall of '87…and I had just met him. Sterling penetrated the lane and got undercut and landed on his head. When I saw him land, I cringed. It was ugly. He picked himself off the floor and walked to the top of the key to check the ball. It was an obvious foul. As he checked the ball, blood was running from his mouth and Kai said in his German accent, "Sterl…you sure you're okay, man? Sterling felt his mouth and realized that he was not only bleeding, but missing a tooth. So…we looked for Sterl's tooth. We found it stuck in the Arena floor. I remember thinking, wow…dudes pretty tough. He was 5'10" at best, with a massive lower half. He had the thighs and calves of a running-back. He was an explosive jumper and used his physical strength to bully opposing guards. Sterling was the player responsible for dubbing Coach Watson with his famous nickname, "Randy Watson…Sexual Chocolate." Mahan is now a member of the SIU Hall of Fame. He was an incredible point guard. Sterling said this about his experience at SIU:

Sterling Mahan: *If I had to do it over again…I would go back to SIU… and do it all again.*

Rick Shipley and I came to SIU in the fall of 1987. Shipley was also inducted into the SIU Hall of Fame and scored more than 1,000 points in his career and grabbed close to 1,000 rebounds. Shipley was a mainstay in the line-up for four seasons and key player in the re-build of the program. He gained the respect of his teammates through his consistent effort and dependability. We were roommates and close friends. Shipley was a Centralia native and was well aware of Coach Herrin before he came to SIU.

Rick Shipley: *Growing up in Centralia…I always knew who he was. As kids, my brother Reid and I always played one-on-one basketball. I was always Centralia and Reid had to be Benton…and of course Centralia always won. I didn't play for Coach at Benton, but we were both from Southern Illinois and we had that commonality and he knew a lot of people from my past and I believe that made us a little bit closer.*

Shipley had this take on Herrin's philosophy during the re-build period:

Rick Shipley: *It is no secret, Coach loved offense and he wanted to run and score points and if you are going to get beat…you have to make it fun to watch. Even during those lean years our teams were competitive. We did have Steve Middleton and he was one of the best players in the conference and I still have the utmost respect for the way he treated me when I came in. I believe Coach knew that he would have a hard time winning early so he went out and got the best local players to generate support…and as recruiting got better the winning came and it just multiplied the interest.*

Erik Griffin was a local high school standout from Carrier Mills, Illinois. Griffin stood at 6'3" and weighed 150 pounds when he arrived on campus in the fall of '86. We hit it off immediately and he became a lifelong friend that I stay in touch with even today. He was affectionately called "Griff" by his teammates. Griff had uncanny jumping ability and a high basketball IQ. Griff was the most articulate of all my teammates and had the greatest sense of humor. When Griff arrived on campus, he was faced with a difficult task.

Erik Griffin: *My experience under Coach Herrin was challenging. I was in a situation that I had been a back-to-the-basket post player in high school and was faced with the challenge of becoming a perimeter player. It was a struggle for me to maintain any level of consistency…I struggled with injuries…especially my junior year when I got my nose broke at Eastern Illinois. I will say this…Coach never gave up on me. When he recruited me, I knew of him and all of the great teams he had at Benton. He was the man in Southern Illinois basketball at that time. When he recruited me…that was a big deal and I made up my mind that I was going to SIU.*

One of my favorite stories involving Griff happened my sophomore year in college. Griff was the master at impersonations. He could do anyone. Griff, Shipley and myself were listening to a late-night talk show that Mike Reis hosted called "Saluki Hoops." The radio show aired every Sunday night at 9:00 p.m. for the purpose of giving SIU fans an inside look at our team. There was a part of the show where fans could call in and ask questions or give their opinions. The show was about to start and Doug Collins was the featured guest. At the time, the Benton native was the head coach of the Chicago Bulls. Earlier that day, I made a big deal about him being on the show. It backfired.

We were living on the third floor of Abbot Hall when the "Collins incident" took place. Again, Ship, Griff and myself were the only ones in the room. As we were listening to the radio show, Mike Reis informed the listeners that after a commercial break the show would take call-in questions for Collins. I was lying on my back in a lofted bed with my eyes closed waiting for the show to start back up. My bed was the furthest from the door. During the commercial break, Griff and Ship quietly snuck out of the room. I was totally oblivious. They scurried down to Griff's room and locked the door from the inside. Griff then picked up the phone and called the show. When Mike Reis came back on the air, he uttered these words, "We have a caller...and its Saluki player and Benton native...Matt Wynn." My heart dropped and my eyes popped open immediately. I sat straight up in bed. At first, I was stunned. I thought, It can't be me...I'm right here. Then, I noticed they were gone. I jumped off my bed and raced down the hall to Griff's room. It was locked so I beat on the door. Through the door, I could hear laughter as Griff did his best Matt Wynn impersonation for all of Southern Illinois to hear. I stood outside the door in fear of what he was saying. I had no answer. Well played! The prank was so genius that I could not bring myself to get mad. I just hated that the joke was on me.

In '88-'89, the team posted a 20-14 record and earned an NIT berth. It was the first time that Southern had qualified for a post season tournament since the NCAA run in 1977 with the stinger Mike Glenn. Newcomers Tony Harvey, Freddie McSwain, Kelvan "Crime-Dog" Lawrence and Jerry Jones boosted the team's athleticism.

The most notable win of the '88-'89 campaign came in the second game of the year against Big East heavyweight, Villanova. The game was played in the San Juan Shootout in Puerto Rico. Villanova was just three years removed from winning the National Championship in 1985 and was led by coaching legend, Rollie Massimino. Rick Shipley scored 21 points to lead the Salukis to victory.

Rick Shipley: *I never remember going into a game thinking we were going to lose. We beat some good teams when I was at Southern; Villanova and Oklahoma State were two big wins. Even my freshman year when Bradley came into the Arena with Hersey Hawkins...we were in the game. That game was within ten points the whole way. Coach always talked affirmatively about winning each game.*

In the NIT, we were beaten badly by the St. Louis Billikens by a score of 87-54. Seniors Randy House, Kai Nurnberger, Todd Krueger and Scott Hesse all played a critical role in moving the program forward.

In '88-'89, I had a great practice year. I was stronger, quicker and played with more confidence. On the floor, I appeared in only eight games and scored five points. I got my old number back…number 22. I had adjusted to college life and loved living in the dorms. Some of my best friends in college were not athletes. Some of the guys from the dorms were Todd Thomas, Steve "Marco" Cotone, Paul Hunley and Joe Campbell. My claim to fame in the '88-'89 season was an air-ball I shot at Bradley in the waning seconds of the game. We were getting drilled and I received a pass in the corner directly in front of our bench. I set my feet and let it fly…it looked good…so I said just loud enough to where my teammates on the bench could hear…"Money." We were losing and I knew it was bush league to say anything in that situation, but I had to. The shot was long…way long. I missed that shot four feet on the opposite side of the rim…an air-ball. The Bradley fans that remained chanted, "A-I-R B-A-L-L!" When the final horn sounded, I felt like a complete buster. Ron Herrin was on the bench that night with us and he printed off some cash with my picture in the middle of it, and passed it around at practice the next day. I deserved it.

The '89-'90 team was the best basketball team I ever played on. Rick Shipley was so steady. He was a solid player in the paint but he could now step out and hit the three. Shipley sometimes played the small forward position when we played a bigger line-up. Shipley was blue-collar and a tremendous leader on the floor. Along with Shipley was newcomer Ashraf Amaya. As a freshman, Amaya played at 6'8" and he was chiseled. Amaya's strength was his desire to compete. He always played hard, a fierce competitor. As a freshman, he was like a bull in a china closet, but later in his career, he evolved into being the most dominant inside presence in the Missouri Valley. Ron Smith tells a neat story about Amaya's journey to SIU.

Ron Smith: *There is no doubt that Doug Collins opened the door for our opportunity to get Amaya. I spent most of one summer in Chicago recruiting Amaya and Bell. At the time, Doug Collins was coaching the Chicago Bulls and Amaya was going to his camps. Doug spotted Amaya and we were able to contact his parents. We were in on Amaya very early…but he would not commit. He attended Walter Lutheran High School which was a small private school and they got upset in the Super-Sectional. If they would have advanced* *to the State Tournament, he would have been seen by so many more schools and we may have lost him. Doug was instrumental in getting Amaya.*

The monster inside in '89-'90 was Jerry Jones. Jones was a specimen. The first time I saw Jerry was a semester break practice of the '87-'88 season. It was around Christmas break. He came strolling into the Arena sporting a bright orange UTEP sock hat. Nobody knew who he was. Coach Herrin was leaning on the basketball stanchion barking out instructions. Jerry grabbed a ball off the rack and walked down to a side goal and proceeded to jam the ball in the basket with such force that he was literally moving the heavy basketball stanchion. It was funny watching Coach Herrin peek over his shoulder at Jones yet still trying to act interested in practice. Every player and coach began looking his direction. It was such a distraction that Herrin gave us a quick water break. Coach went over to Jones and they briefly chatted before practice resumed. Just a few days later, Jones began practicing with us, although he was not eligible immediately. Jones was a quick jumper and a tenacious rebounder. He had the look of an NFL lineman. He was a gentle giant. During pre-game warm-ups, Jerry and I went thru some inside-out drills together. It was our thing.

Mahan's back-court mate in '89-'90 was 6'5" guard Freddie McSwain. McSwain was a junior college transfer from Oklahoma that was high-energy. Unfortunately, many remember McSwain for the made dunk that bounded off the top of his head and back out of the rim in the '89 MVC Tournament finals at Wichita State, against Creighton. I loved Freddie as a teammate because he played so hard every day. He wanted to win. He had a unique look and a raspy voice that set him apart from my other teammates.

Kelvan Lawrence and Tyrone Bell were the first two guards off the bench. Kelvan had a quiet toughness about him that drew in his teammates. Before going onto the floor, Lawrence would cup his hands to his mouth and make a barking noise to get us ready to play. Bell ("Doc") was a crafty guard from Evanston that ended his career as a member of the '93 NCAA team. Bell was a big part of the team's journey to the NCAA Tournament.

The '89-'90 team finished the season with a 26-8 record. I broke into the line-up on the Hawaii trip and scored 13 points against Chaminade to solidify my role as the designated three-point shooter. It was my role for the remainder of my career. We had such a great presence in the paint with Shipley, Amaya and Jones that it allowed me to get wide open looks.

Opponents were always concerned about our inside game. So much so, that some teams played sagging zones to take away our dominant inside game. I was able to hit 36 three-pointers for the season and shoot the three ball at a .444 % clip.

In the last week of the regular season, our team won the final three home games against Illinois State, Bradley and Wichita State to win the Missouri Valley regular season title. Two of those last three games were sell-outs and the excitement around our team was at an all-time high. I'll never forget the night we clinched. Students poured onto the floor to celebrate with us and each of us climbed the ladder to cut down the nets. Just as he had done at Benton, the entire SIU student body was in a basketball trance. It was an important accomplishment for Herrin. Winning the Valley in '90 validated him as a Division I basketball coach. The former high school coaching legend had proven that he was now a legitimate Division I basketball coach. I can remember being happy for him in that moment, as we celebrated. He had arrived. The excitement around our team was incredible.

Sterling Mahan: *My favorite memory was when we won the conference for the first time at home in 1990. That was an exciting time.*

Despite being 26-7 and losing to second place Illinois State in the MVC Tournament championship game in Bloomington, we were snubbed by the NCAA committee. We were left out of the field of 64. It was a devastating blow to all of us. Herrin made it known to the media that he thought the committee's decision to leave us out of the tournament was unfair. Coach was taking up for us, but just days later we laid an egg by getting drilled at home by Wisconsin Green Bay in the first round of the NIT. It was over.

One of the major reasons we were able to enjoy so much success in '89-'90 was the addition of assistant coach Sam Weaver. Weaver had served as Ron Shumate's assistant at SEMO the year before and first met Coach Herrin through Kyle Herrin. Kyle was playing at UT Martin, who played SEMO. Coach and Sue always made it a point to be at Kyle's games and a casual relationship developed between Weaver and Herrin.

In the spring of '89, Bobby McCollum left SIU to go to Kansas State. His departure made room for Weaver. Weaver played at Three Rivers Community College for Gene Bess, who was considered one of the greatest defensive basketball coaches in the country. Herrin needed Weaver for recruiting purposes, but he turned out to be much more. Weaver not only landed great players like Chris Lowery, Marcus Timmons and Chris Carr but he brought with him a sound defensive philosophy that Southern needed in the worst way.

Rick Shipley: *Before Sam came…it was offense-offense-offense. Sam came in with a solid defensive philosophy and even though he worked for coach, he was willing to step up and change some things we were doing defensively. Sam had a bulldog mentality, and he was the perfect ying to yang…to Coach Herrin's freedom on offense.*

Sam Weaver: *Coach told me he wanted to stop people. He always made me understand what he wanted. I had to sell him on the fact that good offenses were based on ball reversal…and back then 90% of the offenses started with a pass to the wing. So we worked on denying the wing. We wanted the opposing offense to start higher on the floor…and then we moved the offside guys to the mid-line. We were forcing the ball baseline and we had the guys that could do it. It was all about keeping the ball out of the middle of the floor. I remember him saying, "That looks good… go do it."*

Weaver's favorite memory of his time at SIU occurred during the '89-'90 season. It took place before a contest against the Creighton Bluejays at the Arena. Tony Barone was the head coach at Creighton, and they had great teams in the early nineties led by Chad Gallagher and Bob Harstead. Anytime we played Creighton, it was a big game. Weaver tells the story:

Sam Weaver: *One of my favorite memories is before we played an 11:00 a.m. game against Creighton. I was walking out of the tunnel behind Coach Herrin and Tony Barone* (Creighton's head coach). *The game was at home and the place was packed and loud. Barone turned around and said, "Well, you are going to kick our *** this morning and you brought all of your friends in to watch." Coach Herrin didn't curse…so he laughed it off and then he looked at me and said, "And you're the one that started all of this with your recruiting." We all just laughed. And that is exactly what happened. We were so dialed in on defense. It was a great win and those were great times.*

After coming close to reaching the NCAA Tournament in '90, expectations were high entering the '90-'91 season despite losing Jones, McSwain and Schafer to graduation. Chris Lowery, Mirko Pavlovich, Marcelo Da

Silva and Ian Stewart were the top newcomers to the team. The three seniors on the team were Rick Shipley, Sterling Mahan and Erik Griffin.

But something else was happening. Herrin had finally created a coaching staff that he was comfortable with. During his 13 seasons at SIU, the Salukis enjoyed the most success with the staff of Weaver, Smith and Watson. As a player, I sensed that all of the assistant coaches got along with each other. Each coach had their own strengths and developed strong relationships with us off the floor.

Rodney Watson: *I think that one of the biggest things that nobody ever talks about was that Coach Herrin wanted to be at SIU…and so did all of the assistants. We weren't looking to go anywhere else. We had a very close staff that worked together well. Sam, myself and Smitty were very tight. Coach Smith had such a good feel with the players and he was a guidance counselor and he used those skills to take care of the players. Sam came in with a great conviction to his defensive philosophy. Coach Herrin let him do his thing. I remember asking Sam about his future and he said something to me that really resonated.… He said, "If we win…everything will take care of itself." Sam was not a self-promoter. He wasn't looking for the next job. Sam wanted to win. He wasn't job hunting…he just wanted to win games. I loved his answer. We all wanted to be at SIU…and I think you guys felt that.*

Ron Smith had spent the most time with Coach Herrin and served as the liaison between Coach Herrin and the players when it came to communication. Smith knew Herrin so well that he could accurately communicate to the players Herrin's message.

Ron Smith: *At practice and games, I watched the players' faces to see if they understood what he wanted done. I served as a filter and a liaison between the players and Coach to make sure they understood. Coach was a passionate communicator…no one could doubt his passion. He adjusted and became a player's coach.*

Coach Ron Herrin also joined the SIU staff after retiring from Benton in the spring of '89. It cannot be overstated how important it was for Coach Rich Herrin to have his brother Ron on staff. This was the one man on staff that Coach could say anything to. If he needed to vent his frustrations, he knew Ron would listen and he trusted his big brother's advice. The players loved Ron Herrin. Ron's job was to take care of the players and he did that on so many levels. Because of his warm demeanor, he is still referred to by the players as "Uncle Ronnie".

SIU Hall of Fame point guard Chris Lowery remembered why Weaver was able to win the recruiting war for his services and the important role he played on the coaching staff. Lowery played his high school basketball in Evansville and was teammates with Indiana stand-out Calbert Chaney.

Chris Lowery: *Sam Weaver recruited me. Sam was so good to talk to on the phone. He always asked about my family first…and he didn't cut me off to get to the basketball. He listened to me and he was easy to talk to. Sam was definitely our defensive coach. When we did defense in practice…it was Coach Herrin's recess. Defense was Sam's baby. Sam was also the outlet for all of the black players and I believe he loved that part of his job. I can still hear him say, "I promised your grandmother you're graduating with a degree." I needed to hear that and it motivated me.*

After his playing days were over, Lowery coached the Salukis from 2004-2012 and led the Salukis to the NCAA Tournament three consecutive years. His team advanced to the Sweet Sixteen in 2007. He now serves as an assistant coach to Bruce Weber at Kansas State. Although Lowery was recruited by Weaver he loved playing for Ron Smith and Rodney Watson as well.

Chris Lowery: *The first thing that comes to mind when I think of Smitty was his open-door policy with all of us at his home. We were able to go to Coach Smith's house and just hang out with his kids and play video games…we were able to do that. I now realize how important that was to a good basketball climate. Another important job that Coach Smith had was that of the "Shoe Fairy", R-Dub (Rodney Watson). He is the most enthusiastic person when there is no enthusiasm. I remember him saying in our pre-season workouts stuff like, "This is going to be the toughest Division I workout in the country." When I first got there, I really didn't understand all that Coach Watson did. He was only part-time. He had a job at the business incubator to supplement his family's income and I'm sure it was something he really didn't want to do. He later moved up the ladder to become an assistant coach through much hard work. Sometimes you've got to be a good soldier to get where you want to be. I have nothing but respect for Coach Watson's journey.*

One of the reasons the staff of Weaver, Smith and Watson worked together so well was the mutual respect and love they shared for Coach Herrin. Yes, they wanted to win but they also wanted Coach to win. It was a special staff in that way. The coaches were all pulling the cart in the same direction and the players sensed the respect and love the coaches had for one another. All of the coaches wanted Coach Herrin to have success.

Sam Weaver: *It was a lot of fun working with Coach Herrin...and that whole staff. You hear these horror stories about head coaches that are so strict... he wasn't like that. Coach had a way of communicating what he wanted done to the players in a non-threatening way. Nothing was ever personal. He let us work. There is an old saying: If you want to be successful...it's who you hire. I think he believed that. His brother, Ron, was there also. I just think he was very comfortable with the whole staff. I used to love Rodney's scouting reports because he could make a really bad team seem like the greatest team there ever was...and as a defensive coach I fed off that.*

Ron Smith: *I had a good working relationship with Coach Herrin and I learned how to approach him. If I had an idea, I couldn't say, "I think we should do it like this...that turned him off. But if I said something like, "Hey, what do you think about this?" He was more receptive.*

Ron Smith also noticed Coach Herrin's willingness to delegate authority to his assistants. This delegation of power is clearly something Herrin had to do and Smith saw the change.

Ron Smith: *I think over time Coach learned to delegate authority. At Benton, everything started and finished with him. He was the authoritarian figure 100%...but he grew to listen to more ideas from his players and coaches. He changed with the times.*

Rodney Watson: *Every person...no matter where they came from, knew that Coach Herrin was a good person. He never used a swear word. He never went there. He always had time for people. Look...Coach Herrin wanted to be at SIU. It was his dream job. He wasn't looking to go somewhere. Think about this...he had seven great years at SIU and three consecutive trips to the NCAA Tournament...he could have left that job for more money.*

Our '90-'91 team finished the season with an 18-14 overall record. In my opinion, the year was a disappointment. I expected to win the Valley, but we finished the year in strong fashion by advancing to the quarter-finals of the NIT before being eliminated by Adam Keefe and the Stanford Cardinals. I appeared in 31 games and netted 31 three-balls. Graduation was hard for me in '91. I lost three of my closest friends and the guys I came in with; Shipley, Griffin and Mahan. Shipley, Mahan and Griffin expressed what an honor it was to play for Coach Herrin.

Rick Shipley: *He was a great coach. But he was just a guy. He never big-timed people…he could relate to all people. He was from Southern Illinois. People identified with him and wanted to see him do well. I respected him. He was totally dedicated to the game. He literally lived it and breathed it. His greatest strength was his drive to win…but at the end of the day…he cared about you as a person. When you have that kind of desire, you can overcome some of your shortcomings.*

Sterling Mahan: *He let me be me. He was a player's coach and he had a great relationship with everybody on the team. We had different personalities on the team…but he brought everyone together.*

Erik Griffin: *Coach was a visionary. Early on we didn't have the talent, but we had great character guys…and then you could just see the pieces being put together for those teams that made the NCAA Tournament. He was going to put a team on the floor that was fun to watch…and he was going to do it with high-character people. Coach Herrin never promoted himself…he never made it about himself…it was always about the players.*

In 2015, Griff led the Meridian Bobcats to a second place finish in the Illinois Class A State Tournament. In his four years at Meridian, he led the Cats to an 80-50 record. But most importantly, he touched the lives of so many young people. Griff credited his experience under Coach Herrin for changing the basketball culture at Meridian.

Erik Griffin: *Coach completely changed the culture of our program at Southern…and I was able to see those changes and use them in my experience as a high school coach.*

My senior year ('91-'92) our team won the Missouri Valley Conference, led by the Valley player of the year, Ashraf Amaya. Amaya had an incredible season in '92, leading our team to a 22-8 record and yet another NIT berth. I did not have a good season. I appeared in 31 games and connected on only 13 three-point field goals. I graduated with teammates Emeka Okenwa, Kelvan Lawrence and team manager, Peter "Woody" Goff.

Every once in a while, I get this question: "What was it like to play for Coach Herrin?" My answer is this; "Coach Herrin had "IT", and "IT" was a lot of things." Let me explain. I believe everybody has an on-switch, but it can be difficult to find on some people. He was very good at finding a player's on-switch and he could find it on the difficult guys too. Also, we knew he was a good person. At the end of the day, you had to respect that fact. His credibility as a person motivated players to play hard. His work ethic was unmatched and he set the bar high. He challenged you. He was going to do it his own way, win or lose. He never backed down from a challenge and when you knew that he believed in you, he could infuse a confidence that could raise your performance to a higher level. He was never somebody he wasn't. He was real. I think as players we all saw that. He liked to jest with you and we sometimes imitated his speech and all his quirks. He could laugh with you. But when it was game time, it was on. He was an intense competitor. Were there times I disagreed with him? Yes, but not many. I always knew that he had everybody's best interest at heart. He had a way to make you trust that. I can also say that after playing for Ron Herrin for two years in high school, he also had "IT". Some guys may have a different definition of "IT" when it comes to Coach Herrin, but this was mine.

I also felt Coach had a very strong moral compass. You just kind of knew that he wasn't going to do anything out of character. He lived his life in the way that he was raised by his parents and mentored by his brother, Ron. As a player under Coach, I've been present in some very tense locker room discussions. I've seen him upset and I've seen him raise his voice. I never heard him say a swear word in all the years I played for him. He never let it slip one time just to get our attention. As I got older, that really made an impression on me. If he tells a story and he uses a word that he may find inappropriate, he would cup his hands around his mouth and speak quietly. I don't believe this was some sort of conscious effort for him not to swear, he just didn't. That was him.

I will be honest. I am forever grateful that I had the honor to play for Coach Herrin. It was five of the best years of my life. I was young and learning my way but most importantly I was part of something much bigger than myself. I loved my teammates and formed life-long relationships with all types of people.

Our season and my college career came to an end when we were defeated by Boston College in the first round of the NIT. The key newcomer of the year was Marcus Timmons, who was a highly touted recruit from Scott County Central Missouri. Chris Lowery took over the reins as the point guard after playing behind Sterling Mahan as a freshman. It was a position he would hold for the next two years.

Chris Lowery: *I really didn't understand what it would be like playing behind one of the top five players in the league…it meant I wasn't going to play much. I took it personal as a freshman. But after my freshman season it got much better.*

Another key happening in '92 was when Paul Lusk decided to transfer from Iowa to SIU. Lusk was ineligible to play in '92 but he played a key role on the three consecutive NCAA Tournament teams ('93-'95). Although Paul didn't first choose to go out to SIU, he had much respect for Coach Herrin.

Paul Lusk: *I've known Coach Herrin since I was probably thirteen or fourteen years old. I'll tell you one quick story that stands out to me. I was a junior in high school and I was being heavily recruited…it was in the fall and we were having open gyms. One big time school came in and one of their coaches actually pulled me out of class and showed me a video of their program and then basically had a full-contact with me. They stayed the rest of the day and watched our workout after school and stayed afterwards to talk to me. I'm from New Baden, Illinois and we didn't know any of the rules back then but that was illegal…you couldn't do that. The next day, Coach Herrin came into our next open gym and when we got done I was in my dad's office with my dad and it was just the three of us. I asked Coach Herrin a question about Kai Nurnberger or one of the players…he stood there and kind of froze for a second and said, "Pauly…I realize some of the other schools are down talking to you and doing some things they shouldn't be doing…I'm not going to do that. It was literally the three of us in my dad's office. That really resonated with me that he was going to do things the right way. I ended up not going there (SIU)* *to start with, but I transferred there and had a great experience. Coach Herrin was always so good to me. I always thought Coach Herrin supported his players and had their backs. I know personally…my senior year I struggled and he stood by me after having a good junior season. I always appreciated that.*

The '92-'93 Salukis finished the season at 23-10 and had a breakthrough season. The top newcomers on the team in '93 were Chris Carr, Jo Jo Johnson and Scott Burzynski. The team had advanced to the NIT the previous four seasons, but SIU fans were growing impatient.

Jo Jo Johnson was the son of former Benton stand-out Danny Johnson. During his high school career ('88-'92), he took Southern Illinois basketball by storm. He remains the leading scorer at Benton High School by amassing 2,575 points in his high school career. He also led his team to a third place finish in the 1992 Class A State Tournament. Jo is one of the greatest high school players I ever saw. My senior year in college, I saw him play at Mt. Vernon. It was a performance I never forgot.

In '92, the Rangers were coached by Rod Shurtz. I sat in the balcony that night with a couple of my college buddies. The talk about Jo had reached our team and several of us made the trip that night to watch him play. Evidently, he was not feeling good that night, but played anyway. Johnson had a kind of rock star popularity, and he attracted attention at all times. The Mt. Vernon fans were taunting Johnson, trying to get in his head. I knew the Mt. Vernon fans were making a mistake. They were poking the bear. The place was just rocking. The tip went to Jo and he took about two dribbles, and then went between his legs. I had played against him in open gym, and I knew when he went between his legs it was going up. This was his rhythm of getting into his shot. Johnson hit a deep three and then pulled out his imaginary pistols from his holster and took a few shots at the Mt. Vernon student section. That place went crazy, and it literally sent chills down my spine. Although Johnson played at SIU just one year, he was a key contributor off the bench in '93. Johnson was the fifth Benton player to play for Herrin at SIU.

Pressure on Herrin to advance to the NCAA Tournament mounted and came to a head before the team left for the Valley Tournament in St. Louis.

Chris Lowery: *In '92-'93… we were supposed to win the league…but we were so up and down. I think we finished second. When we were about ready to go to St. Louis for the Valley Tournament…some fans painted "Fire Rich*

Herrin" on the rocks outside the rec center. I just remember thinking...we have to do this. We knew how much pressure was on Coach.

In the first game of the '93 Valley Tournament in St. Louis, the Salukis found themselves behind late in the game. Rodney Watson remembered the moment well.

Rodney Watson: *We were down in the first game of the Valley tournament to Bradley and it looked like we were going to get beat. I actually remember thinking stuff like...State Farm is a pretty good insurance company. I thought it was over...if we didn't make a comeback...we're on our way out. Mirko Pavlovich tips in a ball off a missed free throw...and then converts a three-point play on the next possession. We came back to win that game. Matt... that series of events may have changed my career path. We won that game... and then beat Missouri State the next day. Doc Knapp took all of us to Ruth's Chris Steakhouse and we all ate $100.00 steaks that none of us could afford. It's those things you remember...it was a great time.*

Lowery remembered the feeling of the team after that must win against Bradley.

Chris Lowery: *That was our chance to fold but we didn't. I remember we took a big breath after winning...thinking, we can do this. We then beat Missouri State to advance to the championship game against Illinois State.*

It was the third time Herrin had a team advance to the Valley Tournament Championship. The winner of the game received an automatic bid to the NCAA Tournament.

Chris Lowery: *I just knew we were going to beat them* (Illinois State)... *we split during the year and the last game at their place they were up like fifteen...their best player shot an unnecessary three-pointer at the buzzer to pour salt in the wound. We remembered it. Before the game, Amaya was so pumped up. He scared me. When the game started, he just exploded.*

With the clock winding down, the Salukis had the lead. A large contingent of SIU fans made the trip to St. Louis and the chant, "S-I-U...S-I-U" echoed from the crowd. Tears welled up in the eyes of Sue Herrin as she watched the closing seconds of what her husband had been fighting to do the last seven years. When the final horn sounded, bedlam ensued. An excited Rich Herrin could not hold back his emotion. It was Mike Reis's favorite memory during the Rich Herrin era.

Mike Reis: *I'll never forget '93. The postgame...it was one of the top five interviews that has ever been on Saluki radio with Shipley and the wireless microphone catching up to Herrin...and the fans just able to hear the sheer joy and the immediate reaction and then when you add on to that the side show that went with everything...they tried to throw water on Herrin but missed him...and hit Rodney. And Shipley trying to catch up to him and Herrin didn't walk real well even when he was healthy and he's sliding all over the place and Shipley is strong enough to hold him up as he is interviewing him as he is celebrating the biggest win of his coaching career. The sheer relief... because it had been a brutal last three weeks...he was snapping at everybody, including me, because they had lost a couple of games in late February and it looked like it was going to be NIT again...and then...three days later...I interviewed him in his office a couple of days later and he said, "I told my wife Sue before the tournamen that if we don't win this tournament, it's going to be the NIT again and we're going to have to face that music again...but that's really not the way it should be. And you know what? We don't have to face that music now. It's my favorite tape and I could quote it verbatim.*

Chris Lowery: *After we won the game, I'll never forget Coach raising both hands in the air and looking towards the sky. Shipley was interviewing us after the game and I can remember Tyrone screaming, "This one's for you, Ship!" We did feel like we were playing for all of the guys that played on those NIT teams. I was glad we won too...because it relieved a lot of pressure on Coach.*

In the '93 NCAA Tournament, the number 14 seeded Salukis were matched with number 3 Duke and Coach K. The Blue Devils made quick work of the Salukis by defeating them 105-70 in the first round of the Midwest Regional, in Chicago. Despite the loss, the '93 team will be remembered as Herrin's first team to advance to the NCAA Tournament.

The loss to Duke was Ashraf Amaya's last game as a Saluki. Amaya was a warrior. He was my teammate and that is always how I describe him. He was a tough guy that played so hard. After leaving SIU, Amaya played two years in the NBA for the Vancouver Grizzlies and the Washington Bullets. He was inducted into the Saluki Hall of Fame in 1998.

The Salukis advanced to the NCAA Tournament the next two seasons. Fan interest was at an all-time high and Herrin had established himself as one of the most respected mid-major college coaches in the country.

During this time, another newcomer to the SIU program was Pinckneyville standout Shane Hawkins. As a youngster, the "Hawk" attended all of the Panther games and he was well aware of Coach Herrin.

Shane Hawkins: *I understood high school basketball in Southern Illinois and our family had season tickets in the first row behind the opponent's bench. I sat behind Coach Herrin many times when the Rangers came to Thomas Gymnasium. I knew what kind of person he was…and that was a major factor in my decision to go to SIU. Coach Herrin and Coach Watson did a great job recruiting me. They made me feel like I was wanted.*

Hawkins remains Pinckneyville's all-time leading scorer and is the most prolific three-point shooter in Saluki History, shooting 314-805 at .390%. He also ranks third in career assists with 435. The "Hawk" could play, but he remembered how tough a transition it was from the prep ranks to Division I basketball. After reflecting on that first year, Shane admitted that Coach Herrin helped him through that period when he was questioning his own abilities.

Shane Hawkins: *I really struggled early with the transition to Division I basketball. I had a lot of self-conversations walking to and from practice. There were times I was thinking, what am I doing here? If I played one-on-one against Johnny Dhadze…I couldn't beat him one out of ten times. There were times that Coach believed in me more than I believed in myself. He loved to be around his guys. He could tell when I was struggling…and he could say something to give me a positive thought.*

Sesser, Illinois native Scott Burzynski was a true stretch four. Burzynski stood at a thin 6'8" and was a knockdown shooter. He worked himself into playing a key role off the bench from '94-'96. Burzynski was easy going and liked by his teammates. He recalled the '94 and '95 teams as two of the best teams he ever played on. Scott loved his time at SIU under Coach Herrin.

Scott Burzynski: *He did care for his players. He loved us. I never doubted that. One common theme that all of us share was being in the locker room with him after a big victory. Those were special moments.*

Burzynski recalled some of the fun moments he had playing for Coach.

Scott Burzynski: *Coach sometimes had trouble with names. Paul Lusk… right? Lusk isn't hard…he would say "Lust." He called Lowery, "Lalerly". He called Ashraf, "Ashroo". Another time, we were at Drake and a guy had a big sign that said, "Coach…where is your neck?" At halftime, he actually said something like, "Hey gang, did you see that sign?"*

Scott Burzynski: *One of the funniest stories involving coach happened at St. Louis in the Marriot Hotel. We were going to play St. Louis the next day in the afternoon…I was rooming with Hawk and he got really sick. Ed* (Thompson) *and Rodney came down to check on him and decided to take him to Barnes Hospital without Coach Herrin knowing. There was a kid at SIU that had a case of spinal meningitis that lived in Hawk's dorm…and Ed was not going to take any chances. After they took Hawk to the hospital…I was the only one in the room…and then my phone rings. It's our manager, John Sims. Sims says, "Hey…Ed wants you to come down here with us and sleep… just in case he has it…he doesn't want you to be exposed in the same room… we're in room 634." So…it's like one in the morning…I'm tired and I grab my things and head to room 634. I knock on the door…no answer. I knock again…no answer. Now I'm getting mad because I'm tired. I start banging on the door….and Coach Herrin answers the door. He has no shirt on…in his pajama bottoms…and he has those glasses on with "SIU Hoops" in the corner. Then I hear Sue say, "Rich…who is it?" About that time, Sims peaks his head out about two doors down…and has this big smile. They got me.*

It cannot be overlooked as to how important the play of Marcus Timmons was during Herrin's glory years from '93-'96. I only played with Timmons one year, in '92. But I knew he was going to be special. Marcus was such a humble person. He never made a big deal about himself. He was a great teammate. Timmons could do it all. He could score, rebound, pass and finish on the break. He was inducted into the SIU Hall of Fame in 2000 and is still considered one of the greatest players in school history. Scott Burzynski made this point about Timmons:

Scott Burzynski: *I thought the '95 team was one of the most talented teams I played on because we had Marcus as a senior. Marcus made the difference... he could really play.*

Mike Reis had this to say about the big five players (Lowery, Lusk, Timmons, Hawkins and Carr) during that great run of success in the mid-nineties.

Mike Reis: *And you know, you had tremendous freedom...but you better be intelligent about the game...or you could take the freedom and mess it up. They didn't mess it up. The most successful teams had the most intelligent players. Lowery, Lusk, Carr, Timmons, Hawkins...they knew the game...and what to do with the freedom.*

One of the toughest losses during Herrin's tenure came in the first-round loss to Syracuse in the '95 NCAA Tournament. Freshman Shane Hawkins scored 21 points and hit his first six three-point attempts, but the Orange Men defeated the Salukis 96-92. Herrin was so disappointed after the game; he accidentally forgot to do the postgame interview with Mike Reis. It was an extremely tough loss.

Mike Reis: *I believe it was Herrin's most disappointing loss in his years at SIU. When you score 92...you expect to win.*

Another key player on the great teams of '94 and '95 was Chris Carr. He was affectionately called C.C. by his teammates. Carr lived and died the game of basketball. He loved it. When the Salukis were idle, he would go to the rec center to work on his game. As a junior, he averaged 22.6 points a game. But like Hawkins, he struggled to make the transition to the D-I level as a freshman.

Chris Carr: *I wanted to leave SIU after the first week. There was so much size and athleticism with Wells, Da Silva, Timmons and Amaya. The level of athleticism and physicality was over my head. I was going to leave so I called my mom. My mom said, "You're not coming here." Coach knew that I was struggling and the one thing that I remember him telling me was, "Chris, if you quit or transfer now it will be easier for you to do that from now on." So I stuck it out. Ashraf Amaya was a great mentor for me. He took me under his* *wing and he told me that if I wasn't in a drill I needed to be doing wind sprints or push-ups. If both of us were not in a drill, he would do them with me.*

Carr admitted that he could be a challenge for the coaches. There were times he sat alone, away from his teammates. To the coaches, he seemed miserable, but C.C. had worked so hard on his game, he didn't want to compromise anything. As time went on, the coaches broke through his hard shell and C.C. adjusted. Carr improved his game so much, that he became the most-feared offensive player in the Missouri Valley Conference. But it took time. Carr remembered when things started to come together for him as a player.

Chris Carr: *In the first game of the season my freshman year…I got a DNP. I did not play. After the game, my mom waited for me and Coach Herrin came by…she didn't say anything about my playing time. But she did ask Coach Herrin this question: "Is Chris working hard?" Coach said, "Well…I think he can work harder." I remember my mom saying to me later, "Don't complain to me about playing time if you're not working hard." Later on, we lost to St. Louis University in double overtime and then we lost to Missouri in triple overtime. I played the last ten minutes of that game and in all of the overtimes…that is when it really started to come together.*

Carr and his teammates advanced to the NCAA Tournament in all of his three seasons at SIU ('93-'95). He had a great college experience and claimed that Coach Herrin had been a big influence on his life.

Chris Carr: *The biggest thing with Coach Herrin was that he was a true builder of men. Our conversations off the floor were never about basketball. He really invested in me on becoming a great young man. I remember one time we were in a hotel my freshman year at Ole Miss…I had a hat on and I was sitting kind of slouched in the chair. He came by and kind of kicked my foot and said, "Sit up…take your hat off and be a respectful young man. He told me one time, "Chris, you are articulate…you have a smile that lights up a room. Basketball is going to stop. You have to live your life." Coach always sent me to the media room after games. If there was a booster event…he made sure I was there. He said, "You are the face of the program…always do the right things…because you don't know who is watching."*

Carr admits that one of his favorite memories at Southern was seeing how happy Coach Herrin was when the team won the Valley Tournament in '93.

Chris Carr: *I'll never forget Coach Herrin raising both hands above his head in the old Kiel Auditorium after we won the tournament. He was crying real tears. The monkey was off his back. I was young at the time. I didn't understand the amount of work it involved to get there.*

Two days after the Salukis were defeated by Syracuse in the opening round of the '95 NCAA Tournament, Carr's father passed away. NBA scouts had made it known to him that he would be drafted. He had a decision to make.

Chris Carr: *I don't think Coach wanted me to leave. I remember him telling me that he would use me the way Duke used Grant Hill...as more of a facilitator to improve my draft stock. But when my father passed away...I was in a state of flux. We didn't have much at home and I felt that leaving was the best decision for myself and my family at the time.*

Carr did get drafted by the Phoenix Suns. He spent eight years in the NBA with five different teams and scored 1,988 points in his NBA career. Carr was inducted into the SIU Hall of Fame in 2006.

As for the Salukis, '95 was the last time they would finish above .500 in Herrin's thirteen-year stint as SIU's head basketball coach. In '95-'96, the Salukis finished 11-18 and were just 4-14 in Missouri Valley play.

In '96-'97, the team improved to 13 -17. The "Dawgs" were led in scoring by Carbondale natives Troy Hudson and Rashad Tucker. Hudson and Tucker combined for a total of 1,054 points, almost half of SIU's point total in '97 (2,188). Hudson was an explosive guard with uncanny handles. He was a tremendous scorer. Tucker was a slasher and knifed through the opposing defenses attacking the rim. They had been high school teammates.

After a stellar college career, Shane Hawkins graduated in the spring of '97. Troy Hudson then left early that same year, making himself eligible for the NBA draft. Hudson played eleven seasons in the NBA with five different teams. He scored nearly 5,000 points in the league and was most productive in his five seasons with Minnesota from 2002-2007. Troy Hudson was inducted into the SIU Hall of Fame in 2011.

Shane Hawkins became a successful high school basketball coach and is presently coaching at Carterville High School in Carterville, Illinois. The Hawk reflected on his time at Southern with Coach Herrin.

Shane Hawkins: *First of all…he treated you like a man. He trusted you on the floor to make the right decisions, but he also expected us to live a life in which we made good decisions off the floor. Whether it be as a father, husband or employee, he allowed us the space to make those decisions. When Ron was on the bus with us, I would listen to Ron and Rich talk about their memories of the game. I appreciated that stuff and it was those moments I cherish the most. What a neat thing to see…two brothers working side by side and having a chance to go to the NCAA Tournament together.*

After two seasons below .500, pressure to win mounted. Unfortunately, the old saying, "What have you done for me lately?" played out. The team could not right the ship. With Ron Herrin's death just five months before the season began, '97-'98 proved to be one of the toughest seasons Herrin ever had to endure. The Dawgs finished the year 14-16. Under pressure from SIU Athletic Director Jim Hart, Herrin resigned on April 9, 1998.

In his thirteen seasons at SIU, Herrin guided the Salukis to a 225-174 record. He led the team to four NIT's and three NCAA appearances. He did it. He rebuilt a sputtering program and brought it back to respectability. Mike Reis believes that Herrin may have saved SIU basketball from falling to the Division II level.

Mike Reis: *I believe if that fourth and fifth year would have been under .500…I believe SIU would have cut ties with him. So that's where it was headed. So, in that case, look we've brought in this local icon and that didn't work either…what business do we have trying to be Division I? I say that to say this…I do believe that the success of the basketball program saved Southern from falling to the Division II level.*

Coach Herrin's 13-year tenure at SIU, and 225 total wins, ranks him fourth among Valley coaches. Coach's teams won the Missouri Valley Conference regular season twice and won the MVC Tournament three times. He had two players receive the prestigious Larry Bird MVC Player of the Year Award: Ashraf Amaya in '92 and Chris Carr in '95.

Herrin will be forever known by his players as someone who never over-coached. He gave his players the freedom to play, which made the game fun.

Rick Shipley: *The end justified the means. If we scored it was good…he was less concerned about the method than the end. His philosophy was offensive freedom. What player doesn't like that?*

Doug Elgin served as the Missouri Valley Commissioner for thirty-three seasons and remains as one of the most respected administrators in the world of NCAA athletics. It was Elgin's job to oversee the conference along with formulating conference schedules and managing the conference tournament.

MVC Commissioner Doug Elgin: *What I respected most about Rich is that he always put his team first – by that, I mean his total focus was preparing his Salukis teams to play their best basketball. Coach Herrin was the proverbial 'ball coach' – he lived to coach basketball, and his players really played hard for him.*

And he was content to be the head coach at Southern Illinois – and from my perspective he never thought much about taking that next step to a 'higher' program. He was from Benton, and what was better than coaching the college basketball team in his home area, and taking them to three consecutive NCAA Tournaments?

When his teams won back-to-back-to-back tournament titles in 1992-94 in a league that was clearly one of the eight or nine toughest in the country, he might have been able to pursue other head coaching openings. And it could be a very long time before any Missouri Valley head coach can match that championship run by Herrin's teams.

Coach Herrin always accepted his conference schedule without complaint. I'd have to say that some coaches were almost never happy about the sequencing of games in the conference schedule that the MVC staff had produced each season, but Rich simply never had any complaints about his Salukis' schedule.

One of my favorite memories involved a day we went fishing in Rend Lake with Kenny Irwin. It gave me the chance to see him away from basketball. I met the two of them at the Rich Herrin Gymnasium at Benton High School, and I remember how cool it was to see the championship banners hanging in the arena. It looked like old Boston Garden, with all the Celtics

NBA championship banners. He was always very proud of his coaching tenure at Benton High.

To the end of his life, Rich Herrin was a friend, a guy I loved and respected. He was a great husband, father, colleague and mentor to the many high school and college players on whose lives he had such a positive and lasting impact. I'll never forget – about a month before he passed – that he called me, and I looped in Mike Reis into a conversation that lasted about an hour. We had an interesting discussion, reminiscing about his years coaching at SIU, and about the great student-athletes that played on his teams.

I know that Rich had the respect of his Missouri Valley coaching peers. Here was a guy who had made the jump from being an ultra-successful high school coach, to leading a collegiate program that played in a very tough mid-major league. And it was clear to see that respect during the annual meetings of head coaches. He had good relationships with the many rival coaches during his thirteen years in The Valley.

Marion (2002-2007)

In the fall of 2002, Marion High School hired Rich Herrin as their new basketball coach. After four years of not being on the sidelines, Coach Herrin could not resist the urge to come back and coach the game he so loved. He was sixty-nine years old when he accepted the job, and the people of Marion were delighted to have his services. Marion native Aaron Mattox served as Herrin's freshman coach and became one of Herrin's closest friends.

Dr. Aaron Mattox: *He was still very high energy. If I heard him say it once… I heard him say it a thousand times, "There's no secrets in basketball…you've just got to outwork people."*

Herrin spent five seasons at Marion compiling a 61-84 record. His best season at Marion was '04-'05 when the Wildcats posted a 20 -11 record. At Marion, Herrin gained his 900th career coaching victory in an upset win over Mt. Vernon, at Changnon Gymnasium.

On February 24, 2006, Coach Herrin and his Wildcats traveled to Centralia for the last game to ever be played in Trout Gymnasium. It was an emotional night. A brief ceremony took place before the game. Herrin thought back to his glory days at Benton when his Rangers won a record six tournament championships. After his name was announced as the head coach of the Marion Wildcats, the people of Centralia stood out of respect and gave the old coach an emotional ovation. There is a panorama picture that hangs in the lobby of the new Centralia Gymnasium showing Herrin on the sidelines on that special night. The picture is in honor of Herrin having the record of most games coached in Trout Gymnasium by an opposing coach.

Coach Herrin resigned as Marion's head coach on October 27, 2007. Although Herrin didn't have the same success he enjoyed at Benton, he was able to bridge the age gap and build relationships with his players. Dr. Aaron Mattox, Herrin's assistant coach, said this about Coach Herrin:

Dr. Aaron Mattox: *I knew of him growing up in Marion. It's really hard for me to put into words what it was like to coach with him. My dad took me to all the SIU games in his heyday. I went to the SIU summer basketball camps when I was a kid. He brought me in and treated me like family. With Coach Herrin…when you're in…you're in. He was a great mentor and friend. The people he introduced me to…he was truly one of a kind. There is nobody else like him. I learned a lot about basketball from him…but probably more about life.*

Morthland College (2012-2017)

In Herrin's final coaching job, he was hired to lead the basketball program of a fledgling Morthland College. Morthland College was a small four-year Christian college in West Frankfort, Illinois. With the hire of Herrin, the school instantly gained credibility. Although Herrin was approaching eighty years of age, he continued to influence the lives of his players.

One of the players that Herrin built a strong bond with was former Eldorado standout, Will Carmickle. In fact, in the later years of Coach Herrin's life there was perhaps nobody closer to Coach Herrin than Will. Carmickle told me how he believes Coach Herrin saved his life.

Will Carmickle: *Out of high school I went to McKendree University and it didn't work out. I wasted a scholarship and came home. When I came back from McKendree, I started plumbing. I got married December 3, 2008, and we had a son named Lucas. He went to Cardinal Glennon hospital immediately after being born…he had a condition that couldn't be treated. We* *talked with the doctors and took him home on April 9th…and he passed away in June. After Lucas passed away…I was not in a good place. There was a part of me that didn't want to be here. I think my parents knew it too. I always wanted to go back and play college basketball. One day, I got a call out of the blue from Coach Herrin. He asked me if I wanted to play college basketball for him at Morthland College. I thought he was kidding me. You have to understand…I really didn't know anything about Coach Herrin. I was unaware of his history. He came and picked me up and he showed me the campus…my attitude then changed. When I got home, I googled him…and then realized who he was. I questioned God for a while…but Coach would say little things like, "God only gives you the things he knows you can handle." Since then, Coach has been like family to me. His whole family just took me in…Sue and Kyle…and everyone. Some of Coach Herrin's friends helped me also…Rich Stein…and Clark Dixon…and Mr. Rudolph. We won the 2015 NCCAA National Championship and I ended up playing on a torn-up knee. I'll never forget Coach Herrin and all of us celebrating after the game. He was crying. I only knew him eight years…but I cherished the times I had with him. He was like my grandpa.*

In 2018, the college closed and Herrin was out of a job. Some people wondered why he didn't just retire and find something else to do, but he loved it. Coach would often say, "I'm pretty fortunate…I didn't work a day in my life."

Later in his life, Coach stayed busy. With the help of Dick Corn and Brad Weathers, he continued his summer basketball camps at McKendree College. He loved being around young people and catching up with many of his former players that were now basketball coaches. There are over one hundred students, players and managers that fall under his coaching tree.

Coach also picked up the game of golf and loved to play with several of his friends. He did continue his golf scramble, with all of the money raised used to form scholarships for various schools around the area. He played with friends; Tom Wheeler, Bob Karnes, Richard Woods, John Jones and others. Tom Wheeler remembered the fun they had on the golf course with Coach Herrin.

Tom Wheeler: *The golf course is where I got to know Rich Herrin as Rich Herrin and not Coach Herrin. I spent a lot of time with him and he didn't talk much about his own success…he talked about other people. I was always amazed at who he knew. I know when you get older it's easier to tell people* *that you love them, and I remember saying one day, "Coach...I love you.... even though you missed some easy putts." He was one of a kind.*

Allen Van Winkle was the head basketball coach at
SIU from 1981 to 1985. *(SIU ATHLETICS photo)*

Dean Stuck (on the right) is shown here with SIU's new athletic director, Jim
Livengood in the fall of '85. Stuck stood strong and advocated for
Herrin to get the SIU job. *(SIU ATHLETICS photo)*

SIU Hall of Fame broadcaster, Mike Reis, and Coach Rich Herrin developed a
friendly relationship built on respect.
(SIU ATHLETICS Photo)

Chuck Oyler was the principal at Benton High School when Rich Herrin left
Benton. Oyler told Herrin, "Don't go Rich." *(Benton High School)*

Coach Rich Herrin is introduced as SIU's new coach in the spring of '85. Herrin is pictured at his first press conference. *(SIU ATHELTICS photo)*

The Herrin boys had all graduated from high school when Herrin took the SIU job. When the Herrin's moved to Carterville, Illinois- it was Coach, Sue and Kristy. *(SIU ATHLETICS photo)*

Coach and Sue during the SIU years. *(SIU ATHLETICS photo)*

Doug Novsek is still considered one of the deadliest three point shooters in SIU history. Novsek played on the great Lawrenceville team that defeated the Rangers and later played for Coach Herrin at SIU. *(SIU ATHLETICS photo)*

Coach Herrin, Coach Ron Smith and freshman, Randy House are pictured on media day in '85. *(SIU ATHLETICS photo)*

Front row, left to right: Scott Hesse, Brian Welch, Steve Middleton, Greg Matta and Thad Matta. Middle row, assistant coach Herman Williams, Grant Martin, Lonnie Spears, Todd Krueger, Ken Dusharm, Billy Ross and Harry Gauthier. Back row, assistant coach Larry Peterson, head coach Rich Herrin, Wayne Harre, Dan Weiss, Doug Novsek, Darrin Carlile, Randy House, assistant coaches Steve Carroll and Ron Smith.

The 85-86 Salukis. Coach Herrin's first team at SIU. The team was 8-20 but Herrin believed it was the best coaching job of his career. *(SIU ATHLETICS photo)*

Coach Herrin instructing the troops in '85. Just above coach Herrin
is Thad Matta. Matta later transferred to Butler and became a legendary
college coach at Ohio State. *(SIU ATHLETICS photo)*

Coach Herrin gives chase to an official to protest a call just
before halftime. (SIU ATHLETICS photo)

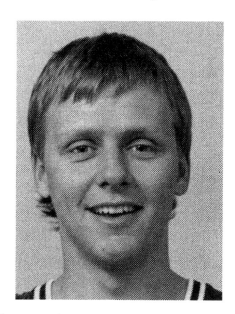

SIU point guard, Kai Nurnberger was one of the best players I ever played with or against. In my opinion, Nurnberger would be a great choice for the SIU Hall of Fame. (SIU ATHLETICS photo)

SIU Hall of Famer Steve Middleton was from Brooklyn, New York. Middleton was a scoring machine and he kept the Salukis competitive in Herrin's re-building years. *(SIU ATHLETICS photo)*

He later went to the University of Southern Indiana and
led the Eagles to a Division II Final Four Appearance in 2019.
(SIU ATHLETICS photo)

Coach Ron Smith encouraged me to walk on at SIU in the spring
of '87. Smith recruited some of SIU's finest players during the programs
rise to prominence. *(SIU ATHLETICS photo)*

Sam Weaver brought a defensive philosophy and the ability to recruit. Coach Weaver was a key factor to the rising success of the Salukis in the early 90's. *(SIU ATHLETICS photo)*

My good friend and teammate, Erik Griffin. Griff later led the Meridian Bobcats to a 2nd place finish in the state in 2015. *(SIU ATHLETICS photo)*

857

Another great friend, Sterling Mahan. Mahan looked like a
fullback but he could really hoop. Sterling is an SIU Hall of Famer.
(SIU ATHLETICS photo)

My roommate and good friend, Rick Shipley. Shipley and Mahan were able to
take the SIU program to another level. *(SIU ATHLETICS photo)*

The great Ashraf Amaya in '92. Amaya was a fierce
competitor that led the Salukis to their first NCAA
appearance in '93. *(SIU Athletics photo)*

The Benton connection in the fall of '88 while doing some pre-season
barnstorming. This picture was taken after a pre-season scrimmage
in Benton. **Front Row-** Herrin, Nurnberger, Wynn, Smith
Back Row- House and Schafer. *(Matt Wynn family collection)*

This is me letting one fly against the St. Louis Billikens.
(SIU ATHLETICS photo)

1989–90 Season — Won 26, Lost 8

Champions of the Missouri Valley Conference in 1990 (10-4, 26-8), Southern Illinois University's Salukis are, front row, left to right, Asst. Coach Rodney Watson, Asst. Coach Sam Weaver, Jay Schafer, Ashraf Amaya, Rick Shipley, Jerry Jones, Erik Griffin, Asst. Coach Ron Smith and Head Coach Rich Herrin. Back row, Trainer Ed Thompson, Grad Asst. Tim Wills, Matt Wynn, Jason Hodges, Oliver Cesair, Freddie McSwain, Kelvan Lawrence, Tyrone Bell, Sterling Mahan and Sports Information Director Fred Huff.

The best basketball team I ever played on; the 89-90 Salukis. In my opinion,
we should have had an at-large bid to the NCAA Tournament.
(SIU ATHLETICS photo)

SIU Hall of Famer Jerry Jones. With Jones, Shipley and Amaya inside,
I was able to get plenty of open looks beyond the arc.
(SIU ATHLETICS photo)

An unforgettable night. Coach Herrin being interviewed after sweeping the last
three home games to win the MVC in '90. *(SIU ATHLETICS photo)*

As a player, Chris Lowery was a fearless leader. Lowery later became
the head coach of the Salukis. He is a member of the SIU Hall
of Fame. *(SIU ATHLETICS photo)*

Paul Lusk was a fierce competitor that played on the three
NCAA tournament teams. Lusk led the Salukis in scoring in '94.
(SIU ATHLETICS photo)

Coach Herrin gets excited as he can see his dream of qualifying for the NCAA Tournament come to a reality. This picture is taken during the MVC Tournament Championship game of '93. *(SIU ATHLETICS photo)*

Chris Carr (CC) was an unbelievable talent that contributed to three NCAA teams and left a year early to turn pro. Carr is a Saluki Hall of Famer. *(SIU ATHLETICS photo)*

The '93 Salukis. The first SIU team to qualify for the NCAA Tournament under Herrin. **Front Row-** Stewart, Timmons, Pavlovic, Amaya, Da Silva, Burzynski, Carr **Row Two-** Lowery, Lusk, Pace, Bell, Piper, Hughey, Johnson, Greathouse **Row Three-** Huff, Herrin, Smith, Herrin, Weaver, Thompson, Knapp, and Watson. *(SIU ATHLETICS photo)*

Sesser native, Scott Burzynski, played a valuable role off the bench for the Salukis from 92-96. Brian Laur and Jamie Veach also played for the Salukis. They were also from nearby Sesser, Illinois. *(SIU ATHLETICS photo)*

The Salukis celebrate their third straight trip to the NCAA
Tournament in '95. *(SIU ATHLETICS photo)*

1992-93 NCAA Final 64
Southern Illinois University
Forward Marcus Timmons and Head Coach Rich Herrin

One of the all-time great Salukis, Marcus Timmons. Timmons could do it all
and he played on three NCAA qualifiers. *(SIU ATHLETICS photo)*

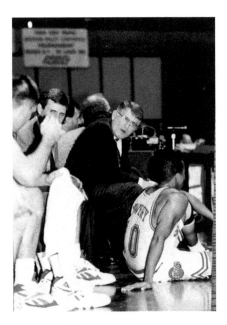

Coach Herrin and Rodney Watson communicate to the bench players in '94. *(SIU ATHLETICS photo)*

The "Hawk" was a high school basketball legend in Southern Illinois and had a stellar career with the Salukis. The Pinckneyville native played on the great '95 team and is one of the most prolific three point shooters in school history. *(SIU ATHLETICS photo)*

This is the way I remember coach Herrin at SIU. Always leaned
on the stanchion barking instructions. He loved practice.
(SIU ATHLETICS photo)

Coach Herrin poses with Shane Hawkins and Rashad Tucker
on media day '97. *(SIU ATHLETICS photo)*

A picture of Coach Herrin in '96. *(SIU ATHLETICS photo)*

I love this picture. Coach Herrin with his big brother in the
background in '97. *(SIU ATHLETICS photo)*

One of Coach Herrin's closest friends, Ernie Reynolds. Reynolds was a high school referee. Here he is back in the day. *(Rich Herrin family collection)*

Coach Herrin and Will Carmickle (in Green) grew to be extremely close when Herrin was coaching at Morthland College. Aaron Mattox (end) coached with Herrin at Marion and they remained close friends. *(Aaron Mattox family collection)*

Doug Elgin served as commissioner of the Missouri Valley Conference. Elgin
believed that Herrin was truly one of the good
guys in College basketball.

CHAPTER THIRTY-TWO

A Life…Well-Lived

"I never worked a day in my life." – Coach Rich Herrin

My entire family gathered at our house for Christmas, 2020. As we told stories and opened presents, I received a text. It wasn't good news. The text read; "Coach may not make it through the night." I didn't mention this to anyone. I quietly separated myself from the noise and took a seat in my recliner. I needed to be alone. In my mind, I visualized a fiery Coach Herrin at Rend Lake Basketball Camp when I was ten years old barking out instructions. I remember him saying, "Matt…lets go…get Freddie!" when I scored the first meaningful points of my college career. I remember his sheer joy after winning the Missouri Valley Conference crown in 1990. He was such a big part of my life. As I reminisced, tears began to stream down my cheeks, so I discreetly left the room. No one noticed.

When everyone left, I told my wife Trudee that Coach wasn't doing well. She took it hard. She loved Coach too. When we were in college, he would say, "Hey…you're not the same girl I saw him with last week." And he would just laugh. Coach always made her smile.

Trudee Wynn: *Coach always made it a point to speak to me. He knew our children and he and Sue were at our wedding. He was just always there… almost like part of our family. You could tell that he was more than just a* *coach by how many players enjoyed talking to him and being around him off the court.*

On that Christmas evening, I hopped in my car and went to Rich Herrin Gymnasium. Ironically, I teach in Coach Herrin's old classroom, in what was the old drivers ed room. The room is also used as the booster club room at Ranger home games. I turned the gym lights on and began to walk the upper concourse. I was in deep thought. As I looked up, the maroon banners hanging from the east rafters reminded me of his dominance at Benton. In the downstairs lobby, I looked at pictures of the great players that were part of his basketball machine. But in the end, it wasn't about Coach's basketball success; it was about his influence. Coach Brad Weathers had these words to say about Coach Herrin:

Brad Weathers: *I saw a quote on a Coach's Twitter account that said, "Judge your success on the amount of lives you've impacted. Not on the amount of wins." Coach Herrin proved that you can do both exceptionally well! His impact on my life, as well as countless others, is immeasurable. My family has been truly blessed to have Coach and Sue in our lives.*

As I walked, my mind was flooded with memories of how Coach touched my life. I thought back to that June day in 2020 when Coach and Sue gave me permission to do the book. It was one of the greatest days of my life. I sat alone with Coach at his home and we discussed intimate details of his childhood and how much he loved his family. Sue came in several times as the conversation turned to how she and Coach first met. I remember the pain he displayed when talking about the death of his brother, Ron. We had spoken almost every day up to this point. Sometimes the phone would ring well past ten at night and it would be Coach. We would talk late into the night. For me personally, those were the times I will cherish the most.

When my son Gehrig was in the eighth grade, his team played in the State Championship at Rend Lake College. We played Centralia. The gym was packed. As the game was beginning to start, Trudee and I were sitting on the front row of the bleachers. The crowd was shoulder to shoulder in the small gym, there was hardly any room. All of the sudden, someone tapped me on my shoulder. It was Coach. He said, "Scoot over…let me in here." He knew my son was playing, and he was there in support. Coach and Sue were at my wedding and my association with him helped me land virtually every job I've ever gotten.

That night, I said a prayer for Coach and his family before I went to sleep. I was still hoping that he might somehow pull through. It didn't happen. When I awoke the next morning, Coach had passed. He was eighty-seven years old.

When the news of Coach's death became public, friends, former players and students began to share Facebook posts about how Coach had touched their lives. The entire Southern Illinois area was in a state of mourning. Local t.v. stations and newspapers did stories about his life.

As a tribute to Coach, Mike Reis and Saluki Radio aired player interviews with former SIU players to get their reaction to Coach's death. Herrin and Reis worked closely together for thirteen seasons at SIU. One of the pieces of memorabilia that Reis treasures the most is a signed picture by Herrin that says, "To Mike Reis: A great friend and best play-by-play man ever." Reis explained why that picture is so important to him.

Mike Reis: *I think I benefitted from the fact that he knew my style to begin with…he also knew that wasn't the style he preferred. It certainly wasn't the style he was used to at Benton. He was used to…everything is always good… and it's we…and if there is something bad…we ignore it. My background was as a reporter…and he knew that because he listened…he listened to sportscasts. That's why when he wrote that…it meant so much. He had never said that to me. To earn his respect when I knew that I didn't do the games the way he preferred…that meant a lot. That's all I ever wanted anyway…was to be respected. I'm no different…I want friends…I want to be liked…but not at the expense of respect. Not at the expense of how I believe the job should be done. I certainly respected what he had accomplished…and I think he had respected what I had accomplished…and I think I grew into more of a Southern Illinois person when he was the coach.*

One of the most heartfelt interviews was from former Saluki and Benton Ranger, Randy House. House played for Herrin a total of seven years (three in high school and four in college). With his voice cracking with emotion, House had this to say:

Randy House: *We knew that it was inevitable…we have been pretty close for the last thirty years and had a lot in common. A few weeks ago he fell…we* *were hoping he could make a recovery but the deck was kind of stacked against him. The thing that I think of...is the...privilege...I got to play for him longer than anyone else. I got to play for him three years in high school and four in college. That is probably the fondest memory I have.*

Some of the best Facebook posts were shared by ex-students at Benton that had Coach Herrin as their drivers education teacher...students that didn't play basketball. One of my best friends, Michael Yarberry, fell into this category. He was a 1987 graduate of BCHS. After high school, he attended the St. Louis College of Pharmacy.

Michael Yarberry: *My mom* (Jan) *was a teacher in Benton for many years and we have talked about this many times. During the years that Coach and Sue were at Benton...we had an inordinate number of students beyond those that played basketball that left Benton...and had professional success in their careers. I've always believed there was a direct line between the basketball team's success and Benton kids having the belief that they were not limited by attending a rural school. Look ...I never scored a point or grabbed a rebound for Coach Herrin...during my first year of pharmacy school...there were many students from larger schools with prestigious academic reputations. More than once, I reminded myself that with hard work and dedication Coach Herrin beat those same schools in basketball...so if we could beat those schools in basketball...then I could compete with them in the classroom. Sue, who was my second grade teacher...and Coach Herrin were very influential in my life. And I don't think my experience was unique just to me. I have always believed that Coach Herrin's influence in the community went far beyond just the basketball players.*

The day after Coach's death, I received a phone call from Kristy Herrin, Coach's daughter. In a conversation filled with emotion, Kristy asked if I would do Coach's eulogy, along with former Ranger Rod Shurtz. I told her that I loved her dad...and that I would gladly speak for him.

   The Herrin family is very close. Yes, Coach was a busy man, but he was never too busy for his family. Although the family shared coach with so many people, he still managed to build special relationships with each of his children and grandchildren. In the end, this is what mattered most.

Randy Herrin: *We did share Dad with a lot of people. Never once growing up did I feel short changed. Dad loved basketball…and I was glad Dad had that love. He had a lot of friends and people in his life, but we never saw it as a conflict. All of us had our own relationship with Dad. He was very firm on us growing up…but he was loving at the same time. He would do anything for us. He came up to St. Louis and built a bathroom on the back of my house. He would drive up to Rod's and mow for him. We are so incredibly proud of our dad. Yes, he was a great coach and person…but he was a great dad. He was of the utmost character. A measure of his greatness was how many people he influenced. That was Dad.*

Close friend Dick Corn helped Coach Herrin continue his summer basketball camps at McKendree College. Coach Corn had this to say about Coach's deep love for his family:

Dick Corn: *Often when the two of us would be in our dorm room at basketball camp late at night, he would tell me how lucky he was to have the love and support of Sue and his family. And he always followed that with how much he missed Ron and wished he could call him. As great a coach as he was…and as passionate as he was toward basketball…his greatest achievements were as a husband, dad, grandfather, and dearest friend to many.*

In my interview with Kristy Herrin, she expressed to me how blessed she was to have Coach and Sue as her parents. Kristy recalled some of the greatest life lessons she learned from her parents.

Kristy Herrin: *No matter where we were…we were never better than anyone else. He didn't care who you were, how much money you had…or what color you were…he taught me that we're all the same. Just because I was Coach Herrin's daughter…I wasn't better. I don't think he saw color or economic status. I don't think Mom did either. He did expect you to work hard and give your best at whatever you were doing. Dad just treated people so well. Now, he could be stubborn…and if he thought something was right…it was hard to change his mind. I always knew that Dad loved me, but he didn't say it as much when I was younger. Dad showed me that he loved me thru his actions…but we got closer as he got older…and he told me he loved me all the time.*

Randy Herrin remembers his dad as having the utmost character.

Randy Herrin: *Dad never cussed. That is such an important part of human-ity…he had the utmost character. Dad wasn't fake…he was real. Dad loved basketball. I've heard him say this several times, "I never worked a day in my life." He absolutely loved what he did. He loved coaching and he loved helping other people.*

The Funeral

Wednesday, December 30, 2020, was a cold, wet and windy day. It was the day of Coach's graveside service. Trudee and I picked up Rod and Tonya Shurtz about 12:15 and we drove to the cemetery. Two large tents were set up near the burial site; one designated for family and the other for the expected crowd of friends and former players. We arrived early at the gravesite and with the weather being so nasty, we decided to sit in the car for a while. The family had not yet arrived. Coach chose to be buried at Masonic and Odd Fellows Cemetery in Benton, Illinois. This is the same place his brother, Ron, was buried. As the time inched closer to 1:00 p.m., we decided it would be best to walk over and take our places inside the tent. A picture of Coach in his younger years sat propped on an easel to the left of the speaker's podium. Former player and close friend Ron Head and his son, Chris, were busy adjusting the sound system that sat in the back of the tent.

At approximately 1:15, the black Hearse pulled up to the gravesite. Sue entered the tent first and sat by herself, while Rod, Randy and Kyle carried their father's casket to its resting place. Ron's wife, Mary Lou, and her family huddled together in the back corner. As the family took their places, Sue Herrin sat front and center with her children and grandchil-dren surrounding her on all sides. My wife and my son Gehrig were with me that day. Gehrig stood next to Trudee and was filled with emotion. He loved Coach too. Everyone sported long overcoats, scarves and gloves for protection against the biting wind and drizzle that ripped through the tent. The wind was so strong that at one point the easel that held Coach's picture toppled to the ground. It was quickly re-assembled.

Pastor Larry Gilbert opened the service with a short message to the family followed by a touching eulogy by Rod Shurtz. Rod played for Herrin in '78 and had remained close with Coach.

Before I said my part of the eulogy, I glanced over at the tent next to us. It was a very surreal moment that I will never forget. They were all there. Yunkus, Semanski, Wills, Frailey, Hammond, Corn, Weathers, Hurley and many more. All of the ex-Rangers came out to say goodbye. The players were now grey and moved slower. They were years removed from filling the lane on a fast break. Many had tears in their eyes. As they took in the moment, they thought about how Coach had touched their lives. Some of the men came from tough home lives and Coach was their closest father figure. Many went to college on basketball scholarships that changed the course of their lives forever…some received jobs because of their association with him…for some of the men, playing for him was the best years of their lives. Many of the men became basketball coaches. One thing is certain; they were all better because of him. As their youthful bodies faded, they knew that Coach had impacted their lives far beyond basketball. They were better husbands and fathers. Better men. In the end, this was Coach's greatest victory.

Near the end of my eulogy, I told the family that one of the things I loved most about Coach was his fun personality. So I told a funny story to lighten the mood. Although I averaged close to eight minutes a game at SIU from my sophomore year on, I spent much of my time on the bench. One night we were playing Illinois State in Bloomington and I was sitting next to teammate Erik Griffin. The game was going on and he turned to me and said, "You know, Matt…have you ever noticed that when you go into the game, you always guard someone that is not very athletic?" It was Griff being Griff and I just kind of laughed it off. Just minutes later, Illinois State subbed in a player by the name of Sam Skarich. Skarich wasn't a bad player but he was not extremely athletic and at the time he was lugging around a heavy knee brace. As soon as Skarich entered the game, Griff leaned over and said, "Get ready." I kid you not, Coach Herrin then said, "Matt…Matt." I remember checking in to the game…just laughing to myself. Coach found somebody I could guard.

I ended the eulogy with a poem that I had written entitled, *The Legend I knew*, which summed up our relationship. I then stepped aside. Ron Head (Class of '61) then sang a beautiful rendition of *Amazing Grace* and Pastor Gilbert concluded the service in prayer.

When the funeral was over, I talked with the family. I knew coach was a Christian and this gave me hope. A friend of mine, Jane Allen, told me that she envisioned arriving in heaven to be much like arriving at an airport after your flight had landed. I can just see it now…God coming over the loudspeaker in heaven's airport" saying, **"Coach Rich Herrin…has just arrived…all those that know Coach Rich Herrin…please come to**

the terminal." Think of that reunion. Coach's parents, Homer and Florence, would certainly be there. I can see many of Coach's former players that died far too young scurrying to the terminal to see him. Rich's former high school coach, Doc Hunsaker, would be part of the crowd along with Coach's most loyal supporters; Mike McCarty, Barnie Genisio, Chubby Rice and Doc Swinney. Long-time assistant coach Harry Stewart, and dear friend Ernie Reynolds would be at the terminal.

But I have to smile when I think of Coach being reunited with his brother, Ron. I can just see the wide grin on Ron's face when he sees his little brother for the first time in years. It gives me great comfort to know that Coach is together with his brother, and I have the hope that they will both someday be at my reunion in Heaven's airport.

My family with Coach after the Rich Herrin shootout in 2004.
Gehrig, Bailey, Trudee, me and coach. *(Matt Wynn family collection)*

One of my favorite pictures. I snuck down in the tunnel before the
BIT Championship G's junior year and got this picture. Gehrig played
on a team that won 31 and 25. A credit to his coaches; Ron Winemiller,
Wade Thomas and Jason Hobbs. *(Matt Wynn family collection)*

Coach Shurtz Coach Herrin and myself watching Rend Lake College play John A. Logan. Randy House was coaching the RLC Warriors at the time. *(Matt Wynn family collection)*

A little get together at Coach's House in the summer of 2020.
L-R Schafer, Wynn, Shurtz, House, Harre, Johnston.
(Matt Wynn family collection)
Wayne Harre played on Herrin's first two teams at SIU.
He later accumulated a 412-77 record in just 15 seasons as
Nashville's head Girls Basketball Coach. He and his Lady Hornets
won a State Championship in 2013.

Me with my lifelong friend, Michael Yarberry, under the goal
in my driveway that we must have shot at a million times.
(Matt Wynn family collection)

A photo of Coach and his grandson Britton watching the Rangers. Coach and
Britton were very close. Coach built a relationship with all of his grandchildren;
Reese, Madison, Jake, Kate, Rachel and Mackenzie,
Mallory and Hunter. *(Matt Wynn family collection)*

This was a great night. Chris Lowery was inducted into the SIU Hall of Fame.
L-R Wills, Wynn, Weaver, Stewart, Coach, Lowery, Griffin,
Watson, Bell and Boston.

Coach Herrin with Brad Weathers (Right) and Brad's son Patrick (Left). Brad
Weathers and Dick Corn were extremely close friends with coach
and helped Coach with his summer camps at McKendree for years.
(Brad Weathers family collection)

Coach pulls one in. *(Rich Herrin family collection)*

Along with Weathers, Dick Corn was very close to Coach.

Coach Herrin at the Curtis Smith Golf Scramble at the Benton Country club. Coach Herrin continued his golf scrambles with the help of Tom Wheeler, John Jones, Hugh Frailey and Dr. Bill Dixon. **L-R** Loyd Stewart, Bob Karnes, Coach Herrin and Tom Wheeler. *(Tom Wheeler family collection)*

What a life!!! *(Rich Herrin family collection)*

The Runnin' Rangers

We were known as the Running Rangers…back in the day,
In the old South Seven…we had our way

The Rangers darted from the tunnel with excitement and flair,
It was the magic circle…the flat top hair

Two-line layups…accompanied by "Sweet Georgia Brown".
It was by far…the greatest show in town

Fancy uniforms lined with maroon and white,
Stars on the shorts…shining bright.

There was Yunkus, Johnson, Smith and Baker,
Collins, Stewart, Dunbar and Tabor.

The gym was loud…the fans on their feet,
A capacity crowd…not an empty seat.

The ball tipped…the game has begun,
Its Friday night with my buddies…too much fun.

The players play hard…they're skilled…they care,
It's all because of Coach on the sideline…out of his chair.

The man with the square jaw…hollers and kicks the bleacher,
It's Basketball 101…and Coach Herrin is the teacher.

The final buzzer sounds…the Rangers win,
Game Saturday night…we'll do it again.

That's what I remember back in the day,
The Rangers were King…that's all I can say

Coach Herrin's Coaching Resume

- 11 South Seven Titles (1966, 1967, 1968, 1971, 1972, 1974, 1975, 1976, 1978, 1982, 1985)
- 21 Regional Titles (1961, 1962, 1963, 1965, 1966, 1967, 1968, 1969, 1970, 1971, 1972, 1974, 1975, 1977, 1978, 1979, 1980, 1982, 1983, 1984, 1985)
- 8 Sweet Sixteen Teams (1961, 1966, 1967, 1971, 1980, 1982, 1983, 1984)
- 6 Elite Eight Teams (1961, 1966, 1971, 1982, 1983, 1984)
- 6 Centralia Championships (1965, 1966, 1970, 1972, 1974, 1982)
- (1956-1960) 95-17 @ Okawville - (1960-1985) 521-192 @ Benton - (2002-2007) 61-84 @ Marion
- **Overall High School Record 34 years (677-293)**
- **@ SIU (1985-1998) Record 13 years (225-174)**
- 4 NIT Appearances (1989-1992); 3 NCAA Appearances (1993-1995)
- 2 MVC Conference Championships (1990, 1992) 3 MVC Tournament Championships (1993-1995)
- **@ Morthland College (2012-2017) Christian College National Invitational Tournament Champions in 2016. TOTAL WINS - 981**

High School All-Americans

- Rich Yunkus   1967
- Billy Smith   1975

Olympians

- * Doug Collins   1972
- * Kai Nurnberger   1992

Centralia Tournament MVP's

- Jim Adkins   1965
- Rich Yunkus   1965, 1966
- Danny Johnson   1968

- * Rob Dunbar   1974
- * Bruce Baker   1982

Benton All-State Players

•	Jim Adkins	1966	Curtis Smith	1980
•	Rich Yunkus	1966, 1967	Rob Williams	1982
•	Danny Johnson	1968	Tim Wills	1982
•	Doug Collins	1969	Kyle Herrin	1983
•	Jim Semanski	1971	Bruce Baker	1983, 1984
•	Dave Lockin	1971	Randy House	1985
•	Steve Stewart	1972	Jay Schafer	1986
•	Rob Dunbar	1975	Jo Jo Johnson	1992 (@ SIU)
•	Billy Smith	1975	Reece Johnson	2021

Benton's Collegiate Players under Herrin from the 1960's

•	Tom Whittington	Middle Tennessee	1962
•	Terry Thomas	Middle Tennessee	1962
•	Wiley Hall	Rice University	1962
•	Bob Orchid	Central Missouri State	1962
•	Robert Crawford	Tulane University	1963
•	Rich Adkins	Sam Houston State	1964
•	Mike Franklin	Southeastern Jr. College	1964
•	Tom Smothers	Southeastern Jr. College	1965
•	Jim Adkins	University of Alabama	1966
•	Terry Heard	Kalamazoo College	1966
•	Dave Woodland	MacMurray College	1966
•	Kenny Payne	McKendree College	1966
•	Rich Yunkus	Georgia Tech	1967
•	Jerry Hoover	University of Florida	1967
•	Greg Fustin	Rice University	1967
•	Bill Lowery	Young Harris Jr. College	1967
•	John Burlison	Mac Murray College	1967
•	Danny Johnson	Western Kentucky	1968
•	Dick Corn	Monmouth College	1968
•	Bruce Taylor	Union University	1968
•	Dennis Miller	Olney Central College	1968
•	Pat Tindall	Hiawassee Jr. College	1968

- Doug Collins   Illinois State   1969
- Joe Milton   Eastern Illinois University   1969
- Laird Wisely   MacMurray College   1969

Benton's Collegiate Players under Herrin from the 1970's

- Don Smith   Rend Lake College   1970
- Brad Weathers   Rend Lake & McKendree College   1971
- David Lockin   Georgia Tech university   1971
- Denny Smith   University of Tennessee Chattanooga   1971
- Jim Semanski   University of Tennessee Chattanooga   1971
- Roger Adkins   Louisiana College   1971
- Rodney Kaspar   Louisiana College   1971
- Steve Stewart   Louisiana College & Rend Lake   1972
- Robert Corn   Memphis State & Missouri Southern   1973
- Chris Moore   Illinois Wesleyan   1973
- Paul Dinkins   Creighton University   1974
- Scott Hall   Baptist College of Charleston   1974
- Billy Smith   Georgia Tech University   1975
- Rob Dunbar   Western Kentucky University   1975
- Roger Smith   Rend Lake College   1975
- Eric Forby   Rend Lake College   1976
- Jay Sandusky   Rend Lake College   1976
- Roger Webb   Rend Lake College   1977
- Rod Herrin   McKendree College   1977
- Joe Durham   St. Louis university   1978
- Rod Shurtz   Missouri Southern   1978
- Dave Fairchilds   Rend Lake College   1978
- Mark Craddock   Rend Lake College   1978
- Ron Brookins   Rend Lake College   1978
- Doug Dunbar   Rend Lake College   1978
- Carl Shurtz   Rend Lake College   1979

Benton's Collegiate Players under Herrin from the 1980's

- Jim Labuwi   Rend Lake College   1980
- Jerry Corn   Rend Lake College   1980
- Steve Shurtz   Rend Lake College   1980
- Curtis Smith   Rend Lake & Missouri Baptist   1980

- Mark Kerley   Hannibal College & Rend Lake   1982
- Rob Williams   Northern Iowa   1982
- Tim Wills   Rend Lake & SIU-Edwardsville   1982
- Clark Dixon   Southern Illinois University   1982
- Kyle Herrin   University of Tennessee Martin   1983
- Mark Peters   Mississippi State University   1983
- Bruce Baker   University of Alabama Birmingham   1984
- Daren Carlile   Rend Lake & SIU   1984
- Kai Nurnberger   Southern Illinois University   1984
- Randy House   Southern Illinois University   1985
- Jeff Thomspon   Geneva College & Blackburn College   1985
- Jay Schafer   Southern Illinois University   1986
- Tony Shell   Freed Hardeman University   1986
- Brad Wills   Rend Lake College   1986
- Matt Wynn   Southern Illinois University   1987
- John Launius   McKendree University   1987

NBA Players under Herrin

1. Doug Collins   Number one Draft pick; Philadelphia '76ers (1973-1981)
2. Ashraf Amaya   Vancouver Grizzlies (1995-1996); Washington Bullets (1996-1997)
3. Chris Carr   Phoenix Suns and others (1995-2001)
4. Troy Hudson   Utah Jazz and others (1998-2008)

Coach Rich Herrin Hall of Fame Inductions

- Member of the McKendree University Hall of Fame
- Member of the SIU Hall of Fame
- Member of the IHSA Hall of Fame
- Member of the Missouri Valley Conference Hall of Fame
- Member of the St. Louis Sports Hall of Fame

**** Acknowledgements****

The process of writing this book has truly been a labor of love. Benton basketball is something that is near and dear to my heart and Coach Herrin was obviously a great influence on my life. My vision for the book was to accurately tell the life story of Coach Herrin through the people that knew him best: family, former players, friends. More than anything, I wanted the book to be accurate and insightful. Also, as I was writing the book, I constantly reminded myself of the book's historical significance. For future generations that will never know Coach Herrin personally, the contents of this book may be their only source. Therefore, it was important that the book be done right.

First and foremost, I would like to thank Coach and Sue for allowing me the honor to write the book. Coach was always available to talk and the book project allowed us a chance to get closer. Those late night phone conversations with Coach Herrin were moments that I will always cherish. We laughed, told stories and gigged each other, great times. Coach gave me access to his yearbooks at McKendree and Okawville and countless phone numbers of people I could contact for interviews. Sue was able to provide two big tubs of old pictures that I used for the book. The Herrin children, Rod, Randy, Kyle and Kristy, were willing to share intimate details of their relationship with their parents. These were some of my favorite interviews.

With that being said, I feel as if Coach Herrin's story was waiting to be written. All of the scorebooks from 1960-1985 were completely intact, resting on shelves in a storage room in Rich Herrin Gymnasium. Many of the players that were a part of Coach Herrin's glory years at Benton and SIU are alive today and scattered across the country. Although I had never spoken to many of the ex-players I interviewed, they gladly jumped on board to share their memories about Coach Herrin. In my opinion, the personal perspectives from the people that knew Coach best give the book its credibility. I want to personally thank the family, ex-players and all of Coach's friends for their willingness to provide their input into the project. For me personally, the phone-call interviews were my favorite part of the project.

I would also like to give a shout-out to Ceasar Maragni and his son, Brett. Ceasar Maragni devoted his working life to the belief "that a picture is worth a thousand words." He worked as a photographer for the Benton Evening News during "the fever" and was able to capture many of the greatest moments in Benton Rangers Basketball History. Ceasar is a life-long friend of mine and it is truly an honor for me to have the opportunity to display his work. We spent more than an hour in my classroom as he walked me through the steps of gathering the pictures for the book. Ceasar.... Thank you!

Brett Maragni is another friend that I must acknowledge. Brett and I grew up together and played on the same little league teams. In fact, I went to my first Saluki game with Brett and his father (Ceasar). Brett is now a preacher in Jacksonville, Florida and is a published author. Along with editing one of my early chapters, Brett gave me honest advice about my writing style. He is most responsible for giving me the idea of adding a meaningful quote underneath the title. Brett.... Thank You!

Also, I want to apologize to anyone that may feel snubbed by not getting an interview. Coach had hundreds of ex-players and many close friends; some that I didn't know. I'm sorry.

A special thanks to Susan Stickel, Pam Teague and all of the ladies at the Benton Public Library for granting me access to past BCHS yearbooks and newspaper articles from the Benton Evening News. I found that the Benton Public Library is one of my favorite places in town. The yearbooks and old newspaper clippings were extremely helpful in telling an accurate account of each season. I would also like to give a shout out to Joey Clinton who now serves as our technology director at Benton High School. Your help with the technology aspect was critical to the process. Thank you, Joey! I would also like to thank Tammy Koelling and all of the crew at Words Matter publishing Company for making my dream of writing a book come to a reality. Tammy and crew- Thank You!

A special thanks to Rod Shurtz for providing me with many player contacts. I would also like to thank my co-worker, Jim Eldridge, for giving me honest input and legitimate ideas about writing the book. Good friend Michael Yarberry suggested Coach Herrin's name be in the title of